MEIN KAMPF

BY ADOLF HITLER

THE FORD TRANSLATION

A new and easy to understand translation.

The first modern, truly complete and uncensored edition in over 65 years and the first translation available in an English language audio format.

Final Translation and Edit by Michael Ford With assistance and support from the Elite Minds Inc. research staff

MEIN KAMPF

BY ADOLF HITLER

THE FORD TRANSLATION

CONTENTS

Listen To Mein Kampf

PREFACE TO THE FORD TRANSLATION

Mein Kampf is one of the most widely known and heavily quoted books of all time. It demonstrates both Hitler's ability to persuade and his ability to instill a sense of heroic destiny.

It is critical that you understand Hitler's reasoning. Short, one-hour video documentaries only provide an abbreviated discussion of *"what Hitler did"*, leaving the viewer clueless about who he was and why he did it. His own words are the best way to understand why.

When most people hear the title, *Mein Kampf*, their first reaction is a growing emotional outburst that finally erupts in a yell of anti-Semitism; however anyone who has read *Mein Kampf* knows there is much more to the work. It is a retrospective on history, politics, and a guide to achieving power from the point of view of Adolf Hitler. It has become a dictators' manual, which has been read by all major dictators since World War II including Sadam Hussein who patterned his political movement, the Ba'ath party, after the Nazi party. The accuracy of the political parts of *Mein Kampf* was proven by Hitler's successful rise to power and by the rise of those who have followed his formula.

Many people think *Mein Kampf* is a long diatribe against Jews and other races. The truth is that only a small part of *Mein Kampf* is anti-Semitic. The majority of the book involves Hitler's discussion of the German people's difficult times after the First World War, his political theories and his organization of the Nazi Party, and it includes an especially large number of attacks against his enemies.

Mein Kampf is a large work that offers an interesting interpretation of politics, people, and foreign policy matters. To characterize it as simply a racist work is to oversimplify its message. Germany did not follow Hitler because he was a racist, they followed him because he promised a great future, and *Mein Kampf* is where he promised that great future.

It is important to understand that reading anti-Semitic passages or passages on race will not turn anyone into an anti-Semite. You do not have to worry about being filled with hatred simply by reading *Mein Kampf;* it is not a magic tome. Some people have so little faith in their own beliefs that they fear any exposure to *Mein Kampf* might twist them into something evil. If their beliefs are so fragile, so easily twisted, then they are already evil.

Unfortunately, many people are afraid that if they do not violently reject anything connected to *Mein Kampf*, and reject it in a showy way so that everyone sees their public display of rejection, then it somehow means they approve of the Holocaust. Of course, that is not logical reasoning and it seems silly when it is spelled out, but people often live by their gut reaction and do not think about *why* they dislike *Mein Kampf*—they just know they "*do*" or that they "*should*". They are driven by fear, which leads to a hatred of *Mein Kampf* without a rational basis and without the need to read it in order to understand what it says. They want to live in a simple world where they can conveniently dismiss Hitler as a raving lunatic along with anyone else who does not immediately jump up at the mention of his name to join in the shouting match.

It is foolish to dismiss Hitler's words as the rantings of a psychopath. To do so is to ignore historical facts. The people of Germany did not follow a ranting crazy man into war. They willingly followed someone they saw as a leader, a father, even a god, because they believed in him. To dismiss his work as lunacy is the equivalent of hiding your head in the sand and pretending the world is a nice place where nothing bad can happen again now that Hitler is gone. To claim Hitler was simply crazy is to over simplify the facts and ignore the obvious. Someone else will appear who uses the same formula to gain power. **If you cannot recognize the signs of Hitlerian Power, if you do not know how to counter their efforts, if you remain confused and uncertain as your opponent makes his moves, step by step with decisiveness and intention, and your inaction allows him to come closer to power, then you have already lost and they have won, for they know the rules of the game and you do not.**

Only through understanding can we come to grips with why the German people followed Hitler and why so many today still follow his example.

The *Mein Kampf* book has had a number of incarnations. The first volume was written while Hitler served a prison sentence in 1924(*Published July 1925*). The second volume was published in December 1926. Later, after 1930, the two volumes were combined into the *Mein Kampf* we know today. Special editions were produced for Hitler's 50th birthday, for wedding gifts, and a special soldier's dition among others.

Mein Kampf is not strictly autobiographical or strictly political; it is a combination of both. *Mein Kampf* has elements that are autobiographical—for instance, the first chapter of *Mein Kampf* is about Hitler's childhood, but even this is a political exposition. Hitler's personal life was so devoted to political ideas that even strictly biographical sections had to be very political in nature.

Hitler never sat down to write *Mein Kampf*. One of the benefits he was allowed in prison was a personal secretary. His secretaries Rudolf Hess and Emil Maurice typed as Hitler paced across the floor and around the desk, dictating what he wanted the Nazi party to know. The second volume was dictated to Hess and Maurice in Hitler's villa on Obersalzberg. *Mein Kampf* was primarily intended as an internal guide for his followers. In it, he reveals more than he might have wanted the public to know.

One of the most marked characteristics of *Mein Kampf* is its emotional tone. It is difficult not to be moved by many passages when Hitler speaks of perceived injustices dealt to the German people. This gave his speeches great power and, though tempered in the written word, this power can still be felt very clearly. The tone can be in part attributed to the environment in which it was composed. Hitler's standing and pacing in his small cell, speaking as his thoughts flowed while Hess frantically transcribed his words, trying to keep up. Hitler increasingly worked himself to frenzy, building on his own fervor, until he became exhausted.

The title Hitler initially wanted to give his work reflects the emotional nature of its content: *Four and a Half Years of Fighting Against Lies, Stupidity, and Cowardice.* His editor found this title to be wordy and asked him to change it to *Mein Kampf*. *Mein Kampf* is most commonly translated as "My Struggle", however, the real meaning is somewhere between "My Struggle" and "My Battle" for the people. It was not intended to describe his own greatness; it was meant to describe his battle for the greatness of Germany and for the preservation of the German race and the world.

Today, many people accept Hitler's contention that human existence is controlled by the laws of an eternal conflict and struggle for a greater good. This is by definition the classic Hero's Struggle. It is not surprising that people followed Hitler. It is surprising that more did not. His words offered the chance for everyone to participate in his personal Hero's journey—to be a part of something greater than they could ever be on their own. He was the hero of his own story, of course, only a fool would write their autobiography any other way. He appealed to very basic human instincts which are still present in everyone and still just as available for another would-be leader to massage and control. Hitler's words have a universal appeal that will continue to resonate among people who seek something greater than they perceive their own life to be.

The world has become so distracted by the later events of World War II and with the handful of racial comments in *Mein Kampf*, it has forgotten about the significance of the Third Reich's other activities. Hitler withdrew from the League of Nations; Hitler marched into the Rhineland; Hitler repudiated German disarmament; Hitler took back the coal mines of the Saar and established a National Socialist government; Hitler joined Mussolini in Spain and marched into Austria; Hitler forced Chamberlain to accept the Munich pact.

With each act, the world covered their eyes and proclaimed, "Thank goodness this will be the last of Nazi aggressions". Yet Hitler's future plans were already spelled out in *Mein Kampf.* Many have criticized world leaders for not taking the words in *Mein Kampf* more seriously and for not using it as a guide to thwart Hitler's plans. Such accusations are the result of hindsight. *Mein Kampf* does lay out very clearly Hitler's plans, however they are only clear in retrospect. It would be foolish to even attempt to predict what decisions a man will make tomorrow. Hitler made many statements in *Mein Kampf* that were open to interpretation, and many of his statements were revised or reversed in his later speeches. Many of his actions were not predictable, such as his alliance with Russia and Japan, which both completely contradicted *Mein Kampf.* Following the exact plan of Mein Kampf would have made those events appear impossible. *Mein Kampf* may have clearly predicted a future in 1925, but there was no way anyone could have used it to see that future no more than if they copied *Mein Kampf* quotes onto Tarot cards and attempted to divine Hitler's plans through a card reading. Even if his individual decisions were not certified and dated, his overall plan was clear and should have been the incitement needed to act much earlier. Unfortunately, the world wanted to wait for proof, more proof, and finally, they wanted to see him act before they felt forced to act against him. Hitler did not have this weakness. He recognized a threat or saw a goal and acted immediately, often even before he had the first piece of proof. That gave him the advantage for many years.

Hitler plays on the common belief of the time in Germany that Jews were responsible for their loss in the First World War: *"...the Jewish financial and Marxist press.*

intentionally incited the hatred against Germany until one state after another gave up its neutrality and joined the World War coalition, ignoring the real interests of their people in the process". This view was easy to accept within the borders of Germany, with limited information and a limited view of world events and a history of anti-Semitism. It ignores the accumulation of economic, political, and military rivalries, and the violation of Belgian neutrality that drove England into the war. It also ignores America's entry into the war which was a clear turning point. These factors, and not the influence of Jewish Germans, turned the tables in The First World War. However, these facts were of no use to Hitler and even the German people were not interested in hearing them.

The mood of the German people in 1933 made them dangerously susceptible to falling under the spell of a strong leader. They tried to return to their normal lives and find some national self-respect, but instead they found the way blocked by other nations and blind misunderstanding. The war victors were interested only in reparations. The German labor parties, which might have helped, were split into half a dozen warring camps. This occurred at a time when the people had become accustomed to a long period of strong nationalism.

Order and security became more important than a political freedom and that was synonymous with violence and bloodshed. Hitler saw these problems and spoke directly to people's fears and desires. The German people wanted a strong leader to solve their problems, a leader who could return their national self-respect.

To the German people, anti-Semitism, concentration camps, and political oppression were byproducts of what was needed to achieve their desires. Following Hitler was not a great leap for the German people. It was what they needed, when they needed it. Understanding how a leader can appeal to and control a nation without being questioned is critical to identifying similar events unfolding today.

Michael Ford
Editor

Adolf Hitler's birthplace at Braunau on the Inn.

Adolf Hitler in school at eleven years old, Royal Staats-Oberrealschule in Linz on the Danube River.

Hitler's home in Lambach. (Corner house on right)

Hitler's school, the Benedictine Monastery, Lambach in Bavaria. Hitler was a student here from 1897 to 1898 and a member of the choir.

Hitler in his prison cell after the failed Putsch.

Prison cell of Adolf Hitler with the desk where *Mein Kampf* was written/typed as Hitler dictated it to his secretary.

Left: French occupation of Ruhr as General de Viry, Commander of the 9th Brigade, French Dragoons, surveys Rathaus Square in Essen (A Ruhr town where Krupp armament works is located). Right: Landsberg on the Lech prison where Hitler was held in Markplatz square, Bavaria, and where he dictated *Mein Kampf*.

Hitler leaving prison in a photo for his followers.

15

William II, German Emperor. Hitler saw William II as the creator of the German Navy.

Leo Schlageter, considered a hero in the Nazi party, was shot by the French for his part in resisting the Ruhr occupation.

An example of Vienna slums around 1900 which Hitler would have experienced.

The Hofburg, former palace of the princes of Vienna. The statue in front is of Empress Maria-Theresa. Hitler would likely have walked through this area often and studied the architecture.

Members of the early Nazi party distribute propaganda flyers in Berlin

Vienna and the Ring-Strasse in the early 1900's which Hitler admired so much. On the left is the Reichsrat (Imperial Council or Parliament), behind it the Rathaus (City Hall).

The Technische Hochschule (Technical High School) in Vienna where Hitler attended school.

Hitler (far left) in Landsberg Prison with visitors, from left to right: Adolf Hitler, Emill Maurice, H. Kriebl, Rudolf Hess, F. Weber

Leopoldstadt showing the Aspern bridge over the Danube Canal.

Ludwig III was the last King of Bavaria, reigning from 1913 to 1918.

A younger Erich Ludendorff. Later, he was a famous German general and was part of the 1923 Putsch.

Dr. Victor Adler, Leader of the Austrian Social Democratic Party.

Joseph II, Emperor of Germany, son of Maria Theresa and Francis of Lorraine, he succeeded his father as German Emperor in 1765 and was known for his reforms.

Dr. Karl Lueger, founder of the
Christian Social Party which battled
against the Social Democrats. He was
mayor of Vienna from 1897 to 1910.

Archduke Franz Ferdinand was
Archduke of Austria. He was
assassinated in Sarajevo Bosnia June 28
1914 which sparked World War I.

Emperor Maximilian of Mexico
was the brother of Francis Joseph
of Austria. He became Emperor of
Mexico in 1863.

Prince von Bismarck. Hitler discussed
his policy and anti-Marxist acts in detail.

The Austrian Reichsrat(Imperial council or Parliment). Hitler refers to the horses pulling away from each other as being symbolic.

The Austrian Reichsrat, interior.

The Ruhr Valley has many coal mines and industrial centers which made it a vital part of Germany's economy and their only hope of paying back any reparations.

Johann Wolfgang von Goethe wrote in poetry, drama, literature, theology, philosophy, humanism and science. He was mentioned a number of times by Hitler.

Hitler (far right) and a terrier dog named Foxl he
adopted in the trenches of the First World War.

Hitler (far left) as a Lance Corporal on the Western Front with his comrades
of the 16th Bavarian Regiment

Retired Colonel Charles Repington, a British war correspondent for the Times, who first coined the phrase World War, and said contemptuously, "Every third German is a traitor".

Supporters of the German Revolution of 1918. An army lorry with soldiers and sailors celebrate the Revolution while Hitler was in the hospital recovering from mustard gas.

Matthias Erzberger was a Finance Minister and he was one of the officials who accepted the Treaty in 1919. He was assassinated in 1921 by two soldiers from a militant organization. Hitler called him "...a fat Mr. Erzberger..."..

Arthur Schopenhauer was a German Philosopher. Hitler said of him "...*in an eternally true statement that is still fundamentally valid where he called Jews "the great master of lies"*.

Gottfried Feder was an economic theoretician who was later a key member and guided the Nazi party. His lectures influenced Hitler.

Kurt Eisner organized the Socialist Revolution that overthrew the Wittelsbach Monarchy in Bavaria in November 1918. He was assassinated in Munich when Anton Graf von Arco auf Valley(commonly known as Anton Arco-Valley) shot him in the back on February 21, 1919, while he was on his way to present his resignation to the Bavarian parliament.

Sterneckerbräu inn Tal. This is where early DAP meetings were held and where Hitler first heard Feder speak.

Hofbräuhaus banquet hall in Munich was the location for the first mass meeting Hitler held.

The only daughter of William II, the ex-German Emperor, Princess Victoria-Louise of Prussia (later Duchess of Brunswick). Here she is in the uniform of a Colonel-in-Chief of the 2nd Regiment of Death's Head Hussars. Hitler refers to this when he says *"How could an ordinary man or woman feel a surge of enthusiasm for a Princess who was riding on horseback and wearing a uniform as soldiers filed past on parade?"*

Theobald von Bethmann-Hollweg, Chancellor of the German Empire until 1917 who was viewed as a moderate. Hitler said *"If instead of a Bethmann-Hollweg, we had a more forceful man of the people as a leader, the heroic blood of the infantry soldier would not have been shed in vain. In the same way, the excessive intellectual refinement of our leadership was the best ally for the revolutionary November criminals"*.

The Hofbräuhaus in Munich. This is the banquet hall part of the building where on the 24th of February, 1920, nearly 2000 people gathered to hear the explanation of the National Socialist Movement's program.

Hugo Stinnes was an industrial magnate and politician with large electrical, mining and shipping interests who was mentioned by Hitler.

Dr. Walther Rathenau was criticized by Hitler for soliciting France's favor.

Dr. Edouard Bernstein (left), was a Socialist Democrat, and Albert Ballin(right), was managing director of the Hamburg-America cruise ships and friends with Wilhelm II. Hitler refers to them when he says, "*His Majesty the Kaiser himself held out his hand to these old criminals offering these disloyal assassins of the nation mercy, protection, and an opportunity to collect themselves for their next strike*".

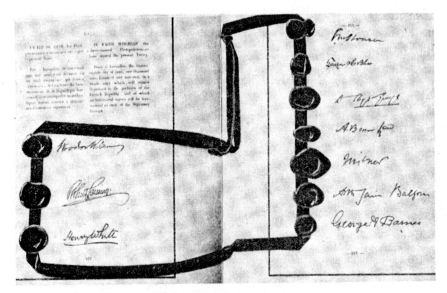

The Treaty of Versailles showing the first two pages of signatures, June 28, 1919.

The signing ceremony for the Treaty of Versailles in the Galerie des Glaces, the Hall of Mirrors, in the Palace of Versailles.

The Polish town of Brest-Litovsk was once the home of Polish kings and it is where the treaty between Germany and Russia was signed in 1918.

Adolf Hitler lecturing his followers in a suit at the Hofbräuhaus Keller in Munich. This is a painting which reproduces a photo taken by an early follower. Hitler ordered the original destroyed.

31

Chief Bailiff Wilhelm Frick took part in the Beer Hall Putsch (November 1923), at which time he was part of the Munich police department. He was arrested and imprisoned for his part in the 1923 Putsch and was tried for treason in April 1924. He was given a suspended sentence of 15 months' imprisonment and was dismissed from the police department.

Julius Streicher(left) published an anti-Semitic newspaper of offensive cartoons and anti-Semitic children's books. Streicher had his own personal followers and merged them with the Nazi party. He also participated in the failed 1923 Putsch.

Moltke the Elder, Helmuth Karl Bernhard von Moltke was a Prussian soldier, Chief of General Staff in 1858 and responsible for the French defeat in 1870.

Laplanders. Two families of Lapps in front of their summer homes in the extreme north arctic region of the Scandanavian Peninsula. Hitler refers to them as Lapps which has become a derogatory term for the people of Sami, the cultural equivalent of Eskimos living in Europe.

Armed members of the Spartacist League on their way to a demonstration in Berlin, January, 1919. Hitler said about them, *"This formed the Independent Socialist Party and the Spartacist League which were the storm troops of revolutionary Marxism"*. The Spartacist League was a revolutionary Marxist group named after Spartacus, leader of the slave uprising.

A group of soldiers celebrate the Naval mutiny at Hamburg outside their temporary headquarters. This photo shows the main leaders, Vogtherr and Sturmer, in the center.

Marxist revolutionaries distributing flyers during the 1918 revolution.

A mass demonstration in Munich against the Law For The Protection Of The Republic, 1922. This is the gathering of the nationalistic societies including the NSDAP Hitler talked about.

The market-place of Coburg with the Rathaus and on the extreme right a statue of Prince Albert. Coburg is a city in Bavaria, which only voted to join Bavaria in 1920 and was previously ruled by a duke in the fief of Saxe-Coburg and Gotha. It lost its ruler as a result of the Revolution.

Philipp Scheidemann was a supporter of the German imperial policy. However, he later joined Erzberger in the campaign for peace without annexation. He was a German Social Democratic politician, who proclaimed the Republic on November 9, 1918, and who became the second Chancellor of the Weimar Republic.

Frederich Ebert was the first president of the new German Republic. Hitler said, *"As long as Frederick the Great's historical memory has not died out, Frederick Ebert will never achieve more than moderate admiration"*.

Dr. Otto Gessler was the First Director of the Reichswehr (Germany's national defense force under the surrender terms). He then became the Minister of Defense and dictator of Germany under President Ebert's emergency proclamation during Spartacist uprisings.

Charles Maurice de Talleyrand-Périgord was an influential French diplomat under Napoleon I and other rulers. He also established many of the borders of the Prussian empire. These borders allowed Prussia to create a powerful position, eventually resulting in German unification, and the borders remained until the start of the First World War. In *Mein Kampf*, the reference to him means Germany does not have such a Frenchman who would act in favor of Germany.

Dietrich Eckart was a founding member of the DAP and involved in the Beer Hall Putsch. After he was released from prison, he died soon after due to a heart attack.

Georges Benjamin Clemenceau was a French statesman and journalist who was the prime minister of France from 1906 to 1909 and again in 1917 to 1920. He strongly influenced the Treaty of Versailles.

Germany announced in July 1922 that she could not pay war reparations demanded by the Treaty of Versailles. France responded by invading the Ruhr, an economically important industrial and mine center. Here troops enter the city of Essen.

Occupying French troops in the main square of Essen around a statue of Emperor William I.

Understanding Hitler

A new video documentary which explains how Hitler was able to rise to power and the part Mein Kampf played in his plan.

Find out more about this video at www.HitlerLibrary.org

Dissecting The Hitler Mind

Sex – Violent Childhood – Fear – Fits of Rage – Belief in Destiny

They all played a part in creating the personality of Adolf Hitler. Psychoanalysis combined with hundreds of interviews with those close to Hitler have reverse-engineered the mind of Hitler in this professional psychological analysis. It reveals many previously unknown characteristics plus answers the question about the "*first more or less political activity.*". Hitler mentions in Mein Kampf. Includes pdf of the original report and almost 7 hours of MP3 audio.

Find out more at **www.HitlerLibrary.org**

A NOTE ON MEIN KAMPF's PRINTING HISTORY

There are a number of editions of Mein Kampf. *Some are very rare and collectible. Some have historical significance and others have none. You can read more about the different editions of* Mein Kampf *plus see what they looked like in the* **Mein Kampf: Collector's Guide** *and download the* **Mein Kampf: Translation Controversy** *which are available at* www.HitlerLibrary.org

AUDIO VERSIONS OF MEIN KAMPF

This is the first complete translation of Mein Kampf *to be made available in an Audio Version. In today's fast paced society, many people do not have time to sit down and read a book. We recognized this problem and that is why the Ford Translation of* Mein Kampf *is available as an audio book for easy listening at home, or while driving. The audio version of* Mein Kampf *with additional bonus material is available at the audio website:* www.Mein-Kampf-Audio.com

As a purchaser of this book, you can download free bonus material at the below website. Grab your bonus material and learn even more about *Mein Kampf* while this special bonus offer is still available.

http://Bonus.HitlerLibrary.com

THE FORD TRANSLATION

This is the new and easy-to-read Ford Translation. It is the first uncensored version to be made available in over 65 years and also the first ever to be made available in an audio format through www.Mein-Kampf-Audio.com. It contains both of the original two volumes—the first published in July 1925, and the second in December 1926, which were later combined into one volume after 1930.

Mein Kampf is not a fixed work. Adolf Hitler made changes throughout the printing history. Sometimes these changes were to make the meaning clearer, to correct the grammar, or to remove names of people Hitler disfavored. Sometimes changes were made to conceal information Hitler felt certain countries were not ready to know (the authorized French version omitted several statements about France being an arch-enemy). This translation adopts the grammar and correction changes in order to provide the clearest and most accurate version that Hitler envisioned for Mein Kampf. In any instance where the change was not made for clarity or correctness, such as the removal of certain people's names, the original writing was used as the source and was not censored.

We have replaced some German words to improve clarity. We have also updated some references which had meaning in Germany or in the 1920s but were confusing and not widely used today. In the original, the phrase "World War" referred to World War One, but it was confusing because we now have more than one World War. Any instance of The World War was replaced by The First World War to make it clear which war is being discussed. The sentences and grammar in the original German Mein Kampf were not perfect and this imperfect style was preserved while still making the text more readable and understandable. Run-on sentences, passive voice, and agreement problems were common in Hitler's dictation and the resulting transcription. Many of these errors have been preserved when they did not make the material unclear. Most of the errors were corrected to make the text easier to understand and to avoid extremely long, confusing and complex sentences.

This translation has corrected over 1000 errors which were present in past translations. Many instances of Hitler's style were omitted from the older English translations and some references to mythology and historical people were censored, while common sayings and rhythmic styles, which often made his words poetic in nature, were removed simply because past translators did not understand their meaning or importance. Past translations, even the ones that claim to be unexpurgated, omitted passages, or simply skipped passages the translator could not understand. Older translations often failed to correctly translate humorous passages or sharp-satirical jokes correctly, resulting in the meaning being lost. All of these elements have been restored in the Ford Translation and all passages past translators found confusing have been researched, deciphered, and included clearly and accurately for the first time. No English reader has been able to appreciate these nuances in any previous English translation, not until this one.

The German word "Weltanschauung" was commonly used by Hitler and is replaced by "World-View" in this translation. The original German word more accurately means an encompassing concept about nature, human life, values, culture, religion, politics, economics, and all of human existence. In the interest of brevity, we will call it World-View.

Social Democracy is used throughout the book, but it can be confusing for modern readers. A social democracy is not equivalent to modern democracy. In Germany, Social Democrat means Marxist. The communists picked the name Social Democrat to appeal to the larger part of the population.

The word "propaganda" should be taken to mean political-advertising. The modern use of the word has negative connotations and is often associated inaccurately with brainwashing. This was not Hitler's intent when he used the word. The word propaganda is maintained wherever he used it, but the reader should keep in mind that it was describing a type of education for the people and was not seen as something sinister or manipulative.

The word "bourgeois" has also been replaced. In a number of places Hitler refers to the bourgeois. This term is very uncommon in the day-to-day language of English-speaking countries so it was updated to "privileged-class" which is reasonably accurate. Bourgeois as used in Mein Kampf means the social class that includes the wealthy, the employers and aristocrats, but not those of royal birth. It can also describe people who make money through education or government service that are considered to be socially above what we would today call the lower-middle-class and above blue collar workers—farmers, factory workers, day laborers—which are referred to as the proletariat or peasants or masses. This term too has been updated to use more accurate terms such as "farmer" or "physical-laborer" as appropriate for the context.

Many German sentences become nonsense when directly translated to English. This was a serious problem in past translations. Based on these poor translations, critics often characterized Hitler as rambling. For instance, a direct translation may start as *"So, if I thus soon became, however.."* which is clearly wordy in English and such unnecessary complexity only confuses the reader. Some of the original German passages have ten or more clauses in one sentence, and many sentences comprise entire paragraphs with only comma or semi-colon separations. This complexity is a result of Hitler dictating his work and not writing it. This has contributed to the idea that Mein Kampf was poorly written. It is not meant to be a great novel but a transcription of a very long speech. It is not meant to be a literary work and it is also not fairly represented by past translations.

We have also added clarifications—any reference to people, places, things or quotes that the modern reader may be unfamiliar with has been explained. Readers of past translations were left confused when obscure references were made to military theorists, Greek stories, or to places that had relevance to Germans but not to the rest of the world. All of those references are now explained in parentheses after the entry. For example, *"My youthful enthusiasm for the master of Bayreuth (meaning the composer, Wagner) knew no bounds"*. The modern reader may not know who the *"master of Bayreuth"* was. The new Ford translation explains the background so any reader will understand what these otherwise confusing references mean.

Previous translations use hundreds of uncommon words like *"propitious"*, *"excrescences"*, *"recalcitrant"*, or *"parvenu"*, which only obscure the meaning of the text. This new Ford Translation uses common and clear words. There was no way to read and understand previous versions of Mein Kampf without a dictionary in one hand and Mein Kampf in the other. Before this translation was made, even a vague understanding was limited to college professors, hence Ralph Manheim's German language footnotes in his translation. The inability to understand the text also caused many readers to dismiss the work as complex nonsense; however, the problem was in the past translations, not the original work.

When making a translation, the translator's own beliefs can color the choice of words. Does a certain passage about a group of people best translate as race, blood, people, nation, or ancestry? Does a passage mean force, or encourage? Some words have stronger connotations than others and the meaning of a passage can be easily influenced by the translator's choice. Any or all may be technically correct as well. Older translations used words like *"populist"* or *"folkish"* when the real meaning was *"ethnic"* or *"race"*. This made the true meaning unclear because confusing and vague words were used. The words populist/folkish are generic in English and the meaning depends on who uses them. In Hitler's case, they mean *"our people"*, *"our Teutonic people"*, *"our Aryan Germans"* or *"our race"*, so racial is more true to the intent. The Ford Translation uses the words *"race-based"* or *"racialist"* which are more accurate translations of the original German word *"völkisch"*. The word *"racist"* was not used because it has a negative modern connotation and that was not Hitler's intention. His use of the word was meant to identify someone who makes decisions based on race and studies race-based issues, and it was not intended to have any negative associations.

You can find more details about how words and phrases were translated to extract their true English meaning, plus learn more about Hitler's style in the eBook **Mein Kampf: A Translation Controversy.**

This ebook is *available for free at **www.HitlerLibrary.org***

This new Ford translation has been heavily researched and every line has been reviewed multiple times to verify it is as accurate and true to the original German meaning as possible, and it has been edited to make it as easy to understand as possible. No other translation of Mein Kampf *has ever been produced that is this thorough or this easy to understand.*

When everyone knows how the trick works, it is no longer magic.

– Michael Ford

And now we begin....

Adolf Hitler's FOREWORD

I began my sentence in the Fortress of Landsberg on the Lech, April 1, 1924 resulting from my sentence handed down from the Munich People's Court.

For the first time in my years of uninterrupted Party work, I was finally able to begin a job that many had asked me to complete and one which I myself felt was useful for the Movement. I decided to write two volumes which would not only explain the aims of our Movement, but also would reveal the birth of the Movement. I believe my story will be more beneficial than a simple historical description.

This work will allow me to describe my own growth in the Movement and assist in crushing the falsehoods about me created by the Jewish press.

My writing is not for strangers, but for those heart-strong supporters of the Movement, and those whose minds need enlightenment.

I know that men are more rarely won over by the written word than they are by the spoken word and that every great movement in this world owes its growth to great speakers, not to great writers.

Still, writing is necessary to create a unified doctrine we can distribute. I must lay down its principles for all time. These two volumes, then, are meant to serve as stones which I hereby add to the foundation of the Movement.

Adolf Hitler
The author
Landsberg on the Lech Prison Fortress

On November 9, 1923 at 12:30 P. M., the following men who believed in the resurrection of their people, fell in front of the Field Marshall's Hall in Munich (*Hitler dedicated the first volume to these men. They were the Nazi Party members who were shot and killed during the failed putsch [putsch means coup d'etat or government overthrow] of 1923 which resulted in Hitler's prison sentence*):

- *Alfarth, Felix, Salesman, born July 5, 1901*
- *Bauriedl, Andreas, Hatmaker, born May 4, 1879*
- *Casella, Theodor, Bank Official, born August 8, 1900*
- *Ehrlich, Wilhelm, Bank Official, born August 19, 1894*
- *Faust, Martin, Bank Official, born January 27, 1901*
- *Hechenberger, Ant., Locksmith, born September 28, 1902*
- *Korner, Oskar, Salesman, born January 4, 1875*
- *Kuhn, Karl, Headwaiter, born July 26, 1897*
- *Laforce, Karl, Engineering Student, born October 28, 1904*
- *Neubauer, Kurt, Servant, born March 27, 1899*
- *Pape, Claus von, Salesman, born August 16, 1904*
- *Pfordten, Theodor von der, Councilor of the Supreme Court(Munich), born May 14, 1873*
- *Rickmers, Joh., Cavalry Master a.D.(Retired), born May 7, 1881*
- *Scheubner-Richter, Max Erwin von, Doctor Engineering, born January 9, 1884*
- *Stransky, Lorenz Ritter von, Engineer, born March 14, 1899*
- *Wolf, Wilhelm, Salesman, born October 19, 1898*

The so-called national, constitutional authorities refused these dead heroes a proper burial ceremony.

Therefore, I dedicate to their common memory the first volume of this work, for their martyrdom shall shine forever on our Movement.

Landsberg on the Lech, Prison Fortress, October 16, 1924.

Adolf Hitler

MEIN KAMPF

VOLUME ONE: **An Accounting**

1. CHILDHOOD HOME

Today, I am pleased that Fate chose the city of Braunau on the Inn of northern Austria as my birthplace. This little town is on the frontier of the two German states whose reunion, at least for those of us from the younger generation, will be the accomplishment of a lifetime. We must do everything we can to reunite these states.

Austria must return to the great German mother country. Not for economic reasons. No, the economics are unimportant. Even if it did not make economic sense, it must still take place because common blood belongs in one common realm.

The German people have no moral right to setup remote colonies when they cannot even unite their own children in a common state. The people will only earn the right to acquire foreign soil when the Reich has expanded to include every German. The plow will become the sword, and the wheat which becomes the bread of posterity will be watered by the tears of war.

This little frontier city has now become the symbol of a great undertaking, but it also has a past that we should take as a warning today. More than a hundred years ago, this humble place had the privilege of being immortalized in German history as the scene of a tragedy which shook the whole German nation. It was the day of our Fatherland's deepest humiliation when the bookseller Johannes Palm, a citizen of Nuremberg, an unapologetic "Nationalist" and hater of France, died for the Germany which he loved passionately even in her time of misfortune. (*Johannes Philipp Palm was a book dealer in Nuremberg and in 1806 sold a pamphlet denouncing France titled* Germany's Deepest Humiliation, *but France previously invaded and was in control of Bavaria at that time. The Bavarian police chief turned him in. He refused to name the author and Napoleon ordered Palm to be shot at Braunau on the Inn, where Hitler was later born and where there is a monument to Palm.*)

Palm stubbornly refused to reveal the names of his fellows who believed as he did. He was very much like our Leo Schlageter (*Leo Schlageter fought in the First World War, joined the Nazi party in 1922, and committed acts of sabotage against the French occupation of the Ruhr, and was betrayed, tried and executed by the French. He was viewed as a hero in the Nazi party*). And, like Schlageter, Palm was betrayed to France by a government representative. An Augsburg police director was responsible, and this act laid down the framework that formed the modern disreputable official German government under the Reich of Mr. Severing. (*Carl Wilhelm Severing was a Social Democrat Official in the Weimar government controlling Germany at that time who refused to make an effort to stop the execution of Schlageter.*)

This little city on the Inn, which was made golden as a result of the German martyrdom I mentioned, was German-Bavarian by blood and Austrian only by borders. It is here my parents lived in the late Eighteen-eighties. My father, a conscientious employee of the state as a custom's official, and my mother, occupied with the household, were both, above all, devoted to us children with unwavering love and care. I do not remember much from that period. After only a few years, my father left the little frontier town he was so fond of so he could take a new post at Passau in Germany itself. In those days, Austrian Customs Officials traveled frequently. Soon afterward, my father went to Linz where he retired from work. This does not mean the old gentleman had a chance to rest.

His family could be called very poor farmers and, even in his earliest days, he had not lived in a happy home. Before he turned thirteen, the small boy packed his knapsack and ran away from his home in the mountainous section of lower Austria. Against the advice of villagers, he chose to go to Vienna and learn a trade. This was back in the Eighteen-fifties, so it was not a simple decision to travel into the unknown with only three crown coins. But by the time the thirteen-year-old turned seventeen, he had passed his journeyman's examination to be a cobbler, yet he had still not found contentment. To the contrary, the long period of economic problems back then, the unending misery and wretchedness he encountered only strengthened his determination to give up his trade and become something better. When he was a poor boy in the village, he thought that the church pastor embodied the highest possible summit of human aspiration. However, his experience in the big city replaced this notion with the dignified possibility of becoming a state official. With the endurance of a man who had grown old through grief and distress while still half a child, the seventeen-year-old mustered up his new determination and became a customs official. When he was almost twenty-three, I believe, he decided that he had achieved the goal he set so long ago. The poor boy had once taken a vow not to return to his native village until he had become somebody. He had reached his goal, but when he returned, no one in the village remembered the little boy of years earlier. As he looked around, he found the village had grown strange to him. It was no longer the village he remembered from childhood.

When he finally retired at fifty-six, he could not stand to live a single day as a do-nothing, so he bought property in the neighborhood of the Upper Austrian market town of Lambach, farmed it, and thus completed the circle of a long and hard-working life by returning to the point where his forefathers began.

I believe it was around this time that my first ideals were forming. My constant romping around outdoors, taking the long road to school, and my association with extremely rowdy boys sometimes gravely worried my mother. It also kept me from being a stay-at-home soul. So, the few serious ideas I had about my future certainly did not point toward my father's career. Even then, my gift for speaking was developing more or less through violent disputes with my playmates. I had somehow become a little ringleader among my group. I had no trouble learning and completing my lessons at school, but otherwise I was fairly hard to handle.

In my free time, I had singing lessons at the Catholic Monastery's Chapter in Lambach, and here I was dazzled by the dignified and magnificent church musical festivals. Just as my father had once looked upon the little village pastor, I now looked at the local religious leader as an ideal to aspire to. At least for a while this was the case. My father did not think very highly of his quarrelsome boy's vocal talents, and he did not see a future in the church for his offspring. He had no appreciation for such youthful ideas either. He must have watched anxiously as my nature clashed with my desires.

My desire for that calling soon disappeared and was replaced by hopes that were better suited to my temperament. In rummaging through my father's library, I found various military books. There was a popular edition of the Franco-Prussian War of 1870-71; two volumes of an illustrated magazine from those years now became my favorite reading. It was not long before the great heroic battle had become my greatest spiritual experience. From then on, I became more and more enthusiastic over anything connected with war or at least with being a soldier.

This was important to me for another reason. For the first time, I was forced to ask myself if there was a difference between the Germans who fought these battles and the Germans around me, and if they were different, how were they different? Why did Austria not fight in the war? Why did my father and all the others in our city not fight? Were we not like all the other Germans?

Did we not all belong together? This problem stirred in my young brain for the first time. I learned that not every German was fortunate enough to belong to the Empire of Bismarck. I could not understand this at the time, so I began my studies.

Based on my character and especially my temperament, my father decided that attending a classical secondary-school (*Gymnasium or high school attended from age 10 to 18 which teaches in Greek or Latin classics, but not vocational subjects*), would conflict with my personality. He thought a vocational school would be more suitable. His opinion was confirmed by my obvious ability to draw. That was a subject which he believed was neglected in the Austrian humanistic schools. Perhaps his own hard-working life made him think less of classical studies, which he considered impractical. Being a man of principle, he had already decided that his son should, no, <u>must</u>, become a state employee. His own difficult youth naturally made his later accomplishments seem even greater because they were the product of his own iron strength and ability. The pride of being a self-made man led him to want the same or better for his son. He believed his own hard work would make it easier for his child to succeed in the same field.

My outright refusal to follow a career that had been his whole life was, to him, quite inconceivable. So, my father's decision was simple, definite, and clear, and, in his eyes, he had an obvious course of action. His lifetime struggle for existence had made him domineering, and he would have never left an important decision to a boy he saw as inexperienced. This would have seemed an unforgivable weakness in the exercise of his parental authority over his child's future. It was impossible for him to reconcile it with his concept of duty. And yet, it was all destined to end differently.

At the time, I was barely eleven, and for the first time in my life, I was forced to oppose my father. Steadfast and determined as my father might be in carrying out the plans that were fixed in his mind, his son was no less stubborn and resistant in refusing this unappealing idea. I would not enter the civil service.

Neither pleading nor reasoning with me had an affect on my resistance. I would not be an official, "no" and again, "no". Every attempt to arouse my interest in that calling through descriptions of my father's experience had the opposite effect. I yawned myself sick at the thought of sitting in a government office, not being the master of my own life, but a slave devoting my entire existence to filling out various forms.

What affect could this possibly have on a young boy who was anything but "good" in the ordinary sense? I did my school work with ridiculous ease and had so much ree time left that I was outdoors more than in.

Today, when my political opponents scrutinize my life with such loving care—searching back even into my childhood for the satisfaction of uncovering some piece of deviltry this fellow Hitler was up to in his youth—I thank heaven for them giving me a few more memories of that happy time. Field and forest were the battleground where my constantly recurring differences in opinion were settled. Even the attendance at the secondary-school which followed did little to restrain me. But now another dispute had to be fought out.

So long as my father's intention to make me into an official clashed only with my general dislike of the career itself, the conflict was quite tolerable. I could withhold my private views and I did not have to make a constant issue of them. My own determination never to become an official was enough to give me an inner calm. I clung to this determination firmly.

The situation became more difficult when I developed a plan of my own that opposed my father. This happened when I was still only twelve. I cannot recall how it happened, but one day it was clear to me that I would be a painter, an artist. My talent for drawing had been clearly demonstrated, and in fact, it was one of my father's reasons for sending me to a secondary-school; however, he would never consider giving me professional art training. On the contrary, when I rejected my father's pet idea once again, he asked me for the first time what I myself wanted to be. Without thinking, my decision suddenly popped out. It was clear my choice had already been firmly planted and would not be changed, and for a moment my father was speechless.

"A painter? An artist?"

He doubted my sanity and then thought perhaps that he had not understood correctly. But when I explained it to him, and he saw I was serious, he was against it completely. Any talents I might have were simply beyond his consideration.

"An artist! Never, not so long as I live". But since his son had inherited, among various other qualities, a stubbornness like his own, my answer was equally stubborn. Both sides stuck to their guns. My father held to his "never", and I redoubled my "nevertheless".

The result was not pleasant. The old gentleman was embittered, and, though I loved him, I was equally bitter. My father forbade me even to hope that I would study painting. I went a step further and declared that in that case, I would not learn

51

anything more. Of course, I came in second with such a declaration since the old gentleman began to ruthlessly assert his authority. I then learned to keep silent in the future, but I did carry out my threat. I hoped that when my father saw my lack of progress in school, he would have to let me pursue the happiness I dreamed of

I do not know whether my calculation would have been correct or not; the only certainty was my obvious failure in school. Anything else I learned was something I thought I would use later as a painter. Whatever I thought was not connected to painting, or whatever failed to interest me, I sabotaged. My report cards from that point on were always in extremes. Next to "Good" and "Excellent" rankings were "Passing", and "Below Passing". By far, my best performances were in geography and particularly in world history. Those were my two favorite subjects.

When I look back now, so many years later, I see two facts that are especially significant. First, I became a nationalist. Second, I learned to understand the meaning of history.

Old Austria was a national state that consisted of many states. At that time, someone who was a subject of the German Reich could not grasp what this fact meant to their daily life. After the great march of triumph by the army of heroes in the Franco-Prussian War, the Germans of the Reich had gradually become separated from German elements elsewhere. They did not understand the value or they were no longer aware of the value in it. The German-Austrians were too easily confused and as a result, the Imperial dynasty decayed along with the otherwise sound and healthy people.

They did not understand that if the Germans had not been of the best blood, they would never have had the ability to impress their character on a state of fifty-two million Austrians. The mistaken idea took root, especially in Germany, that Austria was a German state. This was nonsense and the result had grave consequences, but it was still a brilliant tribute to the ten million Germans in the Ostmark (*The East-Mark or Eastern border lands*), Austria because their small presence was perceived as a total ownership by distant Germans. Very few in the German Reich realized there was a constant struggle to preserve the German language, German schools, and German character in Austria.

Today, this sad state of affairs has been forced upon millions of our people who dream of a common Fatherland while they sit under a foreign thumb and long to preserve the sacred mother tongue. Finally, people are beginning to realize what it means to fight for one's nationality. And now, perhaps, a few here and there can appreciate the greatness of the German population in Ostmark, which through its own resources, shielded the Reich on the east for centuries, then waged an exhausting guerrilla war to maintain the German language frontier in an age when the Reich cared for colonies, but not for its own flesh and blood.

As in any battle, there are three groups in the struggle for our language in old Austria: the fighters, the lukewarm, and the traitors. The sorting process begins in school. The most remarkable thing about a language battle is that its waves beat hardest upon the schools. The war is waged over the next generation, and the first war-cry is to the children: "German boy, do not forget that you are a German", and "German girl, remember that you are to be a German mother".

Anyone who understands the soul of youth will realize that young people will receive this battle-cry with joy. In a hundred ways they carry on the struggle in their own fashion and with their own weapons. They refuse to sing non-German songs; they are more enthusiastic over German heroes; the more they are suppressed, the more they go hungry in order to save pennies for the war-chest of their elders. They have an incredibly sensitive ear for a non-German teacher. They wear the forbidden badges of their own nation and are happy to be punished for it. In other words, they are a faithful image in miniature of their elders, except that their devotion is often stronger and more direct.

When I was small, I too shared in the struggle for German nationality in old Austria. Money was collected for the South Mark German League by school associations. We wore cornflowers and black-red-gold badges proclaiming our beliefs. (*Cornflowers were the symbol of Germans loyal to the Hohenzollern Monarchy and of Austrians who supported the Pan-German movement.*) "Heil" was our greeting, and instead of the Imperial anthem, we would sing the German anthem, "Germany Above All", (The Song of Germany, Deutschland über alles), despite threats of punishment. Young people were politically trained at a time when citizens of a so-called national state still knew very little about their own national character other than their language. I was not among the lukewarm even in those days. I was soon a fanatical German Nationalist. Of course, I do not refer to the present political party using that name.

My nationalistic development was very rapid. By the time I was fifteen, I could easily see the difference between the patriotism shown by those who followed rulers in the Imperial dynasty and the true "nationalism" for the nation and for the people. For me, only nationalism existed.

Anyone who has not bothered to study the Hapsburg Monarchy (*Austrian Royal Family*) may find this strong nationalism puzzling. In Austrian schools, there is very little actual Austrian history worth mentioning. The fate of Austria is so completely intertwined in the Germanic life that it is unthinkable to separate history into German and Austrian. When Germany finally split into two spheres of authority, this very separation was German history.

The insignia of former German Imperial splendor, displayed for all to see in Vienna, continued its spell as a reminder of our common and unending life together.

The cry of the German people in Austria for a reunion with their German mother country when the Hapsburg state collapsed resulted from a deep ache that slept in the people's hearts. They had never forgotten this longing to return to the home of their fathers. This can only be explained through the history taught to German-Austrians, which made those nationalistic feelings grow. Their history is a fountain that never runs dry—a silent reminder in times when it is easier to forget. Though we may be distracted by momentary prosperity, we hear the whispers of a new future by remembering the past.

It is true that the quality of World-History education in intermediate schools is in a sad state. Few teachers realize that to memorize and rattle off historical dates and events is not true history. It is not important for a boy to know exactly when some battle was fought, some general born, or when some insignificant monarch was crowned. No, God knows, that is certainly not what is important.

To truly "learn" history means to open your eyes and discover the forces that cause historical events to happen. The art of reading and of learning means remembering the important parts and forgetting the unimportant.

It is likely that my later life was influenced by the fact that I had a good history teacher. He had a unique ability to teach and test us on principles, not dates. My professor, Dr. Leopold Pötsch of the Linz school, was the very embodiment of this idea. He was an older gentleman. He was kind, but set in his manner. His brilliant eloquence not only fascinated us, but absolutely carried us away. I am still touched when I think of this gray-haired man, whose fiery descriptions often made us forget the present as he conjured us back into days long past, and how he could take dry, historical memories from the mists of centuries and transform them into living experiences. In his class we were often red-hot with enthusiasm, sometimes even moved to tears.

I was luckier than most because this teacher not only illuminated the past by the light of the present, but he taught me to draw conclusions for the present from the past. More than anyone else, he gave us an understanding of the current problems.

He used our national fanaticism to educate us. He would appeal to our sense of national honor, which brought us bad-mannered adolescents to order more quickly than anything else ever could.

This teacher made history my favorite subject. Even then, though he did not intend it, I became a young revolutionary. Indeed, who could possibly study German history under such a teacher without becoming an enemy of a State whose ruling house had such a catastrophic influence on the nation? Who could preserve his allegiance to the emperors of a dynasty that had betrayed the interests of the German people again and again for its own petty advantage? Did we not know, even as boys, that this Austrian state had no love for us as Germans, and indeed it could have none?

My historical insight into the work of the Austrian Hapsburg Monarchy was strengthened by my daily experience. In the north and in the south, foreign people came in and poisoned the body of our nation. Even Vienna became less and less a German city. The House of the Archdukes showed favoritism to the Czechs at every opportunity. It was the hand of the Goddess of Eternal Justice and Retribution that overthrew the deadliest enemy of Austria's German nature when She struck Archduke Francis Ferdinand by the very bullets he had helped to cast. After all, he was the patron who was charged to protect Austria from the northern Slavs.

The burdens laid upon the German people were enormous. They suffered unheard-of sacrifices in taxes and blood. Anyone who was not blind could see their sacrifice would be in vain. What hurt us most was the fact that these activities were shielded by the alliance with Germany. The gradual extermination of German qualities in the old Monarchy was to a certain extent sanctioned by Germany itself. The hypocrisy was evident when the Hapsburg Monarchy worked hard to give the outside world the impression that Austria was still a German state, and this only fanned hatred for that Monarchy into blazing anger and contempt within Austria.

In Germany, the elected members of the government failed to see any of this happening. It was like they were struck with blindness. They could have walked beside a corpse showing signs of decay and proclaim they had discovered signs of "new" life. In the alliance between the young German Empire and the Austrian sham state grew the seeds of the First World War and of the collapse.

Throughout this book, I will more thoroughly detail the problem of this alliance. It will be sufficient now to say that as a boy I arrived at an insight, which never left me, but only grew deeper. This insight was that the safety of German culture in Austria first required the destruction of Austria, and that feelings of nationalism have nothing to do with patriotism to an Imperial dynasty. The house of Hapsburg was destined to bring misery on the German nation.

Even then, this realization created a warm love for my German Austrian homeland and a profound hatred for the Austrian state. I never abandoned how I learned to think about history either. World history became my inexhaustible source for understanding how the present events, that is to say the political situation, came to be. I did not intend to "learn" from history; instead, history was to teach me. If I became a political revolutionary so quickly, then I also became a revolutionary in the arts equally fast.

The Upper Austrian capital had an excellent theater which put on nearly everything. When I was twelve, I saw the heroic William Tell play for the first time. A few months later, I saw my first opera, Lohengrin, (*a Wagner opera about knights*). I was totally captivated. My youthful enthusiasm for the master of Bayreuth (*meaning the composer, Wagner; Bayreuth is where he lived until he died*) knew no bounds. Again and again I was drawn to his works and it seems fortunate to me now that I could attend the smaller performances where I could get up close, and it actually intensified the experience.

Once my painful adolescent years were over, my deep aversion to the calling my father had chosen for me was even clearer. I knew that I could never be happy as a civil servant. My talent for drawing had been recognized at school, and my determination to be an artist was firmly fixed.

Neither prayers nor threats dissuaded me. I was going to be a painter and I would not be an official for anything in the world. It was curious that, as I grew older, I took an increasing interest in architecture too. At the time, I thought it complemented my painting ability and was pleased that my artistic interests had expanded. I never dreamed that it would all turn out quite differently. My calling was to be decided sooner than I could have expected.

When I was thirteen, I lost my father suddenly. A stroke took the vigorous old gentleman, painlessly terminating his earthly career, and plunging us all into the deepest grief. His deep desire to give his child a livelihood and spare his offspring from his own bitter struggle must have seemed unfulfilled. But he had sown the seeds for a future which neither he nor I could have understood then.

There was no outward change yet. My mother continued my education according to my father's wishes, intending that I prepare for a civil service position eventually, while I myself was more determined than ever to avoid becoming an official. I became less and less interested in school and grew more indifferent. Suddenly, an illness came to my assistance. Within a few weeks, my future and the subject which caused constant dispute at home was decided for us. I had serious lung trouble, and the doctor urgently advised my mother against putting me into a closed-office environment. My attendance at the secondary-school was also interrupted for at least a year. What I had secretly desired for so long, what I had always fought for had now, through this illness, become reality almost of its own choosing.

Pressured by my illness, my mother finally agreed to let me go to the Academy of Fine Arts in Vienna instead of the vocational secondary-school. The happy days I expected to follow seemed to me almost like a beautiful dream and a dream they were to remain. Two years later, my mother's death put a sudden end to all my fine plans.

She died at the end of a long, painful illness which had little room for hope of recovery. Even so, the blow to me was terrible. I had honored my father, but I had loved my mother.

I was forced by need and hard reality to make a quick decision. My father was a man of small means, and what he had saved was largely used up by my mother's grave illness. My orphan's pension was not nearly enough to live on. I was compelled to earn my own bread somehow. With a bag of clothes in my hand and an inextinguishable will in my heart, I set off for Vienna. What my father had accomplished fifty years before I hoped to also wrestle from fate. I, too, would be "something important", but never an official.

2. YEARS OF LEARNING AND SUFFERING IN VIENNA

When my mother died, Fate had already made its decision.

During the last months of her life, I went to Vienna to take the entrance examination for the Academy. Armed with a thick bundle of drawings, I was convinced I would find the examination mere child's play. In the secondary-school, I was by far the best draftsman in my class. Since that time, my ability had only improved. My own satisfaction in my ability led me to hope for the best.

There was one single fly in the ointment—my talent for painting was frequently exceeded by my ability as a draftsman, especially in architecture. My interest in architecture kept growing. My interest accelerated when I visited Vienna for a couple of weeks before I turned sixteen. I went to the art gallery of the Court Museum and found I had eyes almost solely for the museum itself. From early morning until late at night, I trotted from one sight to another, but only the buildings really held my attention. I could stand for hours looking at the Opera House and for hours admire the Parliament buildings. The Ringstrasse (*circular street in the old town section of Vienna*) section seemed like an enchantment from the stories out of a Thousand and One Nights.

I was now in the beautiful city for the second time. I waited for the results of my entrance exam as I was filled with excitement, impatience, and proud confidence. I was so certain of success that when I received a rejection, it struck me like a bolt from the blue. And yet, that was it, period. When I called on the head of the Academy and asked the reasons why I had not been admitted to the School of Painting, he assured me that my drawings showed I had no aptitude for painting and that my true ability was in the field of architecture. The School of Painting was out of the question, but the School of Architecture was for me, even though at first they found it difficult to believe that I had never attended an architectural school or had any instruction in architecture.

As I left Hansen's magnificent building on the square, I was at odds with myself for the first time in my young life. What I had just been told about my abilities was like a lightning flash illuminating an unexplainable confusion in me that had been growing for a long time. Within a few days, I knew I would be an architect someday.

I could see the path before me would be enormously difficult. Everything I had been too stubborn to learn in secondary-school was now taking its bitter revenge. Admission to the Vienna Academy School of Architecture required attendance of the Building School of Technology, and admission here was based on graduation and the final exams from an intermediate school. I did not have either. It seemed my dream of art was now impossible.

After the death of my mother, I returned to Vienna, this time to stay for some years. I once again regained my calm and determination. My earlier spirit of defiance had also returned and I was determined to reach my goal. I would be an architect. Obstacles exist to be overcome, and I would overcome those obstacles with the image of my father before my eyes. He fought his way from farm boy and shoemaker to state official, and my soil was richer than his, so my battle should be that much easier. What had then seemed to me to be the unkindness of Fate I accept as the wisdom of Providence. When the Goddess of Trouble embraced me and often threatened to crush me, the will to resist grew, and at last that will was victorious.

That period made me strong. I thank her for snatching me from the emptiness of a comfortable life and for pulling this mama's boy out of the comfortable, cozy bed. I was reluctantly thrown into the world of misery and poverty, which introduced me to those I would later fight for.

That is the point when I saw two dangers approaching. Previously, I did not truly understand their names or their importance to the German people's existence. Their names were Marxism and Jewry.

Vienna is widely considered the very essence of innocence and bliss as the festive home of happy crowds. It has turned into a constant reminder of the saddest period in my life. Even today, the city stirs only gloomy thoughts in me. Five years of misery and wretchedness are encapsulated in the name of this Phaeacian city (*Phaeacia is the final city visited by Homer in the Odyssey; however, it is also a common knowledge reference in Germany and something any German would recognize. The belief is that the people liked to enjoy life and the reference means a city of loafers or do-nothings, or parasites.*). For five years I had to earn my bread, and as a small painter, my bread was meager at best. It was never enough to satisfy my hunger. In those days, hunger was my faithful sidekick who never left me. When I bought a book, he shared it with me. A trip to the opera would give me his company for days. It was a never-ending battle with my unsympathetic friend. In those lean days, I learned faster than I had ever learned before. Besides my architecture and a rare ticket to the opera, books were my only remaining pleasure.

I read voraciously. I used any free time I found to study. After a few years, I was able to lay the foundations of a knowledge which I still live on today. At that time, I formed an image and a concept of the world which had become the rock solid foundation of my present political activity. Since that time, I needed only to learn a little beyond what I had already assembled because I found there was nothing in my image that required changing.

On the contrary, today I firmly believe that all creative ideas usually appear in youth if they exist at all. I must distinguish this from the wisdom of age, which is a thoroughness and caution forced by the experiences of a long life. This is different from the genius of youth who pours out unending thoughts and ideas while their great number prevents them from being developed. This youthful genius furnishes the foundation from which an older and wiser man can build stones into a structure. At least that is the case if the so-called wisdom of age does not choke the genius of youth.

My early home life differed little from the home life of others. I could watch for the next day without a care and without any problems to worry over. My youth was spent in lower middle class circles. That is to say, I was in a world that was not in contact with those who worked at pure physical labor. Strange as it may seem at first glance, economic differences between this level and that of ditch diggers is often deeper than one thinks. This antagonism comes from a social group which has just recently lifted itself from the ranks of physical labor and is afraid it could fall back, or at least be counted as one of them. There is often a repulsive memory of cultural poverty among this lower middle class, so any social contact with physical laborers, which they feel they have outgrown, becomes unbearable.

A man from the higher social levels can mix with worker classes in a way that would be thinkable to the relative newcomers of this lower middle class. A newcomer to a social class is anyone who fights his way by his own energy from one position in life to a higher one. But eventually, this bitter battle kills off human sympathy for the class he escaped. One's own painful struggle for existence destroys his feeling for the misery of those left behind.

In this respect, Fate took pity on me. By forcing me back into the world of poverty and insecurity, which my father had once abandoned, the blinders of a limited lower middle class education were removed from my eyes. Only then did I learn how to distinguish between a hollow or brutal man's exterior and his inner nature.

In the early years of this century, Vienna was among the most socially unhealthy of cities. It was a combination of glittering wealth and revolting poverty. In the center of the inner districts, one felt the heartbeat of an empire of fifty-two million people along with the dangerous magic of this State of mixed nationalities. The blinding magnificence of this cultural and government center was like a magnet to the wealth and intelligence of the State. On top of that came the extreme centralization of the Hapsburg Monarchy. It offered the only possibility of holding this stew of peoples together. The result was an extraordinary concentration of high government offices in the capital and around Imperial residence.

Vienna was not only the political and intellectual center, but also the economic capital of the old Danube Monarchy. In contrast with the army of high officers, officials, artists, and scholars were a larger army of workers who were against the wealth of the aristocracy and their practice of bleeding poverty for all they could.

The palaces of the Ringstrasse (*a circular street in Vienna*), became a waiting room for thousands of the unemployed, and below the arch of triumph of old Austria, the homeless lived in the twilight and slime of the sewers.

There was not one German city where the social situation could have been better studied than in Vienna. Do not be misled. This "studying" cannot be done from above. Someone who has not been in the clutches of this viper cannot truly know its venom. Studying from above results in superficial chatter or the formation of false opinions based on emotion. Both are harmful: one because it can never reach the heart of the problem; the other because it passes by the problem entirely. I do not know which is more devastating—to ignore those who lack the basic necessities such as we see in those who are favored by fortune or live well as a result of their own effort, or is it those who stand tall in their fashionable skirts or trousers and "feel for the people" because it is the latest fad. In any case, these people commit a sin greater than their limited intelligence will ever allow them to understand.

Then, they are astonished when their fashionable "social conscience", which they proudly display, never produces any results. When their fruitless good intentions are resented, they blame the ingratitude of the people. People with minds like this fail to understand that there is no place for merely social activities. When the masses want results, social displays are not enough and there can be no expectation of gratitude for such a show. It is not a matter of distributing favors, but of retribution and justice.

I did not learn about the social problem by observing from the outside. It drew me into its magic circle of suffering and instead of teaching me, it sought to test its strength on me, and it receives no credit if I survived its tests safe and sound. I could never completely relate my sensations from that time; I can only describe the essential and most staggering impressions here along with the lessons I learned.

I rarely had difficulty finding work. I was not a skilled worker but had to earn my bread as best I could, so I did so as a helper or day laborer. I had the attitude of the laborers of Europe who shake the dust from their feet with their determination to build a new life and a new home in the New World. (*The New World means the United States, which was receiving a large number of immigrants at the time.*) They are free from preconceived notions of occupation and social background, of status and tradition, and they grasp any means of support that is offered to them. They go to any job and gradually arrive at the realization that honest labor is no disgrace, no matter what kind of labor it may be. I, too, was determined to leap with both feet into a world that was new to me and to find my way through it.

I soon learned that someone always needs some kind of work, but I learned just as quickly how easy it is to lose that support again. The insecurity of one's daily bread soon became one of the darkest aspects of my new life. The skilled worker is turned out on the street less often than the unskilled, but even he can be pushed out the door. Instead of losing his job because he is not needed, he is locked out or he strikes.

This dependence reveals a weakness in the whole economic system. The peasant boy who is drawn to the big city by the promise of easier work and shorter hours is accustomed to a certain amount of security. He has never left one job without having another or at least the prospect of another lined up. As more boys are drawn to the city, the shortage of farm labor takes its toll and the chance of being unemployed increases. Now, it would be a mistake to think that the young fellow who goes to the big city is made of sterner stuff than the one who stays home and makes an honest living from the soil. No, quite the contrary. Experience shows that emigrant groups are more likely to be made up of the healthiest and most energetic individuals. And these emigrants include not only the man who goes to America, but also the young farm-hand who leaves his native village to move to the distant big city. He is just as prepared for an uncertain fate as the farm boy going to another country. Usually, he comes to town with a little change in his pocket to last him at least a day if he does not immediately find work. However, his situation will quickly worsen if he finds a job then loses that job at the wrong time. Finding a new job as a worker can be almost impossible in winter months. For the first few weeks, he receives unemployment benefits from his union and does his best to survive. But when his last penny is gone and the union benefits expire, he then finds himself in a difficult position.

He walks the street as his stomach growls, perhaps pawns or sells his last possessions. His clothes become fewer in number and worse in condition, which drags down his appearance. Soon he finds himself in surroundings that corrupt him not only physically, but spiritually. If he then becomes homeless in winter, his suffering becomes even more intense. Eventually, he is able to find some sort of work under a union, but then the game begins all over again. He is hit a second time with unemployment in the form of a strike, then the third time may be even worse. Gradually he learns to become indifferent to the constant insecurity of his finances. The cycle changes into a habit that he continues without further consideration.

We now have an otherwise hard-working man whose attitude toward life grows slack and gradually matures him into a tool of those unions who will merely use him to gain their own advantage. He has so frequently switched between working and non-working through no fault of his own that he no longer notices whether the

trike in which he takes part will secure him any economic rights or whether it is
an attempt to destroy the State, the whole social order, and even civilization itself.
He may not like the idea of going on strike, but he is completely indifferent when
he is handed strike papers.

have watched this process a thousand times with my own eyes. The longer I
saw the game continue, the more I disliked this city of millions. It greedily sucks
men in, then cruelly wears them to pieces. When men came to the city, they still
belonged to their nation. When they stayed, they were lost to it.

Life threw me around in the great city, too. I felt the full force of such a fate, body
and soul. I discovered something else as well—quickly switching between periods
of work and unemployment along with the seesawing of income and expenses
eventually destroyed many people's sense of thrift and intelligent planning. The
body becomes accustomed to living high in good times and starving in bad. They
no longer make any effort to plan sensibly in good times, for the bad times they
know will come. Indifference surrounds its victim with a mirage which makes them
see only well-fed prosperity, regardless of their true circumstances. This mirage
grows to such morbid intensity that they give up all self-control the moment wages
begin to flow into their pocket. That is why a man who has difficulty finding any
work stupidly forgets to plan for bad times when he does find work. He, instead,
lives greedily and indulges in the moment. His tiny weekly income is instantly
spent because he does not even plan for the remainder of the week. At first, his
wages last five days instead of seven, then only three, then scarcely a day, to be at
last squandered the first evening.

These men are not all living life by themselves. They likely have a wife and children
at home. Their family is also poisoned by this way of life, especially if the man
is naturally kind to them and even loves them in his way. Before the week's pay
has evaporated in two or three days, they eat and drink as long as the money holds
out. They then go through the remaining days together on empty stomachs. Then,
the wife slinks about the neighborhood, borrowing a bit here and there, opening
charge accounts with the shopkeepers, and trying thus to survive the terrible later
days of the week. At noon, they all sit at a table which does not contain enough
for everyone, if it contains anything at all. They sit, waiting for the next payday,
talking of it, making plans. While they starve, they are already lost in the mirage of
the good fortune which comes on payday.

The children, even in their youngest days, will come to see this wretched life of
empty fantasy as normal. The situation can become worse if the man lives like this
and the wife objects for the sake of their children. Then, there are quarrels and bad

blood, and the more the husband drifts apart from his wife, the nearer he drifts to alcohol. Every Saturday, he becomes drunk. Now, his wife must fight for the few pennies she can snatch from him in an effort of self-preservation for herself and the children. What she can get is only what is left over from his journey between the factory and the bar. When he finally comes home on Sunday or Monday night— drunk, brutal, and penniless—there are likely to be scenes that would wring tears from a stone.

I saw all this going on in hundreds of cases. At first, I was disgusted or outraged. I later came to realize the tragedy of this suffering and to understand its deeper causes. They were the unhappy victims of evil circumstances. The housing conditions of those days were worse. The housing situation of the Viennese laborer was absolutely frightful. I shudder now when I think of those wretched caverns some lived in, of the houses where journeymen of a common trade lived together, and mass dormitories which were sinister pictures of refuse, filled with disgusting filth and worse.

It was bound to happen. The flood of slaves set loose from these squalid caves pours down upon the rest of the world, upon its thoughtless fellow men! It is bound to happen again. This other world lets things drift without thinking about the consequences. It has lost its instinct to tell it that sooner or later, Fate will move toward retribution unless mankind placates destiny before time runs out.

I am indeed thankful to a Providence for sending me to that school of hard knocks in the city. There, I could not sabotage what I did not like. I had to quickly grow up. If I wanted to avoid falling into despair because of the people who surrounded me, I had to learn the distinctions between their outer character and inner life and the circumstances that created their lives.

Only through this understanding could I bear it all without giving up to despair. It was no longer human beings who rose before me out of unhappiness and misery, out of squalor and physical degradation, but the sad products of sad laws. At the same time, my own fight for life, which was no easier than theirs, preserved me from becoming emotionally involved with the products of this ill society and allowed me to remain objective. No, emotional sentimentality will not help understanding here. Even then I saw that only a two-fold path could lead to the improvement of such conditions.

I experienced a deep feeling of social responsibility to establish a better system for our development. I knew it would require brutal determination to destroy this human outgrowth which had no chance of being preserved and corrected. Nature does not focus on preserving what exists; nature concentrates on breeding a new generation to perpetuate the species. It is almost impossible for man to improve those bad things that exist in society, but it is much easier to create healthier paths from the start.

Even during my struggle for existence in Vienna, I realized the task of improving social elements could never be a frivolous welfare scheme. They are ridiculous and useless. Instead, we must overcome the fundamental weaknesses in the organization of our economic and cultural life. The holes in the system are bound to lead to the perversion of individuals, or at least they are capable of doing so.

Wavering judgment is the enemy that will halt our advance when we need to use the most brutal weapons against a criminal group that is hostile to the state. This uncertainty results from a feeling of personal guilt and responsibility for the tragic decline of society. Uncertainty cripples any serious and firm resolve and results in opinions swaying from one side to the other, leaving any decision that is made weak and half done, even when it comes to the most essential measures of self-preservation. Only when there comes an age not haunted by the shadow of its own guilt will there be both the inward calm and the outer strength, which can brutally and ruthlessly prune the dead limbs and uproot the weeds in our society's garden.

The Austrian state had no real social legislation or system for administration of justice at all. Its weakness in suppressing even the worst abuses was obvious to everyone. I do not know what horrified me more—the economic misery of my neighbors, their moral weakness, or the low state of their intellectual development.

How often does our social class rise up in righteous indignation when it hears some wretched tramp say he does not care whether he is a German or not? He says that he is equally happy anywhere so long as he has what he needs to live on! This lack of "national pride" should be deeply condemned and such statements should be loudly admonished. How many have really asked themselves why their own way of thinking is better? How many realize there are countless reminders of the grandeur of the fatherland in every field of culture and art? When these reminders are combined, those affected have a justified pride in belonging to such a fortunate people.

Pride in the fatherland is built on knowing about its greatness in all these fields. Have the members of our social class noticed that this knowledge, which is needed to instill pride for the fatherland, is not available to the people?

We cannot use the excuse that "it is the same in other countries" because the worker in other countries has no difficulty holding onto his nationality. Even if this were so, it would be no excuse for one's own shortcomings. The French people teach France's greatness in every department of culture, or as the Frenchman says, of "civilization", and we foolishly dismiss it as a fanatical glorification in their upbringing.

The young Frenchman is simply not trained to be <u>objective</u>, but instead he is given a <u>subjective</u> attitude of greatness anywhere the political or cultural aspect of his fatherland is concerned. This type of education has to be widespread and, if necessary, it must be pounded into the people's memories and feelings by perpetual repetition.

With us there is both the sin of omission and a destruction of what little we were lucky enough to learn in school. The rats infecting our political system gnaw even the tiny bit we have learned out of the hearts and memories of our people. Poverty and wretchedness have also done their share to crush these memories.

Here is an example: in a basement consisting of two stuffy rooms lives a laborer's family of seven. Among the five children is a boy of three years. This is the age when a child first becomes conscious of things around him. Gifted people carry memories of that period far into old age.

The small, overcrowded space produces an unfortunate situation. The conditions often generate quarrels and bickering. The people are not living <u>with</u> one another; they are merely living in the same place, squeezed together. Every small argument leads to a sickening quarrel. In a larger dwelling, the argument would be easily smoothed out simply by separation. The children may tolerate these conditions because children can quarrel constantly and forget the argument quickly. However, a daily battle between parents slowly teaches the children a lesson. The dispute may take the form of a father's brutality to a mother, of drunken maltreatment. Any person who does not know of this life can hardly imagine it. By the time the boy goes from three to six, he has developed a working idea of the world which must horrify even an adult. Now, he is morally infected and physically undernourished, and the young "citizen" is sent to primary school with vermin living in his poor little scalp.

Now, with great difficulty, he must learn reading and writing, and that is about all he can manage.

Studying at home is out of the question. Father and mother argue and use language that would not be socially appropriate right in front of their own children, making studying impossible. But when the parents talk to teachers and school officials, they are more inclined to talk roughly to them than to turn their young child over their knee and introduce him to reason. Nothing the little fellow hears at home strengthens his respect for his fellow human beings. They never utter a good word about humanity. No institution is safe from their profane attacks, from the school teacher to the head of the state. No matter whether it is religion or morals, state or society, everything is defamed and dragged in the muck. When the boy leaves school at the age of fourteen, it is hard to tell which is greater—his incredible stupidity where common knowledge and basic skills are concerned, or his biting disrespect and bad manners. The immoral displays, even at that age, make one's hair stand on end.

He holds almost nothing sacred. He has never met true greatness, but he has experienced the abyss of everyday life. What position can he possibly occupy in the world which he is about to enter? The three-year-old child has become a fifteen-year-old who despises all authority. Aside from filth and uncleanliness, he has yet to find anything which might stir him to any high enthusiasm.

As he begins the more demanding parts of his life, he falls into the ruts he has learned from his father. He wanders about, comes home Heaven knows when, beats the tattered creature who was once his mother, curses God and the world, and finally he is sentenced to a prison for juvenile delinquents. Here, he gets his final polish.

His fellow-citizens are astonished at his lack of national enthusiasm. They see theater and movies, trashy literature, and yellow press day-by-day pouring out poison. Then, they are surprised at the low morality and the national indifference of the people. They do not realize movie trash, cheap journalism and the like would never produce the skills needed to recognize the greatness of the Fatherland!

I finally realized something I had never even dreamed of before. The ability to "nationalize" a people is primarily a question of creating healthy social conditions that can be used to educate the individual. Only when upbringing and school training have taught a man the political greatness of his own Fatherland will he achieve an inner pride that comes from belonging to such a great people. You can fight only for something you love. You can love only what you respect. You can respect only what you know.

When my interest in social problems was aroused, I began to study it thoroughly. A world that had been so strange to me before suddenly began to open up.

In 1909 and 1910, I no longer needed to earn my daily bread as a laborer. I started working independently as a draftsman and watercolor artist. This line of work was difficult financially; there was barely enough earnings to keep body and soul together. However, it was great in that it was closer to my chosen profession. I was no longer dead tired when I came home from work in the evening, unable to even look at a book without dozing off. My new work paralleled my future profession. As master of my own time, I could now plan it better than before. I painted to earn a living and learned for pleasure.

I was also able to round out my understanding of the social problem by building a necessary understanding of the theoretical background. I studied pretty much every book on the subject I could get my hands on and plunged myself in my own thoughts. My acquaintances must have thought I was more than a little eccentric.

I passionately pursued my love of architecture. Along with music, I thought architecture was the queen of the arts. It was not "work" to spend time on it, but the height of happiness. I could read or draw late into the night and it never made me tired. My faith was strengthened by the dream of a future that would become a reality after all. Even though it took years, I was firmly convinced that I would make my name as an architect.

The fact that I also took great interest in anything having to do with politics did not seem especially significant. On the contrary, I felt that was the duty of all thinking people. Anyone who did not actively learn about politics lost all rights to criticize or complain. In this area, I continued to read and learned a lot.

My definition of "reading" may be different from the average person's definition. I know people who "read" all the time— book after book, word for word—but I would not call them well-read. They do have a mass of knowledge, but their brain does not know how to divide it up and catalog the material they have read. They cannot separate a book and identify what is valuable and what is worthless for them. They retain some in their mind forever, but cannot see or understand the other parts at all.

Reading is not an end in itself, but a means to an end. In the first place, it should help to fulfill an individual's personal framework and give each person the tools and materials a man needs in his job or profession, whether it is for daily necessity, simple physical fulfillment, or higher destiny. In the second place, reading should give a man a general picture of the world.

In either case, what is read shouldn't simply be stored in the memory like a list of facts and figures. The facts, like bits of a mosaic tile, should come together as a general image of the world, helping to shape this world image in the reader's head. Otherwise, there will be a confusion of information learned, and the worthless mix of facts gives the unhappy possessor an undeserved high opinion of himself. He seriously believes he is "cultured and learned" while thinking he has some understanding of life and is knowledgeable simply because he has a stack of books by his bed. Actually, every piece of new information takes him further away from the real world, until often he ends up either in a psychiatric hospital or as a "politician" in government.

No man with this kind of mind can ever retrieve from his jumbled "knowledge" what is appropriate when he needs it. His intellect is not filled with his own life experiences, but is filled with what he has read in books and in whatever order the content happened to land in his head. If Fate reminded him to correctly use what he has learned in his daily life, it would also have to cite volume and page or the poor guy could never find what he needed. But since Fate does not do this, these "knowledgeable" men are embarrassed when it really counts. They search their minds frantically for appropriate comparisons and usually end up with the wrong idea. If this were not the case, then it would be impossible to understand the political achievements of our learned government heroes in high places unless we decided they are mischievous and not mentally disturbed.

A person who has mastered the art of <u>proper and true</u> reading can read any book, magazine, or pamphlet and immediately spot everything he believes he needs to remember, either because it fits his purpose or because it is generally worth knowing. What he has learned then takes its proper place in his imagination concerning the matter at hand. It can then either correct or complete that image to increase its correctness or clarity in his mind. If life suddenly presents some question that requires examination or a solution, the memory stored through this reading method will instantly recall the already imagined picture as a standard and will bring out individual bits of information on the subject which have been retained through decades, and that will be the basis for the intelligence used to clarify or answer the question. Only then is there sense and purpose in reading.

A speaker who does not study the materials to back up the issues he deals with will never be able to fight effectively for his opinion when challenged, even if it is absolutely true. In every discussion, his memory will fail him as he stammers to find someone else's words to repeat. He cannot connect to the reasoning he needs to enforce what he says or argue with his opponent. When the result is just a matter of personal ridicule, as with a speaker, this may not be fatal, but it becomes serious if Fate places one of these incompetent know-it-alls in a high position such as a head of state. Then it is serious indeed.

Even at a very young age, I was careful to read "properly", and this skill has helped me tremendously by improving my memory and understanding. In this light, my time in Vienna in particular was fruitful and valuable. The experiences of daily life stimulated me to constantly study. Being in a position to support reality with theory and to test theory by reality, I was prevented from either suffocating in theories or growing superficial in how I judged reality.

My experiences in daily life guided and encouraged me to make a thorough, theoretical study of two vital questions aside from the social problem. Who knows if I would have ever become absorbed in the doctrines and character of Marxism if my life had not simply rubbed my nose in it!

In my youth, I knew almost nothing about Social Democracy and what I did know was wrong. I thought it was a good thing that the Social Democrats were fighting for the right of all men to vote by secret ballot. Even then my mind told me this had to weaken the hated Hapsburg regime. I was also convinced the Austrian state could never be maintained unless it sacrificed the German element living in Austria. Even at the cost of slowly converting the German element to Slavs, there was no guarantee the empire would survive since their ability to preserve a Slavic society is highly doubtful.

Therefore, I was excited about any development which I thought would lead to the collapse of this unstable state that has condemned to death the Germanism of ten million people. The more the language uproar gnawed at the parliament, the closer the hour of collapse approached for this Babylonian Empire, and the closer the freedom of my German-Austrian people came near. (*Babylonian Empire is a reference to the Tower of Babel story where the people were cursed to speak different languages and scattered around the world.*) This was the only way that a return to the old mother country could someday happen.

The activities of the Social Democrats did not seem unattractive to me at the time. I thought it was also a good thing that they were trying to improve the living conditions of the working man. At that time, I was still innocent and stupid enough to believe this could happen. What did repel me was their hostile attitude toward the fight for the preservation of Germanism and their pitiful wooing of the Slavic "comrades" who were willing to accept this courtship and make concessions. Otherwise, they maintained an arrogance and conceit, which gave these insistent beggars their just reward.

At the age of seventeen, I had become somewhat acquainted with the word Marxism and I thought Socialism and Social Democracy were identical ideas. Again, the hand of Fate opened my eyes to this unprecedented fraud on the people.

So far, I had encountered the Social Democratic Party only as a spectator at a few mass demonstrations without gaining any insight into the mind-set of its supporters or the nature of its doctrine. Now, at one moment, I met face-to-face with the results of its training and who supported its "World-Concept". In the course of a few months, I learned something that otherwise may have taken years—an understanding of a disease masquerading as social virtue and the love of one's neighbor—a disease which humanity must free the earth from or the earth would soon be freed of humanity. My first encounter with Social Democrats was on a construction job.

It was not a good situation from the very beginning. My clothes were still in good shape, my language was cultivated, and my manner reserved. I had so much to do in dealing with my own Fate that I couldn't trouble myself with the world around me. I was looking for work only to avoid starving and so that I could educate myself no matter how long it took. I might not have paid any attention to my new surroundings if an event on the third or fourth day had not compelled me to immediately adopt a new attitude. I was asked to join the organized union.

My knowledge of the trade-union organization at that time was zero. I could not have proved whether or not it was in any way useful. When I was told I must join, I refused. My grounds for refusal were that I did not understand the situation, and I would not be forced to do anything. Maybe this was the reason they did not throw me out immediately. They may have hoped they could convert me or wear me down within a few days. In either case, they were very mistaken. Within a couple of weeks, I had reached the end of my rope. During that time, I gained a better understanding of my surroundings and no power in the world could have forced me to join an organization whose members acted the way they did.

The first few days I was further annoyed. At noon, some of the men went to nearby bars, while others stayed on the lot and ate their pitiful lunch. These were the married men whose wives brought them their soup in heavily-worn bowls. As the week progressed, their numbers grew. I figured out the reason later. When they finished their soup, they would talk politics.

I drank my bottle of milk and ate my piece of bread somewhere out of the way as I cautiously studied my new surroundings or considered my misfortune. Still, I heard more than enough and it seemed that people crept up beside me deliberately, hoping to force me to make my beliefs clear. In any case, what I heard irritated me to the extreme. They were against everything—the nation—because they thought it was an invention of the "capitalistic" classes. I heard that constantly! They were against the Fatherland, as a tool of the privileged-class to exploit the workers;

the authority of law, as a way to oppress the working class; the schools, as an institution to train slaves and slave-owners; religion, as a means of stupefying the people so they could be exploited; morals, as a symbol of stupid, sheep-like patience; etc. There was nothing they didn't drag through the mud.

At first, I tried to stay quiet, but finally I could no longer hold my tongue. I began to express my beliefs and contradict them. Then, I realized this was useless until I knew more about the points under dispute, so I began to go to the same sources where they drew their supposed wisdom. Book after book, pamphlet after pamphlet, I read them all in their turn.

There were often heated arguments on the building lot. I went on struggling, growing more informed than my adversaries were every day, until one day the ultimate method was used that vanquishes reason—terrorism and violence. Some of the opposition spokesmen forced me either to leave the job at once by choice or to fly off the scaffolding on my head. As I was alone and resistance seemed hopeless, I preferred to follow the former advice, richer by one experience.

I left filled with disgust, but at the same time so agitated that it would have been impossible for me to turn my back on the whole affair. No! After the spark of the first indignation, my stiff neck once more got the upper hand. I was absolutely determined to find another construction job just the same. My decision was strengthened by the fact that I had eaten up what little earnings I had saved in just a few weeks. I had no choice but to find work. And so the game began all over again, only to end the same way it had before.

I struggled with all of this. I had to ask, were these human beings worthy of belonging to a great people? It was a painful question. If the answer were "yes", the struggle for a national body was really not worth the effort and sacrifice that the best individuals must make; but if the answer were "no", our people were a poor lot as human beings. I was restless and uneasy during those days of brooding and wondering as I saw the mass of non-nationalistic people grow into a menacing crowd.

With new stronger feelings, I watched the endless rows of Vienna workmen marching in a mass demonstration one day. For almost two hours, I stood breathless, observing the enormous human serpent twisting its way past me. At last, depressed and uneasy, I left the square and walked home. On the way, in a tobacco shop, I saw the Workers' Times, the official socialist newspaper of the old Austrian Social Democratic Party. It was also available at a cheap café where I often went to read the papers, but I had never succeeded in bringing myself to read the trash for more than two minutes at a time. Its whole tone affected me like intellectual poison. Now, under the depressing effect of the day's demonstration, an inner voice pushed me to buy a copy and read it thoroughly, and so I did that evening, fighting down frequent rage at this concentrated essence of lies.

By reading the Social Democratic press daily, I could study the inner nature of its train of thought better than from any theoretical literature. What a difference there was between the glittering phrases in the theoretical writings about freedom, beauty and dignity, and these words in the paper created an illusion of profound wisdom with some difficulty due to the disgusting moral tone, all written with a brazen claim of prophecy. The brutal daily press of this doctrine claimed to be the salvation of a new humanity, but was full of vileness, using every kind of slander, and absolutely full of lies! The theory is intended for stupid dupes of the middle and upper "levels of intelligence"; the more vile and base sections were targeted at the masses.

To me, dwelling on the literature and press of this doctrine and organization meant finding my way back to my own people. What once seemed an impassable gulf now created in me a love greater than ever before. Only a fool, once he knows about this enormous work of corruption, could still condemn the victims. The more independent I became in the next few years, the more my insight grew into the inner causes of Social Democratic success. Now, I understood the meaning of the brutal demand that only Red newspapers be subscribed to, only Red meetings be attended, only Red books be studied, etc. With sparkling clarity, I saw right in front of me the inevitable result of this doctrine of intolerance.

The soul of the great masses of people is receptive to nothing weak or half-way. Like a woman—whose spiritual perceptions are attracted more by the strength of a leader than the reason of a follower—the masses love the ruler more than the follower and they find more inner satisfaction in a doctrine that tolerates nothing that it, itself, has not granted approval and freedom. The masses are seldom able to make much use of such freedom and are likely to feel neglected if given too much. They are as unconscious of the shamelessness that intellectually terrorizes them as they are of the outrageous mistreatment of their human liberty. After all, they have no clue about the doctrine's internal error. They only see the ruthless strength and brutality of its expression, which they always yield to.

If Social Democracy opposes a more truthful, but equally brutal theory, the new theory will win, even if it requires a battle first. In less than two years, I had developed a clear understanding of both the doctrine and the technical methods the Social Democrats used to propagate it.

I realized the infamous intellectual terrorism of this movement targets the privileged-class, which is neither morally nor spiritually a match for such attacks. They tell a barrage of lies and slander against the individual adversary it considers most dangerous and keep it up until the nerves of the group being attacked give in and they sacrifice the hated figure just to have peace and quiet again. But the fools still do not get peace and quiet. The game begins again and is repeated until fear of the villain becomes a hypnotic paralysis.

Since the Social Democrats know very well the value of power from their own experience, their storming is directed mainly at those whose character has this same quality. Conversely, they praise every weakling on the other side, cautiously, then loudly, according to the intellectual qualities they see or suspect. They fear an impotent, weak-willed genius less than they fear a forceful nature with only modest intellect. Their highest recommendation goes to weaklings in both mind and nature.

They are successful in creating the impression that giving-in is the only way to win peace and quiet from them while they quietly, cautiously, but unerringly, conquer one position after another, either by quiet extortion or by actual theft when the public attention is on other things. The public is distracted and either unwilling to be interrupted or they consider the situation too small to worry about and believe it is not worth provoking the angry foe again.

These are tactics planned by exact calculation to exploit every human weakness, and it is almost mathematically sure to be successful unless the other side can learn to fight poison gas with poison gas. To those who are weak in nature, it can only be said that this is a simple question of survival or non-survival.

To me, the significance of physical terrorism toward the individual and toward the masses was plain to see. Terrorism on the job, in the factory, in the meeting hall, and at mass demonstrations, will always be successful unless equal terrorism opposes it.

When the socialist party encounters opposition, it screams bloody murder and yells for help from the state, only to get what they want in the end. That is to say, it finds some idiot of a high official who hopes to befriend the Marxists and is willing to crush the current adversary of the socialist party to gain the party's favor.

The followers' and rebels' success can be understood only by a man who knows the soul of a people, not from books, but from life. While its supporters regard it as a triumph of right for their cause, the beaten opponent usually feels future resistance is pointless. The better I understood the methods of physical terrorism in particular, the more I was able to forgive the hundreds of thousands who had given in to it. This realization is something I am most profoundly grateful for during that period of suffering. It gave me back my people and I learned to distinguish the victims from the deceivers.

The result of this seduction of mankind can only be described as victimization. If in some pictures of life I have drawn the character of these "lowest" humans, that picture would not be complete without my assurance that in these depths I found light in the form of extraordinary self-sacrifice, faithful comradeship, contentment in adversity, and complete modesty, especially among the older workmen. Even though these virtues were gradually disappearing in the younger generation through the influence of the big city, there were still many whose good, healthy blood overpowered the vileness of life. If, in politics, these kind, honest people failed to join together and fill the ranks instead of our people's deadly enemies, it was because they couldn't and didn't understand the vileness of the new doctrine and because nobody else bothered to give them any attention, and, finally, because social conditions were stronger than any rebellion. Sooner or later, the impoverished were bound to be the victims and they would be driven into the Social Democrats' camp.

Many times, the privileged-class in a clumsy and immoral manner, formed a united front to oppose worker demands that were justifiable and based in fundamental humanity, and, they did this without offering any excuse, without any reason. Therefore, even the most decent of workmen was driven from the trade-union organizations into political activity.

Millions of workers were inwardly hostile to the Social Democratic Party at first, but their resistance was overcome by the often pointless and insane way in which the privileged-class parties opposed any social demands. The inflexible refusal of reasonable demands such as to improve working conditions, simple safety devices on machines, prevention of child labor, protection for women—at least during the months of pregnancy—this all helped to drive the masses into the nets of Social Democracy, which gratefully latched on to every case of similar contemptible sentiments. Our politicians, our privileged-class, can never rectify these past sins. By resisting all attempts to cure social ills, it sowed hatred and apparently justified the claim that the Social Democratic Party alone represented the interests of the working people. Above all, the privileged-class furnished the moral excuse for the existence of the unions, which have always been the greatest suppliers for the socialist political party.

During my Vienna apprentice years, I was forced to adopt some beliefs, whether I wanted to or not, regarding the union question. As I considered them an inseparable part of the Social Democratic Party, my decision was swift and wrong. I rejected them without hesitation. In this infinitely important question, Fate itself instructed me and, eventually, I had to overturn my rash judgment. At twenty, I had learned to distinguish between the union as a means to defend the employee's general social rights and to win better living conditions, and the union as a tool of the socialist party promoting the political class struggle.

The Social Democrats realized the enormous importance of the trade-union movement and that assured them a position of power. Because the privileged-class failed to understand this importance, it lost its political position. The privileged-class thought they could sweep aside a logical argument by a bold denial, and through political force, push the issue down and make it look like an unreasonable path. It is nonsense and a lie to say any union movement is in itself hostile to the Fatherland. The opposite is nearer the truth. If union activity envisions and attains the goal of improving the position of a class that belongs to the pillars of the nation, its effect is not hostile to state or Fatherland, but is "national" in the truest sense of the word. It is helping to lay the social groundwork necessary to maintain the nation. Without this groundwork, no education is thinkable. The trade-union movement gains the highest credit for destroying social cancers by attacking both intellectual and physical toxins, and thus contributing to the general health of the body of the nation.

To question whether or not a union is a necessity is really pointless. It is obvious they are necessary. As long as there are employers with little social understanding or even with a faulty sense of justice and an inability to see what is appropriate, it is not merely the right, but the duty of their employees to protect the public interest against the greed or unreasonable acts of individuals. The preservation of honor and faith in a nation is a national interest just as much as the preservation of the people's health. The nation's faith and public health are seriously threatened by unworthy business operators who do not feel themselves to be members of the people's community. The evil effects of their greed or ruthlessness cause serious harm for the future of the nation and the people.

To remove the causes of these problems is a service to the nation. No one can say that every individual is free to walk away from any supposed injustice. No! Such claims must be regarded as an attempt to divert attention from the facts. Correcting bad or antisocial elements is either in the nation's interest or it is not. If correction is in the interest of the nation, we must make war upon the problems with weapons which offer some promise of success. The individual worker is never in a position to defend himself against the strength of a large enterprise. Therefore, this can never be a question of victory for the cause of right versus wrong because the justice of the cause can be determined by the one in the position of power. If the decision were based on how just the claim was, people's sense of justice alone would end the dispute honorably and amicably, and then things would never even reach the point of a dispute.

If poor treatment drives people to resist, then the struggle can only be decided by superior strength if legal and judicial machinery are not created to resolve these issues. An unjust enterprise can only be opposed by a group of employees united into a single person if there is to be any hope of victory. The organizing of a union may lead to stronger social ties in daily life, and then to the removal of problems which continue to produce dissatisfaction and complaints. The existing state of dissatisfaction can be blamed on those who have managed to obstruct all attempts at legal regulation by using their political influence.

The Social Democrats dug their fingers so deeply into the labor movement that the political privileged-class failed to understand, or did not want to understand, the importance of union organization and actively opposed it. In the process of their opposition, they lost sight of their real purpose and began fighting for different objectives.

The Social Democrats had no intention of allowing the union movement to continue its original goal. No, that was not what they had in mind. Within a few decades, their trained hands had turned a method of defending human social rights into an instrument for destroying the national economy. The interests of the workers had no place in their plans. Even in politics, the use of economic pressure is a strong extortion tool as long as one side has little or no conscience, and the other side is sufficiently stupid and has sheep-like patience. Presently, both requirements are fulfilled.

Even by the turn of the century, the labor union movement no longer served its original purpose. From year to year it was drawn more and more into the sphere of Social Democratic politics, until finally it served only as a battering-ram in the class struggle. The Social Democrats assumed that continual blows would make the whole economic structure tumble, then the state—deprived of its economic foundations—would suffer the same fate. The representation of the working people's real interests played less and less a part in the Social Democratic agenda. Eventually, political concerns made relieving the social and cultural problems of the workers undesirable. If the workers were not distressed and were fully satisfied, and their will was no longer fueled by resentment, there would have been a danger that they could no longer be used as an army.

Intuitively sensing this development, the leaders of the class struggle fell into such a panic that eventually they simply refused to bring about any beneficial social improvement and actually took a decided stand against any improvements for the workers. There was no need to be embarrassed by such seemingly incomprehensible behavior. They could avoid it by constantly increasing their demands on businesses, which made the rejection of any proposed improvement appear as if the business was engaged in a diabolical attempt to cripple the workers' most sacred rights. Considering the minimum thinking power of the masses, the Social Democratic success is not surprising.

The privileged-class camp was outraged at these obviously deceptive Social Democratic tactics, but they still based their actions on the statements made by the Social Democrats. The Social Democrats' fear of raising the working class from its abyss of cultural and social misery should have led their opponents to make supreme efforts to improve the workers' lives. This would have gradually twisted the weapons from the hands of the socialist leaders of the class struggle. But this did not happen.

Instead of attacking and capturing the enemy position of the high moral ground themselves, they preferred to be squeezed and shoved. Finally in their negotiation battles with the unions, they relented and gave in to changes that, no matter how far reaching, were insufficient for the socialists. The Social Democrats easily rejected the changes because it was too little too late. Everything remained the same except now there was more dissatisfaction than ever among both the workers and the business owners.

Even then, the "free trade-union" already hung like a menacing storm cloud on the political horizon and loomed over the existence of everyone. It was one of the worst terrorist instruments against the security and independence of the national economy, against the unity of the state, and against the freedom of individuals. This turned the idea of democracy into a ridiculous and disgusting cliché. It was an outrage against freedom and forever mocked the idea of brotherhood as demonstrated in the saying, "If you will not be a comrade too, it means a broken skull for you".

This is how I came to understand mankind. Through the years, my views broadened and deepened but there was no need to change my way of thinking. The more I understood the outer nature of Social Democracy, the more I longed to understand the inner core of the doctrine. The official party literature was not very useful here. It is incorrect in both details and in the proof it offers for economic questions. It is also untruthful in its discussion of political aims. Besides, I was especially repelled by the dishonest and unethical manner in which it was presented. Sentences are written using a lot of vague words with unintelligible meanings that are as clever as they are senseless. Only those unconventional types rotting among us could possibly feel at home in this intellectual maze. They scrape some "spiritual experience" from this artsy literary manure, and the message is assisted by the humility of our people who think something is deep and wise just because they don't understand it.

I gradually built a clear picture of its inner intent by balancing the theoretical untruth and nonsense of this doctrine with its actual outward appearance. When I began to understand, fear and horror crept over me. I saw a teaching compounded by ego and hatred, which according to mathematical law could very well lead to victory, but would then lead to the end of humanity as well. During this time, I learned about the connection between this doctrine of destruction and the nature of a people. Up until now, this was unknown to me.

A knowledge of the Jews is the necessary key to grasping the real intentions of Social Democracy. If a person knows these people, the mask of delusion hiding their aims and the meaning of the party falls from his eyes, and the ape-like face of Marxism grins at him. As it speaks, a fog of social talk flows from the ugly smirk on his face.

Today, I still find it difficult, if not impossible, to remember when the word "Jew" first developed a special meaning for me. I do not remember ever hearing the word mentioned at home during my father's lifetime. I think the old gentleman would have considered it uncultured or antiquated to emphasize the designation at all. In the course of his life, he developed a mixed bag of views, which had survived in me along with my extreme nationalist sentiments and colored my feelings.

At school, there was nothing to change the ideas I received at home. I did meet a Jewish boy in secondary-school whom we all treated with caution, but only because experience had taught us to mistrust him due to his quietness. None of us thought much about this.

I didn't encounter the word "Jew" very often, not until I was fourteen or fifteen, and then primarily in connection with political talks. I felt a slight aversion to it and could not help but have an unpleasant feeling when I became involved in religious arguments. But at that time, I did not see any other significance.

The city of Linz only had a few Jews. In the course of centuries, they had become outwardly Europeanized and looked human. In fact, I even thought they were

Germans. I did not realize the nonsense behind this notion because I believed their only distinguishing mark was a strange religion. Persecution for their religion and hostile comments against them often brought my objection in return. I had no idea that organized hostility against the Jews even existed.

Then I came to Vienna. I was fascinated by the architecture and preoccupied with my own fate. At first I was not concerned with the classes of people in the large city. Although there were already nearly two hundred thousand Jews among the two million people of Vienna, I did not see them. My eyes and mind could not grasp all the values and ideas in the first few weeks. Only when I began to settle in did I begin to look more closely at my new world and see the busy scene more clearly. That's when I encountered the Jewish question.

I cannot say that the way I encountered it was particularly agreeable. At first, I only saw the religious aspect of the Jew and for reasons of human tolerance, I maintained my opposition to religious attacks. The tone of the anti-Semitic press in Vienna seemed unworthy of the cultural tradition of a great people. I was bothered by the memory of certain happenings in the Middle Ages which I did not want to see repeated. (*All through the Middle Ages, Jews were blamed for any bad occurrence and killed by the thousands at a time. Some cities blamed them for the Black Death plague. Some areas exiled them or forced them into ghettos, others required them to wear yellow cloth armbands or buttons, and they were restricted from certain fields of work, all throughout the Middle Ages.*) Since the newspapers in question were not generally considered among the most outstanding quality, I thought they were the product of angry envy rather than the result of a principle, even if it was wrong.

My belief was strengthened by what I considered the infinitely more dignified and commendable way in which the truly great newspapers answered those attacks. They did not even mention them, but responded with silence. Eagerly I read the world press, the "New Free Press" (*a Vienna newspaper*); the Vienna Daily Newspaper (*Wiener Tagblatt*), etc., and I was astonished at how much they offered the reader and at their objectivity. I also admired their dignified tone. Occasionally, I did not like their pretentious style, but I thought it might be more acceptable in the bustle of the cosmopolitan city.

Since I considered Vienna such a city, I thought this amateur explanation might be a sufficient excuse. But the way these newspapers played up stories in the Royal Court's favor did repel me more than once. There was rarely an event at the Hofburg Imperial Palace (*the palace of the Hapsburg Dynasty in Vienna, Austria*), which was not told to the reader in tones of enraptured ecstasy or grief-stricken sorrow. When an event dealt with the "wisest Monarch" of all times, it read almost like a mating dance between lovers.

The whole thing seemed so fake. I thought that such a policy was a stain on the ideal of liberal democracy. The way they would crawl for the Court's approval and betray the dignity of the nation. This was the first bad feeling I developed about the press.

As always, I followed every event in Germany with burning concentration, whether political or cultural. With proud admiration I compared the rise of the Reich with the sickness and decline of the Austrian state. Happenings outside Austria were mostly a source of pure pleasure; the less agreeable events at home often brought worry and gloom. I did not approve of the fight then being carried on against William II (*the German Emperor and King of Prussia until the Revolution*). I saw him not only as the German Emperor, but primarily as the creator of a German Navy. I was extraordinarily annoyed when the German parliament forbade the Emperor to speak in Parliament. The prohibition came from a people who had no reason to object considering the fact that these parliamentary geese chattered more nonsense in a single session than a whole dynasty of emperors could produce in centuries.

I was outraged that the heir of the Imperial crown could receive "reprimands" from the shallowest chattering-institution in a state where every half-wit claimed the right to criticize and might even be turned loose on the nation as a "lawgiver". But, I was even more angered when the Vienna press, which bowed to the lowest member of the Royal Court hoping for some attention, now expressed doubts about the German Emperor. Their apparent concern seemed more like malice in my opinion. They quickly claimed they had no intention of meddling in the affairs of the German Emperor, heaven forbid, but they pretended that by touching a delicate spot in such a friendly way they were fulfilling a duty resulting from the mutual alliance between the two countries, and at the same time, discharging their obligations of journalistic truthfulness. Then the finger pushed into the sore spot and dug ruthlessly into the wound.

Cases like this made the blood rush to my head. This was what gradually made me regard the great press with more caution. I did have to admit that one of the anti-Semitic papers, *The German People's Paper* (*Das deutsche Volksblatt*), was honorable on occasion.

Another thing that bothered my nerves was the revolting cult of France which the big papers were then propagating. It was enough to make a person ashamed of being a German. We were constantly bombarded with praises to the "great civilized nation". More than once, this wretched spell of French-captivation made me lay down one of the "world papers". In fact, I began to turn to *The German People's Paper* more often, which was much smaller, but cleaner in such matters. I disliked the sharp anti-Semitic tone, but I did occasionally read arguments which gave me something to think about.

Such stories eventually educated me about the man and the movement which then governed Vienna's destiny—Dr. Karl Lueger and the Christian Socialist Party. (*Karl Lueger was a member of the Christian Socialist Party which was an anti-Semitic party. He was also the mayor of Vienna in 1897-1910, which made him mayor until Hitler was almost 21 years old.*)

When I came to Vienna, I was hostile to both. In my eyes, the man and the movement were opposed to political and social change. However, a sense of common justice forced me to change my opinion gradually as I learned about the man and his work. Eventually, my opinion grew into admiration. Today, more than ever, I consider the man the greatest German mayor of all times. But, how many of my preconceived views were upset by this change in attitude toward the Christian Socialist movement?!

My opinions on anti-Semitism also slowly changed with the passing of time, and this was the most difficult change I ever went through. It was the most difficult of all my spiritual struggles. Only after battling for months between understanding and feelings did the voice of reason finally win. Two years later, feelings followed understanding, and from then on, understanding was the most faithful watchman and guardian I could have had with me.

During my bitter struggle between emotional ties to what I learned as a child and cold reason, the streets of Vienna offered me priceless first-hand lessons. The time had come when I no longer walked blindly through the vast city as I did at first. I kept my eyes open and looked at people as well as buildings.

Once, as I was strolling through the inner city, I suddenly met a figure in a long caftan with black curls. "Is that a Jew?" was my first thought. Jews did not look like that in Linz. I covertly observed the man, but the longer I stared at that alien face, scrutinizing feature after feature, my question changed from, "Is that a Jew?" to "Is that a German?"

As always, I tried to resolve my doubts through books. For a few coins, I bought the first anti-Semitic pamphlets I had ever purchased in my life. Unfortunately, they were all based on the theory that the reader grasped or at least was familiar in principle with the Jewish question. Their tone made me feel new doubts because of the often shallow and unscientific proofs they offered.

I would relapse to my former way of thinking for weeks, sometimes months. The matter seemed so monstrous and the accusations so unrestrained that I feared it might be unjust for me to decide one way rather than another, and again I became timid and uncertain.

Even I could no longer doubt that this was a question about a people in itself and not about Germans of a particular religious persuasion. Since I had begun to occupy myself with the question and to pay attention to the Jew, Vienna had appeared to me in a new light. Wherever I went now, I saw Jews and the more I saw, the more clearly my eye distinguished them from other people. The inner City and the Districts north of the Danube Canal were especially filled with people who didn't look anything like Germans. If I continued to have doubts, my indecision was ended by the attitude of the Jews themselves. A great movement among many of them, especially in Vienna, sharply emphasized the special character of Jewry as a separate people: Zionism.

Only some of the Jews approved of this movement, and while the great majority condemned and even rejected the very idea, the appearance of the movement melted away in an evil fog of excuses, I could even say lies. So-called liberal Jewry rejected the Zionists as Jews who were impractical and, perhaps dangerous in their public adherence to Judaism. It made no difference; they were all still Jews. There was no real separation and they maintained their internal solidarity.

This fictitious conflict between the Zionists and the Liberal Jews soon disgusted me. It was false through and through and contradicted to the moral dignity and pure character their race had always prided itself upon.

Morality and purity of character were terms that had their own meaning among these people anyway. It was obvious from their unclean appearance that they were not water-lovers. I am sorry to say that this was very clear, even with my eyes closed. I was frequently nauseated by the smell of these caftan-wearers. In addition, their clothes were dirty and they generally looked poor.

All this was unattractive enough by itself, but one was positively repelled when they realized uncleanliness went beyond personal filth and into the moral mud-stains of these people. My greatest concern was the activities of the Jews in certain fields of life. I slowly penetrated this mystery. Was there any shady undertaking, any form of foulness, especially in cultural life, in which at least one Jew did not participate? If you carefully punctured this abscess with a knife, like a maggot in a rotten body who was blinded by the sudden influx of light, you would discover a Kike (*ein Jüdlein*).

I saw a great burden of guilt fall upon Jewry when I came to understand how it controlled the press, the influence in art, in literature, and in the theater. All their slimy declarations now meant little or nothing. It was enough to look at one of the billboard pillars and study the names credited for the awful movie or theatrical presentations in order to be firmly convinced of the Jewish problem.

Here they were, infecting the people with a pestilence—an intellectual pestilence worse than the Black Death of ancient days. This poison was produced and distributed in massive quantities too! Naturally, the more immoral these artists and producers are, the more they grow. Such a fellow flings his garbage in the face of humanity like a windmill. Do not forget their unlimited number. For every one German writer like Goethe, nature plants at least ten thousand of these slimy creatures in the pelt of humanity where they poison the people with their disease. It was a dreadful but inescapable fact that the Jew seemed specially chosen by nature in tremendous numbers for this horrible destiny. Are we supposed to assume that this is the way he is "chosen"?

At that time, I began to carefully examine the names of all the producers of these unclean products in the world of art, and this scrutiny only damaged my attitude toward the Jews more. Though my feelings were outrage times a thousand, I must surrender to my reason and let it draw the conclusions. It was true that nine-tenths of all the literary filth, artistic trash, and theatrical nonsense must be attributed to a people constituting scarcely one one-hundredth of the country's population. It was a plain fact.

I now began to scrutinize even my beloved newspapers from the world press. The deeper I probed, the more my previous admiration shrank. The style grew more intolerable. I objected to the content as flat and shallow. The objectivity was transformed into more of a lie than honest truth—of course the authors were Jews. A thousand things which I had once barely noticed now struck me as remarkably obvious, while others, which had merely given me something to think about, I began to grasp and understand.

I now could see the liberal sentiments of this press in a new light. The dignified tone in replying to attacks, as well as the silent responses, now revealed a trick as shrewd as it was low. Their enraptured theatrical criticisms always favored a

Jewish author, while their disapproval never fell on anyone except a German. The constant and quiet sneering at William II revealed they had a deliberate plan. Their advocacy of French culture and civilization also played into their schemes. The trashy content of the short stories now became an indecency and I heard sounds of an alien people in the language. The general sense was so clearly harmful to everything German that it could only be intentional. But who had an interest in this? Was it all mere chance? Gradually I became unsure.

My development was accelerated by the insights I gained into a series of other matters. This was the general display of manners and morals openly shown by most of Jewry.

The street again offered some truly ugly object lessons. The relationship of Jewry to prostitution and, even more, to white slavery itself could be studied in Vienna more so than in probably any other Western European city, with the possible exception of southern French seaport towns. If a person walked the streets and alleys of Leopoldstadt (Leopold Town) in the evening, all along the way you could see things which remained hidden from the great majority of the German people. (*Leopoldstadt is a district in Vienna separated from the main city by the Danube waterways. The area was heavily Jewish and considered a ghetto.*) These things remained secret until the First World War gave the soldiers on the Eastern front an opportunity, or rather forced them to see similar happenings.

It sent a chill down my spine when I first realized the Jew was the manager of this immoral trade among the scum of the city. He was icy calm and shamelessly businesslike which made me fuming angry. Now, I no longer evaded discussing the Jewish question. Now I wanted to discuss it. I had seen the Jew in every area of cultural and artistic life, then I suddenly encountered him in another spot where I would have least expected to see him, and I recognized the Jew as the leader of Social Democracy, the Marxists, and that is when the blinders fell from my eyes. Suddenly, a long, spiritual struggle came to an end.

I was astonished how easily my fellow workmen changed their minds over a question. Often their opinion changed within a few days, sometimes even within a few hours they turned around. I could hardly understand how people who individually held reasonable views could suddenly lose them the moment they came under the spell of the masses. It was enough to drive a person crazy. I would argue for hours and finally believe I had broken the ice or cleared up some piece of nonsense they had in their heads. I would feel pride in my success and then the next day, I would be stressed to find out I had to begin all over again. It had all been for nothing. Their crazy opinions seemed to always swing like a pendulum.

I could understand how they felt. They were dissatisfied with their place in life. They cursed Fate, which often dealt them such hard knocks; they hated the businessmen, who seemed to be the heartless tools of Fate, and criticized government offices, which in their eyes had no sympathy for the workers' situation. They demonstrated against food prices and marched through the streets in support of their demands. All this I could understand, but what I could not understand was the boundless hatred they felt for their own nation—the way they despised its grandeur, the way they defiled its history, and the way they dragged great men in the gutter.

This struggle against their own kind, their own nest, their own homeland, was as senseless as it was incomprehensible. It was unnatural. They could temporarily be cured of this vice, but only for days or for weeks at the most. Later, if one met a supposed convert, he may have fallen back into his old self against his fellow men. His unnatural tendencies would again have him in their grip.

I gradually came to realize that the Social Democratic press consisted mostly of Jews, but I attached no particular importance to this situation. Circumstances were the same at the other newspapers. One thing was remarkable to me; there was not one paper where Jews worked that I would have considered a proud national voice that was in line with my concept of national pride.

I forced myself to at least make an attempt at reading this Marxist journalism, but the more I did, the more I disliked it. I now tried to get closer to the manufacturers of these mischievous words. From the editor on down, they were all Jews. I picked up every Social Democratic pamphlet I could and looked up the author's name. Jews. I noticed the names of almost all the leaders. Most of them were also members of the "chosen people", the Jews, whether they were representatives in the government or secretaries of the unions, chairmen of organizations, or street agitators. The same uncanny picture was continually repeated. I will never forget the names of Austerlitz, David, Adler, Ellenbogen, and others.

One thing was plain to me now. The leadership of the party whose petty representatives I had to fight my most violent battles with for months consisted almost exclusively of an alien people. I then had the happy satisfaction of knowing for certain that the Jew was no German. Now, for the first time, I became thoroughly familiar with the corrupter of our people.

Living one year in Vienna had been enough to convince me that no worker is too inflexible to yield to greater knowledge and superior enlightenment. I had gradually become an authority on their own doctrine, which I used as a weapon in the battle for my convictions. Success was almost always on my side.

The great mass of people could be saved, even if it was only by the greatest sacrifice of time and patience. But no Jew could ever be freed from his opinion.

In those days, I was still childish enough that I would try to explain the madness of their doctrines to them. In my own little circle, I talked until my tongue was sore and my throat was hoarse and thought I must succeed in convincing them how destructive their Marxist madness was, but the very opposite was the result. Growing insight into the destructive effect of Social Democratic theories only increased these people's determination.

The more disputes I had with them, the better acquainted I became with their arguing techniques. First, they would count on the stupidity of their adversaries, and then, if there was no way out, they pretended to be stupid themselves. If all else failed, they claimed they did not understand, or, being challenged, they would instantly jump to another subject and talk about obvious truths. If these were agreed on, they immediately applied them to entirely different matters. When they were caught off guard, they would avoid the conversation and claim they had no knowledge or understanding of the issue. No matter where you seized one of these apostles, your hand grasped slimy ooze, which spurted through your fingers, only to unite again the next moment. If your argument really gave a man a shattering defeat in front of others, he could do nothing but agree. You might suppose that this was one step forward, but how surprised you would be the following day!

The next morning you will find that Jew has not even the slightest memory of yesterday and continues to repeat his old mischievous nonsense as if nothing at all had happened. When pressed about the previous conversation, he would pretend astonishment and could remember nothing at all except the truth of his statements, which he felt had been proven the day before.

Frequently I was simply paralyzed. It was hard to know what to admire the most: their fluency or their artistry in lying. Gradually, I began to hate them.

There was one good result in all of this. My love for my own people was bound to grow just as fast as the expansion of Social Democracy. After all, considering the diabolical skillfulness of these seducers, who could possibly condemn their poor victims? It was unbelievably difficult for me to master and overcome the contradictory lies of this race! Any success with people who twisted the truth was immediately turned around. They would make a statement one moment to counter your argument, then the next moment use the same reasons they just tried to discredit in order to prove their own point! No. The better I became acquainted with the Jew, the more I could forgive the worker.

In my opinion, those to blame were not the workers. The blame fell squarely on those who did not think it worthwhile to sympathize with their own kinsfolk. With those who would not give to the hard-working son of the national family what was his by the iron logic of justice. The blame fell on the same seducer and corrupter who should be placed against the wall.

Stimulated by the experience of daily life, I now began to search for the sources of the Marxist doctrine itself now that I had come to understand its effect in detail. Every day, its success caught someone's attention, and with a little imagination I could see where the results were leading us. The only question remaining was whether the founders had foreseen the results of their creation in its final form or whether they were victims of error. I felt that both answers were possible.

On one hand, it was the duty of every thinking person to force his way into the front ranks of the cursed movement and try to prevent it from going to extremes. On the other hand, the actual creators of this national disease must have been true devils. Only in the brain of a monster—not a human being—could an organization's plan take shape that would eventually result in the collapse of human civilization and the desolation of the world.

If this were the case, the last hope was battle. A battle by every weapon which the human mind, understanding, and will could grasp, no matter who Fate blessed.

I began to familiarize myself with the founders of this doctrine in order to study the foundations of the movement. I was able to obtain results sooner than I had even dared to hope because of my new, if not yet profound, knowledge of the Jewish question. That alone allowed me to compare its realities with the theoretical shuffling by the founding apostles of this Social Democracy movement. It had taught me to understand the language of the Jewish people, who speak to conceal, or at least veil, their thoughts. Their real purpose is often not in the writing itself, but sleeping snugly between the lines.

This was a time when my spirit experienced the greatest upheaval it has ever endured. I turned away from a weak set of political notions and into a fanatical anti-Semite.

Once more and for the last time, restless, uneasy, and oppressive thoughts came to me in my extreme anxiety.

I had researched the work of the Jewish people during long periods of human history, and suddenly I was struck by the alarming question of whether the mysteries of Fate had irrevocably determined that the final victory was not the destiny of our little people for reasons unknown to we puny humans. The Jews are a people which live for this earth alone. Could they have been promised the earth as their reward? Do we have an objective right to fight for self-preservation or is this just an illusion?

I buried myself in the teachings of Marxism and gave calm, clear consideration to the work of the Jewish people. Fate itself gave me my answer.

The Jewish doctrine of Marxism denies the noble goal of Nature and sets mass and dead weight of numbers in place of the eternal privilege of strength and power. It denies the value of personality in man, disputes the significance of nation and race, and deprives mankind of the essentials of its survival and civilization. As a foundation of the universe, Marxism would be the end of any order conceivable to man. The result of applying such a law could only be chaos. Destruction would be the only result for the inhabitants of this planet. If, through his Marxist faith, the Jew conquers the peoples of this world, his crown will be the death and destruction of all mankind. Earth would again move uninhabited through space as it did millions of years ago. (*Hitler originally said thousands of years ago in the very first edition, but it was changed in the second printing. Although, it could be considered correct either way because he was talking about humanity.*)

Eternal Nature takes revenge for violation of her commandments. I believe I am acting today in the spirit of the Almighty Creator. By standing guard against the Jew, I am defending the work of the Lord.

3. GENERAL POLITICAL CONSIDERATIONS OF MY VIENNA PERIOD

Generally, a man should not be active in public politics under the age of thirty unless he is of extraordinary talent. The reason is obviously that before that age, he has been building a general platform from which he can examine the various political problems and build his own beliefs. Only after he has established a fundamental World-Concept and has stabilized his own way of looking at the individual questions of the day, should the man who is at least achieved an inner maturity be allowed to guide the community politically.

Otherwise, he is in danger of either changing his previous positions on fundamental questions once he realizes he was wrong or clinging to a view which he no longer supports or may even be against. This will make it politically difficult for his followers to maintain their faith in him. Their old unshakable solid belief will be upset because he now appears to be undecided himself. To followers, such an about-face of their leader, means complete confusion in addition to their feeling of shame in front of those they have previously attacked over the issue. The second alternative brings about a result which is particularly common today. The leader continues to publicly claim he believes in what he had previously said. He then becomes more hollow and superficial and eventually becomes more corrupt. He no longer dreams of working seriously for his political ideals; no one dies for something he does not himself believe in, and his demands upon his followers grow greater and more shameless to compensate for his own insincerity until at last he sacrifices his remaining fragment of leadership and begins to play the political game for the sake of politics alone.

He has joined that class of people whose only real conviction is absence of conviction coupled with a bold and shamelessly well-developed skill at lying.

Unfortunately for decent people, if such a fellow moves into big government, the essence of his politics is limited to a heroic battle for permanent possession of his position to maintain his political life for himself and his family. The more his wife and children cling to him, the more stubbornly he will fight for his seat. If only for this reason, he is the personal enemy of every other man with political instincts. In every new political movement he senses the possible beginning of his end. In every greater man he senses a danger which may threaten him. I will have more to say about this sort of Parliament (bed)bug later.

Even a man who is thirty years old will have much to learn in his life, but what he learns will merely fill out and complete the picture which his fundamental World-Concept presents to him. His learning will be more than a mere re-learning of principles. It will mean learning more, understanding better. His followers will not have to choke down the uneasy feeling that up to this time he has misled them on some matter. On the contrary, the visible organic growth of the leader will give them satisfaction since his learning seems to be the deepening of their own doctrine. In their eyes, this is an argument that proves the truth of their views.

A leader who has to abandon the platform of his World-Concept because he realizes it is mistaken is honorable if he admits his view was faulty and is ready to correct his conclusions. He must then give up any further public political activity as well. Since he has already fallen victim to error once in building his fundamentals, the possibility of a second lapse is always present. He has no right to ask for, let alone demand, the confidence of his fellow citizens.

We can judge from the general moral corruption of the group who feel called upon to be politicians that such ideas of honor are not practiced today. Many feel called, but rarely is one truly chosen.

I believe I was more concerned about politics than many others, but I avoided making any public appearances. Only in very small groups did I talk about what inwardly moved or attracted me. This kind of intimate talking helped me a lot. I did not learn much about "speaking", but I came to know people through their primitive views and objections. In doing so, I trained myself and wasted no opportunity to further my education. There was nowhere in Germany that could have provided such a favorable opportunity as I found in Vienna, Austria at that time.

Judging by its extent, general political thinking in the old Danube Monarchy (*the Hapsburg Monarchy of Austria*) was larger and more inclusive than in the old Germany of that period, except in parts of Prussia, Hamburg, and the coast of the North Sea. The Austrian part of the great Hapsburg Empire was settled by Germans and was in every respect the cause of that state's creation. The population alone had the strength to support cultural life for centuries, yet was still politically artificial. The more time passed, the more the existence and future of that state came to depend on the preservation of this German seed of the Empire.

If the old Monarchs were the heart of the Empire—forever sending fresh blood into the circulation of state and cultural life—then Vienna was the brain and strength of the nation. On the outside, this city looked like it had the strength to rule as the queen over a huge group of people. Her splendid beauty caused the deadly signs of mental deterioration to be forgotten.

No matter how the interior of the Empire was shaken by the bloody turmoil between individual nationalities, the world outside, and Germany in particular, saw only the charming image of this city. The illusion was easier to accept because the Vienna of this time seemed to be taking its last and greatest visible rise. Under the rule of a mayor who was a true genius, the inspiring Residence of the Kaisers of the old Empire rose up to a wonderful new life. The last great German born to the colonist people of the Ostmark was not officially included as a "statesmen", but as Mayor of the "Capital City and Imperial Residence" of Vienna; Dr. Lueger, made magic with his achievements in every field, whether it was community, economic, or cultural policy. He strengthened the heart of the entire Empire and as Mayor, he became a greater statesman than all the so-called "diplomats" of the time put together.

The fact that the collection of races called "Austria" went to its doom in no way discredits the political ability of Germans in the old Eastern territories. That was the impossible and inevitable result of trying to maintain a State with fifty million people of various nationalities for any length of time without definite principles being established.

The German-Austrian had always been accustomed to living within the framework of a great Empire and had never lost his feeling for the work this involved. He was the only one who could see beyond his own front yard all the way to the frontier of the Empire. When Fate moved him from the Fatherland, he still tried to preserve for Germany what his fathers had once squeezed out from the East through battle. We must not forget that this is what happens even when a man is separated from his country. The best men's hearts and memories never ceased to feel for the common mother country and always reserved a fragment for the homeland.

Even the general outlook of the German-Austrian was broader than others. Frequently, his economic connections embraced almost the entire Empire. Almost all the really great enterprises were in his hands. He was the source for most of the personnel used for management, technicians, and officials. He conducted the foreign trade because Jewry had not yet laid their hands on this special domain. Politically, he alone held the State together. Even his military service took him far beyond the narrow limits of his homeland. The German-Austrian recruit might join a German regiment, but the regiment was just as likely to be stationed in Herzegovina as in Vienna or Galicia. The officers were still Germans and so were the higher ranking civil servants.

Finally, art and science were also German. Aside from the trash that has come out recently, which could have been made by any negro tribe, the Germans alone possessed the true inspiration for art. In music, architecture, sculpture, and painting

Vienna was the primary source of this artistic wealth which supplied the whole Dual Monarchy and never seemed to run out. (*The Dual Monarchy was the Austrio-Hungarian Monarchy which was the union forming the Hapsburg Monarchy.*)

Germans were the pillar of all foreign policy with the exception of a small body of Hungarians. Nevertheless, every attempt to preserve the Empire was useless since the most essential requirement for its preservation was missing. For Austria there was only one possible way of overcoming the scattering of the individual states. The states had to be centrally governed—an organized internal government—or it would fail.

When the Highest officials were temporarily thinking clearly, they realized this truth, but it was quickly forgotten or set aside because they believed it would be too difficult to accomplish. Thoughts of a more united version of the Empire were bound to go wrong because there was no strong state instigator, no one with dominant authority. The internal status of the Austrian state was very different from that of the German Empire as Bismarck shaped it. In Germany, it was only a question of overcoming political traditions since a common cultural basis was always there. Germany was primarily made up of only one group of people aside from small alien fragments. In Austria, the situation was reversed.

Except for Hungary, the individual countries had no political memory of their own grandeur, and among the people, that memory had been eliminated. Now, nationality and racial forces began to develop again, which was increasingly difficult to overcome as national states began to form along the edge of the Monarchy. The people of these states, racially related or similar to the individual fragments within Austria, now began to exert a stronger attraction than the German-Austrian could. Even Vienna could not hold out for long in this conflict.

When Budapest had grown large enough to rival Vienna, their mission was not to hold together the distant parts of the Empire, but rather to strengthen one part. Within a short time Prague followed the example of Budapest, and later on came Lemberg, Laibach and others. These places were raised from small provincial towns to national cities which created rallying centers for an independent culture. Through this, the local national instincts acquired a spiritual foundation and gained a more profound hold on the people. The time was sure to come when the interests of each country would become stronger than their common imperial interests. Once that stage had been reached, Austria's doom was sealed and the Empire would fall apart.

These developments after the death of Joseph II were plain to see. (*Joseph II was co-regent or co-ruler with his mother, Maria Theresa, for much of his reign. He is known for his efforts to unify the Kingdom, but his diplomatic skills were poor. When his brother, Leopold II, succeeded him, he tried to restore relations by giving concessions to those Joseph II had alienated.*) The rapid growth of these areas depended on a series of factors that included the Monarchy itself and the Empire's position in foreign politics. If the battle to preserve the state was to be fought to the finish, only a central government as ruthless as it was persistent could possibly succeed. In that case, it was necessary to establish a uniform state language that would emphasize the unity of the people and furnish the government with a technical tool necessary to maintain a unified state. Only then could a consistent state awareness be created through the schools. This could not happen in ten or twenty years, it was something that would take centuries; however, in all questions of developing a country, a large goal is more important than momentary efforts.

Both administration and political leadership must be conducted with rigid unity. I learned a lot when I discovered why this was not done and why this did not happen. The person guilty of this omission was the one who was completely responsible for the collapse of the Empire.

More than any other state, Old Austria depended on the greatness of its leadership. The cornerstone of a national state was missing. The basis of a national state is the people and they still have the power to sustain it no matter how bad the leadership is. Thanks to the natural activity of its inhabitants and the power of resistance that results from that independence, a unified national state can often survive the worst administration or leadership without being destroyed. A body like this often seems to have no life at all, as if it were dead and gone, then suddenly what appeared to be a corpse rises up and gives mankind astonishing signs of its indestructible life force.

However, this is not true of an empire composed of different people who are living under a common strong arm of leadership and not connected by common blood. In this situation, governing weakness does not lead to the hibernation of the state, but to an awakening of all the individual instincts which are present in the blood of the various groups. Even if they are unable to grow under the influence of a single dominant will, the individual elements will still rise. Only centuries of common education, common tradition, and common interest can reduce that danger. This is why the younger a state structure is, the more they depend on the greatness of their leadership. In fact, the work of strong, outstanding figures and intellectual heroes often collapses immediately after the death of the great, lonely founder.

Even after centuries, however, these dangers cannot be considered defeated. They are sleeping and often will suddenly awake the moment weakness in a common leadership is felt. The force of education and the grandeur of tradition are no longer strong enough to overcome the native life force in the various races.

It is the House of Hapsburg's fault that this was not understood. Fate gave one of them the opportunity to change the future of his country, but that flame of hope was extinguished forever. In a state of panic, Joseph II, Roman Emperor of the German Nation, saw how his leadership was being driven to the outside edge of the Empire. It was eventually going to disappear in the whirlwind of a corrupt people unless everything that his fathers had failed to do was fixed at the last minute. The "Friend of Mankind", Joseph II, decided he would use superhuman strength and try to correct in a decade the centuries of neglect by his forefathers. If he had been given just forty years for his task, and if only two generations had continued the work he had begun, the miracle would probably have succeeded. But, he died after ruling barely ten years. He was worn out in body and soul and his work followed him to the grave, to sleep forever, without reawakening. His successors had neither the intelligence nor the will to get the job done.

When the first sparks of a new age began to flash through Europe, the revolution set Austria on fire. When things started really rolling, those flames were fanned more by the people than economic, social, or even general political causes.

The Revolution of 1848 (*The European Revolutions of 1848 were known in some countries as the Spring of Nations, Springtime of the Peoples or the Year of Revolution. This wave of revolution caused political upheaval throughout the European continent.*) was a class struggle everywhere else, but in Austria, it was the beginning of a new war between nationalities. At that time, the German man forgot or didn't realize his origin and sealed his own fate by entering the service of the revolutionary uprising. He helped to stir up the spirit of Western Democracy that soon deprived him of the foundation for his own existence. Without first deciding on a common state language, the formation of a parliamentary representative body had laid the foundation for the end of German supremacy in the Monarchy. From that day on the state was lost. Everything that happened after that was the historical liquidation of an Empire.

Watching the Empire dissolve was as moving as it was instructive. The execution of a historical sentence took place in a thousand different ways. The fact that most people walked blindly through the resulting decay only proved that it was God's will to destroy Austria. I do not want to get lost in details; that is not my purpose. I only want to provide information about those processes which still have importance for us today and which helped to establish my political way of thinking, like the unchanging causes of the decay in the people and the state.

The institutions that most clearly demonstrated the decay inside the Austrian

Monarchy was the Parliament or Reichsrat as it was called in Austria, which should have been the strongest institution. This was obvious even to the half-blind, privileged-class Philistine.

The model for this group was obviously in England, the land of classical "Democracy". That excellent parliamentary structure was transferred almost directly to Austria with as little alteration as possible. In the House of Deputies and the House of Lords, the English two-chambers of government were resurrected. Only the "Houses" themselves were somewhat different. When Barry built his palaces, or, as we say the Houses of Parliament, on the shore of the Thames, he could take the inspiration for his work from the history of the British Empire. (*Barry was Sir Charles Barry, an English architect who, after a fire, rebuilt the Palace of Westminster which is the English Parliament building in London.*) In that history he found sufficient material to fill and decorate the magnificent corridors. His statues and paintings made the House of Lords and the House of Commons temples dedicated to the glory of the nation.

Here was Vienna's first problem. When Hansen, the Danish architect, (*Theophilus Hansen was a master of the Historicism of the period, which interpreted in Classicist, Byzantine and Renaissance style in Vienna, where his buildings include the Musikverein concert hall, 1869, the Stock Exchange, 1877, and the Parliament building, 1884.*) finished the new marble house of the peoples' representatives, there was nothing he could do but borrow from Antiquity for decoration. Now, Roman and Greek statesmen and philosophers beautify this theater of "Western Democracy". With symbolic irony, the four-horse chariots above the two houses pull away from each other and toward the north, south, east, and west. This was a perfect expression of what was going on inside at the time.

As an insult and irritant, these "nationalities" objected to any glorification of Austrian history in this building. It was the same in Germany where no one dared to dedicate the Wallot Reichstag Parliament building with an inscription to the German people until the First World War battles were underway. (*Paul Wallot was the architect of the German Reichstag Parliament Building completed in 1894.*)

Before I was twenty, I had mixed feelings the first time I went into the splendid building on the famous Ring Street to see and hear a sitting of the House of Deputies. I had always hated the Parliament. It wasn't the institution I hated because as a lover of freedom, I could not imagine any other kind of government. As a result of my attitude toward the Austrian House of Hapsburg and their ruler, the thought of any sort of similar dictatorship would have seemed a crime against liberty and reason.

One of the main reasons for this was the fact that my constant newspaper-reading as a young man had given me protection without me even realizing it. There was a certain admiration for the English Parliament, an admiration I could not get rid of very quickly. According to the great reports in our newspapers, the dignity with which even the lower House fulfilled its duties impressed me greatly. How could there possibly be any nobler form of self government for a people?

For that very reason, I was an enemy of the Austrian Parliament. The way that the whole thing was carried on seemed to me unworthy of its great model. The following considerations also influenced my attitude: the fate of the German race in the Austrian state depended upon its position in the Austrian Parliament. Until the introduction of secret ballot voting for all men, there was still at least a small German majority in Parliament, even if it was an insignificant one. Even this was dangerous. The national attitude of the Social Democrats was unreliable, and in crucial questions concerning German character, they always fought against German interests to avoid losing their followers among the various alien peoples. Even in those days, Social Democracy could not be considered a German party. The introduction of universal voting, however, destroyed the German numerical superiority. There was no longer any obstacle to the further de-Germanization of the state.

The instinct of national self-preservation made it impossible for me to welcome a representative system where the German element was not represented properly, but was instead betrayed by the Social Democratic fraction. These defects could not be attributed to the parliamentary system as such, but rather to the Austrian State. I still believed that if the German majority could be restored in this representative body, there would be no need to oppose such a system as long as the old Austrian State continued to exist.

This was the opinion I held when I entered those sacred and coveted halls. For me, they were sacred only because of the radiant beauty of that majestic building. A Greek wonder on German soil. Soon, though, I was outraged at the wretched spectacle that happened right before my eyes! There were several hundred representatives present who were expressing their opinions on a question of economic importance.

The events of the first day alone gave me enough to keep me thinking for weeks. The intellectual content of what they said was at an extremely depressing level, that is, if you could understand their chatter at all. Some of the gentlemen didn't speak German. They only sputtered in their Slavic mother tongues or dialects. Now I had a chance to hear with my own ears what I had previously known only from reading the papers. It was a wild commotion with gesturing, yelling, and interruptions in every tone of voice. In the middle of it all was a harmless old man who was trying his best to restore the dignity of the House by violently ringing a bell and shouting in a soothing way, then in warning tones. I could not help laughing.

A few weeks later, I visited the chamber again. The scene was transformed beyond recognition. The hall was almost empty. Down below, people were asleep. A few deputies were in their seats, yawning at one another while one of them "spoke". A Vice President of the House was present and he looked over the chamber with visible boredom.

I had my first misgivings, but I kept looking in on meetings whenever I could possibly find time. I watched what was going on quietly and attentively, listened to as much of the speeches as was understandable, studied the more or less intelligent faces of the chosen representatives of the nations in this sad state, and then gradually formed my own ideas.

A year of calm observation was enough to absolutely change or rather destroy my former opinions on the nature of the institution. I no longer objected to the distorted form Parliament had assumed in Austria. No, now I could no longer acknowledge Parliament as a government body at all. Up until now, I had only seen the ruin of the Austrian Parliament in the lack of a German majority, but now I saw destruction in the whole nature and character of the institution. I saw a whole new series of questions that needed to be answered.

I began to familiarize myself with the democratic principles of majority rule as the foundation of the whole institution, but I was equally attentive to the intellectual and moral values of the gentlemen who were the chosen members of the nations and who were supposed to pursue this goal. I became familiar with both the institution and the men who made it up.

Within a few years, my perception and understanding allowed me to form a clear and well-rounded image of the most dignified figure of modern times, the Parliamentarian. He made an impression on me in a way which had never significantly changed. The object-lessons of this first-hand experience had again preserved me from smothering in a theory which many people find so seductive at first glance, but which is actually a sign of decay in mankind.

The Democracy of the West today is a forerunner of Marxism, and without it, Marxism would be unthinkable. It alone gives this plague the surface on which to grow. Its outer form—the parliament style of government—is a "monstrosity of filth, and fire", but the creative fire seems to me burnt out at the moment. (*Hitler's humorous use of this quote is from J. W. von Goethe's Faust where Faust calls Mephistopheles, "You are the birth/monstrosity of filth/crap, and fire".*)

I am grateful to Fate for approaching me with this question in Vienna. I am afraid that if I had been in the Germany of that time, it would have made the answer too easy. If my first encounter with the ridiculous institution called Parliament had been in Berlin, I might have made the error of believing the opposite. With good reason, I may have joined those who saw the salvation of the people and Empire solely in strengthening the power of the Imperial structure and remained a blind stranger to the current times and to human nature.

In Austria, it was impossible to make this mistake. If Parliament was worthless, the Hapsburgs were worth even less. To oppose the idea of a parliament was not enough because the question of "what now?" would still be there. The abolition of the Parliament would have only left the House of Hapsburg as a governing power. This idea was especially unbearable to me.

This particular case was so difficult it made me as a youth take a closer look than I would have otherwise. What struck me first and gave me the most food for thought was the obvious lack of any individual responsibility. No matter how disastrous the result, no one is responsible or accountable for the passage of a Parliamentary resolution. Is all responsibility nullified when Parliament retires for the evening after making a catastrophic decision? Or perhaps responsibility is dissolved with the election of a new Parliament or formation of a new coalition? Can any majority which is unable to make a decision ever be held responsible? Isn't the very idea of responsibility not firmly connected with people? Can anyone make the head of a government accountable if he acts based on the decision made by a crowd of people?

Instead of developing constructive ideas and plans, is the business of a statesman actually the art of making a flock of sheep understand his plan? Is it his job to explain and coach them on common sense so that they will grant him their generous approval, or is his job instead to improve the nation? Should a statesman possess a gift of persuasion greater than the statesman's ability to conceive great political measures and make them happen? Is a statesman incompetent if he fails to win over a majority of votes to support his policy in an assembly, which has been called together as the chance result of an electoral system that is not always honestly administered?

Has this parliamentary crowd ever understood any idea before it was a success?

Isn't every accomplishment of genius in this world the result of the one genius going against the inertia of the masses? What is the statesman supposed to do if flattery fails to win the crowd's approval for his plans? Is he supposed to accept it? Is he supposed to abandon the tasks which he knows are vital to the people and go home or retire? Does he quit even if he knows failure resulted from the stupidity of his fellow citizens? Or is he to stay regardless? In a case like this, doesn't a man of real character fall into hopeless conflict between his insight and his honorable intentions? Where is the dividing line between duty to the community and duty to one's personal honor?

Shouldn't every true leader refuse to be degraded by acting as a political juggler? On the other hand, shouldn't every juggler feel a call to go into politics since the ultimate responsibility falls on some undefined mob and not him? Must our parliamentary majority lead to the total destruction of the leader concept? Can anyone believe that this world comes from the brain of majorities and not from the heads of individuals? Or does anyone believe that we can someday do without this essential aspect of human civilization, the individual? Can we not say that today more than ever before, the creative brain of the individual is indispensable?

By rejecting personal authority and substituting the mass of the crowd, the parliamentary principle of majority-rule sins against the basic aristocratic idea of Nature. However, we must admit that Nature's idea of nobility is not necessarily represented in the present decadence of our upper ten-thousand government and community leaders.

If he has learned to think independently, the reader of Jewish newspapers can hardly imagine the havoc brought on by the institution of modern democratic parliamentary rule. This rule is the main reason why our whole political life is so overrun with the inferior figures of today. A true leader is bound to withdraw from political activity that consists largely of trading favors and haggling for the approval of a majority rather than creative work and achievement. This kind of activity only attracts small minds, not great thinkers.

The smaller the mind of this petty man who sees politics as a trade, the more clearly he recognizes his own misery and the more loudly he will praise a system which does not demand great strength or genius. He is contented with the slyness which makes an efficient town clerk and probably even prefers this hollow wisdom to the true wisdom of that great democratic creator in Athens known as Pericles. (*Pericles was a great speaker and statesmen in ancient Greece known for a period called the "Age of Pericles".*)

That sort of simpleton shouldn't be plagued with responsibility for his actions. He is far beyond the reach of such worries because he knows that no matter what the results are of his "statesmanlike" confusions, his end has been written in the stars for a long time. Someday, he will have to give in to another and equally "great" mind. It is a sign of decay when the number of "great" statesmen increases as the quality of the individual statesmen declines. The quality of the individual statesman is bound to become less important as his dependence on parliamentary majority grows. After all, great minds will refuse to be the servant of silly incompetents and windbags. On the other hand, the representatives of the majority or the stupid, hate nothing more than a superior brain.

It is always a consoling feeling for one of these select men from some insignificant town to know that they have a leader whose wisdom is equal to their own. This way each man occasionally has the pleasure of letting his intellect sparkle. Besides that, each citizen feels that he has a chance to one day rise to the top. If this other man of limited ability can do it, why not me. If John can be boss, why not Paul?

This new invention of democracy has a quality which recently has grown to a real scandal. The cowardice of our so-called "leadership" is obvious. How lucky for them that when it comes to any decisions of importance, they can hide behind the skirts of the majority! Just take a close look at one of these political doormats. He begs for the approval of the majority for every action in order to guarantee he has an adequate number of accomplices so he can unload all responsibility! That is the main reason why this sort of political activity is disgusting and hateful to any decent and courageous man. It attracts the most contemptible characters. Anyone who will not take the personal responsibility for his actions and runs for cover to avoid responsibility is a cowardly villain.

Once a nation has put despicable leaders like these in place, the people's punishment will be swift. Representatives will no longer have the courage to make any decisions and would rather accept abuse, defamation, even dishonor as long as they do not have to pull themselves together and make a real decision. After all, there is no one left who is ready to take responsibility for himself and carry a difficult decision through.

Never forget that a majority cannot replace a man. A majority always represents stupidity and cowardice. A hundred cowards do not make a hero any more than a hundred fools make a wise man. The less responsibility the individual leader has, the more would-be politicians will feel they are called upon to devote their pitiful "gifts" to the nation. They are not even able to wait for their turn. They stand in a long line, sadly counting the people ahead of them and marking off the minutes until it will be their turn to board this political train. They wait a long time for any change in the office they have fixed their eye on, and are grateful for any scandal which thins the ranks ahead of them. Occasionally, someone refuses to move from his office, which makes the ones in line feel like there has almost been a violation of a sacred promise. Then, they grow spiteful and do not rest until the bold politician holding onto their office is ousted. After that, he won't hold office again anytime soon. If one of these creatures is forced to give up his post, he will immediately try to crowd into the waiting lines again, that is, unless he is prevented by the yelling and abuse from the others.

The result is an alarmingly rapid change in the important posts and offices, and the result is always bad and sometimes catastrophic. Fools and incompetents will not be the only victims of this custom, but the real leader will be affected if Fate can still manage to put a true leader in this position. The moment people recognize him, they form a united front of resistance, especially if someone of any intelligence intrudes on this group without rising from their own ranks. They want to keep every position of power among themselves, and they all hate every mind which might be a "one" among all the "zeros". They may be dimwitted and slow in other areas, but in this one, they are sharp and focused. The result is an ever-spreading intellectual wasteland in the government. For state and nation, the effect can easily be judged by anyone who is not one of these so-called "leaders".

Old Austria had parliamentary government in its purest form. The prime minister was appointed by the Emperor and King, but even this appointment was simply the will of Parliament and the trading of favors, for individual posts was typical just as in Western Democracy.

The intervals between the replacement of one person by another gradually became shorter, finally ending up in a wild relay chase to see who could gain the office first. Each change reduced the quality of the "statesman" until finally only the petty-type of political juggler remained. The qualities of statesmanship in these people were valued according to their skill in piecing together one temporary alliance after another and in their ability to manipulate the pettiest political deals. This is the only kind of political activity suited to the abilities of these representatives.

The city of Vienna became a school which offered the best insights in this field. I was very interested in comparing the knowledge and ability of these popular representatives with the jobs they were supposed to be doing. This was necessary in order to understand the intellectual horizon of these who were chosen by the people. One could not help but think seriously about the processes that discovered these "magnificent figures in our public life". It was worthwhile to thoroughly study how the real talents of these gentlemen were used in the service of their country. In other words, to analyze thoroughly their step-by-step procedure.

We must be objective in considering an institution whose members think it is necessary to refer to "objectivity" in every other sentence as the only just basis for any judgment or belief. Anyone who examines these gentlemen for themselves can only be astonished at the result. The parliamentary life looked more and more desolate as one penetrated its structure and studied the people and principles of the system in a spirit of ruthless objectivity.

If you do consider the matter with absolute objectivity, the parliamentary principle is wrong. There is no other principle as wrong as the parliamentary principle. We can say this without even referring to the way the election of the honorable deputies takes place, the way they get into office, and the way titles are given to them. Only in a tiny fraction of cases are the offices filled based on widespread desire and certainly it does not stem from any need. It is obvious to anyone that the political understanding of the masses has not reached the point where they can arrive at political views on their own. They are incapable of picking out the most qualified person. What we always call "public opinion" is based only on individual experience or knowledge. Most public opinion results from the way public matters are presented to the people through an overwhelmingly impressive system of controlled information. Just as religious beliefs are the result of education, the political opinion of the masses is the result of an often incredibly thorough and determined assault on the mind and soul.

By far the greater part of political "education" or propaganda is the work of the press. It is the press which primarily takes care of the "work of enlightenment" and acts as a sort of school for adults. This means the teaching materials are not in the hands of the state, but in the clutches of characters who are motivated by their own interests. As a young man, Vienna gave me the best opportunities to become intimately acquainted with the owners and manufacturers of this mass-education machine. At first, I was astonished to see how quickly this evil power succeeded in producing a particular opinion among the public, even though the meaning may be twisted or a flat-out false representation of public desire. A few days were enough to turn some ridiculous affair into a momentous act of state, while vital problems were generally forgotten or simply erased from the memory of the masses.

In the course of a few weeks, the press could conjure up names out of nothing and attach the incredible hopes of the public to them. Suddenly they would become more popular than a really important man may ever enjoy in a lifetime. These were names which no one had even heard of only a month before. At the same time, old and stable figures of government or public life simply ceased to exist as far as the world was concerned, or they were buried under such rudeness that their names soon risked becoming symbols of wickedness or dishonesty. If we are to understand this process, we have to study this infamous Jewish way of magically drenching the clean garments of honorable men with the slop buckets of filthy libel and slander from hundreds of directions at once. We must study it if we are to understand the real danger from these journalistic villains.

There is nothing these powerful intellectual newspaper rogues would not do if it allowed him to accomplish his disrespectful ends. He sniffs his way into the most secret family affairs and he does not rest until his nosiness has rooted up some awful situation which will serve to cook the unlucky victim's goose. If he does not uncover anything in public or private life, he resorts to slander. He has a deeply-rooted belief that some of it will stick. Even if there are a thousand contradictions in his claims, after it is repeated a hundred times by all his accomplices, the victim usually can't put up a fight at all. This pack of scoundrels will never admit their actions affect mankind, and they certainly would never admit that they even understand what they are doing. Heaven forbid! These idle and dishonest people are like squids that hide in a cloud of truth, proclaiming "journalistic duty" and other lies while attacking the rest of the world in the sneakiest way possible. They congregate at congressional meetings and conventions to confirm the tedious talk about their journalistic duty and the honor they do to society. Then this species bows to pay their respects to one another and with it they end their meeting. This insidious group manufactures more than two-thirds of all so-called "public opinion", and this is where parliament obtains their strength.

To describe all of this in detail and prove its lies and falsehoods would take volumes. But putting all this aside, if we just look at the product and its effect, I think this will be enough to show how this crazy business works in such a way that even the most innocent and skeptical person will understand.

The quickest and easiest way to understand this senseless and dangerous deviance is by comparing democratic parliament systems with a genuine Germanic democracy.

A body of five hundred men, or even recently, women, is chosen, whose duty is to make a final decision on all kinds of issues. They alone are effectively the government. Even though they may choose a cabinet, which on the outside is supposed to manage the affairs of state, this is only for show. In reality, the government cannot take any step without first getting permission from the general assembly. Consequently, it is not responsible for anything since the final decision does not rest with anyone in the government, but with the majority of Parliament. In any case, the government simply carries out the will of the majority. Its political capacity can really only be judged by its skill in either conforming to the will of the majority or convincing the majority to switch to its side. This reduces it from being a real government to being a beggar at the feet of the majority. Its most urgent job is to gain the favor of the existing majority or to try to set up a more agreeable new majority. If it succeeds, it can continue the political game for a little while longer. If it does not succeed, it must quit. Whether its intentions are right or wrong are not even considered. This eliminates all responsibility for anyone's actions or decisions.

It does not take a lot of thinking to figure out what the results will be. The five hundred representatives of the people present a disjointed and usually a pitiful picture if you look at their dissimilar occupations or their varied political abilities. Surely no one would assume that those elected by the nation are chosen because of their ability to reason or their intellect. I hope no one is foolish enough to think that hundreds of statesmen can emerge from ballot boxes which have been stuffed by those who themselves only posses an average intelligence. We can never denounce sharply enough the silly idea that geniuses are discovered through general elections. The average nation only finds a real statesman once in a blue moon, not a hundred at a time. The masses will oppose any outstanding genius because it is their instinct. A camel can pass through the eye of a needle sooner than a great man can be "discovered" by an election. (*Matthew 19:24 is the Bible verse about a camel passing through the eye of a needle which is referenced by Hitler; similar passages also appear in the books of Mark and Luke.*)

History has always shown that those who rose above the average level did so through the driving force of an individual personality. Now we have five hundred people of mere modest ability voting on the most important issues of the nation and installing a government which requires the approval of the exalted five hundred. This government in turn learns that to secure its position it must carry out the policy of the five hundred. Unfortunately, the policy is actually created by five hundred people and it carries the same shabby appearance.

Even if there were no question about the ability of these representatives, we must remember how varied the problems are that are waiting to be solved and in how many totally separate fields answers and decisions have to be given. We can easily understand how worthless a government institution is that entrusts the right to make a final decision to a mass meeting of people among whom only a few have any knowledge and experience in the matter being discussed. The most important economic measures are presented to a forum where only a tenth of the members have any economic training. This is simply putting the final decision on an important matter in the hands of men who lack the skills to deal with it intelligently.

That is how it ends with every question. Things are always settled by a majority of ignoramuses and incompetents, since the membership of this institution never truly changes. The problems presented extend to almost every field of public life and would require a constant change of parliamentary leaders to judge and vote on them. After all, it is impossible to let the same people deal with matters of transportation and with a question of important foreign policy. Otherwise, they would all have to be geniuses in every area and this does not happen once in centuries. Even worse, they are not "brains" at all, but only narrow, conceited, and arrogant amateurs and intellectual pretenders of the worst sort. In fact, that is the reason for the incomprehensible carelessness these ruling classes display when they make decisions on matters that even the greatest minds would find stressful. Measures of vital importance for the whole state—actually the fate of the people and the entire race—are treated as if they are a game of Sheepshead or Tarot, which would be a more suitable pursuit for such people. (*Schafkopf or Sheepshead is a card game common in Bavaria; Tarot is fortune telling by cards.*)

Of course, it would be unfair to say every deputy in parliament has no sense of responsibility. That is not the case at all. But by forcing the individual member to make up his mind on questions which are not in the realm of his talents, this system gradually corrupts the character of every member. Nobody is going to have the courage to say, "Gentlemen, I do not think we know anything about this matter. I, personally, at any rate, certainly do not". It would not make any difference if he did state his objection because that kind of frankness would not be understood in this crowd and people would not let such an honest ass spoil everyone else's game. Anyone who knows human nature will understand that in such a situation, nobody likes to be the dunce, and in certain circles, honesty is a synonym for stupidity.

So, a representative who begins by being honorable is forced down the crowded path of lies and cheating. He believes that an individual withdrawing from a decision would not make any difference in the eventual outcome of the group decision and this kills every honest impulse that a person may feel. He will end up telling himself that he personally is far from the worst and that by joining in, he might prevent worse things from happening.

Some may object by saying even though the individual deputy may not have any special understanding of a particular matter, his belief is based on the direction given by his party, by his politics. The party has its separate committees, and he feels they are more than sufficiently informed by experts. At first glance, this seems to be true. But then comes the question, why choose five hundred when just a few of them possess the necessary wisdom needed to adopt a policy in important matters?

Yes, there is the true difficulty in the whole system. The basis of our present democratic parliament is not to form an assembly of wise men, but instead put together a herd of nobodies who are dependent on the intellect of everyone around them. They become easier to lead in a certain direction as their abilities decrease. This is the only way party politics can be carried on. This is the only way it is possible for the puppeteer to remain hidden in the background without ever being personally held accountable for what he does. Then, every decision, no matter how harmful to the nation, is blamed on a whole party and not just one mischievous culprit pulling the strings. All responsibility disappears because responsibility can only exist if an individual makes a decision and not an association of parliamentary windbags.

Only an evil creature of the night, fearful of daylight, could approve of this institution, while every honest man who accepts personal responsibility for his own actions must find it disgusting. Consequently, this kind of democracy has become the tool of that race whose real purpose forces it to hide its actions from sunlight where others might see now and forever. Only the Jew can praise an institution as dirty and deceptive as himself.

On the other side, we have the true Germanic democracy consisting of a free election. This leader is bound to assume full responsibility for everything he does. In this format, there is no roll call of a majority on individual questions, but only the rule of an individual who has to support his decisions with his property and his life. To anyone who objects by saying no one would be willing to devote himself to such a risky responsibility under those conditions, there is but one answer: thank God. It is the very purpose of a Germanic democracy to keep every unworthy political climber who might by chance fall into the office from gaining any power in the government of his fellow man through the back door. The very magnitude of this responsibility is meant to scare off weaklings and incompetents.

If such a fellow should try to sneak in any way, it is easier to find and harshly punish him: "Get away, you coward! Step away, you are stinking up the stairway. The front steps to the Pantheon of history are not for cowards, but for heroes!"

I arrived at this opinion after watching the Vienna Parliament for two years. Then, I stopped going. Parliamentary government was largely responsible for the ever-increasing weakness of the old Hapsburg state during the previous few years.

The more its work shattered German supremacy, the more a system of playing one nationality against another gained ground. In the Parliament Building itself, this was always at the expense of the Germans and eventually at the expense of the Empire. By the turn of the century, it had to have been obvious to any fool that the central force of the Monarchy could no longer overcome the individual countries' attempts to break loose. On the contrary, the more terrible the methods became that were used by the state for self-preservation, the more universally the state was hated. In Hungary and in the individual Slavic provinces, the people did not identify themselves with the Monarchy so they did not feel its weakness was shameful to them. Instead, they were rather pleased at the signs of senility because they preferred the Monarchy's death to its recovery.

The complete collapse of Parliament was only prevented by giving in to humiliating concessions that consisted of inappropriate demands. Of course, the Germans had to foot the bill. In Austria, defense of the State depended on playing off the various nationalities against one another. But the general line of development still bore down on the Germans. When the Imperial succession gave Archduke Francis Ferdinand more influence, the increase of Czech authority really began to accelerate with his support from above. This future ruler of the Dual Monarchy used every means possible to promote and encourage the removal of the German element, or at least to cover it up. Through the civil servants, purely German towns were slowly but surely pushed into the danger-zone of mixed language. In Lower Austria, this policy progressed even quicker and many Czechs already considered Vienna "their" greatest city.

The family of the new Hapsburg Monarchy spoke only Czech. The Archduke's lower class wife, a former Czech countess, belonged to a group who held their fear of Germans as a tradition. His primary purpose was gradually to set up a Slavic state in Central Europe built on a strong Catholic foundation as a defense against Orthodox Russia. The Hapsburgs commonly made religion the servant of their political idea and this had a disastrous effect on Germans.

The results were more than sad in several respects. Neither the House of Hapsburg nor the Catholic Church received the expected reward. The Hapsburgs lost their throne and Rome lost a great state. By putting religious elements to work for political purposes, the Crown awakened a spirit that it had not dreamed was possible. When they attempted to completely exterminate German culture in the old Monarchy, the response was the Pan-German movement in Austria. This movement wanted to unify all German language speakers and German ethnic people into a single German state.

By the Eighteen-eighties, the Manchester Liberalism (*a political, economic, and social movement of the Nineteenth-century originating in Manchester, England, which challenged the existing economic system*), which was fundamentally Jewish, had reached the peak of influence in the Dual Monarchy. Like everything in old Austria, the reaction against it was primarily founded on nationalistic and not social considerations. Self-preservation forced German elements to defend themselves with the greatest force. Economic considerations slowly gained an important influence, but only as an afterthought. Two parties emerged from the general political turmoil—one had a nationalistic tendency and the other more social—and both were extremely interesting and instructive for the future.

After the crushing conclusion of the War of 1866 (*also called the Seven Weeks War between Austria and Prussia with Germans on both sides, it gave Prussia control over most smaller German states*), the House of Hapsburg considered retaliation on the battlefield. The death of Emperor Maximilian of Mexico prevented a closer alliance with a France. (*Emperor Maximilian I of Mexico was Austrian born and part of the Hapsburg-Lorraine Royal House. He was installed with the help of the French in 1864 as a monarch of Mexico but was overthrown and executed in 1867.*) His unfortunate expedition was blamed on Napoleon III, and his desertion by the French soldiers aroused universal anger. But even then the Hapsburgs were lying in wait. If the War of 1870-71 (*the Franco-Prussian war, the Prussian victory restored the German Empire*) had not turned out to be such a triumphant march, the Vienna Court would probably still have ventured the bloody game of revenge for Sadowa (*the German name for Sadová, a village in the Czech Republic*). When the first remarkable and unbelievable but true tales of heroism came from the battlefield, the so called "wisest" of all Monarchs realized the timing for revenge was inappropriate and tried to make the best of a bad situation by accepting it with grace.

The heroic struggle of those years produced an even greater miracle. The Hapsburgs showed new attitudes but it never meant there was a change of heart, just pressure from the current situation. The German people in the old Eastern Territories were carried away by Germany's joyful intoxication in victory and were deeply touched by the resurrection of their fathers' dream which became a reality. Make no mistake, even in the Czech city of Koniggratz, the German-spirited Austrian saw the tragic but inevitable need for the resurrection of the Empire, an empire which could not be contaminated with the stench of the old German Confederation. (*Koniggratz is a reference to the Battle of Koniggratz where Prussia defeated Austria and this became the first step in the formation of the German Empire.*) Above all, he learned by bitter personal experience that the House of Hapsburg had at last completed its historical mission, and that the new Empire must only choose the Kaiser as a man whose heroic spirit made him worthy of the title "Crown of the Rhine". The spirit of Fate, which bestowed this honor upon the descendant of a House that in the distant past had given the nation a shining symbol of national praise in Frederick the Great—a symbol to last forever—that Fate deserves great praise.

After this great war, the House of Hapsburg began to slowly and with desperate determination exterminate the dangerous German element in the Dual Monarchy. Without any doubt, this was the purpose of the policy which eliminated the German element in favor of Slavs. At that moment, the resistance of these people who were marked for total destruction flamed up in a way new to German history.

For the first time, patriotic and nationally-minded men became rebels. They were rebels against a way of government that would lead to the destruction of their own nationality and not rebel against state or nation. For the first time in recent German history, the customary patriotism for a dynasty was distinguished from the patriotism of national love for the Fatherland and its people by open conflict.

The Pan-German movement of German-Austria in the Eighteen-nineties receives credit for clearly and unmistakably realizing that a state has the right to demand respect for its authority only when it is for the protection and in the interest of its people, or at least will not cause any harm. State authority cannot exist as an end in itself or any kind of tyranny would become sacred and untouchable.

If the government is driving a nationality to its destruction, the rebellion of every member of that people is not merely a right, but a duty. Whether or not this condition exists is not shown by theoretical stories, but it is shown when force is used against the people and in the success of effort to suppress the nationality.

Of course, every governing power claims their responsibility is to uphold the authority of the state no matter how badly they have abused that authority, even though it has betrayed the interests of a nationality a thousand times over. In fighting such a power and in winning freedom or independence, the peoples' instinct for self-preservation will have to use the same weapon used by its adversary. That is to say the battle will be carried on by "legal" means as long as the power which is being overthrown also uses legal methods, but the insurgents should not hesitate to use illegal means if the oppressor employs them.

Never forget that the highest purpose of man's existence is the preservation of his own kind and not the maintenance of a state or government. The question of legality is secondary if the survival of the race is at stake and they may be pushed aside or destroyed. Even though the methods used by the ruling power are a thousand times "legal", the self-preservation of the oppressed is always the most noble justification for a struggle using any and every weapon. The truth of this statement can be seen by anyone, and this earth's history shows tremendous examples in the wars of independence against inward or outward enslavement of peoples.

The law of humanity is above the law of the state. However, if a people are defeated in their struggle for human rights, this means those people are not favored on the scale of Fate and they are not slated to remain on this world. The world will not be possessed by those who are weak-willed.

Using Austria as a clear and striking example, it is easy to see how a tyranny can wrap itself up in so-called "legality". The legal power of the state once rested with the anti-German foundation of the Parliament with its non-German majority and on the equally anti-German ruling House. These elements embodied the entire authority of the state. Any attempt to change the German-Austrian people through these groups would have been nonsense. Consequently, our admirers of the "legal" way as the only "permissible" one, and those admirers of the state's authority itself were bound to think that all resistance must be abandoned because it could not be carried on by legal means. This would have inevitably meant a quick end to the German people under the Monarchy. The German element was saved from that Fate only by the collapse of the state.

The theorist with his thick glasses hanging off his nose would rather die for his doctrines than for his people. He believes that since men made laws for themselves, men should thereafter exist for the laws. To the credit of the Pan-German movement in Austria, and to the horror of all amateur theoreticians and other state worshipers, the Pan-German movement swept away this nonsense.

While the Hapsburgs were trying to close ranks on the German element by whatever means possible, this party struck back and ruthlessly attacked the "exalted" ruling House itself. The party was the first to dig into the rotten state and open the eyes of hundreds of thousands. The Pan-German movement deserves the credit for rescuing the love of the Fatherland from the embrace of this sorry dynasty.

When it first began, the party had such an extraordinary following that it threatened to become a regular landslide, but its success did not last. By the time I arrived in Vienna, the movement had long since sunk into complete insignificance and was overtaken by the Christian Socialist Party. The whole process of the Pan-German movement's growth and decline and the Christian Socialist Party's unheard-of rise was a classical example for study and of great importance to me.

When I came to Vienna, my support was totally on the side of the Pan-German movement. The fact that people had the courage to stand up in Parliament and shout "Heil Hohenzollern!" (*Hail to the Hohenzollern Prussian Dynasty!*) impressed and delighted me. I felt a happy confidence because they continued to regard themselves as only temporarily separated from the German Empire and not a moment passed without announcing the fact. It seemed to me that the only remaining road to salvation for our people was to speak out without hesitation on every question concerning the German element and never to compromise. But I could not understand why, after its first magnificent rise, the Pan-German movement could collapse. I understood even less how in the same period, the Christian Socialist Party (*which focused on the privileged-class and Catholic priests*) had built an enormous power base. It was just then reaching the peak of its fame.

While I was attempting to compare the two movements, Fate gave me the best instruction I could have hoped for and helped me to understand the reason behind this puzzle.

I began my deliberation with the men who must be considered the leaders and founders of the two parties: Georg von Schonerer and Dr. Karl Lueger. (*Georg Ritter von Schonerer was a well known nationalist politician in Austria who was Anti-Semitic, Anti-Slav, Anti-Catholic and Pro Pan-German. He formed the Pan-German Party.*) In purely human terms, they both tower above any so-called parliamentary figures. In the swamp of general political corruption, they remained pure and above reproach. My personal compassion was on the side of the Pan-German, Schonerer at first and gradually extended to the Christian Socialist leader, Dr. Karl Lueger. Schonerer's ability seemed to be much better and he was a more solid thinker on problems of principle. He realized the inevitable end of the Austrian State more clearly and more correctly than anyone else. If the German Empire had listened to his warnings about the Hapsburg Monarchy, the catastrophe of Germany's First World War against all of Europe would never have happened.

Schonerer could grasp the inner nature of a problem but was completely unsuccessful as a judge of men. This was Dr. Lueger's strong point. He was a rare judge of human nature and was careful to never view men as better than they are. Consequently, he primarily dealt with the practical possibilities of life of which Schonerer had little understanding. Everything the Pan-German Schonerer thought was theoretically true, but he did not have the strength or ability to explain this theory to the masses. He could not express it in a way that the common people, with limited understanding of the issue, could comprehend. Therefore, all his insight was just the wisdom of a seer and could never become a reality.

This lack of understanding when it came to human nature eventually led to errors in judging the strength of the movements as a whole and the old traditions. Lastly, Schonerer recognized that these were questions worthy of a World-Concept , but he did not realize that only the broad masses of people can be the foundation of such, almost religious, convictions. He did not see how the fighting spirit in the privileged-class circles was so badly limited. They had no fighting will because of their economic position. The individual who is afraid may lose too much will and hold himself back and avoid risk. In general, a World-Concept can only hope for victory if the broad masses—the foundation of the new doctrine—are prepared to fight the necessary battle.

His inability to understand the importance of the lower classes gave him an inadequate understanding of the social problem. In this way, Dr. Lueger was Schonerer's opposite. Lueger's thorough knowledge of human nature allowed him to judge the possible forces of men, and, at the same time, prevented him from judging the power of existing institutions. This may have been what led him to use the masses as a means to accomplish his goals. He very well understood that the political fighting strength of the upper level of the privileged-class in modern times was small and not sufficient to assure victory for a great new movement. In his political activity, he put the most emphasis on winning over the population whose daily life was threatened. This stimulated rather than paralyzed their fighting spirit. He was also willing to use every instrument of power available to win the favor of powerful existing institutions and derive the greatest possible advantage for his own movement from the old sources of power. He aimed his new party chiefly at the middle-class, which was threatened with destruction, and thus assured himself of an almost unshakable following—a following that was ready for great self-sacrifice and full of stubborn, dogged-fighting determination. His relation to the Catholic Church was built up with infinite shrewdness, and soon attracted so many of the younger clergy that the old clerical side of the party was forced to either abandon the field of battle or, a wiser choice, to unite with the new party.

We would be doing the man a serious injustice if this was the only characteristic we saw in him. Besides being a shrewd tactician, he had the qualities and the genius of a truly great reformer, but all these were limited by the resources he believed were available and also by his own capabilities.

This truly outstanding man set himself a completely practical goal. He wanted to capture Vienna. Vienna was the heart of the Monarchy. The last remnants of life went out from this city into the sickly and aging body of the rotten Empire. The healthier the heart became, the more quickly the body could heal. The idea was right in principle but could only be put in practice for a limited time. That was the weakness of the man. What he achieved as Mayor of the city of Vienna is immortal in the best sense of the word, but that did not enable him to save the Monarchy. It was too late.

His opponent, Schonerer, had seen this more clearly. Dr. Lueger was extremely successful in putting his plans into practice, but this did not give him the result he hoped for. Schonerer did not have the ability to accomplish what he wanted. What he dreaded most finally happened and to a frightening degree. (*The Prime Minister proclaimed civil servants were to be required to speak Czech as the official language in Bohemia which excluded German speakers from applying for government jobs. Soon thereafter Schonerer lost support due to his strong views and active opposition.*)

So neither man reached his ultimate goal. Lueger was too late to save Austria, and Schonerer was too late to preserve the German people from destruction. It is extremely enlightening for us today to study the causes of both parties' failure. It is particularly useful for my friends, because today conditions are not very different from conditions then. By looking back, we can avoid the same mistakes that brought about the end of one movement and made the other sterile.

In my opinion, there were three reasons for the collapse of the Pan-German movement in Austria. First, there was only a vague idea of the importance of the social problem, which is particularly bad for a new and revolutionary party. Schonerer and his followers primarily focused on the privileged-classes so the result was bound to be tame and weak. Although its individual members would never suspect it, the German privileged-class, especially the upper privileged-class, is opposed to war to the point of self-surrender in matters of nation or state. In times when the government is functioning well, this inclination is the reason why this class of people is extraordinarily valuable to the state. However, in times when the government is functioning badly, they become absolutely catastrophic. In order to fight a serious battle, the Pan-German movement would have to devote itself to winning over the masses. It did not do this. From the beginning, it was deprived of the basic drive needed to support a wave of momentum and allow it to build. Without this support, it subsided quickly. If you do not realize this principle and carry it out from the beginning, the new party can never recover from this omission later. When a large, moderate, privileged-class element is captured, the movement's beliefs will always be directed along their pre-existing ideas, and then any chance of winning strength from the common people is lost. After that, the movement can never progress beyond weak arguing, pale wrangling, and criticism. We can no longer find a religious-like faith and a willingness for self-sacrifice. They are replaced by a process that gradually wears away the rough edges of the questions in dispute resulting in "constructive" collaboration, which in this case means acknowledging the existing state of affairs. Ultimately they wind up in a satisfyingly-corrupt peace.

That was what happened to the Pan-German movement. It did not start by recruiting its followers from the great mass of common people. It became "privileged-class, respectable, and restrained". This mistake gave birth to the second cause of swift decline. By the time the Pan-German movement arose, the German element's situation in Austria was already desperate. From year to year, the Parliament had strengthened its intent to slowly destroy the German people. Any hope of rescue lay in the removal of this institution.

This raised a question of fundamental importance for the movement. In order to destroy the Parliament, should it be done from the inside or the outside? They went in and came out beaten. They had no choice but to go in because fighting such a power from the outside means being armed with unshakable courage and ready for infinite sacrifice. In this situation the bull must be seized by the horns. We will take a lot of sharp blows and are often knocked down in this kind of fight. We may even have shattered limbs, but we must stand up again. Victory rests with the bold attacker only after an extreme struggle. The magnitude of the sacrifice is the only way to attract new fighters for the cause. This must continue until determination is rewarded with success. For that purpose, the children of the great masses of the people are needed. Only they would be determined and persistent enough to fight the battle to the bloody end. The Pan-German movement did not control these great crowds. There was no choice but to go into Parliament.

It would be a mistake to think that their decision was the result of a long spiritual consideration. No, they never considered any other option. Being a part of this nonsense was just the concrete result of vague ideas concerning the importance and meaning of taking part in an institution which they recognized as wrong in principle. In general, they probably hoped it would be easier to enlighten the broad masses of the people by grabbing the opportunity to speak in front of a "forum of the whole nation". Also, it seemed obvious that an attack from inside the root-of-the-evil would be more successful than an outside. They believed the screen of parliamentary immunity would add to the safety of the individual fighter and the force of the attack would only be increased.

What actually happened was quite different. The forum the Pan-German deputies spoke to had become smaller, not larger. No one can speak and reach a larger audience by using reports and summaries. The only audience they will reach is the circle which can either hear or already accepts them. The greatest direct forum of listeners is not found in the chamber of a Parliament, but in great, public mass meetings.

Public meetings provide thousands of people who have come simply to hear what the speaker has to tell them. In the Chamber of Deputies, there are just a few hundred listeners and most are there just to receive extra pay and not to be enlightened by the wisdom of some "honorable representative of the people". It is always the same audience and they will never learn anything new because they lack the intelligence and the desire to open their minds.

Not one of these representatives will bow by choice to superior truth and then adopt it as his cause. No, nobody ever does this unless he hopes that by changing, he can save his seat for another session. These "models of manhood" make it their business to move over to the other party only if they suspect they could be more successful and then only when there are noises that the previous party is not going to do well in the upcoming election. The shift usually takes place in the middle of an explosion of loudly-voiced moral concerns to explain the reason for their change. Consequently, a great migration always begins when an existing party seems to be disliked so much that a crushing defeat is threatened. The parliamentary rats abandon the party ship.

This has nothing to do with superior knowledge or intentions. It is just a clairvoyant gift that warns the parliamentary rodents in time to fall into a new, warm, party bed. Speaking in front of such a "forum" is really just casting pearls before swine (*Matthew 7:6, meaning, it is a wasted effort to reveal pearls of wisdom to people who plan to reject us or do not appreciate the value*). It is really not worthwhile and the result is nothing. The Pan-German deputies could talk until their throats were sore without effect.

The press either responded with dead silence or they distorted the speeches from the parliament floor so much that any meaning was twisted or lost. Public opinion consequently formed a very bad impression of the new movement's purposes. What the individual gentlemen said made no difference because the meaning depended on how it was written up in the newspaper. Only a small portion of their speeches were covered, and this was so disjointed, it seemed like nonsense. That is exactly the impression that was intended by the press. The only forum they really spoke to consisted of barely five hundred parliamentarians and that explains why they never reached the public. The worst part was that the Pan-German movement could only count on success if it understood from the beginning that the problem was about a new World-Concept and not about a new party. Nothing less could stir up the necessary inner strength to fight this gigantic battle to the end. Only the best and bravest minds were of any use as leaders. Unless they are heroes, ready to sacrifice themselves and lead the fight for a new concept, there will be no soldiers ready to follow them and die for the cause either. A man who is fighting for his own existence has nothing left over for a common cause.

While the new movement may offer fame and honor among generations to come, today it can offer nothing because it is nothing. The more a movement has open posts and positions which are easy to obtain, the more people who are zeros will step forward to fill them. Finally, these political day-laborers overrun a successful party so much that the honest fighter of the early days no longer recognizes the old movement, and the new arrivals strongly object to him as an intruder. And thus ends any such movement's "mission".

The moment the Pan-German movement sold its soul to Parliament, it naturally gained "parliamentarians" instead of leaders and fighters. It sank to the level of one of the ordinary political parties of the day and lost the strength to courageously fight to the death. Instead of fighting, it learned to "speak" and "negotiate". The new parliamentarian soon preferred and believed it was less risky to fight for the new World-Concept with the "intellectual" weapons of parliamentary eloquence rather than to throw himself into a battle whose result was uncertain, possibly risking his own life. With this mindset, nothing could be gained.

Now that the party had people in Parliament, the followers outside began to hope for and expect miracles, but that of course, never happened and never could happen. They quickly became impatient. Even what they heard from their own deputies didn't satisfy the voters. This was easy to explain since the hostile press was careful not to give the people a truthful picture of the Pan-German deputies' work.

The more the new representatives acquired a taste for the gentler style of "revolution" in Parliament, the less they were willing to return to the more dangerous work of enlightening the large masses of the common people. For this reason, the mass meetings that were truly effective, directly personal, and a way of exerting influence and possibly winning over a large number of the people, were abandoned.

When the beer table of the meeting hall was finally exchanged for the auditorium of Parliament, and the speeches were poured into the heads of the so-called "chosen" and not to the people, the Pan-German movement ceased to be a people's movement and quickly sank into a club for academic discussions. The bad impression given in the newspapers was no longer corrected by personal testimonies at meetings and finally the word "Pan-German" left a very bad taste in the mouths of the common people.

One thing all the champions with ink-stained fingers and fools of today should take to heart is that the great upheavals in this world have never been guided by a pen. The only job of the pen has been to explain them in theory. Since the beginning of time, the force that started the great religious and political landslides of history has been the magic power of the spoken word alone.

The great masses of a people yield only to the force of speech. All great movements are people's movements. They are volcanic eruptions of human passions set off either by the cruel Goddess of Desperation or by the torch of the word as it is thrown to the masses. They are not the sweet words of smooth-talk, literature, and heroes. Only a storm of hot passion can change the "Fate of a People". Passion can only be aroused by a man who feels it inside himself. Only the possessor of passion can give the words that will open the gates to a people's heart like a hammer.

A man who has no passion and whose mouth is closed has not been chosen by Heaven as a Messenger of its Will. Let writers stick to their ink-pens and do "theoretical" work if their intelligence and ability will let them. He has not been born or chosen to be a Leader.

A movement that hopes to achieve great things must be alert and keep its connection with the common people. Every question must be considered from that standpoint and decided with that view. A movement must avoid anything that might reduce or even slightly weaken its ability to influence the masses. Without the mighty force of a great people, no great ideas, however noble and exalted, can possibly be achieved. Harsh reality alone must determine the path to the goal. An unwillingness to take difficult roads in this world too often means abandoning the goal. When the Pan-German movement emphasized its activity in Parliament and not among the people, it lost the battle for the future and received a cheap, momentary success in its place. It chose the easier battle which made it no longer worthy of the final victory.

I thought through these particular questions very thoroughly in Vienna. In my effort to understand them, I saw one of the chief causes of the movement's collapse, which I previously believed was destined to assume the leadership of German elements in Austria at that time.

The first two mistakes which wrecked the Pan-German movement were closely related. The Pan-Germans did not understand the inner, driving forces of great upheavals and they failed to understand the importance of the great masses of people. Their interest in defining the social problem was small, their attempts to capture the soul of the lower levels of the nation inadequate, and their positive attitude towards Parliament only increased their inadequacy.

If they had realized the enormous power inherent in the masses as their greatest supporter, they would have approached propaganda issues differently. Their emphasis for the movement would have been put on the factory floor and the street and not in Parliament.

Even their third mistake had its origin in the fact that they did not recognize the value of the masses. The masses are set in motion like a toy car that is pointed along a path by superior intellects, and, as it travels, it then maintains its momentum after it is in motion. From that point on, the founders provide encouragement and determination right up to the attack. The hard struggle the Pan-German movement fought against the Catholic Church can be explained by its insufficient understanding of the people's spiritual nature.

The new party's violent attack upon the center of Catholicism, Rome, also had a number of causes. When the House of Hapsburg finally decided to transform Austria into a Slavic state, it resorted to whatever means were necessary to accomplish that goal. With very little conscience, this ruling house unscrupulously put religious institutions to work for the new "State Idea". Employment of Czech priests and their spiritual shepherds was just one of the many ways used to obtain what they wanted—the conversion of Austria to a Slavic state.

The process took place something like this. In purely German church parishes, Czech pastors were installed. They in turn gradually began to place the interests of the Czech people above the interests of the churches, and this made them focal points in the process of removing German elements from society.

The German clergy failed to counter these tactics. Not only were similar tactics completely useless in any struggle on the Germans' part, but they could not resist the attacks of the other side. By misusing religion on one hand and providing an inadequate defense on the other, German elements were slowly and consistently pushed under the rug. This is how it happened on a small scale, and things were not very different on a large scale. The anti-German efforts of the Hapsburgs were not resisted as they should have been by the higher clergy and the upholding of German interests was pushed entirely into the background.

The general impression was that the Catholic clergy had committed a serious infringement on German rights. In other words, the Church did not seem to feel any loyalty to the German people, but unjustly took the side of its enemies. In Schonerer's opinion, the root of the whole trouble was that the Catholic Church did not have control in Germany and because of this, it was hostile to the interests of our nationality wherever they were found.

In this, as in almost everything in Austria, cultural problems were moved almost entirely into the background. What determined the Pan-German Party's position toward the Catholic Church was more about its insufficient efforts on behalf of German rights and its constant support of Slavic interests and greed and not so much about the Church's attitude toward science.

Georg Schonerer was not the kind of man who would do things halfway. He took up the struggle against the Church with the conviction that this struggle alone could save the German people. The "Freedom-from-Rome" movement (*also called the Away-From-Rome movement*) he founded seemed the most violent, but also the strongest way of attacking the problem and one that surely would destroy the enemy strongholds. He believed that if it succeeded, the unhappy split between the two Churches in Germany would end and they would come together resulting in the creation of inner strength for the Empire and this would give the German nation a huge victory.

But neither the premise nor the conclusion of this struggle was correct. Without a doubt, the power of nationalist resistance from German Catholic clergy members concerning German society was less than that of their non-German counterparts, especially their Czech colleagues. Only an ignoramus would fail to see that the German clergy never took the offensive on behalf of German interests. Anyone except a blind man was forced to admit this was due to Germans who were in distress over the thought that the objectivity of our attitude toward our own nationality might not be objective.

The Czech priest's attitude toward his people was subjective and his attitude toward the Church was objective. On the other hand, the German pastor was subjectively devoted to the Church and remained objective toward his nation. This is a phenomenon that can be observed in a thousand other cases. It is by no means exclusive to Catholicism either. This obsession with objectivity has quickly contaminated almost every one of our institutions, especially state or intellectual institutions.

We only have to compare our civil servants' attitude toward a national revival with the attitude of civil servants from another nation. Would any army officers anywhere in the world put aside the interests of the government of their nation as ours have done for the past five years? They are even praised for doing so. Do not both Churches today take a stand in the Jewish question that is against the interests of the nation or the real needs of religion? Consider the attitude of a Jewish Rabbi towards any question, even one of quite insignificant importance concerning the Jews as a race, and compare his attitude with that of the majority of our clergy, whether Catholic or Protestant.

We see the same thing whenever there is a question about maintaining an abstract idea. "Governmental authority", "democracy", "pacifism", and "international solidarity", are ideas that we almost always turn into rigid, totally theoretical concepts and we use them to judge vital national matters from the point of view they give us.

This disastrous way of looking at issues from a preconceived opinion kills the ability to think subjectively about anything which objectively contradicts one's own doctrines. It eventually leads to a complete reversal of the means and the – ends; people cannot tell the difference between the procedure used to reach a goal and the goal they want to achieve. People resist a national revival when it depends on the removal of a bad and destructive regime because they would say this is an offense against "governmental authority". "Governmental authority" in the eyes of one of these fanatics clinging to objectivity is not a means to an end but the end itself, and that end is sufficient to fill his whole, sorry life.

Such people would loudly object if anyone attempted to set up a dictatorship, even if the leader was to be Frederick the Great, who we know would be an outstanding leader. They would still object to this replacement even if the Parliament was filled by a majority of politicians who were small minded and incompetent or maybe even worse. They do this because these sticklers for abstract principles hold the law of democracy more sacred than the welfare of the nation. Some of them will defend the worst tyranny, destroying their own people in the process, because the tyranny embodies "governmental authority". They will oppose even the most beneficial government if it does not fit in with their idea of "democracy".

In the same way, our German pacifists will ignore this bloody rape of the nation, and no matter how bloodily it is carried out by the most evil military forces, they will still ignore it if the only way to avert this fate is by resistance and force. (*This is a reference to the Treaty of Versailles' reparations and the Ruhr-Area occupation by France.*) Resistance would violate the spirit of their peaceful society. The German International Socialist can be robbed by his comrades in each country of the world and the Socialist returns the favor with brotherly love. He would never dream of using force or even make any effort toward defense simply because he is a German who could never consider using force.

This may be a sad fact, but before we can change anything we must recognize the problem first. The same holds true for the weakness in the clergy who fail to uphold German interests. It is not malicious ill will in itself nor compelled by orders "from above". What we see is the result of inadequate training in the love of German culture from childhood along with complete subjection to the idea that we should not control our national destiny.

Training that is dished out for democracy, for International Socialism, for pacifism, is so rigid, exclusive, and completely subjective that it influences how we see the rest of the world. From childhood on, the attitude toward German culture has always been very objective. The pacifist, subjectively surrendering himself altogether to his idea, will, if he is a German, look for the objective justice in every serious threat to his people and will never join and fight in the ranks of his people not even from a pure instinct of self-preservation.

We can see in the Catholic and Protestant churches how this principal has taken hold. By nature, Protestantism upholds the interests of German culture better. This has to do with its origin and later tradition, but it fails the moment it is called upon to defend national interests which are not in the sphere of its ideals and traditions or which, for some reason or other, may be rejected by the Church.

Protestantism will always take some role in promoting German ideals as long as it concerns moral integrity or national education, or when the German spiritual being or language or spiritual freedom need to be defended. This is only because these represent the principles on which Protestantism itself is founded. This same Protestant attitude will violently oppose every attempt to rescue the nation from the grasp of a mortal enemy. This same Protestant attitude towards the Jews is rigid and fixed in their dogma. This is also the first problem which has to be solved. Without a solution, all attempts to bring about a German resurgence or to raise the nation's standing are destined to end in rubbish and will become impossible.

While I was in Vienna, I had the opportunity to look into this question without having a previously formed opinion on the matter. My daily contacts with people confirmed my view a thousand times over. In this mixture of nationalities, it was quickly proven that only a German pacifist will always try to look objectively at the interests of his own nation, while the Jew never does this with the interests of the Jewish people. Only the German Socialist is "international" in a sense where he considers outside interests to be equal with his own nation's interests, and this prevents him from winning justice for his own people except by whimpering and bawling to his international comrades. It is never true of the Czech or the Pole. I saw even then that the spreading harm was only partly in the doctrines themselves, and our weak devotion to the nation was the result of our inadequate training in our own nationality.

This disproves the first purely theoretical argument for the Pan-German movement's struggle against Catholicism. We should train the German people from childhood to exclusively recognize the rights of their own nationality and not infect the children's hearts with our curse of "objectivity", especially in matters of self-preservation. The result of this would be that the Catholic element in Germany, just as in Ireland, Poland, or France, will be a German first and foremost. Of course, all this assumes a radical change in the national government. Our strongest proof of this argument is in the period when our people last appeared before the judgment-seat of history for a battle of life and death. As long as leadership representing the Heavens was present, the people did their duty overwhelmingly. Protestant pastor and Catholic priest both contributed enormously to continuing our resistance, not only at the front, but at home. During those first years there was really only one Holy German Empire for both camps and everyone turned to his own Heaven to sustain that future.

There was one question that the Pan-German movement in Austria should have asked itself: Is the preservation of German-Austrian culture possible with a Catholic faith or not? If so, the political party had no business bothering with religious and confessional matters. If not, then a religious reformation was necessary and not a political party. Anyone who thinks he can arrive at a religious reformation by way of a political organization shows that he doesn't have the faintest idea how the growth of religious ideas or teachings build a Church.

Here, one truly cannot serve two masters. Make no mistake, I believe the founding or destruction of a religion is a far greater matter than the founding or destruction of a State, let alone of a political party. It is not an argument to the contrary for someone to say that the attacks were only defensive measures against attacks from the other side.

Down through the ages, men lacking conscience have not hesitated to make religion a tool in their political business. When they turn it into a tool, it is almost always the sole aim of such characters to use it as nothing more than a tool and they have no true beliefs. It would be wrong to hold a religion or a Church responsible for the scoundrels who abuse it. That type of person would use anything that served his purpose.

Nothing could be better suited to one of these worthless parliamentary tricksters than finding a scapegoat for his political juggling. The moment religion or any sect is made responsible for his personal bad behavior, the lying scoundrel shouts to the whole world so they can witness how justified his behavior has been, and how he alone has been the salvation of religion and Church through his eloquence. The rest of the world, as stupid as it is forgetful, usually does not recognize or remember him amid the shouting as the original source of the problem. By this time, the scoundrel has achieved his objective.

These crafty foxes know perfectly well that their misdeeds have nothing to do with religion. He will hide his face and laugh so none may see his sick joy when his honest but unskilled adversary loses the game and, some day afterward, he loses all faith in humanity and retires from the activities of public life.

In other respects, it would also be unfair to make religion or even the Church responsible for the misdeeds of individuals. If we compare the greatness of its visible organization with the imperfection of men in general, we will have to admit that the balance of good to bad is better in religious institutions than almost anywhere else. Without a doubt, there are some priests who see their holy office as just a stepping stone for their political ambitions. Amid the political battle, they forget that they are the guardians and not defenders of a higher truth. But for every unworthy figure, there are a thousand honorable shepherds of souls faithfully devoted to their mission who stand out like little islands from the swamp of the present corrupt and deceitful age.

I do not and must not condemn the Church if some corrupt creature wearing a priest's collar happens to commit a moral offense. I also must not condemn the whole group if one among the many soils and betrays his nationality, especially in an age when this is a daily occurrence. We should not forget that for every public traitor like the famous Greek betrayer Ephialtes, there are thousands who feel the misfortunes and have deep sympathy for their people. These great men long for the moment when Heaven will once more smile on us. (*Ephialtes was a soldier who betrayed the Spartan army. He is said to have told the Persians about the pass of Thermopylae around the mountains which they used to attack in the Battle of Thermopylae in 480 B.C., so this reference means a traitor.*)

If anyone feels these are not petty, everyday problems but questions of fundamental truth and beliefs in general, we can only answer him with another question. Do you think you are chosen by Fate to proclaim this truth? Then do it. But have the courage not to do it through a political party. This is a deception and a betrayal of your vocation. Instead, replace the bad parts with something better, something that will last and improve the conditions for future generations.

If you do not have the courage or if you are not sure about the alternative you are supporting, then let things alone. In any case, do not try to sneak into a political movement that you would not dare to reach for openly. As long as religious problems do not undermine the morals and ethics of one's own race like an enemy of the people does, political parties have no business meddling with them. Just as religion should not identify itself with political party mischief, political parties should not meddle in religion.

If dignitaries of the church use religious institutions or even doctrines to injure their own nationality, we must never follow them or try to fight them with their own weapons. To the political leader, the religious beliefs and institutions of his people must be sacred; otherwise, he has no right to be a politician. He is in danger of becoming a reformer if he has the right stuff for it. Any other attitude, particularly in Germany, would lead to catastrophe.

After studying the Pan-German movement and its struggle against Rome, I came to the following belief and that belief only became stronger through the years. The movement's failure to see the importance of the social problem cost it the capable fighting masses of the people. Its entrance into Parliament deprived it of this mighty force and infected it with all the weaknesses found in parliament. Its struggle against the Catholic Church made the fight impossible in many lower and middle-class groups and robbed it of many of the nation's best elements. The practical result of the Austrian Culture Struggle (*Kulturkampf*) was effectively zero.

They did succeed in taking almost a hundred thousand members from the Church, but failed to inflict any real damage. The Church did not shed any tears over the lost sheep. The only losses were those who had not really belonged to the Church for a long time in their hearts. There was an important difference between this new Reformation and the old Reformation. During the old Reformation, many of the Church's best members left because of religious convictions. In the new Reformation, only the lukewarm left and that was for political reasons. From the political standpoint, the result of this attempted reform was as sorry as it was ridiculous.

Once again, a movement that showed promise for the political salvation of the German nation had gone to pieces because it was not conducted with the necessary ruthless clear-sightedness and it lost itself in squabbles. One thing is true: the Pan-German movement would never have made this mistake if it had sufficiently understood the character of the broad masses. If its leaders had known that to succeed at all, for purely psychological reasons, they must never show two or more adversaries to the masses. If they do, then the fighting force is completely divided. If they had realized this, the Pan-German movement would have directed their full fighting force at one single adversary. Nothing is more dangerous for a political party than to let itself be led back and forth hither and yon between decisions because this means it can never accomplish anything visible.

No matter how many things may actually be wrong with a particular religious persuasion, a political party must never, not even for an instant, lose sight of the fact that no purely political party in a similar situation has ever succeeded in a religious reformation. This is well established in history. We do not study history to forget its teachings; we study it to put those teachings to practical use. We should not think that things are different now and that its eternal truths no longer apply. On the contrary, from history, we learn what we should do today. No one who cannot learn from history should imagine himself as a political leader. He is actually a shallow and usually very conceited simpleton, and all the goodwill in the world does not excuse his deficiencies.

In any age of history, the qualities of a truly great and popular leader consisted of focusing on a single adversary and not distracting the people's attention. The more unified the people's will to fight a single object, the greater the magnetic attraction a political movement will have and the more tremendous its impact. It is part of the genius of a great leader to make even widely separated adversaries appear as if they belonged to just one category. Weak characters who have difficulty making decisions will begin to doubt whether their own side is right when they see a variety of enemies.

When the wavering masses see themselves fighting against too many enemies, objectivity immediately appears with the question of whether all the others are really wrong and just one side is right. That is the first sign of one's own strength weakening. Therefore, a number of opponents must always be lumped together so that in the eyes of one's own followers, the battle is fought against one single enemy.

This strengthens their faith in their own cause, and increases their bitterness against anyone who attacks it. This cost the Pan-German movement their success when they failed to realize the importance of a single front. The Pan-German goal was correct and its will was pure, but the road it took was wrong. It was like a mountain climber who keeps his eye fixed on the peak to be scaled and takes the obvious trail while he is filled with great determination and energy. As he walks, he pays no attention to the path and he doesn't see where it truly leads because his eye is always on the goal. He finally wanders astray.

The position of its great competitor, the Christian Socialist Party, seemed to be reversed. The road it took was clever and correctly chosen, but a clear understanding of the goal was missing. In almost every matter where the Pan-German movement was lacking, the attitude of the Christian Socialist Party was right and was deliberately planned to achieve results.

It realized the importance of the masses and secured at least part of them by clearly emphasizing its social aspect from the very start. By adjusting itself to win the middle and lower-middle classes, it obtained a following as faithful as it was stubborn and self-sacrificing. It avoided fighting any religious institution and secured the support of a mighty organization in the Church. Consequently, it only had one truly great adversary. It recognized the value of large-scale propaganda and was skilled in working on the human instincts of the broad mass of its followers. However, it also failed to reach its dream of saving Austria.

There were two shortcomings in its method: the means they employed, and the lack of a clear goal. The anti-Semitism of the new movement was founded on a religious concept instead of a racial insight. The reason this mistake occurred was the same reason that caused the second error. If the Christian Socialist Party was to save Austria, the founders felt it must not take its stand on the race principle because they feared the State would collapse from the pressure. In the party leaders' view, the multi-ethnic situation in Vienna made it necessary to put aside anything that divided people, and in their place, emphasize anything that united the public.

By that time, Vienna was already so thoroughly impregnated with foreigners, especially Czech elements, that they had to be extremely tolerant when it came to race questions otherwise they could not keep these elements in a party that was not anti-German from the beginning. If Austria was to be saved, the people in Austria could not be tossed aside. An attempt was made to win the great number of Czech lower classes in Vienna by a drive against Manchester Liberalism (*a political, economic, and social movement originating in Manchester, England*). It was presumed that this attack would be seen as struggle against Jewry on a religious basis, which would bridge all the national differences of old Austria. Such an attack would only create a small amount of worry among to the Jews. At worst, a dash of baptismal water would always save his business and Judaism both.

With a superficial argument like this, they never achieved serious scientific treatment of the whole problem and so they repelled anyone who did not understand this sort of anti-Semitism already. The attractive power of the idea was limited almost exclusively to intellectual circles. The leaders failed to go from that point to developing a real insight by using a pure emotional experience. The political elite remained hostile. The whole affair looked more and more like a mere attempt at a new conversion of the Jews or even envy of competitors. The struggle lost the appearance of a movement born from devout conviction and seemed to many average people immoral and reprehensible. There was no reason to believe that this was a vital question for all of humanity or that the Fate of all non-Jewish people depended on it.

This half-hearted attempt destroyed the value of the Christian Socialist Party's anti-Semitic attitude. It was a movement that made no pretenses to anti-Semitism, and that was worse than having no leaning towards anti-Semitism at all. The people were being lulled into a sense of security and thought they had the enemy by the ears, while in reality, they were being led around by the nose.

The Jew, however, soon became so accustomed to this sort of anti-Semitism that he probably would have missed it more if it wasn't there than he was bothered by its presence. Submitting to a State of mixed nationalities demanded one great sacrifice, and the upholding of German culture demanded a greater sacrifice. The party could not be "nationalistic", and if they were, they would lose the ground under their feet in Vienna. By gently evading any question of nationalism, they hoped to save the Hapsburg State and that is what ruined the movement. At the same time, the movement lost a great source of inner strength—a strength that can fill a political party with an inner driving force for the long run. The Christian Socialist movement became a party no different from any other.

I followed both movements closely. One was from the urging of my own heart and the other was because I had so much admiration for the rare man who even then seemed to be a bitter symbol of all Austrian-German culture.

When the tremendous funeral procession carried the dead mayor (*Lueger*) from the City Hall out toward the Ring Street of Austria (*Ringstrasse*), I was among the many hundreds of thousands who watched the tragic scene. Feelings were stirred, and I knew this man's work was in vain because Fate was inevitably leading the State towards its doom. If Dr. Karl Lueger had lived in Germany, he would have been ranked among the great minds of our people. Having lived in this impossible State was unfortunate for him and for his work.

When he died, the flames in the Balkans were already greedily flickering higher every month, and Fate had mercifully spared him from seeing what he still believed he could prevent. I tried to understand the reasons for the failure of one movement and the misdirection of the other. Aside from the impossibility of fortifying the State in old Austria, I came to the definite conclusion that the mistakes of the two parties were the following:

The Pan-German movement was on the right track in principle as it desired the goal of a German revival, but its choice of weapons was unfortunate. It was nationalistic but did not have the social appeal needed to conquer the masses. Its anti-Semitism; however, rested on a correct realization of the importance of the race problem and not on religious concepts. On the other hand, the attack on a particular religious persuasion was wrong.

The Christian Socialist movement had vague ideas about the goal of a German renaissance, but it made an intelligent choice in its weapons to carry out the party policy. It realized the importance of the social aspect but was mistaken in the principles it used to fight Jewry, and did not understand the strength of the nationalistic idea.

If the Christian Socialist Party had taken their shrewd knowledge of the broad masses and adequately understood the importance of the race problem as the Pan-German movement did and been nationalistic, or if the Pan-German movement had adopted the practical insight and attitude toward Socialism of the Christian Socialist Party along with its true insight into the goal of the Jewish question and the meaning of the nationalist idea, the result would have been that one of these movements might have successfully changed the fate of Germans. The nature of the Austrian State was the reason this did not happen.

Since my convictions were not represented clearly in any political party around me, I could not make up my mind to join or fight for one of the existing organizations. Even then, I thought all the political movements were failures and incapable of carrying out a national renaissance for the German people on any large scale.

My distaste for the Hapsburg State continued to grow. The more attention I began to pay to questions of foreign politics, the more my conviction strengthened that this State structure could only lead to serious misfortune for German culture. More and more clearly, I saw that the fate of the German nation was being decided here in Austria as well as within the German Empire itself. This was true in cultural life and in questions of politics.

Even in the field of purely cultural or artistic affairs, the Austrian State showed every sign of weakening and it was losing its importance to the German nation as a cultural resource. This was especially true in the field of architecture. Modern architecture in Austria could not be successful because after the Ring Street (*Ringstrasse*) was built in Vienna, the rest of the jobs were insignificant when compared to the plans being developed in Germany. I began to lead a double life more and more. Reason and reality made me go through a bitter though useful apprenticeship in Austria, but my heart was elsewhere.

An uneasiness came over me as I realized the emptiness of this State and that it was impossible to save it. At the same time I felt perfectly certain that it would bring misfortune to the German people if Austria collapsed. I was convinced that the Hapsburg State would balk and hinder every German who might show signs of real greatness, while at the same time it would aid and assist every non-German activity.

This conspicuous mix of races in the capital of the Dual Monarchy, this motley collection of Czechs, Poles, Hungarians, Ruthenians (*Ukranians*), Serbs and Croats, and always that infection which dissolves human society, the Jew, were all here and there and everywhere. The whole scene was repugnant to me. The gigantic city seemed to be the embodiment of mongrel depravity.

The German I learned to speak in my youth was a dialect which is also spoken in Lower Bavaria. I never forgot that particular style of speech, and I could never learn the Viennese dialect. The longer I stayed in the city, the hotter my hatred burned for the promiscuous alien people who began to gnaw away at this ancient seat of German culture. The idea that this State could be preserved much longer seemed absolutely ridiculous.

Austria was like an old mosaic where the cement holding the separate bits of stone together had become old and started to crumble. As long as it is not touched, the work of art still appears solid, but the moment it is shaken, it falls into a thousand fragments. The only question was when the jolt would come.

Since I had never loved an Austrian Monarchy, only a German Reich, the moment of the State's collapse seemed to be the beginning of the salvation of the German nation. For all these reasons, my desire grew stronger to go where my secret wishes and secret love had been pulling me since early youth. I hoped some day to make a name as an architect and to work hard for the German nation on either the large or small scale as chosen by Fate.

Lastly, I wanted to enjoy the happiness of living and working in the place where the greatest desire of my heart must someday be fulfilled: the union of my beloved homeland with its common Fatherland, the German Empire.

Even today, many people will not be able to understand my deep desire, but I appeal especially to two groups of people. The first are all those who have been denied the happiness I have spoken of, and the second are those who once enjoyed that happiness but had it torn from them by a harsh Fate. I speak to all those who are separated from the mother country and must fight for even the sacred possession of their native language, those who are pursued and tormented for their faithfulness to the Fatherland and who long in anguish for the moment that will bring them back to the heart of the beloved mother. I speak to all of these and I know they will understand me!

Only those who know by bitter experience what it means to be a German without the privilege of belonging to the dear Fatherland can measure the deep longing, which always burns in the heart of the children who are away from the mother country. It torments its victims and denies them happiness and contentment until the doors of the paternal house open and common blood will find rest and peace in a common realm.

Vienna was and has remained the hardest and most thorough school of my life. I had entered the city as a young boy and I left it as a quiet and serious man. There I laid the foundation for a general World-Concept and a particular way of political thinking which I later completed in detail. Only now can I fully appreciate the real value of those years of apprenticeship.

I have addressed this period of my life at some length because it gave me my first object lessons in issues that form the basis of the Party, which had tiny beginnings and in just five years has started to develop into a great mass-movement. I do not know what my attitude would be today toward Jewry, toward Social Democracy, or toward Marxism as a whole, and toward the social question if a cornerstone of personal views had not been laid early by the pressure of Fate and by my own self-education.

Even though the misfortunes of the Fatherland may stimulate thousands upon thousands to think about the inner causes of the collapse, such could not lead to a thorough knowledge and deep insight that a man develops on his own, who has fought a difficult battle for many years so that he might be master of his own Fate.

4. MUNICH

In the spring of 1912, I moved to Munich for good. (*This was written by Hitler in 1924.*)

The city was as familiar to me as if I had lived within its walls for years. My studies were the reason for this because they repeatedly turned my attention towards German art. If you haven't seen Munich, you haven't seen Germany or German art. This time before the war was the happiest and by far the most contented of my life. My living was still meager because I only painted enough to meet my living expenses and so I could continue my studies. I believed that someday I would still reach the goal I had set for myself. This in itself made it easy for me to tolerate the small worries of daily life. I had a deep love that possessed me for this city ever since I first arrived, more than any other town I knew. It was a true German city! What a difference after Vienna! Thinking back to that corrupt Babylon-like city of races turned my stomach. The dialect in Munich was also much more natural to me. When I talked to the Lower Bavarians, it reminded me of the days from my youth. There must have been a thousand things which were or became dear and precious to me in this city. I was most attracted by the wonderful mix of natural vigor and a fine artistic temper, the unique line from the architecture of the Hofbräuhaus (*Court Brewery*), to the music house (*named the Odeon and built by Ludwig I*), and the September-October Festival (*Oktoberfest*) to the beautiful Art Museum (*Pinakothek was also built by Ludwig I*). Today, I am more attached to that city than to any other spot in the world, no doubt partly because it is so firmly intertwined with the development of my own life. The happiness of true inner contentment that I enjoyed then could only be attributed to the magic spell that the wonderful capitol of the Wittelsbachs casts on every person. (*Wittelsbach is the name of the German-Bavarian Royal Dynasty.*) Visitors who are drawn here are clearly blessed with a sharp intelligence and with a sensitive spirit.

Aside from my professional work, what attracted me the most was the study of the day's political events, especially matters of foreign policy. I was attracted to matters of foreign policy through the German Alliance Policy, which even in my Austrian days I had considered absolutely wrong. But in Vienna, I had not fully realized the extent of the German Empire's self-deception. I had been inclined to assume that people in Berlin knew how weak and unreliable their ally would actually be, but were withholding this knowledge for more or less mysterious reasons. At least, this is what I told myself. They might be trying to support an alliance policy, which Bismarck himself had originally introduced and thought it was not a good idea to break it off suddenly. They may want to avoid arousing other foreign countries, which were lying in wait for their chance to strike or perhaps it might alarm the citizenry at home.

I was soon horrified to discover from my contacts that my belief was wrong. To my surprise, everywhere I looked, even the most well-informed circles were clueless about the nature of the Hapsburg Monarchy. The common people were especially victims of the idea that their ally could be considered a serious power that would support them in their hour of need. The masses still considered the Monarchy a "German" state and thought they could depend on it. They believed that strength could be measured by the millions of people in Germany itself. They completely forgot that Austria had long since ceased to be a German state and the inner structure of this Empire was moving closer to dissolving by the hour.

I understood this state structure better than the so-called "official diplomacy" did. As usual, they were spinning blindly toward disaster. The opinions of the people resulted from what had been poured into their heads by the leaders. But the leadership was nurturing a cult like following of our "ally" similar to the historical golden calf. They probably hoped to make up for the lack of honesty on the other side by being exceptionally friendly, so everything the other side told them was always taken at face value.

In Vienna, I was furious when I saw the occasional difference between the speeches of the official statesmen and what was printed in the Vienna newspapers. Even then Vienna at least appeared to still be a German city.

The situation was totally different if one traveled from Vienna, or German-Austria, into the Empire's Slavic provinces! A person only needed to look at the newspapers to see how the deception of the Triple Alliance was judged there. They had nothing but bloody sarcasm and contempt for this "masterpiece of statesmanship". During this period of peace, while the two Emperors kissed each other on the brow as a token of friendship, the people made no bones about the fact that they knew the Alliance would collapse as soon as this glimmering glory of a Nibelungen ideal was tested in reality. (*The reference to Nibelungen is from Wagner's opera and Germanic mythology. Here it is a reference to a mythical royal family which was the supposed origin of the some royal bloodlines or to the royals of that area.*)

The people were very unhappy a few years later when the moment came for the Alliance to prove itself, and Italy broke away from the Triple Alliance leaving her two allies on their own. Italy then became an enemy herself! How the people ever believed for a moment such a miracle was possible—that Italy would fight on the same side with Austria—was absolutely incomprehensible to anyone not blinded by diplomacy. But the situation in Austria was identical.

The sole support for the alliance in Austria came from the Hapsburgs and the German-Austrians. The Hapsburgs supported it because it was in their own interests and they had no choice. The Germans supported in good faith and out of political stupidity. The good faith of the Triple Alliance came from the fact that they thought they were doing the German Empire a great service by helping to strengthen and defend it. The political stupidity was because their belief was mistaken and they were actually helping to chain the Reich to a dead state. This was bound to drag both into a bottomless pit and most of all, this very Alliance sacrificed them to the very efforts aimed at destroying German culture. The alliance gave the Hapsburgs reason to believe that the German Empire would not interfere in their domestic affairs, which left them free to carry out their domestic policy of gradually eliminating the German element without risk.

Not only were they shielded from any protest of the German government by the well-known "objectivity", but by referring to the Alliance, they could always silence the dirty mouth of Germans in Austria if it became too objectionable in its threats to stop some method being used to convert the area to a Slav region. After all, what could a German in Austria do when the German Reich itself expressed admiration and confidence for the Hapsburg regime? Was he to resist and be branded as a traitor to his own nationality throughout the German-speaking world? He, who for decades had made the greatest sacrifices for his nationality?

What value did the Alliance have once the German elements in the Hapsburg Monarchy were exterminated? Was the value of the Triple Alliance for Germany not absolutely dependent upon the preservation of German elements in Austria? Or did they really think they could live in alliance with a Hapsburg Empire of Slavs? The official attitude of German diplomacy, as well as that of the general public towards internal problems affecting the Austrian nationalities, was not merely stupid, it was insane. The Alliance destroyed any level of security and erased the possibility that a nation of seventy million could continue to exist, while at the same time, they allowed their partner to continue his policy of undermining the sole foundation of that Alliance. Eventually, all that will remain is a formal contract with Vienna diplomats. The Alliance itself would be useless and Germany could never depend on the Allies for any form of support.

Italy knew this from the beginning. If the people in Germany understood history and national psychology a bit more clearly, they never would have believed that the Princes of Rome and the Vienna Hofburgs (*the Hofburg is the Imperial Palace of the Austrian Hapsburg Royal Family*) would ever fight together. Italy herself would explode before the government would have dared send a single Italian to the battlefield for the hated Hapsburg State, not unless the soldier was sent to fight against the Hapsburgs. More than once in Vienna, I saw absolute contempt and unending hatred flare up between the Italians and the Austrian State. The sins of the House of Hapsburg against Italian freedom and independence stretching over centuries was too great to be forgotten. This kind of hatred ran too deep, neither the people nor the Italian government wanted to forget.

For Austria, there were only two options available when it came to facing Italy, either alliance or war. By choosing alliance, she was able to take her time in preparing for the second. The German alliance was both senseless and dangerous, especially since Austria's relations with Russia came closer and closer to armed conflict. Here was a classic example of the total lack of deep or profound thinking in foreign policy. Why did they decide on an alliance at all? Was it only to assure a better future for Germany than she could manage with her own resources? But the future of Germany depended on the preservation of the German people's existence. So, the question becomes, what position should the German nation take in the face of this predictable future, and how can we guarantee security for this development while living in the European balance of power?

After carefully looking at the requirements for German statesmanship to be successful in foreign politics, we must come to the following conclusion: The yearly increase in Germany's population is almost 100,000 people. The difficulty of feeding this army of new citizens is bound to grow from year to year and will eventually end in catastrophe unless we find a means in time to avoid starvation.

There were four ways to avoid this frightening development.

1. Using the French model—pregnancies could be aborted and therefore over-population avoided.

It is totally true that in times of great trouble, bad climate conditions, or a poor crop yield, Nature herself takes steps to limit a population's increase in certain countries or races. She does it both wisely and with no mercy. She does nothing to destroy actual reproduction, but prevents the survival of what is reproduced by exposing the new generation to such difficulties and deprivations that all the weaker and those that are less healthy are forced to die. Everything that Nature allows to survive faces the trials of existence a thousand times over, which makes life difficult and only the well-equipped continue to reproduce. This allows the process of separating the good from the bad to start all over. By brutally and immediately eliminating the individual that can't handle the storms of life, she keeps the race and species strong and even pushes them to supreme achievement.

Reducing the numbers creates stronger individuals and, in the end, improves the species. The result is different when man begins to limit his own number. He is not carved from the granite of Nature but wants to be "humane". He believes he knows better than the cruel Queen of all wisdom. He limits reproduction itself, not the survival of the individual. He always sees himself as an individual and never as the race. He believes this road is more humane and better justified.

Unfortunately, the results are also reversed. Nature puts a severe test upon survival while allowing free reproduction, then chooses the best among a lot of individual creatures to remain alive and propagate their species. Man, on the other hand, restricts breeding, but takes frantic care that every creature that is born will survive at any cost. This correction of divine purpose seems wise and humane to him, and he is delighted to have outwitted Nature and proven her inadequacy. The Heavenly Father's pet ape hates to acknowledge the fact that the individual's value is reduced when their numbers are restricted.

The moment reproduction is restricted and the number of births reduced, we have a craving at any cost to "save" even the weakest and most sickly instead of allowing the strongest and healthiest to survive naturally. These seeds of a new generation are bound to become more and more pitiful the longer this mockery of Nature and her will continues. If this policy continues, the nation will eventually terminate its own existence on this earth. Man may defy the eternal laws of Nature's procreation for a short time but vengeance will follow sooner or later. A stronger race will push aside the one which has grown weak. The divine will shatters all the absurd chains of this so-called humane consideration for the individual and replaces it with the humanity of Nature. She has no hesitation and wipes out what is weak in order to give a rightful place to the strong. Anyone who attempts to assure a people's existence by limiting birth rates is simply robbing the nation of its future.

2. A second way to avoid a frightening future might be the one we constantly hear recommended today: internal colonization. Those who suggest this idea mean well, but they don't have a clue what they are talking about and this would ultimately cause the greatest harm that could be imagined.

Without a doubt, the yield of certain areas of soil can be increased. However, this is only possible within certain limits and cannot continue indefinitely. For a time the increase in the number of German people can be balanced by increased crop production without the danger of starvation. But, ultimately, the demands made on life will increase faster than the population. People's requirements for food and clothing grow from year to year, and that cannot even be compared to the meager needs of our forefathers say a hundred years ago. In other words, it is a mistake to believe that increases in productivity make an increase in population possible. No, this is only true to a certain extent, since at least part of the increased crop production must go to satisfy the increased needs of men. Even with great sacrifice on one hand and constantly running industry on the other, the earth itself is bound to set a limit. All the diligence in the world can't squeeze any more out of it. Disaster still comes, even if it is somewhat delayed. For a while, starvation will only happen occasionally, when crops fail or something of that sort occurs, but as the number of people increase, it will come more and more often until the only time it doesn't happen is when bumper crops fill the grain storehouses. Finally, the time comes when the pain can no longer be alleviated and starvation is constant. Now, Nature must come to the rescue again and decide who will live or else man resorts to artificial restriction to slow the population increase.

Some may still believe that sooner or later this future must come over the world and, as part of Nature, no one can escape it. At first glance, this is absolutely true. Nevertheless, we must consider the following:

Someday, balancing the crop production with the population growth will be impossible and will force all mankind to stop expanding the human race. Either they will have to leave the decision to Nature or strike the necessary balance by solving the problem themselves, but by a method better than those available today. This will be true for all people, while now, only those races that no longer have the strength and energy to assure themselves of the land they need in this world are in trouble. At present, large areas of land still exist in the world that are being unused and just waiting to be broken by the cultivator. It is also true, however, that Nature is not holding this land in reserve for the future of a particular nation or race. The land is for the people who have the strength to take it and the diligence to till it.

Nature knows no political boundaries. She simply deposits life on this globe and watches what happens. The boldest and most industrious of her children becomes her favorite and is made the Lord over Creation.

If a group of people confines itself to internal colonization while other races are grabbing greater areas, their options will be limited when the other races can constantly increase in number. Someday this will happen and the smaller the people's living space, the sooner it will be. The best nations, which are the only truly civilized races, decide in their pacifist blindness to make no effort to expand their land and are content with internal colonization while inferior nations succeed in taking large livable areas of the world. A smaller and densely populated territory may be better from the cultural standpoint of these less ruthless races, which are limited by land and restricted in their population's growth, but people of lower civilizations, which are simple-minded and cruel, would still be able to increase without limit because of all their territory. In other words, the world will someday be dominated by the culturally inferior but more energetic part of humanity.

Some day in the future, there will be two possible outcomes. Either the world will be governed according to the ideas of our modern democracy and the equality of every decision will lie with the more numerous races, or the world will be ruled by the natural laws of relative strength, and the people possessing brutal will power will triumph over the nations that have denied themselves what they need to survive.

There is no doubt that the world will someday be the scene of huge battles for the existence of mankind. In the end, the craving for self-preservation alone will triumph. That stupid and cowardly group of humanity that thinks they know more than everyone else will find their humanitarianism melts like snow in the March sun when they face destruction. In eternal battle, mankind can find greatness; in eternal peace, it will find destruction.

For Germans, the slogan of "internal colonization" is damnation, if for no other reason, it immediately confirms the belief that we have found a peaceful existence that allows us to lead a gentle dreamlike life, by working for our living. If we ever took this idea seriously, it would mean the end of any effort to maintain our rightful place in the world. Let the average German become convinced that his life and future can be guaranteed and it will extinguish any effort to protect German vital necessities. If the whole nation took this attitude, we could regard any useful foreign policy as dead and buried along with the German people.

It is not an accident that the Jew is the one who first plants such deadly ideas among our people. He knows his wimps too well not to realize that they will be willing victims of any swindler who tells them he can snap his fingers causing Nature to jump to attention, and that he can alleviate the hard struggle for existence while still allowing them to ascend to lordship over the planet by working only when a pleasing chance presents itself, but mostly by it just happening.

I cannot emphasize enough that all German internal colonization must serve primarily to correct social abuses by those who do not make good use of land, especially by withdrawing the land from public control which prevents its use, or to release it from the grasp of speculators who only buy it without using it; but, internal colonization can never adequately assure the future of the nation without acquiring new land. If we follow any other path, we will soon be at the end of our territory, as well as at the end of our strength.

If we pursue internal colonization alone, we will soon reach a point beyond which the resources of our soil can no longer sustain us, and at the same time, we will reach a point beyond which our manpower cannot expand.

The size of a people's home territory is an important factor in its outer security. The greater the space at a people's disposal, the greater their natural protection. The decision to use military force can be made more quickly, more easily, more effectively, and more completely against people who live in small, restricted territories, but such force cannot be used so easily against the same people occupying a larger territory. The large size of a state's territory does offer a certain protection against off-handed attacks because any battle would require a long and intense struggle. The risk involved in a malicious assault will seem too great unless there are extraordinary reasons for it. That is to say, the very size of a state allows its people to more easily preserve its freedom and independence, but on the other hand, a small country invites an invader.

The first two options for striking a balance between the rising population and the fixed amount of land were opposed by so-called nationalist circles in Germany. The reasons for this attitude were different from those just given. When the idea was proposed, people were hostile to the idea of limiting births mostly because of their morals. They indignantly condemned internal colonization because they felt it was an attack against the great land owners and saw this as the beginning of a general attack against ownership of private property. Considering the way this second doctrine of salvation was supported, they were probably exactly right in their assumption. As far as the great masses were concerned, the defense was not very skillful and in no way reached the heart of the problem. Now there were only two ways remaining that could assure the rising population would receive their fill of work and bread.

3. Either new land could be acquired, purchased or taken, that would support the extra millions year by year and keep the nation self-sustaining, or

4. Industry and commerce could focus on producing goods for export and extract a living from the profits. In other words, use either a territorial or a colonial and commercial expansion policy.

These options were reviewed from various angles, discussed, argued, and opposed until finally, the option of internal colonization was definitely followed. The more solid decision would have been one that was not properly considered, the third, expansion. Additional new land for the overflowing population has countless advantages, particularly if we look to the future and not just at the present.

Preserving a healthy farming class as the cornerstone of the whole nation and can never be over-valued. Many of our current troubles result from the unsound relationship between country and city people. A solid nucleus of small and medium-scale peasant-farmers has always been the best protection against the kinds of social issues we have today. This is the only solution which allows a nation to obtain its daily bread through its own domestic economy. Industry and commerce would withdraw from their unhealthy position of leadership and take their places in the general scheme of a nationally balanced consumption economy. They are no longer the basis of the nation's livelihood, but only an aid to it. By confining themselves to this balanced role between home production and consumption in every field, they make everyone's livelihood more or less independent of foreign countries and help to assure the freedom of the state and the independence of the nation, especially in time of stress.

It has to be said that this territorial policy cannot be carried out in a place like the African Cameroons, but almost without exception will have to take place in Europe. We coolly and calmly realize there is no way it can be the intention of Heaven to give one group of people fifty times as much of the world's soil as another group controls. We must not let political frontiers distract us from the frontiers of Eternal-Justice. If this Earth really has room for everyone, we should have under our feet the land we need to exist.

No one will give up land willingly. But here, the law of self-preservation comes into play, and what is denied in peaceful friendship must be taken by force. If our forefathers had made their decisions using the same pacifist nonsense we see today, we would only possess a third of our existing territory. There would barely be any German people left to suffer in Europe. No, we owe our existence to the natural determination to fight for our own survival which gained us the two Eastern boundaries of the Empire (*the Ostmark areas bordering Poland*). This inner strength has gained us a large state and territory for our race, which alone has allowed us to survive to the present day.

There is another reason this is the correct solution. Many European states today are like inverted pyramids. The territory of some European countries is ridiculously small compared to their load of colonies and their level of foreign trade, etc. We can correctly say that the apex is in Europe and the base is all over the world. In contrast, the American Union's base is still on its own continent and only the apex touches the rest of the earth. The enormous strength of the American State comes from their size and the reverse is true for most European colonial powers which contributes to their weakness.

England does not disprove this because in front of the British Empire, we have a vast community linked by a common language and culture throughout the world. Because of its linguistic and cultural ties with the American Union, England's position cannot be compared with that of any other state in Europe.

For Germany, the only territorial policy was acquiring new land in Europe itself. Colonies are useless for this purpose unless they are suitable for large-scale settlement by Europeans. In the nineteenth century, that sort of colonial territory could no longer be obtained by peaceful means. Any attempt at a colonial expansion outside of Europe would have required a large military effort. It would have been more practical to undertake that military struggle in Europe and gather land there instead of spreading abroad.

A decision of this magnitude requires absolute, single-minded devotion once it is made. There must be no half-hearted efforts or hesitation in attacking a task which can only be achieved by using every last ounce of strength. The political leadership of the Empire must be devoted exclusively to this purpose. Everything done must be done to accomplish this task without distractions. The goal could only be achieved by force, and that knowledge should be taken to the battle with determination, peace, and calm.

Any alliance with another country should have been considered and assessed based on its usefulness from this standpoint alone. If European soil was the objective, it could be acquired primarily at the expense of Russia. The new Empire must once again march the road of the ancient Knights of the German Order and use the sword to provide land for the German plow which can then provide our daily bread.

For this kind of policy, there was only one ally in Europe—England. Only with England covering our rear could we have begun a new Germanic migration. Our justification would have been as strong as our forefathers. None of our pacifists refuse to eat food from the East, and they ignore the fact that the first plowshare there was actually a sword!

No sacrifice should have been too great to win England's friendship. We should have given up all thought of colonies and sea power and avoided competition with British industry if that is what was needed. Only absolute clear-sightedness could bring success along with abandoning world trade, colonies, and a German navy.

The State's power must be totally concentrated on the army. The result would have been a temporary setback, but a great and mighty future.

There was a time when we could have discussed this plan with England. England understood very well that Germany had a growing population with growing needs. Those needs would be filled either with England as an ally in Europe or by another ally in the world. At the turn of the century, London itself tried to establish a relationship with Germany. For the first time, people were upset thinking we might have to pull England's chestnuts out of the fire. This attitude was unfortunate and caused them to act as if an alliance did not require mutual give-and-take! Such a deal could easily have been made with England. British diplomacy was at least smart enough to know that nothing can be expected without something in return.

If a wise German foreign policy had taken over Japan's role in 1904 (*in the Russo-Japan War, also called the Manchurian Campaign, where Japan was victorious over Russia and gained large territories*), we can hardly grasp the impact it would have had for Germany.

Things would never have reached the point of "The First World War". The bloodshed in 1904 would have saved bloodshed in 1914 to 1918 by ten times. And what a position Germany would hold in the world today! The alliance with Austria would then have been nonsense. This dead state was only allied with Germany to preserve a continued peace, which could be cleverly used for the slow but sure extermination of German culture in the Monarchy. The alliance could never have been used to fight a war. If for no other reason, this alliance was impossible because there were no German national interests to be upheld. How could we expect a state that did not have the strength and determination to put an end to the destruction of German culture on its own frontier to be a true ally in time of war? If Germany didn't have enough national common sense or ruthlessness to maintain control over the fate of ten million of its own race and protect them from the Hapsburg State, it could not be expected to take on such a daring and future-focused plan. The attitude of the old German Empire toward the Austrian problem might have been seen as a test of its stamina where the destinies of the whole nation were at stake.

In any case, they had no business watching idly while German culture was whittled away year after year. The value of Austria's alliance depended totally on the preservation of the German element in Austria, but they made no effort to preserve or protect our people. They feared falling into a struggle more than anything and were finally forced into the battle at the worst time. They hoped to flee Fate and were overtaken by it. They dreamed of preserving world peace and ended up in a

World War.

Here is the main reason the expansion necessary for a German future was not even considered. They knew that the acquisition of new territory could only be accomplished by going East through Russia. They understood the battle that would be necessary and they wanted peace at any price. The song of German foreign policy had long since changed from "Preservation of the German nation by every means" to "Preservation of world peace by any means". How "well" they succeeded, everyone knows. I will have more to say on that subject later.

Then there was the fourth possibility: industry and world trade, sea power and colonies. At the beginning, this development was easier and quicker to achieve. True colonization of territory, however, is a slow process and often takes centuries. Indeed the strength of colonies results from the fact that they take a long time to build and are not the result of a sudden burst of energy like industrial growth. Industrial growth bursts can be built within a few years. Unfortunately, the industrial result is not of great quality but is frail, more like a soap-bubble. It is much easier to build quickly than to follow through with the difficult task of settling a territory with farmers and establishing farms. It is also true that the easy path is more quickly destroyed than the slow one.

When Germany chose to maintain peace at any cost, she had to realize that this choice would lead to battle someday. Only children could expect pleasant and mannerly behavior, and a constant emphasis on peaceful intentions would give them their "bananas" in the "peaceful competition of nations". These people talked as if they were groveling diplomats hoping war would never come.

No. If we took this road, someday England was bound to be our enemy. Our innocent assumptions fit nicely with pacifism, but it was silly to resent the day England would violently oppose what they saw as an attempted expansion. Obviously they would enforce their self interests. Of course, we would never have done such a thing; how could we protect our self-interests with pacifists at the helm?

A European territorial expansion policy could be carried on strictly against Russia and in-league with England as our ally. On the other hand, if we allied with Russia against England, then a colonial and world-trade policy would be possible against England and her colonies only with the support of Russia. In that case, the most important conclusion must be drawn here: that Austria must be sent packing at once.

Considered from any angle, the alliance with Austria was sheer madness, even by the turn of the century.

Germany never dreamed of allying with Russia against England any more than siding with England against Russia, because in either case, the result would have been war. It was only to avoid war that the commercial and industrial policy was chosen in the first place. By using the "peaceful economic conquest of the world" policy, they thought they would break the neck of the old policy of force once and for all. There may have been some doubts about Germany's conviction to this policy, particularly when England began to utter incomprehensible threats. We then responded by building a navy. However, this navy was not meant to attack and annihilate England, but to defend the "world peace" and the "peaceful" conquest of the world. The fleet was kept within modest limits, not just in the number and size of vessels, but in armament. These limits were set as proof that our intentions were merely to maintain peace.

The fine talk about "peaceful economic conquest" of the world was probably the greatest nonsense ever included in a guiding principle of state policy. The nonsense was made even worse by the fact that people pointed to England as an example of how this type of conquest was possible. Our part in the teaching and concept of history was the reason for this error and is the most striking proof of how many people "learn" history without even understanding it. People should have recognized England as the most crushing disproof of the theory. No people have ever used the sword more brutally in the service of its economic conquests or more ruthlessly defended them afterward than the English. Is it not the most characteristic feature of British diplomacy to obtain economic gain from political power and then to turn around and immediately transform every economic advance into political strength? What a mistake to think that England was too cowardly to back up its economic policy with its own blood! The fact that the English people lacked a "national army" was no proof. This is not a question of the form of their military, but of the will and determination to exert whatever force is needed. England always had the armament she needed. She always fought with the weapons that were necessary for success. She fought with mercenaries as long as mercenaries were enough. She dipped deep into the best blood of the whole nation when such a sacrifice was essential to bring victory, but the determination for the struggle and the stubbornness and brutality with which it was conducted, always remained the same.

The German schools, press, and comic books gradually created an image of the Englishman and his Empire, which was bound to lead to fatal self-deception. Everyone was gradually affected by this nonsense and the result was to underestimate our enemy; for that we paid dearly. The misrepresentation was so overwhelming that people firmly believed the Englishman was a business man whose sharp negotiation skill was equaled only by his incredible personal weakness. Unfortunately, it did not occur to our dignified teachers and dispensers of wisdom that a world empire the size of England's could not be built by stealing and swindling. The few men who sounded a warning were ignored or met with a conspiracy of silence. I can still remember the astonishment on my comrades' faces when we clashed in person with the Tommies (*English soldiers*) in Flanders. After the first few days of battle, it began to dawn on everyone that these Scotsmen were not the men they had been led to believe and were not like the ones depicted in comic books and newspaper articles. That was when I first began to understand some of the most useful forms of propaganda.

These false representations had one advantage for its perpetrators. The example could be used to show that the economic conquest of the world was a sound idea. If the Englishman could do it, so could we. Our greater honesty and the lack treachery, which was so English in itself, was considered a great advantage for us. People hoped to win sympathy from the smaller nations as well as the confidence of the great ones.

Because we took it all seriously, we never dreamed that our honesty was an outrage to the rest of the world. They considered our behavior an extremely cunning form of dishonesty. It was not until our Revolution that they realized our "honest" intentions were sincere to a point beyond stupidity which they no doubt found astonishing.

Only this rubbish of "peaceful economic conquest" of the world could make the foolishness of the Triple Alliance clear and understandable. What other state could Germany possibly become allies with? They could not obtain territory from any state in Europe when allied with Austria. This was the inside weakness of the Alliance from the beginning. Bismarck could allow this as a temporary solution, but that did not mean every inexperienced successor should do the same, especially in an age when the basis of Bismarck's alliance had long ago ceased to exist. Bismarck still believed in his time that Austria was a German state. But, with the gradual introduction of the general right to vote, the country had sunk to a parliament controlled, un-German state of confusion.

As a matter of race policy, the alliance with Austria was also disastrous. The growth of a new strong Slavic power was tolerated right on the borders of the Empire. They should have seen that the attitude of this power toward Germany would sooner or later be very different from that of Russia. At the same time, the Alliance itself was bound to grow empty and weak from year to year because the sole supporters of the idea lost influence in the Monarchy and were crowded out of the most influential positions.

By the turn of the century, 1900, Germany's alliance with Austria had reached the same stage as Austria's alliance with Italy. We had to make a choice: Either side with the Austrian Hapsburg Monarchy or openly protest the oppression of German culture in Austria. Once a decision of this sort is made, it usually ends in open battle.

Even psychologically, the Triple Alliance had only a modest value since the strength of an alliance declines as soon as it begins to limit itself to preserving an existing situation. On the contrary, an alliance increases in strength when it offers both parties the hope of territorial expansion. It is true everywhere that strength is not in the defense, but in the attack.

This was recognized in many places, but, unfortunately, not in the so-called "competent" circles of the elected officials. Colonel Ludendorff, Officer on the Great General Staff at that time, pointed to these weaknesses in a paper written in 1912. Of course the other "statesmen" attached no value or importance to the situation. Clear common sense is apparently only needed for ordinary mortals and it can always be dispensed with in the case of "diplomats".

Germany was lucky that Austria was the cause of the war in 1914. This required the Hapsburgs to participate. If war had come from the other direction, Germany would have been alone. The Hapsburg State could never have taken part, or even wanted to take part, in a struggle started by Germany. If Germany was the cause of war, Austria would have done what Italy was later so loudly condemned for doing. It would have remained "neutral" in order to at least protect the State from a revolution at the very start. The Austrian Slavs would rather have broken up the Monarchy in 1914 than offer to help Germany.

Very few people at that time realized how great the dangers were or the added problems that the alliance with the Monarchy brought with it. In the first place, Austria had too many enemies who hoped to inherit the decaying State. During that time, Germany was bound to be exposed to some hatred because Germany was the obstruction to the dismemberment of the Monarchy which was almost universally desired. In the end, nations came to the conclusion that Vienna could only be reached by way of Berlin.

In the second place, Germany lost its best and most promising chance of forming an alliance with another country. Instead, tensions increased with Russia and with Italy. The general feelings in Rome toward Germany were favorable and equally hostile toward Austria, but tensions still built against Germany politically.

Since the commercial and industrial expansion policy had been established, there was no longer any reason for Germany to struggle with Russia. Only the enemies of both Germany and Russia could have any real interest in a conflict between them. In fact, it was chiefly Jews and Marxists who used every way they could think of to stir up war between the two states.

Third and lastly, the Alliance concealed one huge threat to Germany. Any great power that was hostile to Bismarck's Empire could easily mobilize a whole string of states against Germany by promising spoils at the expense of the Austrian ally.

All of Eastern Europe, especially Russia and Italy, could have been raised up against Austria and the Monarchy. The world coalition started by King Edward would never have happened if Germany's ally, Austria, had not been an irresistibly tempting prize. This promise was the only way to unite these states that otherwise had such varied desires and goals. In a general advance against Germany, everyone could hope to benefit at the expense of Austria. The danger was actually even greater because Turkey also seemed to belong to this unlucky alliance as a silent partner.

The forces behind International Jewish World Finance needed this bait in order to carry out its long-cherished plan of destroying Germany. At this time Germany had not yet given in to general international control because of its finance and economic structure. It was the only way to forge a coalition which would be strong and bold enough and would have the numbers of marching millions, which could battle with the armored skin of Siegfried at last. (*A Wagner opera reference where Siegfried bathes in the blood of a dragon, which forms scales on him as protection, similar to Achilles. Here Siegfried is another name for the Germanic race.*)

Even in Austria, I was completely unhappy with the Hapsburg Monarchy alliance, and it was now the subject of a long, inward analysis which ended by confirming my earlier opinion even more strongly.

In the humble circles in which I moved, I didn't hide my conviction that this unhappy treaty was with a state marked for destruction, and it must lead to a catastrophic collapse of Germany too if we did not get out in time. My solid conviction never wavered, even when the storm of the First World War seemed to have cut off all sensible thinking and the flood of enthusiasm had swept away those who could coldly look at reality with total objectivity. Whenever I heard these problems discussed, even while I was at the front, I maintained my opinion that the alliance must be broken off, and the sooner the better for the German nation. It would be no sacrifice at all to deliver up the Hapsburg Monarchy if Germany could limit the number of her adversaries. Millions strapped on the steel helmet to save the German nation, not to preserve a wicked dynasty.

Once or twice before the war, at least one camp would have some doubts about the soundness of the alliance policy. From time to time, German-Conservative circles began to warn about being too trusting. Their warnings were ignored along with all other common sense. People were convinced they were on the high road to a world "conquest". All they could see was the enormous chance of success without any cost whatsoever. Once again, there was nothing for the average man to do but watch in silence while the "elected officials" marched the country straight to damnation, with the good folk following after them like rats, following the Pied Piper of Hamelin. (*The Pied Piper of Hamelin is the subject of a Middle Ages legend where he led a great many children from the town of Hamelin, Germany to their death after he was not paid for his services leading rats away from the town.*)

The general state of our entire political thinking was the main reason it was possible to make a group of people accept the nonsense of "economic conquest" as a political goal, and this same weak thinking caused them to accept the preservation of "world peace" as a political goal.

With the victorious march of German industry and invention and the growing successes of German trade, people could no longer see that the whole thing was based on the assumption that the state was strong. In many circles, people went so far as to argue that the state itself owed its existence solely to the industry, and that the state was primarily an economic institution which should be governed based on economic interests. They thought its existence depended on the economic life—a condition which was praised as the healthiest and most natural form of being.

This is wrong. The state has nothing whatsoever to do with any particular economic concept or development. The state is not a union of economic contracting parties within a definite limited area to perform economic tasks. It is the organization of a community. A collection of physically and spiritually similar people who, together, make the preservation of their species possible, as well as the accomplishment of the goal which Providence has set for their existence. That and that alone is the purpose and meaning of a state.

The economic system is one of the many methods needed to reach this goal. It can never be the purpose of a state unless it is set up on an incorrect and unnatural basis from the beginning. That explains why a state should not assume any territorial limitations as a requirement of its founding. Expansion is necessary for people who want to assure their species continues with their own resources and who are ready to fight in order to live from their own efforts. People who succeed in sneaking in among the rest of mankind like loafers—letting the others work for them while making all kinds of excuses—can form states without any definite living boundaries of their own. This is especially true of those people that the rest of honest humanity is suffering from today, the bloodsucking Jews.

The Jewish State has never been limited by space. Their one race has universally unlimited territory. Therefore, these people have always formed a state within the state. It is one of the most brilliant tricks ever invented to have this State sail under the colors of a "religion". The tolerance by the Aryan is assured because he is always ready to make allowances for a religious group. The Mosaic Law religion (*commonly known as Halakha, which is the collective body of Jewish law*) is nothing but a doctrine for the preservation of the Jewish race. This is why it includes almost every field of sociological, political, and economic knowledge that could possibly serve that purpose.

The instinct for preservation of the species is the original reason for the formation of human communities. The state is a race oriented organization and not an economic organization. As great as the difference is between them, it is still totally incomprehensible to the "statesmen" of today. They think they can build up the state by purely economic means, but in reality, the state comes from the will of a species and race to survive. These qualities are always heroic traits and never the ego of a businessman. After all, the survival of a species depends on its willingness to sacrifice the individual. The words of the poet, "And if you do not stake your lives, life shall never be your prize" (*quoted from the song Curassiers in Schiller's Wallenstein*), signify that giving up personal existence is necessary to assure the survival of the species. The most essential requirement for the formation and maintenance of a state is a community of similar character and a species who believe in that community, and are willing to back it up by whatever means are necessary. People protecting their own soil become heroes. With parasites, it is different. It leads to lying hypocrisy and malicious cruelty.

The initial formation of a state can only take place by applying these heroic qualities. In the resulting struggle for self-preservation, some people who lack these qualities will fall victim to the parasites and become economic slaves who will be defeated and eventually die. These are not heroes; they can't resist the methods of the hostile parasites. But even here, it is almost never a lack of wisdom, but more a lack of courage and determination which tries to hide under the cloak of humane principles.

There is only the slightest connection between economics and state-building and state-preserving. This is best demonstrated by the inner strength of a state which only rarely coincides with its economic success. We can also find countless examples that show prosperity is a sign of approaching decline. If the formation of human communities were primarily for economic forces, strong economic development would mean the greatest strength of the state and not the other way around.

Faith in the state-building or state-preserving power of economics is particularly hard to understand when it holds influence in a country that clearly demonstrates the opposite from its history. Prussia wonderfully proved that ideals and virtues alone make the creation of a state possible and not material qualities. Only under their protection can economic life flourish. When the elements that were responsible for state-building collapse, the economic structure also topples. This is a process we are now seeing in a sad way. The material interests of mankind always flourish best when they are shadowed by heroic virtues, but when economics attempts to take center stage, they destroy the essential part of their own existence.

Whenever a strong political power has existed in Germany, economic life has always progressed. Whenever the economic system has become the only substance of our people's life, it smothered the virtues of idealism, and the state collapsed and carried the economic benefits with it into the ground.

If we ask ourselves what forces preserve a state, we can lump them all in one category: the ability and willingness of an individual to sacrifice himself for the whole. These virtues have nothing at all to do with economics. We can see this from the simple fact that man never sacrifices himself for economics. People don't die for business, but for ideals. Nothing showed more clearly the Englishman's superior ability to look into the psychology and into the soul of his people than the motivation he demonstrated in his struggle. While we were battling for bread, England was fighting for "freedom" and it was freedom for the little nations, not even for herself. We laughed and were annoyed by this audacity. We showed the same thoughtless stupidity the German statesman demonstrated so well before the war. Men lost the slightest desire to die of their own free will. As long as the German people in 1914 still believed they were fighting for ideals, the battle continued; when they were told to fight for economic survival, they gave up. When something finds itself fighting simply for the production of daily bread, it prefers to give up.

Our intelligent "statesmen" were astonished at this change in public sentiment. They never understood that from the moment a man begins to fight for an economic interest, he avoids the death that would prevent him from ever enjoying the rewards of his struggle. The most delicate mother becomes a heroine to save her own child.

The battle for the preservation of the species and of the home or state that shelters it is what always made men willing to go to war.

We offer the following as an eternal truth: No state has ever been created by establishing a peaceful economy. Only through the instincts that preserve the species, whether they are heroic virtue or shrewdness, have states been created. Heroic virtue produces true Aryan, working, civilized states while shrewdness produces Jewish parasite colonies. When instincts in a race or a state are overrun by economics, the economic structure itself releases the causes that lead to defeat and oppression.

The belief before the First World War that Germany could open up or even conquer the world through peaceful colonial means and commercial policy was a sign that the state-building and state-preserving virtues had been lost. Also lost was the insight, strength of will, and determination needed to take decisive action. The law of Nature brought the First World War and its results as revenge upon our heads. Anyone who failed to look below the surface would only see an unsolvable puzzle when considering this universal attitude of the German nation. After all, Germany herself was the most wonderful example of an empire created by power and military valor. Prussia, the nucleus of the Empire, was created by brilliant courage, not by financial operations or business deals. The Empire was missing the magnificent reward of a leadership based on power politics and based on the courage to risk death. How could the political instincts of the Germans become so diseased? This was not a one-time occurrence, but a matter of destructive forces in frightening numbers that spread among the people and attacked the nation like a cancerous ulcer. It seemed as if a constant stream of poison was being injected by some mysterious unseen power into the very blood vessels of what had once been a hero's body. As this poison spread, it crippled common sense and the simple instinct of self-preservation.

My attitude toward the German economic policy and Triple Alliance policy from 1912 to 1914 forced me to review these questions over and over. Through the process of elimination I found the solution to the puzzle; it was a power which I had already come to know in Vienna from a different standpoint. The source of the problem was the Marxist doctrine and their resulting actions throughout the nation.

For the second time in my life, I dug into this doctrine of destruction. This time I was guided by my observations of what was happening in the nation's political life and not by the impressions and effect of my daily surroundings. I became absorbed again in the theoretical literature of this new world and tried to understand its possible consequences. I compared these with the actual events and their effects in political, cultural, and economic life. For the first time, I also devoted my attention to those efforts made to stop this plague.

I studied the purpose, struggle for, and effect of Bismarck's emergency legislation. (*Bismarck passed laws in 1878 to curb Social Democrat and Marxist activities.*) Gradually, I laid a rock-solid foundation for my own belief and I have never had to revise my views on this issue. I also examined the connection between Marxism and Jewry more closely. While in Vienna, I had believed Germany was an unshakable Colossus, but now, uneasy doubts began to build in me. In my own mind and in the small circle of my acquaintances, I argued German foreign policy and discussed what I believed to be the incredibly negligent treatment of the most important problem that then existed in Germany at that time, Marxism. I really could not understand how they could stagger so blindly towards a horrible danger whose aims were clearly and openly discussed by the leaders of Marxism. Among my acquaintances, then and now, I warned against the smooth talking, soothing slogan of all cowardly wretches who said, "Nothing can happen to us!" A similar troublesome attitude had destroyed one giant empire already. Did everyone believe Germany alone was going to be exempt from the laws that governed all other societies?

In 1913 and 1914, I announced my conviction that the future of all Germans depended on destroying Marxism. Some of the circles where I spoke are now faithfully part of the National Socialist movement today. In the destructive German Triple Alliance policy, I saw the result of the Marxist doctrine's destructive hand. The fearful teachings of this poison almost invisibly destroyed every foundation of a healthy economic policy and every healthy state concept. This occurred in such a way that the victims' who were contaminated did not even realize the acts and desires that resulted were actually part of a World-Concept which they were otherwise strongly against.

The inner decline of the German people started long before they recognized the destroyer of their existence was growing among them. Now and then, there was some treatment of the disease, but the symptoms were too often confused with the cause. As people did not or would not look at the cause, the struggle against Marxism was as effective as a long-winded quack's miracle cure.

5. THE FIRST WORLD WAR

What depressed me more than anything when I was a wild youth was that I had been born into an age that honored only tradesmen or civil servants. The surge of large waves seen in history seemed to have calmed down so much that the future belonged only to the "peaceful competition of people" or to quiet, mutual swindling where any aggressive method of self-defense had been abandoned. More and more, the individual nations began to resemble businesses that mutually undercut one another, stole customers and orders, and tried to outwit each other in every way, while making protests as loud as they were harmless. This development not only seemed to progress, but it was generally hoped it would someday transform the world into one huge department store where the reception area would for all time display statues of the most skillful manipulators and most harmless executives. The English could then furnish the businessmen, the Germans would furnish the administrative officials, and the Jews would have to sacrifice themselves as managers since they speak the most languages, and, by their own admission, they never make a profit, but "keep paying" forever.

Why couldn't I have been born a hundred years sooner? Say at the time of the Wars of Liberation (*The Napoleonic War of the Sixth Coalition 1812-14 against France*) when a man had some value apart from the "business" which he operated.

It often annoyed me when I thought that my life started too late. I believed the age of "peace and good order" in front of me was an undeserved cruel strike of Fate. Even as a boy, I was no "pacifist" and every attempt to push me in that direction was a failure.

Then, the Boer War (*fought between Britain and two African Boer republics 1889-1902*) appeared like a bright light on my horizon. Every day, I anxiously waited the newspapers. I devoured news reports and letters. I was happy to witness this heroic struggle, even if it was from a distance. During the Russo-Japanese War (*commonly called the Manchurian Campaign in 1904-1905 between Russia and Japan over Manchuria and Korean territories*), I was more mature and more observant. Here I took sides for more rational reasons and supported the Japanese in every discussion we had. I saw the defeat of the Russians as a defeat of the Austrian Slavs.

Years had passed since then, and what I had thought was slow-moving weakness as a boy, I now believed to be the calm before the storm. Even in my Vienna days, the Balkans (*the peninsula territories east of Italy*) were burning under the feeble heat that usually predicts the approach of a hurricane. Flashes of light were already beginning to flicker, only to be lost again in the strange darkness. Then came the

Balkan War (*1912-13*) and with it, the first puff of wind whipped across a nervous Europe. The approaching events weighed on men like a nightmare—like feverish, brooding tropical heat—and it continued until the constant worry finally turned the feeling of approaching catastrophe into desire. Let Heaven give in to the destiny that could not be avoided. Then, the first mighty flash of lightning struck the earth. The storm broke and the thunder of the sky was mixed with the roar of the artillery in the First World War.

When news of the murder of Archduke Francis Ferdinand arrived in Munich, I was sitting at home and caught only bits and pieces of what happened. (*The assassination of Archduke Francis Ferdinand sparked the First World War when Austria-Hungary declared war against Serbia.*) At first I was afraid and worried that the bullets had come from the pistol of a German student. They were angry at the Crown Prince over his constant work to convert the nation to a Slav region, and they wanted to free the German people from this enemy within. It was easy to imagine what the result would have been; a new wave of persecution against German elements in Austria which would have been "thoroughly justified" by the whole world. But immediately afterward, I found myself dumbfounded at the way Fate played her game of mysterious revenge when I heard the names of the suspected assassins. They were Serbians.

The greatest friend to Slavs was brought down by fanatical Slav patriot's bullet. Anyone who had watched the relationship between Austria and Serbia in previous years could have no doubt that this act started boulders rolling that could never be stopped.

It isn't fair to criticize the Vienna government today for the method and theme of the ultimatum it presented then. No other power in the world could have acted differently in a similar situation. On her Southeast border, Austria had an unyielding, deadly enemy that kept provoking the Monarchy more and more often and would have never stopped until their time came to shatter the Empire.

There was good reason to fear this would happen with the death of the old Kaiser. By then, perhaps the Monarchy would not be in any position to offer serious resistance. In its last years, the whole State rested completely on Francis Joseph and the broad masses felt that the death of this aged incarnation of the Empire meant the death of the Empire itself. More than that, it was one of the sly tricks of Slavic policy that they were able to create the impression that the Austrian State owed its continued existence exclusively to the Monarch's marvelous and unique skill. This piece of flattery pleased the Austrian Hofburg Imperial Palace even more because the Emperor didn't deserve it. The sting hidden in this eulogy was not noticed. People either did not see or did not want to see that the more the Monarchy depended on the "outstanding governing skill" as they called it, of this "wisest Monarch" of all times, the more catastrophic the situation was destined to be when Fate finally knocked at the door to demand its due.

Could old Austria even think without the old Kaiser? Would not the tragedy of Maria Theresa be repeated? (*Maria Theresa was an Archduchess of Austria and the only ruler until 1765 when she recognized her son, Joseph II, as co-regent. She unified the Hapsburg Monarchy, but after the death of her husband withdrew and was no longer active as a Monarch even though she had made many civil reforms earlier.*)

No, it is really unfair to Vienna government circles to blame them for starting a war that otherwise might have been avoided. It could no longer have been avoided— possibly postponed for one or two years—but not avoided. The curse of German and Austrian diplomacy was that it had always tried to postpone the inevitable reckoning until it was finally forced to strike at the most inopportune moment. We can be sure that another attempt at peace would only have brought on the war at an even more unfavorable time.

Anyone who did not want this war must have the courage to accept the consequences of their past refusal. This consequence could have only been the sacrifice of Austria. The war would still have come, but probably not with everyone against us. Instead, it would have meant the separation of the Hapsburg Monarchy. It was necessary to decide whether to take part or simply to gawk empty-handed while Destiny took its course. The very people who today curse the loudest and pass judgment about the starting of the war were the ones who took the most fatal part in leading us into it.

For decades, the Social Democrats had been sneaky in their efforts to spark war against Russia. The German Centrist Party (*a Catholic political party*), on the other hand, had made the Austrian State the pivotal point of German policy for religious reasons. Now, the results of this craziness were upon us. What came next was inevitable and could no longer be avoided under any circumstances. The German government's share of the guilt was that in its effort to preserve peace, it missed all the best moments to fight. It became wrapped up in the alliance to preserve world peace and finally became the victim of a world coalition, which was absolutely determined to oppose a World War and to preserve world peace at any cost. Even if the Vienna government had given an ultimatum in more palatable terms, it would not have changed the situation but, instead, it might have generated public outrage if the masses saw the ultimatum as too moderate and certainly not extreme or excessive. Anyone who denies this today is either a forgetful blockhead or an intentional liar.

The First World War of 1914 was not forced on the masses, but was demanded by the people. They wanted to finally put an end to the lingering uncertainty. Only on that ground can we understand how more than two million German men followed the flag into this supreme struggle, ready to protect it with their last drop of blood.

To me, those days seemed like deliverance from the anger of my youth. Even now, I am not ashamed to say that I fell on my knees overcome by a wave of enthusiasm, and thanked Heaven from an overflowing heart that it had granted me the good fortune to live in this time.

A battle for freedom had begun whose unparalleled greatness the earth had never seen. Destiny had barely begun to take its course before the great masses started to realize that this time it was not just Serbia's or Austria's fate at stake, but the existence of the German people itself.

After many years, the people could finally see the future. At the very outset of the monstrous struggle, the intoxicating, extravagant enthusiasm was quickly replaced by the necessary serious undertones. Only this realization made the nation's exaltation more than just a passing fad. This was necessary because the majority of the people did not have the slightest idea how long the battle would be. They dreamed of soldiers being home again by winter so they could return to their peaceful jobs.

What man wants, he also hopes for and believes in. The overwhelming majority of the nation was sick of the eternal uncertainty, so it was understandable that no one believed in a peaceful solution of the Austrian-Serbian conflict and instead hoped for a final settlement. I was one of these millions.

The news of the assassination had barely reached Munich when two ideas flashed through my mind. First, war was now unavoidable, but beyond this, the Hapsburg State would now be compelled to stick to its alliance. What I had always feared most was the possibility that some day Germany itself might be involved in a conflict that was not caused by Austria. Then, for domestic, political reasons, the Austrian State would not have the resolution to back up its ally. Even though the alliance had already been made, the Slavic majority of the Empire would have sabotaged it at once and would have preferred to shatter the whole State rather than given help to their ally. This danger was now removed. The old Austrian State had to fight whether it wanted to or not.

My own attitude toward the conflict was perfectly clear and simple. What I saw was not Austria fighting for some satisfaction against Serbia, but Germany fighting for her all. The real battle was the German nation fighting for its existence or non-existence, for its freedom and future. Bismarck's creation must now go out and fight. What its fathers had once conquered in battle with their heroic blood—from Weissenburg to Sedan and Paris—young Germany had to now earn back. If the battle was victorious, then our people would rejoin the circle of great nations once more. The German Empire could prove itself again as a mighty stronghold of peace without having to put its children on short rations for the sake of maintaining peace.

As a boy and young man, I had often wished I could demonstrate that my nationalistic enthusiasm was no empty obsession. It often seemed to me almost a sin to cry out in joy with the crowd without having any real right to do so. Who could rightfully shout *hurray* without having tried it, when all pettiness is over and the Goddess of Fate's cruel hand begins to test the strength of everyone's convictions? Like millions of others, my heart overflowed with happiness now that I could be free of this paralyzing feeling. I had sung *"Deutschland über alles" ("Germany ahead of all", the actual song title is "The Song of Germany")* and shouted, "Heil" so often at the top of my lungs. Now it seemed to me almost like Heavenly grace granted retroactive justice by allowing me to testify to the truth of my convictions and prove they were real. I knew from the first moment that in the face of an inevitable war, I would abandon my books immediately. I also knew that my place must be where the inner voice of conscience sent me.

I left Austria primarily for political reasons. Now that the struggle was beginning, it seemed natural that I should review my convictions. I would not fight for the Austrian Hapsburg State, but I was ready at any time to die for my people and for the German Empire they belonged to.

On the third of August 1914, I presented a petition to His Majesty King Ludwig III, requesting permission to join a Bavarian regiment. During those days, the Cabinet Chancellery had a lot to deal with, but I was overjoyed when I received an answer to my request the very next day. I opened the letter with trembling hands and read that my petition was granted and I was instructed to enroll in a Bavarian regiment. My gratitude and joy was unbelievable. In a few days, I was wearing the uniform that I would wear for the next six years.

For me, and probably for every German, the greatest and most unforgettable period of my earthly life now began. Compared to the events of this incredible struggle, everything in my past paled as if it was nothing. Now, as the tenth anniversary of the great event approaches, I think back with melancholy pride about those weeks at the beginning of the heroic struggle of our people, where Fate graciously allowed me to take part.

It seems like just yesterday. Image after image goes through my mind. I see myself uniformed and with my beloved comrades we are marching out for the first time, drilling until the day our departure finally came. I and many others were worried whether or not we would arrive too late at the front. This often kept me awake at night. In the victorious delight we took when we heard about each new heroic deed, there was also some irritation since each new victory seemed to increase the danger that we would arrive too late to play our part.

At last, the day came when we left Munich to fall in and do our duty. I saw the Rhine River for the first time as we were traveling beside its gentle waves on our way west to protect it. The Rhine—the German river of rivers—we were now going to protect it from the greed of our old enemy. When the gentle rays of the dawn sun first beamed down on us through the delicate veil of morning mist from the Niederwald Monument (*a statue that commemorates the founding of the German Empire after the Franco-Prussian War*), the old song "Wacht Am Rhein" ("*Guard on the Rhine*") roared from the long transport train into the morning sky, and my heart was ready to burst in patriotic pride. Then came a cold, wet night in Flanders and we marched through it in silence. When day began to break through the mist, we were suddenly met with an iron greeting as it hissed over our heads. With a sharp crack, it hurled the little pellets of shrapnel through our ranks, splashing up the wet soil. Before the little cloud was gone, the first "hurray" came from two hundred voices in response to this greeting by the Angel of Death. Then the crackling and thunder began; singing and howling, and with feverish eyes, everyone marched forward, faster and faster. At last, across beet-fields and hedges, the battle began—the battle of man against man. From a distance, the sound of song reached our ears, coming closer and closer, and jumping from company to company. Just as Death began to busy himself in our ranks, the song reached us too, and we in turn passed it on: "Deutschland, Deutschland über alles, über alles in der Welt!" ("*Germany before all, Germany ahead of everything in the world*".)

Four days later, we went back to camp. We even walked differently. Seventeen-year-old boys now looked like men. Maybe the volunteers of the List Regiment (*The Second Infantry Bavarian Regiment*) had not really learned to fight, but they did know how to die like old soldiers.

That was the beginning. That's how it went on year after year, but horror had replaced the romance of battle. Enthusiasm gradually cooled down and the wild excitement was smothered in deadly fear. For each man, the time came when he had to struggle between the instinct of self-preservation and the obligations of duty. I was not exempt from this struggle. Whenever Death was close, a vague something in me tried to revolt and tried to disguise itself as reason to the weak body, but it was still just that sly cowardice laying sneaky traps. A great tugging and warning would begin, and only the last remnant of conscience would get me through the day.

But the harder this voice worked to caution me and the louder and more piercingly it spoke to me, the stiffer my resistance became, until finally, after a long inner struggle, duty won. This struggle was decided for me by the winter of 1915-1916. My will had finally become the absolute master. The first few days I ran to the fight laughing and gloating, but now, I was calm and determined. That was the frame of mind that would endure. Now, I could proceed to the final trial of Fate without nerves cracking or the mind failing. The young volunteer had become an old soldier.

This transformation had taken place throughout the army. They had come out of the perpetual battle older and stronger, and whatever could not stand up to the storm was simply broken.

Only now was it fair to judge this army. After two or three years of fighting one battle after another—always fighting a force greater in numbers and weaponry, starving and suffering hardships—then was the time to judge the value of that unique army.

Thousands of years from now, no one will speak of heroism without mentioning the German Army in the First World War. Through the veil of history, the iron front of gray steel helmets will appear, unswerving and unyielding, a monument of immortality. As long as there are Germans, they will remember that these were sons of their forefathers.

When I was a soldier I did not want to talk politics. That was not the time for it. To this day, I am convinced that the last stable-boy was more valuable to the Fatherland than the first "parliamentarian". I had never hated these windbags more than now as every quiet, truthful lad said what he had to say point blank in the face of the enemy, or else left the small talk at home and focused on doing his duty in silence. Yes, at that time I hated all these "politicians", and if I had my say about it, a parliamentary pick-and-shovel brigade would have been formed at once. There, they could have chattered between themselves to their hearts' content without annoying or harming decent, honest humanity.

I wanted nothing to do with politics, but could not help adopting attitudes toward things that affected the whole nation, and especially to things that affected us soldiers.

There were two things which annoyed me at that time that I thought were harmful to our interests. After the very first report of victory, a certain section of the press began slowly, and possibly unnoticed to some, to sprinkle a few drops of bitterness into the general enthusiasm. This was done behind a false front of benevolence, good intentions, and concern. They did not believe in celebrating victories "too much". They claimed they were afraid that such celebrations were unworthy of a great nation and out of place. The bravery and heroism of the German soldier were to be taken for granted because they were accepted facts which did not justify such jubilation. They said outbursts of joy should not be encouraged because foreign countries may view quiet and dignified rejoicing as more attractive than unrestrained excitement. Finally, we Germans, should not forget that the war was not our creation and that we shouldn't be ashamed to admit openly as men that we were ready at any time to do our share in the reconciliation of mankind. It was, therefore, not wise to tarnish the purity of the army's deeds by too much shouting. The rest of the world might not understand such behavior. They said nothing was more admired than the modesty and restraint with which a true hero calmly and silently forgot his deeds. That was basically their warning to the people.

Instead of bringing these fellows to the forefront and pulling them high on a pole with a rope, so that the victorious enthusiasm of the nation should no longer offend the sensibilities of these knights of the pen, people actually began to follow their lead and issue warnings against the "unsuitable" character of the victory celebrations.

The politicians never realized that once the enthusiasm was stopped, it could not be revived when it was needed. It is a state of intoxication and must be maintained as such. Without this sort of enthusiasm, how could the nation endure a struggle which would make enormous demands on their spiritual stamina?

I knew the nature of the broad masses well enough to realize that a "showy" display of moral superiority was no way to fan the flames needed to keep the iron hot. I thought officials were crazy when they did not act to raise the boiling point, increase the heat of passion, but I surely didn't understand why the government would push policy to restrain the little excitement that existed.

The second thing that annoyed me was the attitude that Marxism was acceptable. In my eyes, this just proved that people had no idea how dangerous this disease truly was. They seemed to sincerely believe that by no longer recognizing any political party distinctions during the war, they had brought Marxism to reason and restrained it.

Marxism is not a matter of a political party, but of a doctrine which is bound to lead to the utter destruction of humanity. This was not widely understood because that side of Marxist theory was not taught at our Jew-ridden universities. Too many people have been trained to think that if something is not taught in their university then it is not important enough to pick up a book and learn about it, which is silly, especially among the higher level government officials and civil servants. This revolutionary trend passed over these "intellectual-official-heads" without them paying any attention to it, which is the reason why state institutions usually drag behind private ones.

Heaven knows the German proverb is truer of those intellectual-officials than of anyone else: "What the peasant doesn't know, will not bother him". (*The English idiom is "What you don't know can't hurt you", a variation of "Ignorance is bliss", "If you do not know about a problem then you cannot make yourself unhappy by worrying about it."*) The few exceptions just prove the rule.

It was an unparalleled mistake to identify the German workman with Marxism in August of 1914. When the time came, the German workman chose to free himself from the grasp of this poisonous epidemic or he could never have taken part in the struggle of the war. But people were stupid enough to think that, now, perhaps, Marxism had become "nationalistic". This was a stroke of "genius", which proves that for many long years, none of these official heads of the State had ever bothered to study the nature of the Marxist doctrine. If they had done their homework, such a crazy idea would have never survived.

Marxism's ultimate goal is and always will be the destruction of all non-Jewish national states. It was horrified to see that in July of 1914, the German working class, which it had previously trapped, was waking up and quickly entering the service of the Fatherland. Within a few days, the whole smoke screen of this deceit, of this infamous fraud on the people, was blown away and suddenly the Jewish leaders were alone and deserted. It was as if there wasn't a trace left of the nonsense and insanity which they had been pouring into the masses for sixty years. It was a bad moment for the deceivers of the German working class people. But, the instant the leaders recognized the danger that threatened them, they dawned their tarn-caps and boldly pretended to take part in the national revival. (*A tarn cap, or Tarnkappe, means a magical cap that allows the wearer to take any form they wish. Siegfried uses one in Wagner's operas and the reference is common in Germanic stories. Other stories give it the power of invisibility and strength;, however, it is likely Hitler was referring to Wagner's version meaning the people put on the trappings and took the form of a nationalist as if by magic.*)

This would have been the time to take a stand against the whole fraudulent brotherhood of Jewish pests hiding among the people. Now was the time to give them a severe penance without the slightest consideration for any protest or consequence that might have arisen as a result. In August of 1914, the Jewish chant of international solidarity was gone with a single blow to the heads of the German working class. A few weeks later, this nonsense was replaced by American shrapnel as it poured the blessings of worker-solidarity over the helmets of the marching soldier's columns.

Now that the German workman had returned to his own nationality, it should have been the duty of any responsible national government to unmercifully annihilate the agitators who stood against it. If the best men were falling at the front, the pests assaulting national spirit could at least have been exterminated at home.

But instead, His Majesty the Kaiser himself held out his hand to these old criminals offering these disloyal assassins of the nation mercy, protection, and an opportunity to collect themselves for their next strike. (*The old criminals refers to Dr. Edouard Bernstein, a Socialist Democrat, and Albert Ballin, managing director of the Hamburg-America cruise ships and friends with Wilhelm II.*) The serpent could then go on working, more cautiously than before, but this made him more dangerous. While honest people dreamed of peace and security, the lying criminals were organizing a revolution. I was more than dissatisfied with the fact that officials had settled on a set of terrible half-measures to deal with the problem, but I didn't even realize how horrible the result would eventually be.

Then what should have been done next? The leaders of the whole movement should have been put under lock and key immediately. They should have been put on trial and the nation freed from them. Every resource of military power should have been used to brutally exterminate this epidemic. The Marxist parties should have been dissolved and the Reichstag brought to reason at the point of a bayonet if necessary. Or better still, it should have been immediately abolished. Just as the Republic dissolves parties today, they had even more reason to resort to this means then. After all, the existence or destruction of an entire people was at stake!

This would certainly have raised another question: Can intellectual ideas be destroyed by the sword at all? Can violence be used to combat a "World-Concept"? I asked myself these questions more than once at that time.

If we think through similar cases found in history, especially cases of religious matters, we arrive at this principle: After a certain point in their development, concepts and ideas as well as movements of a spiritual nature, whether true or not, can never be broken by force. The only exception is when force is used to replace these ideas with a fresh, new idea, thought, or World-Concept that burns even brighter and stronger than the one it replaces.

The use of force alone without the driving power of a strong spiritual or intellectual concept can never destroy an idea or even slow how fast it spreads, not unless force is used for the complete extermination of every last supporter and the absolute destruction of all related traditions that may linger. This usually means the disappearance of this state from the realm of political power for a long time and sometimes, forever. The state can never stand beside other nations, nor will they allow it after such an exercise of power. Experience shows that a blood sacrifice of this sort hits the nation in the best part of the people. Any persecution carried on without an intellectual or spiritual basis appears morally unjustified and the people will react. This incites the most valuable part of a population to become champions of the ideas by adopting the beliefs of the unjustly persecuted movement. Many people do this simply out of a feeling of opposition toward the state's attempt to kill an idea by brutal violence.

The number of movement followers grows at the same rate that the persecution increases. A complete destruction of the new teaching can only be carried out by a tremendous and ever-increasing extermination until finally, the people or state in question loses all the valuable blood it has. All the people of value are gone. Retribution is then at hand. Such an internal purge may indeed take place, but the price is the loss of the nation's strength. This process will always be useless from the beginning if the doctrines to be fought have gone beyond a certain small circle.

As with all growing movements, destruction is only possible when the movement is young. While resistance increases with the passing years, the movement will grow and then yield to fresh and younger members who will sprout new groups in a different form and with slightly different motives.

Almost all attempts to uproot a doctrine and its related organizations by violence with no intellectual or spiritual basis are failures. Frequently in fact, such efforts produce the opposite result from the one intended.

When sheer force is used to combat the spread of a doctrine, then that force must be used systematically and persistently. Only regular and steady suppression of a doctrine can possibly be successful. The moment there is any hesitation and violence alternates with mercy, the doctrine being overcome will not only recover, but it will gain new value from each following persecution. This happens because when pressure is eased, resentment at what has been suffered brings new followers to the old doctrine, and existing supporters cling to it with greater defiance and deeper hatred than ever. In fact, after the danger is gone, even those who renounced and betray their movement will try to return to their old beliefs. The only way to achieve success is through a constant and regular use of violence. This persistence can only happen with a definite intellectual and spiritual conviction backing it up. All violence not founded on a solid spiritual or intellectual basis is indecisive and uncertain. It lacks the stability that can only live in a fanatically intense world concept. It flows from the energy and brutal determination of an individual. This dependence on the individual also makes it subject to changes of its nature, personality, and strength as it changes hands.

There is still another consideration. Any World-Concept , whether religious or political in nature—though it can be difficult to tell when one ends and the other begins—strives less for the negative destruction of hostile ideas than to positively affirm its own ideas. Its battle must be more offense than defense. This is an advantage because the movement knows its own goal. The aim is victory for its own idea. On the other hand, it is hard to decide when the negative aim of destroying a hostile doctrine can be considered accomplished and certain. If for no other reason, the World-Concept 's attack should be better planned and also more forceful than its defense. As in everything else, victory is decided in the attack, not with the defense. A struggle by violence against an intellectual power is mere defense unless the battle is also upholding, proclaiming, and spreading a new intellectual teaching.

To summarize, remember this: Every attempt to fight a World-Concept by violence will eventually fail unless the struggle is fighting for a new way of thinking. Only in a struggle between two World-Concept s can the weapon of brute force be used persistently and ruthlessly to bring victory to the side it supports. So far, the attempts to combat Marxism had always failed for that reason.

This was why even Bismarck's anti-Socialist legislation fell short and was destined to fail. There was no new platform, no new World-Concept that the battle could have been fought for. Only the proverbial wisdom of high ministerial officers could have managed to believe that so-called "governmental authority" or "peace and good order" or the intellectual driving force was a suitable basis behind a life-and-death battle.

Because there was no real intellectual concept backing up the legislation, Bismarck handed over the development of his anti-Socialist plan to the judgment and "good will" of the very institution that was born of the Marxist way of thinking. When the Iron Chancellor left his war on Marxism to the "good will" of Social Democrats (*Marxists*), he was asking the goat to watch the garden. This was the inevitable result since there was no new authoritative, fundamental World-Concept , that could drive a strong conquering will into champions who would rebuild this new cause where Marxism was and drive it out. The only result of Bismarck's struggle was a severe disappointment.

Were conditions at the beginning of the First World War in any way different? Unfortunately, no, they were not. The more I thought about the necessary change in the attitude of the government toward Social Democracy as the temporary personification of Marxism, the more I recognized there was no workable substitute for this doctrine. What could they have offered the masses if Social Democracy had failed? Not one movement existed that could successfully draw the great crowds of workers under its influence once their leaders were gone. It is silly and more than stupid to presume that the international fanatic, having left his working-class political party, will suddenly join a privileged-class party or any new class organization at all. As disagreeable as it may be to various organizations, there is no denying the fact that privileged-class politicians believe separation of classes is important as long as it does not result in a political disadvantage. Denying this fact proves the audacity and stupidity of these liars.

In general, we must avoid thinking that the masses are more stupid than they actually are. In political matters, decisions are based more on feeling than understanding. The belief that this feeling on the part of the masses somehow proves stupidity towards international matters can be immediately disproved by simply pointing out that a pacifist democracy is equally insane because its supporters are almost exclusively from the intellectual privileged-classes. When millions of citizens continue to reverently worship their Jewish democratic press every morning, it looks bad for the upper class to make fun of the stupidity of the common "comrade" who, in the end, is swallowing the same dirt, just presented differently. The manufacturer is one and the same in both cases, the Jew.

We must be careful not to deny things whose existence is obviously a fact. It is an undeniable fact that class questions have nothing to do with ideals, though that tripe is commonly served up at election time. The class arrogance of many upper class people and the low regard of the manual laborer is not in the imagination of a lunatic, but a well-known fact. Apart from this, it shows the small thinking-power of our so-called intellectual elite when they assume that circumstances that failed

165

to prevent the rise of Marxism can now somehow find a way to recover what has been lost to it.

The privileged-class parties can never bring the lower class masses into their camp. These are two worlds that are divided in nature and artificially. When they stand together, there will be battle, but no matter what, the younger one, Marxism, will be victorious.

A war on Marxist Social Democracy in 1914 would have been conceivable. It is, however, questionable how long that fight could have been maintained considering the lack of any practical substitute. I believed this long before the war and that is why I could never make up my mind to join one of the existing parties. During the First World War, my opinion was strengthened more by the obvious impossibility of declaring a brutal war on Social Democracy. There was no movement available that was anything more than a "parliamentary" party.

I openly expressed my beliefs to my close army friends quite often. That is when it first occurred to me that I might someday enter politics. This was why I often assured my circle of friends that after the War, I would become a speaker in addition to my profession. I believe I was very sincere about it.

6. WAR PROPAGANDA

Pursuing all political events with interest like I did made me very interested in propaganda. In it, I saw a tool that the Socialist-Marxist organization understood well and used with masterful skill. I realized early that the proper use of propaganda is a true art and one that remained practically unknown to the privileged-class parties.

Only the Christian-Socialist movement achieved a certain skill with this tool and its success was owed to Lueger's contributions in his day. Not until the war was there a chance to see the enormous results that focused propaganda can produce. Here again, unfortunately, the other side was the sole subject of study because our side's understanding and use of propaganda was insignificant. This negligence was obvious to every German soldier. It was an absolute failure of the entire German information system. This now led me to investigate more thoroughly the use of propaganda.

Often there was more than enough time for consideration and reflection, but, unfortunately, it was the enemy who gave us this great practical lessons. What we failed to do, our adversaries did with extraordinary skill and calculation amounting to genius. Even I learned an infinite amount from the enemy's war propaganda. But of course, time passed without a trace of understanding raining on the politicians' heads. Some of them thought they were too clever to take lessons from the enemy, and the rest were unwilling to learn. Did we have any propaganda at all?

Unfortunately, no. Everything that was tried in this area was so inadequate or wrong from the start that, at best, it did no good and was often actually harmful. After a careful review of German war propaganda, it was inadequate in form, and it was psychologically wrong in fundamentals. Anyone could see this was true, even with a cursory inspection. Officials were not even clear in their own minds about whether propaganda is a means or an end.

It is without question a *means* and has to be judged based on how it accomplishes the ends. Its form has to be adapted to accomplish the desired result. It is also obvious that the importance of the end may vary. The ends may even stray from the general needs of the public. The propaganda must also adjust to match the value of the ends desired. The end that we struggled for during the war was the most glorious and tremendous that a man could imagine: the freedom and independence of our people, security of income for the future, and the nation's honor which is something that does exist despite those with contrary opinions. It must exist because people without honor lose their freedom and independence sooner or later. This, in turn, agrees with a higher justice because generations of scoundrels without honor deserve no freedom. No one who is willing to be a cowardly slave can or should possess any honor because that kind of honor would quickly become an object of universal hatred.

The German people were fighting for their very existence, and the purpose of propaganda in the war should have been its goal to back up the fight and victory.

When people are fighting for their existence on this planet and are faced with the fatal question, "to be or not to be", all considerations of humaneness or appearances crumble into nothing. These concepts are not floating in the air, but are born in man's imagination where they will cease to exist when he ceases to exist. Man's departure from this world dissolves those concepts into nothing because Nature does not know them. They are limited to the men in a handful of countries or rather a few races, and their value is only to the degree they unfold from these men's feelings. Humaneness and showy-idealism for the sake of appearances would disappear from the inhabited world if the races that created and upheld these concepts were lost.

In a peoples' struggle for its existence in the world, these concepts are of only minor importance. They are not important in determining the form of the struggle. If the time comes when they might cripple the drive for self-preservation in a struggling people, they must be discarded.

As far as the question of humaneness is concerned, even Moltke (*known as Moltke the Elder, Helmuth Karl Bernhard von Moltke was a Prussian soldier, Chief of General Staff in 1858 and responsible for the French defeat in 1870*) pointed out that in war it is essential to make a decision as quickly as possible, and that the most ruthless methods of fighting are at the same time the most humane.

If anyone should try to improve us with nonsense about putting on airs of moral superiority for appearance's sake or showy-idealism because it is what they think other people believe we should do, there can only be one answer: Any question of destiny that is as important as a people's struggle to survive immediately disposes of any duty to demonstrate "proper" appearances or to be concerned in any way with how we appear to outsiders. The least beautiful thing that can exist in human life is the yoke of slavery. Or do these touchy-feely people find the present lot of the German nation only an appearance to be viewed by others? We have no need to discuss the matter with the Jews. They are the inventors of this perfume of civilization which makes people more concerned with appearances than with survival. Their whole existence is a denial of the beauty of God's creation.

Since these ideas of what is humane and showy-morality for the benefit of others have no place in warfare, they are not to be used as standards for war propaganda.

Propaganda in the war was a means to an end. The end was the German people's successful struggle for existence. Therefore, the propaganda should have only been considered based on how it achieved that goal. The cruelest weapons were humane if they brought quicker victory, and the only showy-morality to be used was that which helped assure the dignity of freedom for the nation. This was the only attitude possible when facing the question of war propaganda in such a life-and-death struggle.

If the so-called competent authorities had understood this, the form and use of propaganda as a weapon would never have been a matter of confusion. Propaganda is merely another weapon, a very frightening one, in the hands of an expert.

The second question of absolutely central importance was this: Where should propaganda be directed? At the educated intellectuals or at the less-educated masses? It must be aimed continuously at the masses alone!

For the intellects, or those today who think they are intellectuals, we do not offer propaganda, but scientific teaching. Judging by its substance, propaganda is no more science than an advertising poster drawing is art. The art of the poster is in the designer's ability to attract the attention of the crowd with form and color. A poster advertising an art exhibition only has to draw attention to the art in the exhibition. The better it succeeds, the greater is the art of the poster itself. In addition, the poster should show the masses the importance of the exhibition, but it should never be a substitute for the art there on display. Anyone who wants to involve himself with actual art must study more than just the poster. In fact, for him, a simple walk through the exhibition is not enough. Only after a detailed study of the exhibits can he be expected to give a thoughtful examination to the individual works, and then slowly form a sound opinion.

The situation is the same today with what we call propaganda. Propaganda's purpose is not scientific training of the individual, not to give details or to act as a course of instruction, but directing the masses' attention to particular facts, occurrences, and necessities. The importance of these facts can only be brought in their view by the means of propaganda.

The art of propaganda consists in putting a matter so clearly and forcibly before the minds of the people that it creates a strong conviction in everyone. It is essential to success that propaganda reinforces the reality of the facts that are promoted, the necessity of what is being promoted, and the just or rightness of its character.

This art is not an end in itself. Its purpose must be identical to the advertisement poster—to attract the attention of the masses and not to distribute instructions to those who already have an educated opinion on things or who prefer to form their opinions based on objective study. That is not the purpose of propaganda. It must appeal to the feelings of the public rather than to their reasoning ability.

All propaganda must appeal to the common people in tone and in form and must keep its intellectual level to the capacity of the least intelligent person at whom it is directed. In other words, the intellectual level must be lowered as the mass of people it is intended to reach grows. If it is necessary to reach a lot of people, as in the case of national propaganda for the continuation of a war, you can never be too careful about controlling the intellectual level of the propaganda.

The less science is involved and the more emotions are involved, the more complete the success will be. Success is the best proof of the effectiveness of propaganda, and not the fact that it satisfies a few scholars or "image-conscious, sickly apes" who are concerned more with appearances and feelings.

Understanding the emotional patterns of the great masses and using proper psychology to get their attention and touch their hearts is the true art of propaganda. The fact that those who supposedly have their intellect and wits enhanced by education fail to understand this proves their mental laziness or their conceit.

Once we understand the importance of targeting the art of propaganda advertising to the broad masses, we have the following consequence:

It is a mistake to try to create propaganda in the same way you would create a document for scientific instruction. The great masses' capacity to absorb information is very limited; they have little understanding and they are very forgetful. For these reasons, any effective propaganda must be confined to a very few points, and these must be expressed in simple stereotyped formulas. They must be used repeatedly until the very last man cannot help but know the meaning instantly. The moment we forget this principle, and try to vary the approach, try to be general or abstract, we minimize the effect. The crowd cannot understand what is being offered. Therefore, the greater the scope of the message, the more necessary it is for the propaganda to follow a simple plan of action, which is also the most effective and targeted psychologically.

For instance, it was a fundamental error to make the enemy look ridiculous as was done in Austrian and German comic book propaganda. It was a fundamental error because when soldiers came face to face with the enemy, he saw something different. The result was terrible because now under the direct pressure of his enemy's resistance, the German soldier felt like he had been deceived by the ones who were supposed to have enlightened him. Instead of his war spirit or his commitment being strengthened, the opposite happened. The soldier lost his will to fight.

The war propaganda of the British and Americans, on the other hand, was psychologically on target. By portraying the Germans to their people as brutal and destructive barbarians, they prepared the individual soldier for the horrors of war and helped protect him from illusions. Even the most terrible weapons used against him only confirmed what he had already learned. This strengthened his belief in the truthfulness of his own government and stirred up his anger and hatred against the evil enemy. The effect of the enemy weapons, which he now discovered through first-hand experience, gradually proved the barbaric and already familiar brutality of the "Huns" was real. He was never led to believe that his own weapons might be more dreaded. Consequently, the English soldier never felt he was being lied to at home.

This was not the case with the German soldier. Eventually, German soldiers refused any information from home because they saw it as deceitful and a fraud. This happened because officials thought they could assign any convenient jackass to propaganda duty. They failed to understand that propaganda demands the most skilled minds that can be found. German war propaganda was a unique research project whose desired effects were reversed because of a complete lack of any understanding of psychology.

The enemy, however, had a tremendous lesson to teach anyone who was willing to open their eyes and learn. There was plenty of opportunity when we sat through a four-and-a-half year tidal wave of enemy propaganda.

What the people never understood was the first requirement for any propaganda activity: an intentionally biased and one-sided attitude toward every question discussed. The failure in this area, from the very beginning of the war, and from the top down, was so bad that it made me question whether this much failure could all be credited to pure stupidity. For instance, what would people say about a poster which advertised a new brand of soap, but which at length described the good qualities of other soap brands? The viewer would simply shake their heads in disbelief.

The same is true of political advertising. It is the responsibility of propaganda to emphasize exclusively the one cause it represents and not to evaluate other causes. It must not objectively explore any truth that favors the other side or fairly weigh the options, and then present the masses with a strict doctrine. It must not argue matters based on theoretical rules of justice. Propaganda must constantly endeavor to present only the aspect of the truth that is favorable to its own side.

It was a fundamental error to discuss who was responsible for starting the First World War and then declare that Germany was not totally responsible. The right way would have been to pile the guilt totally on the enemy, even if this wasn't true, but in this case, it was.

What was the result of this half-and-half propaganda? The great masses of people are not made up of diplomats, professors of law, or even people capable of making a judgment based on reason and logic. They are human beings—indecisive and subject to doubt and uncertainty. The moment our own propaganda admits even the faintest glimmer of justice is due to the other side, the seeds of doubt have been planted and they will begin to question whether our own side is just. The masses cannot tell where the enemy's wrongs end and their own begin. In these cases, they become uncertain and suspicious. This is especially true when the enemy does not commit the same foolishness, but puts the guilt, lock, stock and barrel, on his adversary.

It was natural for our own people to believe the more intense and focused hostile propaganda of our enemy instead of their own people's words. This is easily seen in those who have a mania that craves objectivity, like the Germans! Everyone preferred to be fair to the enemy rather than to risk injustice. Even willing to destroy his own people and State in the process.

The masses never realized that this outcome was not the leaders' intention but it was their failure to understand which was the cause. The overwhelming majority of the people tend to be so feminine in their leanings and beliefs that emotion and feelings rather than serious logical reasoning determine thought and action. This feeling is not complicated. It is simple and firm. There is no gray area. There are not many different shadings, but a positive or a negative, love or hate, right or wrong, truth or lie, but never half-and-half, never part of one and part of the other.

These are all things English propaganda did in an excellent manner. They never allowed two sided arguments which might have raised doubts. They realized the broad masses' emotional state was primitive. They proved this by publishing horror story propaganda that met the masses on their level. They ruthlessly and brilliantly reinforced their moral position, which strengthened endurance at the front despite great defeats. They were equally vivid in their "festival" nailing-down of the German foe, portraying him as the sole guilty party for the outbreak of the War. This was a lie, which because of the complete and one-sided colossal boldness of its presentation, appealed to the emotional and extreme attitude of the common people, and therefore it was totally believed.

The effectiveness of this sort of propaganda was most noticeably shown by the fact that after four years, it was still holding the enemy to his guns and had started to eat away at our own people.

It was really no surprise that our propaganda was unsuccessful. It carried the seed of ineffectiveness in its deep ambiguity. Its content alone made it highly unlikely that it would create the impression on the masses that was necessary for success. Only our irresponsible "statesmen" could have hoped to generate enthusiasm in men to the point of dying for their country with this stale, watered down pacifist tea.

This sorry product was not just useless, but harmful. All the brilliant presentations in the world will not lead to the success of propaganda unless one fundamental principle is always kept clearly in view. Propaganda must limit itself to saying a very little, but saying it a lot. First and foremost, that is the absolute important prerequisite for success.

In the field of propaganda, we must never be guided by the beauty of propaganda itself because the expression and form of what was said would soon only attract literary tea-parties of intellectuals instead of being suited to the masses. Neither must it be guided in a carefree manner because the lack of emotional freshness makes it weak and people are constantly seeking new stimulants. Intellectuals quickly become bored with everything. They cannot imagine themselves in the same place as their fellow man or even understand his needs. These intellectuals are always the first to criticize propaganda's content, which they think is too old-fashioned, too stale, and too worn out. They are always looking for something new, seeking variety and are the death of any effective political mass recruiting. As soon as party propaganda is organized and its substance focuses on the intellectuals' needs, they lose their unity and become scattered.

The purpose of propaganda is not to be a constant source of interesting diversion for unconcerned, smart gentlemen, but to convince the masses. The masses are slow-moving, and it may take a long time before they are ready to even notice something. Only constant repetitions of the simplest ideas will finally stick in their minds.

Any variations in the propaganda message must never change the purpose of the propaganda, but should always reinforce the same conclusion. The main slogan must be highlighted from various angles, stated in different ways, but every discussion must end with the conclusion itself. Only then can and will propaganda produce a unified and concentrated effect.

Only this broad approach, through steady and consistent use, will ever pave the way to final success, and this steadfast course must never be abandoned. It is astonishing to discover the enormous results which such perseverance can accomplish.

The success of any advertising, whether in business or politics, depends on perseverance and consistency. The enemy war propaganda was a perfect model because it was restricted to a few points, targeted exclusively at the masses, and continued with tireless perseverance. When those basic ideas and methods of presentation were seen to be solid, they were used throughout the war without even the slightest change. At first, the propaganda seemed idiotic in its use of disrespectful statements. Later, it became unpleasant, then it was finally believed.

After four and a half years, a revolution whose slogan originated in enemy war propaganda broke out in Germany. The English understood that the success of this weapon lies in extensive usage, and once it is successful, it more than pays for the cost.

The English saw propaganda as a primary weapon, while with us, it was the last resort of employment for jobless politicians and a comfy job for those who avoided the role of hero-soldier. All in all, its success was zero.

7. THE REVOLUTION

Enemy propaganda first came to us in 1915. From 1916 on, it became more and more intensive and swelled until the beginning of 1918 when it grew into an absolute flood. The effects of "dangling the bait" were seen at every step. The army gradually learned to think the way the enemy wanted it to.

The German counter-efforts were a complete failure. The so-called "leader" who guided the army had those around him who possessed the drive and desire to take up the struggle of counter-propaganda, but the necessary tools were not there and they had no means to distribute anything even if they had produced it. It would have been a mistake psychologically for the army to give this enlightenment to the troops. If it was to be effective, it had to come from home. Otherwise, it was impossible to count on it being successful among men who had suffered starvation and whose immortal deeds of heroism and endurance had been performed for that very homeland for nearly four years.

But what did come from home? Was the failure a result of stupidity or evil? In mid-summer of 1918, after the retreat from the southern bank of the Marne (*a river in northern France*), the German press started to demonstrate not only incompetence, but criminal stupidity. I asked myself with daily and increasing disappointment if no one at home was going to put an end to this intellectual sabotage of the army's heroism.

What happened in France when we swept into the country in 1914 in an unparalleled whirlwind of victory after victory? What did Italy do while her Isonzo front (*along the Isonzo river in eastern Italy*) was collapsing? What did France do in the spring of 1918 when the assaults of the German divisions seemed to be unhinging the

French positions, and the long-reaching arm of the German heavy artillery was pounding on the gates of Paris? They raised the boiling point of national passion, and stoked the fire of weakening courage and hurled it in the faces of the retreating regiments! How wonderfully their propaganda skills inspired and influenced the masses as they labored to pound into the hearts of the broken front soldiers a belief in the final victory, now more than ever!

And what was happening on our side? Nothing! I was often overcome with outrage and fury when I received the latest newspapers and saw the psychological mass murder they were committing. More than once, I was tortured by the thought that if Providence had put me in place of these criminal incompetents and do-nothings in our propaganda service, the War would have ended in a different fashion.

During those months, for the first time, I felt the full force of cruel Fate, who was holding me at the front in a spot where any negro could by chance point his rifle in the wrong direction and shoot me down; while if I had been in another place, I could have performed a very different service for the Fatherland.

Even then, I was presumptuous enough to believe I would have succeeded. But I was a nameless one among eight-million, so it was better to stay quiet and do my duty as well as possible where I was.

In the summer of 1916, the first enemy leaflets fell into our hands. With only minor variations, their substance was almost invariably the same: "Distress In Germany Was Growing Ever Greater"; "The War Would Last Forever, While The Chance Of Winning It Was Vanishing"; "People At Home Were Longing For Peace, But 'Militarism' And The 'Kaiser' Would Not Consider Peaceful Solutions"; "The Whole World Was Making War On The One Guilty Foe Called The Kaiser And Not On The German People"; "The Struggle Would Not Come To An End Until This Enemy Of Peaceable Mankind Was Eliminated"; "After The War Ended, The Peaceful And Democratic Nations Would Receive The German People Into The League Of Eternal-World-Peace, A Peace That Was Guaranteed To Spring Forth The Moment 'Prussian-Militarism' was destroyed".

To illustrate these claims, they included "Letters From Home" which appeared to confirm these statements. At that time, everybody just laughed at these attempts. The leaflets were read and then sent to the rear for the commanders to inspect, then they were forgotten until the wind blew another load down into the trenches. They even sent special airplanes just to drop the leaflets.

There was one striking element in this kind of propaganda. In every sector where there were Bavarians, an attack on Prussia was pushed with extraordinary persistence. It said that Prussia was solely responsible for the whole War, and there was not the slightest hostility against Bavaria, but they could not come to the assistance of Bavaria as long as it served Prussian interests and kept pulling Prussia's chestnuts out of the fire.

This technique actually began to have a certain effect as early as 1915. Bad feelings against Prussia noticeably increased among the troops without producing the slightest counter-measures from our leadership. This was more than a mere sin of omission. Sooner or later there were bound to be serious repercussions, and not for the "Prussians", but for the German people of which Bavaria is a considerable part.

Enemy propaganda began to have definite success in this area by 1916. The real letters from home were filled with complaints which had also started to take effect. It was no longer necessary for the enemy to drop leaflets into our trenches; the letters were delivered by post. The "government-in-charge" did nothing except issue a few foolish warnings while the front was constantly flooded with this poison sent from home by thoughtless women. They never dreamed that this would strengthen the enemy's confidence and increase the sufferings of their loved ones at the front lines. The silly letters from German women eventually cost hundreds of thousands of men their lives.

Even by 1916, several alarming signs became apparent. The men at the front were cursing and complaining—they were discontented and justifiably resentful in many respects. While they were starving and suffering and their families at home were in misery, they could still see places where there was abundance and festive living. Even at the front itself, everything wasn't as it should have been in this respect. There were faint warnings of crisis, but these were all still internal matters. The same man who growled and cursed would silently do his duty a few minutes later as if it were habit. The same company that was feeling discontented would dig into the section of trenches it had to defend, as if Germany's Fate depended upon this hundred yards of mud and shell-holes. This front line was still formed by the old, magnificent "Army of Heroes!"

I would soon experience the difference between it and home in glaring contrast. At the end of September, 1916, my division entered the battle of the Somme (*one of the largest battles in the First World War with over 1.5 million casualties at the river Somme in northern France*). For us, it was the first of the huge battles that now followed, and the impression it created is hard to describe. It seemed more like Hell than a war. The German front held out against the whirlwind drumming of the guns for weeks at a time. Sometimes, they were pushed back; then they would advance again, but they never gave up.

On October 7, 1916, I was wounded.

I arrived safely at the rear and was ordered to Germany by transport vehicle. Two years had passed since I had seen home, which was an almost endless stretch of time to be away. I couldn't even imagine how Germans who were not in uniform would look. When I was in the base hospital at Hermies (*a farming village in France at the time*), I was startled when the voice of a German woman, a nurse, addressed a man lying next to me. It was wonderful hearing a sound like that for the first time in two years!

The nearer to the border the train approached—which was bringing us home—the more restless each man became. All the towns moved past that we had ridden through two years before as young soldiers: Brussels, Louvain, Liege. Finally, we thought we recognized the first German house by its high gables and its striking shutters. It was the Fatherland!

In October, 1914, we had been on fire with wild enthusiasm when we crossed the border. Now, stillness and reverence ruled. We were all happy that Fate allowed us to once again see what we were defending so fiercely with our lives.

Almost on the anniversary of my departure, I arrived in the hospital in the Brandenberg town of Beelitz near Berlin. What a change! From the mud of the Battle of the Somme into the white beds of this amazing structure! At first, one hardly dared lie on them. Unfortunately, this world was new in other ways too.

The spirit of the front-line army wasn't here. For the first time, I heard something we didn't know about at the front: someone boasting of his own cowardice. One did indeed hear cursing and grumbling at the front, but never to encourage the neglect of or the dereliction of duty, let alone to glorify the coward. No, the coward was still a coward and nothing more. On the front, he was treated with a contempt as strong as the admiration that was felt for a true hero. But here in the hospital, conditions were almost the reverse. The most dishonest trouble-makers and unprincipled trouble-seekers took the floor and tried in every way with every resource of their sorry eloquence to make the decent soldier appear ridiculous and the coward's lack of character a model to be emulated.

A few disgraceful fellows were the ringleaders. One said that he had stuck his own hand into the barbed-wire entanglement so he would be sent to the hospital. Despite the minor nature of his injury, he appeared to have been here a very long time and was planning to stay. It appeared that an arrangement was struck as the result of a swindle or bribe, which allowed him to stay here, and another such act was the only reason he made it on a transit train for Germany at all. This filthy pest of a fellow actually had the nerve to display his own cowardice shamelessly and claim it was the result of a bravery higher than the heroic death of the honest soldier. Many listened in silence; others walked away; a few actually agreed.

I was disgusted within an inch of my life, but the troublemaker was calmly tolerated in the hospital. What could anyone do? Surely the hospital office knew who and what he was, yet nothing happened.

When I could walk again, I was allowed to go to Berlin. Hardship was obviously very severe everywhere. Millions were suffering from hunger. Discontent was all around. In different shelters where the soldiers visited and in pubs the tone was the same as at the hospital. It seemed like these fellows deliberately sought out such spots in order to spread their views.

But things were even worse, much worse, in Munich itself. When I was discharged from the hospital after my recovery and was assigned to the reserve battalion, I hardly recognized the city again. Anger, disgust, and abusive talk were everywhere. In the reserve battalion itself, the spirit was absolutely beneath contempt. One factor was the total incompetent treatment of the active soldiers by non-commissioned training officers who had never spent a single hour on the battlefield. For this reason, they were only able to establish a working relationship with the battle-experienced soldiers. The old front-line soldiers did have certain peculiarities, which were the result of their own experience at the front lines, but these were incomprehensible to the inexperienced officers of the reserve troops. An officer who had himself come from the front was not puzzled by them. Such an officer received a very different sort of respect from that given to the officers who served at the rear away from the action or at headquarters. Besides this, the general temper was awful. Avoidance of military service began to be considered a sign of higher wisdom while the faithful endurance of service became the earmark of inner weakness and partial blindness. The government offices were full of Jews. Almost every clerk was a Jew and every Jew a clerk. I was astonished at this multitude of "chosen people" and could not help comparing it with their sparse presence at the front lines.

The situation in business was even worse. Here the Jewish people had actually become "indispensable". This spider was slowly beginning to suck the blood from the people. In the business of "War Companies", an instrument had been found to gradually sweep away the national, free economy. The necessity of creating centralized suppliers without restrictions was emphasized. In fact, by 1916-1917, almost all production was under the control of financial Jewry.

But at whom did the people now direct its hatred? I was horrified to see a doom approaching which was bound to lead to a collapse if it wasn't avoided in time. While the Jew was plundering the whole nation and forcing it under his domination, people were being turned against the "Prussians". At the front lines and at home, nothing was done by the leadership to curb this poisonous propaganda. Nobody seemed to understand that the collapse of Prussia would not mean the rise of Bavaria. On the contrary, the fall of one would inevitably drag the other with it into the abyss.

This behavior caused me infinite pain. I could see no purpose in it except that it was the Jew's most inspired trick to distract general attention from themselves to others. While Bavarians and Prussians were quarreling, the Jew was sneaking the income from under their noses. While the Bavarians were damning the Prussians, the Jew organized the Revolution and with one blow shattered both Prussia and Bavaria.

I could not stand to watch this doomed feud among the German clans and preferred to return to the front lines. I asked to be transferred there immediately after my arrival in Munich. By the beginning of March, 1917, I was back with my regiment again.

Toward the end of 1917, the deepest point of the army's depression seemed to be past. After the Russian collapse, the whole army had new hope and courage. The belief that the struggle would end with a German victory began to grow in the troops more and more. Singing was heard again and there were fewer grumblers. People believed in the future of the Fatherland again.

The Italian collapse in the Autumn of 1917 had a wonderful effect. In this victory, the troops saw proof that it was possible to break through other fronts beside the Russian campaign. A magnificent faith flooded back into the hearts of the millions and made it possible for them to hold out for the spring of 1918 with relieved assurance of victory. The enemy, on the other hand, was visibly miserable. That winter, things were somewhat calmer than usual. It was just the calm before the storm. As the front was making the final preparation to conclude the endless struggle, and as endless lines of transport-trains filled with men and supplies were rolling toward the Western Front and the troops were being groomed for the great attack, the greatest treachery, the most foul trick of the War broke out in Germany.

Germany must not win the War. At the last moment when the German victory flag threatened to wave, a calculated blow was made to stifle the German spring attack at birth, making victory impossible. The weapons manufacturing strike was organized among the labor unions.

If it was successful, the German front would break and the wish of the Social Democratic newspaper, Vorwärts (*"Forward"*), that Germany would not be the victor this time would be fulfilled. Without weapons, the front would collapse in a few weeks. The offensive would be prevented, the political agreement saved, and the international capital made ruler of Germany. Cheating the people was the inner goal of the Marxist and they succeeded. It was the destruction of the national economy in order to establish the rule of international capital and it happened thanks to the stupidity and gullibility of one side and the enormous cowardice of the other.

The munitions strike was not as successful as was hoped and did not deprive the front line of weaponry and armaments. It collapsed too early for the weapons shortage alone to condemn the army to destruction according to plan. However, the moral damage that was done was so much worse! First, what was the army fighting for if people at home did not even want victory? Who were the enormous sacrifices and hardships for? The soldier is sent out and told to fight for victory, and at home they strike against it! Second, what was the effect upon the enemy?

In the winter of 1917-18, dark clouds rose for the first time on the Allied sky. For almost four years, the Allies leaned against the German giant and had been unable to topple him. He had only one arm holding a shield for defense in the West which left his sword arm free to swing to the East and the South. Now, the giant was finally free from his battles behind. Rivers of blood had flowed before he succeeded in smashing one of his adversaries. Now, this giant could turn and let the sword join the shield in the West. The enemy had not succeeded so far in breaking down the defense; the attack would now fall completely on him. The enemy dreaded him and feared the imminent victory.

In London and Paris, there was one meeting after another, but on the front line, a drowsy silence reigned. The insolence of the allied leaders suddenly sank. Even the enemy propaganda was struggling. It was not as easy to prove the impossibility of a German victory. The same thing was also true on the front lines. They too began to see a strange light. Their inner attitude toward the German soldier had changed. Up until now, they might have thought he was a fool marked for defeat, but now, they were facing the destroyer of their Russian ally. The necessary confinement of German offensives to the East now seemed to be part of an inspired strategy.

For three years, the Germans had charged against Russia and appeared to have no effect. People almost laughed at these pointless attempts. After all, the Russian giant with his superior numbers must be the ultimate winner while Germany would surely collapse from loss of blood. The evidence seemed to justify this hope.

Starting in September, 1914, when the endless masses of Russian prisoners from the battle of Tannenberg (*a decisive battle between Russia and Germany in the early days of the First World War*), began to march into Germany along highways and railroads in long caravans; the stream appeared to continue forever, but for every Russian army that was beaten and annihilated, a new one arose to take its place. The vast Empire kept giving the Czar new soldiers and fed the war its new victims. How long could Germany last in this race? Wouldn't the day come, after a great German victory, when the Russian army reserves would prepare themselves for the final battle? And then what? In all human probability, Russia's victory might be postponed, but it would eventually come.

Now, all these hopes pinned on Russia were lost. The ally who had laid the greatest blood-sacrifices on the altar for the Allies was at the end of his strength and lay at the feet of the merciless attacker. Fear and horror crept into the hearts of the soldiers who, up until now, had filled their minds with blind faith. They now feared the coming spring. If they had not succeeded in breaking the German line when he could give only part of his energy to the Western Front, how could they expect victory against the entire strength of the mighty land of heroes which was gathering itself for an attack?

The shadows of defeat from the South Tyrolean Mountains (*the Alto Adige mountain range in Italy*) sank uneasily on the imagination. As far away as the fog of Flanders (*in France*), the beaten armies of General Cadorna created gloomy spirits and their belief in victory crumbled as they saw a future filled with fear and defeat. (*General Luigi Cadorna led 250,000 Italian soldiers to their death in the early days of the First World War along the Isonzo River and he achieved little or no military gains.*)

Just as people thought they could hear the steady rumble from advancing shock troops of the German army in the cool of the night and when they were anxiously expecting the coming judgment day, suddenly a glaring red light blazed from Germany, throwing its flare into the last shell-hole of the enemy front. At the moment the German divisions were making their final preparations for the great assault, the general labor-strike broke out in Germany.

For a moment, the world was speechless. But then, with a sigh of relief, the enemy propaganda grabbed this opportunity for a reprieve in the twelfth hour. In one strike they found ways to restore the diminishing confidence of the Allied soldiers, to call the chance of victory a certainty again, and to change the uneasy dread of what was coming into confident determination. Now, the regiments waiting for the inevitable German attack could go into the greatest battle of all time with the conviction that the end of the War would be decided not by the bravery of the German assault, but by the persistence of its own defenses. Let the Germans win as many victories as they pleased. At home, the Marxist Revolution was welcomed as it marched in, not the victorious army.

The English, French, and American newspapers began to plant this belief in the hearts of their readers, while a substantial and skillful propaganda movement fed the morale of their troops at the front.

"Germany on the eve of Revolution! Victory of the Allies inevitable!" This was the best medicine to set the wavering French and English on their feet. Now, German rifles and machine-guns could be fired again, but instead of fleeing in panic and terror, they met determined resistance and confidence.

This was the result of the strike at weapons factories. It strengthened the enemy's faith in victory and swept away the paralyzing hopelessness of the Allied front. Afterward, thousands of German soldiers paid with their lives while the originators of this dishonorable wickedness were slated to move into the highest State offices of Germany as a result of the Revolution.

The visible effects of this act on the German troops could be overcome for now, but on the enemy's side, the results had a long lasting effect. The resistance was no longer an aimless army that has given everything up for lost, but instead the bitter intensity of a struggle for victory appeared. In all human probability, victory would come if the Western Front could just hold out for a few months against the German attack. The parliaments of the Allies recognized this future chance for victory and approved the use of astonishing, stupendous amounts of money to continue the propaganda which would eventually undermine Germany.

It was my good fortune to have a part in the first two and the last offensives. They are the most tremendous impressions of my life. They were tremendous because this was the last time the struggle lost the character of defense and took on that of attack, as it felt in 1914. The men in the trenches and dugouts of the German army drew a deep sigh of relief now that the day of revenge was here at last after more than three years of stubbornly resisting the enemy inferno. Once more, the victorious battalions shouted, and they hung the last immortal laurel wreaths on the battle flags amid the lightning flashes of victory. Once more the songs of the Fatherland roared toward heaven along the endless marching columns and for the last time, and, the Lord's mercy smiled.

In Mid-summer of 1918, stifling heat covered the front. At home people were quarreling. Over what? Many stories circulated through the various divisions of the army in the field. The War was now hopeless, they said, and only fools could still believe in victory. The people had no more interest in continuing in resistance; only the capitalists and the Monarchy wanted to continue. That was the story from home and it was discussed on the front as well.

At first, there was scarcely any reaction. What did we care about general voting rights? Was that what we had fought four years to gain? It was a piece of evil robbery to steal the war's goal from the graves of dead heroes. The young regiments that died in Flanders did not cry, "*Long live general voting rights*", but they shouted, "*Germany ahead of all*". The difference was "*small*", but not insignificant. Those who were shouting for general voting rights were never there when the fighting was going on. The whole political party rabble were strangers to the front. One only saw a fraction of the "Honorable Parliamentarians" in places where decent Germans were found.

The old soldiers who were the backbone of the front had no interest in this new war aim of Ebert, Scheidemann, Barth, and Liebknecht (*Social Democrats who were key figures in the German Revolution of 1918*). We could not see why these slackers should suddenly have the right to inappropriately claim State authority for themselves over the army's leadership.

My personal attitude was settled from the start. I hated the whole pack of wretched, nation-swindling party scoundrels intensely. I had realized for a long time that with this gang it was a question of filling their empty pockets and not of the nation's welfare. For this purpose, they were now willing to sacrifice all the people, and if necessary, let Germany go to her doom. In my eyes, it was time to string them up. Giving in to their wishes meant sacrificing the interests of the working people in favor of a set of pickpockets. Those wishes could only be fulfilled if one were ready to give up Germany, and this is what the great majority of the fighting army still thought. The reinforcements from home quickly grew worse and worse. Their arrival weakened instead of strengthened the fighting power. The young reinforcements in particular were mostly worthless. Often, it was hard to believe that these were sons of the same people who had once sent out their youth to the battle of Ypres (*the First battle of Ypres, also called the Battle of Flanders in 1914*).

In August and September, the symptoms of disintegration quickly increased. The enemy attacked with terrible effect, but it was mild when compared to the past defensive battles of Somme and Flanders (*battlefields in France*), which were blood curdling.

At the end of September, my division re-took for the third time places which we had once stormed as young volunteer regiments. Those were some great memories! For there, in October and November of 1914, we had received our baptism of fire. With love of the Fatherland in its heart and a song on its lips, our young regiment had gone to battle as if to a dance. The most precious blood was joyfully given in the belief that this would preserve independence and freedom for the Fatherland.

In July of 1917, we walked on this ground, sacred for us all, for the second time. Here slept the best of our comrades, children almost, who had given their lives for the Fatherland, their eyes glowing with enthusiastic love. We veterans, who had marched out with the regiment long ago, stood with deep reverence at this altar of "faithfulness and obedience unto death". The regiment had stormed this ground three years before. Now, it was to defend it in a bitter battle of resistance.

With three weeks of continuous artillery, the English prepared for the great Flanders offensive. Now, the spirits of the dead seemed to come alive. The regiment braced itself in the filthy mud and dug into the shell-holes and craters, unyielding, unwavering, and grew smaller and thinner, just as they had once before at this spot. Finally, the English attack came on July 31, 1917.

Early in August we were relieved by fresh troops. What once had been the regiment was now a few companies. They staggered back, covered with mud, more like ghosts than men. Except for a few hundred yards of shell-holes, the Englishman had only won death.

Now, in the fall of 1918, we stood for the third time on the ground we had stormed in 1914. The small town of Comines (*in Belgium*), where we once had been stationed on a base, was now our battlefield. The battleground was the same, only the men had changed. The troops now talked politics, too. The poison from home began to take effect here, as it was everywhere else. The younger reinforcements were absolutely useless because they came from home where they had succumbed to its effects.

On the night of October 13th to 14th the English attacked with gas on the southern front south of Ypres (*a Belgian municipality in West Flanders*). They used yellow-cross gas (*yellow crosses were painted on gas shells to show they contained mustard gas producing liquid*), whose effect was unknown to us as far as personal experience was concerned. I found out about it firsthand that very night. The evening of October 13th, on a hill south of Wervick (*a Belgium municipality in West Flanders*), we were subjected to a pounding of gas bombs lasting several hours, and it continued more or less violently all night. By midnight, half of us were knocked out of action, some of our comrades forever. Toward morning, I was gripped by more and more violent pains as the minutes passed. By seven o'clock in the morning, my eyes felt like they were on fire. I fumbled and staggered to the rear, taking with me my last messenger report I was destined to deliver in the War. Within a few hours, my eyes had turned to red-hot coals and everything around me was dark. I was sent to the hospital in the German city of Pasewalk (*on the Uecker river*) in Pomerania (*an area now split between Germany and Poland*) and there I had to experience the greatest disgrace of this century. The Revolution.

There had been something vague and repulsive in the air for some time. The gossip was that "things" were going to pop in the next few weeks. I could not imagine what they meant by "things". My first thought was of a strike, like the one in the spring. Unpleasant rumors were constantly coming from the Navy, which was supposed to be in a state of confusion. To me, this seemed more the creature of a few scattered rascals' brains than any concern of a large mass of people. In the hospital, everyone talked about the ending of the War, which they hoped would be soon, but no one counted on it being immediately. I could not read newspapers because of my eyes.

In November, the general tension increased. Then one day, suddenly and unexpectedly, the disaster was upon us. Sailors came in trucks inspiring and rousing us to join the Revolution. A few Jew-boys were the "leaders" in this struggle for the "freedom, beauty, and dignity" of our national people. None of them had been at the front lines or seen any action. Three Orientals who were sent home from behind the lines by way of the so-called "clap hospital", that is to say venereal disease, left Marxist flags behind, and these red rags were now hoisted up in the hospital.

By that time, my condition had begun to improve somewhat. The pain in the hollows of my eyes lessened and I could distinguish rough outlines of my surroundings again. I had hopes of getting my eyesight back at least enough so that I would be able to find some useful occupation. I did not, however, hope to be able to draw again. Still, I was on the road to recovery when another monstrous thing happened.

My first hope was that this high treason was only a local affair. I tried to cheer up some of my comrades with that reassurance. My Bavarian hospital-mates in particular were willing to accept this outlook. Their temper was anything but "revolutionary". I could not imagine that the craziness would break out in Munich because I thought the respect for the House of Wittelsbach (*the Royal House of the German State of Bavaria*) was sure to be stronger there than the will of a few Jews. I could not help but tell myself it was just a matter of a revolt in the Navy which would be put down in the next few days.

The next few days came, and with them the most horrible information I have received in my life. The rumors grew even more alarming. What I thought was a local matter was a general Revolution. On top of it all, the shameful news came from the front: They were going to surrender. How could this be possible?

On the 10th of November, the pastor came to the hospital for a short speech and we found out the whole story. Those around me were extremely excited as we listened to his brief speech. The dignified old gentleman seemed to be trembling like a leaf as he informed us that the House of Hohenzollern (*the noble families of Prussia, Germany, and Romania*) could no longer wear the crown of the German Emperors. The Fatherland had become a "Republic", and our Fatherland would certainly be under the control of other people in the future. He said we must beg the Almighty not to withhold His blessing of the transformation and not to forsake our people in the times to come. He could not refrain from saying a few words about the Royal House. He tried to speak in appreciation of what it had done for Pomerania, for Prussia, for the German Fatherland, and here, he began to weep softly. Profound unhappiness came upon every heart in the little hall, and I do not believe there was a dry eye at this point. The old gentleman tried to continue and began to tell us that we would now have to end the long War and that the future of our Fatherland would face heavy burdens. The War was lost and we were throwing ourselves upon the mercy of the victors. He also said the Armistice was to be accepted and our trust was put in the generosity of our enemy. By that time, I could stand it no longer. It was impossible for me to stay in the room. Everything went black before my eyes again and I staggered and stumbled my way back to the dormitory, flung myself upon my cot, and buried my burning head in the blanket and pillow.

I had not cried since the day I stood beside my mother's grave. In my youth, whenever I was gripped by the hard and cruel hand of Fate, my stubbornness increased. When Death took dear comrades and friends from our ranks in the long years of the war, I would have thought it almost a sin to complain. Were they dying for Germany or not? When I fell victim to the creeping gas that began to eat into my eyes during the very last days of that frightening struggle, and I suffered the horror of going blind forever, there was a moment when I was ready to lose courage, but then the voice of conscience thundered at me: "You miserable wretch! Who are you to whimper while thousands of souls are a hundred times worse off than you?" So, I bore my fate in silence. I had realized for the first time how personal suffering disappears in the face of the misfortune of the Fatherland.

It had all been in vain. All the sacrifices and starvation were in vain; the hunger and thirst that stretched for months without end were in vain; the hours gripped by deathly terror in which we still did our duty were in vain; and the death of the two million who gave their lives, it was all in vain. Surely the graves would open up returning all the hundreds of thousands who had marched out believing in the Fatherland? Surely they must open and send forth the silent heroes, covered with mud and blood, as avenging spirits to the homeland which had so outrageously cheated them of the highest sacrifice that a man can offer to his people in this world? Was this what the soldiers of August and September, 1914 (*referring to the Battle of Tannenberg where the Germans decimated the Russians*) had died for? Was this why the volunteer regiments followed their old comrades in the fall of the same year? Was this why these boys of seventeen had died on the soil of Flanders? Was this the meaning of the sacrifice that the German mother made for the Fatherland when, with an aching heart, she sent her dearest boys out, never to see them again? Was all of this so a mob of miserable criminals could dare to lay hands on the Fatherland?

Was this why the German soldier, exhausted by sleepless nights and endless marches, hungry, thirsty, and frozen, had stood fast through burning sun and driving snow? Was it for this he had gone through the inferno of continuous artillery fire and the fever of gas attacks, never yielding, always remembering the single duty to guard the Fatherland from enemy invasion?

Truly, these heroes deserved a monument that says: "Stranger, when you travel to Germany, tell them that we lay here, faithful to the Fatherland and obedient to duty". (*These words are paraphrased from the monument erected at Thermopylae in Greece to the memory of Leonidas and his Spartan soldiers.*)

But was the supreme sacrifice all we must consider? Was the Germany of the past worthless? Do we have any obligation to our own history? Were we still worthy enough to take on ourselves the glory of the past? And how could this deed be justified to the future? These are immoral and miserable criminals! The more I tried to understand this outrageous event, the more my cheeks burned with indignation and shame. The pain of my eyes was nothing compared to this wretchedness. Awful days and worse nights followed. I knew that all was lost. Only fools or these liars and criminals could hope for the enemy's mercy. During those nights, hatred grew—hatred for the perpetrators of this deed.

In the next few days, I became aware of my own Fate. I had to laugh when I thought of my personal future, which had caused me so much worry only a short a time ago. It was funny to think of building houses on this ground. Finally, I realized that the thing I had dreaded so often, the thing which was inevitable had happened, but I did not have the heart to believe it.

Emperor William II had been the first German Emperor to offer the hand of reconciliation to the leaders of Marxism, not dreaming that those crooks have no honor. While they grasped the Imperial hand with their left hand, the other hand was reaching for the sword. With the Jew there can be no understanding or agreement, but only the unyielding "either-or". I resolved to become a politician.

8. BEGINNING OF MY POLITICAL ACTIVITY

By the end of November, 1918, I was back in Munich. I went to the reserve battalion office of my regiment, which was in the hands of the new "Soldiers' Councils". The whole administration was so disgusting to me that I decided to leave as quickly as possible. With a faithful friend of the campaign at my side, Ernst Schmidt, I traveled to Traunstein (*a town in the south-east part of Bavaria Germany*) and remained there until the camp was broken up.

In March of 1919, we went back to Munich. The situation there was shaky which threatened to continue the Revolution. Eisner's death only hastened the development and it finally led to the dictatorship of the Councils. (*Kurt Eisner, the Bavarian Socialist politician, journalist, and organizer of the Socialist Revolution, died in February of 1919. He was killed by a lone assassin not associated with the Nazi movement. He previously led the Munich Revolution and became Premier of Bavaria.*) Or, more accurately put, to a temporary Jewish domination which was the original goal of those who created the Revolution.

At that time, plans bounced back and forth in my head. For days, I considered options and thought about what could possibly be done, but the result of every train of thought was the sober realization that no one knew me and I did not have the means to actually do anything. Later I will explain the reason why I could not even make up my mind which of the existing political parties to join.

During the new Revolution of the Councils, for the first time, I behaved in a way that the Central Council found annoying. The later result was that I was to be arrested early in the morning of April 27, 1919, but the three fellows who came for me did not have enough courage when facing the muzzle of my rifle to complete their task and ran off as quickly as they came.

A few days after the "liberation" of Munich, I was ordered to appear before the Commission of Investigation to discuss the revolutionary events in the Second Infantry Regiment. This was my first, somewhat, purely political activity.

Within a few weeks, I received orders to attend a "course" or a series of lectures which was being held for members of the military forces. Here, a soldier was supposed to receive a definite foundation for his thinking as a citizen. The only value in the performance to me was that it gave me a chance to meet like-minded comrades with whom I could discuss the real situation at hand. We were all firmly convinced that Germany could no longer be saved from the coming catastrophe, certainly not by the parties who committed the November crime (*the surrender and formation of the Weimar Republic*), the Center Party and the Social Democratic Party. Even if they had the best intentions in the world, the so-called "privileged-class Nationalist" organizations could never correct what had already been done. They lacked the full set of necessary fundamentals and without them, such a task could not succeed. Time has shown that our view was correct.

In our little circle, we discussed the formation of a new Party. The basic ideas we had in mind were the same that were later realized in the "German Workers' Party" (*the DAP, precursor to the Nazi party*). The name of the movement to be founded must help us reach the broad masses from the very beginning. Without the ability to reach the masses, the whole task would be senseless and unnecessary. We hit on the name "Social Revolutionary Party" because the social views of the new organization actually constituted a revolution.

But there was also a much deeper reason for the name. Attentive as I had always been to economic problems, my focus had been confined to the social problems. Only later were the bounds of my attention extended as I examined the Triple Alliance (*the Alliance was between Germany, Austria-Hungary, and Italy which Hitler detested*). This alliance was mostly the result of a poor assessment of the economic system, as well as a vagueness about the basis on which the German people could be sustained in the future. All these ideas rested on the opinion that money was only the product of labor, and finances could be corrected by adjusting issues that helped or hurt human activity. In fact, this unexpectedly revealed the true role of money because it depended completely on the greatness, freedom, and power of the State and people. This dependency requires financial sectors to actively support the State and people. It is a matter of instinct and self-preservation for the improvement of its own development. The necessary dependence of finances upon the independent free State would compel financial sectors to work for this freedom, power, and strength of the nation. This made the duty of the State toward finances comparatively simple and clear. It only had to be certain that capital remained a servant of the State and did not become the master of the people. The expression of this attitude could then remain within two boundary lines: preservation of a healthy, independent national economy on one side, and the safeguarding of the wage-earner's social rights on the other.

Previously, I did not realize there was a difference between capital as the result of work and a capital derived from speculation investments—not until I received a push in the right direction. This push was by one of the various gentlemen who lectured in the previously mentioned course, Gottfried Feder (*an economic theoretician who was later a key member and guided the Nazi party*).

For the first time in my life, I heard a basic outline explaining the workings of international finance and loan capital. When I heard Feder's first lecture, the idea instantly flashed through my mind that I had now found my way to accomplish one of the key essentials needed in the foundation of a new party.

In my mind, Feder's merit was demonstrated in his ruthless and vigorous method of describing the double character of the finances used in stock-exchanges and loan transactions. He laid bare the fact that this capital is always dependent on the payment of interest. His explanations of all the basic questions were so sound that from the start, his critics did not dispute the theoretical correctness of the idea but they doubted the possibility that it could be carried out. What others considered a weakness in Feder's arguments, I thought was the strong point.

The task of the plan's creator is not to lay out the details needed to fulfill the plan, but to explain the plan. He should be concerned less with the method and more with the goal. The essential truth behind an idea is the deciding factor, not the difficulty in carrying it out. The moment the plan's creator attempts to consider so-called "convenience" and "reality" instead of absolute truth, his work will no longer be a star seeking humanity and will become nothing more than an everyday procedure. The program-maker of a movement must determine its goal; the politician must attempt to reach it. Accordingly, the thinking of the plan's creator is determined by Eternal-Truth and the action of the politician is determined by the practical reality of the moment. The greatness of one man lies in the truth behind the theory of his idea and in his proper approach to the given facts. The greatness of the other lies in his practical use of them. The goal set up by the plan's creator must serve as a

Guiding-Light to others. The test of a politician's importance is the success of the plans and actions as they become a reality, even though the final intention of the plan's creator can never be realized. Human thought can indeed grasp truths and set up goals as clear as crystal, but their complete fulfillment will be prevented by the universal imperfection and inadequacy of man. The truer the theory and the more tremendous the idea, the more impossible it is to achieve as long as it depends on human beings. For that reason, the importance of the plan's creator cannot be measured by the achievement of his goals, but by their rightness and the influence they have on the development of humanity. If this were not true, the founders of religion could not be considered to be among the greatest men on this Earth since the fulfillment of their moral goals are not even close to being achieved. Even that, which is called the "Religion of Love", is only a shadow of the Will of its Righteous Creator, but its importance is in the attempt to convey ethics and morals to the general development of Human Culture.

This fundamental difference between the tasks of the political philosopher or plan's creator and the politician is also the reason why the two are almost never the same person. It is particularly true of the so-called "successful", or more accurately the unimportant politician whose actions are limited to "the art of the possible", as Bismarck defined politics. The more such a "politician" avoids great ideas and sticks to that which he can easily accomplish, the easier his job becomes, the more obvious his small victories, and always the quicker his successes will be. These successes have an Earthly and brief life and often do not live longer than the author. The work of this sort of politician is of no importance to future generations since its present success depends solely on avoiding crucial problems and ideas. The solutions to larger problems are actually valuable for later generations as well as the current one.

The accomplishment of goals which will have value and meaning for distant generations is usually unrewarding for their champions today and are rarely accepted or understood by the great masses. The masses understand reductions in beer and milk prices better than deep plans for a distant time where the benefits will only be seen by their future generations.

A close relative of stupidity is vanity, and vanity is the reason the great majority of politicians will distance themselves from any difficult plans for the future. They want to avoid losing the momentary favor of the crowd. The success and importance of such a politician then lies entirely in the present and their actions have no meaning for the future. This doesn't bother the small minded; they are satisfied with immediate results.

The political philosopher is a different matter. His importance almost always lies totally in the future since he is frequently what we call a dreamer. If the art of the politician is considered the art of doing the possible, then the political philosopher is one whom it is said pleases the Gods only when he demands the impossible. He will almost always have to give up fame in the present, but in its place, if his ideas are immortal, he receives glory from future generations.

Once in a very long time, a politician and political philosopher may be one and the same, but the more intimate this fusion, the greater the resistance will grow to the politician's efforts. He is no longer working for necessities obvious to the average person, but for goals only a few can understand. His life is torn between love and hate. The protests of those presently around him who do not understand the man will battle against his struggle to accomplish something important for posterity. The greater the future will be for a man's work, the less the present can grasp it, the harder the battle will be, and the rarer success will be found. If success does smile on one man in centuries, a glimmer of the coming glory may possibly surround him in his old age.

Even so, these great men are just the marathon runners of history. The glory of the present only rests upon the brow of the dying hero. We must count these men as the great warriors of this World. Those are the men who are not understood by the present, but who are nevertheless ready to fight to the end for their ideas and ideals. They are the ones who will someday be closest to the people's hearts. Each of these individuals felt it was his duty to repay the wrongs which great men have suffered at the hands of their contemporaries. Their lives and their work are then studied with touching and grateful admiration. In dark days of distress, such men have the power to heal broken hearts and elevate the people from their despair.

To this group belong not only the genuinely great statesmen but all the great reformers as well. Besides Frederick the Great (*Friedrick II, from the Hohenzollern dynasty, who united much of the Prussian dynasty*) we have such men as Martin Luther (*the monk and Protestant Church reformer)* and Richard Wagner (*the famous anti-Semitic German composer*).

When I heard Gottfried Feder's first lecture on "Breaking the Slavery of Interest", I immediately knew that this was a theoretical truth which was of huge importance for the future of the German people. The separation of finance capital from the national economy made it possible to oppose the internationalization of the German economy without threatening national self-preservation. I saw Germany's development much too clearly not to have known that the hardest struggle would have to be fought against international capital and not against hostile people. In

Feder's lecture, I heard a mighty rallying cry for this coming struggle.

Subsequent developments showed how right our feeling was. Today, we are no longer laughed at by our deceptive, privileged-class sly-boots politicians. Today, if they are not deliberate liars, even they see that international finance capital not only took the lead in nurturing the War, but especially after the struggle has ended it is doing everything possible to make the Peace into a Hell.

The struggle against international finance and loan capital interest has become the most important point in the program of the German nation's economic independence and freedom. For those practical people who may object, I offer these answers: All apprehensions about the economic consequences that would follow the abolition of the slavery that results from interest-based financing capital are not valid because in the first place, the economic principles that we have previously followed already proved to be quite disastrous to the interests of the German people.

The comments by the authors of those plans on questions of self-preservation strongly remind us of the past verdicts passed out by similar "experts" such as the Bavarian Medical Faculty regarding the question of introducing the railroad. We now know that none of this exalted body's fears have happened since riders of the new "steam-horse" did not become dizzy, spectators watching the train pass were not made ill, and the board fences intended to hide the new invention are gone. All that is left are invisible blinders on the so-called "experts" and those will always be there.

In the second place, we should remember that any idea becomes dangerous if it presumes to be an end in itself, but in reality, it is just a means to an end.

For me and all true National-Socialists, there is only one doctrine: *Folk and Fatherland*. We must fight to assure the existence and the growth of our race and our nation. We must feed our children and keep our blood pure. We must fight for the freedom and independence of the Fatherland so that our nation may grow and fulfill the mission given to it by the Creator of the Universe.

Every ideal and every idea, every teaching and all knowledge must serve this purpose. It is from this perspective that we must judge everything and use it or discard it according to its suitability for our purpose. In this way, a theory can never harden into a deadly doctrine since it must all serve the common good.

The insight of Gottfried Feder led me to deep study in a field where I previously had little knowledge. I resumed the process of learning and came to realize for the first time the purpose behind the life work of the Jew, Karl Marx. Now, I really began to understand his currency, the capital he used, as well as the struggle of Social Democracy against the national economy—a struggle that was meant only to lay the groundwork for the rule of true international finance by interest-based money.

In another respect, these courses had a great effect upon my later life. One day during the course, I asked for the floor in a discussion after one of the men attending the course felt compelled to break a lance for the Jews and defended them at great length. This aggravated me so much I had to reply. The overwhelming majority of those present were on my side. The result was that a few days later I was assigned to a Munich regiment as an "education officer".

The discipline of the troops at that time was still fairly weak. They suffered from the after-effects of the Soldiers' Council. The introduction of military discipline and subordination in place of "voluntary obedience", a term for the filth under Kurt Eisner (*who led the Marxist revolution in Bavaria and was Premier until 1919*), had to be implemented very slowly and cautiously. The troops themselves had to learn to feel and think as Nationalists and be patriotic. My new focus was pointed in those two directions.

I happily began my task. Suddenly, I had an opportunity to speak before large audiences. What I had always felt and assumed to be true was now being proven—I could "speak". My voice had improved enough so that people could always understand me, at least in the small squad room.

No task could have made me any happier. Now, before being discharged, I could do a useful service for the institution which had been so close to my heart, the army. I can say my talks were a success. During the course of my lectures, I led hundreds, probably thousands, of my comrades back to their *Folk and Fatherland*. I "nationalized" the troops and was able to help strengthen the general discipline.

In the process, I became acquainted with a number of comrades, who believed as I did and later formed the center of the new Movement.

194

9. THE "GERMAN WORKERS' PARTY"

One day, I received orders to find out about a political organization going under the name of "The German Workers' Party", which had scheduled a meeting in a day or two where Gottfried Feder was to speak. I was to attend, check out the group, and then make my report.

The army's curiosity in regard to political parties was more than understandable. The Revolution gave the soldiers the right to take part in politics, and it was the most inexperienced men who were now making full use of it. Until the Center Party (*a Catholic-based party*) and Social Democratic Parties (*the Marxists*) realized to their distress that these men were beginning to turn away from the Revolutionary party aims and turn toward the national movement; did they think it was appropriate to deprive the troops of their right to vote and forbid their involvement in political activity?

It was obvious that the Center Party and Marxism would resort to this measure because if they had not cut off "civil rights", which is what they called the political equality of the soldier after the Revolution, then within a few years, there would have been no November State left and no more national shame and humiliation that came with it. The troops at that time were well on the way to freeing the nation from its blood-suckers as well as the politicians inside the government who were tools of that political agreement. The fact that even the so-called "nationalist" parties voted enthusiastically for this doctrine of the November criminals (*to reverse soldiers' right to vote*), without regard to its true meaning, and thus helped to squelch the tools of a national revival, which should have been the nationalists' goal, showed once more that the inflexible attachment to an idea that is purely abstract can lead the gullible away from their own goals. Suffering from total intellectual deterioration, this privileged-class party seriously believed the army would again become a stronghold of German bravery. The real goal of the Center Party and Marxism was to cut out the dangerous nationalist fangs of the military. But without the ability to bite, an army becomes the police, not a body of troops that can do battle with the enemy. This is something which later events proved fully.

Did our "national politicians" think the army could have developed in any way other than becoming nationalistic? That would be just the style of these gentlemen. That is what happens when someone spends the war as a windbag parliamentarian and not as a soldier. They lose any sense of what is going on in the hearts of men. The hearts in the army are filled with a stupendous past reminding them that they were once the best soldiers in the world.

So, I resolved to attend the previously mentioned party meeting since I was not familiar with them and had not heard of them before. When I arrived that evening and went to the back room of the former Sternecker Brewery beer-hall, which is now a place of historical significance, there were about twenty or twenty-five people, mostly from the lower class.

I was already familiar with Feder's lecture through the courses I had taken, so I focused primarily on observing the society itself. It did not make a good or bad impression on me. It was just another new organization. Those were the days when anyone who was dissatisfied with previous developments and had lost confidence in the existing parties thought he should start a new party. Such societies sprang up like mushrooms everywhere, but disappeared without a squeak after a short time. Most of the founders did not have the slightest idea what it meant to turn a social gathering into a political party, let alone a movement. So, the groups they founded almost always drowned in their own ridiculous pettiness.

After listening for about two hours, I decided that the "German Workers' Party" could be lumped in with the rest. I was glad when Feder finally finished speaking. I had seen enough and was getting ready to go when they announced there would be an open discussion. With that, I was persuaded to stay awhile longer. Nothing of any consequence happened here until suddenly a "professor" took the floor. He first questioned the soundness of Feder's reasoning and then, after an excellent reply from Feder, suddenly took his stand and argued about the "facts" of the issue. But, before they continued he strongly urged the young party to adopt the "separation" of Bavaria from "Prussia" as an important point in the party program. The man brazenly continued to insist that German-Austria would immediately unite with Bavaria, that the peace would then be much better, and he continued with similar nonsense. At this point I could not resist asking for my turn on the floor and telling the learned gentlemen my opinion on the subject. I spoke with such success that before I had even finished, my predecessor on the floor left the hall with his tail between his legs. People looked astonished as they listened to me talk. When I was saying goodnight to the group and starting to leave, a man came running after me to introduce himself and handed me a booklet that was evidently a political pamphlet. He begged me to read it. I did not catch the man's name.

I thought this was very convenient because now I could become acquainted with the tiresome society without having to attend any more of their tiresome meetings. The man, obviously a workman, did leave a favorable impression on me though. Then, I left.

At that time, I was still living in the barracks of the Second Infantry Regiment in a little room which plainly showed the traces of the Revolution. I was away all day, usually with the 41st Light Infantry or at meetings or giving lectures to some other part of the troops. I was only in my quarters to sleep at night. Being in the habit of waking up at 5 o'clock every morning, I was accustomed to amusing myself by putting a few hard bread crusts on the floor for the tiny mice that played in the room. I would watch the comical little animals scramble for these morsels. I had endured enough starvation in my life that I could well imagine the hunger and also the delight of the little creatures.

The morning after the meeting, I was laying awake in bed at five o'clock watching the mice scurrying about. I couldn't go back to sleep and I suddenly remembered the night before, and then the booklet that the man had asked me to read. So, I began to read it. It was a small pamphlet in which the author—this very workman who gave it to me—described how he had escaped the Marxist and trade-union slogans and returned to thinking on nationalistic lines. The title was "My Political Awakening". Once I started reading, I consumed the pamphlet with interest all the way through. It described a process which reminded me of the one I had gone through twelve years before. I recalled my own development again. I thought about the matter several times throughout the day and was ready to put it aside again, when, less than a week later, I received a post-card stating that I been made a member of the German Workers' Party. The card asked what I thought about this and would I please come and share these thoughts at a committee meeting of the party the following Wednesday.

I must say, I was more than astonished at this method of "recruiting" members, and did not know whether to be annoyed or amused. I would not have dreamed of joining an existing party; I intended to found my own. This request was really out of the question for me. I was about to send my answer to the gentlemen in writing when I was overcome with curiosity and I decided to go on the scheduled day to explain my reasons in person.

Wednesday came. The pub where the meeting was to take place was the Altes Rosenbad (*the Old Rose*) in the Herrnstrasse (*Road of Gentlemen*) area, a very shabby place where somebody might wander by mistake once in a blue moon. That was not surprising in 1919, at a time when the menus of even the larger restaurants had only the most humble and sparse offerings. But this particular pub, I had never even heard of before.

I went through the dim front room, discovered the door to the back room, and found myself in the presence of the "meeting". In the faint glow of a half-functioning gas light, four young men were sitting around a table. Among them was the author of the little pamphlet, who immediately and excitedly greeted and welcomed me as a new member of the German Workers' Party. I was rather surprised at this. I was told that the real "national chairman" had not yet arrived and I decided to save my explanation for everyone at once. Finally, he showed up. He was the chairman from the meeting at the Sternecker Brewery when Feder had lectured.

While waiting, I had become curious again and waited to see what would happen. Now, at least, I found out the names of the various gentlemen. The chairman of the "national organization" was Karl Harrer and, the Munich chairman, Anton Drexler (*a machine and railway worker and a member of the völkisch movement offshoot which was anti-Semitic. He, together with journalist Karl Harrer, founded the German Workers' Party (DAP) in Munich with Gottfried Feder and Dietrich Eckart in 1919*).

The minutes of the last meeting were now read, and a role call of confidence in the secretary was passed. Then it was the treasurer's turn to read his report. The finances of the organization totaled all of seven marks and fifty pfennigs and for this, general confidence was expressed for the treasurer. This was also recorded in the minutes. Then, the chairman read aloud letters they had prepared in reply to past correspondence. One was a letter to Kiel, one to Dusseldorf, and one to Berlin. These were unanimously approved. Then the incoming mail was recorded and consisted of a letter from Berlin, one from Dusseldorf, and one from Kiel, whose arrival seemed to be received with great satisfaction. This increasing correspondence was declared to be an excellent and visible sign of the spreading importance of the "German Workers' Party". Then, there was a long discussion regarding the reply letters to be written in answer to the newly received correspondence.

Awful, just awful! This was a small-town club of the worst kind and this was what I was supposed to join? The new members were offered the floor for consideration of their membership. In other words, my capture in their trap was complete.

I began to ask questions, but I found that other than a few guiding principles, there was nothing—no program, no printed material at all, no membership card, not even a humble rubber stamp of the party seal. All I saw was good faith and good intentions.

I had lost my desire to laugh at these happenings. This was all a sign of total confusion and complete discouragement, which was common to these parties with their programs, purposes, and their activities. The deep feeling that drew these few young men together into this ridiculous meeting was a result of their inner voice which, more instinctively than consciously, made all past party activities seem useless for the nationalist revival of Germany or for the cure to its inner ailments, which were caused by those controlling the internal affairs of the State. I quickly read over the basic principles, which were in typewritten form, and I thought they revealed that these souls were searching and longing for answers rather than showing any knowledge of the battle that needed to be fought. Much of it was vague or uncertain and a lot was missing, but it was obvious they were looking for truth. What inspired these men was something that had been deep inside me too. It was the longing for a new movement which should be more than a party in the old sense of the word.

When I went back to the barracks that evening, my opinion of the organization was clear. I was faced with probably the most difficult question of my life: Should I join or should I decline? My reason advised me to refuse, but I had a restless feeling and the more I tried to convince myself the whole club was nonsense, the more I felt inclined to favor it. I could not rest for the next few days.

I began to argue back and forth with myself. I had decided to become politically active a long time ago. I was also convinced that a new movement was necessary, but my impulse to act had been lacking. I am not one of those who start something today, then forgets about it the next day or switches over to something new. My very conviction was the main reason it was so hard for me to decide to join a new organization. This organization either had to grow to be everything I saw it should be or else was better left alone. I knew I was making a decision forever and there could be no turning back. For me, it was no temporary plaything, but a deadly serious undertaking. I have always had an instinctive dislike for people who start everything and finish nothing. To me, such a jack-of-all-trades was to be loathed. I thought what they did was worse than doing nothing.

This was one of the main reasons why I could not decide as easily as others when it came to start something because it must either become everything or otherwise be conveniently left undone. Fate itself now seemed to give me a sign and point me down the right road. I would never have joined one of the existing large parties, and will explain my reasons in a moment. I felt this ridiculous little creation with its handful of members had one advantage in that it had not yet hardened into an "organization". Instead, it still gave the individual a chance for real personal input and activity. Here, a man could still accomplish some effective work, and the smaller the movement was, the greater the chance of forming it into the right shape. Here, in this group, its character could still be formed, which was out of the question from the start with the existing big parties.

The longer I considered, the more convinced I became that a small movement like this would serve as an instrument of national resurgence. This could never happen with one of the parliamentary political parties which clung far too tightly to old ideas, because they profited in the structure of the new regime. What must be declared here was a new World-Concept , and not a new election slogan.

Still, it was a frightening and difficult decision to try to turn a purpose into reality. What tools could I bring to the task? Being poor and without resources was the least of my troubles. A greater problem was that I was unknown. I was one of the millions whom Chance could let live or die without even his nearest neighbors noticing. In addition, there was the problem that I had never completed my schooling.

The so-called "intelligent people" look down with unlimited condescension on anyone who has not been dragged through the required schools so that he has the necessary knowledge pumped into him. After all, nobody ever asks, "What can the man do?" but, "What has he learned?" The "educated" people will like the greatest idiot if he is covered in enough diplomas while they will care nothing for the brightest boy who does not have those precious wrappings. So I could easily imagine how the "educated" world would receive me. My only mistake was in thinking men are a little better than they actually are. True, the exceptions shine even brighter because of who they are. For my part, I learned to distinguish between those who are endlessly preparing for the real world through schooling and the men of real ability who can take action.

After two days of painful pondering and consideration, I was finally convinced I must take this step. It was the hardest decision of my life. There could and must be no retreat if I went forward. I applied for membership in the German Workers' Party and received a provisional membership certificate bearing the number seven!

10. CAUSES OF THE COLLAPSE

The fall of any group is always measured by the distance between its present position and its original position. The same thing holds true for the downfall of races and states. This makes the original position highly important. Only what rises above the ordinary limits can be noticed in its fall. The collapse of the Second Reich was so hard and so horrible to every thinking and feeling person because the fall came from a height which today, in the face of our disastrous present humiliation, is hard to even imagine.

The very founding of the Reich seemed to be made golden by the magical happenings that elevated the whole nation. After a victorious and unequaled journey, an Empire grew for their sons and grandsons as the ultimate reward for immortal heroism. Whether consciously or unconsciously, the Germans felt that the noble way it was founded raised this Empire higher than any other state. Its existence was not due to parliamentary maneuvers to jockey above the standing of other states. It was not in the small talk of a parliamentary argument, but in the thunder and roar of the battlefront around Paris that the solemn act took place. This was a demonstration of the will of the Germans, princes and common people, who sought to form one Empire for the future that would once more exalt the Imperial Crown as a great symbol. It was not done by a knife in the back. Deserters and traitors were not the founders of Bismarck's State; it was built by regiments at the front lines.

This unique birth and fiery baptism alone were enough to surround the Empire with a glow of historic glory that few of the oldest states could claim. What a rise began from that point!

Freedom from the outside world gave us independence and a means for creating our own daily bread on the inside. The nation grew in number and in wealth. The honor of the State and the people was guarded by an army, which was the most powerful demonstration of the difference between the new unified Empire and the old German Confederation.

The downfall which has overtaken the Empire and the German people is so deep that everyone seems dizzy and dumbfounded. People can barely see in their mind's eye the old heights of the Empire because today's disgrace is such a contrast to the unreal dreams of yesterday's greatness and magnificence. It is natural enough for people now to be so blinded by the past splendor that they forget to look for the reason behind the great collapse. There must have been a symptom in some form that caused the collapse.

This is true only for those to whom Germany was more than just a place to live and make and spend money. Those who truly valued the Empire can feel the present state of collapse. To the others, it is the fulfillment of their long-hoped-for silent wishes.

The warning signs predicting the collapse were present and clearly visible in the early days. Few people tried to learn anything from them. Today, this is more necessary than ever. A disease can only be cured if it is diagnosed. The same is true when it comes to curing political ills. The visible symptoms of a disease, which is easy to see, is more easily identified than the inner cause. This is also the reason why so many people never move beyond the recognition of symptoms. They confuse the symptoms of the political disease with the cause. They may even try to deny the existence of the cause. Even now, most of us see the German collapse as the cause of our general economic distress, but that is actually the result which came with the German collapse. To truly understand this catastrophe, almost everyone has to personally suffer his share of the burden, and that is why every individual looks upon the current economic troubles as the cause of the State's problems. The great masses are far less capable of recognizing the collapse in its political, cultural, and moral aspects. This is why many people's instinct and understanding are both at a complete loss.

Some might say that this is only true of the great masses, but the fact that even in intellectual circles, the German collapse is primarily seen as an "economic catastrophe" and can be fixed by economic means is one of the reasons why no recovery has yet been possible. Only when we realize the economic element occupies a second or third place in the line of responsibility—while political, moral, and racial factors occupy the top—can we begin to comprehend the means required for a cure.

The search for the causes of the German collapse is of primary importance, especially for a political movement whose goal is to overcome this disaster. While searching the past for the cause of this disaster, we must be careful not to confuse the obvious effects or symptoms, which are easily spotted, with the less obvious causes, which are easily overlooked.

The easiest and most popular explanation of the present disaster is to say it results from the loss of a war. Obviously, that must be the cause of the whole problem. No doubt there are many people who honestly believe this nonsense, but there are more who know better and deliberately spread this lie. Those now feeding at the government trough are fed this slop. Wasn't it the heralds of the Revolution who kept telling the great masses how the results of the war would not effect them? Did they not solemnly vow that only the "great capitalists", the high financiers, had an interest in the victorious end of the war, but the German people, the German worker had no interest whatsoever in the outcome? Did these apostles of world reconciliation not declare quite openly that a defeat would destroy only "militarism", while the German people would experience a wonderful resurgence and prosperity. Weren't these the same men who raised the flag of the Entente, the flag of surrender, and laid blame for the whole bloody struggle upon Germany? Could they have done this without their announcement that a military defeat would have no special consequences for the nation? Wasn't the whole Revolution dressed with bright, pretty colors to block the march of German victory flags? Did they not say only in this way the German people would advance toward its inner and outward freedom? Wasn't this so, you disgraceful, lying scoundrels?

It requires a disrespect unique to the Jews to blame the German collapse on the military defeat now while the official mouthpiece of this high treason, the Berlin Vorwärts (*the Forward, which was the newspaper of the Social Democrats*), wrote that the German people must not bring its victory banner back this time! And now, the defeat is supposed to be the cause of our collapse?

Of course it would be quite pointless to argue with such a group of forgetful liars. I would not waste words on it if this nonsense were not unfortunately repeated by so many thoughtless people who have no real hatred or intention to deceive. They merely parrot what they read. This discussion is intended to furnish our followers— our warriors of enlightenment— with the weapons which will be necessary when the spoken word is twisted in its meaning, often even before one can get it out of his mouth.

Here is the reply that should be given to anyone who says that the loss of the war was responsible for the German collapse: True, the loss of the War had dire consequences for the future of our Fatherland. Yet, the loss is not a cause but only a result of other causes. It was always perfectly clear to every intelligent and honest person that failure would be the outcome of this life-and-death struggle. Unfortunately, there were also people who failed to see this at the right time. There were also those who first questioned then denied the truth. These were the ones who suddenly understood too late the catastrophe their collaboration had helped to cause. And there were those who denied the truth after their secret wish was fulfilled even though they knew better. All of these people were guilty of causing the collapse, not the lost war, as they suddenly chose to say or pretended to know. The loss of the war was the result of their activity and not the result of "bad" leadership as they now try to claim. The enemy was no coward; he, too, knew how to die. He had more soldiers than the German army from the start, and the arsenals and armory factories of the whole world were available to him.

Therefore, the German victories that were steadily gained through four long years against the world were due solely to superior leadership as well as the heroism of our soldiers. The organization and direction of the German army were the most tremendous things the world had yet seen. Their faults were no more than the limits of human fallibility. The army's collapse was not the cause of our present misfortune, but only the result of other crimes. This result ushered in another and more visible collapse.

This collapse is shown from the following analysis: Does a military defeat automatically mean a complete breakdown of a nation and a state will be the result? Since when has this been the result of an unsuccessful war? Are nations ever destroyed by lost wars and that alone? The answer in short is "yes", if their military defeat reflects these people's inner rottenness, cowardice, lack of character, and unworthiness. If this is not the case, the military defeat would instead be the drive that leads to a new and greater advancement rather than the gravestone of a people's existence. History offers endless examples to prove this statement.

Unfortunately, the military defeat of the German people is not an undeserved catastrophe, but a deserved punishment of Eternal revenge. We more than earned that defeat. It is simply the obvious outward symptom of decay resulting from a series of inner problems. They may have been hidden from the eyes of the average men or those ostrich-like people who refused to see the obvious and stuck their heads in the sand.

Consider how the German people received this defeat. Didn't many groups welcome the misfortunes of the Fatherland joyfully and in the most shameful ways? Who could act like this without bringing down vengeance on his head for his attitude? Didn't they go even further and boast that they finally made the war-front collapse? It was not the enemy who disgraced us. Oh no, the German's own countrymen put this shame on our heads! Was it unjust for disaster to follow them after their actions? When has it ever been customary to take full blame for a war oneself? What people would accept such guilt even though they have better sense and know the truth to be different!

No, and again no. How the German people received its defeat is the best sign that the true cause of our collapse has to be found somewhere other than in the military loss of a few positions on hilltops or the failure of an offensive. If the front lines had really given way and if a military misfortune had caused the Fatherland's catastrophe, the German people would have received the defeat in a completely different way. They would have borne the disaster that followed with clenched teeth or have grieved about it, overpowered by agony. Their hearts would have been full of rage and anger against the enemy that was victorious merely through the double-cross of Chance or the will of Fate. Like the Roman Senate, the nation would have gone to meet the beaten divisions carrying the thanks of the Fatherland for their sacrifice and begging them not to lose hope for the Empire. Even the surrender would have been signed with the calm intellect of the brain, while the heart would have pounded as it already looked toward the revival to come.

That was how a defeat would have been received that was due to Fate alone. There would have been no laughing and dancing, no boasting of cowardice and no glorifying defeat, no jeering at the fighting troops and dragging their flag and medals in the mud. Above all, things would never have come to pass which caused an English officer, Colonel Repington (*retired Colonel Charles Repington, a British war correspondent for the Times, who first coined the phrase World War*), to say contemptuously, "Every third German is a traitor". No, this disease would have never risen to the choking flood that for the past five years has drowned the last remnants of the world's respect for us.

This is what best proves the statement that the lost war is the cause of the German collapse and is totally false. No, the military collapse itself was the result of a disease whose germs had attacked the German nation even before the war broke out. This was the first universally visible catastrophic result of moral poisoning, of a loss of the self-preservation instinct, and all that goes with it which had started undermining the people and the Empire many years before. It took all the enormous lies of Jewry and its army of Marxists to put the blame for the collapse on the very man who was trying single-handed with super-human energy and will-power to prevent the catastrophe he had foreseen, and to spare the nation from its deepest degradation and shame. Ludendorff (*a well known German general who created the Dolchstoßlegende, the Stab-in-the-back theory that Germany was betrayed and because of this lost WWI; he was also a proponent of propaganda, an anti-Marxist and anti-Semitic who held Adolf Hitler in high regard*) was branded as guilty for the defeat and with this act, the weapon of moral righteousness was snatched from the hand of the only accuser who was dangerous enough to have risen up against the betrayers of the Fatherland and brought them to justice. Here they were acting on the true principle that within a big lie, a certain fraction of it is always accepted and believed. At the bottom of their hearts, the great masses of a people are more likely to be misled by their emotions than to be consciously and deliberately bad. In the primitive simplicity of their minds, they will more easily fall victim to a large lie than a small lie, since they sometimes tell petty lies themselves, but would be ashamed to tell a lie that was too big. They would never consider telling a lie of such magnitude themselves, or knowing that it would require such impudence, they would not consider it possible for it to be told by others. Even after being enlightened and shown that the lie is a lie, they will continue to doubt and waver for a long time and will still believe there must be some truth behind it somewhere, and there must be some other explanation. For this reason, some part of the most bold and brazen lie is sure to stick. This is a fact that all the great liars and liars' societies (*meaning the Jewish press*) in this world know only too well and use regularly.

Those who have known this truth about the possibilities of using lies and slander best have always been the Jews. Their whole existence is built up on one great lie: that they are a religious community when they are actually a race, and what a race! As such, one of the greatest minds of humanity(*Arthur Schopenhauer, the German Philosopher*) forever "nailed-down" an eternally-correct and fundamental truth when he called the Jews "The Great Masters of the Lie". Anyone who refuses to see or declines to believe this can never help truth become victorious in the World.

We may almost consider it a stroke of good fortune for the German people that the extent of its creeping disease was shortened by such an awful and sudden catastrophe. Otherwise, the nation would have been destroyed, perhaps more slowly, but even more surely. The disease would have become chronic. In the seriousness of the collapse, it is now visible to the eyes of the crowd. It is not by chance that man mastered the plague more easily than tuberculosis. One disease comes in dreadful waves of death which shake humanity; the other creeps slowly. Plague leads to fear; tuberculosis leads gradually to indifference. The result was that men faced the plague with ruthless energy, while they tried to keep tuberculosis in check by weak methods. Man became master of the plague, while tuberculosis became master over him.

The same thing is true of the diseases of nations. If they do not take the form of a catastrophe, men slowly adapt to their presence and the damage is much greater because it is gradual. It is strangely a piece of good luck, though a bitter one, when Fate decides to interfere in this slow process of decay and suddenly inflict the final stage of the disease on the sufferer. Such is the result of such a catastrophe; it forces the development of a cure to be carried through with total determination. Even in this case, the recognition of the inner causes which produced the sickness must come first before we can look for a cure.

Here too, the most important thing is to distinguish the germs from the conditions they produce. This becomes more difficult the longer the virus has existed in the political body and the more it is taken for granted to be part of the body. It may easily happen that after a length of time, someone will regard clearly harmful poisons as an integral part of one's own people, or at least will come to tolerate them as a necessary evil so that they no longer feel it is necessary to search for the poisonous germ.

In the long years of peace before the war (*the First World War*), certain evils had definitely shown themselves and been recognized as such. With only a few exceptions, no one paid much attention to what caused them. Here again, the exceptions were primarily in aspects of economic life, which effected and caught the attention of the individual more than problems in other areas. There were many signs of decay that should have been food for serious thought.

From the economic angle, there is this to be said: The amazing growth of the German population before the war brought the problem of receiving an adequate supply of daily bread more sharply to the forefront. Unfortunately, those "responsible people" could not make up their minds to adopt the one correct solution. Instead, they preferred to accomplish their purpose in a cheaper way through industry. The decision to give up acquiring new land and its place to become entangled in the ghost of an industrial world economic conquest was bound to eventually lead to an industrialization that was as uncontrollable as it was harmful.

The first consequence which had a major impact was the weakening of the farming or peasant class. As fast as this class declined, the number of working class people in the large cities grew until the balance was entirely lost.

Now, the intense contrast between poor and rich also became evident. Abundance and filth lived so close together that the results were bound to cause conflict. Distress and frequent unemployment began to take their toll on men and left discontent and bitterness behind. The result was a political division of classes. Despite spreading prosperity, dissatisfaction grew and became more intense. Circumstances reached the point where many believed that "this division could not continue much longer". However, people weren't able to see what was going to happen.

These were clear and visible signs of the far-reaching discontent. Worse yet were other consequences which the commercialization and industrialization of the nation brought with them. Just as economics became the ruling mistress of the state, money became the God all had to serve and before whom all had to bow down. More and more, the Gods of Heaven were put on the shelf as antiquated and worn out. Incense was not burned to them, but to the false God, Mammon (*the false God of greed*). A very destructive collapse began—destructive especially because it came at a critical time for the nation, a time when it needed the noblest of heroic spirit more desperately than ever. Germany should have realized that some day it would need to back-up its acquisition of daily bread by "peaceful economic work" with the sword.

The rule of money was authorized in the very place where it should have been most strongly resisted. His Majesty the Kaiser mistakenly allowed the new financial moguls to rise to the level of nobility. It must be admitted in his defense that even Bismarck unfortunately did not recognize the danger this elevation would have.

It meant that the virtues of idealism had moved to second place behind the value of money. It was clear that once we set out on this path, the warrior nobility must soon take a secondary position to the financial nobility.

It is easier to find success in financial operations than military operations. There was no longer any attraction for the real hero or statesman who did not care to be thrown together with the first stray Jewish banker. The really deserving man no longer had any interest in being presented with cheap decorations (*civil medals and awards for economic accomplishment*). Instead he declined them with a simple thanks. The purity of blood was an even more gloomy matter in this decline. More and more, the nobility lost the essential racial element required for its existence. For many of them, the name "ignobility" would have been far more suitable(*not being noble in quality or character*).

A serious sign of economic decay began with the slow disappearance of personal control over property and the gradual transfer of the entire economic system into the hands of stock-controlled corporations. Labor had become an object of exploitation and speculation for deceitful stockbrokers with no conscience. The transfer of property from the wage-earner to the financiers grew out of proportion. The stock exchange began to triumph, and slowly but surely, started to take the life of the nation under its protection and control.

The German economic system had already started down the road of internationalization when it began issuing shares of stock. German industrialists made a determined effort to save the system, but it eventually fell before the united attack of money-grabbing financiers who fought this battle with the help of their most faithful friend, the Marxist movement.

Marxism launched a constant and visible war on German heavy industry to turn it into an international business. This could only be accomplished through the victory of Marxism in the Revolution. As I write this, the attack has succeeded against the German Government Railways, which are now being handed over to International financiers. This "International Social Democracy" has once more accomplished another of its great objectives.

We can see how far this attempt to make "economic animals" of the German people succeeded from the fact that after the war, one of the leading minds of German industry, and especially of commerce, said that only economic improvement could possibly put Germany on her feet again. This nonsense was spouted at the same time by France who was restoring the German education system, a "humanitarian" gesture, in order to promote the belief that the nation and the State owe their survival to economics and not to eternal values. This remark of Stinnes (*Hugo Stinnes, a German industrialist and politician of extensive wealth*) regarding commerce as the only savior for Germany caused incredible confusion. It was picked up at once by all the babbling and idiotic bums Fate had unleashed on Germany as "statesmen" after the Revolution.

One of the worst signs of decay in Germany before the war was the habit of doing everything halfway. It comes from people being timid in their actions as well as from a cowardice growing out of this and other causes.

The disease was made worse by the education system. German education before the war had an extraordinary number of weaknesses. It was very one-sided and aimed to produce pure "knowledge" to the exclusion of teaching practical ability. Even less value was attached to the development of individual character, at least as much as it is possible to teach character, and there was little encouragement to learn responsibility and no cultivation at all of will and determination. The result was not to produce strong men but passive "Polymaths" (*intellectuals who know a little about everything*). This is how the world saw and treated Germans before the war (*the First World War*). The German man was popular because he was very useful as a result of his knowledge, but he was not respected because of his weak character. For this reason, he was the quickest of almost all peoples to lose or forget his nationality of the Fatherland when he traveled outside the country. The common saying, "He who travels with hat in hand can go the whole width of the land" tells the entire story (*meaning a man who is humble, humbly holds his hat in his hand, can go anywhere and be welcomed; the saying does not mean a beggar*).

This submissive nature became positively dangerous to the country when it was used to determine how one could act in the presence of the Monarch. This social etiquette dictated that one never contradict the Monarch, but instead must approve anything and everything His Majesty appeared to like.

This was the very place where free expression of manly dignity was most needed and not subservience. The institution of the Monarchy would be destroyed by such false flattery. Flattery is what it is and nothing more. It is suited for sorry, self-serving beings who are more interested in securing a place for themselves in circles of royalty. This whole corrupt crew of flatterers always felt more comfortable around the Royal thrones than among frank and honorable people. With all their humility toward their Lord and meal ticket, these "humble servants" of his majesty have always displayed extreme arrogance towards other mortals. This was especially true when they chose to display themselves to the other sinners as the only true believers who supported the "Monarchy". This gross impertinence was so extreme that it could only exist among the newly-nobled or yet-to-be-ennobled.

These types of fellows have always been the gravediggers of a Monarchy and especially patriarchal ideas. It could not have ended differently. A man who is ready to stand up for his cause can never grovel in front of its representative. A man who is really serious about preserving and promoting his cause will cling to it with every fiber of his heart, and will never lose faith when his representative begins to show any faults or confusion. He will never run through the streets as the democratic "friends" of the Monarchy did, acting in an equally deceptive and backstabbing fashion. Instead, he will urgently and seriously warn the wearer of the Crown and try to convince him of the need to act. As a true believer in a cause, he will not and must not take the standpoint that His Majesty is free to act as he pleases, when he pleases, if he pleases, especially when his current course of action is clearly leading to disaster. On the contrary, the man of conviction will be forced in that case to protect the Monarchy against the Monarch itself at any personal risk. If the value of the Monarchy were limited to the person at the head—the Monarch at that moment—then one could not imagine a worse institution than a Monarchy. It is truly rare that monarchs are the flower of wisdom and reason or even of character, even though people may choose to pretend they are. Only the professional boot-lickers who win favor through flattery believe this, or at least pretend it is true. Upright men are the ones most valuable to the State and they cannot help but be repelled by the nonsense of such "wise-monarchs". For them, history is history and truth is truth, even where monarchs are concerned. The people are rarely fortunate enough to have a great man as a great monarch and if they do, they must realize they are lucky that the cruelty of Fate has spared them from the absolute worst monarch.

The value and meaning of the Monarchy concept cannot lie in the monarch himself unless Heaven decides to put the crown on the brow of such an inspired hero as Frederick the Great or such a wise character as William I. Such leaders may find their way to the top once in centuries, but rarely more often. The idea of a Monarchy should be above the person, then the system exists totally in the institution. This means the monarch himself is one of those who must serve the Monarchy. He is but a wheel in the machine and must do his duty to it. He must also adjust to the office so he can follow the higher purpose. Therefore, the true "monarchist" is not the man who silently allows the wearer of the crown to violate it, but prevents any violation. If the significance of the Monarchy were not in the idea but in the "sacred" person who wears a crown, the establishment of an obviously insane prince could never be questioned and he could never be removed.

It is necessary to establish this as a fact because lately, those figures whose sorry attitudes were in part to blame for the Monarchy's collapse have come out of hiding again. With a certain naive shamelessness, these people start talking about "their King". This is the same king they disgracefully deserted at a critical moment only a few years ago. Now they call anyone who refuses to join in their chorus of lies a bad German. Yet these are the very same chicken-heart cowards who scattered and fled in 1918 to the red arm-band of Marxism. They left their King to look out for himself as they hastily exchanged their sharp weapon for a walking stick, put on neutral neckties, and vanished without a trace or tried to mix in among peaceable civilians. In an instant these royal champions were gone. It was only after the revolutionary hurricane had begun to die down that they could shout "Hail to the King, all Hail". These "servants and counselors" of the Crown begin to make a cautious appearance again but only after others had suppressed the Revolution and taken a bloody nose for it. Now, they are all here again, gazing longingly at the luxurious life. They are once more filled with excitement, energy, and devotion for their King. At least until the day when the first red arm-band appears again and the whole crew of profit seekers from the old Monarchy once more scatters like mice from a cat!

If the monarchs were not responsible themselves for these things, we could only pity them heartily. But the monarchs themselves must realize that thrones can be lost with knights such as these, but never won.

Such slavish submission was a weakness of our whole system of education and the results in this situation were especially disastrous. Thanks to it, these sorry figures could maintain themselves at all the royal courts and gradually undermine the foundation of the Monarchy. When the pillar started to shake, the entire structure collapsed and was gone with the wind. Naturally, belly crawlers and selfish flatterers are not going to wait to be killed for their master. Monarchs never see this and almost never bother to learn it; this has always resulted in their ruin.

One of the worst signs of this corruption was the growing cowardice. No one wanted to face responsibility for anything and the resulting weakness and indifference in dealing with the problems that resulted only accelerated the downfall.

The source of this epidemic is primarily in the parliamentary institution, where irresponsibility is positively cultivated and nurtured. Unfortunately, the disease slowly spreads to all life outside the Monarchy, especially to governmental life. Everywhere, people started to dodge responsibility. To avoid any responsibility, they resorted to insufficient, ineffective, halfway measures that reduced their personal responsibility to a minimum.

We only have to consider the attitude of the individual governments toward a series of damaging occurrences in our public life, and we will easily recognize the dreadful impact of this universal half-heartedness and fear of responsibility.

I will cite only a few cases from the enormous number of examples known to me:

Journalistic circles are particularly fond of describing the press as a "great power" in the State. Indeed, its importance is truly enormous. It simply cannot be overestimated. It continues the education of adults which is important.

Readers can be divided into three groups: Those who believe everything they read; those who no longer believe anything they read; and those minds which critically examine what they read and then form their own judgments about the accuracy of the information.

The first group who believes everything they read is the largest and strongest because they are composed of the broad masses of the population. These great masses of the people represent the most simple-minded part of the nation. It cannot, however, be divided by occupation, only by general degrees of intelligence. This group includes those who have not been born with the gift of, or trained for independent thinking and who believe anything which is printed in black and white. This is partly because of inability and partly through incompetence. This group also encompasses a class of lazy people who could think for themselves, but who gratefully accept anything someone else has already put any thinking-effort into on the humble assumption that he worked hard for his opinion so it must be right. All these groups represent the great mass of the people and the influence of the press on them will be enormous. Since they are unable or unwilling to weigh what is offered to them and evaluate it for themselves, their approach to every daily problem is totally determined by how they are influenced by others. This may be an advantage if their understanding is fed by serious and truth-loving persons, but it will be disastrous if they are led by scoundrels and liars.

In number, the second group who does not believe anything they read is considerably smaller. It is partially made up of those who once belonged to the first group of total-believers. Then, after continued disappointments, they have switched to the opposite extreme and now believe nothing in print. They hate all newspapers and either do not read them at all, or fly into a rage over the contents which they believe to be nothing but lies and deceptions. These people are very hard to deal with because they will always be suspicious, even of the truth. They are useless when it comes to accomplishing any positive work.

The third group who reads and evaluates for themselves is by far the smallest. It consists of those really fine minds, which have been educated and through training or maybe are naturally capable of independent thinking. They try to form their own judgments on everything and they subject everything they read to a repeated, thorough scrutiny and further develop the implications and meaning for themselves. They never look at a newspaper without mentally taking part in the writing and then Mr. Writer's task is no easy one. Journalists have a reserved, perhaps limited appreciation for such readers.

To the members of this third group, the nonsense which a newspaper may choose to scribble is not dangerous or even significant. They have usually become accustomed in the course of a lifetime to regard every journalist as a rogue who happens to sometimes tell the truth. Unfortunately, the importance of these splendid figures is only in their intelligence and not in their number. There are too few of them to have a significant impact. It is unfortunate that during this age wisdom means nothing and majority means everything! Today, when the voting ballots of the masses are final, the deciding factor is the highest number——that is the largest group and this is the first group I discussed. This is the crowd of the simple-minded or most gullible citizens.

The State has a prime interest in preventing these people from falling into the hands of bad, ignorant, or evil-intentioned gurus. It is, therefore, the State's duty to supervise their education and prevent any mischief from being performed. In doing so, the State must keep a particularly sharp eye on the press. The press' influence on such people is by far the strongest and most penetrating because it is exerted continuously and not just momentarily. It is the continuous, consistent repetition of this educational instruction that makes it enormously important. The State must also remember that all means must point towards the same end. It must not be misled by chatter about so-called "freedom of the press" into neglecting its duty. The State must never deprive or allow others to deprive the nation of the nourishment it needs and can thrive on—the nourishment that is good and can accomplish good. The State must use ruthless determination to keep control of this instrument of popular education and make certain it is placed in the service of the State and the Nation.

What was it that the German press fed people before the war? Wasn't it the most virulent poison imaginable? Wasn't the heart of our people injected with acute pacifism at a time when the rest of the world was preparing slowly but surely to pounce on Germany? Even in peace time, didn't the German press fill the minds of the people with doubts about the just cause of its own State which reduced the choice of weapons the State could select for defense from the very beginning? Wasn't it the German press which succeeded in offering the nonsense of "Western Democracy" in an appetizing way to our people, until at last, captured by all the enthusiastic fluff, the people believed it could entrust its future to a League of Nations? *(The League of Nations resulted from the Treaty of Versailles after the First World War and was meant to maintain peace.)* Didn't it help bring a state of moral degradation upon our people? Didn't it portray morality and decency as ridiculous, calling them old-fashioned and narrow-minded, until at last our people renounced them to become "modern?" Didn't the continuous assault by the press undermine the foundations of government authority until one push was enough to collapse the institution? Didn't the press oppose at every turn the movement to give to the State that authority which is the State's, and degrade the army by constant criticism, sabotage the universal military draft, and urge the refusal of military funding increases until eventually the campaign of the press was assured to be a success?

The liberal press' activity dug the grave of the German people and the German Empire. This does not even include the small Marxist lie-sheets which were handed out. They cannot live without lying any more than a cat can live without catching mice. Their primary goal is to break the national backbone of the people in order to prepare it for the burden of international financiers and their master, the Jew.

What did the State do against this mass poisoning of the nation? Nothing, nothing at all. A few ridiculous rules, a few sentences about not being too violent, not being too evil, and that was all. They took no serious action because they hoped to win the favor of this pest by flattery, by recognizing the "value" of the press, its "importance", its "educational mission", and other such nonsense. All of this the Jews accepted with a sly smile, giving devious thanks in return.

This shameful powerless display by the State was not so much due to its failure to recognize the danger as it was to a cowardice that cried to Heaven for relief and the resulting half-hearted effort behind every decision. No one had the courage to use a radical remedy that would completely solve the problem. Here, as everywhere, people fooled around with weak half-cures. Instead of stabbing the heart of the problem, they merely provoked the viper. This resulted in the countermeasures staying the same, but the power of the groups that should be combated grew from year to year.

The resistance of the German government in those days against the mostly Jewish press, which was slowly corrupting the nation, lacked any direct determination, and above all, it had no visible goal. The officials completely failed to understand the situation because they did not properly estimate the importance of the struggle and failed to choose the means to combat the problem. They did not create a definite plan. They tinkered aimlessly, and sometimes, if they were bitten too hard, they would lock up one of these journalistic vipers for a few weeks or months, but the snakes' nest itself was left undisturbed.

This was partly the result of the endless, crafty tactics of Jewry on one side and a stupidity or naivety on the other. The Jew was far too shrewd to allow a simultaneous attack to occur against the entire press. Then when one part of the press was attacked, the other members would give cover to protect their stronghold. The Marxists were taking the field in the lowest way possible to attack and revile all that man holds sacred and wickedly attacking both State and government, and setting social classes of the people against each other. The Jewish propaganda newspapers, which were aimed at the privileged-class, knew exactly how to make themselves appear to be the heralds of objectivity and carefully avoided all strong language. They knew that the empty-headed can only judge what is on the outside and are never able to look deeper; avoiding strong language concealed their true message by hiding it in a pretty box. So, for them, the value of something is measured by the exterior instead of by the substance, a human weakness that the press has carefully studied and understands well.

For such empty-headed people, the Frankfurter Zeitung (*the Frankfurter Newspaper, a German Newspaper in Frankfurter which openly supported the Treaty of Versailles*) was and is the very essence of "decency". It never uses rude language, opposes all physical brutality, and urges war only with "intellectual" weapons, which oddly enough is always the favorite idea of the most unintelligent people. This is a result of our half-way education system, which teaches students to separate themselves from natural instincts and pumps them full of certain information without leading them to the ultimate knowledge or true understanding. Diligence and good intentions alone are useless if they fail to provide the necessary understanding of what is being taught. This final combination of intelligence and natural instinct is indispensable. Ultimate knowledge consists of intellectually understanding the causes which are already instinctively perceived.

Man must never be so misguided that he believes he has ascended to the position of lord and master over Nature. The conceit of half-education has made men think this illusion is possible. He must understand the fundamental law of necessity rules in Nature's domain, and realize how completely his existence is subject to these laws of eternal battle and the struggle for dominance. Only with this understanding will he see that in a universe where planets revolve around greater suns, moons revolve about their greater planets, where the strong are masters over the weak;

there can be no separate law for mankind. Man must be subject to these laws or be crushed by them. This supreme wisdom must dominate man. He can try to understand these principles, but he can never free himself from them.

It is for those who choose to be kept, like a seedy harem among the followers of this press, that the Jew writes his so-called newspapers he writes for that "intelligent" reader. The Frankfurter Zeitung (*Frankfurter News*) and the Berliner Tageblatt (*The Berlin Daily, a major liberal newspaper in Berlin*) are made for this intellectual crowd because their tone is chosen so that it speaks to them and influences these people the most. Carefully avoiding any seeming harshness and never speaking in a crude manner, they nevertheless pour their poison into the hearts of their readers by other means. With a steady flow of pretty words and phrases, they lull their readers into believing that these lovely words are a fountain of knowledge and moral principles which are pouring from their pages. In truth, theirs is the brilliant and crafty art of disarming any enemy who might oppose the Jews and their press. As one group of newspapers drips with decency, the half-wit followers are all the more ready to believe that the other newspapers speak the same truth only in a slightly more crude fashion. It is a question of degree. The offenses of one group does not seem as serious or extreme when compared to this journal of "decency". These abuses then appear to be small, and being of such a perceived minor nature, would never lead to any restriction upon "freedom of the press". That is the loophole that allows such newspapers to escape legal punishment for this harmful poisoning and lying to the people. Therefore, the government hesitates to take action against these journalistic bandits for fear they will immediately have the "decent" press line up against them too. This fear is well founded. The moment anyone attempts to take action against one of these scandal sheets, all the others immediately rush to its defense. It is not because they approve of its method of fighting, Heaven forbid. It is said to be a matter of freedom-of-the-press and a matter of free expression of public opinion. That alone is what is being defended. Even the strongest men will fall down, weakened under this uproar, because the outcry comes entirely from the mouths of "decent" newspapers.

This poison was allowed to enter and do its work in the blood stream of our people without interference and without the State exercising the strength needed to control the disease. In the ridiculous half-measures it employed, one could see the pending downfall of the Empire. An institution, which is no longer determined to protect itself with every available weapon, has effectively surrendered its existence. Every half-hearted act is a visible sign of inner decay which will eventually be followed by outward collapse.

I believe that the present generation, with proper guidance, will more easily conquer the danger. This generation has gone through various experiences which have strengthened the nerves of everyone who did not lose their nerve altogether. In the days to come, the Jew will raise a terrible protest in his newspapers when a hand is laid on his favorite den to stop his journalistic mischief, and the press is set to work as a means of forming public opinion through education for the State. This valuable messenger can no longer be left in the hands of aliens and enemies of the people. This necessary action will not disturb us younger men as much as it would have our fathers. A ten-inch shell hissing overhead is louder than a thousand Jewish newspaper snakes. Let the vipers hiss!

Another example of weakness and half-hearted actions on the part of the government of pre-war Germany concerning the most important questions to the nation is this: For many years a horrible physical poisoning of the people has run its course along side the political and moral infection of the citizens. Syphilis began to spread in the large cities, while tuberculosis gathered its harvest of death almost uniformly throughout the country.

In both cases, the effects on the nation were horrible yet the government could not make a decision to take action and stop them. Toward syphilis, the attitude of the State and race-focused leaders can only be described as absolute surrender. Any serious attempt at stamping it out needed to go farther than anything that was actually done. The invention of a questionable remedy and its commercial exploitation did little good against this disease. Here, too, the only possibility was a fight—a fight against the cause, not the removal of the symptoms. The primary cause is our prostitution of love. The mixing of blood (*mixing of races*) through prostitution is the corruption. Even if it did not result in this disease of nature, it would still damage the people morally. The devastation that follows this perversion is enough to lead our people slowly but surely to ruin. This Judaism of our soul by commercializing our natural instinct will sooner or later corrupt our future generations. Instead of vigorous, emotionally healthy children, we will have only the sorry products of a quick financial deal for selfish pleasure. Financial considerations have become the foundation and sole requirement for marriage. The result is that love looks elsewhere to find itself.

Man may defy Nature for a certain length of time, but eventually she will call her due, and payback will come. When man recognizes this truth, it is often too late.

We can see in our noble class the disastrous results of long and continued neglect of the natural fundamentals for marriage. Nobility are paired according to their status and how the marriage can improve their standing. We observe the consequences of a reproduction which is focused partly on social pressure and partly on financial considerations. One leads to general weakening, the other to blood-poisoning because any Jewish daughter of a department store owner is thought good enough because they can increase the standing of His Grace's descendants financially. Even the privileged-classes now follow this example. In both cases, complete degeneration is the result.

With no concern for the consequences, people ignore this unpleasant truth as if ignoring it would make the problem go away. No, our metropolitan population is prostituting its love life more and more, and growing numbers are falling victim to the plague of syphilis. This fact will not disappear if we close our eyes to it. It is there. The clearest results of this mass sickness can be found in the insane asylums, and, unfortunately, in our children. Children in particular are the sad products of the poisoning of our sexual life. In the sickness of the children we see the immoral habits of the parents.

There are various ways people deal with this unpleasant, horrible fact. Some people see nothing at all, or rather choose to see nothing. This is by far the simplest and cheapest "attitude". Others wrap themselves in the saintly garments of a prude and pretend to have modesty, which is nothing but a deception. They speak of the whole subject as if they were talking about a great sin, and express profound righteous anger toward every sinner who is caught. They close their eyes in self-righteous loathing to this godless plague, and pray to the good Lord that He will pour fire and brimstone upon this Sodom and Gomorrah to make an example, preferably not before their own natural death of course. This would then provide an educational lesson to the rest of shameless humanity. A third group sees the awful consequences which this plague can and will someday bring with it, but they merely shrug their shoulders, convinced that they can do nothing against the coming danger. They stand aside and allow events to run their course.

All of these people choose the simple and easy path. The problem is that such apathy will have fatal consequences for the nation. The excuse that other nations are no better off will make little difference when our nation is the one to fall. The only benefit to that claim is the sympathy toward others makes our own misfortune slightly more bearable. The most important question is which nation will step forward and defeat the epidemic, and which nations will submit and be smothered by it. That is what it comes down to in the end. This is just a measure of racial excellence, a test of racial values. The race that cannot stand the test will simply die and make room for healthier, stronger races which can endure hardships more easily. Since this question primarily concerns future generations, it is about them that it is said with such frightening truth: "The sins of the fathers will be visited on the tenth generation" (*paraphrased from Deuteronomy 23:2 and Exodus 20:5*).

This holds true only for crimes against blood and race. The sin against blood and race is the original sin of this world and it will bring the end of any humanity which surrenders to it.

The attitude of pre-war Germany concerning this one question was truly sad! What did they do to stop the infection of our young people in the great cities? What was done to attack the disease and selfish commercialization of our love life? What was done to combat the spread of syphilis that resulted? The easiest way to find the answer is to point out what should have happened.

The question should not have been taken so casually. Authorities should have understood that a solution, or lack of a solution, would impact the happiness or unhappiness of generations to come. The existence of a solution might decide the future of our people. To admit this would have required action. Action would have meant the enactment of ruthless measures and intervention efforts. The conviction and attention of the whole nation should be concentrated on this dreadful threat first, above any other consideration, so that every individual would be aware of the importance of the struggle. Imposing obligations of character can be difficult to implement unless the public is thoroughly instructed on the importance. This commitment would require obligations and burdens which are necessary and sometimes hard to manage. These obligations can only be universally effective if the individual is made to feel the need as well as the motivation to carry them out. This requires a tremendous process of explanation, and any other problems that arise from day to day would have to be put in the background.

In every case where there appear to be impossible demands on the nation, the full attention of a people must exclusively be concentrated on this one question at hand without distraction. It should be approached as if the existence or non-existence of everyone actually depended on its solution. Only then will people's emotions be stimulated to such a pitch that they become willing and able to voluntarily accomplish great achievements and efforts.

This principle also holds true for the individual if he wishes to accomplish great things. He can accomplish great goals only by taking one step at a time. He must concentrate all his efforts on the accomplishment of a certain limited task, and he must not waiver to another task or weaken in his resolve until it has been achieved, and only then can the next stage be attacked. The man who cannot divide up the road into individual stages and work towards achieving each step, one at a time, by focusing all his energy, can never reach his final destination. Instead he will fall somewhere along the road or veer off the track entirely. This process of working toward an objective is an art and demands supreme effort at every stage in order to cover the entire distance step by step.

The very first requirement in attacking such a difficult stretch of the human road is for the leadership to present the immediate, partial goal, which must be achieved as the one and only goal, which should be considered or given any attention, and the outcome must be presented as if it will decide everything about their existence. The great mass of the people can never see the entire long road in front of them without becoming tired or weary and falling into despair before giving up. They may see their long-term goal in the far distance ahead, but they only recognize the immediate goal as they follow the path one section at a time. It is like the traveler who knows his destination, but can only make the long trip when he divides it up into sections and attacks each one as if it were his only journey. This is the only way he can maintain his determination to reach the ultimate objective without losing faith in his ability to achieve the final goal.

Every type of propaganda should have been used to fight syphilis. It should have been presented as the main and most important responsibility of the nation, not just as a task. For this purpose, its ill effects should have been hammered into people by every available method and shown as the most awful of all disasters until the whole nation became convinced that future depended a solution to this problem. They must be faced with the unavoidable choice between a healthy future or absolute national decay. This kind of education and preparation should have continued for years if necessary. Only then will the attention and the determination of all of the people be aroused to such a level that even severe measures involving great sacrifice can be used without danger of being misunderstood or suddenly neglected by the masses. Everyone must know that enormous sacrifices and equally enormous efforts are necessary in attacking this plague.

A successful battle against syphilis requires a battle against prostitution, against prejudices, against old customs, against pre-existing ideas, and against public opinion, such as the false pretense of extreme modesty in certain circles.

Before the State can claim any moral right to attack these things, it must allow and encourage people to marry earlier. (*At this time in Germany, women could marry at age 18 but men could not marry until age 21, Many also waited until later in life to marry.*) Allowing marriages to only take place for older generations forces us to preserve a system that is dysfunctional and causes shame to humanity. The custom of late marriage, which causes so much trouble, is a creature that misrepresents itself as the "image" of God.

Prostitution is a disgrace to humanity, but it cannot be abolished by moral lectures or pious intentions. Its restriction and eventual disappearance presumes the removal of a whole series of preexisting causes. The first of these is to make early marriage possible, particularly for the man so he can fulfill the dictates of his human nature. As for the woman, she is only a passive party in the matter.

We can see how misguided and totally confused some people have become when we hear mothers in so-called "proper" society say they would be thankful to find their daughter a husband who has "already sown his wild oats". There is no shortage of this type of man either. So the poor girl is sure to find such a Sigfried, stripped of his protective skin, for a husband, and the children will be the visible result of this "wise" marriage. (*Siegfried refers to the Wagner opera character and his invulnerable skin. The reference means the husband has been compromised, his protection weakened, his strength gone, and he is not a true man any longer.*) When we consider that procreation in itself is reduced by these actions, we see that natural selection takes no part since every creature that is produced, no matter how sorry, must be preserved due to its scarcity. There is only one question left to ask: Why do we allow such a convoluted marriage institution to exist at all, and what is its purpose supposed to be? How is this type of marriage different from prostitution? Does duty to future generations no longer count at all? Or do people not know what curses they are inflicting on their children and their children's children by such criminal failure to maintain the rights and duty of Nature? Following this path is how civilized nations deteriorate and gradually perish.

Not even marriage can be an end in itself. It must serve the greater purpose of increasing and preserving the species and race. That alone is its meaning and its purpose.

Knowing this, we see the quality of marriage can only be measured by the way that it fulfills that purpose. For this reason, early marriage is good. The young couple will still have the vigor which alone can produce strong and healthy children. To encourage earlier marriages, a whole series of social changes are necessary. Without these changes, we cannot imagine early marriages being possible. The solution to even this small question cannot take place without radical and heroic social changes. This need is especially important today when the incompetence of the so-called "Social" Republic in solving the housing shortage and has prevented many marriages, which in turn assisted the spread of prostitution. The wage levels are nonsense. Paychecks fail to consider what is required to support a family. Low wages makes many early marriages impossible. A real attack on prostitution can be made only by reforming social conditions to make earlier marriage possible. This is the very first essential requirement for a solution to this prostitution problem.

In the second place, education and training among the youth will have to eliminate a whole series of evils and false ideas that no one has worried about before. Above all, a balance must be struck in education between intellectual instruction and physical development. What is called a Gymnasium or secondary school today is a mockery of the Greek school it was supposedly modeled after. We have completely forgotten in education that in the long run, a sound mind can only live in a sound body. If one takes into consideration the great masses of a people, this statement is clearly true with only a few exceptions.

Before the First World War in Germany, absolutely no attention was paid to this truth. People simply continued sinning against the body while believing that training only the "mind" guaranteed the greatness of the nation. This was a mistake and the results were felt sooner than expected. It was not by accident that the Bolshevist wave found a place to grow and develop where the population had deteriorated through hunger and long-term conditions resulting from malnourishment. This is common in Central Germany, Saxony, and the Ruhr district. There has been no serious resistance, even from the so-called "intellects", to this Jewish disease in any of these districts. The simple reason for this is that the intellects are physically unhealthy as a result of education and not hardship or starvation. The approach intellectuals take when they focus exclusively on education in the upper classes makes them incapable of surviving during times when the strong arm, and not the mind, makes the decisive strike. Physical ailments are usually the precursor to personal cowardice.

Excessive emphasis on purely mental training and the neglect of physical development only promotes the risk of sexual thoughts much too early in youth. The boy who has been strengthened by sport and gymnastics is less subject to the need for physical indulgence than is the bookworm fed exclusively on mental nourishment. This is something a sensible education system has to consider. It must also not forget that the healthy young man's expectations of a woman are different from those of a prematurely corrupted weakling. Education and class time should be scheduled so that a boy's free time is used to strengthen his body. During these years, he has no right to loaf around or make a nuisance of himself in the streets and movies houses. After his day's other work, he must strengthen his young body like steel so that when life puts him to the test, it will not find him too delicate. It is the responsibility of those educating youth to prepare their bodies and not just pour knowledge or so-called wisdom in their heads. This system must also sweep away the impression that the responsibility of training one's own body should be left to the individual. There can be no such thing as allowing the freedom of choice to sin against posterity and therefore against the race.

Along with physical training, the fight against poisoning the soul must begin. Today, our society is like a garden where sexual fantasies and stimulations are nourished and forced to grow. When we look at the selection of our movies, theaters, and vaudeville houses, it is obvious that these are not providing the proper examples for anyone and especially not for young people. In store windows and on posters, the lowest, most vulgar methods are used to attract the attention of the crowd. Anyone who has not lost the ability to recall their own adolescence can see that this trash will do serious damage to young people. This seductive, sensual, physical atmosphere generates fantasies and stirrings in the heads of boys which they should not even know about. We can study the results of this sort of filth-education in the youth of today and the result is not pleasant. Our youth have matured too quickly which has made them prematurely old. The courts sometimes remind the public ear of this danger and give horrible insights into the spiritual life of our fourteen and fifteen-year-olds. How can anyone be surprised that syphilis has begun to pick its victims at that age? Isn't it a crying shame to see a physically weak and spiritually undone young man receive his introduction to the mysteries of marriage through some big-city whore?

No, he who seeks to strike at the root of prostitution must first remove its spiritual cause. He must sweep out the garbage of our moral infection of city "culture" and do so mercilessly without wavering when the protests and screaming start from the outcry that will surely follow. If we do not lift youth from the disgusting mess of its present surroundings, it will sink deeper into that filth. The man who refuses to see these things is supporting them, and through his inaction he assumes a share of the guilt for the slow prostitution of our future which grows in the coming generation. This purification of our culture must expand into almost every area. Theater, art, literature, cinema, press, advertisements, and store windows must have the pollution which is rotting our world removed, and they must be forced into the service of a moral idea of State and culture. Public life must be free from the overpowering perfume of eroticism and also of all unmanly elements and false prudishness. In all these things, the goal and road to that goal must be carefully considered then set in stone for the preservation of our people's health in body and soul. The right of personal freedom is secondary to the duty of preserving the race.

Only when these educational measures are complete can the medical assault on the disease itself begin and still have some chance of success. There can be no half-way measures. We have to make the most serious and most radical decisions. It would be a half-measure to allow those who cannot be cured the chance to infect others who are in good health. This sort of humaneness avoids causing suffering to one individual while it sends a hundred to the damnation of death. It must be made impossible for diseased persons to produce equally defective children. This requirement is simply common sense. This would be humanity's most humane deed if it were consistently carried out. It will save millions of unfortunate souls from undeserved suffering and in the end, lead to an overall improvement in national health. The determination to proceed with this plan will also halt the further spread of venereal diseases. We may have to resort to harsh segregation of those who cannot be cured. This is a savage measure, especially for the unhappy victim of the disease, but it is a blessing for the rest of the country and for posterity. The temporary suffering of one century can and will free thousands of future generations from suffering.

The battle against syphilis and its distributor, prostitution, is one of humanity's greatest tasks. It is enormous because it does not involve just one single solution, but the removing a series of evils which lead this disease into the veins of our society. The disease of the body is simply the result of diseased moral, social, and racial instincts.

If this battle is not fought because of laziness or cowardice, imagine what the nation will look like in five hundred years. There will only be a few men left in God's image, the rest will be a blasphemy against the Almighty.

How did people try, in the old Germany, to deal with this disease? Calm consideration returns a truly sad answer. The havoc caused by the disease was known to the government, though they may not have fully comprehended its consequences. In fighting it, they were a complete failure, and instead of making thorough reforms, they preferred to resort to miserable and ineffective controls. They concentrated their efforts on fixing the results of the disease and left the causes alone. They subjected the individual prostitute to medical examinations and supervised her as well as they could. If disease was discovered, they shoved her into some hospital and when she no longer showed signs of disease, she was once more let loose on mankind.

The government did introduce "protective legislation". According to this law, anyone who had venereal disease or who was not entirely cured was prohibited from engaging in sexual intercourse under penalty of law. This in itself was a proper measure, but when it came to implementing the plan, it was almost a complete failure. When the woman suffers such a misfortune, in most cases she will probably refuse to be dragged into court as a witness against the miserable poisoner who corrupted her health. This can be the result of her limited education or understanding of the system and often can result in the answering of hurtful or embarrassing questions. The woman is the one who benefits the least. In most cases, she will suffer the worst anyway. The hatred of her unkind neighbors will fall on her much more heavily than it would with a man. Finally, imagine her position if the carrier of the disease is her own husband. Is she to bring a complaint against him or what else is she to do?

In the case of the man, he may encounter this disease when he is drunk. In that condition, he is the least able to judge the quality of his "beautiful one". The diseased prostitute realizes this stupor only too well and they have learned to fish for men in this ideal state. The result is that no matter how the unpleasantly surprised man may later rack his brains, he cannot remember his kind-hearted benefactor's name or face. This is scarcely surprising in a big city like Berlin or even Munich. The prostitute's catch is often an unsophisticated visitor from the provinces who is confused and bewildered by the magic charms of a great city.

Ultimately, who can tell whether he is infected or healthy? There are many cases where a person appears cured and then has a relapse and does the most dreadful damage without even realizing it. The result of this legal penalty for the act of infection is actually zero. The same is true of control over prostitutes—even the value of the cure is still uncertain and it may not even work. Only one thing is sure: all of these measures have failed to keep the disease from spreading. This is the most conclusive proof of the ineffectiveness of these measures. Everything that was done was inadequate and ridiculous. The spiritual prostitution of the people continued and nothing was done to stop it.

If anyone is inclined to take this matter casually, let him study the statistics on the spread of this disease. Compare its growth in the last hundred years and imagine where it will go from here. He must be as simple-minded as a donkey if he does not have an unpleasant shiver running down his spine when faced with these facts. The weakness and half-hearted attitude adopted, even in old Germany, toward this terror is a visible sign of our people's decay. When the courage no longer exists to fight for one's own health, the right to struggle in this life is at an end. True strength belongs to the vigorous "whole" man and not to the weak "half" man.

One of the clearest signs of decay in the old Empire was the slow decline in culture and I do not mean civilization. Civilization seems to be more of an enemy who raises the standard of living and woos the mind. Even before the turn of the century, a previously unknown element began to intrude into our art. Even in earlier days, there were sometimes offenses against good taste, but these were rather artistic eccentricities to which future generations could at least attach a certain historical value. Then came products of degeneration to the point of senselessness, not in art, but in the spirit. These were cultural signs of the political collapse which became clearly visible later.

The Bolshevism of art is the only possible cultural form of life and intellectual expression that Bolshevism is capable of.

Anyone who thinks this is unclear or strange need only look around those "fortunate" Bolshevized States. This official and State-recognized art is looked at with horror. I speak of morbid disfigurements produced by lunatics and degenerates which we have become acquainted with since the turn of the century as Cubism and Dadaism (*these were abstract types of art using distorted images; however, the content especially of Dadaist art was often an attack on Nationalists; it promoted pacifism and was often political in nature*). Even during the short life of the Council's Republic in Bavaria (*Marxist control in Bavaria*), this phenomenon began to appear. One could see how all the official posters and propaganda cartoons in the newspapers bore the stamp of political and cultural decay.

Sixty years ago, a political collapse as extensive as we are now experiencing would have been unthinkable. Equally unthinkable would have been a cultural collapse like we see in Futurist and Cubist art creations. Sixty years ago, an exhibition of so-called Dada type "experiences" would have been absolutely impossible and its promoters would have been sent to the insane asylum. And yet today, they are made presidents of art associations. This disease could not have made its appearance at that time because public opinion would not have tolerated it, nor would the State have sat idly by. It is the responsibility of government to prevent its people from being driven into the arms of intellectual insanity. Today we would see complete intellectual madness if this type of art had been accepted. On the day that this sort of art was accepted and found its place in harmony with the public senses, that would be the most momentous and horrible transformations of mankind that would ever occur. The human brain would regress from normality, which would lead to an end that could hardly be imagined.

If we review the last twenty-five years of our cultural life from this standpoint, we would be horrified to see how far we have already declined. Everywhere we look, we find seeds that sooner or later grow and destroy our civilization. Here is where we see the symptoms of the decay. We see a slowly rotting world. Woe to the nations who can no longer master this disease and fail to halt its spread!

Such disturbed thought processes could be seen throughout art and culture in Germany. Everything seemed to have passed its prime and to be accelerating toward the abyss. The theater declined visibly and would probably have disappeared as a cultural factor even earlier if the Royal Court theaters had not stood their ground against the prostitution of art. Aside from them and a few other praiseworthy exceptions, the offerings of the theater stage was in such a shambles that patrons would have benefited more if they quit attending completely. It was a sorry sign of inner decay that one was no longer allowed to send young people to most of these alleged "shrines of art". This decline was openly admitted with shameless candor in the warning signs seen outside cinemas which proclaimed "for adults only".

Remember that such cautionary signs were hung outside the very places which should have existed primarily for the education of young people and should not exist for the amusement of sophisticated adults. What would the great dramatists of past ages have said about the need for this kind of regulation and to the deplorable conditions which made it necessary? How Schiller (*meaning Friedrich Schiller: German poet, philosopher, historian, and dramatist*) would have blazed! How Goethe (*meaning Johann Wolfgang von Goethe, a German writer and scientist*) would have turned away in disgust! How do Schiller, Goethe, or Shakespeare compare to the heroes of modern German literature? Old, thread-bare, and worn out, actually you can say they have been discarded. In this age you only see the production of filth, but it does not stop with its own creations. In addition, this generation slandered everything truly great from the past. This is, of course, not an unusual historic occurrence. The more vile and contemptible the products of an age and its men are, the more they despise and disparage the achievements of past greats. These people would prefer to destroy mankind's memory of these past works so they could eliminate any chance that their own filthy spatters might be compared to true greats. Only by removing this standard for comparison can they make their own trash appear to be "art".

The more despicable and wretched a new movement is, the more it will try to extinguish every last trace of the past. Any truly innovative movement that is for the benefit of mankind will stand undisturbed beside the achievements of past generations. The existence of the monuments or great works of the past will enhance and encourage the acceptance of the modern productions if they are worthy. In fact, comparison with the greats may even show for the first time the full value of these new products. True quality works have no reason to fear that they will fade when compared to works of the past.

A new work contributes to the general fund of human culture by preserving the memory of earlier achievements, and only through that history can its own value be fully recognized. This history assures the full understanding of the new advance by its audience. He who has nothing of value to give the world and tries to pass off Heaven knows what as art will hate all existing contributions, which have value and will seek to oppose or even destroy them.

This is not just true of new cultural developments, but it applies in politics as well. New revolutionary movements will despise and discredit older movements. The more worthless they are, the more they will attack the past movements. Here we can see how the desire to make one's own trash seem great, and how it can lead to blind hatred of past superior movements. As long as Frederick the Great's historical memory has not died out, Frederick Ebert (*the first president of the Weimar period*) will never achieve more than moderate admiration. When we compare the former Bremen saloon-keeper (*meaning Ebert, who was actually a saddle maker before coming into politics but kept bar at meetings; this reference is also made later*) to the hero of Sans Souci (*location of the summer palace built by and burial place of Fredrick the Great*) it is like comparing the sun to the moon. Only after the rays of the sun are gone does the moon shine, and then they only shine as a result of the sun. All new moons of humanity have a deep hatred for the fixed stars which shine on their own. If Fate throws one of these nobodies into temporary leadership, they immediately dishonor and slander the past with diligent enthusiasm. Blaming the past leaders for problems on their watch takes them out of the line of fire for public criticism. As an example, we can look at the Legislation to Protect the Republic which was passed in the new German Reich.

If some new idea, doctrine, new World-Concept , or political or economic movement tries to deny the accomplishments of the past by calling it bad and worthless, we must be extremely careful and suspicious, and we must question their reason for such slander. This hatred sprouts from its own worthlessness or because its true intention is to cause harm. A truly productive movement will always begin to build on the spot where the last good foundation stopped. They will not be ashamed of using those truths which already exist as their cornerstone. All of human culture and man himself are only the product of one long continuous development in which each generation has added a new stone to the structure. The purpose of revolution is not to tear down the whole building, but to remove only those parts, which are poorly attached or unsuitable for their purpose and to build a better structure onward and upward from the spot that is left bare.

Today we can talk about the progress of mankind because it is built on past accomplishments. Otherwise, the world would never be rescued from chaos and each generation would reject the past and destroy its works to make way for the creations of the new generation.

The saddest thing about the condition of our German civilization before the war was not only the absolute weakness of artistic and cultural creative power, but how the memory of a greater past was polluted, befouled, and smothered by hatred. At the turn of the century (*1900*), in almost every area of art, particularly in theater and literature, people began to defame the best of the old, saying it was inferior and worn out. They were more interested in trashing the old works than in creating new works. This was a disgraceful and inferior era that was unable to produce anything new or significant and had no right to belittle the great works!

Their striving to put the past out of sight of the present revealed plainly and distinctly the evil intent of these apostles of the future. People should have been able to see this was not a matter of something new, even if it was wrong. It was part of a process meant to destroy the foundation of our civilization. The confusion that then surrounded what was previously a healthy art community made it possible to lay the intellectual groundwork for political Bolshevism. If the Age of Pericles was embodied in the Parthenon, the Bolshevist era was embodied in the travesty of the Cubist grimace.

At this point we must focus our attention on the cowardice among those of our people who, by virtue of their education and position, had the responsibility of standing firm against this cultural outrage. They chose to avoid a confrontation on the chance the Bolshevists might raise a commotion. The Bolshevist art-apostles violently attacked everyone who failed to recognize them as the peak of creation, branding opponents as old-fashioned and a Philistine. No one would stand up against these Bolshevist art-apostles out of fear. They surrendered themselves to what seemed to be the inevitable. These people trembled, frightened that they might be accused of being simple minded or worse, lacking artistic appreciation by these half-lunatics or frauds as if it were a disgrace not to understand the products of these mental degenerates or sly imitators! These apostles of culture did have one very simple way to stamp their nonsense with the illusion of high quality and greatness. All their incomprehensible and obviously insane garbage was presented to an open-mouthed public and labeled as what they called an "inner experience". In this cheap method, they kept the people's criticism silent. Of course, no one had the slightest doubt that these inner experiences could be from their Bolshevist minds. However, one must seriously doubt that there could be any justification for exposing the hallucinations of crazy men or criminals to the healthy minded public. The works of a Moritz von Schwind (*an Austrian painter born in Vienna who painted highly detailed, realistic works*) or a Böcklin (*Arnold Böcklin, a Swiss painter known for Mythology and Renaissance styles who later influenced Surrealistic painters*) were inner experiences too, but these were the experiences of artists favored by Heaven, not clowns.

This was a fine demonstration of the pitiful spinelessness of our so-called intellectuals who did not resist this poisoning of our people's sound instincts and left it to the people to formulate their opinion about this disrespectful nonsense. To avoid being considered artistically illiterate, people accepted any mockery of art and eventually became unsure in their own judgment. They could no longer determine what was good or bad. Taken together, these were signs of an evil time to come.

Another suspicious sign is the following: In the nineteenth century, our cities began to lose their character as centers of culture and declined into mere human settlements. The working class has a very small emotional connection to the place where they live. This is because their living quarters is an accidental abode, a collection of people in a place and nothing more. This is mostly because they must frequently move due to social conditions and a man has no time to develop a close relation to his city. Another cause is the general cultural insignificance and the poverty of modern cities themselves.

At the time of the Wars of Liberation (*part of the Napoleonic Wars 1813-14*), German cities numbered very few and those were small. Most of the really big cities were royal residences which gave them a certain cultural value and usually a definite artistic impression. The few towns of more than fifty thousand inhabitants were rich in treasures of science and art compared to cities of the same population today. When Munich reached sixty thousand in population, it was already on its way to being one of the leading German art centers. By now, almost every factory town has reached that size or larger, but often without having the slightest elements of true value to call its own. They are collections of tenement houses and dwellings that are like barracks and nothing more. It is no wonder why the people do not become emotionally attached to the meaningless place where they live. No one is going to be particularly attached to a city which offers nothing more than any other city and which lacks any individuality and where everything that might so much as resemble art has been painstakingly avoided.

If this were not enough, as the population increases, the number of artworks dwindle. They seem more and more to have been suppressed down to a level where art appears to be dead. The larger cities have the same look as a poverty-stricken little factory town, just on a larger scale. Modern times have added almost nothing to the cultural substance of our great cities. All our cities are living on the glory and the treasures of the past. Take everything away from present-day Munich, everything that was created under Ludwig I, and you will be horrified to see how little remains. (*Ludwig the First is well known for creating a cultural center in Munich of great classical architecture.*) Almost nothing has been produced since that time. The same thing is true of Berlin and most of the other great cities.

Here is the essential point. Our modern great cities have no monuments towering above the skyline that represent symbols of the whole age. In the old cities of antiquity, almost every town had some special monument to show its pride. The characteristic feature of each city was not the private buildings, but the monuments of glory to the community. These were not created for the moment but for eternity because they were intended to reflect the greatness and importance of the community instead of the wealth of an individual owner. These monuments were calculated to bind citizens to their own city in a way which sometimes seems incomprehensible to us today. Visitors did not see the shabby houses of private owners but the splendid structures of the whole community. By comparison, individual homes were only of a secondary importance, actually trivial.

It is necessary to compare the size of ancient public buildings with the private houses of their time to understand the overwhelming force and impact of this emphasis on the public structures. These buildings were given first place ahead of all others. What we admire today among a few remaining giants rising from the rubbish-heaps and ruins of the ancient world, are not former commercial palaces, but temples of the gods and government buildings. These buildings were owned by the community. Even in late Rome, it was not the villas and palaces of individual citizens that were most important, but the temples and baths, the stadiums, the circuses, bridges, and cathedrals of the state, of the whole people.

Even the Germanic Middle Ages maintained the same guiding principle, though their approach to art was entirely different from the Romans. What had been expressed in the Acropolis or the Pantheon now took on the form of the Gothic cathedral in Germany. Like giants, these monumental structures towered above the little hive of half-timbered, wooden or brick buildings in the medieval city. They became landmarks, which stamp the character and the skyline of these towns even today, while apartment houses are sprouting up all around them and obscuring their greatness. Cathedrals, town halls, granaries and defense towers are the visible signs of an old idea, and outward expression which had its counterpart in the ancient world but which is missing today.

The relation between public and private buildings today is truly sad! If Berlin should suffer the fate of Rome, future generations would admire the department stores of a few Jews and the hotels of a few corporations as the mightiest works of our age believing those to be the characteristic expression of this civilization. Compare the obvious imbalance between the buildings of the Reich and the finance and commerce buildings in a city like Berlin.

The amount of money spent on government buildings is inadequate and ridiculous.

These buildings are not made for eternity, but only to satisfy the need of the moment. No one thinks about greatness when they commission a building. When the Castle at Berlin was built, it was a great work possessing a significance that is lacking in the new library of our time. That great show-place cost about sixty million marks while less than half that amount was spent on the Reichstag. This is the most imposing structure, yet built for the Reich, and it should have been built to last through the ages. Then, when the question of the interior came to a vote, the Exalted House voted against the use of stone and ordered the walls be covered with plaster. Fortunately, for once, the parliamentarians did the right thing. Plaster statues are certainly out of place among stone walls.

Our present-day cities lack any towering landmarks to represent the people's community and we cannot be surprised if the community does not see its cities as a representation of itself. Unhappiness is the result and we can see this in the complete disinterest toward the concerns of the citizen's city.

This is also a sign of our declining civilization and our general collapse. This generation is smothered in the pettiest practices or in slavery to money. It is hardly surprising that there is no sense of heroism under this deity. Today we reap what the recent past has sown.

All these symptoms of decay result from the lack of a definite, universally recognized World-Concept . We have no plan and this results in general uncertainty when it comes to handling the great questions of the time. This is why everything, beginning with education, is half-hearted and indecisive because it shies away from responsibility and winds up in cowardly tolerance of obvious abuses which are known to be destructive. The desire to be humane—this craze—has become fashionable. By weakly submitting to this deviance and sparing the feelings of individuals from hurt, we have sacrificed the future of millions.

The spread of disunity can be seen in the religious conditions before the war. Here, the various parts of the nation had long abandoned their unified convictions which might have amounted to a World-Concept . In this matter, it is important to note that the small number who officially left the church were not as important as the much larger number who were simply indifferent. Both Churches (*Protestant and Catholic*) maintained missions in Asia and Africa to gain new converts for their Faith. In Europe, they were losing millions upon millions of followers who had either given up on religious life or preferred to follow their own interpretation. The consequences definitely impacted the moral life of the country. On a side note, the progress made by the missions spreading the Christian Faith abroad was only modest when compared to the spread of Islam. The results from a moral perspective are especially poor.

There is something else that is important to note. Violent attacks upon the basic principles of Church teachings have increased steadily. It would be unthinkable to live in a world without religious faith. The broad masses of a people are not made up of philosophers, so the faith of the masses is often the sole foundation for any moral World-Concept they may have. The various proposed substitutes have not shown any results that would indicate they could be useful replacements for religious denominations. But if any religious-type teachings are actually to take hold of the broad groups, as they successfully have in the past, the basic teachings of existing religion would be a necessary foundation in order for a new teaching to be effective. There may be a few hundreds of thousands of superior men who can live wisely and morally without depending on the general standards of religion, but the millions of others cannot do so and need daily guidance. The way people live ordinary life, by following religious principles, can be compared to the way governments follow principles of the state and Churches follow their own dogma. The purely intellectual idea of how one should conduct oneself can change and may be reinterpreted endlessly. It is the religious doctrine alone which binds the idea and puts it into a form that makes it a faith. Otherwise, the moral idea would never grow beyond the status of an abstract concept or a philosophic opinion. Accordingly, the attack on a religious doctrine is very similar to an attack against the constitution that founded the State. Just as the State would fall into chaos from such an attack, so would religion become worthless and end in emptiness with the annihilation of the core church beliefs.

A politician must not judge the value of a religion by its faults. Instead he should ask if there is an available substitute which fits his needs more closely. As long as there is no substitute for religion, only a fool or criminal would consider abolishing an existing religion.

The Church must take its share of responsibility for those who overload religion with purely earthly concerns and unnecessarily battle against exact science. They spend too much time arguing about physical matters when they should be focused on the spirit. After a difficult struggle, science will almost always win. In the eyes of people unable to see through the superficial nature of science, religion will be severely damaged. The worst chaos is created when religion is used for political purposes. Such miserable deceivers who see religion as a means for gaining themselves political, or rather business power and should be harshly condemned. Of course, these bold liars shout their claims of faith to all the world in a very loud tone so that the other sinners will have no choice but to hear their proclamation clearly. Their smiles do not express a willingness to die for their beliefs, but instead their aim is to improve their own lives. For enough money or political favors, they would sell the meaning of an entire faith and they would do it for a single fraudulent gain if they felt the value was a fair exchange. For ten seats in Parliament, they will join the deadly Marxists who are enemies of all religions. For a seat in the Cabinet they would marry the Devil himself, that is, if he was not prevented by some trace of decency which is more than these charlatans possess.

Religious life in pre-war Germany had left an unpleasant taste in many people's mouths because of the abuse of Christianity by "Christian" political parties and as a result of boldness from those who attempted to associate the Catholic faith with a political party. This bold attempt to connect Catholicism with politics was a fatal stroke that gave a number of good-for-nothings seats in Parliament and the political games seriously damaged the Church.

The whole nation suffered the consequences. The weakening of religious ties spread at a time when morality and culture were beginning to waver and give way too.

These faults and cracks in our political body might not have been dangerous if there was no strain placed on its back, but they were bound to be disastrous when the internal solidarity of the nation turned into a storm of violent events.

In the realm of politics, an observant eye saw evils that could be, and had to be, considered signs indicating a coming collapse of the Empire if no changes or improvements were made immediately. The aimlessness of German domestic and foreign policy was clear to anyone who was not deliberately blind to it. The system of compromises at first seemed to follow Bismarck's concept of politics as "the art of the possible". But Bismarck was not like later German Chancellors. There was one small difference; Bismark knew how to make his goals into a reality while still working within the political limitations of the time. When the mouths of his new successors spoke of the art-of-the-possible, it had an entirely different meaning. Bismarck meant to say that every possible effort must be made and exercised to the fullest extent to attain a given political objective. In the same words, his successors saw an excuse to avoid any political aims or principles at all and limited themselves to doing what was easily accomplished. Political aims in the government of the Empire at that time no longer existed. They needed a definite World-Concept and required a grasp of the inner laws of political evolution, which is necessary for any political leadership. There were many who foresaw what was coming and criticized the lack of a plan and complete absence of forethought in the Empire's policy. It was clear they plainly recognized its inner weakness and hollowness. Unfortunately, these were only outsiders in political life and their words did not carry much weight.

Government officials were and still are indifferent to principles of those like Houston Stewart Chamberlain (a British political philosopher whose work affected Nazi racial platforms and pan-German movements. He was a German supporter in the First World War, and he also married the daughter of composer Richard Wagner). These people are too stupid to think of anything themselves and too conceited to learn what they need from others. Oxenstierna (Axel Gustafsson Oxenstierna, a Swedish Chancellor who played an important role in the Thirty Years War and was later Governor-General of occupied Prussia) expressed this well when he said, "The world is ruled by only a fraction of all Wisdom", out of a tiny particle, almost any Ministerial Counselor represents only one atom. Since Germany has become a Republic, even this small amount of wisdom is left un-exercised. That is why the Law to Protect the Republic forbids anyone to talk about or even to believe their leaders are unwise. (The Republic passed the Law To Protect The Republic forbidding membership in any organization that sought to assassinate officials or overthrow the government and prohibits insults to officials and the flag. The law was passed after Walter Rathenau, the Weimar Foreign Minister, was assassinated.) It was lucky for Oxenstierna that he lived when he did, and not in our "wise" Republic.

Even before the First World War, many people recognized the primary element of weakness in the very institution which should have symbolized the strength of the Empire, the Parliament, the Reichstag. Here, cowardice and irresponsibility were perfectly matched.

One of the most thoughtless statements heard today is that the parliament in Germany has been "a failure since the Revolution". This implies that before the Revolution, things were different. In reality, this institution never functioned except to cause damage to the country. Most people were still wearing blinders and either could or would see nothing that was happening. This institution is to blame for Germany's downfall. The fact that the catastrophe did not occur even earlier cannot be credited to the Reichstag, but is due to the resistance of those who opposed this institution. During the years of peace, those in the Reichstag took up the job of gravediggers for the German nation and the German Empire.

Out of the enormous list of devastating evils committed either directly or indirectly by this institution, I will pick out just one single calamity which shows clearly the inner nature of this irresponsible institution. The terrible evils I refer to resulted from the half-hearted actions and weakness of the political leadership of the Reich in the Reichstag, which became one of the chief causes of the political collapse.

Everything connected to or influenced by this parliament was done with weakness or in a half-measure. No matter how we look at it, this is true. The Empire's policy for forming foreign alliances was willy-nilly. By trying to preserve peace, they steered us straight into war.

The Polish policy was a perfect example of these half-way measures. The policy caused irritation without ever taking any serious action or exerting any control. The result was not a victory for Germany, not the appeasement of the Poles, but the arousal of Russia's hostility. Russia became an enemy.

The question of Alsace-Lorraine (*a territory created by German annexation in the Franco Prussian War and lost to France with the Treaty of Versailles*) was only half solved. Instead of brutally crushing the head of this French monster once and for all, and then giving the right of German statehood to the Alsatian, they did neither. They were unable to do either because among them were the greatest traitors of the Center parties, for instance, Mr. Wetterlé. (*The Center party in the Reichstag and the separatist Center Party of the Alsace-Lorraine territory were partly but never fully merged, then they completely split over the Alsace-Lorraine constitution passed by the Reichstag.*) (*Mr. Wetterlé referrs to Abbé Wetterlé, the leader of the Alsace-Lorraine Center party who was forced to flee to France in 1914.*) All this would still have been bearable if the general half-heartedness had not also sacrificed the power of the army, on which the existence and survival of the Empire depended.

Those who were supposed to be the "German Parliament" were forever cursed by the German nation for their crimes. For the most disgraceful, contemptible reasons, the party henchmen stole from our people's hands the weapon they needed for self-preservation, the sole protection of our people's freedom and independence, and by various means they destroyed the army. If the graves spread over the Flanders plains were to open today, the bloody accusers would rise from them to point the finger of blame at the Reichstag. Hundreds of thousands of the best young Germans, who were sent poorly trained and half-prepared into the arms of death by these conscienceless parliamentary criminals, paid dearly. The Fatherland simply lost these poor souls. These and millions of others were crippled and killed, lost to the Fatherland, lost solely to allow a few hundred deceivers and swindlers of the people to carry out their political maneuvers, enforce their excessive demands, or even test their theories of political doctrine. They are traitors.

The Jewry, through its Marxist democratic press, shouted the lie of "German militarism" to the world, hoping to paint Germany as an aggressor. They tied

Germany's hands by every means available. The Marxist and Democratic parties refused to approve funding for comprehensive training of the German defense forces. Yet this monstrous crime must have been immediately clear to anyone who saw that in a war, the whole nation may have to take up arms. Consequently, the mischief of these fine "representatives of the people" would drive millions of Germans into the face of the enemy while they were only half-trained and poorly equipped. Even if we set aside the result of the crude and brutal lack of principles in these parliamentary fancy-men, anyone could see the absence of properly trained soldiers at the beginning of war might easily lead to defeat. This result was frighteningly confirmed in the course of the First World War.

The German nation's loss of the struggle for freedom and independence was the result of half-way measures and weakness. It began during peace-time by the employment of crippling policies that stripped away the organization and training needed to defend the Fatherland.

There were too few recruits being trained on land and the same half-hearted effort was sabotaging the navy to make that weapon of national self-preservation worthless. Unfortunately, the naval command itself was infected with the spirit of half-way measures. The tendency to always build the ships smaller than the English ones being launched at the same time was short sighted and not exactly a demonstration of genius. A navy that does not have the same numbers as its likely opponent must make up for that lack by the outstanding fighting effectiveness of the individual ships. Superior fighting effectiveness is what counts and not a mythical superiority in "merit". Modern technology has progressed so far and is so nearly uniform in the civilized states that it is impossible to give ships of one power a greater fighting value than the ships of the same size belonging to another state. It is even more unthinkable that superiority can be achieved by a smaller size ship over a greater size vessel. The smaller tonnage of the German ships was bound to be at the expense of weaponry and engine power. The excuse used to justify smaller ships showed a very serious logical failure by the naval office in charge during times of peace. (*British ships were allowed by treaty a larger tonnage based on the argument that they needed to carry more fuel to reach colonies The German Navy was also kept small to avoid an appearance of threatening England.*) The available German naval artillery equipment was declared to be superior to the British guns. The performance of the German 30.5 centimeter (*12 inch.*) gun was in no way inferior to that of the British 30.5 centimeter (*12 inch.*) gun! (*The British gun suffered from accuracy and weapon-longevity problems, and the German guns also had better penetration.*)

For this very reason it should have been their duty to change over to the 30.5

centimeter gun instead of using smaller weapons on the fleet. They absolutely should not have been seeking equal fighting strength but superior fighting strength.

If superior strength were not of concern, then why were 42 centimeter field artillery pieces adopted in the army? Larger field pieces would have been unnecessary if they were seeking equality, since the existing German 21 centimeter field artillery was far superior to any French artillery existing at that time. Any fortresses would probably have crumbled for the 30.5 centimeter field artillery, but the Command of the army was logical and reasoned correctly when they chose their artillery, while the navy, unfortunately, was not so logical.

The navy's rejection of superior artillery and of superior speed was based on the completely mistaken so-called "concept of risk". (A *military term describing the level of danger or risk in an engagement versus what is required to counter that danger.*) The Naval Command assessed their needs based on the idea of defense and completely abandoned offensive planning. From the beginning of the war they were surrendering any chance of success, of victory, because those can only come from attacking, from offense, not defense.

A ship of slower speed and inferior weaponry will be quickly blown out of the water by its faster and better-armed adversary who can fire effectively from a greater distance. A considerable number of our cruisers discovered this to their bitter sorrow. The peace-time views of the Naval Command were completely mistaken as shown by the war. This forced the re-equipment of old ships and the use of better weapons on new ships whenever they had the chance. If in the battle of the Skagerrak (*The strait of Skagerrak between Norway and Sweden was strategically important to Germany*) the German ships had had the same tonnage, the same armament, and the same speed as the English ships, the British navy would have gone to a watery grave under the hurricane of accurate and more effective German 38 centimeter shells.

Japan chose a different naval policy. Their entire emphasis was put on building a fighting strength in each new ship that was superior to their eventual adversary. The offensive capabilities of the fleet in battle was their reward.

While the Army Command still kept itself free from such fundamentally erroneous reasoning, the navy had more "parliamentary" representation and succumbed to the spirit of Parliament. The navy was organized and run using their method of doing everything half way, and it was later used in the same way. The immortal glory the navy did earn can only be credited to the good work of German weapon manufacturers and the competent and incomparable heroism of individual officers and crews. If the former Supreme Command of the navy had been equally brilliant, all the sacrifices would not have been in vain.

Perhaps the navy's very undoing resulted from the parliamentary skills which influenced its leading brains in peace-time. Even in its building-up period, they relied on parliamentary instead of purely military considerations when making decisions. The half-hearted weakness and illogical thinking which characterize the parliament, contaminated the Command of the Navy.

As I have said, the army kept away from such fundamentally mistaken trains of thought. Ludendorff, who was then a Colonel in the General Staff, fought especially hard in a desperate battle against the criminal half-hearted weakness and opposed the Reichstag when they waffled and wavered over questions vital to the nation. If the struggle that this officer fought was unsuccessful, one must lay half of the blame on the Parliament and the other half with the, if possible even more pitifully weak, Imperial Chancellor, Bethmann Hollweg. This does not prevent those who are responsible for the German collapse from trying to put the entire blame on Ludendorff, the one man who stood his ground against the fatal neglect of national interests. At this point, one deception more or less means nothing to these born liars.

Anyone who thinks about all the sacrifices forced on the nation by the criminal neglect of these utterly irresponsible individuals, anyone who reviews in his mind's eye all those who were unnecessarily killed and crippled, the boundless disgrace and shame poured on our heads, the immeasurable misery which we sink into more and more every day, and anyone who knows that this all took place just to open a few seats in Parliament for a gang of political climbers and position-hunters with no conscience, anyone will understand that these creatures can be described only by words such as wretch, scoundrel, liar, and criminal. If it were not for these men, the meaning and reason for the existence of these expressions in the language would be incomprehensible. In comparison to these national traitors, any common swindler is a gentleman of honor.

It was most peculiar that the dark faults of old Germany were only exposed when doing so had the potential to harm the inner stability of the nation. In such cases, the unpleasant truths were shouted at the great masses while many other things were bashfully kept quiet and hushed up or simply denied. Denial or silence were the clear choices when the open discussion a problem might have brought improvement. The competent members of the government understood next to nothing about the value and nature of propaganda. Only the Jew knew that the clever and persistent use of propaganda could make Heaven seem like Hell and

Hell appear as Heaven itself, or make the most miserable type of life seem like a paradise. The Jew knew what to do and he acted on that knowledge. The German, or rather his government, didn't have the faintest idea how to use propaganda or what it truly was. As a result, we saw the most severe results during the War as penance for such ignorance.

In German life before the War, we experienced the problems I have discussed but there were also many advantages. To evaluate things fairly, we must recognize that most of the problems we experienced were also present in other countries and peoples. Their problems were sometimes so great that it often put us in the shade of their gloom because we enjoyed advantages they lacked.

The leader among these virtues was the fact that, when compared to almost all European peoples, Germany tried the hardest to preserve our national economic character. This gave Germany a clear superiority. It reduced our exposure to the control of international finance, though there were symptoms to indicate its presence. This virtue turned out to be dangerous because it became a major cause of the First World War. Putting this and other things aside, three institutions must be pointed out that were unequaled in their perfection. They helped us stand apart from the other great nations and made it possible to restore the nation when it was damaged.

The first was the form the State took and the special way it developed in the Germany of modern times. We may reasonably overlook individual monarchs who, as human beings, were subject to all the weaknesses common to humans and shared with the children of this earth. If we were not understanding and indulgent to these weaknesses, we would be in total despair at the present time because there would be very few people left to run the country. The representatives of the present regime are considered as no more than celebrities, personalities, and are morally and intellectually probably the least developed that one can imagine. Anyone who measures the "quality" or merit of the German Revolution by the merit and stature of the people it has given to the German nation as leaders since November 1918 (*the end of the First World War and start of the Weimar Republic, a reference to the November Criminals*) will hide his head in shame before the judgment of future generations. Future generations will not be bound by the Law for Protection of the Republic and cannot be silenced by such protective laws. They will say what we all realize even now; that the brains and virtues of our new German leaders are a lot smaller than their big mouths and their big vices.

Many people, especially the common people, lost touch with the Monarchy. This was because the Monarchy was not always surrounded by the, shall we say, most alert and especially not the most upright characters. The Monarchy preferred flatterers above straight-talking, honest men. The flatterers were the ones who kept the Monarchy "informed". This caused serious damage at a time when the world was undergoing a transformation and many old opinions were cast off while new ideas replaced them to sit in judgment upon a variety of ancient Royal Court traditions.

By the turn of the century opinions had shifted. How could an ordinary man or woman feel a surge of enthusiasm for a Princess who was riding on horseback and wearing a uniform as soldiers filed past on parade? Apparently, no one in these upper circles had any idea as to how this sort of flamboyancy looked to the people. If they did, such awkward performances would have never happened. The pretentious trend for showing insincere humanitarianism in these circles also repelled more than it attracted. For instance, at one time, if Princess X descended to sample the product of a soup kitchen, of course finding it to be excellent as expected, so she could show how strongly she felt a familiarity with the people, it might have made a perfectly good impression in the past, but the current result was the opposite. It is safe to assume that Her Highness never dreamed that on the day she tasted the soup, it was just a little different from what it usually was, but it was enough that everybody else knew this to be the case. What may have been the best of intentions became ridiculous, if not absolutely offensive.

Descriptions of the proverbial frugality of the Monarch generated many ominous conversations. We were told how he woke up much too early, how he absolutely slaved till late at night, and of the ever-present danger of pending undernourishment resulting from his devotion to duty. Nobody wants to know what and how much the Monarch ate. Nobody begrudged him a "square" meal. No one was trying to deny him a full night's sleep. People were satisfied if he honored the name of his House and his nation as a man and a public servant who fulfilled his duties as a ruler. The telling of fairy tales about him did more harm than good.

All the flamboyancy and fairy-tales as well as other events like them were insignificant compared to the spreading lethargy. Growing throughout a large part of the nation was the terrible belief that governing was taken care of from above automatically, and that the individual didn't need to think about it. As long as the government was really a good one, or at least had the best of intentions, they could continue without anyone objecting. But, beware! When the fundamentally well-meaning old government was replaced by a new gang of lower quality leaders, then the existing meek, docile obedience and child-like faith became the most fatal evils that could possibly be imagined.

To offset these and many other weaknesses, there were undeniable positive effects of the Monarchy. One was the stability of rule imposed by a Monarchy form of government. This removed the highest posts in the State from the reach of ambitious politicians. Further, there were the respect and authority of the institution in itself that elevated government civil servants by association with the Monarchy, especially the army, above the level of mere political party obligations.

There was the further advantage that the Monarch himself was a person who held the head of the State position, and the example set by the Monarch in bearing sole responsibility is more than that which is assumed by the chance mob of a parliamentary majority. The proverbial honesty and integrity of the German administration was due primarily to this responsibility of the man-at-the-top.

The cultural value of Monarchy to the German people was great and this alone easily offset other disadvantages. Residential cities of the German princes have remained a stronghold of artistic senses, but now they are threatened more and more to die out in our materialistic age. What the German princes did for art and science, particularly in the nineteenth century, was a model for advancement. The present day cannot, in any way, show accomplishments of equal value.

At the beginning and during the slowly spreading collapse of the political body, the greatest asset was reclaiming the army. It was the greatest school the German people had available to teach them lessons they were not receiving elsewhere. Those who wished to harm Germany despised the army and for just cause. The hatred of every enemy was directed squarely at this shield representing national self-preservation and freedom. There can be no more splendid monument to this unique institution of the Monarchy than the fact that it was slandered, hated, and resisted, but also feared by every one of the inferior elements that wanted to attack Germany. The fury of the international profiteers and exploiters of Versailles (*Versailles Treaty*) was directed primarily at the old German army, and this shows the army was the stronghold of our people's freedom against the power of the international stock exchange. Without this force standing guard and sounding the alarm, the intentions of Versailles profiteers toward our people would long since have been fulfilled. What the German people owe to the army can be summed up in a single word: Everything.

The army taught a sense of duty at a time when this quality had already become very rare, and avoiding responsibility was the order of the day. This example was set by that model of irresponsibility, the Parliament. The army also taught personal courage in an age when cowardice threatened to become a raging disease. Readiness to sacrifice oneself for the general good of the nation was considered to be stupid and weak-minded while the only man who seemed sensible was the man who could shield and advance his own self interests. The school of the army still taught the individual German to seek salvation in the nation, not in the lying insincerity of international brotherhood among negroes, Germans, Chinese, Frenchmen, Englishmen, etc., but in the strength and unity of his own nationality.

The army bred decisiveness, while everywhere else in life, indecision and skepticism determined men's actions. In an age when the smart-alecks everywhere set the tone, it meant something to maintain the principle that doing something is better than doing nothing. This one principle symbolized a vigorous healthy force that would have been lost in our lives a long time ago if the army and its training had not constantly renewed this fundamental concept. One only has to look at the horrible inability of our present leadership to make a decision. They cannot shake off their mental and moral lethargy to decide on a definite action except when they are forced to sign some new order for the exploitation of the German people. In that case, they decline all responsibility and sign with the speed of a court stenographer anything that is put in front of them. In this case, the decision is easily made because they do not have to reach a decision; the decision is dictated to them.

The army bred idealism and devotion to the Fatherland and its greatness, while in civil life, greed and materialism were out of control. The army trained a united people and united the classes. Perhaps its only fault was the institution of one-year military service for high-school graduates (*Those who completed higher education only had to serve one year instead of the full military term.*) This was a fault because it broke through the principle of absolute equality and put the better-educated individuals outside the circles of their more common comrades. Actually, the very opposite policy would have been better. Our upper classes are so isolated from the real world and they are becoming more and more alienated from their own people, that the army could have had a beneficial effect if it had avoided any preferential treatment in the ranks of the intellectuals. The failure to treat everyone equally was a mistake, but where can you find any institution in the world that doesn't make a mistake? In any case, the good aspects of the army greatly outweighed the defects. The few flaws that existed were far below the average level of human imperfection.

We must consider it a great credit to the army of the old Empire that it placed the individual above mob-rule at a time when majorities were everything, and everyone based their beliefs on the mob's conscience. The army's teaching was in direct opposition to the Jewish Democratic idea that one should blindly worship whatever the greatest number of people believed. Instead, the army upheld faith in the personal values of the individual above the collective values of the mob. It even trained what was most urgently needed: real men. In the swamp of a universally spreading softness and femininity, three hundred and fifty thousand young, well-trained men sprang every year from the ranks of the army and mixed with the population. In two years of training, they had lost the softness of youth and gained bodies as hard as steel. The young man who practiced obedience during this time was now ready to command. One could distinguish a soldier who had done his service by the way he walked.

The army was the great school of the German nation. This was the reason for the fierce hatred of all those who, through envy and greed, wanted and needed to make the Empire weak and defenseless. The world could see what many Germans in their blindness or evil intentions chose not to see; the German army was the mightiest weapon that served to defend the freedom of the German nation and guard the livelihood of its children.

Along with the Monarchy and the army, there was a third foot to the tripod: the incomparable body of civil servants in the old Empire.

Germany was the best organized and best administered country in the world. It was easy to criticize the German civil service because of bureaucratic red tape, but other nations were no better off and many were actually worse. But what the other nations did not possess was the wonderful strength of the machine and the incorruptible, honorable spirit of those who served. Better to wade through a little red tape with honest and faithful men, than suffer through enlightened and modern characters who were ignorant, exercised poor judgment, and incompetent. To those who like to pretend now that pre-war German administration, while unarguably bureaucratically efficient, was bad at dealing with business matters, I can only reply: What country in the world had a better-managed and better-organized business than German government railroads? It was left for the Revolution to destroy this model business structure and then, after it was thoroughly trashed, they decided it was ready to be taken from the hands of the nation and socialized. "Socialized", according to the meaning given to it by the founders of this new Republic, actually meant it now served international finance capital, who were themselves the controllers of the German Revolution.

The trait that distinguished the body of German civil servants and the German administrative structure was its independence from the sudden and unfortunate changes in individual governments. Their momentary politics could have no influence on the position of German State civil servants. Since the Revolution, there has been a complete change. Adherence to party policy has replaced ability and aptitude, and a self-reliance, an independent capability, with an attitude that is more a hindrance than a help.

The wonderful strength and energy of the old Empire rested on the Monarchy, the army, and the State officials of the civil service. These were the foundation of a great strength, a quality completely lacking in the State today: the State's authority. Strength depends on the universal confidence that can be placed in the administration of a commonwealth and not on the babbling in Parliaments or legislative assemblies (*Landtags in some German states*), or on laws to protect the State, or on court sentences passed to frighten those who boldly deny State authority. This confidence is the result of an unshakable inner conviction that the government and administration of a country is driven by an impartial and honest desire for the good of the nation and on a general consistency among the laws which are in harmony with the moral beliefs of the people. Government systems are maintained by the people's faith in their government's goodwill and honest sincerity. In the long run, this belief will uphold and promote the interests of a people and thereby maintain the government, not force or terror.

As strongly as certain evils of the pre-war days may have threatened to eat away and undermine the inner strength of Germany, it must not be forgotten that other nations suffered from most of these diseases, some even more than Germany, and yet they did not collapse and suffer similar destruction at the critical moment when they were tested by crisis. When we consider that for every German weak point before the war there was an equally great strong point, the final cause of the collapse can and must lie in another direction. That is indeed the case.

The deepest and most profound cause of the downfall of the old Empire lay in its failure to recognize the race problem and to see its importance for the historical development of peoples. The events in the life of nations are not expressions of chance, but processes of natural law, of the need for self-preservation and to increase the species and race. Even though men may not see in their mind's eye the motives behind their actions, those actions affect the course of nations.

11. PEOPLE AND RACE

There are certain truths which are so completely obvious that, for the very reason that they are so common, the average person does not see them or at least does not recognize them. A man may often pass blindly by such obvious truths and be utterly astonished when someone suddenly discovers a fact that everybody should have already known. Columbus' eggs are lying around by the hundreds of thousands, but a Columbus is rare indeed. (*The egg of Columbus refers to an idea or discovery that appears obvious after it is made; the reference is based on a common story about Christopher Columbus.*)

All men, without exception, stroll about the garden of Nature, arrogantly assuming they know and are familiar with all of it. Yet, with few exceptions, they pass blindly over one of the most striking principles of Nature's rule: the inner separation of the various species of all earth's living creatures.

Even the most casual observer can see a firm, basic law that rules all the countless creatures in which Nature expresses her will to live. All of the different forms of animals keep within specific boundaries, within their own species, when propagating or multiplying their kind. Every animal only mates with another of the same species. The titmouse pairs with the titmouse, the finch with the finch, the stork with the stork, the field-mouse with the field-mouse, the house-mouse with the house-mouse, the wolf with the she wolf, etc.

Only extraordinary circumstances can alter this boundary rule and then it only happens under the pressure of captivity or for some other reason that makes mating within the same species impossible. But, even then, Nature begins to resist with all her might. Her clearest protest is demonstrated in the infertility of the bastard creature or in restricting the fertility of later descendants. In most cases, she deprives them of the ability to resist disease or deprives these unfortunates the means to defend against attacks from enemies. This is natural.

Every breeding between two creatures that are not from the same level produces a result mid-way between the levels of the two parents. The offspring will be on a higher level than the racially lower one of its parents, but not as high as the higher one. Consequently, in battle, it will eventually yield to the higher species because of its deficiencies. That sort of mating runs counter to Nature's will to breed life upwards. Nature's will is accomplished by complete victory of the higher species, not by uniting superiority and inferiority. The stronger must rule. It must not unite with the weaker, thus sacrificing its own higher nature. Only those who are born as the weaker being can think this cruel and that is why he is a weak and defective man. If this Law did not hold, the evolution of life would be unthinkable.

The consequence of this instinct for race purity, which is found universally throughout Nature, is not only the sharp outward difference between the separate races, but their uniform nature within themselves of their character that is unique to each species. The fox is always a fox, the goose a goose, the tiger a tiger, etc. The only possible difference is in varying degrees of health, strength, understanding, cleverness, and endurance among individual specimens. We will never find a fox which naturally has moments of kindness toward geese, just as there is no cat with a friendly affection for mice.

The battle is born out of hunger and love, not because of any native hostility. In both cases, Nature watches with calm satisfaction. The struggle for daily bread conquers the weak, sickly, and undecided, while the males who win the contest for the female win the right or at least the opportunity of reproduction for the healthiest individuals. Struggle is the means that improves the health, strength, and stamina of the species and the reason for its evolution to a higher quality of being.

If any other process were the choice of Nature, all development and evolution would cease and the progress so far achieved would reverse. There are always more inferior beings than the best examples of a species. This is simply a matter of numbers and the fact that only some can be the Best among them. Given equal opportunities for survival and reproduction, the worst part of a species would increase so much faster than the smaller number of quality members until eventually the best would be crowded into the background. A correction that favors the dominance of the better individual must take place. Nature takes care of this by subjecting the weaker part to difficult living-conditions. That alone is sufficient to restrict their number to some degree. But these cannot be allowed to increase in number randomly. A new, ruthless selection method is made and only the strongest and most sound will make the cut.

Nature does not desire the mating of a weaker species with stronger individuals. Even less does she desire the mixing of a higher race with a lower race. If this were allowed to happen over thousands of years, the efforts of natural selection would be for nothing.

History shows us countless examples which prove this law. It shows with alarming clarity that every time Aryan blood has mingled with inferior races, the result has been the end of the greater civilization whose members were the flag-bearers of superiority. The North American population consists overwhelmingly of Germanic elements which have mingled very little with inferior colored peoples and this shows a very different sort of civilization and culture from Central and South America. In Central and South America, the mostly Latin (*meaning people of Italian, French, Spanish, and Portuguese origin*) settlers mingled, sometimes on a large scale, with the people who were native to the area. This one example by itself clearly and distinctly shows us the effect of racial mixture. The racially pure and almost unmixed Germanic peoples on the American Continent have risen to become the master of their land. He will remain the master as long as he does not yield to blood pollution by mixing with lesser races.

The result of any crossing of races is this:

A. A decline in the level or quality of the superior race.
B. A slow but certain wasting disease of physical and intellectual degeneration begins.

To commit such a deviation is nothing more or less than to sin against the will of the Eternal Creator. This action is rewarded with vengeance.

In attempting to rebel against the iron logic of Nature, man comes into conflict with the principles to which he owes his very existence as a human being. His defiance of Nature is bound to lead to his own downfall.

To this we always hear the arrogant objection of the modern pacifist which is truly Jewish in its inspiration, and correspondingly stupid: "But, man can conquer Nature!"

Millions thoughtlessly babble this Jewish nonsense and end by imagining themselves as conquerors of Nature, but their only weapon is an idea, and this is such a preposterous one that it would be impossible to imagine the world could exist if it were true. Man has never once conquered Nature, but at most has caught hold of and tried to lift one corner of her giant veil which conceals her eternal mysteries. He is never able to create anything. He can only discover things. He does not rule Nature, but has only learned to dominate some of Nature's creatures who lack the knowledge he has gained. An idea cannot conquer the foundations of mankind's growth and his being since the idea itself depends completely on man. Without man, there can be no human idea in the world. Therefore, the idea is always dependent on the existence of men, and he in turn is subject to all the laws that created the conditions essential for that existence.

There is more to the matter. Certain ideas cannot be separated from the man who conceived them. This is particularly true of thoughts which are not based on science but based on feelings or an "inner experience". All these ideas are chained to the existence of the men whose intellectual imagination and creative power spawned the idea and have nothing to do with pure logic. Such ideas represent mere manifestations of feeling, such as ethical and moral concepts, etc. The preservation of those particular races and men is the essential element for the existence of the ideas they have created. If someone should truly desire, with all his heart, for the pacifist idea to be victorious in this world, he would have to do his best in every way to help Germans conquer the world. If the reverse should happen and Germany should be extinguished, the last pacifist would very likely die out with the last German. I say this because the rest of the world has not been so completely fooled as our own people have been by this unnatural and unreasonable pacifist nonsense. Anyone who seriously intended to follow pacifist ideology would have to make up his mind to wage war in order to keep pacifism alive. In fact, this and this alone was what the American world savior, Wilson (*Woodrow Wilson who was elected President on a peace-at-all-costs platform, but was forced to join the First World War later*), intended, or at least what our German prophets thought he intended, and they believed that through his plans their ideals would be attained.

The humane-pacifist idea may be a perfectly good one but only after the most advanced race of men has first conquered and enslaved the world on a scale which makes him the only master of the earth. The idea will then have no chance to cause harm. At least it cannot cause harm any greater than the level it is applied, which will become rare and then impossible once the master race has conquered all. Battle first, then afterwards, perhaps we will see if pacifism works. Any other course that does not lead to the strongest race ruling mankind means mankind has passed the peak of its development and the end will not be the reign of any supreme moral idea, but degeneration into barbarism and eventually chaos. Some may laugh at that statement, but our planet moved through space for millions of years without men walking on the surface. Someday, it may do so again if people forget Nature's laws after they have achieved a higher level of existence. They must not forget that their achievement was due to the recognition and brutal application of the laws of Nature and not to following the ideas of a few crazy ideologists.

Everything we admire on this earth today, science and art, industry and invention, is the creative product of just a few peoples and perhaps originally, all of one race. The survival of this whole civilization depends on them. If they are destroyed, the beauty of this earth will be buried with them. No matter how much the soil may influence mankind, the result of that influence will always differ according to the races in question. The infertility of a territory may encourage one race to strive for supreme achievement. Another race may accept bitter poverty and starvation along with all the consequences. The ultimate outcome is determined by the inner natural tendencies of a people and the way they deal with external influences. What brings one race to starvation will train another to work hard.

The great civilizations of the past have all been destroyed simply because the original creative race died out as a result of pollution of their blood lines.

In every case, the original cause of the downfall has been the failure to remember that all civilization depends on men, and not vice-versa. In order to preserve a particular civilization, the type of men who created it must also be preserved. But this preservation is dependent on the inflexible law that it is necessary and just for the best and strongest men to be the victor and only they have the right to continue. The many, who would desire to live, must fight. Any man who will not fight for his place in this world of constant struggle, does not deserve to live.

Even though this may sound harsh, it is the way things truly are. It will be an even harsher fate that befalls the man who believes he can conquer Nature, for he only insults her. Suffering, disaster, misfortune, and disease will be Nature's response to him.

The man who makes the mistake of ignoring the law of race cheats himself of the happiness which is fated to be his. He blocks the triumphant advance of the greater race, and thus the *sine qua non* (*Latin meaning "indispensable ingredient or requirement for"*) of all human progress. Burdened with humanitarian interests and human sentiment, he falls back among the helpless beasts.

It is useless to argue over what race or races were the original flag-bearers of human civilization and the real founders of everything we consider as the world's humanity. It is simpler to ask this question about the present time. Now, the answer is plain and simple. All human culture, art, science, and invention which surround us are almost exclusively the creative product of the Aryan race. This very fact justifies the deduction that the Aryan alone was the founder of a superior type of human life and is the prototype of what we mean by the word "man" today. He is the Prometheus (*the intelligent Titan of Greek myth who brought fire to earth for man*) of humanity from whose brilliant mind the divine spark of genius has always sprung, ever rekindling the fire which, in the form of knowledge, has illuminated the night of unspeakable mysteries, and thus sent man up the road to lordship over the other creatures of this earth. Take him away, and perhaps within a few thousand years, profound darkness will descend again upon earth, human civilization will vanish, and the world will become a desert.

If we were to divide humanity into three classes, the founders of civilization, the maintainers of civilization, and destroyers of civilization, the Aryan would be the only possible representative of the first class. He laid the foundation and built the great walls of all human creations, and only the outward shape and color are determined by the particular characteristics of the individual peoples. It is the Aryan who furnished the great building-stones and plans for all human progress, and only the execution depends on the character of the various races. Within a few decades the whole of Eastern Asia, for example, will call a single culture its own, however this culture is not its own creation but was built on the foundation of Hellenistic spirit (*built on Greek achievement*), but it was also built with Germanic technology, just as in our own case. Only the outward form will show traits of Asian character; the foundation is Aryan. It is not true that Japan is superimposing European technical progress on her own civilization as many people assume. Original European science and technology have long been decorated with Japanese style. The basis of life in Japan is not the product of a purely native Japanese civilization, but it is instead built on the tremendous scientific and technical work from Europe and America, that is to say from Aryan peoples. However, this civilization does choose the color of their contemporary life, which because of the inner difference of the culture, is more obvious to the European who sees the outside. Only by integrating these Aryan achievements can the Orient take a place along with other countries in general human progress. Aryan scientific and technical achievements provide the foundation that supports their general life and struggle for daily bread in Japan. Only the outward decoration has gradually changed to fit the Japanese character.

If, starting today, all future Aryan influence on Japan were to end, as if Europe and America were both destroyed, Japan's present advance in science and technology might continue for a short while, but within a few years, the well would run dry. The Japanese internal character would gain hold again, and the present civilization would become stagnant and would sink back into the sleep that it was awakened from seven decades ago by the wave of Aryan civilization. Just as the present Japanese development and culture owes its existence to the influence of Europe and America, we can also be assured that in the distant past an outside influence, an outside culture, brought into existence the Japanese culture of that day. The best proof of this is the fact that their culture later suffered stagnation and paralysis when the influence stopped, and it remained this way until it was revived seven decades ago. This can happen to a race if the original creative racial core has been lost, or if the outside influence which supplied the stimulus and the materials for the first cultural development is removed. If it is known that a race receives and absorbs the fundamental substance of a civilization from alien races, and progress comes to a halt each time the external influence ceases, the race may indeed be called a "sustainer" of civilization, but never a "creator".

Examination of the various peoples around the world from this standpoint shows that almost none of them are creators; they are nearly always sustainers; they are merely the recipients of another culture.

This is usually how their development occurs:

Often, amazingly small groups of Aryan tribes overpowered other peoples and caused the dormant intellectual and organizing powers of the conquered people to surface. These abilities were unexercised until the Aryans awoke these abilities in the lesser race. The benefits of the particular living conditions in the new territory, such as the fertility of the soil, climate, etc., made it possible for them to accomplish this cultural reawakening by using the large number of available workers from the inferior race. Often in a few thousand or maybe just a few hundred years, they built up civilizations which originally displayed every inner mark of their founder's character but were adapted to fit within the special qualities of the local area and the characteristics of the subjugated people.

But eventually, the conquerors violate the first principle, keeping their blood pure and not mixing with lower racial stock. They begin to interact with the conquered inhabitants and in doing so, put an end to their own existence. Even for the original sin of man, the penalty was expulsion from Paradise.

After a thousand years or more, the last visible trace of the former ruling people appears only in the lighter skin coloration that its blood bestows on the subjugated race. It is a stagnated culture of which the Aryans had been the true founder. Just as the physical and spiritual aspects of the conqueror were submerged and lost in the blood of the conquered race, so too was the fuel for the torch of human cultural progress extinguished. The blood of the former masters has left a faint glow in the complexion as a sign, and the night of the inferior cultural life is gently illumined by the surviving creations of the ancient bringers of that light. They shine throughout the uncivilized state and can easily make the observer who passes by think he is looking at the image of the present people, but he is just looking into the mirror of the past; he actually sees the glow radiated from the original bearers of the fire of culture.

It may be that throughout history such a people have come into contact a second time, or even more often, with the race that once brought it civilization, without any surviving memory of this past. Unconsciously, the small shred of the old master's blood which remains will be drawn toward the newly arriving race, and what had originally been possible only by force may now happen through free will. A new wave of civilization explodes and lasts until those who carry the mantle of progress are adulterated and again go down in the blood of alien peoples.

It will be the responsibility of those who study future cultural and world history to make their discoveries from this point of view and not to smother themselves in descriptions of outward events, as our present historical scientific education does too often.

Even this short sketch of the development of "culture-sustaining" nations also reveals the growth, work, and decline of the real culture-founders of this earth, the Aryans themselves.

Just as in daily life, the one we call a genius needs a special occasion or even a regular jolt to cause him to shine. A race of people also need such a jolt to bring out the dormant genius. In the monotony of daily life, even outstanding men may appear insignificant. They never rise above the average level of those who surround them. But take that same person and let him face a situation where others would give up or freeze in fear and the genius rises visibly out of this unnoticed, average man, often to the astonishment of everyone who knows him in his everyday life. This is why the prophet is seldom thought about much in his own country. There is no better opportunity to observe this than in war. In times of testing and trial, when others surrender to despair, those who are apparently innocent children spring up into heroes, headstrong in determination and ice cold in judgment. If the hour of stress had not been inflicted, no one would have dreamed that inside that beardless boy was a young hero. Some sort of impact is almost always necessary to arouse the genius. The hammer-blow of Fate will knock one man down and strike against steel in another. Once the everyday outer shell breaks, the hidden core is exposed to an astonished world. Then the world cringes, refusing to believe that what had seemed to be a man of its own average rank is now, suddenly, a greater being. This process occurs almost every time an outstanding son of the race appears.

Although an inventor does not establish his greatness until the day his invention is created, it is a mistake to think that genius itself had never taken hold of the man until then. The spark of genius exists in the brain of a truly creative and gifted man from the hour of his birth. True genius is always present from birth and never taught or learned. This applies, as I have already emphasized, not only in the individual, but in the entire race. Actively creative peoples have fundamental creative gifts from the beginning, even though the outside observer may not recognize it. Outward recognition only results from the accomplishment because the rest of the world is not capable of recognizing genius by itself. They only see its visible expression in the form of inventions, discoveries, buildings, pictures, etc. Even then, it may be a long time before the world recognizes the genius that drove the accomplishment. Just as the genius or the outstanding individual man with extraordinary talent is unable to bring out his ability until it is set in motion by particular stimuli, a race is only able to bring out its creative powers and abilities when the right conditions stimulate the peoples into action.

These abilities are the clearest in the race which has been, and is, the bearer of human cultural development: The Aryans. The moment Fate imposes special conditions on them, their inborn abilities surface at a quicker pace and their genius is shown through the physical result. The cultures they create are almost always determined by the soil, the climate, and the conquered people. The last of these elements is the most important. The more primitive and the greater the technical limitations of any acquired culture, the more effort will be required for the civilizing activity and therefore the more man-power will be needed. When the man-power is organized, concentrated, and applied, it can substitute for the power of mechanical machines. Without the availability of lower ranked men, the Aryan could never have taken the first step toward his later civilizing of those people. It is the same as if he had never tamed and used various domesticated animals to help build the foundation of civilization. Then he would have never arrived at a level of technical development which now is gradually permitting him to do without these very animals. The saying, "The Moor has finished his job, so let him now depart" (*possibly a paraphrase from Shakespeare's Othello, also attributed to the German poet Schiller*) has an unfortunate meaning which is deeply true today. For thousands of years, the horse was forced to serve man and help him lay the foundations of a civilization. Now, thanks to the automobile and mechanical devices, the horse himself has become unnecessary. Within a few years, the horse will no longer be used, but without his help in days gone by, man would have had difficulty in arriving where he is today.

Therefore, the availability of inferior races was one of the most important elements in the formation of higher cultures. Their labor could compensate for the lack of technical tools and machines, without which advanced development is unthinkable. Without question, the first civilization of humanity depended less on domesticated animals and more on the use of racially inferior human beings.

It was the enslavement of conquered races which occurred first; only later did animals find the same fate and not the other way around, as many people would like to think. First, it was the conquered man who drew the plow and only later did the horse take his place. Only whining fools and pacifists can consider this fact a sign of human degradation. This progression had to take place in this order so man could finally arrive at a point where these apostles can stand up and make the world listen to their crowing.

Mankind's progress is like climbing an endless ladder. To climb higher you must first climb over the lower rungs. Therefore, the Aryan had to follow the road required by reality and not that road dreamed up in the imagination of the modern pacifist. The road of reality is harsh and difficult, but it is the only one that finally leads where the pacifist dreams mankind should be, but in reality he is removing the possibility of achieving that dream. The real truth is that those dreamers only lead man away from his goal, not towards it.

It is no accident that the first civilizations arose where the Aryan encountered and conquered lower races and made them do his will. The inferior races were the first mechanical tools to serve a dawning civilization.

The road which the Aryan must travel was clearly marked. As a conqueror, he defeated the inferior peoples and controlled their physical labor under his orders, according to his will, and for his own purposes. In putting them to a useful, but hard task, he not only spared the lives of the conquered, but gave them a fate that was actually better than their previous so-called "freedom". As long as he ruthlessly maintained a master's attitude, he remained not only the real master, but he preserved and advanced the new civilization. This new civilization depended entirely on his inborn abilities and on the survival of the Aryan race. When those who had been conquered began to advance themselves, possibly to the level of using their conqueror's language, the sharp split between master and servant disappeared. The Aryan surrendered the purity of his blood by intermingling, and lost the right to the Paradise which he had made for himself. His racial purity declined as it mixed with the native races and gradually he lost more and more of his cultural creativity until finally, he began to resemble the natives more than his own forefathers, both mentally and physically. For a time, he could still live on the cultural substance he had built, but then stagnation set in and finally, oblivion claimed his race.

The ultimate result is that civilizations and empires collapse to make way for new structures. Mixing of blood and the decline in racial quality that it causes is the main reason for the dying-out of old cultures. Civilizations are not destroyed by war but because they lose that stamina inherent in a pure bloodline. Anything in this world that is not of sound racial stock is a useless husk which is blown away in the wind. Every event in world history is an expression of the racial instinct for self-preservation, whether for prosperity or suffering.

The question of why the Aryan is so important is found in how his instincts are expressed and not because he has a stronger instinct for self-preservation. The individual's will to live is equally great everywhere. Only the actual form it takes will vary. In the most primitive creatures, the instinct of self-preservation does not go beyond caring for itself. This selfishness extends to include time, so that the immediate moment is the most important and nothing is planned for the future. In this state, the animal lives for itself alone, seeks food when it is hungry, and fights only when forced to defend its own life. As long as the instinct of self-preservation takes this form, there is no basis to form a community or even a primitive family.

Once the partnership between male and female becomes a true partnership, not just for the purpose of mating, it then requires that the self-preservation instinct be extended. The care and struggle for only self now extends to protect the mate. The male often hunts for food, but when a child is produced, they will both work to feed their young. One will almost always fight to defend the other. This exemplifies the first forms of self-sacrifice, even though this is infinitely primitive. When this feeling spreads beyond the limits of the immediate family, we have the essentials required for the formation of larger groups, and finally, of nations.

In the most primitive men on earth, this quality is present only to a very limited degree, often not going beyond the formation of the family. As the willingness to put aside purely personal interests increases, the more advanced the ability to set up extensive communities will become.

This will to sacrifice, to devote personal labor and, if necessary, life itself to others, is most highly developed in the Aryan. The Aryan's greatest power is not in his mental qualities necessarily, but in the extent of his readiness to devote all his abilities to the service of the community. In him, the instinct of self-preservation can reach its noblest form because he willingly subordinates his own ego for the prosperity of the community and is even willing to sacrifice his own life for it, if necessary.

The reason for the Aryan's constructive ability and especially his ability to create civilizations does not lie in his intellectual gifts. If he only had intellectual abilities, they might easily be destructive and he would never be able to organize and build. The essential character of the individual depends on his ability to forfeit his personal opinions and interests and to offer them instead for the service of the community. Only by serving his community and assuring its prosperity does he receive his own rewards. He no longer works only for himself, but takes his place within the structure of the community, not only for his own benefit, but for the benefit of all. The most wonderful demonstration of this spirit is through Work. He understands that his labor is not just for his livelihood, but his labor serves the interests of the community without conflicting with community's interests. Otherwise, the goal of his work is only self-preservation without consideration for the welfare of the community. In such a case his work for his own self-interest would be properly called theft, robbery, burglary, or usury.

This spirit of placing the community's prosperity before the self-interests of one's own ego, is the first essential element for every truly human culture. This spirit alone has brought about all the great works of humanity. It brings only a small reward to the originator, but rich blessings to future generations. This alone makes it possible to understand how so many people can bear a shabby but honest life filled with nothing but poverty and insignificance; they know they are laying the foundation for the existence of the community. Every workman, every peasant, every inventor, and every civil servant who labors without ever attaining happiness and prosperity is a pillar of this high ideal, even though the deeper meaning of his actions are forever hidden from him. What is true about work as the basis of human survival and of all human progress is true to an even higher degree when it is done for the protection of man and his civilization. The surrender of one's own life for the existence of the community is the height of all self-sacrifice. Only in this way can we assure that what we have built is not destroyed by Nature or human hands.

Our German language has a word that precisely and splendidly describes that principle: Pflichterfüllung or performance of duty. That means service to the common good of the community ahead of personal self interests. The fundamental spirit that creates this action is what we call idealism. It is the opposite of egotism or selfishness. It means exclusively the individual's ability to sacrifice himself for the community, for his fellow-men. It is necessary for us to realize that idealism is not superficial emotional gut-reaction or humanitarianism, but that it is, was, and always will be the necessary precondition for what we call human civilization. It is the source that provides meaning to the word "human". To this spirit, the Aryan owes his position in this world, and to the Aryan the world owes the creation of "mankind". For this spirit alone shaped a creative force from a pure mind, which was a unique marriage of muscular power and great intellect and this built the monuments of human civilization.

Without its idealistic spirit, all the mental capabilities of the mind, no matter how brilliant, would remain mere inner thoughts or technical knowledge without any outward expression of the inner value and therefore it would never become a creative force.

True idealism is the subordination of one's self, of the individual's interest and life to the community; which is in accordance with the ultimate will of Nature. This is the first essential element for the development of any kind of organization. It leads men voluntarily to recognize the dominance of power and strength and makes them into grains of sand within the realm of creation from which the whole universe is made. The purest idealism unconsciously becomes the perfect counterpart to the most profound wisdom.

We can immediately see how true this is and how little genuine idealism has to do with a fantasy-utopia by asking an unspoiled child, a healthy boy, for instance.

This boy can listen to the rantings of an "idealistic pacifist" without understanding a word he says, but the same boy will immediately be ready to turn on his heel and sacrifice his young life for the ideal of his people.

This willingness results from an instinct in the unconscious which obeys a deeper understanding, a need to preserve the species at the expense of the individual if necessary. He naturally protests against the prophetic speech of the pacifist, who tries to disguise himself as something other than the selfish coward that he is, and is constantly seeking ways to violate the laws of Nature. It is a necessary part of human evolution that the individual has a spirit of self-sacrifice which favors the prosperity of the community and not on the disgusting dreams of cowardly wise guys and critics who pretend to know more than Nature and seek to violate her decrees.

When self-interest threatens to replace idealism, we notice an immediate weakening in the force that maintains the community. When the community breaks, so falls civilization. Once we let self-interest become the ruler of a people, the bonds of social order are broken. When man focuses on chasing his own happiness, he falls from Heaven straight to Hell.

Future generations do not remember the men who pursued their own self-interests, but they glorify the heroes who sacrifice their own happiness.

The most extreme contrast to the Aryan is the Jew. The self-preservation instinct is developed more strongly in the so-called "chosen people" than in any other people in the world. The best proof of this is the mere fact that the race still exists. What other people have undergone so few changes of mind and of character in the last two thousand years as the Jew? What people have gone through greater upheavals and yet always come through the most tremendous catastrophes of humanity unchanged? An infinitely tenacious will to live and to preserve one's species is demonstrated by this fact!

The intellectual qualities of the Jew have been trained through thousands of years. He is considered "cunning" today and, in a certain sense, always has been. But his intellectual ability is not the product of his own evolution, but of object-lessons from others. The human mind cannot climb without steps on which to stand. The spirit requires successive steps to climb upward. Every upward stride needs a foundation, one which is laid in the developments of the past, and this can only be found in a civilization of people. Knowledge rests only to a small degree on one's own experience and predominately relies on the accumulated past experiences and knowledge of others. The general level of civilization provides the individual with this wealth of preliminary knowledge which allows him to easily take further steps of progress on his own. This is primarily done without the individual even being aware of it. The boy of today, for instance, grows up surrounded by an absolute multitude of technical achievements from past centuries. He takes these achievements for granted, without noticing things that only a hundred years ago were a mystery to the greatest minds. However, these achievements are critically important to him if he is ever to understand our progress in a certain area or to improve on it. If a genius from the 1820's were suddenly to return from the grave today, he would encounter a monumental intellectual adjustment before he could hope to understand present time. Facing a new piece of technology would be more difficult and confusing for the genius than it is for a modern average fifteen-year-old boy. This genius would lack all the endless preliminary knowledge which the present day population absorbs automatically, as they grow up among the technological products of their particular civilization.

For reasons which will immediately be apparent, the Jew has never possessed a culture of his own and the basis for his knowledge has always been furnished by the civilizations of others.

In every age, his intellect has developed by using the civilization surrounding him. The reverse of that process has never taken place. The self-preservation instinct of the Jewish people is greater than that of other peoples. Even if their intellectual powers at first appear to be equal to other races, they completely lack the all important requirement of a civilized people, the spirit of idealism.

The Jewish people's willingness to self-sacrifice does not go beyond the basic instinct of individual self-preservation. Their strong feeling of racial solidarity is based on a very primitive "herd" instinct like you see in many other forms of life. It is worth mentioning that this herd instinct leads to mutual support only as long as a common danger makes it seem useful or unavoidable. The same pack of wolves which a moment before was united in devouring its prey breaks up into individuals once their hunger has been satisfied. The same is true of horses. They will band together in order to defend themselves against attack and then scatter again when the danger is past.

The same holds true for the Jew. His apparent will to self-sacrifice is deceptive. It exists only when the life of each individual is at stake and an alliance becomes absolutely necessary for the preservation of the individual. The moment the common enemy is defeated, the common danger avoided, or the plunder secured, the apparent harmony of the Jews' pact among themselves comes to an end, giving way once more to their original natural tendencies. The Jews are in agreement only when a common danger forces them, or when a common prey tempts them. When they are not faced with either case, their most insensitive selfish qualities take over and in an instant, these united people become a swarm of rats carrying on bloody battle, bitterly fighting against each other.

If the Jews were alone in the world, they would smother in filth and slop and would try to outwit and exterminate one another in a bitter battle. However, the lack of any willingness for self-sacrifice and the expression of their own cowardice turns even this battle into a pretense.

It is a complete mistake to assume an idealistic self-sacrifice is seen in the Jews when they come together to fight, or rather, when they come together to exploit their fellow-men. Even here, the Jew is guided by nothing but blatant individual selfishness. For that reason, the Jewish "State", which should be a vital organization aimed at the preservation and increase of a race, has no boundaries. In order to have definite borders for a state, which give it structure, one must have an idealistic spirit within the state's race and a proper understanding of the idea of labor. Any attempt to form or even to preserve a state that has no boundaries will fail if this attitude towards work is missing. Without a State, the sole foundation which a culture needs to grow disappears. Despite the Jewish people's apparent intellectual qualities, they still have no true civilization, at least not a civilization of their own. Whatever pretense of a civilization the Jew possesses today, comes from the contribution of other races, mostly those who were damaged by them.

In order to judge the place Jewry holds in human civilization, we must always remember that there has never been any Jewish art and there is none today. The two Queens of the Arts, architecture and music, owe nothing original to Jewry for it has contributed nothing and created nothing. What Jewry accomplishes in the field of art is either a shorter and simpler version of existing works or outright copies of the intellectual products of others. In other words, the Jew lacks those qualities which distinguish that creative and culturally favored race who are the founders of civilization, the Aryans.

We can see the extent the Jew's usurp a civilization created by others, or to be more accurate how they corrupt it, if we look where he is seen most frequently, in the art which depends the least on personal originality and requires no original invention, by which I mean the dramatic arts. Even here, he is really only using tricks to re-arrange the work of others, he can more correctly be called a monkey-grinder (M*eaning the organ-grinder man of the time period, a street performer of questionable morality who cranks a barrel-organ playing a repetitive tune as his monkey collects tips from the crowd*.) He lacks the final touch of greatness or flair which is necessary to produce a truly great work. He is not the brilliant creator, but the superficial imitator, and all his retouching and little tricks cannot hide the fact that everything he produces lacks energy or life.

Then the Jewish press provides its loving aid and shouts such high praises over every clumsy and inadequate performer, no matter how mediocre, as long as he is a Jew. The press makes him sound so amazing and wonderful that the rest of the world is fooled into believing it is in the presence of a real artist, but in truth, the man is nothing more than a low-class mime. The Jew possesses no civilization-building power. He has none and never did have the idealism required to improve and develop mankind. Consequently, his intellect is never constructive, but will always be destructive. In very rare cases, his intellect may seem, at best, a stimulus, but even then we see how it becomes twisted into the model for the poet's words: "The power whose will is always evil but who ends up doing good". (*Originally in German:* kraft, die stets das böse will und stets das gute schafft, *is a paraphrase of a riddle from Faust which, based on what is happening in the play where Mephistopheles makes this statement, appears to imply here that Jews do bad things which have the unintentional result of producing something good.*) It is not through the Jew's assistance that humanity progresses, but in spite of him.

Since the Jew has never had a state with definite territorial boundaries and could never call a civilization his own, some have said they are nomads. That idea is a deceptive mistake. The nomad definitely has a clearly defined territory, although he does not cultivate; however, he is unlike the farmer who settles on a piece of land. Instead he lives off his herds which he follows as they wander about his territory. The reason he wanders is because the soil is infertile and therefore cannot support a settlement. The deeper cause, however, lies in the lack of a technical civilization which is needed to compensate for the sparse resources. There are areas where development has taken place over more than a thousand years, and it was only possible because of the technology of the Aryan, who is able to make himself the master over large areas and establish solid settlements that can support him. If he did not have this technology, he would either have to avoid these areas or live as a constantly wandering nomad. That is if, after thousands of years of living with his technical developments, the idea of a sedentary nomadic life was not intolerable to him. We must remember that at the time when the American continent was being settled, many Aryans struggled for a livelihood as trappers and hunters etc. They were often in large groups with their wives and children and always on the move. Their existence was exactly like that of nomads. But, as soon as their numbers grew to a certain point and better equipment made it possible to tame the land and resist the natives, more and more settlements sprang up throughout the country.

The Aryan was probably the original nomad and, over the course of time, settled in one place. But even so, he was never a Jew! No, the Jew is not a nomad. Even the nomad had a definite concept of "work", which would serve as the basis which he built his civilization on. There is a certain amount of idealism in the attitude of the nomad, even though it is primitive. His whole nature may be foreign to the Aryan, but it is not disgusting to him. However, this attitude simply does not exist in the Jew. Therefore, the Jew has never been the nomad, but instead has always been a parasite fattening himself on the body of other peoples. The fact that he has abandoned previous regions was not by choice. He was driven out by his hosts who had become tired of having their hospitality abused by these "guests". Jewish expansion is an act typical of all parasites. He is constantly looking for a new land for his race. This has nothing to do with being a nomad because the Jew never dreams of leaving an area or vacating a territory once he is there. He stays where he is, and he holds on to it so intently that he is very hard to get rid of even by force. He only spreads to new countries when conditions necessary for his existence attract him. However, unlike the nomad, he doesn't change his previous residence. He remains a typical parasite, spreading like a harmful bacteria wherever he finds a suitable place to grow. The effect of this parasite, wherever he happens to be, causes the host nation to die off sooner or later.

The Jew has always lived in the states of other races and within that state he has created his own state. This state within a state sailed under the colors of a "religious community" and continued to do so as long as he was not forced to reveal his true nature. Once he thought he was strong enough and no longer needed to hide, he would drop the veil and suddenly all would see what so many had refused to see and to believe previously, the real character of the Jew.

The Jew's life as a parasite within the body of other nations and states is the origin of an unusual characteristic which caused Schopenhauer (*Arthur Schopenhauer, the German philosopher*) to describe the Jew as the "great master of lies". This kind of existence drives the Jew to lie and to lie regularly and methodically in an orderly, businesslike way which comes as naturally to them as warm clothes to those who live in cold climates.

His life within a nation can only continue if he convinces the people that Jews are not a separate people, but merely a "religious community", although an unusual one. But this itself is the first great lie.

In order to carry on his existence as a parasite among other nations, he must conceal his inner character. The more intelligent the individual Jew is, the more successful his deception will be. This deception may even convince parts of the host nation that the Jew is really a Frenchman, an Englishman, a German, or an Italian, just a person of a different religious persuasion. Government offices are particularly easy victims of this notorious trick because bureaucrats have little sense when it comes to history and only react to a fraction of actual history. In such circles, independent thinking is often considered a sin against sacred rules that determine who is promoted and who is not. Because of this, we must not be surprised that the Bavarian State Ministry, for instance, even today doesn't have the faintest idea that the Jews are members of a separate people and not of a simple "religious group". One glance at the world of Jewish newspapers immediately proves this, even to someone of the most ordinary intellect. Of course, the Jewish Echo (*a Jewish newspaper*) is not yet an official government journal, so in the mind of these government officials they have no need to read it.

Jewry has always been a nation with definite racial characteristics and it has never been identified solely as a religion. Their need to advance in the world caused the Jew to search for a method that would distract undesirable attention from its members. What could have been more effective and more innocent in appearance than a religious community? Even here, everything is borrowed, or rather stolen. The Jew could never create a religious institution on his own because he lacks any form of idealism which would be needed to create such a cover. The lack of idealism means that a belief in any life hereafter is absolutely foreign to him. According to the Aryan concept, no religion could be conceived that lacks a belief in some form of life after death. In fact, the Talmud (*the record of Jewish Law, ethics, customs, and history*) is a book that explains how to prepare for a practical and prosperous life in this world and it says nothing about preparation for the hereafter.

The Jewish religious teachings consist mainly of rules to keep the blood of Jews pure and to regulate the dealings of Jews among themselves and even more with the rest of the world, with the non-Jews. Even here, their rules consist of extremely petty economic guides and are not concerned with ethical problems. For a long time, there have been very detailed studies made which reviewed the moral value of Jewish religious teachings. These studies were certainly not made by Jews because the Jews twist their statements to suit their own purpose. The Aryans who conducted these studies found this kind of "religion" to be detestable. The clearest indication of what this religious education can produce is the Jew himself. His life is only concerned with this world and his inner spirit is as foreign to true Christianity as his nature was two thousand years ago to the great Founder of the new teaching Himself, Jesus Christ. Jesus made no secret of His feelings toward the Jewish people, and even used the whip to drive this rival out of the Lord's temple. Even then, the Jewish religion was just a means to make money as a business. Christ was nailed to the cross for his intolerance of the Jews, while our present Christian political parties lower themselves in elections by begging for Jewish votes. Afterwards, they try to hatch deceitful political plots with the Jewish atheist parties and against its own nationality.

On this first and biggest lie, that Jewry is not a race but a religion, the Jew builds subsequent lies. To him, language is not a way to express his thoughts, but a way to conceal them. When he speaks French, his thinking is Jewish. While he is fabricating German rhymes, nothing he says can be believed because he is just expressing the nature of his own race, that of the lie. As long as the Jew has not become the master of the other peoples, he must speak their languages, but the instant they become his slaves, they will have to learn an artificial universal language like Esperanto (*Esperanto is an artificial international language based on word roots common in Europe*) so that Jewry could rule them more easily.

The whole existence of these people completely depends on one continuous lie and this is uniquely proven in the "Protocols of the Elders of Zion" (*which is an anti-semitic work outlining a plot by Jewish and Masonic elements to achieve world domination. Today the manuscript is known to be a forgery*)that is so bitterly hated by the Jews. The Frankfurter Zeitung (*the Frankfurt Newspaper*) keeps groaning to the world they are a forgery which is the best proof that they are genuine. What many Jews wish to do unconsciously is consciously made clear here. It does not matter what Jewish mind these revelations come from. What matters is that they uncover the nature and activity of the Jewish people with absolutely horrible accuracy and show their inner connections, as well as their ultimate goal. This book shows how the Jewish mind works, and the activities described, as well as the methods, are characteristic of the Jewish people. The best test of the authenticity of these documents is by studying current events. Anyone who examines the historical development of the last hundred years with the revelations in this book will immediately understand why the Jewish press is so upset and denounces it constantly. Once the contents of this book have become general public knowledge, the Jewish threat can be considered destroyed.

In order to know the Jew properly, it is best to study the road he has taken through other nations during recent centuries. It will be enough to follow through one example in order to fully understand. Since his career has always been the same, just as the peoples he devours have remained the same, in the interest of simplicity we will break up his development into definite steps, which I will indicate by letters of the alphabet.

The first Jew came to what is now Germany during the advance of the Romans. As always, they came as traders. During the turmoil resulting from the great migration of German tribes, they seemed to disappear again. Jews reappeared with the first formation of a Germanic state and this may be considered the beginning of the new, and this time permanent, Jew infiltration of Central and Northern Europe. The same process has occurred wherever Jewry came into contact with Aryan peoples.

Letter A. With the foundation of the first permanent settlement, the Jew is suddenly "there". He appears as a trader at first and does not bother to hide his nationality. He lives openly as a Jew. This is evident because of the extreme physical racial difference between him and his hosts. His knowledge of the local languages is minimal, and the clannish nature of the local people is too strong for him to risk appearing to be anything but a foreign trader. With his cunning he knew his lack of experience in the host nation was no disadvantage, but rather an advantage, so it was in his interest to retain his character as a Jew. The stranger finds a friendly reception among his hosts.

Letter B. Gradually he begins to take an active role in the local economy, but not as a producer. He acts solely as a middleman. His skillfulness has been a thousand years in the making, which altered his commercial cunning and negotiation skills so that they were far superior to the Aryans. The Aryans are still inexperienced and clumsy when it comes to business, but their honesty had no limits. Within a short time, trade threatens to be monopolized by the Jews. He begins by lending money at extremely high interest rates. He actually started the practice of charging interest on borrowed money. The danger of this new method of borrowing was not recognized at first and it was even welcomed for it provided short term advantages.

Letter C. The Jew settled down by this point and he now occupied a special section, his own market-places in the cities and towns, forming more and more of a state within a state. He viewed all trade and all money related business to be a privilege provided exclusively by him and he ruthlessly exploited it.

Letter D. Finance-related businesses and trade in goods have now become his private monopoly. His ridiculously high interest rates finally begin to arouse opposition. His growing boldness became offensive and his disrespect stirred resentment. His display of wealth further ignites envy. It is the last straw when he begins to include the very soil of the earth in his realm of profit and degrades land into a commodity to buy, trade and sell. He never cultivates the soil himself and regards it only as an object of development for profit. He allows the peasants to continue to live upon "his" property, but they must submit to the most wicked and excessive demands from their new master. The dislike of the Jew gradually rises until it becomes open hatred. His blood-sucking domination grows so extreme that the people ultimately resist his tyranny with violence. People scrutinized the alien more and more closely and they continued discovering new, disgusting traits and characteristics until the gap between the Jews and their hosts is too wide to be bridged.

In times of great public distress, we see the hatred and rage against the Jew surface. The robbed masses take the law into their own hands and recover their property from the Jew which ruins him and frees themselves of what they believe is an affliction sent by God. In the course of centuries, they have come to know the Jew and in times of trouble, they saw his very existence as a danger like the plague.

Letter E. Now the Jew begins to reveal his true character. Using the disgusting tool of flattery, he pays homage to governments, puts his money to work to dig deeper into the community, and in this manner keeps his license to rob his victims. Even though the people's rage against the perpetual leech often blazes up, that does not stop him from returning again a few years later in the same town and resuming his old life all over again. No amount of persecution changed his ways and he continued taking advantage of men. No matter how loudly the people shouted and yelled, no one could run him off. Every time the Jew is chased away, he soon returns and is up to his old tricks again. To prevent the very worst from happening, Jews were forbidden by law from possessing land.

Letter F. As the power of the princes and kings grew, the Jew elbowed his way closer and closer to them. He begs for deeds to property and for special privileges. The noble lords were always facing financial problems which made it easy for him to obtain these courtesies once he has made satisfactory payment. It did not matter what this cost him because, within a few years, he knew he would receive his money back with interest compounded many times. This Jew is an absolute leech who fastens himself to the body of the unfortunate people where they cannot remove him. There he feeds until the princes need money again and, with their own dignified hands, they draw off the blood he has sucked from the people.

This game keeps repeating itself. The role the German princes played is just as disgraceful as that of the Jews themselves. These rulers became the punishment of God on their dearly beloved people and we can still find their kind among the various government ministers of today. It is because of the German princes that the German nation could not free itself from the Jewish troublemaker. Unfortunately, this never changed, so they received a reward from the Jew that they had earned a thousand times over for the sins they committed against their people. They associated with the devil and later found themselves in his power.

Letter G. The Jewish entanglement of the princes soon leads to their own destruction. Slowly, but surely, their support among the people grows weaker as they cease to represent the people's interests, and spend their time exploiting their subjects. The Jew carefully watched for the time when the princes would fall and when he sees it coming close, he does all he can to speed up the collapse. He feeds their constant financial problems by preventing them from honoring their true duty to the people, by boot licking and using the most blatant flattery, by introducing them to vices, and in the process he makes himself more and more indispensable. His skillfulness, or rather deceitfulness, in all financial matters succeeds in sweeping, no, I should say horsewhipping, new funds from the robbed subjects. These exploited subjects find themselves driven down the road to poverty faster and faster. Each court has its "Court Jews", as the monsters are called, who torture the people to the point of hopelessness and arrange the endless pleasures of the princes. How can anyone be surprised that these "assets" of the human race receive official honors and climb into the upper class by joining their families, they not only make nobility look ridiculous, but they actually contaminate it from the inside.

Now the Jew is in a better position, politically and socially, to push his own advancement forward. Finally, he allows himself to be baptized and in doing so he gains all the opportunities and rights of the native people. This act of "business" delights the churches which believe they have a new son of Faith among their flock, and this business also delights Israel (*the Jewish people, not the country, the country did not exist yet*) when they see the successful fraud they have accomplished.

Letter H. In the world of Jewry, a transformation now begins to take place. Up until now, they have been Jews. That is to say that they had no interest in appearing to be anything else, and, in fact, could not have done so considering the very pronounced racial characteristics which differentiated them from the native race. As late as the time of Frederick the Great (*in the mid to late 1700's*), everyone regarded Jews as an "alien" people. Even Goethe(*Johann Wolfgang von Goethe, a famous German writer*) was horrified at the thought that someday, marriage between Christian and Jew may no longer be legally forbidden. Goethe, Heaven knows, was no extreme conservative and not against progress and certainly not a blind follower of philosophy. What he felt was nothing but the voice of blood and reason. His race's blood and common sense spoke the truth to his ears. Even without all the disgraceful actions occurring in the Royal Courts, the people instinctively saw the Jew as a foreign substance in its own body and formed an appropriate attitude in response.

Now was the time for a change to take place. Over the course of more than a thousand years, the Jew has learned the language of his hosts so well that he shows his Judaism less and dares to put his "German" side in the foreground. As ridiculous and stupid as it may at first seem, he has the audacity to transform himself into a "Teuton" (*an ancient German or a speaker of the German language*) or an actual "German". This was the beginning of one of the most notorious deceptions that can be imagined. Since he possesses none of the qualities of German character and can only abuse and twist its language and otherwise has never mixed with the Germans to absorb their character traits, his ability to pretend to have a German identity depends on his ability to emulate the language alone. A race is not bound by their language, but entirely by their blood. This is something the Jew knows better than anyone. The Jew doesn't care about the preservation of his own language, but he does care deeply about the purity of his blood. A man may change languages and easily learn a new one, but his new language will only express his old ideas. His inner nature is not changed. The best proof of this is the Jew, who can speak a thousand languages, and yet his Jewish nature remains intact; he is the same Jew. His characteristics have always been the same, whether he spoke Latin two thousand years ago as a grain merchant at Ostia (*Ostia Antica, an ancient Roman trading harbor city*) or mumbles German gibberish today as a middle man pushing adulterated flour. It is still the same Jew. It can be taken for granted that this obvious fact is not understood by an average clerk's supervisor at any government office or by a police administrator today since there is hardly anything with less instinct and intelligence running at large than these civil servants chosen by our present model of a government.

The reason why the Jew suddenly decides to become a "German" is obvious. He feels the power of the princes slowly beginning to waver, and acts to strengthen his own standing. His financial domination over the entire economic system has already advanced to a point that it can grow no further until he gains the full rights of a citizen. He can no longer support the entire enormous structure and his influence cannot increase anymore without this critical piece. But not only does he want to preserve what he has, he wants to expand further. The higher he climbs, the more tempting his old goal becomes, just as it was promised to him in ancient times. With intense greed and wide eyes, his alert mind sees the dream coming within reach again; the dream of ruling the world. All his efforts are directed towards becoming a full citizen which gives him full possession of civil and political rights.

This is why he cleansed himself from the Jewish Ghetto--so he could become a full citizen.

Letter I. Through this process the Court Jew gradually developed into the people's Jew. This does not mean he lives among the people; no, it means that the Jew remains among the noble lords as always and, in fact, tries more than ever to worm his way deeper into their ruling circle. At the same time, another part of his race begins to use flattery as their tool to gain approval with the good, common people. When we consider what sins the Jew has committed against the masses throughout the centuries, how he has persistently squeezed and sucked them dry, how the people gradually learned to hate him for it, and how the people finally came to see his existence as a punishment on them from Heaven, we can understand how difficult this transformation must be for the Jew. Yes, it is hard work to suddenly stand in front of those victims you whipped raw and present yourself as a "friend of humanity".

He begins by attempting to make amends in the eyes of the people for his previous crimes. He starts his transformation by donning the cloak of a "benefactor" to humanity. Since his new benevolence is very evident, he is obviously unable to follow the teachings of the old quote from the Bible that the left hand should not know what the right hand is giving (*Matthew 6:3, meaning do not flaunt generosity, not even in your own mind.*) He feels compelled to let as many people as possible know how deeply he feels the sufferings of the masses and what personal sacrifices he is making to help them. With his innate "modesty" , the Jew drums his virtues into the minds of the rest of the world until they actually begin to believe it is true. Anyone who does not accept this belief is considered to be bitter and unfair to him. Within a very short time, he begins to twist things to make it appear as if, up until now, it was he who had suffered all of the wrongs and not the reverse. There were many particularly stupid people who believed him and could not help pitying the poor "unfortunate" Jew.

This, incidentally, is the place to remark that with all his fondness for self-sacrifice, the Jew never becomes poor himself. He understands how to manage his money. His benevolence can be compared to the manure that a farmer spreads in the field. The farmer does not spread the manure because he loves the field, but in anticipation of future benefits. In any case, everyone knows within a fairly short time that the Jew has become a "benefactor and philanthropist". What a transformation!

Generous actions are taken for granted in others but they cause astonishment and frequently even admiration in this case because it is so unusual for a Jew. People give him much more credit for these deeds than they would give to any other member of humanity. More than this, the Jew will suddenly become liberal and then he begins to babble about the necessary progress of humanity and how it should be encouraged. He slowly makes himself the herald of a new age.

It is also true that more and more, he completely undermines the pillars of the economy which the people need the most. He used the stock exchanges to buy shares of the national companies thereby breaking in to the cycle of national production. He then changes production into an object to be bought and sold by barter and exchange. This robs the factory workers of personal ownership. With the introduction of the Jew, the split between employer and employee occurs for the first time. This later leads to political class resentment. Jewish influence on economic affairs through the stock exchange grows with tremendous speed. He becomes the owner or at least the controller of the nation's labor force.

To strengthen his political position, he tries to break down the racial and civil barriers which still restrict him wherever he goes and which hamper his advancement. For this goal, he fights with all his native stubbornness to champion religious tolerance. Freemasonry has fallen entirely into his hands and through it, he has found an excellent instrument to fight for his purposes openly or gain them by secrecy. Governing circles, as well as the higher levels of the political and economic privileged class, have fallen into his Masonic trap without them even realizing it.

The particular group of people who were beginning to become aware of their own power and fight for their rights and freedom are the only ones who cannot yet be controlled by Jews and their deep level of influence across a wide range of society. Implementation of this control is necessary more than anything else because the Jew can only hope to be elevated to a ruling position if there is someone ahead of him to lead the way, and he believes he sees this forerunner in the privileged-class, as long as he can sweep large numbers of them in. However, the glove manufacturers and fabric manufactures were not caught with the delicate net of Freemasonry as the Jew had planned. Here, more coarse, but no less penetrating means were required. To Freemasonry, a second weapon is added in the service of Jewry: the press.

He pursues it with all the determination and skill he can muster. With the press in his pocket, he slowly begins to control all of public life. He traps it, guides it and pushes it. He is in a position to create and direct a force that is more familiar to us today than it was a few decades ago and we know it as "public opinion". At the same time, he claims he is infinitely thirsty for knowledge and praises all progress, but he especially praises that which leads to the ruin of others. He judges all knowledge and every development based on what advantage it gives his own people. Where there is no advantage to him, he becomes the unyielding, deadly enemy of all light and the hater of all true culture. He uses all the knowledge he has learned from others exclusively in the service of his race.

He guards the Jewish nationality more than ever before. While he seems to be overflowing with "enlightenment", "progress", "freedom", and "humanity", etc., he practices the strictest isolation of his own race so they do not mix with others. He may sometimes give one of his women to an influential Christian, but as a matter of principle he always keeps his male line pure. He poisons the blood of others, but preserves his own purity. The Jew almost never marries a Christian woman while the Christian takes the Jewess wife. But the bastards that result from this union always claim their place on the Jewish side. As a result, part of the higher nobility has deteriorated completely. The Jew knows this very well and they steadily use this method to deceive and confuse the leading intellectuals of his racial enemies. To disguise his actions and to soothe his victims, he talks more and more about the equality of all men, regardless of race and color. Eventually, the simpletons start to believe him.

The whole character of the Jew has the stink of a foreign being; therefore, the great masses of the people do not fall into his snare so easily. He responds by having his press paint a picture of him that is completely false yet useful for his purpose. In comic journals, for instance, great pains are taken to represent the Jews as a harmless little people who have their own unique peculiarities just like everyone else. The comics portray a humorous, but always kind and honest soul. In the same way, they are always careful to make him seem insignificant rather than dangerous.

His goal at this stage is the victory of democracy, or rather, establishing total dominance and rule by parliament which is democracy as the Jew understands it. This is the system which is best fitted to his needs. It does away with the personal element and puts a majority of stupidity, incompetence, and cowardice in its place. The final result will be the downfall of the Monarchy, which will eventually happen.

Letter J. The enormous change in economic development leads to a change in the social levels of the people. The small craftsmen slowly disappear as they are replaced by factory workers. This makes it impossible for the individual workman to win any independence in his existence. As a result, he sinks to the level of a day-laborer. The industrial factory-worker finds himself in an existence where he is rarely ever in a position to create a livelihood that he can live off in his later life. He is deprived of his future and destitute in the truest sense of the word. His old age is miserable and can hardly be described as any sort of life.

We faced a similar situation once before. It urgently demanded a solution and so one was found. A new social class had surfaced to join the manual laborer and the craftsman. It was the officials and professional employees, particularly of the State. They too were a destitute class in the truest sense of the word. The State finally found a way out of this unhealthy condition by providing to the State employee that which he could not prepare himself for in his old age. They introduced pensions and retirement pay. Private enterprises slowly followed this example. Today, almost every regular employee, who is not a manual laborer, eventually draws a pension if the firm he worked for has grown. By providing for the old age of the State civil servant, the State instilled in him an unselfish devotion to duty, which was the finest characteristic of German officials before the war. An entire class who had no property was wisely saved from social misery and assigned a proper place in the social structure of the nation.

Now this question rises to face the State and nation again, this time on a much larger scale. Masses of people, even numbering into the millions, moved from farming communities into the large cities to earn their living as factory workers in the newly founded industries. The working and living conditions of the new class were worse than miserable. The mechanical transfer of the previous work methods used by the old craftsmen or farmers to the new factory style was totally unsuited to their habits or how they think. The daily activity these groups were accustomed to was completely different from the intense and constant output effort required from the industrial factory worker. Time previously played a small role to the craftsman, but with the new methods of factory work, time was more important than ever. The takeover of the old working hours by the large industrial enterprise was absolutely catastrophic. Past daily production had been small because present day intensive production techniques were not used. It was possible for a person to complete a fourteen or fifteen hour work day in the past, but the new system is beyond human endurance where every moment is used to the maximum. In fact, the result of this senseless transfer of old working hours to the new industrial activity was disastrous in two directions. First, worker health was shattered and faith in a higher justice was destroyed. Finally, there was the pitiful amount of worker pay on one hand which gave a superior financial position to the employer on the other.

In the country there could be no social problem since the master and worker did the same work together and even sat together as they ate the same food. But this changed as a new system gave a different status to masters and workers.

The separation of employer and employee now seemed complete in every field of life. The inner Judaization of our people can be seen by the lack of respect, if not contempt, given to manual workers. This is not the German way. The loss of national respect in our lives, which resulted from Judaization, transformed the old respect for the work of craftsmen into a definite contempt for any physical labor at all. From the economic and social change grows a new group of laborers and factory workers who receive very little respect and some day we must ask whether the nation will have the strength to make a place for the new group in society or whether the class differences will grow into a gap that can never be bridged.

One thing was certain, the new social group did not include the trouble-makers of the community; it included the strongest and most spirited part of our nation. As society became more complex, and as a result, more adulterated, the decaying and destructive effect failed to reach this class. The great masses of the new group were not yet touched by the poison of pacifist weakness, but were robust and even brutal when necessary.

The privileged-class paid no attention at all to this significant problem and without showing any concern they let events take their course. All the while, the Jew realized the limitless possibilities offered to him for the future. On one hand, he organized capitalistic methods of human exploitation down to the last detail. Then on the other, he crept up on the victims of his spirit and activity to overcome them and gain their favor. Soon the Jew became the leader of the battle against himself. I am speaking figuratively when I say "against himself" because the "great master of lies" always succeeds in making himself seem innocent and throwing the blame on others. Since he had the audacity to lead the masses himself, it never occurred to the people that this could be the most legendary fraud of all time. And yet, it was.

The new class barely had time to develop out of the economic transformation before the Jew clearly recognized it as the new forerunner that he could use to blaze the trail for his own further advancement. First, he used the privileged-class to strike against the farm-based economy which created the factory worker. Now, he uses the factory worker against the privileged-class. Just as his craftiness helped him acquire civil rights in the shadow of the privileged-class, now he hopes to find the road to his own power in the workers' struggle for existence.

When the time arrives, the workers' only responsibility will be to fight for the future of the Jewish people. Without being aware of it, the laborer is put to work for the very power that he believes he is fighting against. He is led to believe he is acting against capitalism, and therefore he is easily made to fight for capitalism. The cry is heard against international capital, but the real target is the national economy. The current economy must be destroyed so that the international stock exchange can replace it on the corpse-strewn battlefield, with Jewish financial world interests.

To achieve his goal, the Jew proceeds as follows: he creeps up on the workers in order to win their confidence, pretending to have compassion for their poverty and circumstances or even anger at their miserable lot in life. He is careful to study all the real or even their imagined problems. Then he arouses the desire for change. With infinite shrewdness, he stirs up the urge for social justice, an innate desire that is sleeping within every Aryan. Once the fire is burning, the Jew turns it into hatred toward those more fortunate and puts the stamp of a very special World-Concept on the battle; he builds a philosophy designed to correct social injustice. He founds the Marxist doctrine.

By representing it as part of a series of socially justified demands, the Jew is able to spread his message and inspire the people all the more easily. But at the same time he provoked the opposition of decent people who rejected these demands after they recognized the fake philosophy, and distorted form used to present the concepts. To these good people, it seemed fundamentally unjust and a goal that was impossible to accomplish. Under this covering of purely social ideas we find that extremely evil intentions are present. In fact, they are openly presented, in full public view, with the most bold insolence. This doctrine is an inseparable mixture of reason and absurdity, but it is always arranged so that only the absurd parts could be put into practice and never the parts of reason. By its absolute denial of the personal value of the individual and of the nation and its racial substance, it destroys the basic foundations of all human civilization which depends precisely on those factors. This is the true core of the Marxist World-Concept , if this creature of a criminal mind can be called a "World-Concept ". The destruction of individuality and race removes the primary obstacle that prevented domination by the inferior man, the Jew.

The very absurdity of the economic and political theories of Marxism give it an unusual characteristic. These pseudo-theories prevent intelligent people from supporting the cause, while the intellectually challenged and those who lack any understanding of economics rush to it waving their flags furiously. Even this movement needs intelligence in order to exist, but the intelligence driving the movement is "sacrificed" by the Jew from his own ranks as a glorious service to the masses. A movement made up of laborers was thereby created but under Jewish leadership. It gives the impression that it aims to improve the conditions the worker lives under, but its true intent is to enslave him and thus totally destroy all non-Jewish peoples.

In the circles of the so-called intellectuals, Freemasonry spread their pacifist teaching which paralyzed the instinct for national self-preservation. This poison was then spread to the broad masses of workers as well as the privileged-class by the mighty and unceasing Jewish press. A third weapon of disintegration is added to these two and is by far the most fearful. It is the organization of brute force. Marxism plans to attack and storm any shreds of social order it has not yet undermined and to complete the collapse which was started by the first two weapons.

The coordination of these forces is a work of art in itself. There is really no reason to be surprised if those very institutions that are always so fond of posing as the embodiment of the somewhat mythical authority of the State fall to Marxism. With only a few exceptions, the Jew has always found the most willing tools for his work of destruction in our high and highest State officials. These officials possess an attitude of crawling submissiveness towards those above them and arrogant haughty disdain for "inferiors". Those are as much marks of this class as its reprehensibly slow ability to understand, and that is exceeded only by an absolutely astonishing conceit which occasionally borders on amusing. But these are qualities which the Jew needs in our government offices and therefore appreciates the most.

In rough outline, the practical battle which now begins to take place is as follows: in order to manage the ultimate goals of the Jewish struggle better, the Jew divides the Marxist organizations into halves. The Jew is not satisfied with economic world conquest but also demands political control. These two halves seem to be separate, but are really one indivisible whole: the political movement and the trade union movement.

The purpose of the trade union movement is to assemble the recruits. In the hard battle for existence, the worker wages war against the greed and short-sightedness of many employers, while the movement offers help and protection and the possibility of forcing others to provide the worker with better living conditions. At a time when the State ignores him, the worker cannot leave the defense of his human rights to the blind whim of officials who are irresponsible and heartless, so he must take his defense in his own hands. The so-called nationalistic upper-middle and privileged classes, blinded by their own financial interests, put serious obstacles in the way of this life-and-death fight by the worker. The employers of the middle and upper class not only resist, but often actually sabotages attempts to shorten inhumanely long working hours, end child labor, provide security and safety to women, and improve sanitary conditions in factories and homes of the working class. While the middle and upper classes impede the worker at every step, the shrewd Jew sides with the people who are oppressed. He gradually becomes the leader of the trade union movement. This happens easily because he is not interested in a real and honest correction of social abuses, but only in forming a blindly devoted economic fighting force that will shatter national economic independence. The direction of a sound social policy will always balance between the necessity of preserving the people's health on the one hand and of assuring an independent national economy on the other hand. These two considerations are not part of the Jew's plan, they are not even considered in this struggle, only their complete elimination is the purpose of his life. He does not want to preserve an independent national economy; he wants to destroy it. Consequently, as leader of the trade-union movement, he has no conscience or doubts to prevent him from making demands that go beyond their declared purpose, or making demands that are either impossible to fulfill or would mean the ruin of the national economy. He does not want to create a solid and tough race of people as followers. He needs a decayed herd ready for submission. This ultimate objective allows him to make the most absurd and senseless demands because he knows that accomplishing them is unrealistic or impossible. Making these demands, which cannot be accomplished, will never produce any change in the status-quo. At best, it would only create unrest and turbulence among the masses. This, however, is what he is after and not a real and honest improvement in social conditions.

The Jew's leadership in trade unions will continue until either a massive education campaign opens the eyes of the broad masses and enlightens them to the true source of their unending misery, or the State disposes of the Jew and his work. As long as the masses lack the ability to understand, and the State remains as indifferent as it is today, the masses will follow anyone who makes the boldest promises in economic matters. In this, the Jew is a master and he has no moral hesitations to interfere with his activities!

In the trade unions, he soon defeats every competitor and drives them away. His inner nature of greedy brutality leads him to teach the union movement the most brutal use of force. If anyone with sound judgment has been able to resist the Jewish traps, his defiance and wisdom are broken by terrorism. The success of this tool is tremendous.

By using the union, which might under other circumstances be a blessing to the nation, the Jew actually destroys the foundations of the national economy.

The political organization works together the with trade union side. The trade unions prepare the masses for political organization by using violence and pressure to force them into joining. Unions are also the financial source from which the political organization feeds its enormous machine. Trade unions are the instrument of control for the political activity of their members and it recruits new members at large political demonstrations. In the end, it abandons any interest in economic concerns and puts its primary weapon at the disposal of the political arm: refusal to work, a general mass strike.

Through the formation of trade-unions and a political press, whose content is tailored to the limited intellectual scope of the least-educated people, the political and trade-union organizations have created an instrument they can use to stir up the lowest level of the nation and drive them to commit rash actions. It is the task of the press to cater to the masses' lowest instincts; they make no effort to lead people with positive ideals which might lift their minds above the swamp of their daily lives and lift their spirit to a higher level. This is a gamble which ultimately proves to be successful with the lazy-minded and often self-important masses.

It is this kind of press which attacks anything that might support national independence, cultural values, and economic self-reliance using an absolutely fanatical war of slander. It pounds away with particular hostility at all those honorable characters who will not bend to the Jewish assumption that they should be dominated, or at those whose naturally inspired ability could threaten the Jew. In order to be hated by the Jew, it is not necessary to challenge him. The mere suspicion that a man might someday stumble on the idea of opposition, or because of his superior genius, he might add to the strength and greatness of a nation which the Jew finds hostile, is enough for the Jew to act against him.

The Jew has a reliable instinct in such matters which will always sense the innermost thoughts of those he deals with. His hostility toward anyone who does not share his thoughts, anyone he does not consider a kindred spirit, will flare, and they will be judged as his enemy. Since the Jew is not the victim but the aggressor, he sees his enemy not only in the man who attacks, but also in any man who is capable of resisting him. The methods that he attempts to use to break down such bold, but respectable souls are not the methods one would consider part of honorable battle. His choice of weapons are lying and slander.

The Jew is not frightened by anything and his cruelty becomes enormous. As a result of this, we shouldn't be surprised if our people someday view the personification of the Devil, the symbol of all evil, as the Jew himself. The ignorance of the broad masses when it comes to the inner nature of the Jew, and the blindness and stupidity of our upper classes, makes the people an easy victim of this Jewish campaign of lies. While natural cowardice makes the upper classes turn away from any man the Jew attacks with lies and slander, stupidity or simple-mindedness makes the broad masses believe everything they hear. The State authorities either hide behind a wall of silence or prosecute the victim of an unjust attack just to put an end to the Jewish journalistic campaign, and that is what usually happens. The procedure of quieting down any such trouble, which in the eyes of one of these jackasses-in-office, is supposed to maintain governmental authority and safeguard peace and good order. Gradually the Marxist weapon in the hands of the Jew becomes a constant bogey-man to decent people. Fear looms like a nightmare on the mind and soul of decent people. They begin to tremble in front of the fearful enemy and in that moment they become his doomed victims.

Letter K. The Jew's domination of the State government seems so assured that he can now openly admit his basic racial and political beliefs and publicly call himself as a Jew again. One part of the Jewish race quite openly admits to being an alien people, though not without lying again, even here. When Zionism (*a movement to create an independent Jewish State*) tries to convince the world that the racial self-determination of the Jew would be satisfied with the creation of their own State in Palestine, the Jews are once again craftily pulling the wool over the eyes of the stupid goyim (*Goyim is an offensive Jewish word meaning gentile or a non-Jew, also a reminder to the audience that the Jews had an offensive word for them.*) They never intended to build a Jewish State in Palestine, not for the purpose of living in it anyway. They just want an organization headquarters for their international swindling and cheating with its own political power that is beyond the reach and interference from other states. It would be a refuge for crooks who were exposed and a college for future swindlers.

It is a sign of their growing confidence and security that some proclaim themselves as part of the Jewish race and others are still falsely pretending to be Germans, Frenchmen, or Englishmen. This impudence and the horrible way they engage in relations with the people of other nations makes it obvious that they see victory clearly approaching.

The black-haired Jewish boy waits, with Satanic delight on his face, for the hour when he can corrupt the unsuspecting girl with his blood, and in seducing her, steal her from her people. The Jew will attempt to undermine the racial foundations of the nation to be conquered using every means possible.

The Jew steadily works to ruin women and girls so that he can break down the barriers of blood on an even larger scale. It was the Jews who brought the negro to the Rhine. The motive behind this is clear and his intention is always the same. He wants to destroy the hated white race through bastardization. He continues to bring negroes in as a flood and force the mixing of races. This corruption puts an end to white culture and political distinction and raises the Jew up to be its masters. A racially pure people, which is conscious of its blood, can never be defeated by the Jew. In this world, the Jew can only be the master of bastards. This is why he continually tries to lower the racial quality by poisoning the blood of individuals among the targeted peoples.

The Jew begins to replace the political idea of democracy with that of a dictatorship for the working class. In the organized masses who follow Marxism, the Jew finds he is holding a weapon that allows him to do without democracy and permits him instead to conquer and rule the people through the iron hand of a dictatorship. The Jew works systematically in two directions for the revolution: economically and politically. Any nation that violently resists his internal attack is surrounded by a net of countries which fall more easily. This ring forms a network of enemies around his target and incites the nation into war, and finally, if necessary, when the troops are on the battlefield, he raises the flag of revolution, right when the country is least prepared.

Economically, the Jew shakes the State until its social services begin to sway. They become so costly that they are transferred away from national control and put under his financial control. Politically, he blocks funding and denies the State access to the resources it needs for self-preservation, he destroys the foundations of any national resistance or defense, he destroys faith in the government leadership, he ridicules the nation's history, and he drags everything that is truly great into the gutter.

Culturally, the Jew corrupts art, literature, and theater. He makes fun of national sentiment, upsets all ideas of beauty and nobility and idealism and anything good. He drags people down into the realm of his own lowest nature. Religion is made ridiculous and morals and decency are represented as old and worn out. He continues his attack until the last support on which the national being must rest, which the nation needs if it is to fight for survival in this world, is gone.

Letter L. Now the Jew begins the great and final Revolution. As he battles his final few steps to political power, he tosses aside the few veils he still wears. The democratic Jew, the popular Jew, become the "Bloody Jew", and he reveals himself as a tyrant over the people. Within a very few years, he attempts to eliminate the intelligent classes of the nation, and by robbing the peoples of their natural, intellectual leadership, prepares them for the slave's destiny under his tyrannical dictatorship.

The most horrible example of this tyranny is Russia, where the Jew has killed or starved close to thirty million people, sometimes using inhuman tortures to enforce his savage fanaticism and assure domination over a great people. This is done to satisfy a crowd of Jewish intellects and financier bandits. The end does not mean just the end of the freedom for the people oppressed by the Jew. It also means the end of the Jew himself as these national parasites begin to disappear. After the death of the victim, the leech itself also dies sooner or later.

If we review all the causes of the German collapse, the failure to recognize the race problem and especially the Jewish menace, remains the ultimate and decisive factor. Standing up under the defeats on the battlefield in August of 1918 would have been child's play. They were nothing when compared to the victories of our people in past battles. It wasn't those military defeats that led to our downfall. We were brought down by a power that had been preparing us for decades to suffer these defeats. They systematically robbed our people of the political and moral instincts that allowed us to survive, the very qualities that give a people the right to exist.

By neglecting their responsibility to preserve the racial foundations of our nationality, the old Empire also discarded the only right that can give a people their authority to live in this world. Nations who become mongrels or allow their people to be bastardized, have sinned against the will of Eternal Providence. Their collapse at the hands of a stronger force is not an injustice done to them, instead it is the restoration of justice. If a people no longer respect the qualities given to it by Nature, qualities which are deeply rooted in its blood, it surrenders its right to complain when its earthly existence is at an end.

Every negative event in the world can be turned into a positive one. Every defeat may father a later victory. Every lost war may be the cause of a later resurgence. Every distress may inspire a new surge in man's willpower. A new spiritual rebirth may spring from every oppression, but this can occur only as long as the racial blood is kept pure. The loss of blood purity by itself will forever destroy inner happiness and forever lowers man. The result of impurity can never be eliminated from man's body and spirit.

If we compare all the other problems we face in life against this one question of race, we immediately realize how small those daily problems are. Those problems are all temporary and limited, but the preservation of blood purity continues for as long as there are men on this earth. All the significant symptoms of decay before the war can be traced back to these basic racial causes. Whether the question is one of universal justice, or of a massive wart on economic life, or signs of cultural decline, or indications of political degeneration, or one of defective school teachings, or one of negative influences through the press, there is one truth that is present always and everywhere— the bottom line is that the source of our problems is a neglect of our own people's racial concerns and a failure to see an approaching alien racial threat.

Therefore, all attempts at reform, all social work and political efforts, all economic advancement, and all apparent increases in spiritual knowledge have ultimately failed to produce any results of value. The nation and that being which makes it possible, the State, have failed to build inner strength. They have not grown healthier, but have visibly wasted away from this disease. All the false prosperity of the old Empire could not hide the inner weakness, and every attempt to strengthen the Empire was abruptly halted when this, the most important question, was ignored and set aside.

It would be a mistake to think that all of those who doctored the German political body with various political ideas and their leaders were bad or malicious men by nature. No matter what they did, their work was condemned to fail because, at best, they only saw the symptoms of our general sickness and tried to combat those obvious signs. They then walked blindly past the root cause of this disease. Anyone who has calmly and systematically traced the old Empire's line of political development cannot help but realize that even when the German nation was unified and on the rise, its inner decay was already in full swing. Despite all the political successes that seemed to occur and an increasing economic wealth, the general situation grew worse from year to year. Even the rising tide of Marxist votes at the Reichstag elections foreshadowed the ever-approaching inner and outer collapse. The successes of the middle and upper class political parties meant nothing. This was not only because they could not prevent the numerical growth of the Marxist flood, even when they had so-called victorious middle-upper class elections, but mostly because they already carried the seeds of degeneration within themselves. The upper class world itself had no idea it was infected with the rotting flesh virus of Marxist ideas. The occasional visible resistance to Marxism was usually due to envy and competition between ambitious leaders and not based on principals or beliefs by those determined to fight to the bitter end. One figure alone fought throughout those long years with unshakable perseverance, and this figure was the Jew. The Star of David rose higher as the will for the self-preservation among our people disappeared.

In August of 1914, the battlefield was not stormed by a solid nation with a determined spirit. Only a small glimmer of the nation's self-preservation instinct remained as a result of the Pacifist-Marxist paralysis inflicted on our political body. In those days the enemy within remained unrecognized. This failure to see the inner cause meant all outer resistance was useless. That is why Providence did not deliver a sword of victory as the reward, but instead followed the law of eternal retribution. From this realization came the guiding principles and the tendency of our new Movement. We were convinced that, only by recognizing these truths could we alone stop the decline of the German people, and lay a solid foundation on which a new state may someday exist. A state that will not be part of an alien machine of economic concerns and interests, but a being of the people. A Germanic State in a German nation.

12. EARLY DEVELOPMENT OF THE NATIONAL SOCIALIST GERMAN WORKERS' PARTY.

At the close of this first volume, I want to describe the early development of our movement and briefly discuss a number of the problems we faced. I do not intend to make this a full dissertation on the intellectual aims of the movement. The intent and mission of the new movement is so tremendous that they will have to be discussed in their own volume. In that second volume, I will discuss at length the foundations of the movement's program and attempt to explain what we mean by the word "State".

By "we", I mean all the hundreds of thousands who see the same fundamental goal in their mind's eye, but can't find the perfect words to describe what is in their heart. All great reforms have a unique aspect where, at first, one man steps forward as a champion to represent many millions of supporters. His goal is the same as the heart's desire inside hundreds of thousands of men from centuries before. The world waits until someone finally appears as the herald of the masses to raise the flag of their deepest desire and lead them to victory with a new idea.

Millions have a strong desire in their hearts to see a radical change in the present condition of our nation. This fact is proven when we see the unhappiness suffered by our people. This discontent is expressed in a thousand forms. For one man, it is manifested as discouragement and despair. In another, it appears as disgust, anger, and resentment. Still others may become indifferent as a result of their profound discontent or their feelings may be expressed as violent wrath. We can see even more of this inner discontent in the people who have become election-weary and have quit dropping their ballot altogether, while others may seek refuge in fanatical left-wing extremes. Our young movement will appeal to all of these. Our aim was not to be an organization of the contented, satisfied and well-fed, but instead to unite the suffering and the discontented, the unhappy, and the dissatisfied, those who could not find peace. Above all, our organization must not float on the surface of the political body, but must have its roots in the foundation of the people.

Taken purely from a political standpoint, the nation had been torn in half by 1918. One half, which was by far the smallest, includes the classes of the intellectuals and nobles. This class excludes all those who do physical labor. It is outwardly a nationalist group, but they cannot understand the meaning of nationalism except as a very flat and feeble method to defend so-called State interests. These interests seem to be identical with the interests of the Monarchy. This class tries to defend its ideas and aims with intellectual weapons that are both incomplete and shallow with only a superficial effect. Such weapons proved to be a complete failure when pitted against the enemy's brutality. With one violent blow, the ruling class of intellectuals was now struck down. Trembling in cowardice, it swallowed every humiliation from the cruel victor.

The second class is the great mass of the workers united in, more or less, radically Marxist movements. These movements are determined to break down any intellectual resistance using brute force. The Marxist movement does not have any intention of being nationalist, but deliberately opposes any advancement of national interests, and equally supports all foreign oppression. This group is the largest in number and strength. It, most importantly, includes those elements of the nation required for a national revival. Without them, a revival is unthinkable and even impossible.

By 1918, it was obvious that any recovery of the German people could only be possible by restoring the nation's strength and then regaining outside power. This does not require arms as our leader class of "Statesmen" keep babbling, but strength of will. At one time the German people had more than enough weaponry. Those tools were not enough to protect our freedom because the national instinct for self-preservation and the will to survive were missing. The best weapon is a useless, lifeless clump if there is no spirit ready, willing and determined to make use of it. Germany became defenseless because the will to preserve the people's survival was absent and not because they lacked the weapons.

Today, when our left-wing politicians, in particular, try to point to disarmament as the unavoidable cause of their cowardly, weak-willed, submissive, or more accurately traitorous foreign policy, there is only one answer to their claim: No. The truth is the other way around. Your anti-national, criminal policy of surrendering national interests, was the reason you delivered up our arms. Now, you try to claim that a lack of arms is the reason why you behaved like disgraceful wretches. This, like everything else you do, is a lie and a bogus claim.

This reproach must fall equally on the politicians of the Right. Thanks to their miserable cowardice, the Jewish gang that came into power in 1918 could steal the nation's arms. They have no reason or right to refer to the present disarmament as the reason they are forced to exercise wise caution, which is pronounced "cowardice", when dealing with foreign policy matters. The nation's defenselessness is the result of their cowardice.

The question of regaining German power is not "How do we manufacture arms?" the real question is, "How are we to produce the spirit that enables our people to bear arms?" When a strong will rules the spirit of the people, they will find a thousand ways, each of which ends with a weapon. Give a coward ten pistols and, in an attack, he will still be unable to fire a single shot. A wooden stick in the hands of a courageous man is worth more than ten pistols in a coward's hands.

Regaining our people's political power is mainly a matter of recovering our instinct for national self-preservation. If for no other reason, this instinct is necessary because, as shown by experience, any foreign policy decisions of the state are guided less by the armaments on hand, and more by the real or supposed moral strength of a nation. A nation's value in an alliance is determined by the existence of an intense national will to survive and a heroic courage in the face of death, not by lifeless piles of armaments. An alliance is not made between arms, but between men.

The British will be the most valuable ally in the world as long as its leadership and the spirit of the great masses permit the brutality and determination needed to fight a battle once it has begun, all the way through, to a victorious end, and using every means available, with completely reckless disregard for the length of a commitment or the great sacrifices required. As long as this spirit stands strong, then the actual military armament available can be completely inadequate when compared to that of other nations and it will not matter.

If we realize that the restoration of Germany is a matter of regaining our political will for self-preservation, then it is also clear that this can only be accomplished by converting those who are deliberately anti-national into nationalist masses and not by winning over elements which are already nationalists.

As a young movement whose goal is the resurrection of a sovereign German State, we will have to direct our battle totally toward winning the great masses. Our so-called "nationalist leading class" is so pitiful in general and even though its nationalist spirit may seem inadequate, there is no reason to expect serious resistance to a strong nationalist domestic and foreign policy from them. Even if the German privileged-class, for narrow-minded and short-sighted reasons, should persist in passive resistance, as it did toward Chancellor Bismarck when the hour of deliverance was at hand, we still have no reason to fear an active resistance because they are admitted and notorious cowards.

The situation is different with the masses of our international finance-minded fellow Germans. Not only does their more primitive roughness naturally draw them toward violence, but their Jewish leadership is more brutal and ruthless, which means they would not hesitate to use violence. They will strike down any German revival just as they broke the backbone of the German army. They will not only do all they can to block any national foreign policy, thanks to their large numbers in this State of parliamentary government, but they will block any effort to regain German strength and with it any possibility of beneficial alliances. We are not the only ones who recognize that our fifteen million Marxists, Democrats, Pacifists, and Centrists, are a weakness. This same obstacle is seen even more by foreign countries, who measure of the value of a possible alliance with us according to the weight of this handicap. No one is going to ally himself with a state in which the active part of its population is, at the very least, passively against any decisive foreign policy.

We must also face the fact that an instinct of self-preservation will make the leadership of these parties of national treason hostile toward any solution; otherwise they would lose their current positions. A short look into history makes it simply unthinkable that the German people could ever regain the nation's status without holding those who were responsible for the collapse of our State accountable for their actions. When future generations sit in judgment, November of 1918 will not be seen as mere rebellion, but as high treason against the nation. Any recovery of German sovereignty and political independence is linked to our people's ability to recover their unified will.

Even from a purely technical standpoint, the idea of a German liberation from outside control is obviously nonsense until the great masses are also ready to support this idea of freedom. From a purely military point of view, it must be clear, especially to any officer who gives it a little thought, that we cannot carry on a foreign battle with student battalions. We need the strength and might as well as the brains of the people. We must also keep in mind that any national defense built solely on intellectual ranks is a waste of an irreplaceable treasure. The young German intellectuals who joined the volunteer regiments and met their deaths in the fall of 1914 on the plains of Flanders were missed deeply later. They were the dearest treasure the nation had and their loss was never made good during the war.

The battle itself cannot be fought unless the working masses are part of the storm battalions. The technical preparation is also impossible to carry out without the inner unity of will in the nation itself. Our people, in particular, are living without a true military, completely disarmed, under the thousand eyes of the Versailles Peace

Treaty. The nation cannot make any practical preparations to win its freedom and human independence unless the army of spies on the inside is cut down to the nub. Only those whose native lack of character allows them to betray anything and everything for the proverbial thirty pieces of silver will remain. Those people can be taken care of; however, there are millions who oppose the national recovery based on their political convictions. Those people are not so easily overcome. They cannot be defeated until the cause of their opposition, the international Marxist World-Concept, is combated and its teachings are torn from their hearts and minds.

From any standpoint where we examine the possibility of recovering our independence as a state and a people or from the standpoint of establishing foreign policy as an equal state among states, technical armament, or the struggle itself, the one indispensable element we need is to win over the broad masses of our people to the idea of national independence.

If we do not regain our freedom from the clutches of other nations, we cannot hope to gain anything from inner reforms. Any changes that do occur will only make us more profitable as a colony to our occupiers. The surplus from any so-called economic improvement will go into the pocket of our international masters, and any social improvement will increase our productivity, which in turn benefits only them. Cultural progress will not be the fortune of the German nation at all. Progress depends too much on the political independence and dignity of a nation.

We can only obtain a satisfactory solution for the problem of Germany's future by winning over the broad masses of our people so they support a national idea. Therefore, the work of educating the masses must be considered our top priority. This priority must be pursued by a movement which is not out to meet the needs of the movement itself but is forced to consider the consequences of what it does, or does not do, based on what the future result will be.

We realized as early as 1919 that the new movement's highest aim must be the nationalization of the masses. From that tactical point of view, a series of requirements resulted:

1. No social sacrifice would be considered too great if it meant winning the masses to our side for a national revival. No matter what economic concessions are made to our wage earners today, they cannot compare to the ultimate gain for the whole nation if they help bring back the common people to their nationality. Only narrow-minded, short-sighted people, like those found all too often among our employers, can fail to realize that in the long run, there can be no economic improvement for

them and no further economic profit if the inward solidarity of our nation is not restored.

If during the war, the German trade-unions had ruthlessly protected the interests of the workers, the war would not have been lost. Even if during the war, they had fought the money-hungry employers for the demands of the workers they represented by constant strikes, the war still would not have been lost. At least this would be true, and the war would not have been lost. If they had been as fanatical in their German nationality toward the nation's defense and had equal ruthlessness for the Fatherland and given what is due the Fatherland, then the war would not have been lost. How trivial even the greatest economic concession would have been when compared to the enormous significance of winning the war!

A movement that intends to restore the German worker to the German people must realize that economic sacrifices are no consideration at all as long as they do not threaten the independence of the national economy.

2. The national education of the broad masses can only take place through social improvement. This alone will create the general economic conditions that allow the individual to share in the cultural treasures of the nation.

3. The nationalization of the broad masses can never be accomplished by half-way measures or by weakly arguing the so-called objective merits of your position. It can only happen by ruthlessly and fanatically concentrating on achieving a one-sided goal. A people cannot be made "nationalist" in the sense of our modern upper and privileged-class; their arguments have too many limitations and reservations. The people can only be made truly nationalistic with the intensity that comes from taking an extreme position. Poison is driven out only by counter-poison and only the shallowness of the privileged leader-class spirit could ever think the middle road is the path to Heaven; the Kingdom of Heaven is not obtained by compromise.

The broad masses of a people do not consist of professors or diplomats. Their weak ability to understand abstract ideas makes them driven by the world of emotion rather than intellect. Their attitudes are formed by emotional impulses and can be positive or negative. Their opinions will only be swayed by those extremes and never by a half-way idea floating between the two. This emotional basis for their attitude also brings with it extraordinary stability. It is always harder to battle against Faith than to battle knowledge. Love is less susceptible to change than esteem. Hatred is more long lasting than mere dislike. The driving force behind the most tremendous turnovers on this earth has never resulted from an intellectual insight directing the masses, but instead from a fanaticism dominating them and hysteria hurling them onward. He who wishes to win the broad masses must understand that the key to the gates of their hearts is not objectivity, which is nothing more than weakness, but a determined and strong will.

4. The soul of the masses can be won only if those who lead the movement are determined not merely to carry through the side of our struggle for the good just to achieve their own aims, but they must also be absolutely determined to destroy the enemy that opposes them. When the people see brutal and unceasing attacks upon an opponent, they also see the truth behind their own just cause. If the attack fails to destroy the enemy, if the battle is ended early, before the aggressor has completely dominated the enemy, the people will see uncertainty in their own cause; they will see this incomplete vanquishing as a sign that their side may in fact be unjust.

The great masses are themselves part of Nature and therefore subject to her passions. Their feelings do not allow them to understand how a handshake can be made between men who have declared themselves as enemies. What they want is absolute victory. They demand to see the stronger raise the banner of the conqueror and the complete extinction of the weaker or his unconditional surrender to the dominance of the superior. The nationalization of our masses and the struggle to save the soul of our people will only succeed if the international poison spread among them is exterminated.

5. All the great problems we face today are short-term difficulties that result from simple origins which have clear and definite causes. But among them all, there is only one with truly great importance. It is the problem of preserving the nation's race. The strength or weakness of man is deeply rooted and dependent on his purity of blood. Nations that do not recognize and respect the importance of their racial stock are like men who foolishly try to train a poodle to be a greyhound. Such a man fails to understand that the speed of the greyhound and the intelligence of the poodle are not qualities that can be taught, but they are qualities which are inherent in race. A nation that fails to preserve their racial purity also sacrifices the unity of their soul in every way. The disunity of their nature is the inevitable result of the disunity of their blood. The change in their intellectual and creative force is similarly the result of the change in their racial foundations. The man who would free the German people from those bad characteristics, characteristics which are not part of its natural makeup and come from foreign sources, that man must first release the nation from the origin of these foreign characteristics. Until we clearly recognize and accept the race problem and the Jewish problem, the German nation can never rise again. The race question is the key to world history and to all human civilization.

6. Assigning the great mass of people who are now in the internationalist camp to their proper place in a national community does not mean that we will sacrifice the protection of their class interests; we will not abandon the worker. Differing interests among labor and trade groups are not the same as class division, but these differences are natural consequences of our economic life. The grouping together of trade members and workers does not interfere with the concept of a true national community. A national unity is one that unifies all problems concerning the life of the nation so that no one is left out.

In order to bring into the national community or into the State one of the new trade or worker classes means we must not lower our current upper classes, but instead must raise the lower classes to a higher level. The higher class can never be the one who starts this process. It must be the lower class who is fighting for equal rights. The present privileged-class did not gain their position within the State by legislation or action of the aristocracy. They achieved their position through their own energy under their own leadership.

A movement cannot help the German worker take his place among the German community if that movement depends on weak displays of brotherhood, with everyone patting each other on the back as they talk about the problems of society before ending their meeting with a handshake. No, the movement must deliberately improve the workers' social and cultural position, and this active role must continue until the greatest and most difficult to bridge differences can be considered overcome. A movement which has this kind of positive development as its aim will have to gain its supporters primarily from the workers' camp. It can recruit the intellectual only if that person completely understands the goal the movement is working toward. This transformation process will not be finished in ten or twenty years. Experience shows that it will take many generations.

The obstacle that prevents today's worker from taking his place in the national community is not his worker interests, but rather the obstruction comes from his international leadership and his attitude which is hostile to the people and the Fatherland. If the very same trade unions had a leader who was fanatically nationalist in political concerns, that leader would turn millions of workers into precious members of their nationality. This would happen regardless of individual battles over purely economic concerns.

A movement that aims to restore the German worker to his people in an honorable way, and to relieve him from the internationalist madness his head has been filled with, must make a forceful stand against a certain common attitude in business circles. This attitude preaches that national community means a complete surrender, without resistance, of all economic rights of the wage-earner to the employer. This belief furthermore claims every attempt by the workers to defend themselves, even when it comes to rightful and necessary economic interests of the wage-earner, are attacks on the national community. Those who uphold this attitude are deliberate liars. In a community, all obligations for one side must be equally subject to the other side.

If a worker sins against the spirit of a real national community by making excessive and unreasonable demands or makes demands without considering their effect on the common welfare and the survival of a national economy, that worker has acted against the national community. And so does the employer who relies on his power to violate this community. If he misuses the national labor power by exploitation, and inhumanely treats workers under his management, and through these unjust actions makes millions by profiteering on the sweat of others, then he has no right to call himself a nationalist and no right to speak of a national community. He is a rogue who pursues his own self interests and by introducing social discontent, he provokes later struggles that will hurt the nation one way or another.

The young movement must draw its supporters mainly from the reservoir of the masses, of our wage-earners. We must snatch them from their internationalist madness, relieve their social distress, lift them above cultural misery, and lead them into the national community as a united, useful element, who are nationalist in feeling and intent.

If we find in the circles of the nation's intellectuals that there are men with a warm heart for their people and its future, who realize deeply how important the struggle for the soul of the masses is, then they will be welcomed in the ranks of the movement as a valuable intellectual backbone. But winning the privileged-class, voting cattle, must never be the movement's aim. If we targeted the intellectual set, we would be burdening ourselves with a group whose existing thought process and nature would paralyze our efforts to recruit among the common people. The idea of uniting the great masses, both the upper and lower classes, within the movement has a certain theoretical beauty; however, it is also an obstacle. We must face the fact that the ability to influence the minds of those who already have a certain spirit and to spread our message among the privileged-class masses at public demonstrations can gain some recruits, but no amount of discussion or influence can change certain qualities or vices of their character, attributes which have been around for centuries, and make those undesirable qualities disappear from this privileged-class group. Differences in cultural levels between the privileged-class and working class, as well as differences in their attitudes toward economic questions are still so great, that the moment the excitement of the demonstration had died out, their presence and nature would immediately become an obstacle to the movement.

Finally, the purpose of the Movement is not to produce a new set of levels within the existing group of nationalists, but to win over those who are anti-national. It is this perspective and strategy that will guide the whole movement.

7. This one-sided, but clear attitude must also be expressed in the movement's propaganda.

If the movement's propaganda is to be effective, it must aim in one direction only, that is to say at one class only. If it attempts to aim at both upper and worker classes, the difference in their intellectual preparation, their educational background, would either prevent the message from being understood by one side, or be rejected because it appears to simply state obvious and uninteresting truths by the other class.

Even the wording and the tone could never be equally effective on two classes which are so noticeably different. If the propaganda sacrifices primitive words and sharp expressions, the broad masses will not connect with the message. But if the propaganda includes straightforward statements that appeal to the masses' feelings and uses expressions they commonly use, the intellectuals will object and declare it to be coarse and vulgar. Among a hundred public speakers, there wouldn't even be ten who can speak with equal effect in front of an audience of street-cleaners, mechanics, and sewer workers today and tomorrow, give a lecture with the same intellectual substance in front of an auditorium of college professors and students. In a thousand speakers, there may be one who can address mechanics and college professors at the same time, and in a style that not only speaks on both their levels, but can influence both of them equally, or possibly even captivate them so strongly that the result is a roaring storm of applause. We must never forget that the greatest idea which embodies a noble spirit and supreme worth can only be circulated to the public through the smallest of minds. The most important point is not what the inspired vision of the creator of an idea was when he set out to spread his message, but what the announcement of this idea to the masses translated into, how those who spread the message shape its meaning and how successful they are in leading the masses to accept the idea.

The ability of the Social Democracy movement, and the whole Marxist movement, to attract followers depended on the unity and the one-sidedness of the public it targeted. The more limited and narrow their argument's line of thought was, the more easily it was accepted and digested by masses whose intellectual ability was on the same level with what they were told.

As a result of this knowledge, our new Movement laid down a clear and simple guideline. The theme and form of the propaganda used to promote our message is to be aimed at the broad masses exclusively and the quality of propaganda can only be measured by its success.

The best speaker at a popular meeting of the common people is the one who captures the heart of the masses and not the one who is able to harmonize with the spirit of the intellectuals who attend. If an intellectual attends this kind of meeting and complains about the low-brow level of the speech, even though he can clearly see the lower class has been rallied and moved by the speech, it proves that he is incapable of thinking and worthless to the young movement. The only intellectual who is valuable to the movement is the one who understands the mission and purpose so completely that he has learned to judge the work of propaganda totally by its success and not by the impression it makes on him personally. The purpose of propaganda is to completely win over those who are against nationalism and not to entertain intellectuals who are already nationally-minded.

In general, those lines of thought which I briefly summed up in the "War Propaganda" chapter should be considered critical guiding rules for the young movement. These concepts proved to be of great value when deciding on the type of propaganda and how it would be distributed to best accomplish its work of enlightenment. Success has proved these methods to be sound.

8. The aim of a political reform movement can never be attained by explaining their views to the public or by influencing the ruling powers. A movement can only obtain political reform by taking political power into its own hands. Every idea that is meant to shake the world has the right and duty to secure the means necessary to carry out its aims, and it must continue until they are accomplished. Success is the only earthly judge of right and wrong in such an undertaking. Success does not mean, as in 1918, the victory of gaining power in itself. True success must be for the benefit of a nation. It must serve the common interests of the people. Therefore, a coup d'état cannot be considered successful, although thoughtless State's Attorneys in Germany today believe it should, merely because the revolutionaries have succeeded in seizing governmental power. It is only successful when the basic purposes and goals of the revolutionary action prove they can do the nation more good than the previous regime did when they have been placed in practice. This is something which cannot be claimed by the German Revolution, as that bandit raid in the fall of 1918 called itself.

If the conquest of political power is what is required to accomplish the movement's goals and reform the state, then the movement must consider from the very beginning that it is a movement of the masses, and that it is not assembled for a tea party or a bowling game.

9. The young movement is by nature and inner organization anti-parliamentarian. That means that both in general beliefs and in its own inner structure, it is against majority rule where the leader is only a figurehead and a puppet-executor of the will and opinion of others. When dealing with the smallest and greatest problems, the movement upholds the principle of absolute authority for the leader, who also carries the highest degree of responsibility.

Here is how the results of this principal are applied in the Movement:

The chairman of a local group is appointed by the next higher leader. He is the director of the local group and responsible for them. All the committees in the local group are under his authority-- he is not under their authority. There are no voting committees, but only working committees. The director is the chairman over the committees and he divides up the work for them. The same principle holds true for the next superior organizational level above, the district, the county, or the city. The leader is always appointed from above and endowed with absolute power and authority. Only the leader of the entire party is elected by the general assembly for the purpose of organization law. He is the exclusive leader of the movement. All the committees are under his authority; he is not under the authority of any committee. He dictates and bears the responsibility on his shoulders. The followers of the movement are free to hold him accountable before a new election and to relieve him of his office if he has not upheld the principles of the movement or has not served its interests. He is then replaced by the new and more able man, who has the same authority and the same responsibility.

One of the most important tasks of the movement is to put this principle in force, not just within its own ranks, but throughout the entire State. The man who would be leader has supreme and unlimited authority but also carries the final and greatest responsibility. A man who is incapable of this kind of responsibility or who is too cowardly to face the results of his action is worthless as a leader. Only a man of heroic quality has the true talent for leadership.

The progress and civilization of mankind are not products of the majority, but they depend totally on the inspiration and strength of a single personality. To encourage and promote this progress is one of the essentials for regaining the greatness and power of our nationality.

Because of our principles we must be anti-parliamentary and any participation in a legislative organization can only be for the purpose of ultimately destroying it from within and thereby eliminate an institution where we see one of the most serious symptoms of mankind's decay.

10. The movement definitely refuses to take a stand on questions that are outside the limits of its political work or immaterial to its aims because they are of no importance in achieving our principle goals. The movement's job is not religious reformation but a political reorganization of our people. It considers both religious denominations to be equally valuable and acknowledges that they provide vital support for the existence of our people. Therefore, the movement will attack those parties that try to degrade this foundation by turning religious institutions into a tool for their own party interests. Those institutions provide our political body with religious and moral support.

Finally, the movement's job is to create the foundations which are necessary for any republic or any Monarchy to survive. Our job is not the restoration of one particular form of government or the destruction of another form. The movement's mission is not to found a Monarchy or to strengthen a republic, but to create a Germanic State. The question of what form a State government should take is not important in principle, the form is merely chosen based on whatever type is the most practical and useful.

Once the people realize the great problems and duties of its existence, they will be able to work together as a State and the question of outward formalities, such as governmental structures, can no longer lead to inner struggles, so such matters can be easily worked out.

11. The movement's inner organization is about convenience, not principle.

The best organization is the one that places the fewest middle men between the leadership of a movement and its individual supporters. The job of an organization is to communicate a specific idea that has originated in the mind of an individual to a large group of people and to supervise how that idea is transformed into reality. The organization structure itself is just a necessary evil. At best, it is a means to an end; at worst, it becomes an end in itself.

Because the world produces more mechanical beings than it produces intelligent minds with ideal natures, the forms that an organization can take are more easily constructed than the ideas themselves. It is easier to build the structure itself than it is to build its substance of ideas which the structure is built to support.

The path of every idea that strives to be fulfilled, especially one that involves major reforms of an existing system, is outlined as follows: It begins when some inspired idea springs from the brain of a man who feels he is called upon to share his insight with the rest of mankind. He preaches his views and gradually wins a certain circle of supporters. This process of direct and personal communication of a man's ideas to the world around him is the most natural and by far the most ideal method. As the number of followers increases, it becomes impossible for the founder of the original idea to carry on directly with the innumerable followers while trying to both lead them as a leader and guide them in the doctrine. When the group grows to a point where it can no longer support one-on-one interaction, an organizational structure is required. The ideal condition comes to an end and in its place we have the necessary evil of organization. Small sub-units are formed by the creation of local groups of members, for instance, and these represent the nuclei for the growth of the political movement's later organization.

However, if the unity of the doctrine is to be maintained, sub-groups cannot be created until the authority of the intellectual founder and his beliefs are accepted absolutely and completely. The next requirement is a centrally-located headquarters and its importance for a movement cannot be over-estimated. The location should be chosen such that it is surrounded by the magic spell of a Mecca or a Rome. This place can give a movement a particular strength that only comes from inner unity because it provides recognition that there is one creator and leader who represents this unity.

In forming the first nuclei of the organization, it is critical to maintain the importance of the place where the idea originated. This place must be preserved and the importance must continue to ramp up until it is paramount to the movement. This growth of the theoretical, moral, and actual dominance of the place where the movement began must occur at the same rate that new nuclei-groups are added and as they, in turn, demand new interconnections between their cells. The increasing number of individual followers make it impossible to continue direct dealings with them and that lead us to the formation of our lowest level groupings. Eventually the number of followers will increase dramatically, and the lowest form of organization will grow which forces us to establish higher units, which may be politically described as an area or district division.

It may be easy to maintain authority of the original headquarters over the lowest local groups, but it will be very difficult to preserve this position when the organization becomes more developed and has various levels of upper management. However, maintaining the authority of the original headquarters is the first essential for a unified movement. Without a unified movement, the continuation of the organization and the ultimate accomplishment of the idea becomes impossible. When these larger middle management groups must be united into still larger and higher units in the organization, maintaining the absolute supremacy of the original place of foundation, its school of teachings, etc., above them becomes more and more difficult.

Consequently, the mechanical shape an organization takes must not be expanded beyond the point where the spiritual authority of headquarters is guaranteed. With such political entities, this guarantee can only be given through strength of force.

From this, we established the following guidelines for the movement's inner structure:

A. Initially, we must concentrate all work in a central location, in one single city, this will be Munich. We must train a group of followers who are absolutely reliable and, with them, develop a school we can use to circulate the movement's doctrine. In order to gain authority which will be needed later, it is essential that we secure the greatest possible number of visible successes in this one city. Such prestige will be beneficial for subsequent expansion. In order to make the movement and leaders well known, it is necessary not only to publicly shake the faith in the invincibility of the Marxist doctrine, but to prove that a contrary doctrine is possible.

B. Local groups can be formed only after the authority of the central management in Munich is absolutely recognized and acknowledged.

C. Establishing district, area, or national groups is to take place only when needed, and then only after the absolute recognition of headquarters as the seat of authority has been achieved. Also, the creation of subordinate cells depends on the availability of possible leaders who are qualified to lead the cells.

Here there are two solutions:

1. The movement must acquire the necessary funds to train capable minds who can become leaders. It then becomes possible to systematically use these resources in whatever manner they are needed. This method is easier and quicker, but it requires much greater financial resources. These leaders, who are trained, can only work full-time for the movement if they are paid a salary.

2. Because of the financial limitations of a young movement, it is not in a position to employ such leaders. Instead it must initially rely on those who will serve on an honorary basis. This method is slower and more difficult.

Under these particular limitations, the movement's leadership must let large districts remain fallow and inactive if a man does not emerge from among its followers who is able and willing to put himself at the disposal of the central authority and to organize and lead the movement in that particular district.

There may be some regions where no leader steps forward at all. Other regions may have two or three potential leaders who are equally qualified. This unequal distribution of potential leadership is frustrating and it will take years to overcome. The essential element for the creation of any cell organization is always finding a leader who is able to lead it. All the military companies of an army are worthless without officers. In the same manner, a political organization is equally worthless without the appropriate leader. It is better for the movement not to form a local group than to allow it to be created and then fail because a guiding and forceful leader's personality was missing.

The desire to be a leader is not an adequate qualification. A leader must have ability. Energy and a strong will are more important than intellectual genius. A combination of ability, determination, and perseverance is the most valuable of all.

12. The future of a movement depends on the devotion, or more correctly, the intolerance for other beliefs that its followers exhibit in defense of it as the only true cause. They must be convinced and enforce the belief that their own cause, as opposed to other similar causes, is the only just cause.

It is a huge mistake to believe that the strength of a movement can be increased by uniting with another similar movement. Growth by merger means an immediate increase in numbers which appears to outside observers that the organization has increased in power and resources. In truth, the organization has simply absorbed germs which will be a source of inner weakness and this will cause suffering later on. No matter what anyone says about the similarity of two movements, such closeness never really exists. If they were truly so similar, there would be only one movement and not two. It doesn't matter where the differences are. Even if the difference is in the inconsistent abilities of the leadership alone, then we have found the difference. The natural law of all development never accepts the joining of two unequal beings. True joining only occurs when the stronger gains victory over the weaker. When this natural selection happens, the strength and energy of the victor is increased by the struggle itself.

Uniting two similar political party structures may produce momentary advantages, but in the long run, any success gained in this way will cause inner weaknesses to appear later. The greatness of a movement is only guaranteed by the unhampered development of its inner strength, the protection of that strength, and the constant increase of that strength until it achieves final victory over all rivals. More than that, we may say that a movement's strength and its right to exist increases only when it recognizes that adherence to the principle that struggle is necessary for growth and that it will only reach the peak of its strength when complete victory is finally achieved. The movement can never attempt to accomplish this victory through instant or short term gains, but only through perseverance and absolute intolerance of any opposition. Only in this way will the movement enjoy a long stretch of growth.

Movements which have expanded from the union of similar organizations, where each made compromises to achieve the joining, are like plants grown in a hot-house. They shoot up quickly, but they lack internal strength and are not substantial enough to stand the test of time or to resist violent storms. The greatness of any powerful organization, which embodies an idea in this world, depends on the absolutely religious fanaticism with which it establishes itself when compared to others. It must be fanatically convinced that it is right and just, and it must be absolutely intolerant of any idea or organization that is counter to its own teaching. If an idea is right and it takes up the sword of battle with this mind-set, it is invincible and any persecution only strengthens it.

The greatness of Christianity was not established through compromise. They had no reason to engage in negotiations of appeasement with those who had roughly similar, ancient philosophical opinions. It was created through unyielding and fanatical declaration and defense of its own teachings.

The apparent head-start that movements gain by uniting with similar movements is more than offset by the steady increase of strength that occurs when a doctrine and its organization remain independent and fight for themselves.

13. As a matter of principle, the movement must train its members to regard struggle as something that they are actually striving for and not as something casually to engage in out of necessity. They must not fear the hostility their enemy directs towards them, but must regard it as the justification for their own right to exist. They must not try to avoid the hatred of the enemies to our nationality and our philosophy, but they should embrace that hatred.

Enemies will use lying and slander as expressions of their own uneasy frustration. Anyone who is not attacked, lied about, and slandered in the Jewish newspapers is no decent German and no true National Socialist. The best measuring stick for the value of a man's principles, the honesty of his convictions, and the strength of his determination is how much deadly venom his name arouses from the enemy who hates him deeply.

Followers of the movement, and in a broader sense all of the people, must be reminded again and again that in his newspapers, the Jew always lies. Even an occasional truth is only intended to cover a bigger lie; therefore, even a truth becomes a deliberate untruth. The Jew is the "Great Master of Lies" and he uses his weapons of lying and deceit in battle.

Every Jewish slander and every Jewish lie is a scar of honor on the body of our warriors. The man they insult the most is closest to us in spirit and the man they have a mortal hatred for is our best friend.

Any one of our followers who picks up the Jewish newspaper in the morning and does not see himself slandered in it, has accomplished nothing the previous day. If he had served any purpose, he would be persecuted, insulted, slandered, abused, and attacked by the Jew. Only the man who effectively opposes this deadly enemy of our nationality and who is also an enemy of all Aryan humanity and civilization can expect to find the slanders of the Jewish race and the war of these people pointed at him.

When these principles become second nature to our followers, the movement will be unshakable and invincible.

14. The movement must encourage respect for individual personalities using every means possible. The movement must never forget that all human values are based on personal values. Every idea and every achievement is the result of the creative power of one man, but the public's admiration for great men is not only a tribute of gratitude to that man, that same reverence is the factor that binds them together into one group with a strong unifying bond.

Individuality is irreplaceable, particularly if that individual possesses the vital cultural and creative elements and not the purely mechanical elements where a man goes through the motions as if he were a puppet.

No student can replace a master painter and successfully complete his half-finished painting. Neither can the great poet and thinker, the great statesman, or the great general be replaced by another. Their activity is an art in itself. What they accomplish cannot be taught mechanically, but such talent is inborn and a gift of Divine grace. The world's greatest revolutions and achievements, its greatest cultural accomplishments and immortal deeds in the field of statesmanship are all forever linked and inseparable from the name that history has chosen to represent each achievement. If we do not give proper respect and reverence to one of those great spirits, then we lose the great source of strength that emerges from speaking the names of any and all great men and women.

The Jew knows this better than anyone. Those they call great men are only great at destroying humanity and its civilization, but the Jew is careful to make certain those figures continue to be admired and idolized. Yet, when any other group of people shows reverence for those of their own who have outstanding minds or made fantastic accomplishments, the Jew tries to represent those great souls as unworthy and brands such reverence as a "cult of personality". (*A cult of personality occurs when the state uses the press to create a heroic image; it can also be called manufactured hero worship.*)

When a people become cowards and yield to such Jewish claims and disrespect, they surrender the mightiest force for inner strength they possess. This force is founded in reverence for genius, and it comes from teaching and adoration of these men as examples of what we can be. Such reverence does not come from dictating to the masses whom they should adore.

When human hearts break and human souls fall into despair, they find a great conqueror of distress, of shame and misery, of intellectual bondage and physical force who looks upon them from the twilight of the past and extends their eternal hands to encourage men of despair. Woe to the people who are ashamed to grasp those hands!

In the early days, when our movement was emerging, we suffered the most from insignificance. Our names were unknown. We began to doubt the chances of our success because of our obscurity. The hardest thing was at the beginning, when there were sometimes only six, seven, or eight who met to listen to the speaker. Back then, it was difficult to awaken and maintain a faith in the tremendous future of the movement within this tiny circle.

There were only six or seven men and they were all poor, nameless devils who were joining together with the intent of forming a movement. Someday, this movement must succeed where the great and powerful mass parties had failed. They must resurrect a German Empire with even greater might and magnificence. At that time, if we had been attacked or even just laughed at, we would have been happy. The most depressing fact was the complete indifference we encountered. This was what weighed on my mind the most at that time.

When I entered the circle of a handful of men, there was neither a party nor a movement to speak of. I have already described my first impressions of this little group. In the weeks that followed, I had the time and opportunity to study the appearance of this so-called Party, although, at this point, there was nothing to see. Heaven knows the picture was uncomfortably distressing. There was simply nothing there. Absolutely nothing whatsoever. There was the name of the party and the leading committee which consisted of all of the party members. This felt like the very thing we wanted to combat, a miniature parliament. Here too, as in parliament, voting was the course to reaching a decision. While the big parliaments shouted until they were hoarse for months, at least they argued about large problems. In this little circle, even the reply to a letter received great attention and such a wonderful event, as having someone write to the party would initiate endless dialogue.

The public knew absolutely nothing of all this. Not a soul in Munich knew the Party even by name, except for its handful of followers and their new acquaintances.

Every Wednesday, there was a committee meeting in a Munich café, and then once a week there was an evening where the group listened to a speaker. Since the entire membership of the "movement" was represented in the committee, the same people naturally showed up at both meetings. What we had to do was finally break out of the little circle, gain new followers, and above all, make the movement's name known at all costs.

We used the following technique to accomplish this: We decided to hold monthly meetings for the public. Later, we began meeting every two weeks. The invitations were written on a typewriter or some were even written by hand. We distributed or delivered them ourselves the first few times. Each of us contacted his circle of acquaintances and tried to persuade some of them to visit one of these meetings. The result was pitiful.

I can still remember how once, during those early days, I had delivered close to eighty invitations and, that evening, we waited expectantly for the crowd of people to come. After waiting for an hour after our regular starting time, the chairman finally opened the meeting. There were seven of us, the same old seven.

We began having the invitations typed and duplicated at a Munich stationary shop. The result was that at the next meeting there were a few more listeners. The number gradually rose from eleven to thirteen, to seventeen, to twenty-three, to thirty-four listeners. By taking up little collections among us poor devils, we were able to raise enough money to publish an advertisement about the meeting in the Munich Observer, which was still an independent newspaper. The result this time was astonishing. We had arranged to hold the meeting in the Munich Hofbräu house cellar, not to be confused with the Munich Hofbräuhaus Banquet Hall, which was a small hall with a capacity of barely a hundred and thirty persons. To me, the room seemed like a huge auditorium and all of us were afraid the great building would have noticeable gaps in the crowd that night. At seven o'clock, there were a hundred and eleven persons in attendance and the meeting was opened.

A Munich professor delivered the main address, and I, as second on the program, was to make my first public speech. To Mr. Harrer, chairman of the party at that time, having me speak seemed very risky. This gentleman, otherwise a good gentleman beyond any doubt, was convinced that I might be able to do a lot of things, but speaking was not one of them. Afterwards, he was still of the same opinion.

The matter of my speaking ability turned out quite differently, however. This was my first time to speak in public and I was allowed twenty minutes to speak. I spoke for thirty minutes. This event proved what I had felt all along: I could speak. At the end of thirty minutes, the people in the little room were electrified. The first expression of their enthusiasm was demonstrated following my appeal for the self-denial of those present. That appeal resulted in the contribution of three hundred marks. This was a great relief. At that time, our finances were so strained that we could not even afford to have the doctrine of the movement printed, let alone distribute leaflets. Now we had a small fund that could finance the most urgent and necessary expenses. The success of this first and largest public meeting was important in another way too.

I began adding some fresh and younger members to the committee's strength. During my years of military service, I had met a large number of faithful friends who slowly began to enter the movement in response to my urging. They were all energetic young men who were accustomed to discipline. They had grown up during their military service and learned the principle that "absolutely nothing is impossible, and where there is a will, there is a way".

After only a few weeks of working with the new members, I realized how necessary this new blood was. The chairman of the party at that time, Mr. Harrer, was a journalist and as such he had a good background in general cultural knowledge. But he had one great handicap that was detrimental for a party leader. He was no speaker. He was a man of conscience and exact in every detail, but he could not motivate with driving passion. This was probably because he was not gifted as a speaker at all. Mr. Drexler was the chairman of the Munich local group at that time. He was a simple working man. He was also not impressive as a speaker and had never served in the army, not even as a soldier during the war. His whole nature was weak and uncertain. He had missed the one school that could turn soft and undecided natures into men. Therefore neither man was made of the stuff that would have enabled him to carry in his heart a fanatical belief in the victory of a movement. Neither man could break down whatever barrier his opposition might use to block the rise of the new idea using unshakable strength of will and with the most brutal ruthlessness. The only characteristics suited for this task were those acquired in the military where men learned virtues of mind and body and such men can best be described as swift as greyhounds, tough as leather, and hard as Krupp steel. (*Krupp is a German family of steel and munitions manufacturers known as Krupp Works who incidentally assisted in rearming Germany after the First World War.*)

At that time I was still a soldier myself. I had been polished on the inside and outside for almost six years. At first, the others must have felt as if I was a stranger in this circle. I had forgotten the words, "you can't do it", "it won't work", "we can't risk that", or "it's too dangerous". This matter was dangerous. The entire undertaking was by its very nature dangerous.

In 1920 a nationalist meeting that dared to appeal to the broad masses and to issue a public invitation was simply impossible in many parts of Germany. Those who attended were disbursed and sent home with broken heads. True, this was no great trick and conducting diplomacy based on a big stick was a feat anyone could accomplish. If a dozen Communists showed up, even at the largest privileged-class mass meetings, they would scatter and run like rabbits being chased by dogs. The Reds hardly noticed meetings filled with nothing more than privileged-class chatter. Those "clubs of the harmless" presented no danger to the Reds and they realized that fact better than the actual members of these organizations. However, they were much more determined to wipe out a movement that seemed dangerous to them and were willing to use any means possible. The most effective tool for them to use at these times was always terrorism and violence.

To the Marxist betrayers of the people, any movement that announced it planned to win over the masses, which had previously been in the exclusive service of the international Marxist Jew and the Stock Exchange parties, was a threat. The very name "German Workers' Party" had the effect of issuing a challenge. It was easy to see that conflict with the Marxist agitators, who were still drunk with victory from the Revolution, would begin at the first opportunity which presented itself to them.

At that time, the entire circle of the movement had a certain level of fear when it faced the prospect of this kind of struggle. They wanted to appear in public as little as possible because they were afraid of being beaten. In their mind's eye, they already saw the first large meeting being broken up and the movement, perhaps, shattered forever. I had a hard fight for my argument that we must not avoid this struggle, but must go out and meet it. We must equip ourselves with the only shield that gives protection from violence. Terrorism is not overcome by intellect, but by terrorism. The success of the first public meeting strengthened my position in this respect. They courageously planned for a second one on an even larger scale.

About October, 1919, the second large meeting took place in the Eberlbräu cellar. The subject was Brest-Litovsk (*meaning the 1918 Treaty of Brest-Litovsk, which marked Russia's exit from the war*) and Versailles(*the Treaty of Versailles which ended the First World War*). Four men spoke. I spoke for nearly an hour and my success was greater than at the first demonstration. The number attending had risen to more than a hundred and thirty. An attempted disturbance was foiled by my friends. The would-be troublemakers were "helped" downstairs with the benefit of broken heads.

Two weeks later, a second meeting took place in the same hall. The attendance rose to more than a hundred and seventy. It was quite a good crowd for the room. I spoke and again, my success was greater than at the previous meeting.

I pushed for a larger hall. Finally, we found one at the other end of the city in the German district of the Dachauer Road area. The first meeting in the new hall was not attended as well as the previous ones. There were only a hundred and forty people. Hope in the committee began to sink again. The eternal doubters thought they knew why attendance was poor and claimed that we were having too many demonstrations too frequently. There were "spirited" disputes about the matter. During these disputes, I maintained the position that a city of 700,000 inhabitants could handle not just one meeting every two weeks, but ten meetings every week. I told them that we must not be discouraged by setbacks, that the path we had chosen was right, and that sooner or later, success was bound to come if we were persistent and stayed strong.

Through the whole winter of 1919-1920 we faced one continuous struggle to strengthen the victorious force of the young movement and to raise the level of passion to the level of faith, a faith that is strong enough to move mountains. The next meeting in the same hall proved I was right again. The attendance rose above two hundred. The publicity was excellent and it was also a financial success. I urged that we immediately arrange for another meeting. It took place barely two weeks later and the crowd of listeners rose to over two hundred and seventy.

Two weeks later, we called the followers and friends of the young movement together for the seventh time. The same hall could barely hold all the people. There were over four hundred. At that time, the inner shaping of the young movement took place on a more serious level. The discussions often caused some more or less violent disputes in the little circle. The various sides discussed whether or not the young movement should even be called a Party. I have always seen this attitude as proof of the incompetence and intellectual pettiness of the critic. These are, and always have been, the people who cannot distinguish outward appearance from inner strength and who try to judge the merits of a movement by how pompous and pretentious the name is. The last straw was when they suggested we use the archaic vocabulary of our forefathers (*the old Germanic language of Roman times*).

They had trouble understanding that even if a movement has not accomplished its ideas and goals, it is still a party no matter what it calls itself.

When someone wants to carry out a bold idea that would benefit his fellowmen, he must begin by finding followers who are ready to stand up and fight for his goals. Even if this purpose is just to destroy the other parties that exist at the time and to therefore end the disunity among them, the supporters of this view and announcements of this decision form a party in themselves until the objective has been achieved. Playing with words like this is splitting hairs and shadowboxing for some advocate who likes to theorize about the popularity of the party's name, and whose practical success is inversely proportional to his wisdom. It is ludicrous for him to imagine he can change the character of every young party movement by simply changing its title.

On the contrary, if there is anything unnatural to people, it is tossing around ancient Germanic terms that don't fit the present day and have no significance to the modern listener. Reviving such terms can easily mislead people into thinking the important element in a movement is in its outward vocabulary instead of the internals of the party. This is a truly destructive tendency, but one which is seen countless times today.

I have repeatedly warned our followers about these German tribal wandering scholars who cannot show a single positive accomplishment except for their ability to inflate their own abundant egos. The young movement had and still has to beware of a number of such men who are known to say that they have been fighting for this same idea for thirty or forty years. Well, if anyone who has stood up for a so-called idea for forty years without producing any results or without even preventing advancement of the enemy, then he has spent forty years proving his own incompetence.

The primary danger from people of this character is that they do not want to take their place as parts of the movement, as regular members fighting for a cause. Instead they ramble on about circles of leadership that they see as the appropriate place for their contribution based on their long-continuous labors. It is disastrous and regrettable when a young movement hands itself over to such people! A business man who has systematically driven a great business into the ground through his forty years' work is not up to the task of founding a new one. Neither is a supporter of people's rights who is as old as Methuselah, and who has spent the same amount of time messing up a great idea, until eventually he caused it to seize up so that it no longer worked or made any progress. That person is not the right man to lead a new, young movement!

On top of that, only a fraction of all these people come into the new movement to be a useful part that spreads the doctrine and serves the idea of the new doctrine unselfishly. They are usually attracted by the chance to bother the public once again with their own ideas under the protection of the movement or through the opportunities it offers. They generally seem to be incapable of describing exactly what these ideas are.

People with this kind of nature characteristically rave about ancient Germanic heroism. They talk about the old times of primitive ages, stone hatchets, a spear and buckler shield, but in reality, they are the most craven cowards that can be imagined. The very people who wear bearskin tunics and a helmet with the horns of oxen on their bearded heads and swing through the breeze German tin swords made to carefully imitate the ancient ones in every detail, preach nothing but an intellectual battle, and they quickly scatter when faced with the first Communist rubber club. Future generations will have little reason to glorify the heroic epics of these "warriors".

I know these people well enough to be profoundly disgusted with their pitiful play-acting. They are the subjects of ridicule among the broad masses, and the Jew has every reason to spare these comedic champions-of-people's-rights from criticism and even to prefer them to the real warriors of a coming German State. Yet these buffoons are infinitely proud of themselves, claiming to know what is best about everything despite all proof of their complete incompetence. They become an absolute pest to all those straightforward and honorable fighters. Not only do they dilute the heroism of the past, but they attempt to hand down to future generations a picture of their own acts as heroism.

It is often difficult to tell which among these people are acting out of stupidity or inability and which are, for some special reason, only pretending to be stupid and actually have a hidden motive. This is especially true in the case of the so-called religious reformers whose beliefs are based on ancient Germanic customs. I always have the feeling they are sent by forces that do not want the resurrection of our nation. Their activities actually lead the people away from the struggle against the common enemy, the Jew. They allow their strength to be sapped by inner religious disputes that are as senseless as they are damaging.

For these very reasons, it is necessary to set up a strong central power with absolute authority for the movement's leadership. Only this strength can put a stop to such harmful elements as these rabble-rousers. One of the greatest enemies of a unified, strictly conducted and guided movement are these activist Ahasueruses. (*Ahasueruses means wandering Jews, a reference to the mythological story about a Jew who taunted Christ and was cursed to wander the world until the second coming.*) What they truly hate about the movement is that it has the power to put an end to their mischief.

There was a reason the young movement settled on a definite program and avoided using the word "Racialist" in it. (*A Racialist is someone who is interested in race or makes decisions based on race or studies race, usually informally.*) The concept of "racialism" is unclear and indefinite which makes it impossible as a basis for a movement. It also does not offer any standard to judge what the members actually stand for. The more vague this concept is and the more open to interpretation it becomes, the more it appeals to everyone. Anyone can see whatever they want in the movement. Injecting an idea into a political struggle that is vague and capable of many interpretations will ultimately destroy the solidarity and lead to harsh fighting within the fellowship. A political movement cannot survive if the individual is allowed to decide on his own what he believes the movement stands for. It is outrageous that people are running around today with the "Racial" symbol on their hats and how many of them have created their own definition of what the idea means.

There is a well-known professor in Bavaria (*in early Mein Kampf editions he was listed as Professor Bauer but the name was removed from later editions*) who is famous for fighting with intellectual means and very successful in marches on Berlin, that is to say, intellectual marches on Berlin. He has decided the racialist concept is synonymous with a Monarchy. This educated mind has so far forgotten to explain in more detail the identity of our German Monarchies of the past which can be associated with the modern "racialist" concept or which monarchies were for-the-people. I fear the gentleman will become confused if he is required to give a precise answer. For it is impossible to imagine anything more non-racialist than most of the German monarchical states of the past. If they had been race-aware, if they were representative of the people, they would never have disappeared or their disappearance would furnish the proof of the instability of the race-based World-Concept .

Everyone interprets the idea as he happens to understand it. Such a wide variety of opinions is unacceptable as a basis for a fighting political movement. I am not even referring to their separation from reality and particularly the ignorance these people display when it comes to the soul of the nation which is commonly seen in these racialist movements, these John the Baptists of the twentieth century. (*satirically meaning prophets of what is to come*.) The value of these people is clearly illustrated in the way they are treated by the Left-Wing parties. They find them ridiculous so they let these people rant and rave and just laugh at them.

Anyone in this world who is not hated by his enemies is worthless as a friend to me. Therefore the friendship of these people for our young movement was not only worthless but downright dangerous. In fact, that was the main reason we chose the name "Party" in the first place. We hoped that this would scare off a whole swarm of racialist sleepwalkers. This is why we also described ourselves as the National Socialist German Workers' Party.

The word Party scared off the fanatics who live in the past, as well as the big talkers who spout meaningless phrases about the "racial idea". The other part, National Socialist German Workers, freed us from a whole parade of knights of the "intellectual" sword and all the ragged misfits that carry "intellectual weapons" as a shield to cover their cowardice.

Naturally the most violent "attacks" on our new movement came from these racialists. Of course the attacks were not physical, but only with their favorite weapon of pen and ink, just as you would expect from such racialist pen heads. To them, there was something revolting about our principle which stated, "If a man offers us violence, we will defend ourselves by violence". They criticized us profusely claiming we possessed a rude type of worship for the rubber club and that our ranks lack any form of intellect. These quacks fail to realize that in a meeting of racialists, a Demosthenes can be silenced by just fifty idiots who rely on nothing but their lungs and their fists if those idiots do not want to let him speak. (*Demosthenes was a Greek statesman and orator who was a major political speaker; here, meaning even a great speaker can be easily silenced.*) The inborn cowardice of the racialist always keeps him out of any such danger. He does not make noise when he works and he never steps out of the crowd--he is always careful to stay silent.

Even today I cannot warn our young movement strongly enough against falling into the trap of these "silent workers". They are not only cowards, but they are all incompetents and do-nothings. When a man knows something is going to happen, and he realizes it is a real danger, and he sees, with his own eyes, the mere possibility of solution, he damned well has the duty and obligation to act. He must make a public stand against evil and openly work for its cure, not work "silently". If he does not do so, he is a miserable weakling who has forgotten the meaning of duty and a failure either through cowardice or through laziness and inability. The great majority of the "silent workers" merely pretend to know what Heaven knows. None of them has any ability, but they all try to fool the whole world with their smoke-screen. They are lazy, but with their alleged "silent" work, they appear to be enormously active and productive. In a word, they are swindlers and political day-workers who find the honest work of others disgusting. When one of these racialist moths prefers the darkness in the valley of "silence", you can bet a thousand to one that in the dark, he is not producing but stealing and stealing from the fruit of others' work.

In addition, there is the arrogance and conceited disrespect that this lazy, night owl crowd dumps on the work of others. They constantly complain about the works of others in a condescending way, and in so doing they actually help the deadly enemies of our nationality.

Every last follower who has the courage to stand on a table in a tavern surrounded by his enemies and boldly and openly defend his views accomplishes more than a thousand of these lying, treacherous sneaks. He definitely will convert and win over one man or another to the movement. His achievement can be tested and proved by the success of his activity. However, the cowardly frauds who boast of their "silent" work and hide themselves in disgraceful anonymity are worthless and may be considered in the truest sense of the word useless when it comes to working for the revival of our people.

At the beginning of 1920, I urged the scheduling of our first great mass meeting. This resulted in differences of opinion in our group. Some of the leading Party members thought the event was premature and would result in disaster. The Marxist press had begun to show an interest in us and we were fortunate enough to gradually to win their hatred. We started attending the meetings of other parties and to speak during the discussion period at their meetings. Of course, we were all shouted down immediately. But it did have one good result. People learned about us. As the familiarity grew, their anger and hatred for us rose. This gave us good reason to hope for large scale attendance of our friends from the Red camp at our first great mass meeting.

I also realized that there was a real chance that our meeting would be dispersed by the Marxists. But the battle had to be fought. If it wasn't fought now, then it would be a few months later. It was up to us to immortalize the movement on the very first day by standing up for it blindly and ruthlessly. I knew how the minds of the supporters of the Red camp worked too well, and I was certain that an extreme resistance is the best way to make an impression and maybe even to win followers. We only needed the determination to make that resistance happen.

The chairman of the party at that time, Mr. Harrer, felt that he could not come to an agreement with my views about whether or not the time was right for our first mass meeting and, as an honorable and upright man, he withdrew from the leadership of the movement. Mr. Anton Drexler moved up into his place. I remained in charge of the organization of propaganda myself and I carried it through without compromise.

The date of this first great public meeting of our previously unknown movement was set for February 24th, 1920.

I personally directed the preparations. They were very brief. The entire organization was set up to make lightning-fast decisions. On questions concerning the attitude we should display and the purpose of the meeting, we had to reach the final answers before the mass meeting occurred which was within twenty-four hours. These points were to be announced by posters and leaflets based on our doctrine. I have already laid down the broad outlines in my discourse on propaganda and these were now used. These guidelines include effectiveness with the broad masses, concentration on a few points, perpetual repetition of these points, self-assured and self-confident wording of the text in the form of a positive statement. We circulated the leaflets with great urgency and then waited patiently for results. For a color, we deliberately chose red. It is the most inflammatory and was bound to provoke and enrage our enemies the most, thus making them aware of us in one way or another.

In Bavaria, the connection between Marxism and the Center political party was plain to see when one looked at how the ruling Bavarian People's Party (*which had splintered from the Center party*) tried to weaken and later to destroy the effect of our posters on the masses of workers who had been swayed to the Marxist side. If the police could find no reason to take steps against us, then our rivals would ultimately complain about the "traffic conditions". Finally, so they could silence their Red spiritual ally, the rival German National People's Party was able to have these posters completely forbidden. It was too late. The posters had already given hundreds of thousands of misled and misguided Red workers a chance to return to their German nationality. These posters are the best proof of the tremendous struggle which the young movement went through at that time. These posters will also bear witness to future generations of the determination and justness of our principles and the illogical response of so-called national authorities when they blocked an unwelcome nationalization and, in doing so, blocked a redemption of the great mass of our nationality.

Our flyers will also help to destroy the misconception that there was a nationalist government in Bavaria at the time and will document for future generations the fact that the government in Bavaria during 1919, 1920, 1921, 1922, and 1923 was not the product of a nationalist inclinations, but was compelled to take into consideration the mass of people who were gradually becoming more nationalist-minded which forced the government to appear nationalist as a result. The government did everything to hinder this process of revival and make it impossible.

There are two outstanding men who we must acknowledge as exceptions:

The Police Chief at the time, Ernst Pöhner (*a radical anti-Semite who participated in the 1923 Beer Hall Putch*), and his devoted advisor, Chief Bailiff Frick (*Wilhelm Frick, who was also part of the Beer Hall Putch in 1923*), were the only high-level state civil servants who had the courage to be Germans first and officials second. Ernst Pöhner was the only man in a responsible position who did not ask for the approval of the masses, but felt himself answerable to his nationality and was ready to risk everything and to sacrifice everything, even his personal existence if necessary, for the resurrection of the German people, which he loved most of all. He was always a thorn in the side of those bribe-seeking officials who acted against the interests of their people and the necessary advancement of its freedom, and who instead acted on the orders of their employer, without considering the welfare of the people or the national property entrusted to them. Above all, Pöhner was one of those rare men with a personal nature which, in contrast to most of our so-called governmental guardians, did not fear being hated by traitors of the people and of the country, but he instead hoped for that hatred and saw it as the natural property of a decent man. The only happiness for him amid the misery of our people was the hatred he received from Jews and Marxists, who fought their entire battle using lies and slander.

Pöhner was a man of rock solid honesty, of Roman simplicity, and German straightforwardness. To him, "better dead than a slave" was not a catchword but the personification of his whole character. I consider him and his colleague, Dr. Frick, as the only men holding positions in state government who have the right to be called co-founders of a nationalist Bavaria.

Before we held our first mass meeting, we had to prepare the necessary propaganda material and to have the guiding principles printed in the program. The guiding principles that we had in mind when drawing up the program is something I will discuss at great length in the second volume. Here, I will merely say that the program was made to give form and substance to the young movement and to present its aims in a manner that could be understood by the broad masses. In intellectual circles, there have been sneers and jokes about our program and attempts to criticize it. But the soundness of our ideas were proven by the effectiveness of the program.

During those years, I saw dozens of new movements come and go without a trace. Only one survived: the National Socialist German Workers' Party. Today, more than ever, I am convinced that even though people may fight it and try to paralyze it and that petty party ministers may block our free speech, it does not matter because they cannot prevent the ultimate victory of our ideas. When the very names of the current State administration and parties are forgotten, the foundations of the National Socialist program will be the basis of a future State.

Our four months of meetings before January 1920 had slowly allowed us to save up the money we needed to print our first leaflet, our first poster, and our first program.

I will end this volume with the first great mass meeting of the movement because that is when the Party burst through the narrow confines of being a small club and extended its influence by reaching into the most tremendous factor of our time, public opinion.

I had only one concern: Would the hall be filled or would we speak to an empty room? I was firmly convinced that if the crowd came it would transform the day into a great success for the young movement. So, I anxiously looked forward to the evening.

The meeting was to begin at 7:30 P.M. At 7:15, I entered the banquet hall of the Hofbräuhaus on the Place in Munich and my heart nearly burst with joy. The meeting hall that before seemed so very large to me was now overflowing with people, shoulder to shoulder, a mass of almost two thousand. Most importantly, the very people we wished to reach were there. More than half of the people in the hall seemed to be Communists or Independents. They already expected our first great demonstration would come to an abrupt end. But the result was not what they expected.

After the first speaker had finished, I took the floor. Within a few minutes, there was a flood of interruptions from shouts and there were violent episodes in the hall. A handful of devoted war comrades and other followers removed the trouble-makers and gradually succeeded in restoring some semblance of order. I was able to resume speaking. After half an hour, the applause slowly began to drown out the yelling and bellowing. Now I took up the task of explaining our program for the first time.

As the minutes passed, the taunting was drowned out more and more by shouts and applause. When I finally presented the twenty-five ideas, point by point, to the crowd, asking them to make their own judgment on each one, they accepted one after another amid growing cheers, unanimously and unanimously again. When the last point had found its way to the heart of the crowd, I had in front of me a hall full of people united by a new conviction, a new faith, a new will.

After almost four hours, the hall began to empty. The mass of people rolled, pushed, and crowded shoulder to shoulder like a slow river toward the exit. I knew they were going out into the German people and spreading the principles of a movement that could no longer pass into oblivion.

A fire had been started and from this flame, a sword would someday be forged that would win back freedom for the Germanic Siegfried and life for the German nation. (*Siegfried is both a German male name meaning peace by victory and an opera by Wagner where a strong sword is forged and the main character is named Siegfried; it also means the average man or a German John Smith.*)

In step with the coming revival, I could feel the marching of the Goddess of Revenge who would bring vengeance for the treasonous deed of November 9th, 1918. The hall gradually emptied. The movement had started.

MEIN KAMPF

VOLUME TWO: The National-Socialist Movement

1. World-Concept And Party

On the 24th of February, 1920, the first great public mass demonstration of our young movement took place. In the Banquet Hall of the Munich Hofbräuhaus (*an extension of the famous beer maker Hofbräu brewery*), the twenty-five points of our program were presented to a crowd of almost two thousand and every single point was received with enthusiasm.

We finally had an opportunity to make the first principles clear and explained our plan for action that would lead our struggle to clear away the chaos of traditional views and ideas and the vague even harmful aims that were ever present. A new force had appeared to split the corrupt and cowardly privileged-class world and this force would shatter the Marxists' wave of conquest. This new movement would ride the chariot of Fate in front of the Marxists' march to triumph and halt it at the last moment, before it reached its goal.

It was obvious that the new movement's only hope to achieve the necessary significance and the required strength for the gigantic struggle ahead was if it succeeded from the beginning in filling the hearts of its followers with the sacred conviction that we were not simply spouting a new election slogan into the political arena, but this new movement was placing a new World-Concept , one of great importance, in front of the people. Think about how pitiful the programs of these other so-called "party platforms" are. They are usually stuck together and shined up or reshaped from time to time, but one platform is basically the same as the next. To understand them, we must look at the motives which drive their construction. These motives, especially of the privileged-class "platform committees", must be put under the microscope so we can truly understand and judge how valuable these outrageous beliefs they call platforms are.

There is only one reason which leads to the re-writing of party platforms or the modification of existing ones: the concern over who will win the next election. Whenever it begins to dawn on these parliamentary craftsmen that the good old common people are about to abandon the party and slip out of the harness of the old party bandwagon, the leaders repaint the bandwagon's wheels. Then, come the so-called "experienced" and "shrewd", usually old, parliamentarians. These are the star-gazers, the party astrologers, who can recall a similar crisis, in their "long political apprenticeship", when the people's patience ended and mass defections loomed. They feel the same kind of calamity drawing dangerously near. So, they resort to the standard formulas: form a "committee", listen to what the good old common people are saying, sniff at the newspapers and gradually smell out what the common people want, what they hate, and what they hope for. Every trade and business group and every class of employee is carefully studied as its most secret wishes are examined. Even the "empty catchwords", which are used by the now dangerous opposition, are suddenly reexamined. Frequently, to the surprise of those who first coined these phrases, they suddenly appear quite innocent, as if the ideas were taken for granted or obvious. Some of them are even found in the intellectual library of the old parties.

So, the committees meet, "revise" the old platform, and write a new one in a way that gives everyone what he wants. This parliamentary class changes their convictions just as the soldier changes his shirt in the field, whenever the old one wears out. No one is left out, the farmer's agriculture is protected, the industrialist's products are protected, the consumer is guaranteed stable market prices, the teachers' salaries are raised, and the civil servants' pensions are improved. The State is to take good care of widows and orphans, commerce is promoted, prices are to be lowered, and taxes are to be practically abolished. Sometimes, one group may have been forgotten or a new demand among the people was not discovered by the party in time to add this revision. Any overlooked concessions are stuck on, wherever there is space, at the last moment. The patches are put in place until the party can faithfully hope that the army of middle-class Philistines and their wives are soothed and satisfied once again. Now, armed with faith in the Lord and the unshakable stupidity of the voting citizens, the party can begin the struggle for "reshaping" the Reich, as it is called.

When election day is over and the parliamentarians have held their last mass meeting for five years, with no further need to consider the commoners, they focus on fulfillment of their higher and more pleasant duties. The committee that created this new platform disbands again and the struggle for reshaping assumes the form of a battle for one's daily bread. Maybe this is why gatherings of parliamentarians are called diets (*an alternate meaning of diet is a formal legislative assembly*.) The parliamentarians draw their daily pay by simply showing up and the "struggle" degrades into a humdrum "daily routine".

Every morning the Honorable Gentleman, the Deputy of the parliament, goes to the House and though he may not make it all the way in, he at least goes as far as the entryway where the attendance lists are kept. He labors strenuously for the people by entering his name there and receives his well-deserved reward in the shape of a small payment for his long and exhausting efforts.

After four years, just about the time their term of service is to expire, or during other critical periods when the end of session for the parliamentary body draws nearer and nearer, these gentlemen suddenly feel an irresistible urge come over them and they have a desire to take action. Just as the caterpillar cannot help turning into a butterfly, these parliamentary worms leave the home of their species and flutter out on new found wings to the good old common people. Once more they speak to the voters, telling them about their own tremendous accomplishments and the stubbornness of their opponents. But sometimes they encounter rude and unfriendly expressions thrown at them from the stupid masses instead of grateful applause. If this lack of gratitude from the people rises beyond a certain level, there is only one thing that can save the day. The glory of the party must be shined up again and surely the party platform needs more repairs. The party platform committee is set up and the charade begins all over again.

Considering the rock solid stupidity of the public, we cannot be surprised at the resulting success of these tactics. Steered by its newspapers and blinded by the attractive new party program, the privileged-class and the working class combine into a united voting herd as they go back into their old stalls and elect the same old deceivers. Then the "man of the people" and the "candidate of the working class" is transformed back into a parliamentary caterpillar where he can continue gorging himself as he clasps to the branches of State life, where he will only to be transformed into a glittering butterfly again four years later.

There is nothing more depressing than watching the whole process in sober reality and seeing the never-ending fraud for oneself.

The privileged-class camp of politicians cannot draw enough spiritual strength from this kind of self-indulgent dealing to fight a battle with the organized power of Marxism. These upper class people never seriously thought of battling them at all. With the admitted limitations and intellectual inferiority in these parliamentary snake-oil-salesmen, who are supposed to represent the white race, how can they seriously expect to make any progress using Western Democracy against a doctrine that, at best, is designed as the means to destroy Democracy. Marxism is the means to an end, and that end is the destruction of Western Democracy by paralyzing the political body, which in turn leaves the path open for itself. For now, one part of Marxism very shrewdly tries to pretend it is connected to the principles of democracy, but we must never forget that when the critical moment is upon us and Marxism is breathing down our necks, these privileged-class legislators did not think a penny's worth of their time could be sacrificed to reach a majority decision on the protection of Western Democratic principles. These privileged-class parliamentarians believe the security of the Reich is guaranteed by the monumentally superior numbers on their side so they remain blind while Marxism snatches power with a crowd of thugs, deserters, political evangelists, and Jewish amateur intellects; these legislators are giving the current democracy a resounding slap in the face through their failure to act. Only a legislator with the devout spirit of a witch-doctor could possibly believe that the wicked determination of those who support and profit from this Marxist plague could be halted simply by uttering the magic spell of Western Democracy.

Marxism will march along side democracy until it indirectly succeeds in gaining support for its criminal intentions from the very nationalist intellectual world which Marxism has marked for extermination. If Marxist leaders became convinced today that, somewhere in the witches cauldron of our parliamentary democratic system, a numerical majority might suddenly be brewed which would furiously combat Marxism, the parliamentary hocus-pocus would be over in an instant. Instead of appealing to the democratic conscience, the flag-bearers of the Red International movement would send out a fiery call to action to the working class masses and their battle would jump from the stuffy air of our Parliamentary chambers into the factories and spill onto the streets. Democracy would immediately be over. What the intellectual prowess of these parliamentary apostles-of-the-people had failed to accomplish in the Parliament would now be accomplished by the crowbar and the sledgehammer wielded by the excited working class masses who would achieve the Marxist goals in a flash, just as in the fall of 1918. With one crushing blow, they would teach the privileged-class world how crazy it was to think that one can resist the Jewish world-conquest with the tools of Western Democracy.

As I have said before, it requires a trusting soul to honor the rules of the game, when he is faced with an opponent who sees the rules only as a masquerade for his own benefit and then the instant he no longer finds those rules give him advantage, he throws them overboard. In all political parties of privileged-class orientation, the entire political struggle consists of a scramble for individual seats in Parliament. During this time they adhere to convictions and principles until those principles begin to weigh them down, and then they are tossed overboard as easily as bags of sand. Naturally, their political platforms and programs are setup in a similar way so they can be discarded just as quickly. The party's strength is measured by that scale, but in reverse, the more weight they discard, the more bogged down they become and hence the weaker they become. They don't have that powerful magnetic attraction which the great masses want to follow, that aura of an irresistible impression, of great and outstanding principles, and of the convincing force of unconditional faith in those principles, along with the fanatical fighting courage to defend them.

At a time when one side, armed with all the weapons of a World-Concept , even though it is absolutely criminal, prepares for the attack on an existing order, the other side can successfully resist only if it covers itself in the form of a new, and in our case political, faith, and exchanges the catchwords of a weak and cowardly defense for the battle-cry of a bold and brutal attack.

If someone, especially one of the so-called nationalist privileged-class ministers like a Bavarian Centrist, accuses our movement of working for an "upheaval", there is just one possible answer to such a political Tom Thumb: "Right you are. We are trying to make good what you in your criminal stupidity failed to do. You and your principles of parliamentary position-jockeying helped to drag the nation into a black pit, but we will aggressively set up a new World-Concept and with fanatical fervor, unshakably defend its principles. We will build the steps that our people will one day be able to again climb to the Temple of Freedom".

When our movement was founded, we devoted our primary efforts toward preventing our army of fighters, for a new and high conviction, from turning into a mere society for the furthering of parliamentary interests. The first preventive measure was the creation of a program that urged the development of a party whose inner greatness was designed and calculated to frighten off the petty and weak minds of our present party politicians. The soundness and necessity of our idea, to establish a sharp definition of our program's aims, was best shown by those fatal problems which led to Germany's collapse. The recognition of the problems faced by Germany was bound to give a shape to the new State-concept, which, in turn, is an essential element in a new World-Concept .

In the first volume, I dealt with the word "racialist", pointing out that this designation is too obscurely-defined as an idea to allow it to form a solid fighting group. There are many groups that are as different as night and day floating around at this time under the blanket name "racialist". So before I go on to explain the aims of the National Socialist German Workers' Party, I would like to clarify the idea "racialist" and its relation to the Party movement.

The word "racialist" is vague. It does not clearly express any specific idea and it is subject to many interpretations, and it is as limitless in practical application as, for instance, the word "religion". It is also difficult for us to create a clear picture in our mind about what it means, either for theoretical or practical descriptions. The term "religious" becomes concrete only when it is connected with a sharply defined form which is actually practiced. It sounds very pretty to say someone is "deeply religious", but that is usually a hollow statement, for it says nothing about a man's character. There may be a very few individuals who feel themselves satisfied by such a general term and others who may even assign to it a definite picture of a particular spiritual state. But the great masses are not made up of philosophers or saints. An absolutely general and non-specific religious idea like this will be turned into the listener's personal interpretation. It does not lead to an effective inner religious craving that one possesses when the purely abstract and unlimited world of ideas shapes itself into a clearly defined faith. This is not an end in itself, but only a means to the end. However, the means is the essential way of attaining the end. This end is by no means solely a theoretical ideal, but the bottom line is that it is extremely practical. In fact, we must realize that generally, the highest ideals always correspond to a profound vital necessity in our lives, just as the nobility we see in beauty is ultimately determined by a form that is logical and useful in the end; [the beauty of form follows its function.]

Faith helps to raise man above the level of a mere animal existence, and it contributes to strengthening and safeguarding his existence. His religious training includes religious doctrine, but in practicality also includes morals, ethics, and the principles it supports. If you eliminate this religious training, it will result in a critical weakening of the foundations of his existence. It is safe to say that man lives to serve higher ideals, but that these higher ideals also are the essentials for his existence as a man. The circle is complete.

Even the general term "religious" implies certain basic ideas or convictions. Some of these are the immortality of the soul, the belief in eternal life, and the existence of a higher Being. These ideas, though firmly believed as factual by the individual, are still subject to the interpretation of that individual and subject to his acceptance or rejection of them if the emotional power behind them does not take on the force of an undeniable law that is the doctrine that defines a clear faith. More than anything else, this doctrine is the fighting element which breaks through the outer appearance of fundamental religious views and pushes those superficial, theoretical trappings aside to clear the path for a deep and committed faith. Without a clearly defined faith, the multiple vague forms of religious feeling followed by individuals would not only be worthless for human life, but probably would contribute to general disintegration.

The same analysis for "religion" is true for the term "racialist". It too embodies certain basic ideas. But these, even though of outstanding importance, are so vague in form that they have no value beyond an opinion more or less deserving of recognition. The ideals of a World-Concept and the requirements deduced from them are not understood by pure feeling or men's inner will any more than freedom is conquered by a universal desire for it. No, only when the idealistic longing for independence is organized to fight in the form of military force can the compelling desire of a people be transformed into a splendid reality.

Even a World-Concept that is totally sound and of the utmost value for humanity will never have any practical value and will never shape the people's lives until its principles have become the banner of a fighting movement. The movement will remain a party until its work has been completed by bringing its ideas victory, and its party doctrines form the new State whose principles shape the community.

If an abstract intellectual concept is to serve as the foundation for future development, the first requirement is to create a clear understanding of the nature, the character, and the extent of this idea. This is the only way a movement can be founded so that it maintains the inner cohesion and uniformity of its convictions and from this uniformity it will develop the necessary strength for the battle. General concepts must be molded into a political program, a general World-Concept into a definite political faith. Since its aim must be one that is within reach and can be accomplished in the real world, this faith must not only serve the idea, but must include the means that will be used to fight and to win victory for the idea. Along with the theoretically sound intellectual idea which was originally declared by the program maker, the politician must use his practical insight to shape the idea into an achievable plan. An eternal ideal that is the guiding star of humanity must adjust itself so that it takes into account the weaknesses inherent in man because of general human imperfection, and only then can it avoid failure the instant it begins. The founder of the idea, the explorer of truth, must be joined by the man who knows the people's spirit, and they must work together in order to extract what is humanly possible for tiny mortals from the realm of ideals and eternal truth and to give it a shape that can be used in the fight.

This transformation of a general and idealistic World-Concept into a definite, tightly organized, political, fighting brotherhood of faith, which is unified in both mind and will, is the most significant achievement we can hope for. Any chance of victory for the idea depends completely on this successful transformation of an idea into a practical plan. Out of a crowd of millions who individually have at least some understanding of these truths, and a few who may fully understand them, one man must arise who can form clear and rock solid principles. This man will create a force out of the shifting tide of understanding that exists in the broad masses, and this force will be so strong it cannot be doubted. He must fight to make the truth of these ideas exclusive so that no others can be considered and continue in his fight until he creates an unshakable rock out of man's will and a single solid belief rises from a world of free flowing and shaky ideas. The right to take such action comes from necessity and the right of the particular man to take this action is justified by his success.

When we try to find the inner core meaning of the word "racialist", we come to the following conclusion:

The ordinary concept that exists in politics is that the State, in itself, has creative and cultural energy it can use to build a civilization, but it has no understanding of the essentials of race in the creation of a State. The State is thought to be more of a product of economic necessities, or at best, the natural result of a political lust for power. If we extend this view to its logical conclusion, it leads to a misconception of racial forces, and it leads to the idea that the individual is of little importance. If we deny that the different races vary in respect to their general powers of creativeness in their own culture, then this must mean that when we evaluate the individual person, he too does not vary in his powers of creativity. The assumption that the races are alike leads to a similar attitude toward peoples, and thereby toward individual men. Consequently, international Marxism itself is just the transformation, by the Jew Karl Marx, of a long existing World-Concept into a definite political profession of faith. Without the widespread pre-existing foundation of such a poison, the amazing political success of this doctrine would never have been possible. Among millions of people, Karl Marx was the one man who, with the sure eye of the prophet, recognized the poisons essential to his plan were already in the swamp of a slowly decaying world. He separated and identified those poisons, like a black-magic wizard, to make a concentrated solution he could use to speed the destruction of the free nations on this earth. All this was done to serve his race.

Marxist doctrine is the extract of the intellectual soul of today's universal World-Concept that is boiled down into a concentrated form. For that reason alone, any struggle against it by our privileged-class is impossible and I would even say such a fight would be ridiculous. The privileged-class world is already saturated with all these Marxist poisons. It has already declared its devotion to a similar World-Concept which differs from the Marxist concept only in its degree and in the character of the privileged-class people who hold those beliefs. The privileged-class world is Marxist, but they believe they can somehow dominate and keep the privileged-class in control. However, true Marxism works day and night to deliver the world into the hands of the Jew.

The racialist World-Concept , on the other hand, recognizes the importance of the racial component of humanity. In principle, it sees the state only as a means to an end and its end is the preservation of the racial existence of mankind. In other words, racialist theorists are far from believing all races are equal, but understand different races have inferior or superior merit along with their differences. This understanding obligates racialism to honor the universal Will of Nature that rules the universe and assists in the victory of the better and stronger and to demand the subjugation of the inferior and those weaker. In principle, it acknowledges the aristocratic idea of Nature and believes in this law's authority down to the last individual creature. Racialism recognizes that races have different values and there are different values of individual men. Out of the masses we see the significance of the individual emerge, and this effect results in the organizing force of racialism and not the disorganizing force of Marxism. It believes the ideal of humanity is a necessity since it regards the achievement of this ideal as the sole essential element for the existence of mankind. However, it cannot allow an ethical idea to prevail if that idea represents a threat to the racial life of those who maintain a higher ethical ideal. In a world that has become bastardized and negroid, any concept of what is beautiful in humanity and noble and any image of an idealized future for our part of humanity would be lost forever.

Human culture and civilization on this planet are inseparable from the existence of the Aryan. His extinction or downfall would bring the barbaric uncivilized ages on the globe once more. In the eyes of any race-based World-Concept , undermining of the existence of human culture by destroying the one group that sustains it, is the most repulsive crime possible. He who dares to harm the highest likeness of the Lord on this Earth offends God, the Creator of this miracle, and is the cause of our expulsion from this Paradise.

Therefore, the race-based World-Concept agrees with the profound will of Nature. It restores that free play of natural forces which lead, stage by stage, level by level, to a continuous improvement of the race by natural selection until the best of humanity acquires its rightful possession of this earth and finally wins a free hand to rule which will extend throughout the world and even beyond this world. We all have a feeling that in the distant future, man may be faced with problems that are so big, only an outstanding race and a powerful ruling nation which is supported by the entire world will be capable of solving.

It is obvious that attempting to impose such a general definition on the extensive meaning of a race-based World-Concept may lead to a thousand different interpretations. In fact, there is hardly even one of our newer political organizations that does not in some way fall back on this concept of the world. The very existence of racialism, as opposed to the multitude of other variations, proves there is a difference in their concepts. The Marxist World-Concept , which is led by a unified head organization, faces a jumble of opposing views which makes little impression on the enemy's united front. Victory cannot be achieved by such weak weapons. Only when the international World-Concept that is politically led by organized Marxism is opposed by a race-based concept that is equally unified and equally organized and equally well led, will these two camps meet on even ground, and that is when victory will stand with the camp that has eternal truth on its side. However, this is only possible if both sides possess equal fighting energy from their members.

The organized embodiment of a World-Concept can exist only if there is a precisely defined formula that lays it out. What doctrines are for religious faith, the party principles are for the political party. Therefore, a tool must be made for the race-based World-Concept , just as the Marxist party organization clears the road for internationalism, the racialist movement needs a party organization that will allow it to take its rightful place in battle. This is the aim of the National Socialist German Workers' Party.

The party's ability to embrace and integrate the racialist idea into its own organization is indispensable for the victory of the race-based World-Concept . The best proof is a fact that it is admitted, at least indirectly, by those who oppose the integration of race-based ideas with party principles into a party unit. The very people who never become tired of insisting that the race-based World-Concept is not the "hereditary property" of an individual party, and cannot be claimed by a single party because it sleeps or "lives" in the hearts of millions of people, are proving themselves wrong because the fact that this idea exists in millions has not stopped the approaching victory of the opposing World-Concept of Marxism. If this concept did exist in a clear way in their hearts, the German people today would have already won a tremendous victory, and they would not be standing on the brink of an abyss. What brought success to the internationalist World-Concept of Marxism was the fact that it was maintained by a political party organized as an offensive militant storm troop. What defeated the opposing World-Concept was a lack of the uniform and united support needed to fight for their cause. A World-Concept doctrine cannot fight and win if it allows the unlimited freedom for anyone to interpret its meaning. It can only fight and win if it is clearly defined in the limited and consolidated form of a political organization.

For this reason, I took it upon myself to sort out the extensive and unformed substance of a general World-Concept and to remodel those central ideas into a rigid dogmatic form. These clearly defined doctrines are capable of unifying the people who pledge themselves to these principles. In other words, the National-Socialist German Workers' Party adopts the essential elements from the race-based World-Concept . These principles form a political declaration of faith by taking into consideration practical realities and limitations, the times we live in, and the available human resources as well as their weaknesses. This creates a closely-knit organization consisting of the greatest mass of people possible, and it provides the basis for a fight to victory on behalf of this World-Concept .

2. THE STATE

Even in 1920-1921, the now exhausted privileged-class world continued to criticize our young movement by saying that we had a hostile attitude toward the present State. Party gangs representing a collection of political views assumed they were justified in attempting, by any means possible, to suppress the young and unpleasant message of our new World-Concept . In the process, they somehow forgot that the present-day privileged-class world itself no longer had any uniform concept of what the State meant, they have no uniform definition for it, and they cannot reach an agreement among themselves. After all, those who do the explaining are often employed at our institutions of higher learning as professors of civil law. Their highest duty is to find explanations and interpretations that support those officials who currently provide their bread and butter through State support. The more impossible a state's make-up becomes as it grows and grows, the more artificial and unintelligible the definitions that try to give a purpose to its existence become. What could an Imperial-Royal University professor write about the meaning and purpose of the State in a country whose State's existence embodied the greatest monstrosity of the twentieth century? This was a difficult task because the present-day professor of civil law has less of an obligation to be truthful than to face pressure to serve a specific purpose. This purpose is the preservation of that particular horror, the monstrous human machine now called the State, which he must salvage at any cost. No one should be surprised if, in the discussion of this problem, realistic considerations are avoided as much as possible, and in their place a jumble of "ethical", "moral", and other intellectual values, tasks, and aims are substituted.

In general we can distinguish three approaches used by these theorists:

A. The group which believes the state is simply a voluntary association of human beings under a governing power.

This group is the largest. In its ranks, we find the worshipers of our present-day principle of authority, in whose eyes the will of the people plays no part at all. To them, the fact of a state's existence in itself makes it sacred and invincible. To accept this craziness of the mind, one would need an absolutely dog-like adoration of so-called state authority. In such people's heads, the means is turned into an end in the twinkling of an eye. The state is no longer there to serve men. The men are there to worship a state authority that embodies the ultimate and somehow the official spirit. To prevent this condition of silent, ecstatic worship from being transformed into one of disorder, the state authority itself exists only to maintain peace and good order. In this fashion it is no longer a means or an end. The state authority must guard peace and civil order, and peace and civil order in turn must make possible the existence of the state authority. Between these two poles all of life must revolve.

In Bavaria this approach is represented primarily by the state craftsmen of the Bavarian Center party, which goes under the name "Bavarian People's Party" (*the party that splintered from the main Center Party in 1919*). Formerly in Austria the Black-and-Gold Monarchy supporters carried this stasis-of-state attitude. (*Black and Gold were the royal colors of the House of Hapsburg and the Legitimists, who supported a Monarchy system and believed in a succession of kings based on fixed rules.*) In the Reich itself, it is often the conservative element whose concept of the state follows this same path.

B. The second group is somewhat smaller in number. It includes those who at least attach a few qualifications to the existence of a state. They want a uniform administration and a single language, if only to make day to day administration easier. The maintenance of state authority is no longer the sole and exclusive purpose of the state. The welfare of the subjects is also included. Ideas of "freedom", which are mostly based on misunderstandings of the word, intrude themselves into the idea of what constitutes a state. The form of government no longer appears sacred by virtue of the simple fact that it exists, but it is tested to show that it has some use and is good for something. The mere fact that the government has existed a long time does not protect it against the criticism of the present. Beyond that, this concept expects the state to provide economic stability and advantages for the individual, and, therefore, the state is judged from the standpoint of how well it promotes economic productivity. We find supporters of this view among our ordinary German privileged-class, particularly the members of our liberal democracy.

C. The third group is the smallest in number. It sees the state as a way to achieve political power. This power is mostly imagined in a vague and distant way as an ethnic group of people within the state that is defined and unified by a specific race and language. They desire a single state language to direct nationalization in their own direction. However, this idea is completely mistaken.

In the last hundred years, it has been a disaster to watch how the word "Germanization" has been played with by those circles just mentioned, even though they often did so with the best of intentions. I myself can still remember how, in my youth, this particular term conjured up a host of extremely mistaken ideas. Even in Pan-German circles at that time, one often heard the opinion that Austrian Germans might, with the assistance of the government, succeed in Germanizing the Austrian Slavs. They never realized for a moment that Germanization can only be applied to a country and never to a group of people. What most people thought the word meant was the forced use of the German language. But it is an unimaginable mistake to think that a negro or a Chinese can become a native German simply because he learns the German language and speaks it in the future and perhaps will cast his vote for a German political party.

The fact that any such Germanization is in reality a de-Germanization was never clear to our privileged-class nationalist world. If forcing a common language could today bridge and eventually wipe out previously obvious differences between various races, it would be the beginning of bastardization and, in our case, it is not a Germanization, but a destruction of the Germanic element in our people. This has happened all too often in history when a conquering people successfully force their language on the conquered, but then a thousand years later, when its language is spoken by a different people, they find the conquerors have really become the conquered.

Nationality, or rather race, is not in the language, but in the blood. It could only be possible to speak of Germanization if this process succeeded in changing the blood of the inferior. But this is obviously impossible. A mingling of blood would produce a change, but that change would mean a decline in the quality of the superior race. The final result of such a process would be the destruction of those very qualities which once made victory possible for the conquering people. Cultural abilities would disappear if they were mated with a lower race, even though the resulting mixed breed spoke the language a thousand times better than the previous superior race. For a time, there will still be some struggle between the differing spirits of the original races. It may be that the declining people, in a last effort, produce surprising cultural achievements. But these are only single products belonging to the remaining elements of the higher race, or bastards of the first generation in whom the better blood still predominates and strives to break through. Such cultural masterpieces are never the products of the final descendants of such hybrids. These mixes will always exhibit a cultural quality that moves backwards and does not progress.

Today it is fortunate that the Germanization of Austria by Joseph II never took place. (*Joseph II, Holy Roman Emperor over Austrian lands until 1790 imposed as part of the Age of Enlightenment the requirement that German be spoken instead of Latin or local languages; it was not well-accepted especially, with the massive number of reforms accompanying it.*) Its result would probably have been the survival of the Austrian State, but the price would have been the lowering of the racial quality of the German nation from sharing the same language among several peoples. Over the course of centuries, a certain herd instinct would probably have crystallized, but the herd itself would have been inferior. A people constituting a state might have been born, but the civilizing element in those people would have been lost.

It was better for the German nation that this process of mixing didn't happen, even though it was not due to any noble insight, but to the narrow-minded, short-sightedness of the Hapsburgs. If it had occurred, the German people today could not be described as a cultural factor any longer.

In Austria as well as in Germany itself, so-called Nationalist circles were and are influenced by similar false reasoning. The often demanded policy of Germanizing the Polish East unfortunately always rested on the same myth. Here, too, they believed the Polish element could be Germanized by simply changing the language. This would have had a fatal result. A people of an alien race would express their alien thoughts in the German language, thereby compromising the nobility and dignity of our nationality by its own inferiority.

Our Germanity is seriously damaged when a Jew, chattering in their version of the German language, sets foot on American soil. They are labeled as Germans because many Americans are unaware of conditions in Germany. No one in Germany would ever consider these unclean immigrants from the East as Germans just because they speak a language that is mostly German.

Historically, the soil that our forefathers conquered with the sword and settled with German farmers has been the most useful Germanized element. Unfortunately, this colonization introduced alien blood into the body of our people, and this contamination created that destructive idea which disconnects our people called German hyper-individualism. (Laissez faire is *the belief in pursuing economic goals free from any government regulation.*) This unfortunate quality is frequently even praised. Even in this third group, many consider the state as an end in itself and they believe the preservation of the state is the highest duty of human existence.

To sum up, the deepest roots of these views fail to tap into the understanding that the true power which creates culture and substance of character depends on racial elements and that the state's primary task is the preservation and improvement of the race. It is the race which is the essential element for all human cultural development. The ultimate conclusions from these false concepts about the nature and purpose of a state were drawn by the Jew, Marx. He separated the state concept from racial obligations, without offering any other acceptable substitute, and used the privileged-class to smooth the path for a doctrine which nullified the value of the state.

Even here, the struggle of the privileged-class world against the International Marxist was bound to be a failure from the beginning. It had long ago sacrificed the foundations which would be necessary to provide a solid footing for their ideas and beliefs. The cunning adversary, recognizing the weaknesses of its enemy's structure, is rushing to the assault with weapons furnished by that same enemy, even if those weapons were handed over unintentionally to the Marxists.

It is, therefore, the first duty of a new movement, which is standing on the foundation of a race-based World-Concept , to explain the nature and the meaning of the State in a clear way.

We can conclude that the state is not an end in itself, but a means to an end. The State is indispensable when it comes to forming a higher human civilization, but the State is not the cause of that higher civilization. The civilization depends exclusively on the existence of a race capable of creating that culture. There might be hundreds of states on earth which are excellent models of government, but if the Aryan bearer of civilization were to die out, no culture could continue to exist, at least not a culture that would match the intellectual level of the advanced peoples of today. We may go further and say that because we can form states, that in itself does not mean the human race cannot be destroyed if their superior intellectual ability and flexibility are lost as a result of the disappearance of the race which possesses the critical cultural creation elements.

If, for instance, the surface of the earth were turned upside down today by a massive earthquake and a new Himalaya mountain range were to rise from the ocean, the civilization of mankind would be destroyed in one cruel catastrophe. No state would continue to exist; all the bonds of order would be dissolved; the documents of a thousand years' development would be destroyed; the world would be one huge corpse-strewn field covered with water and mud. Yet, if from this chaos of horror just a few men of a definite race who were capable of creating civilization had escaped, the earth would once more show signs of human creative power when calm was restored, even if it took a thousand years. Only the destruction of the last civilized race and its individual members would permanently devastate the earth. On the other hand we can see, even from present-day examples, that state structures which are founded by races that lack this cultural intellectual element in their tribal beginnings cannot protect the members of their race from eventual extinction. Just as certain species of great prehistoric animals became extinct, so man must give way if he lacks that certain intellectual strength which is required to find the weapons necessary for his self-preservation.

The state does not advance cultural progress. The state can only preserve the race which does bring about the advancement. Otherwise, the state may continue to exist for centuries without taking any actions, while, as a result of the state's failure to prevent the mixture of races, the cultural capacity and the resulting general quality of life among the people have suffered profound change. The present state, for instance, may still maintain its own existence in a mechanical way for a considerable length of time, but the racial poison of inbreeding allowed by our political body produces a cultural decline that is already horribly apparent today. The existence of a higher level of humanity does not depend on the State, but on the race which is the nationality capable of creating that improved level of humanity.

This capacity always exists and only needs to be awakened by certain outside conditions. Culturally and creatively gifted nations or races have these abilities hidden within them, even though, at the moment, unfavorable outside circumstances do not allow the development of these tendencies. It is an unbelievable outrage to represent the native Germans of pre-Christian times as "uncivilized" or as barbarians. They were never barbarians. The rugged climate of their northern home simply forced conditions on them that prevented the development of their creative powers. If they had come to the more favorable regions of the south, their previously undeveloped capabilities would have blossomed just as what happened with the Hellenes (*the early Greek tribes*). This would have occurred even though there was no old history to build on and as long as they were able to obtain basic mechanical assistance in the form of lower races as workers. This inborn culture-building power did not come about just because of their presence in the northern climate. Had the Lapps (*meaning Laplanders which is a derogatory term for the people of Sami, the cultural equivalent of Eskimos living in Europe*) been brought to the South, they would have had no more culture-building capacity than the Eskimo. No, this magnificent creative capacity and growth capacity was granted to the Aryan. It may be dormant within him or it may be awakened in his life. It depends on how favorable the circumstances are, or whether an inhospitable force of Nature prevents it.

Therefore, the following conclusions result:

The state is the means to an end. This end is the preservation and advancement of a community which consists of physically and spiritually similar beings. Part of this preservation includes assuring the survival of the race and permits the free development of all the forces sleeping within that race. The greatest part of the power of the state will always be devoted to preserving the physical life and only the remaining power assists in further intellectual development. We must remember that the one is always vital to the other, physical and intellectual must both be maintained. States that do not serve this purpose are faulty, even outrages that cannot justify their existence. The fact that these monstrosities do exist is not a justification for their existence any more than the success of a crew of pirates can be a justification for high seas piracy.

We National Socialists, as the supporters of a new World-Concept , must never take our stand on the celebrated "basis of facts", and we must be especially careful of mistaken facts. If we did so, we would no longer be the supporters of a great new idea, but rather slaves of the existing system. We must make a sharp distinction between the State as a bottle and the race as its contents. The bottle has a purpose only as long as it can preserve and protect the contents. If it fails in its purpose, it is worthless. The highest purpose of the race-based state is to care for and preserve those racial elements which are the creators of culture. They produce the beauty and dignity of a higher humanity. As Aryans, we can view the state only as a living organism made up of people. It does not merely assure the preservation of this nationality, but the state must lead the people to the highest freedom possible by continuing to develop its spiritual and intellectual capacities.

But what is forced on us as a state today is in truth the tainted result of profound human error that brings with it unspeakable suffering as its consequences.

We National Socialists know that this attitude is revolutionary in the modern world and we are branded as revolutionaries for it. However, our thoughts and actions are not determined by the applause or disapproval of our contemporaries, but by our inescapable duty to a truth we have recognized. We must believe that future generations with the benefit of hindsight will not only understand our present course of action, but will also confirm it is the right one and praise those who followed this path.

From this we National Socialists set our standards for the evaluation of the state. The state value will be relative when viewed from the standpoint of the individual nations, but it is absolute when viewed from the standpoint of all humanity. In other words, the merit of a state is not found by looking at the cultural level of the state or by comparing the importance of this state's power relative to the rest of the world, but the only value of a state is in how successfully it serves the race of the nation in question.

A state may be described as a model of its kind if it serves the vital needs of the race it represents and if by its own existence the state actually keeps this national race alive. How this nation is viewed by the rest of the world does not matter; that is not a criterion for its success. It is not the task of the state to create abilities but simply to clear the road for those abilities that already exist within its people. On the other hand, a state may be called bad no matter how high its cultural level if it condemns those who carry the cultural ability to destruction by allowing the corruption of its racial make-up. The state, in practice, destroys the essential element needed for the survival of this culture. This culture is not the creation of the state, but is the fruit of a culture-building race protected by its unification as a state. As I said, the state is not the substance of culture but the form. The cultural level of development seen in a specific group of people is not the scale that should be used to measure the goodness of the state in which that race lives. It is obvious that an extensive and deep cultural wealth would appear superior to that of a negro tribe. However the lifeless mechanical state of the culturally-endowed country may be worse than that of a negro nation if you judge by the way each state performs its task, how efficiently and effectively that state meets the needs of its peoples. The best state and the best form of government can never bring out capabilities from a people if those abilities are not and never were present in those people, however, a bad state is certainly able to gradually kill off abilities that originally did exist through the destruction of the culture-sustaining race. A bad state will tolerate or even encourage this destruction of their culture bearing members. Consequently the value of a state can primarily be judged by its relative usefulness to a definite race and not by its importance in the world at large.

This relative judgment can be formed quickly and correctly. A determination of the absolute value is more difficult since absolute value is judged by not only the state but even more by the cultural value and the people's high level racial quality of the country in question.

If we speak of the higher mission of the state, we must never forget that the actual higher mission essentially belongs to the race. The state only has to create circumstances that allow the free development of those people by using the natural organizational strength of the state. When we ask how the state that we Germans need should be constructed, we must first build a clear idea of the kind of people it is to include and the purpose it is to serve.

Unfortunately our German nationality no longer has a unified racial core and the process of fusing the various original races has not progressed to a point where we can talk about the formation of a new race. On the contrary, the various poisonings of blood which have afflicted our political body, especially since the Thirty Years' War, have rotted not only our blood, but our national soul. (*The Thirty Years' War ended in 1648, and was a devastating war in which a large percentage of the population of Europe, especially Germany, was wiped out and many refugees moved to new areas or congregated in cities.*) The open frontiers of our Fatherland, the contacts with non-Germanic foreign people along the borders, and especially the continuous strong influx and constant renewal of foreign blood into the interior of the Reich itself, allows no time for a complete blend. No new race has come from the jumble. The racial elements remain within their own groups, side by side. The result is the German people scatter in all directions, particularly at those critical moments when crisis looms and they should be gathering together instead of separating. The basic racial elements are distributed in various ways. This is not only by territory, but racial distribution can also vary within a small area. With Nordics, we find they mix with East-Europeans; with East-Europeans, they mix with Dinarics (*Croatian and Bosnian races*); there are Westerners with both; and there are mixtures among them all. In one way, this has been very harmful. The German people lack that group instinct which is rooted in uniformity of blood and which protects nations from destruction, particularly in moments of danger. When people face danger, all the small internal differences among them disappear instantly and they form a united front as the similar-group turns to face the common enemy.

The jumble of our still unmixed, extremely different basic racial elements gives rise to what we know as hyper-individualism (*or* laissez faire). In peaceful times, it may occasionally do a good service, but overall, it has cheated us of world domination. If in its historical development the German people had possessed an instinct for group unity which has benefited other peoples, the German Empire today would probably be master of the globe. World history would have taken a different course. No man can tell whether that dream of the blind pacifists might not have already been achieved without having to plead for it by whimpering and weeping. That dream could be realized in the achievement of a peace that is not supported on the luxuries of tearful, pacifist, mourning women, but founded on the victorious sword of a dignified people; a sword that puts the world to work for the purposes of a higher culture and a greater civilization.

The fact that there did not exist a nation united by blood has brought us indescribable suffering. It gave glorious capital cities to many petty German rulers, but the people of Germany were deprived of their right to rule. Our people suffer from this lack of unity still, but what has brought us hardship in the past and present may become a blessing for the future. We have been held back because our race failed to come together and unify; however, it has been equally fortunate because our dispersed people stayed mostly within their own groups, and at least part of our best blood has remained pure, escaping racial degeneration.

There is no doubt that a complete merger of our racial elements would have produced a unified national body, but as any crossing of races proves, the resulting mixed breed race would have had a smaller cultural capacity than that originally possessed by the highest of the ingredient races. This is a fortunate aspect which results from the lack of complete intermingling. Even today, within our German nation's body, we have a great stock of pure and unmixed Nordic-Germanic people who we can consider our most precious possession for the future. In the dark days when we were ignorant of all racial laws, it was believed that a man was simply a man and all men were of equal value. The understanding that there are different merits among the individual racial elements may have been missing back then; however, today we know that a complete intermingling of the elements of our national body would have given us unity and might have brought us external power, but the cost would have been the loss of the highest aim of humanity. This highest aim would have become unreachable since the one foundation, the one race whom Fate has obviously chosen for this achievement, would have been lost in the unified people's motley mixture.

Previously kind Fate has prevented our race's destruction in spite of our ignorance, but now that we understand, we must examine and use this knowledge. Anyone who talks about a mission of the German people on earth must know that such a mission can only begin by developing a state that sees the preservation and advancement of the noblest surviving element of our race and of all mankind as its primary responsibility. This is the only way the state can take on a high inner purpose. Compared to the ridiculous slogan that claims a state's only purpose is in assuring peace and good order that allows quiet, mutual transactions so everyone may dupe everyone else, yes, jumping away from that nonsense, the responsibility of preserving and advancing a supreme humanity bestowed on this earth by the goodness of the Almighty Himself seems to be a truly exalted mission. From our current lifeless mechanical state that claims the right to exist for its own sake, we must form a living being with the sole purpose of serving a higher idea.

The German Reich as a state must include all Germans and must pursue its duty of gathering and preserving the most valuable racial elements among our people so that they may be raised slowly and surely to a dominant position in the world. We must replace this stagnate state with a period of battle. As always and everywhere in the world, the saying will still hold, "rest not, rust not". Victory is always won by the man who attacks. The greater the goals which are fought for and the less the masses understand them, the greater the ultimate success will be. This is the lesson learned by world history. The prominence of this success is increased if the goal has been formed correctly and the battle is fought with unshakable persistence. It may be more comforting for our present leaders of the State to work for the preservation of an existing condition than to fight for a future one. For them, it is much easier to see the state as a mechanism which exists simply to keep itself alive because their lives "belong to the state", as they are in the habit of saying. They say this as if anything originating in a national state being could logically serve any other purpose than that of the nationality, or as if man could work for anything except mankind! It is naturally easier to see the State authority as just the formal mechanism of an organization rather than to regard it as the sovereign embodiment of the instinct for self-preservation of a race. For the weak minds of politicians, the State and State authority are the end in themselves, whereas for us, they are just a mighty weapon in the service of the great eternal fight for life. It is a weapon that everyone must adopt, not because it is a mechanism or tool, but because it is the deceleration of our common will to exist.

In the struggle for our new idea, an idea that is in perfect accord with the original meaning of life, we will find only a few fighting allies in that society of officials which is decrepit in mind and body. The only exceptions are the old men who still have young hearts and fresh spirits. They will come to us from the ruling classes, but those who believe the ultimate goal of their life's-work is the preservation of existing conditions will never join our ranks.

Opposing us is the endless army of the deliberately evil and, even more, the mentally lazy and indifferent. Then there are those who have an interest in the preservation of the existing situation and want to maintain the status-quo forever. It is on the obvious hopelessness of our tremendous struggle and the magnitude of our task ahead that we base the possibility of success. The war-cry that frightens away or discourages weak spirits is the same call that summons the nature of true warriors. We must understand that if a group of men rise above the apathy of the masses, and their total energy and strength is concentrated towards one goal, that these few percent will rise to be the overlords of all. World history is made by small groups when this numerical minority embodies the will and determination of the people as a whole.

What may seem like an obstacle to many people is in reality the first condition for our victory. The very scale and the difficulties of our task mean that only the best warriors will join in the battle. This very separation of the strong from the weak is a guarantee of our success.

In general, Nature takes steps to correct the racial purity of ordinary living beings. She has little love for mongrels. The products of such cross breeding, especially the third, fourth and fifth generation, suffer bitterly. Not only are they deprived of the qualities which were present in the original highest element in the mixture, but due to the disharmony in their blood, they have lost the focus of will and determination that is necessary to live at all. At critical moments, the racially pure being will make sound and single-minded decisions, but the racially mixed one grows uncertain or settles on safer half-way measures. This shows that not only does a certain inferiority exist in the racially mixed being as opposed to the racially pure, but also the mixed race being faces the possibility of becoming extinct more rapidly. In countless cases we see where the pure race stands strong, while the mongrel breaks down. This is where we see the hand of Nature making adjustments, but sometimes she goes even further. She makes some of the offspring sterile, reducing the possibility of further reproduction and preventing further crossbreeds. This ultimately causes their extinction.

If an individual member of a given higher race were to breed with one racially inferior, the result would be a being of a lower level than the upper race. More than this, there would be a weakening of the offspring when compared to the racially pure neighbors who had not intermingled. If more blood mingling with the higher race is completely prevented, the mongrels will constantly interbreed and either die out as a result of their reduced resistance to disease, which is Nature's wise decision, or over the course of many thousand years, they would form a new mixtured race in which the original individual elements, a thousand times crossed, would become completely mixed and no longer be recognizable. This would mean the formation of a new race with a kind of herd resistance, but they would possess considerably less intellectual and cultural ability in comparison with the higher race that took part in the original cross-breeding. Even in this case, the mixed breed product would be defeated in the struggle for existence as long as a higher and unmixed racial group still existed as an adversary. All strength that this new racial group built up through unity with its own kind, over the course of a thousand years, would still not be enough to lead to victory in a struggle with an equally united, but intellectually and culturally superior pure race. This happens because of the general lowering of the racial level and the consequent decrease in spiritual resilience and creative capacity of the mongrel race.

We can, therefore, state the following principles:

Any mixing of races will sooner or later, out of necessity, lead to the downfall of the mixed offspring if the superior element in this crossing still exists as a pure racial group. The danger to the mongrel group is eliminated only when the last racially pure superior individual has disappeared, or when the higher race, which has kept its blood pure otherwise, intermingles with the small number of mongrels. This is the beginning of a slow process of natural regeneration that gradually clears up racial poisoning as long as an element of racially pure beings remain and there is no further blood mixing with lower races.

This process may take place on its own among beings with a strong racial instinct, who have simply been driven from the path of normal, racially pure reproduction by special circumstances or some outside coercive force. When this pressure ceases, however, the racially pure part that remains will again immediately strive to mate with its equal and this will put a stop to further intermingling. The mongrel offspring naturally move into the background again, except in a case where their number may already have increased and become so numerous that any serious resistance to mixing on the part of the racially pure survivors is out of the question.

The man who has lost his instincts and does not recognize the obligation Nature has given him cannot hope for any corrective action on Nature's part until he restores his lost instincts by clear intellectual awareness. Once he understands, then he must face the task of making the necessary amends by bringing back what was lost. There is a great danger that once a man no longer sees his duty clearly, he will continue to tear down the racial barriers until the last remaining shred of his best part is finally lost. Then there would be nothing left but a uniform racial mush, which appears to be the ideal sought by our "wonderful world-reformers" today. However this puree mix would soon drive all ideals from the world. True, a group of great size might be formed in that way because a herd animal can be unnaturally combined, but no such mixture can ever produce a man who can carry a culture or a man who can be a cultural founder and creator. The mission of mankind could then be considered at an end.

Anyone who does not want the earth to approach that condition must accept that it is the task, especially of the German State, to be sure, above everything, that all further bastardization is stopped.

The current generation of notorious weaklings will immediately yell, scream, and complain about interference with the most sacred rights of man. No, there is only one most sacred right of man and this right is also the most sacred duty. It is to guard the blood and keep it pure, thus preserving the best part of humanity and giving these human beings the possibility of a more noble development of humanity. A race-based nationalist state, will, therefore, have to first raise marriage from the level of constant racial contamination and to bless it as the institution that is appointed to reproduce mankind in the image of the Lord, not monsters that are half man and half ape.

Those who protest against this plan on humane grounds corrupt the generation where, on the one hand, every degenerate has the chance to reproduce, bringing untold suffering upon their offspring as well as upon society. On the other hand, contraceptives are offered for sale in every drugstore and by street vendors even to the healthiest would-be parents. The courageous privileged-class nationalist supporters of our present State, which has the highest goal of maintaining peace and good order, they regard halting reproduction among those who are afflicted with syphilis, tuberculosis, hereditary defects, cripples, and the mentally retarded as a crime. Yet the prevention of procreation among millions of the best and most healthy persons is not regarded as evil and is not an offense against the morals of this pious group, but it is convenient for their short-sighted mental laziness. Otherwise they would have to wrack their brains for the answer to how we maintain the conditions necessary to sustain and preserve the healthy members of our nationality who will someday have to perform the same task of sustenance for the coming generation.

How worldly and lacking in ideals and shameful this whole system is! People no longer strive to do their best for the future race, but rather let things just happen. Our churches also sin against the Lord's image, and then they turn around only to preach the importance of the Lord's image. This attitude matches what they are doing; they keep talking about the spirit, but let mankind, the possessor of that spirit, sink into a corrupt and ever lower class. In light of this, people gaze stupidly at how ineffective the Christian faith is in their own country and at the horrible "Godlessness" of this physically degenerate and spiritually ragged group of riff-raff and filthy people. To try and correct the balance, they attempt to convert the Hottentots (*offensive term for Khoikhoin people in South Africa*) and the Zulus (*Bantu people of southeast Africa*) and the Kaffirs (*offensive term used in South Africa meaning Black African*) to their religious cause and to bestow on them the blessings of the Church. While our European people are abandoned, thanks and praise to God for that much, by the missionaries and our people are left to become physical and moral outcasts, the pious missionary travels to Central Africa and sets up negro missions so that our "higher culture" may turn healthy, but primitive and low-grade human beings into a corrupt brood of bastards even there.

It would be more in agreement with the spirit of this world's noblest Man, Jesus, if instead of annoying the negroes with missions that they do not desire and do not understand, our two Christian churches would teach Europe something very important in a kindly, but serious way. Teach them that when parents are themselves not healthy and sound, it is more pleasing to God for them to take pity on a healthy little poor orphan and adopt him than it is for these unhealthy parents to bring a sickly child of their own into the world, which would only cause suffering and misery to itself and everyone around it.

In this area, the race-based Nationalist state must correct what is not being done in any way shape or form by the powers in place. We must make race the central point of public life and the focus of the community. We must take steps that assure the race of our people is kept pure. We must establish the child as the people's most precious possession. We must make certain that only healthy parents have children. There is only one thing that is truly shameful, and that is for the sick and weak to bring children into the world. But even they can reach for the one highest honor and that is to refrain from giving life to an unhealthy child. On the other hand, however, it must be considered extremely reprehensible to refuse the nation healthy children by withholding them. Here, the state must become the defender of a thousand years' future and supersede the desires and the selfishness of the individual with the greater needs of the people. The State must press for the use of the latest advances in medicine to make this realization happen. It must identify and actually make sterile all those who are visibly sick and suffer hereditary taint and those who are severely infectious so they are incapable of reproduction. On the other hand, it must assure that the fertility of the healthy woman is not restricted by financial considerations resulting from poor management of a state government that can make the blessing of children a curse for parents. We must sweep away the lazy, criminal indifference officials of today show towards the social needs of a large family. Instead, the State must take on the role of supreme protector of this greatest of a people's blessings. Its concern must be devoted to the child more than to the adult.

The person who is not physically sound and unworthy in mind must not extend the line of his suffering by inflicting it into the body of his child. The racial state must do an amazing amount of improvement in the area of education. Someday this work will emerge as a greater deed than the most successful wars of our present privileged-class age. Through education we must teach the individual that it is no shame to have an illness, but merely a regrettable misfortune to be weakly and sick. We must also teach them that it is shameful and also a crime to defile this misfortune by giving in to personal selfishness and piling this suffering on innocent beings. It is a symbol of the highest nobility of spirit and admirable humanity for a man who is innocently sick to go without a child of his own and instead to devote his love and tenderness to a young, poor, and unknown child of our nationality whose health offers the promise to someday become an energetic member of the community. It is equally contemptible to produce a child whose health promises to someday disease an energetic member of our strong community. In this work of education, the state provides practical assistance to improve the moral quality of our people. The state must act on this education principle without regard for whether the public will understand or misconstrue the message or even whether or not the public will approve.

If physical degenerates and mental cases were denied the ability and chance to reproduce for just six hundred years, it would not only free humanity from a vast misfortune, but it would also contribute to an improvement in overall health that today seems almost inconceivable. If the fertility of the nationality's healthiest members is encouraged and brought out through a deliberate and systematic campaign, the result would be a race that has eliminated the present day germs which cause physical and spiritual decay. Once a people and a state have traveled this road for a time, they will naturally continue to direct their attention toward increasing the valuable racial core of the people and especially encouraging its fertility so that finally, the entire nationality may share in the blessings of a high-bred body of great racial quality.

A state must not leave the settlement of newly acquired territories to chance but must instead set down specific rules. It must establish race commissions which will issue permits for those individuals wishing to settle the new areas, but these permits will be issued based on the racial purity of the individuals. Using this method, border colonies can gradually be formed whose population consists exclusively of those who possess the highest racial purity and are of the highest racial ability. These colonies become a precious national treasure for all of the people. Their growth will fill every individual member of the people with pride and satisfying confidence. After all, these colonies are the final seeds which will be needed for the great future development of his own people and of mankind.

Our race-based World-Concept will eventually succeed in creating a noble age where people's primary concern is not the improved breeding of dogs, horses, and cats, but the exaltation of man himself. It will be an age when one race with full comprehension of its achievement will silently sit back while the other races joyfully sacrifice and give for the benefit of the higher race.

It can't be denied that this is clearly possible in a world where hundreds of thousands upon hundreds of thousands voluntarily take a vow of celibacy under no pressure or obligation other than their willing acceptance of a religious command. Is the same surrender not possible when the religious idea is replaced by the reprimand to end the original sin of race poisoning, whose affects last forever, and to give to the Almighty Creator beings which are in His own image and return to Him that which He Himself has made?

True, the pitiful army of our present-day lowbrow leaders will never understand this. They will laugh at it or shrug their stooping shoulders and groan their standard excuse, "That would all be very nice, but it can't be done!" It could never be done by you. Your privileged-class world is incapable of accomplishing such an idea. You have only one concern, your personal luxuries and you have only one God, your money! But we are not speaking to you lowly leaders. We are speaking to the great army of those who are too poor to think that their personal luxury is the key to real happiness in the world, to those who do not see gold as the ruler of existence, but to those who believe in other gods. Above all else, we are speaking to the mighty army of our German youth. They are growing up during a great turning-point in history and their fathers' sins of apathy and indifference will force them to fight for their survival. Someday German youth will either be the architect of a new racial state, or it will be the last witness to the complete collapse and end of the privileged-class world.

This generation suffers through mistakes which it sees and is fully aware of, but satisfies itself, as our privileged-class world today does, with the cheap excuse that nothing can be done about it. This is a society which is marked for extinction. Our privileged-class world can no longer deny the evil conditions that exist. It is forced to admit we are surrounded by corruption and evil, but it cannot decide to fight against the evil and it cannot muster up its grim energy to unite a people of sixty or seventy millions strong so that we can make a stand against the threat facing us.

On the contrary, if anyone makes an effort toward change, these leaders make silly, petty comments, and from a safe distance, they try to prove the idea is theoretically impossible and declare any practical success unthinkable. No argument is too half-witted to support their nitpicking claims or serve their moral attitude. If, for instance, an entire continent were to declare war on the poison of alcohol and attempt to free its people from the clutches of this devastating vice (*refers to American Prohibition of 1920*), our European privileged-class world only would only respond with a blank stare and then a superior know-it-all condescending shake of the head, which is particularly becoming to this ridiculous segment of society. But if these foolish declarations are not heeded, and the noble society seeking to improve itself continues in its effort, and the good old way of doing things is successfully discredited because somewhere in the world someone achieved success by another method, then the success itself is questioned or the value of the original objective is declared as unimportant by these privileged-class fools. The privileged-class leaders do not even consider entertaining a discussion of the measures for a moral struggle which could possibly sweep away the greatest of immorality among out people.

We must not fool ourselves. Our present privileged-class is already worthless to mankind when it comes to any dignified task simply because it has lost all values it may have possessed and is evil. It is not evil because it desires to be evil, but rather because these people are too lazy to rise up against the evil attacking our people. For that reason, those social clubs that float around under the general name of "privileged-class political parties" are nothing more than an association with an interest in select professional groups and social classes. Their most noble aim is only to represent their selfish interests as much as possible. It is very plain that this sort of political privileged-class society is not suited for battle, that is to say they are unprepared for a battle where the opposing side is not made up of cautious shopkeepers, but instead is built from working class masses that have been incited to extremes, are highly enraged and are determined to fight to the bitter end.

If we recognize that the first task of the State is in working for the welfare of this nationality and for the preservation and development of its best racial elements, it is natural that this concern goes beyond the birth of the little new member of our people. This concern must extend to training the young descendants into valuable members of our society who can subsequently propagate the race further. The racial quality is the first essential for intellectual capability, and following that, education must begin by promoting physical health. A sound, energetic mind is only found in a sound and energetic body. The fact that geniuses are often physically handicapped and sometimes diseased does not disprove this principle. These are exceptions that only prove the rule. When the masses of a people are made of physical degenerates, we will rarely see a great mind rise out of this swamp. If such a mind does exist, his work will never be fated for great success. The degraded mob will either be unable to understand him at all or their determination and will-power will be so weak that they cannot follow the soaring flight of such an eagle.

Realizing this, the race-based state must direct its primary educational effort toward training sound and healthy bodies and not just pumping in knowledge. Development of the intellectual abilities takes second place. The development of character and especially strength of will and determination, comes first. Together with this we must teach the joy that comes from readily accepting responsibility. Scientific education comes last.

The race-based Nationalist state must operate from the belief that a man with little academic schooling, but who is physically sound and has a good, solid character, who is filled with determination and strong will is more valuable to the people's community than a brilliant weakling. If a nation is led by scholars who are physically degenerate, weak-willed, and cowardly pacifists, they will not conquer anything under Heaven nor even be able to assure their own existence here on earth. In the fierce battle of Destiny, the one who is conquered is not usually the least educated, but is the one who is too weak-willed to put his decisions into action.

There must be a certain harmony maintained between mind and body. A decayed body is not made even a tiny bit more beautiful by a brilliant mind. In fact, the highest intellectual training could not be justified at all if it were possessed by one who was physically degenerate and crippled, weak-willed, indecisive, and cowardly in character. What makes the Greek the ideal of immortal beauty is the marvelous pairing of magnificent physical beauty with a brilliant mind and noble soul.

If Moltke's words are true, "In the long run, only the able man is lucky", they must certainly be true for the relation between body and mind. (*Moltke means Moltke the Elder, Chief of the Prussian General Staff 1857-1871.*) The mind that is healthy will only dwell in a body that is sound.

Physical training in the race-based Nationalist state is not just the concern of the individual or the parents and should not be second or third place in the public interest. It is indispensable for the self -preservation of the nationality and should be upheld and protected by the state. As far as formal education is concerned, the state currently supersedes the individual's right to choose and imposes community-based education by compelling the child to go to a particular school without concern for the parents' wishes. To an even greater degree, the race-based state in the future will have to establish its authority ahead of the ignorance or the misunderstanding of the individual when it comes to preserving the nationality. The state must arrange its educational work so that the bodies of youngest children are suitably tempered and toughened so they can meet the demands they will face in later life. Above all, the state must take care not to create a nation filled with stay-at-home individuals.

The job of care and training must begin by teaching the young mother. It was possible through decades of careful work to achieve antiseptic cleanliness during childbirth and to reduce birth related fevers to just a few cases. In the same manner, it must and will be possible by thorough training of nurses and mothers to introduce a training system for the child in his earliest years that will be an excellent basis for later development.

In a race-based Nationalist state, the school must set aside much more time for physical training. It is not acceptable to weigh down the young brains of students with heavy loads of book learning. Experience has clearly shown that these students will remember only a small fraction of what they are exposed to and the part they do retain usually consists of unnecessary and trivial facts instead of the essentials they will need for later life. The young person is not capable of sifting through the mountain of material and separating out the important from the unimportant parts in this sea of knowledge poured into him. Today, the secondary schools only schedule two hours a week for gymnastics and even those two hours are not mandatory. This is a glaring imbalance of the importance between purely intellectual and physical training. A single day should not go by without the young person's body being trained for at least an hour in the morning and an hour in the evening. This training should be in all kinds of sport and gymnastics. One sport in particular that must not be forgotten is boxing. Many "racialists" regard this sport as brutal and vulgar. The current false opinions in "cultivated" circles about boxing are quite astonishing. If a young man learns to fence with a sword and then goes around dueling, it is socially acceptable and even considered honorable, but for him to box is thought to be rough. Why is this? No other sport approaches boxing when we look at how it builds up aggressiveness, demanding lightning-speed decisions, and training the body in strong agility. It is no rougher for two young people to fight out a difference of opinion with their fists than with a piece of sharpened iron. The man who defends himself with his fists when he is attacked is not less honorable than the man who runs away, yelling for a policeman. Above all, the young healthy boy should learn how to stand up to hard knocks and rise again when he is beaten. Naturally our present-day intellectual warriors regard this as savage. But it is not the purpose of a race-based Nationalist state to breed a colony of pacifists who are more interested in appearances than substance or to breed physical degenerates. The state ideal is not the honest lowbrow or the virtuous old maid, but the defiant individual representing manly strength and women who can bring strong men into the world. Sports exist not only to make the individual strong, agile, and bold, but also to toughen and teach people to endure the difficult world around them.

Our entire intellectual upper class was exclusively brought up by being taught the refined lessons of manners. If they had all learned to box instead, a German Revolution consisting of dandy-men, deserters, and rabble would have never been possible. The Revolution was made a success by the cowardly, miserable indecision of those who guided the State, and its success was not due to the bold and courageous energy of the revolutionaries. Our entire intellectual leadership had been educated with "intellectual weapons" and was defenseless the moment the adversary picked up a real physical weapon. The revolution was possible only because our schools of higher learning preferred to train civil servants, engineers, technicians, chemists, lawyers, literati, and did not train men to be real men. They were more concerned that they would run out of professors. Our intellectual leadership has always been brilliant in itself, but when it comes to will-power and accomplishment, our leadership has been beneath contempt.

No amount of training will make a coward into a courageous man. It is equally certain that a man with some amount of courage may be paralyzed in his development if his education is inferior from the outset and does not encourage his strength and agility. The confidence one gains from physical excellence greatly increases a man's courage and even awakens his aggressiveness. This can be judged best by the army. Our military men were not all heroes here any more than anywhere else. Overall, they were average. But the superior training given to the German soldier in peace-time injected the giant military being with a hypnotic faith in its own superiority and this faith was built up to a degree its enemies never thought possible. The immortal spirit and courage displayed by the onrushing German army in the summer and fall of 1914 were the result of the tireless training through the long, long years of peace. This training led men to achieve the greatest of deeds and out of feeble bodies it produced a self-confidence that was never lost, not even in the horror of the greatest battles.

Our German people are broken and crushed. They lie exposed to the kicks of the world, and they need the hypnotic strength inherent in self-confidence before they can restore themselves. This self-confidence must be trained into the young members of our people from childhood. Our children's entire education and training must be planned to give him the certainty that he is absolutely superior to all others. Through building his physical strength and agility, he must regain his faith in the invincibility of his entire nation. What once led the German army to victory was the sum total of the confidence that each soldier felt in himself and soldiers' common confidence in their leadership. In order for the German people to stand on their feet again, they must restore their conviction to re-conquer their freedom. This can only be achieved when conviction exists equally in the hearts of the grand total of all the millions of our people. We must not allow ourselves to be deceived in this.

The collapse of our people was overwhelming, and the effort to bring this agony to an end must be equally overwhelming. Anyone who believes that our people can obtain the strength to shatter the present world structure and throw the broken chains of slavery in the faces of our enemies from our present privileged-class education, which teaches us peace and good order, is bitterly mistaken. This path would lead to our destruction. Only an extra dose of national will-power, a thirst for freedom, and the utmost passion can correct what we have lost.

Even the clothing youth wear must be suited to this purpose. It is sad to see how our young people are already subject to a fashion-madness that does its share to turn the old saying, "Clothes make the man", into a disastrous one.

Youth is the time when clothing must work for education. The boy who wears long trousers and is wrapped up to the neck in the summer, loses any desire for physical exertion just because of his clothing. To solve this problem we must appeal to ambition and vanity. Not vanity of fine clothes, which obviously not everyone can afford, but vanity of a beautiful, well-formed physique, which everyone can create.

A strong body will be useful in later years too. A young girl must have the opportunity to become acquainted with her knight. If physical beauty were not completely pushed into the background and hidden by our fancy world of fashion, the seduction of hundreds of thousands of girls by bowlegged, disgusting Jew bastards would not be possible. It is also in the best interest of the nation that the most beautiful specimens should find one another and help create new beauty for the nation.

This is more necessary than ever today because military training is no longer required. That was the one institution that at least partly compensated during peace times for what the rest of our education system failed to do, and now it is gone. The success of military training was not exclusively in the development of the individual, but in its influence on the relations between the sexes. The young girl prefers the soldier to the civilian.

The racial state must not only carry through and supervise physical education during the official school years, but must also take responsibility after school is completed. As long as a boy is still developing physically, this development needs to be encouraged and it will be to his benefit. It is nonsense to think that the state's right to supervise its young citizens immediately terminates with the end of school life and suddenly resumes during military service. This is a right just as much as it is a duty. The present-day State, which takes no interest in healthy people, has criminally neglected its duty. The current state policy allows young people of today to experience damnation on the streets and in brothels instead of maintaining control and continuing their physical development until they become healthy men and healthy women.

At this time, the state cares nothing about continuing this training. What should be important is the goal to make these training regiments a reality and research the best methods for such training. The race-based state will also have to consider the intellectual training and the physical development of post-school years as the state's job and maintain this training through state institutions. This education can be the preliminary training for later army service. The army should not have to teach the young recruit the simplest drill instructions. At this point the military will no longer receive recruits as such, but they will simply turn the already physically trained young man into a soldier.

In the race-based state, the army will no longer need to teach the recruit how to stand and to walk, but its job will be that of the final and highest school of training for the Fatherland. The young recruit in the army will receive the necessary training at arms, but he must also be molded further so that he is prepared for his later life. The crowning point of military training must be that which was the greatest merit of the old army. In this school, the boy is to be turned into a man. In this school, he must learn to obey and through this experience he will gain the fundamentals which will later enable him to command. He must learn to be silent when he is rebuked justly, and also learn to suffer unfairness in silence when it is necessary. Fortified by faith in his own strength and carried away by the intensity of *Esprit de Corps* (*common morale or team spirit*), he must become convinced of the invincibility of his nationality.

When he has finished his army service, he is to be given two documents: his diploma of state citizenship, a legal document which permits him to enter into public life, and his health certificate, proving his physical fitness for marriage.

The racial state can also carry on the education of the girl using the same principles as the boy's training. The main emphasis must be placed on physical lifestyle above all, secondly on the development of spiritual and mental aspects, and lastly on intellectual beliefs. The unshakable aim of female education must primarily be on her future as a mother.

The second consideration of the racial state must be to foster character building in every way. Of course the most essential qualities of character are already present in the individual person. The man who is selfish will always remain so and at the other end of the spectrum, the idealist will always be an idealist. But in between those extremes, there are millions of people who seem to have vague and indistinct characters and they can benefit from such education. The born criminal will always be a criminal, but people who have a limited criminal inclination can still become valuable members of society through proper education. On the other hand, bad training may create truly bad people from those who were previously only indecisive characters.

There were many complaints during the war about the fact that our people could not keep their mouths shut! This weakness made it very difficult to keep the enemy from learning important secrets! We must ask ourselves the question, "What did the German education system do before the war to train individuals to be discrete and keep quiet?" Unfortunately, even in school, the little tattle-tale was often favored over his more discreet comrades. Then and now, gossiping is regarded as praiseworthy "frankness" and silence as shameful stubbornness. Did anyone make any effort to represent discretion as a manly virtue? No, because in the eyes of our current school administrators, these values are of little importance. But these "trifles" cost the State countless millions in judicial expenses because ninety percent of all lawsuits for slander are caused solely by a lack of discretion.

Irresponsible statements are blabbed about without considering the consequences. Our economic life is constantly harmed by those who recklessly reveal important manufacturing techniques. The secret preparations for national defense are turned into an illusion simply because the people have not learned to hold their tongues, but are happy to talk about everything to anyone. In war this easy flowing chatter may lead to the loss of battles and contribute to the disastrous outcome of the overall struggle. We must realize that if the youth are not taught something, they will not do it when they are older. That is why the teacher must not try to find out about silly boyish pranks by encouraging unpleasant tattling. Youth forms a mini-state of its own and faces the adults with a certain solidarity, which is perfectly natural. The bonds between the ten-year-old and his friends of the same age are stronger than those with adults, which is also natural for children. A boy who tells on his friends is betraying his friend, and when this tattling suddenly occurs on a large scale, it exposes a nature that is equivalent to high treason. This kind of boy cannot be considered as a "good, well-behaved" child, but as a boy who lacks the quality of character needed to care about others. It may be convenient for the teacher to increase his authority by making use of such failings, but a spiritual seed has been planted in this youthful heart that may later have disastrous results. It frequently happens that a little tattletale has grown up into a great villain.

This is just one example. There is no deliberate effort to develop good, noble qualities of character in the schools today. In fact they practically teach against them. In the future, a much stronger emphasis must be placed on this kind of character building education. Loyalty, self-sacrifice, and discretion are virtues which a great people must possess. The teaching and repetition of these values in the schools is more important than much of what students are taught today. Breaking the habit of complaining, tearful whining and of howling when hurt etc., would also come under this heading and must be taught as well. If an educational system forgets to start out by teaching the child that even pain and hard knocks must be handled in silence, it must not be surprised if at some later crucial moment, like when the man is at the front lines of battle, the entire postal service is devoted exclusively to delivering whimpering and wailing letters filled with complaints back and forth. If there had been a little less knowledge poured down the throats of our children in primary school and a little more self-control, that effort would have been rewarded from 1915 to 1918.

In its educational work, the race-based Nationalist state must attach the greatest importance to character-development along with physical development. Many moral disorders in our present political body can be lessened, if not altogether eliminated, by proper moral education. The development of strength-of-will and determination, as well as the development of a willingness to assume responsibility, should be of the utmost importance.

The army has a principle that: A command is always better than no command. With young people, this should be taught as: An answer is always better than no answer. Not to answer for fear of saying the wrong thing should be more embarrassing than to give an incorrect answer. Starting from this primitive basis, youth must be trained to have the courage to act.

There is a common complaint that in November and December of 1918, every single person in authority was revealed as a failure and that no one, from the Monarch on down to the last divisional commander, had the strength to make a responsible decision on his own. This terrible fact is the handwriting on the wall for our education system. The cruel catastrophe of 1918 was the result, on an enormous scale, of what already existed on a small scale all around us. It is this lack of will which makes us incapable of resistance today and not a lack of weapons. It affects our entire people and blocks every decision involving any risk. No great decision can be made which does not involve great risk; the greatness of a deed consists of its boldness. Without knowing it, a German general succeeded in finding the classic formula for this pitiful lack of will when he said: "I act only when I can count on a fifty-one percent probability of success". (*General Otto von Lossow is who said he would join the 1923 Putsch only if there was a 51% chance of success*) The tragedy of the German collapse is found in this "fifty-one per cent". He who demands a guarantee of success from Fate renounces the significance of a heroic deed. Heroism exists only where one is convinced deadly danger is a condition of action and one still takes the step which may perhaps bring success.

A victim of cancer, whose death is a certainty otherwise, does not need to calculate a fifty-one percent chance of success in order to risk an operation. Even if this operation offered only a one-half of one percent chance of success, a courageous man will not hesitate to risk surgery, and if he chooses not to take the risk, he should not whimper for his life.

Our present disease of cowardly indecision and lack of will results mainly from our incorrect education during our youth. The devastating effect of this education error continues into later life finding its conclusion and its crowning form in the lack of moral courage seen in our leading statesmen.

The same source produces the cowardice that rages today, and it can be seen when one is faced with responsibility. The origin of this mistake can be traced back to the education our youth receives. It saturates all of public life and is immortally perfected in the institution of parliamentary government.

Unfortunately, even in school, instructors attach more importance to remorseful confessions and to the promises "not to do it again", by the little sinner than they do to an honest admission. To many a popular educator today, the honest admission is considered to be a sign of habitual delinquency. As incredible as it may seem, the prophecy of the gallows has been foretold for many a young boy simply because he displayed some of the qualities that would be of great value if they were common among all of our people.

The race-based Nationalist state of the future must concentrate on training the will and the decision making ability in our youth. Beginning with infancy, the state must implant the idea in the hearts of our youth that one should be ready to accept responsibility and to make an honest confession. Only if the education system recognizes this need and how much the impact will benefit the nation, and then only as the result of centuries of education, a national body will exist that is no longer subject to those weaknesses that disastrously contributed to our present collapse.

The State's educational job of academic school training can be taken over by the new race-based state which only needs to make slight modifications. These changes are in three fields.

In the first place, children's brains should not be burdened with things they will not need or with things that they will forget. Almost ninety-five percent of what they are taught is forgotten. The classes taught in primary and grammar schools are an unusual mixture. In many of the individual subjects, the volume of material to be learned has increased so greatly that only a fraction can be remembered and only a fraction of that can be used. On the other hand, what is learned is not enough to train a man to make a living in a certain trade. Take, for instance, the ordinary civil servant who has graduated from secondary school or from the upper secondary school. When he is thirty-five or forty, he is tested to determine how much school learning remains, knowledge that he once so painfully acquired. Then we see how little of all the stuff that was drummed into his head can be remembered! One answer offered is: "Maybe, but the purpose of learning so much was not simply to instill tons of information for later use, but to train his memory and his thinking power and the brain's ability to reason". This is true in part. But still there is a danger that the youthful brain may be drowned in a flood of impressions that it rarely has the ability to master, and the child cannot filter or judge what is of greater or lesser importance among the individual elements in that flood. On top of that, the essential parts of knowledge are the ones which are forgotten and lost, the unnecessary parts of knowledge are retained. Therefore the main purpose of learning so much is lost. The brain cannot be made to learn by dumping unmeasured piles of educational instruction on it, but it can learn by supplying it with knowledge which the individual needs for later life. Through him, then, society benefits.

The justification for the current method is misleading because when such an excessive mass of material is thrown on a person in his youth, in his later life he retains none or only non-essential parts. I see no reason why millions of students over the course of years should be forced to learn two or three foreign languages that they can only rarely use, languages they mostly forget. Out of one hundred thousand pupils who learn French, for instance, scarcely two thousand will have the chance to use any of this knowledge later. The other ninety-eight thousand never use it in their entire lives. Children spend thousands of hours learning something which has no value or meaning to them later. Even the objection that this is part of a general education of the mind is false. This claim would only be valid if students retained what they learned throughout their lives. So it is really for the benefit of the two thousand people who will use this knowledge of the language that ninety-eight thousand are weighted down with useless information and sacrifice valuable education time.

Also the "language" I have used as an example, French, is not one that gives training in "logical thinking" like Latin does. It would therefore be much more appropriate for students to learn only the general outlines of a language. Provide the student a simple sketch of the essentials that would give him some knowledge of the characteristics of the language and perhaps introduce him to the origins of grammar and illustrate pronunciation and sentence structure by examples. This would be enough for average students and it would be easier to understand and retain. Ultimately it would be more valuable than the usual method of cramming the entire language into a student's mind, especially when the language is never really mastered and is later forgotten. We would no longer risk that only a few disconnected fragments of the overwhelming quantity of materials would by chance stick in their memory. This way, the young person would be given only the most noteworthy parts to learn and only the important aspects of the language would be taught.

The basics of a language would be enough to last most people the rest of their lives. Anyone who really needed the language later would have a basic understanding to build on and, by his own choice, he could practice and learn it thoroughly. This would make the necessary time available to schedule physical education and for the increased requirements in the fields already mentioned.

The methods currently used to teach history need to be changed. Very few people have such a strong need to learn from history as the Germans do, but there is scarcely any other nation that makes a poorer use of historical knowledge than Germany. If politics is history in the making, then our historical education is already impaired by the nature of our political leadership. There is no point in complaining about our political performance if we are not determined to improve the political education our people receive. In ninety-nine out of a hundred cases, the result of our current history education is disgraceful. A few scraps consisting of a handful of dates and names are usually all the student can remember, while any clear line of historical development is completely missing. The essential elements from history, the ones that really count, are not taught at all. It is left up to the brilliance of the individual student to figure out inner motives behind actions and the causes of events by sifting through the flood of facts and looking at the sequence of events.

One may resist the idea that this unpleasant state of affairs exists among our politicians, but we only have to carefully read the speeches that are delivered by our parliamentarians on political problems during a single session on any topic, such as foreign policy, to see the truth for ourselves. Remember that foreign policy is, or at least is claimed to be, the flower of the German nation. A great section of these politicians wore out the benches of our secondary schools; some even attended institutions of higher learning. Yet their speeches demonstrate that the historical education these people received was totally inadequate. If they had never studied history at all but simply had a little common sense, the country would have followed a better course and they would have been more useful to the nation.

We must reduce the amount of material students are required to learn, especially in history classes. The main reason anyone learns history is to grasp the big picture and understand historical development and how it affects current events. The more we focus what is taught, the more hope there is that the individual's knowledge will later create a return that will benefit the entire community. We do not learn history in order to know what has happened in the past, but we learn history so that it may be our guide for the future. We use that knowledge for the preservation of our own nationality. This is the real purpose behind learning history, and educational instruction is only a means toward that end. Even here the means has become the end in itself and the true end no longer exists. Don't let anyone tell you that a thorough study of history requires consideration of all these individual bits of information and only their sum total make it possible to determine the broad outlines. To determine these broad connections is the task for a specialized researcher. The ordinary average man is no professor of history. For the common man, a history education exists to give him a measurement for the current political landscape and a historical reference that he needs in order to make up his mind about the political events in his own nation. Anyone who wishes to become a history professor may give the subject profound study later on his own. Naturally when he chooses this course, he will have to concern himself with every detail, even the smallest. For that even our present day historical instruction is not enough. Our current system is too broad in scope for the average man and far too limited in scope for the scholar.

It is also the task of a People's State to assure that a world history will be written in which the race problem is elevated to a dominant position.

Summing up:

The people's race-based state will have to put general education into a form that focuses on the essentials. Outside of that, we must offer opportunities for more detailed, specialized, scholarly training to those who desire this detailed education. The individual person only requires a store of general knowledge in a broad outline, and he will receive a thorough detailed and specialized training only in the field that will be his occupation in later life. General training should be required in all fields, while specialization should be left to the choice of the individual.

This will allow current school schedules to be shortened by reducing the number of classes that would then make additional time for the development of the body, the character, the will, determination, judgment, etc. Our present day school instruction, especially in secondary schools, gives no importance to the training of people for their jobs later in life. This is easily seen in the fact that people may attend three completely different sorts of schools but still end up in the same career. What counts is general cultivation and not the specialized knowledge that has been poured into students. When specific knowledge is needed by a student, it cannot be obtained within the curriculum of our present-day secondary schools. It is the job of the People's race-based State to someday eliminate this sort of half-way measure.

The second change for the People's race-based State in the scholastic program must be the following:

It is the nature of our materialistic age that education is focused more and more toward the subjects of pure science, such as applied mathematics, physics, chemistry, etc. Though these are necessary for an age in which technology and chemistry are kings and they are the most visible characteristics of daily life, it is, however, dangerous for the general education of a nation to be aimed exclusively at pure sciences. On the contrary, education must always focus on teaching ideals. Our system should be adapted to focus on studies of the literature, art, and civilization of Greece and Rome, offering only the basics needed to prepare people who will later follow vocational training. If education is not changed in this way, we will be sacrificing an inner strength that is more important for the preservation of the nation than any technical skill. Specifically, the study of ancient times must not be left out of historical teaching. Roman history is the best teacher when it is properly understood in a broad sense, not only for today, but probably for all time. The marvelous beauty of the ideal Hellenistic (*Ancient Greek*) culture, must also be preserved. The differences between individuals must not be allowed to break down the greater racial community that they share. The struggle raging today has a great goal: a culture is fighting for its existence; a culture that covers thousands of years of history and encompasses the Germans and Greeks.

We must create a sharp distinction between general educational and the specialized knowledge of higher level studies. Higher level knowledge threatens to sink more and more into the service of Mammon (*the false god of greed*) and material wealth. General education must be a counter-weight of ideals against specialized knowledge education. One principle must be constantly pounded home: that industry and technology and trade and commerce can grow only as long as a national community, founded on ideals, provides the necessary conditions for them to flourish. These ideals are based on self-sacrifice and denial and not on materialistic selfishness.

The present education system's main objective is to pump into young people the knowledge they will need for advancement in later life. It is expressed this way: "The young man must one day become a useful member of society". By this, they mean his ability to earn a living in an honorable way. The superficial training as a good citizen they receive, which is mostly accidental and on the side, is feeble from the beginning. Since a state is just a form, it is very hard to train people to see this form as an ideal to be served, let alone make them feel any commitment toward it. A form is too easily broken. But, as we have seen, the idea of a State has no clear meaning today anyway. There is nothing left but the generic "patriotic" education. The old Germany placed a strong emphasis on the glorification of insignificant leaders, even small local leaders. This emphasis was often not very clever and usually appeared very stupid. There were so many of these minor figures that it became impossible for our people to know who were the truly great men and who were nothing. As a result, our broad masses had a very deficient knowledge of German history. Here too the sweeping line of historical development and meaning of history was missing.

It is obvious that this limited historical education provides no opportunity to ever generate any true nationalist enthusiasm. Our educational administrators lacked the skill to pick out a few names from the historical blob of our people and make those great figures part of the entire German people. This would have held together the entire nation by giving them a firm, uniform bond of knowledge and enthusiasm that would have become a shared rallying point. Educators were not able to make the really important men of our people seem like towering heroes in the eyes of the present day. They were not able to point everyone's attention towards them and produce a united state of mind. They were unable to pick from the various school subjects what was glorious for the nation and what would help education rise above the level of a matter-of-fact description and to kindle the national pride with such shining examples. To them, elevating important individuals would have seemed like an unfair exercise of judgment of the worst sort when placing one individual above another. This would not have been well received because today everyone believes both sides of any argument should be given equal status, and one side can never be favored above another. Paying attention to the patriotism felt for a succession of royal dynasty rulers seemed more pleasant and easier to bear than the blazing passion of strong national pride. Patriotism for minor monarchs could always be used by the current administration when it was needed; however, strong national patriotism might some day take control itself. Monarch patriotism ended in veterans' associations where they would hear none of it. Nationalists' passions followed a course that would have been hard to predict and this frightened monarchs away from it. Nationalism is like a temperamental thoroughbred horse which will not allow just anyone in the saddle. It's no wonder rulers preferred to keep away from such a menace. No one seemed to think it was possible that some day a war might come whose artillery fire and gas attacks would put this kind of patriotism to a radical test of endurance. But when a war did come, the lack of supreme nationalist passion was avenged in a terrible way. People had little inclination to die for their imperial and royal sovereigns and most of them did not even recognize the "nation" as a nation.

Now that the Revolution has swept over Germany and monarch patriotism was automatically extinguished, the purpose of teaching history has become nothing more than to pass along factual knowledge. The current state has no use for "nationalist" enthusiasm and what patriotism it does want, it will never have. There could be no patriotism backed by the ultimate strength of a nation's people in this age of a dynasty that is influenced by international interests first. There is even less possibility of building enthusiasm and patriotism for a parliamentary government. There isn't much doubt that the German people would never stay on the battlefield four and a half years under the motto, "For the Parliament". Those who created this miracle structure of government would be the least likely to stay.

As a matter of fact, this Parliamentary Republic owes its disorderly survival to its willingness to voluntarily pay any reparations and to sign any territorial waiver placed in front of it. The Parliamentary Republic is pleasing to the rest of the world in the same way a weakling seems more agreeable than a strong, solid man to those who meet him. The fact that the enemy is fond of this particular form of government is also the most devastating criticism of it. They like the German Parliamentary Republic and let it live because they could never possibly find a better ally for the job of enslaving our people. The "splendid" parliamentary institution owes its present survival to this fact and this fact alone. That is why it can abandon any nationalist education and why it is satisfied with the current Reich flag heroes. Of course those "heroes" would run like little rabbits if they had to protect this flag with their blood.

The new Nationalist state will have to fight for its existence. It will not gain its existence by signing a Dawes Plan (*an unsuccessful attempt by the allies to collect war reparations from Germany by the Dawes Committee*), and it will not be able to defend its survival by signing papers. For its existence and its protection, it will need the very thing that the current administration believes they can abandon. The more precious and worthy the form and substance of the new Nationalist state are, the greater the envy and resistance from the enemy will be. The best protection will not be in its weapons, but in its citizens. Fortress walls will not defend the State; it can only be saved by a living wall of men and women who are filled with supreme love of Fatherland and fanatical nationalist enthusiasm.

The third point to consider in the education system is that the new Nationalist state must find a way to advance national pride in the sciences as well. World history and the entire history of civilization must be taught from this standpoint.

An inventor must not be presented as great just because he is an inventor, but he must be shown to be greater still because he is an inventor who is a member of our people. Admiration for any great deed must be transformed into pride for the lucky achiever as a member of one's own race. From the myriad of great names in German history, the greatest must be selected and so impressively presented to the youth that they become towers of strength and create an unshakable feeling of national pride.

The school curriculum must be systematically built up from that standpoint. Organized education must be shaped so that the young person leaves school as a complete German and not as a half-pacifist, democrat, or something else. For this national feeling to be genuine from the very beginning and not just an empty pretense, one inflexible principle must be hammered into the still malleable minds of youth: He who loves his people proves it only by his willingness to sacrifice for them. There is no such thing as a national-feeling that aims only to benefit personal interests. There is no such thing as a nationalism which includes only certain social classes. Cheering and shouting prove nothing. Yelling the loudest doesn't give a person the right to call himself a nationalist unless a great, loving care for the preservation of a common, healthy nationality stands behind those hoots and hollers. One cannot truly be proud of one's people if they are ashamed of any social class within those people. If one half of a people are miserable, oppressed, and destitute, how can anyone be proud of such a state. Only when a nationality is solid physically and morally can the joy in belonging to such a people rightfully rise in everyone's heart to that height of feeling which we call national pride. But only the man who knows the greatness of his nationality will feel this highest pride.

A personal spirit of nationalism and a sense of social justice must be combined in the hearts of the youth. If that is done properly, someday a nation of citizens will arise that will be committed to one another and forged together by a common love and a common pride, unshakable and indestructible forever.

The fear of showing unfair preference for a side has become our age's symptom of its own weakness. Everyone wants to give equality to both sides without making a decision, without commitment. Fate will never choose our era for any great deed because we lack any overflowing energy. To the contrary, any display of such exuberance is considered totally inappropriate. The greatest changes in this world would not have been imaginable if their driving force had been limited to the privileged-class virtues of peace and good order. Great change is accomplished only when driven by fanatical and hysterical passions. There is no doubt that this world is moving toward a great disturbance and revolution is coming. The only question is whether this change will benefit the Aryan or if it will be for the profit of the wandering Jew.

By appropriate education of our youth, the race-based Nationalist state will have to form a generation that is prepared to face the decisions that will be the last and greatest and will decide the destiny of the globe. The people who travel this road first will be the victors.

The fulfillment of the racial state's educational work includes burning an appreciation of race into the hearts and minds of the youth entrusted to preserve it. Youth must be imprinted both through instinct and understanding with the importance of their race. No boy and no girl should leave school without possessing an ultimate understanding of the importance in maintaining the purity of their blood. This will create the basis which will preserve our nationality's racial foundations and assure the conditions for further cultural development are kept intact. All the physical and intellectual training in the world would be for nothing if that training were given to a being who was not ready and determined to preserve the characteristic qualities of its race.

If we fail to instill this racial appreciation, we would have a widespread problem, a problem that we Germans already regret, yet perhaps without fully understanding the extent our tragedy has reached today. In the future we would become cultural manure to fertilize other civilizations. In the common mind of our present privileged-class, they see only a lost citizen when they look at a lost individual member of our people. They fail to see a lost member of our race who can never be recovered. There is a painful realization that, despite all our knowledge and ability, our blood line is still headed for oblivion. By continually mixing with other races, we lift them from their lower cultural level to a higher one, but we ourselves fall forever from our own race's great heights.

This racial education will be completed in military service. The military is the final state of the regular education for the average German.

Just as important as the physical and mental training in the new race-based state will be, so too is the importance of classifying people and their abilities so the right people may be selected for positions in the State. Today we take this selection for granted. In general the children of upper-class parents or those who have become wealthy are the ones considered worthy of higher education. Here talent is a secondary consideration. A peasant boy may have far greater gifts of talent than the child of parents who can trace their lineage through generations of upper class families. The peasant child may not have the knowledge of the city child, but the city child's greater knowledge has nothing to do with the quality of his talents. This knowledge comes from the abundance of feelings, experiences and images that the wealthy child is exposed to as a result of his more well-rounded education and his abundant surroundings. If the talented peasant boy had grown up from infancy in similar surroundings, his capacity for intellectual achievement would be altogether different.

Today there is one single field in which a man's origin matters less than his natural gifts and it is the field of art. In art one cannot simply "learn", but rather must have talent born in him. His parents' money and property mean nothing. This natural ability is only later subject to how wisely the existing gift is developed. This is the best proof that genius is not confined to the upper classes or to the wealthy. The greatest artist frequently comes from the poorest home. Many a village has seen their small boy later become a celebrated master.

It does not speak well for the wisdom of our age that we do not take advantage of this truth for our collective intellectual life. People foolishly believe that what applies to art is not true of the sciences. There is no doubt that a man can be trained in certain mechanical skills, just as an expert can teach a poodle the most astonishing tricks. But in animal training, it is not the animal's own intelligence alone that creates such tricks. The same is true of man. Even a man who has no talent can be taught certain scientific tricks, but the process is just as lifeless and as uninspired as teaching a dog to jump through a hoop. It is even possible by using a certain intellectual hammer to pound above average knowledge into an average person, but it still remains lifeless and unproductive knowledge. The result of such knowledge cramming is a man who may be a walking encyclopedia, but who still fails miserably in every situation and at every crucial moment in life when he needs to apply that knowledge. He has to be given special, intensive new training for every task, no matter how simple, and is unable to make the slightest contribution on his own to the development of mankind. Knowledge that is drilled into a man by this sort of mechanical method is only adequate for filling a present day state civil service job.

It is obvious that among the nation's population, there will be people with talents in every possible field. It is also obvious that the value of knowledge is greater when even the simplest information is brought to life by the appropriate talent of the individual. Creative leaps in achievement can occur only when talent and knowledge are joined.

The sins of modern mankind against this rule are never ending and can be seen in another example. The illustrated newspapers occasionally show the privileged-class how a negro for the first time has become a lawyer, a teacher, perhaps even a minister, or a heroic opera tenor somewhere or other. The feeble-minded privileged-class looks at such a miracle of animal training with admiration and astonishment before overflowing with respect for this marvelous result of modern education. At the same time the Jew is very shrewd about using this as new proof of the theory that "all men are equal", which he is forcing down the peoples' throats, is valid. It never dawns on the weary middle-class world that such a news article is actually a sin against all reason. It is criminal insanity to train a born half-ape until one believes he has been turned into a lawyer, while millions of members of the highest of civilized races must remain in a position totally unworthy of them. It is a sin against the will of the Eternal Creator to let hundreds and thousands of His most gifted creatures decay in the modern worker-laborer swamp while Hottentots and Zulus are being tamed for intellectual professions. As with the poodle, it is just animal training and not "scholastic" education. The same care and pains spent on intelligent races would prepare every individual for similar achievements and each would be a thousand times more adept.

This state of affairs would be intolerable if these reports were about anything other than the rare exceptions. It is already impossible to tolerate today because talent and aptitude are not what are used to qualify for higher education. The thought is positively insufferable that hundreds of thousands of absolutely untalented persons are thought worthy of higher education every year, while other hundreds of thousands who are highly gifted go without any advanced education at all. The loss the nation suffers because of this discrepancy is immeasurable. The wealth of important inventions created during the last few decades has shown an extraordinary increase, particularly in North America, because many more talented people from the lower classes have a chance at higher education there than they have in Europe.

Knowledge merely ladled out is not enough to spark discoveries. This spark must be brought alive by talent combined with knowledge. But we attach no importance to this gift of talent. Today good grades are all that count.

The new people's state will have to intervene in education here as well. However it is not the state's job to preserve the educational dominance of an existing class in society. The state's job is to find the most capable minds among the entire nation and to drape them with honor and dignity. It is not just the state's obligation to give the average child a basic education, but its duty is to place talent on the road where it belongs. Above all, its highest concern must be to open the doors of the schools of higher learning to every talented person, no matter what social class he comes from. We must do this because it is the only way we can grow inspired leadership for the nation from a class that is currently only filled with unproductive knowledge.

There is another reason why the state must look ahead to our future and help aspiring talent. Especially in Germany our intellectual classes are so isolated and fossilized that they have no living connection with those in the social classes beneath them. This has evil results in two ways. In the first place, the intellectuals have no understanding of and no sympathy for the broad masses. Their connection to the people has been broken too long, they no longer have the necessary psychological understanding needed to relate to them. They have become strangers to their own people. Secondly, these upper class intellectuals do not have the necessary strength of will. Strength of will is always weaker in intellectual social classes than in the primitive mass of the people. God knows, we Germans have never lacked academic scientific education, but strong will and decisiveness have totally eluded us. The more "intellectual" our statesmen have become, the more deficient their accomplishments have been.

The political preparations and military equipment for the First World War were inadequate. This was not because those who governed our people were insufficiently educated, but because they were over-educated, stuffed with knowledge and intelligence, but they had no sound instinct and lacked energy and boldness. It was a catastrophe that our people had to defend themselves in this battle under a weakling philosopher Chancellor. If instead of a Bethmann-Hollweg(*Theobald von Bethmann-Hollweg, Chancellor of the German Empire until 1917 who was viewed as a moderate*) we had a more forceful man of the people as a leader, the heroic blood of the infantry soldier would not have been shed in vain. In the same way, the excessive intellectual refinement of our leadership was the best ally for the revolutionary November criminals. By shamefully holding back the national budget, which the public entrusted to them, instead of risking it in its entirety to build defenses, these intellectuals themselves made the success of the Allies and the Revolution possible.

The Catholic Church is a splendid counter example. The fact that its priests are unmarried forces it to draw the new generation of the clergy from the great masses of the people instead of from its own ranks. This significant effect of celibacy is not usually recognized. It is the reason for the incredibly vigorous strength in this ancient institution. Because the giant army of priests is constantly recruited from the lowest classes of the peoples, the Church not only remains instinctively close to the emotional world of the people, but assures itself of the energy that is always available from the broad masses of the people. This accounts for the amazing youthfulness, intellectual adaptability, and iron strength of will in this giant beast.

The new race-based state will make sure the educational system provides a constant supply of new blood from the lower social classes to the existing intellectual classes. It is the state's duty to carefully and thoroughly sift through the population and discover those of obvious innate talent and put them to work for society. State offices do not exist to provide posts for special social classes, but to accomplish the tasks they are given. That will only be possible if capable and strong-willed personalities are trained for service in these offices. This selection process is true for the intellectual leadership of the nation in every field and for all those who take part in intellectual and moral leadership, not just civil service. The greatness of a people is revealed by how well they succeed in training the most able minds for the fields that they are best suited to and how they are put to work for the national community. If two nations of basically equal resources are competing, the one whose best talents are represented throughout its intellectual leadership will be victorious and the one whose leadership is just one big common feeding-trough for certain groups or social classes, which does not consider the natural ability of individual members, will be defeated.

In our present-day world, this seems impossible. There will be immediate objections from some, if for example, the son of a high state government official is expected to become a craftsman simply because another son of craftsman, seems more capable as a civil servant than the official's son. That may be true given the present social status of manual labor. For that reason, the new race-based state will have to encourage a new attitude toward the idea of labor. Through centuries of education, it will have to break the bad habit of sneering at physical labor as a lowly occupation. The state will have to judge the individual man on how he contributes, not by the nature of his work, but by the form and excellence of his performance. This may seem shocking to an age in which the dullest bum newspaper writer is thought of more highly than the most intelligent precision mechanic, simply because the writer works with the pen. This incorrect evaluation is not part of our nature, but it has been artificially taught. This attitude has not always existed. The present unnatural state of affairs results from the general diseased condition of our materialistic age.

Every kind of work has two types of value: a purely material value and an ideal value. The material value lies in the practical importance of a job for the life of the community. The more the members of the nation benefit from someone's work, the higher the material value of that job. Consequently, this job's value is shown by how much someone is paid for his work. In contrast to this purely material value, is the ideal one. The ideal value does not depend on the importance by material standards, but on the degree of its fundamental necessity, how important is the work to the country as a whole. Certainly, the material advantage of an invention to the country may be greater than that of an ordinary mason's assistant job, but society depends as much on the small service as it does on the great one. Society makes a concrete evaluation of a job's value to the community by varying the rate of pay, but society must establish that every worker is equal whenever each individual does his best in his own field, whatever that may be. The evaluation of a man depends on his contribution to the community and not on his wages.

In a reasonable state where individuals are directed in their vocations, each must be assigned to the activity that suits his ability. In other words, able minds must be trained for the work they can do best. Ability, however, is not taught but born. It is a gift from Nature and not a developed skill that can be attributed to man. Consequently, one's social position should not force a job on the individual. His job should be determined by the abilities he was born with and by the education the community has provided to him. A man's value must be based on the way he handles the job he has been made responsible for by society. The vocation that an individual follows is not the purpose of his existence but only the means to his livelihood. He should continue cultivating and refining himself to reach a higher level as a human being, but he can only do this within his cultural community, which must always rest on the foundation of a state. He must make his contribution to preserving this foundation. Nature has already decided the form of his contribution. All he must do is return to the national community, zealously and honestly, what it has given him. The man who does this earns the greatest esteem and the highest respect. A material reward may be given for achievements that are beneficial to society. However, the individual reward comes from the appreciation he receives; an appreciation that everyone who devotes what Nature has given him and returns what national community has trained him for back to the service of his nationality is entitled to. That means it is no longer shameful to be a good craftsman, but it is shameful to waste God's days and the nation's bread and butter as an incompetent state official. It will then be taken for granted that a man will not be assigned to a duty if he does not have the gifts for it from the start.

Personal effectiveness in one's job is the sole standard that will determine his right to general participation and his right to participate in legal or civil affairs on an equal level.

The present age is cutting its own throat. It introduces universal voting and chatters about equal rights but cannot find any foundation for this equality. It sets a man's value based on how much he earns, which destroys the basis for the most noble equality that can possibly exist. Equality does not and cannot depend on individual achievement; instead equality exists only in the way everyone fulfills his obligations to the community. That is the only way natural chance can be eliminated in judging the value of a man and the individual be made the architect of his own importance.

In the present age, when entire groups of people judge one another by their income, they are incapable of understanding this idea. But this is no reason for us to abandon the idea. On the contrary, the person who wants to heal this inwardly sick and rotten age must first gather the courage to expose the causes of the disease. The National-Socialist Movement must take this as its duty and go beyond any narrow-minded elitism to gather and sort out those people who are the willing forces in our own nationality, ones who are willing to champion a new World-Concept .

There is no doubt that objections will be made saying it is difficult to separate the opinion one has, from the amount of pay, and therefore the lower esteem associated with physical labor comes from the lower rate of pay. This lower rate of pay means a man is less able to participate in the cultural wealth of his nation. This inability to improve his cultural knowledge damages the man's personal culture and has nothing to do with his work in itself. The most understandable reason that someone would find physical labor objectionable is because the lower pay necessarily means the cultural level of the manual laborer must be lower and that, in turn, justifies the lower value people hold for manual labor.

This idea is commonly believed to be true. Because of this, it will be necessary in the future to avoid excessive differentiation in wage scales. Let no one say that this would cause accomplishment to end as pay scales were equalized. It would be the saddest sign of an age's decay if higher intellectual achievement was only driven by the desire to receive higher pay. If this point of view had been the prevalent one in the world previously, mankind would be without its greatest scientific and cultural possessions. The greatest inventions, the greatest discoveries, the most revolutionary scientific work, and the most splendid monuments of human civilization were not given to the world out of a compulsion for money. On the contrary, their creation frequently represented a rejection of the earthly pleasures of wealth.

It may be true that money has become the exclusive ruler of life today, but the time will come when man will kneel to higher gods again. Many things around us today may owe their existence to the desire for money and property, but there is also very little of it that mankind would truly be any poorer without.

Another task of our movement is to work for the day when the individual will receive what he needs to live on, but at the same time will uphold the principle that man does not live exclusively for material pleasures. This will be illustrated in a wisely constructed universal pay scale that will allow every honest working man a respectable and decent existence as a human being and as a member of the nation.

Don't let it be said that this perfect condition is an ideal that this world could never withstand in practice and would never actually achieve. We are not so simple as to believe that a perfect age can ever happen. But this does not relieve anyone of the obligation to fight against the faults we see, to overcome weaknesses in the system, and to strive for the ideal. Harsh reality will always limit what we seek to accomplish. For that very reason, man must do the best he can and aspire to reach the ultimate goal. Failures must not distract him from his purpose, for he cannot abandon a judicial system simply because errors slip through, and he would not condemn all medical science just because there is still sickness in spite of our best efforts.

We must never fail to uphold the strength of an ideal. If anyone is faint-hearted at the thought of upholding ideals, I would like to remind him, especially if he has been a soldier, of a time when heroism was the most overpowering testimony to the strength of idealistic motives. Men did not die over concern for their daily bread, but for love of the Fatherland, belief in its greatness, and national patriotism. When the German people abandoned these ideals to follow the practical promises of the Revolution and exchanged the rifle for a knapsack, our people found themselves, not in an earthly Heaven, but rather in a purgatory of unending contempt and distress. This is why it is necessary to establish a faith in an idealistic Reich to battle against the reckoning imposed by the present materialistic Republic.

3. STATE MEMBER VS. STATE CITIZEN

The structure that is today erroneously called the State, identifies only two kinds of men: citizens and aliens. Citizens are those who possess the right of citizenship either by birth or by later naturalization. Foreigners are those who enjoy the same right in another country. In some places there are also comet-like beings that are considered stateless, who simply wander the universe. These are persons who have the "honor" not to belong to any of the present-day states and possess no right of citizenship anywhere.

Today, the right of citizenship is acquired primarily by birth within the boundaries of a country. Race or membership in the nation plays no part at all. A negro who used to live in the German protected territories and now has a residence in Germany brings a "German citizen" into the world if he has a child. In the same way any Jewish, Polish, African, or Asian child can be declared a German citizen.

That is one kind of naturalization, by birth within an extended territory and there is another possibility for later naturalization, by paperwork. There are various qualifications required to become naturalized like this. For instance, the prospective candidate will preferably not be a burglar or a pimp; he will be politically safe, which is to say he is a harmless political fool; and finally, that he will not become a burden on his new national home. In the present "materialistic" age, this means he will not be a financial burden. In fact, if one is believed to be a potentially good taxpayer, his state citizenship can be rushed. Racial considerations play no part whatsoever.

The whole process of acquiring citizenship is pretty much like joining an automobile club. A person sends in his application, it is checked and approved, and one fine day, he is informed on a slip of paper that he has become a citizen. The information is even put in a humorous and joking manner. The applicant who was previously a Zulu or Kaffir is notified: "By these presented, you are now become a German Citizen".[sic]

This magic trick is accomplished by the signature of a State official. What Heaven could not attempt, one of these Theophrastus Paracelsus officials can do with a scribble of his hand (*Theophrastus Paracelsus was a Swiss alchemist, astrologer, physician in the 1500's who traveled in Germany and was connected to Lutheranism; he is meant to be a magician in this reference, even though Theophrastus disliked that label.*) One scratch of the pen and a Mongolian Wenceslaus is suddenly turned into a real "German". (*Mongolian Wenceslaus appears to refer to a Czech Saint Wenceslaus but here means a Mongolian Saint, not of the Germanic race.*)

No attention is paid to the race of one of these new "citizens". His physical health is not even considered, though he may be crawling with syphilis. Nevertheless, to the modern state he is welcome as a citizen, as long as he is not a financial burden or a political menace.

Every year, these structures we call states, absorb poisons which they can barely survive.

The citizen is different from the alien because all public offices are open to the citizen; he may be required to serve in the military; and he is allowed to take part in elections. Those are his main benefits. The foreigner enjoys protection of personal rights and personal liberty the same as a citizen and sometimes, even more. At least this is how it plays out in our present German Republic.

I know that people will not enjoy hearing all this, but there is nothing more empty-headed and insane than our present naturalization law. Currently there is one state that is making at least a feeble effort to create a better system. Of course, it is not our model German Republic where this good sense has taken hold, but the United States of America. By excluding all immigrants who are unhealthy and outright refusing entry to certain races, the Americans are showing at least faint signs of a common attitude in the race-based Nationalist state idea.

The race-based Nationalist state divides its population into three classes: State Citizens, Subjects of the State, and Foreigners.

One becomes a State Subject by simply being born in the State. State Subject status does not entitle its possessor to hold public office or to be politically active, such as participating in elections, either actively or passively, nor running for office or voting. The race and original nationality of every State Subject must be proven. The State Subject is free at any time to relinquish his Subject status and become a citizen of whichever country is his own. The foreigner is distinguished from the State Subject by the fact that the foreigner already holds citizenship in a foreign state.

The children who are State Subjects of German nationality are required to go through the school system, which is established for every German. Through the school system, he undergoes the training to make him into a race conscious and nationally aware member of the people. Then when he leaves school, he has to go through the additional physical training prescribed by the state, and finally he enters the army. The army training is of a general nature. It will include every single German, and provide training that will make him useful to the military based on his physical and intellectual abilities. On completion of his military duty, state citizenship is solemnly granted on the healthy young man of faultless character. This is the most valuable document of his entire earthly life. He then becomes a full state citizen and is able to enjoy all those rights and privileges. The state must make a sharp distinction between two groups of the people, the ones who support and maintain the existence and greatness of the state, and the ones who simply live here as "gainfully employed" elements within a state.

When a person receives his certification of state citizenship, he must take a solemn oath to the national community and State. This oath must be a common bond that brings together all social classes. It must become a greater honor to be a street-cleaner and a citizen of the Reich than to be a King in a foreign state who is not a citizen of the Reich. The state citizen is a privileged gentleman who enjoys advantages not available to the alien. The citizen is the master of the Reich. But this higher dignity comes with its obligations. The man without honor or character, the common criminal, or the traitor to the Fatherland, may have this honor taken away at which time they become a mere State Subject again.

The German girl is a State Subject and only becomes a citizen when she marries. Citizenship may, however, be granted to female German State Subjects if they have independent careers.

4. PERSONALITY AND THE IDEA OF THE PEOPLE'S STATE

If the race-based National-Socialist State achieves its main interest, the development and preservation of the human strength of the state, then it will not be enough to simply promote the racial aspects of society and then to educate society, and finally prepare individuals for practical life. It will have to also make adjustments in its own organization so that it reflects the same values it promotes.

It would be insane to judge man's value by his race and then turn around and declare war on the Marxist claim that, "all men are created equal", if one were not determined to follow through to the logical conclusion. Once we recognize how important the purity of blood is and the importance of race in ability, then the logical conclusion is that these tests must be applied to the individual person. Just as I must assess nations differently based on the races that fill them, I must assess the individual person within that national community race. The fact that a nation is not simply a nation carries over to the individual within a national community. The value of a nation varies based on those races in it, and the value of a man varies based on the racial elements within him. It's the same thing when we say a mind is not simply a mind, the same as any other! Even when the elements of blood are the same within a race, their qualities are subject to a thousand subtle variations.

The first thing we see from this understanding is what I would call the more crude realization. It is that we must promote the qualities found to be racially valuable within the national community and to encourage them to multiply.

This task may be considered crude because it can be recognized and accomplished almost "mechanically". However, it is more difficult to recognize the most valuable minds that have the intellectual and idealistic qualities needed by the community and to grant them the influence which is not merely given out due a superior brain, but most importantly, granted based on their ability to be useful to the nation.

This separation according to ability and capacity cannot be accomplished by unemotional, unthinking mechanical means. It will be part of the constant struggle that is decided through the daily labors of life.

A World-Concept that rejects the idea of blind rule by democratic masses and gives the world to the best people, to the highest quality human beings, must obey the same noble principle it follows within its people and make absolutely certain that the best minds become the leadership and those great minds are the predominant influence over the people. This World-Concept does not build on the idea of majority, but rather on that of character.

Anyone who today assumes that a race-based National-Socialist state is only differentiated from other states by emotionless qualities, such as better construction of its economic system, does not have the faintest idea what a World-Concept really is. If they think it is created through a better balance of wealth and poverty, or a greater voice in the economic process for the broad masses, or by more equal pay through the elimination of excessive wage differences, they have been blinded by the superficial aspects. Everything I have just described offers no security and does not guarantee our permanent survival. It offers even less of a claim to greatness. A people who become bogged down in these outward reforms would not have the slightest chance of victory in the struggle for the nation's existence. Any movement that believes balancing the social classes and promoting equal economics, though noble, are the sole core of its mission, will not produce any great results or any true reform of existing conditions. All of its activity eventually becomes wrapped in showiness and totally preoccupied with appearances, without giving the people the inner preparation that they need to finally overcome this I say with certainty, those weaknesses we suffer from today.

To understand this more easily, it is useful for us to look back at the real origins of human cultural development.

The first step man took that visibly removed him from the animals was his ability to invent. The very first invention was the discovery of tricks and strategies that were used to make the fight for life easier against other creatures and sometimes were the sole reason a struggle had a favorable outcome for man. These primitive inventions do not reveal the character of their creators because these inventions or strategies are only seen by present day man and then only as a mass phenomenon, a collection of hunting methods and defensive actions spanning a long period. There are also certain tricks and shrewd precautions that can be observed in animals. Man is unable to determine or explore the origin of these actions, so he simply resorts to describing these actions as "instinctive". In the present case, this word means nothing. Anyone who believes in a higher development of living creatures must admit that every impulse and every act in their battle for life must have had a beginning at some time. One individual must have done it first, then it was repeated, then others repeated it more widely until, at last, it became a part of the subconscious of all the members of a given species and appeared as an instinct.

This is easier to understand and easier to believe in the case of man. Man's first clever steps in the battle to control other animals must surely have been made by members of his own civilization who were particularly gifted. Even here, character was once the absolute source for good decisions and conduct that were later adopted by all mankind until they were finally taken for granted. In the same way, all common military strategy originated in one particular mind, and it then spread and came to be generally taken for granted after many years. Sometimes it may have taken hundreds of years to become widespread.

Man supplements his first invention by a second invention. He learns to use other things. He puts objects and even living creatures, to work in the struggle to preserve his own existence. This is where the inventive nature of man, as we see it everywhere around us today, begins. We can see from these material inventions that character is a component in such creations more and more clearly. This started with the use of the stone as a weapon and continued to the domestication of animals, the artificial production of fire by man, and on to the various and admirable inventions of our day, and each of these sprang from the mind of an individual. This becomes clearer as we look at more recent inventions, or if we look at the more significant and decisive inventions of history. We know that everything we see around us in the way of material inventions was produced by the creative energy and ability of individual persons. Fundamentally, all these inventions help raise man higher and higher above the animal world and they definitely remove him from it. They serve humanity's constant progress in the effort to reach higher levels. Even those things that made life easier, such as a simple trick for the man hunting in the jungle long ago, helps now, because it is the basis for brilliant scientific understanding, to make mankind's battle for its present existence easier, and to forge the weapons for the struggles of the future. In its ultimate results, all human thinking and invention serve man's fight for life on this planet. This is true even if the so-called practical use of an invention or a discovery or a profound scientific insight into the nature of things may not be immediately obvious. All things together help to raise man more and more above the living creatures around him. They strengthen and consolidate his position so that he expands and becomes the dominant being on earth in every respect.

All inventions result from the work of one person. Intentionally or unintentionally, all these persons are great contributors to mankind. Their work later gave tools to millions, even thousands of millions of human beings, to make their life-struggle easier.

From the beginning of the present material civilization, we see individual persons as inventors who complement one another and each builds on the work of the one before. The same thing is true when we look at how those inventions are used in new ways. All the processes of production are in themselves inventions and depend on individuals to think them into existence. Even purely theoretical mental work is the exclusive product of an individual person. This is impossible to measure in detail yet still indispensable for all further material inventions. The masses do not invent and the majority does not organize or think. No, it is always from the character of the individual man.

A community must be organized so that it assists as much as possible the work of these creative forces and makes good use of them in the community. Whether the invention is material or mental, the most valuable part of the invention is the inventor's character. The first and highest concern of a national organization is to place him in a position where he is most useful to the community. It is the organization's purpose to put this very principle into practice. Only in this way is it released from the curse of mechanization so the community may take on life of its own. It must endeavor to set leaders where they manage the masses, and consequently to make sure the masses are led by the leaders.

The organization must encourage these leaders to emerge from the masses and remove all barriers that could possibly interfere with their rise. In doing so, it must follow the principle that the blessings of mankind have never come from the masses, but they have come from the creative minds of individuals. In the real world, these creative minds are the founders and providers of the human race. It is in the best interest of the community to make certain these men have the dominant influence and to assist them in their efforts. Unquestionably, the interests of the community are not satisfied and not served by the rule of the masses, but only by the leadership of those whom Nature has equipped with special talents for that purpose. The masses are not experts, the masses do not possess thinking power, and certainly the masses are not Divinely gifted. Only individuals have these powers.

These great minds are revealed mainly through the hard battle of daily life itself. Many are broken and destroyed in the process, which only proves they are not destined for the ultimate positions of responsibility. At last, only the chosen few remain. This process of selection still goes on today in the areas of education, theory, creative art, and economics. However, in the area of economics particularly, it is already subject to severe handicaps. The same idea rules the civil service state administration and is also seen in the power of the military defense forces of the nation. In all these areas, the idea of character, its authority over those of lower rank, and its responsibility to those of higher rank, still dominates. Today, only the area of politics has completely turned its back on this most natural principle. All of human civilization is the result of the creative activity of individual persons who direct the national community and especially those who act as leaders. But in politics, the most important principle becomes the strength of the majority. From the top it trickles down, and it gradually begins to poison all life and ultimately dissolves it. Even the destructive effect of Jewry's activity, which we can see in other nations, result from its constant effort to undermine the importance of the individual person in those nations hosting their presence. The Jew seeks to replace the power of the individual by the domination of the masses. The organizing principle of Aryan humanity is replaced by the destructive principle of the Jew. The Jew becomes the festering rot of nations and races and, in a larger sense, the solvent of human culture.

Marxism is the pure essence of the Jew's attempts to eliminate the importance of character in every aspect of human life and replace it with the numerical power of the masses. Its political counterpart is the parliamentary form of government whose disastrous work we can see going on from the tiny nucleus of the village all the way up to the top of the Reich. Their economic counterpart is the system of trade union movements, which do not serve the true interests of the wage-earner, but only the destructive purposes of the international world Jew. The farther our economic system moves away from the influence of the character principle, the more it surrenders itself to the effects of the masses. The national economy should be productive and provide a valuable service to the community, but it will gradually become involved in the inevitable decline as the power of character is replaced by the influence of the masses. All work councils, which were established by the unions, try to gain influence over production instead of protecting the interests of employees, so they serve the same destructive purpose. They harm the total production system and, in turn, harm the individual worker. The members of the nation cannot be satisfied in the long run by fancy theoretical phrases. They will only be satisfied when they receive the goods they need to carry on their daily lives, and through this process they create a collective conviction among the national community that results in the interests of the community being guarded by the individual, and the interests of the individual being upheld by the community.

It would not matter if Marxism was able to implement its mass-rule theory and happened to take over today's existing economic structure because it would not prove anything. The reliability or myth of this principle is not determined by its ability to take over and manage a system that already exists. The only valid test is whether or not it has the creative power to build up such a culture based on its own principles. If Marxism were to take over and continue the present economic structure under its own leadership, even if it tried a thousand times over and was successful in taking control every time, it would prove nothing. Marxism would not be able to use this principle to create a system like the one it takes over today, not one that works at any rate. Marxism has given practical proof of this. Not only has it never succeeded in creating a civilization or even an economic structure, but it has been unable to continue the operation of existing structures according to its principles. When it had the opportunity, it was forced to almost immediately make concessions and return to the ideas of the character principle. It cannot do without these principles even in its own organization.

What most clearly distinguishes the new race-based World-Concept from the Marxist World-Concept is the fact that the new race-based World-Concept recognizes the value of race and the importance of the individual and makes these the pillars of its whole structure. These are the most important factors that carry its World-Concept .

If the National-Socialist movement failed to understand the fundamental significance of this essential principle-of-character and instead only outwardly patched up the present State or actually considered the mass-rule standpoint as its own, it would then be nothing more than another party competing with Marxism on its own principles. It would no longer have a right to call itself a World-Concept . If the National Socialist program sought to crowd out individuals and replace them with the masses, that would mean National Socialism itself was already eaten away by the poison of Marxism, just as the world of our privileged-class political parties are today.

The new race-based state can best care for the welfare of its citizens by recognizing the importance of the individual's value in anything and everything relating to the operation and leadership of the community. Maximizing production in every field assures that every individual receives the maximum possible share of that overall output. For that reason, the new race-based State must remove the current obscene political leadership, especially the highest leadership positions, from the grip of majority rule by parliament. This will assure that it will be replaced by the right of the individual, and personal responsibility will be placed there instead.

From that, we can draw the following conclusion: The best state constitution and form of state government are those that give the greatest importance and governing influence to the best minds of the national community.

Those men who are most capable in the economic world cannot be appointed by someone in a high position. They must fight their own way up the ladder of success. They provide themselves with endless training, from the smallest business deal all the way through to the greatest industry, and the challenge of life alone does the testing. Similarly, political brains cannot be suddenly "discovered". Geniuses with an extraordinary ability cannot be judged by the same rules we use for normal humanity.

The individual principle must be anchored in the state's organization, from the smallest city council through the head of the government of the entire Reich.

There must be no decisions made by a majority, but only decisions made by responsible persons. The word "council" must be brought back to its original meaning. Every man will have "counselors" to assist him, but ultimately one man makes the decision.

The principle that made the Prussian army a marvelous instrument of the German people must someday be transferred to form the basis of the state, and that principle is this: Every leader will be invested with full authority over those below him, and he will carry full responsibility toward those above. Even then we will not be able to do without parliaments, but their counselors will only provide counsel, and one man alone will have the responsibility, authority, and the right to command.

Parliaments are necessary to identify those minds that will gradually emerge and can later be entrusted with positions of great responsibility.

The general picture of how this will work follows:

From the village up through the government of the Reich, the new race-based state will not have a representative body that decides anything by majority vote but only advisory bodies that assist the chosen leader. The leader divides up duties among them, and as needed, they resume absolute responsibility in certain fields, just as the leader or chairman of the particular body has the responsibility on a larger scale.

On principle, the new race-based state will not tolerate the practice of asking advice or accepting advice on matters that require special knowledge, for instance in economic matters, from people who lack that knowledge and cannot possibly understand the matter due to a lack of training and experience. From the beginning the state must divide its representative bodies into political and occupational chambers.

The cooperation between the two will be assured by a special Senate that will have authority over them.

No vote will ever be taken in either of the Chambers or in the Senate. They are working institutions, not voting machines. The individual member has an advisory voice, but never a decisive voice. Decisive action belongs solely to the particular chairman who is responsible for the matter being considered.

This principle of directly connecting absolute authority with absolute responsibility will gradually cause a group of leaders to emerge. This would be quite unthinkable in our present irresponsible parliament. The nation's state constitution and political structure will then be brought into harmony with the laws of nature to which the cultural and economic fields already owe their greatness.

For those who may question the practicality of these principles, I would ask that you not forget the system of parliament, which uses democratic majority rule, has not always controlled mankind. On the contrary, majority rule is only found in very brief periods of history, and those have always been periods of decline for the people and nations.

Such a transformation cannot be produced by purely theoretical measures decreed from the top down, since logically it cannot be limited to the constitution of a state and expected to propagate, but it must penetrate all other legislation and all of civil life. A radical change like this can and will occur only through a movement which is built up in the spirit of these ideas and bears the principles of the coming state within itself. Therefore, the National-Socialist Movement even today should make itself completely at home with these ideas and put them into practice within its own organization. That way, in the future, it may not only lay down the same guidelines for the state, but may put the perfected body of its own organization at the state's disposal.

5. World-Concept AND ORGANIZATION

I have tried to draw a general picture of the new race-based State; however, it will not be realized by simply understanding what is necessary to construct a state. It is not sufficient to know how a race-based state should look. Much more important is the problem of where to start. We cannot expect the existing political parties, which are mainly landlords of the present state, to take any action themselves toward change or to voluntarily alter their present attitude. This is impossible because they are being directed by Jews, Jews here and Jews there and Jews everywhere. If current events are allowed to develop unhindered, the final result will be the realization of the Pan-Jewish prophecy, and the Jew would devour the peoples of the earth and become their master.

In contrast to the millions in the German privileged-class and workers who amble to their destruction mainly out of cowardice coupled with apathy and stupidity, the Jew follows his chosen path without hesitation, fully conscious of his future goal. A party led by him can fight for only Jewish interests, and these have nothing in common with the needs of the Aryan.

To transform the ideal image of a race-based Nationalist state into reality, one must seek new forces that are willing and able to undertake the battle for such an ideal, and one must especially avoid forces related to the current system. And a battle it must be, because the creation of a new race-based state first requires the elimination of the present Jewish concept of a state. It often happens in history, that the greatest problem faced is not the formation of a new state of affairs, but in clearing out room for it. Bias and self-interests form a solid front and use every means to prevent the victory of a new idea they find disagreeable and menacing. The champion of such an ideal, with all his positive intentions for it, is forced to fight first in order to wipe out the existing state of affairs.

As unpleasant as it may be to the individual followers, a young doctrine of great importance and new significance must use the tool of criticism in all sharpness as its first weapon of assault.

It shows little historical insight when the so-called racialists of today keep declaring that they have no intention of indulging in negative criticism but only in constructive work. This nonsense is as childish and as idiotic as it is truly indicative of the "racialist", and it proves how little they know of their own history. Marxism has an aim also, and it is no stranger to "constructive work", even if that work is nothing more than the creation of a tyranny of international world finance, by which I mean Jewry! Nevertheless, it began its constructive work by practicing criticism and has continued for seventy years. And how destructive it was! This corrosive criticism continued until the constant gnawing of the acid undermined the old State and brought it to collapse. Only then did the so-called "constructive work" of Marxism begin.

However, this was actually natural, right, and logical. You cannot abolish the current system by simply emphasizing and insisting on a future one. Explaining the necessity for change will not win over followers of the present system and it certainly will not convert those with an interest in the existing state of affairs. Unfortunately, it may easily happen that both conditions will exist side by side, so that the new World-Concept becomes a political party, and once that happens, it can never escape from its own limitations. World-Concept s are intolerant and cannot be satisfied with the role of being a "party among others". They arrogantly demand complete and exclusive recognition for themselves and a complete transformation of public life so that it follows their views. A true World-Concept cannot tolerate any continuing existence of a previous state of affairs side by side with their views.

This is equally true of religions. Christianity could never be content with building its own altar. It was driven to destroy pagan altars. The faith could only grow when there was no controversy, and it did grow out of this fanatical intolerance. In fact, intolerance is absolutely indispensable for the growth of any faith.

Now one may object and say such occurrences in world history are related mainly to Jewish ways of thinking, and it is true that this kind of intolerance and fanaticism are common symptoms of Jewish nature. This may be right a thousand times over; however, it is part of all history, and though deeply regrettable, and though we may only grudgingly admit it is part of history, and you can even say this intolerance is not part of human nature, yet it does not change the fact that this is how the world exists today. The men who want to rescue our German people from the current troubles cannot dwell on how wonderful it would be if things were different, but they must determine how those current conditions can be wiped away. A World-Concept full of hellish intolerance cannot be shattered, except by an idea that is promoted with a similar spirit of intolerance, an idea that is defended by the same intense will, and at the same time is pure and absolutely true in itself.

People today may be troubled to discover that the first intellectual terrorism was inflicted by Christianity on the unrestricted ancient world. However, he will not be able to dispute the fact that since that time, the world has been driven and dominated by Christian forces. Force can only be broken by force, and terrorism can only be broken by terrorism. Only then can a new order be created.

Political parties are inclined to compromise; World-Concept s never compromise. Political parties adjust their views to match those of their adversaries; World-

Concept s proclaim their own infallibility.

Political parties almost always start off by planning to achieve total and dictatorial domination. They almost always have some small tendency toward becoming a World-Concept . But the very limits of their program rob them of the heroism that a World-Concept demands. This spirit of compromise and placation attracts small and feeble souls who could never champion any crusade. The result is that very soon they are stuck in their own miserable pettiness. This is how they give up the fight for a World-Concept and resort to using so-called "constructive cooperation" to secure a place at the feeding-trough of the existing regime. Once they have squeezed into their place, they will stay there for as long as possible. This is their whole aim. If they are ever pushed away from the common trough by some brutally-inclined feeder, they simply strain and scheme, whether by force or slyness, to push to the front again and feed among the hungry drove. They will use whatever means are necessary to again eat from the cherished fountain of nourishment, even though they sacrifice their most sacred convictions. They are the jackals of politics!

No World-Concept is ever prepared to share its place with another. It can never be ready to help in an existing regime that it condemns, but instead, it feels obligated to fight the current state-of-affairs and the entire world of hostile ideas belonging to that order by every means possible until it achieves the enemy's downfall. This battle of destruction to collapse the adversary, which they instantly recognize as a threat and oppose with united resistance, requires determined warriors. The positive battle to build and establish its own new ideology also requires determined warriors. Therefore, a World-Concept can lead its ideas to victory only if it unites the most courageous and energetic elements of its age and has the best people in its ranks, solidly shaping them into a vigorous fighting organization. To accomplish this, it is necessary to keep these elements in mind and to pick certain ideas from its World-Concept that can be wrapped up in brief, precise, slogan-like qualities that make them suitable as a doctrine of faith for a new fellowship of men. While the platform of a strictly political party is a formula for success in the coming election, the program of a World-Concept is a formula that declares war on an existing order, an existing state of things, and an existing World-Concept .

That does not mean it is necessary for every individual who is fighting for this World-Concept to have a complete understanding and knowledge of the ultimate ideas and reasoning of the movement's leaders. It is more important that a few fundamentals are made clear to him and the most essential basic lines stamped permanently in his mind so that he is absolutely convinced of the need for the victory by his movement and his doctrine.

The individual soldier is not instructed in high level strategic planning. Instead, he is trained for rigid discipline and a fanatical belief in the justice and strength of his cause, and this makes him totally devoted to the cause without any reservations. The same thing must be taught to the individual follower of a movement so that he knows it is important, and he is fighting for a great future and a supreme purpose.

An army would be worthless if it only consisted of generals. A political movement that upholds a World-Concept is equally worthless if it tries to be a reservoir of "thinking" people. No, it needs the discipline of the simple soldier as well. The survival of any organization depends on the service of a broad and emotionally driven mass of people who are willing to serve a supreme intellectual leadership. It is more difficult to maintain discipline with a company of two hundred equally intelligent men than to maintain discipline with a company of one hundred and ninety with less intellectual capacity and only ten educated men among them.

In the past, the Social Democracy Marxist movement has used this fact to their great benefit. It recruited from the masses our discharged soldiers who were already accustomed to discipline. The Marxists took them under its own equally rigid discipline. Its organization was an army that consisted of both officers and soldiers. But here, the German laborer, who was now discharged from the army, was the soldier and the Jewish intellectual became the officer, and the German trade union officials could be considered the non-commissioned officers. Our privileged-class was always shaking their heads in confusion when they saw that only the so-called uneducated masses belonged to Marxism. They failed to realize this was the reason for its success. While the intellectual privileged-class parties formed a useless and undisciplined mob, Marxism used the non-intellectuals to form an army of party soldiers who blindly obeyed their Jewish masters as they had once obeyed their German officers. The German middle-class thought they were above worrying about the mental reasoning of the "ignorant" lower classes so they paid no attention to them. They also failed to consider the potential consequences or to realize the deeper meaning, and they certainly failed to see the danger that existed in this recruitment of the masses. On the contrary, they believed that a political movement that consisted only of intellectuals was superior simply because it was an intellectual movement. They assumed a group of intellectuals had more of a right and a greater chance of gaining power than the uneducated masses would possibly have. They never realized that the strength of a political party is not found in the great intelligence of individual members, but rather strength is in the disciplined obedience of the members who follow their intellectual leadership. What counts is the leadership itself. If two bodies of troops are fighting, the victor will not be the one whose individual members have the most advanced strategical training;

the winner will be the one with the superior leadership and with better-disciplined, more blindly obedient, and better-drilled troops. This is a basic principle that we must constantly keep in view when testing the possibility of moving a World-Concept into action and making it a reality.

Now that we know we must transform a World-Concept into a fighting movement in order to lead it to victory, it is logical that the movement's program must consider the human resources at its disposal. On one hand, the ultimate goals and guiding ideas of the movement must be firmly fixed and immovable. On the other hand, the propaganda of the recruiting program must adapt to appeal to those whose help is necessary for success. This propaganda must be brilliant and psychologically sound when adapted to the target audience. Without them, even the most brilliant idea would always remain just an idea.

If the race-based nationalist idea is to grow from a vague thought into a clear success, it must carefully select certain guiding principles and ideas calculated by nature and substance to attract and hold a great mass of men. Only this mass can guarantee these ideas in the form of a World-Concept that will be fought for. This mass is the German working class.

For this reason, the program of the new movement was summed up in a handful of guiding principles, twenty-five in all. They are intended to give a rough picture of the movement's intent to the ordinary man of the people. They are, to a certain extent, a political profession of faith. On the one hand, they are to gain followers for the movement and on the other hand, they are to unite those followers by welding the recruits together by giving them a common obligation.

The following realization is important and must always be remembered: The program of the movement is beyond questioning and is absolutely sound in its ultimate aims. But, since it has had to be written down based on what was thought at the time, the opinion may eventually arise that perhaps certain principles should be worded differently and better formulated. This is usually disastrous because it takes something that should be unshakably firm and opens it to discussion. If we allow a single point to be dragged outside the realm of a strict doctrine, discussion will not produce a new, better, and unified formulation. It is far more likely to lead to endless debate and general chaos. In such a case, the alternatives must always be weighed. Which is better? A new and more succinct formula that causes a dispute within the movement, or a form that is less than perfect, but establishes a logical, unshakable, inwardly unified entity? If carefully considered, the unshakable entity will always be preferred. Since changes are only a matter of outward form, making corrections may seem desirable or even possible over and over again. Due to men's focus on the outward appearance, there is great danger that they may see this external re-formatting of a program as the main business of a movement and assume the goal is to tinker with the program. But if that is the focus, the will and strength to fight for the idea will diminish, and the energy that should be directed against the outside world is consumed by internal battles over the program.

If the broad outline of the doctrine is actually sound and it has, up to this point, been considered a rock solid law, it is not nearly as harmful to keep a formula that is less than ideal or may not agree exactly with the truth than to try improving it by opening it up to discussions that may have damaging consequences. Revisions must be absolutely avoided as long as the movement itself is still struggling for victory. How are we to fill men with blind faith in the truth of a doctrine if we spread uncertainty and doubt by constantly making changes to it? We must always seek the inner meaning of the doctrine and not become distracted by the outer shape. This inner core is unchangeable, and for its own sake, we can only hope that by keeping away all actions that can divide and create doubt, the movement may gain the strength necessary to maintain itself.

Here, too, we can learn from the Catholic Church. Although its dogma unnecessarily conflicts sometimes with science on many points, the Church is not willing to sacrifice one syllable of this dogma. It rightly realizes that its strength is not in adjusting to match the scientific results of the moment, which are constantly changing, but in firm devotion to doctrines that are established and form its character of faith. It is more solid today than ever because of this. We may safely foretell that as events become more fleeting and they begin to change faster, the strong and stable fixed pole of the Church will attract even greater numbers of the blindly devoted.

Anyone who truly and seriously desires the victory of a new race-based World-Concept must realize that only a movement that is capable of fighting is equipped to succeed and that such a movement can hold its own only if it is built on an unshakable, impregnable, and solid program. In formulating its program, the movement must never dare to make concessions to the passing spirit of the times, but must always maintain the form that has been decided as the right one, or at least maintain it until the movement is victorious. Until this has happened, any attempt to introduce arguments about the suitability of some point of the program will shatter the unity and fighting strength of the movement in the same degree its followers participate in such inner discussions. An "improvement" carried out today might be subjected to renewed critical scrutiny tomorrow and possibly another better substitute found the day after. Anyone who allows this to happen opens up a road whose beginning he knows, but whose end is lost in a boundless expanse.

This important realization had to be used in the young National-Socialist movement. In the program of the Twenty-Five Points, the National-Socialist German Workers' Party has a foundation that must remain unshakable. The movement's present and future members must never feel it is their task to rework these guiding principles but must feel duty bound to them as they stand. Otherwise, the next generation might waste its strength on similar purely formal work within the party instead of bringing new followers and new power to the movement. For the great number of followers, the essence of our movement will be less in the words of our doctrine and more in the meaning we give them.

The young movement originally owed its name to these considerations. The program was later drawn up in accordance with these and that was how the circle of ideas became rooted. To bring victory to the new race-based ideas, it was necessary to create a people's party, a party consisting not just of intellectual leaders, but of manual workers too.

Any attempt to accomplish the new racialist lines of thought without this forceful organization would be useless today and forever, just as it has proven to be in the past. Therefore, it is the movement's right and its duty to consider itself the champion and the embodiment of these ideas. The basic ideas of the National-Socialist movement are race-based--racialism is National-Socialism. If National Socialism is to conquer, it must declare this set of ideas absolutely and exclusively as its own. Here too it has the duty and the right to stress that any attempt to maintain the race-based idea outside the confines of the National-Socialist German Workers' Party is pointless and impossible, and in most cases, such claims are outright fraud.

If anyone today accuses the movement of acting as if it "owned" the race-based idea, there is just one single answer: We not only own it, but for all practical purposes, we created it.

Nothing that previously existed under the name racialist was fit to influence the destiny of our people in the slightest because these ideas all lacked clear, unified formulation. In most cases, these ideas were a collection of mere isolated, disconnected convictions, which varied in their soundness. They often contradicted one another and never had any cohesion among themselves. Even if this cohesion had existed, it was too weak to build a movement from. This is what the National-Socialist movement accomplished alone.

Today, all kinds of societies, big and small, even "great parties", lay claim to the word racialist. This is a result of what our National-Socialist movement has accomplished. If it had not been for our work, none of these organizations would ever have dreamed of even of saying the word "racialist". The word would have meant nothing to them and been incomprehensible to their leaders. It was only the work of the NSDAP (*National Socialist German Workers' Party*) that made this concept into a meaningful word, and now everyone uses it. Our party's successful work in enlisting support through its propaganda has shown the power of racialist ideas. Others are forced, if only by their greed, to gain new members, to at least pretend they want something similar.

It is the same old story. They exploited our work to help their party at the elections. For them, the word "racialist" is just a superficial, empty catch-word that they use to counter the attraction their members have for our National-Socialist movement. They are concerned for their own movements and fear our movement, which is carried by a new world-view of universal significance, a significance which is so great that they can only speculate about the true meaning, and they can only suspect how dangerous it is for one party to be the exclusive torch bearer of this idea. It is only this fear for their own survival and alarm at the rise of a movement supported by a new World-Concept that makes them use this new word of "racialist". Eight years ago, they didn't even know this word. Seven years ago, they laughed at it. Six years ago, they called it stupid. Five years ago, they fought it. Four years ago, they hated it. Three years ago, they put it on trial. Finally, two years ago, they added it to their vocabulary as their own war-cry for their battle.

Even today we have to keep pointing out that none of these parties has any clue what the German people actually need. The most striking proof of this is the superficial way they use the word "racialist". All those fake-racialists roaming around with hybrid ideas are just as dangerous. They build fantastic plans based on nothing more than a concept. It may sound like a good idea, but alone, it is totally meaningless and cannot be used to lead a great, unified fighting fellowship, and it is certainly unfit to build one. These people who brew together a program, partly from their own thinking and partly from what they have read in other programs, are often more dangerous than those who admit they are enemies of the racialist idea. The best among these fake-racialists are unproductive theorists, but even here, most of them strut arrogantly towards disaster. They often believe they can cover up their spiritual and intellectual nonsense and their instability by hiding behind a flowing beard and a distracting people with primitive Germanic gesturing.

To contrast all these unsuccessful attempts, it is a good time for us to recall when the young National-Socialist movement began its struggle.

6. THE STRUGGLE OF THE EARLY DAYS
- THE IMPORTANCE OF SPEECHES

The first great meeting on February 24th, 1920 in the Hofbräuhaus Banquet Hall was still fresh in our mind when we began preparing for the next meeting. Previously, we thought it was a bad idea to hold a small meeting once every two weeks, or even once a month in a city the size of Munich, but we were now planning to have a great mass-meeting once a week. One fear and one alone kept troubling us: Would people come and would they listen to us? I personally was unshakably convinced, even then, that once people are there, they will stay and listen to what we had to say.

During those days, the Munich Hofbräuhaus Banquet Hall became almost sacred to us. It was the place where we had a meeting every week, and every week it was filled with more attentive people than the time before. We started with "War Guilt" about the responsibility for the war, and at that time the general public did not think about it much--they did not care. We went through the Peace Treaties. Almost everything that was discussed seemed to stir the crowd, which made it appropriate material for campaigning. With strong interest all around, we paid particular attention to the Peace Treaties. Again and again, our young movement had been foretelling to the great masses of people what would fall on their heads and now, almost every prophecy had been fulfilled.

Today it is easy to talk or write about those things, but in those days before our first big meetings, a public mass-meeting that embraced the irritations of the working classes, instead of demonstrating privileged-class weaknesses, and dealt with "The Peace Treaty of Versailles" was viewed the same as an attack on the Republic and a sign of die-hard, Monarchy supporters. At the very first sentence that criticized the Versailles Treaty, the speaker could expect to be the target of the stereotypical interruption: "And Brest-Litovsk? Brest-Litovsk!"
(*Meaning the 1918 Treaty of Brest-Litovsk, which marked Russia's exit from the war with extremely harsh terms and massive losses of territory and resources for Russia; here the crowd appears to mean "But the Treaty of Versailles was the result of our abuses in the Treaty of Brest-Litovsk, so we brought this hardship on ourselves; anyone who attacks the Versailles Treaty must want to bring back the Monarchy".*)

The crowd would keep roaring this again and again until it gradually became hoarse or the speaker gave up trying to convince them of whatever his point was. One could have beaten his head against the wall sympathizing with the misery of these poor people! The crowd would not listen and would not understand that

Versailles was a shame and a disgrace, and the demands it made amounted to an unheard of plundering of our people. The Marxists had worked their destruction, and the enemy propaganda poisoned our people beyond the reach of reason. We were not even allowed to complain about this disgrace openly. Who were we "little" Germans to complain about anything when there was such immeasurable guilt on the other side! What had the privileged-class done to stop this dreadful collapse, to oppose it, and to clear the path for truth by better and more complete understanding? Nothing and nothing! In those days, the great racialist apostles, which we see all around today, were nowhere to be seen. They may have been talking in clubs or at tea parties among their own like-minded circles, but they never ventured among the wolves where they should have been. The only time they were with the wolves was when they had an opportunity to howl with them.

I realized that the question of War Guilt must be clarified through historical truth for the small group that made up the Party. Providing an understanding of the Peace Treaty to the great masses was an indispensable step toward the movement's success in the future. In those days, the masses still saw the Peace as a success for democracy. It was necessary to make a stand against the treaty and the first step was burning ourselves into the people's minds forever as an enemy of that Treaty. Later, when bitter reality revealed the real deception and exposed the hatred concealed in the Treaty, the memory of our earlier attitude would win us the confidence of the masses.

Even then I always advocated making a stand against misguided public attitudes, regardless of whether it was popular at the time or even if it generated hatred; I was ready to start the battle. The NSDAP must not be a follower of public opinion, but must become the master of public opinion. It must not be the masses' servant, but their lord. When a movement is still weak, there is naturally a great temptation to follow the crowd and join in the shouting by using the slogans and battle-cries of the enemy. This temptation comes at a time when an overwhelmingly superior challenger has already succeeded, through seductive deceit, in forcing the people to make crazy decisions or form incorrect beliefs. This is true especially when the young movement believes there are a few obvious slogans used by the enemy that seem to speak for the new movement equally well. Human cowardice accepts such arguments eagerly if it believes they give it justification for expressing "its own point of view", even if it is following in the criminal footsteps of the enemy.

Several times I have been in situations where it took extreme energy not to let the ship of the movement drift into artificially created currents or from actually sailing right into them. The last time was when our hellish press, the Hecuba of the existence of the German nation, succeeded in blowing the problem of South Tyrol out of proportion, which could be disastrous to the German people.

(*Hecuba of ancient Greece had a vision that she would give birth to the destruction of Troy, here the reference means the press will cause the destruction of the German nation.*)

(*South Tyrol was an Austrian province lost to Italy with the Treaty of Saint-Germain, which dissolved the Austrian-Hungary Empire at the end of the First World War. Hitler believed the German population in Southern Tyrol was insignificant, and it was not part of his original Pan-German plan; he was willing to let Italy keep it while many people wanted it back.*)

Without stopping to think about exactly who they were working for, many so-called "nationalist" men and parties and societies joined the general outcry out of weakness when they were faced with the public opinion that had been thoroughly inflamed by the Jews. This helped to senselessly strengthen the attack against a system that we Germans should regard as the one ray of light in a corrupt world. (*The ray of light is the fascist Italian government of Mussolini even though it is not explicitly stated.*) While the international-world Jew slowly but surely strangles us, our so-called patriots lash out against the man and the system that have dared to withdraw from the Jewish-Freemason embrace and to resist this spreading poison. (*The unnamed man and the system are Mussolini and his government, which took control of the Italian press.*) But these weak characters could not avoid being blown in the wind of public opinion, and so they surrendered to its call. And a surrender it was. Though these people, in their wretchedness and lies may not admit it, maybe not even to themselves, it is nevertheless the truth that only weakness and a fear of the temper of the masses, which was only stirred up by the Jew, made them take part in the outcry. All other explanations they offer are disgraceful excuses from the guilty little sinner himself.

It was now necessary to yank the course of our movement around with an iron hand in order to preserve it from ruin by following this misguided trend. When the flame of public opinion is being fanned by every force that could drive it and is burning bright in one single direction, it is unpopular to follow a course in a different direction and, in fact, often dangerous to the life of anyone who dares attempt such a course correction. Many men in history have been stoned for actions that future generations fell to their knees and thanked them for carrying through.

That is why a movement must count on posterity to be its judge and not the raging applause of the passing minute. Undoubtedly, we will find the individual suffering torment at those times when he must maintain a true course, but he must never forget that every such instant will be followed by redemption. A movement that is trying to reshape the world must serve the future and not the passing hour.

We can easily say that some of the greatest and most long lasting successes in all of history were the ones that were the least understood at their outset because they were in sharp opposition to general public opinion, its views, and even its desires.

We learned this for ourselves at our first public appearance. We did not "court the favor of the masses" at our appearances but instead we opposed the foolishness displayed everywhere by the people. During those years, I would appear before a group of people who believed the opposite of what I was saying and wanted the opposite of what I wanted. It would take two hours to lift two to three thousand people out of their former convictions, to shatter the foundations of their established understanding, until, blow by blow, I finally led them to stand on the firm ground of our convictions and brought them to the side of our World-Concept .

I quickly learned that it was important for me to knock the weapon of reply from my opponent's hand at the very beginning. We soon noticed that those who challenged us in open-forums shared a very definite "repertoire" of constantly recurring objections. The uniformity of their replies made it obvious they had received special training from their masters. This is how we were able to recognize the incredible discipline in our adversaries' propaganda methods. I am very proud, even today, that I was able to effectively counter their propaganda and eventually to best its creators at their own work. Within two years, I had become the master in the art of propaganda.

It was important in every single speech to determine in advance what objections would be raised by the crowd. This way, these objections can be totally torn to pieces in the speech before discussion is even possible. It was always a good idea to bring up possible objections oneself and then to prove how they were invalid or show that they did not apply. The listener who came in an honest spirit, even though he was filled with the objections he had been trained to use, was then more easily won over by the preemptive rebuttal of the objections that had been stamped on his memory. Everything that had been drilled into him was automatically countered, which meant he was attracted more and more to the speech.

When I was still an instructor for the military troops, I delivered my very first lecture on "The Peace Treaty of Versailles". After that experience, I altered my speech by calling it "The Peace Treaties of Brest-Litovsk and Versailles". As I learned from the discussion after my first lecture, people knew nothing whatsoever about the Treaty of Brest-Litovsk, but they had been indoctrinated by their parties' skilled propaganda machine to ridicule this treaty because they were taught it was one of the world's most shameful acts of rape that Germany had committed against Russia. The constant insistence of this lie meant that millions of Germans saw the Peace Treaty of Versailles as the revenge for the crime we had committed at Brest-Litovsk, and they felt that any struggle against Versailles was a moral outrage. They were often deeply honest in this belief. This was one of the reasons why the disrespectful and horrible word "Reparations" was adopted into Germany's language. This hypocritical lie seemed to be a fulfillment of higher justice to millions of our misled fellow nationals. It was horrible, but that is what they believed. The best proof of this was the success of the propaganda I initiated against the Peace Treaty of Versailles, which was now introduced by a discussion of the Treaty of Brest-Litovsk. I compared the two Peace Treaties, point by point, and showed how absolutely humane Brest-Litovsk was when compared to the inhuman cruelty of the Versailles Treaty. My success was incredible. I then spoke on that subject in meetings of two thousand people where I was often met by thirty-six hundred hostile eyes. Three hours later, I would have in front of me a surging crowd filled with solid resentment, righteous anger and absolute rage. Once again, a great lie had been uprooted from the hearts and minds of a crowd of thousands and a truth planted in its place.

At that time, "The True Causes of the First World War" and "The Peace Treaties of Brest-Litovsk and Versailles" were the two lectures I considered my most important ones. I repeated them dozens of times in various ways until a clear and unified attitude was established among the first members of the movement.

For me, these meetings had another advantage. I gradually became a mass-meeting speaker and grew skillful in evoking feelings and developing gestures that are needed in a great room holding thousands of people. Except for some small circles, no one seemed to understand the need for good speech making skills. Many of those parties now throw out their chests and act as if they were the ones responsible for the change in public opinion. If a so-called nationalist speaker did give a similar lecture somewhere, it was only for groups that already shared his opinion and, at best, did nothing more than reinforce their existing beliefs.

There was no need to convince those who were already believers. What was more important was to use explanation and propaganda to recruit those who were on the enemy's side of the fence as a result of their training and opinions. We used leaflets to explain this. While I was still in the army, I had written a leaflet that compared the Peace Treaties of Brest-Litovsk and Versailles. That leaflet was widely distributed. Later, I used elements of it for the Party, and it proved to be very effective. The first party meetings were memorable because the tables were covered with all kinds of leaflets, newspapers, and pamphlets. Even then, however, the main emphasis was on the spoken word. Only the spoken word is capable of producing truly great revolutions, and this is based on sound psychological reasons.

As I have said before, every great and world-shaking event has been produced by the spoken word and not by the written word. This claim was followed by a long discussion in some of the press. They naturally took a very sharp stand against my assertion, especially the privileged-class smart-alecks. The reason for this confused many of my skeptics. The privileged-class intellects protested my confidence in the power of public speaking because they lacked the strength and ability to influence the masses with the spoken word. They concentrated on purely literary activities, abandoning the real campaigner's weapon of public speaking. The necessary result of this habit led to what distinguishes our privileged-class today. They lost the instinct needed to influence or motivate the masses.

The speaker receives constant feedback from the crowd he is speaking to, and he can constantly judge from the faces of his audience whether they understand his message, and if his words are having the desired effect on them. The writer does not know his readers at all. Therefore, he will not address any specific group of people but will keep his writing general. Writing in this way causes him to lose the psychological delicacy and adaptability he needs. In general, a brilliant speaker will write better than a brilliant writer can speak, unless he too practices the art of speaking constantly. There is also the fact that the masses of people are lazy by nature. They will not pick up and read something unless it goes along with their own existing beliefs or offers what they hope for. Therefore, a written work about a specific issue is usually only read by people who already belong to that movement. A poster or a leaflet may be short enough to be quickly read by one who thinks differently. There is a better chance for response from a picture in all its forms, up to and including the motion pictures or movies. Here, man depends even less on his brain. It is enough simply to look or, at most, read very short captions. Many people are much more willing to take in a pictorial representation than to read a longer written work. The explanation a picture can give in one quick look would require a lot of tedious reading. So a picture is worth a thousand words.

The most essential point is that you never know whose hands the written material will fall into and no matter who picks it up, its form remains the same. In general, it will be more effective if this form agrees with the intellectual level and character of those who are reading it. A book intended for the broad masses must, from the start, use a different style and mental level than would be used in a work destined for readers in the higher intellectual classes.

Written matter approaches the spoken word only when it is adapted to exactly match the audience. The speaker may discuss the same topic as a book, but if he is a great and inspired speaker, he will rarely repeat the same argument twice in the same way. He will always allow himself to be influenced by the listeners so that his feelings will give him precisely the words he needs to move his audience at that moment. If he makes even the slightest mistake, he has a living admonishment constantly in front of him. As mentioned earlier, he can read from the expressions of his listeners to see whether, firstly, they understand what he is saying, secondly whether they can follow it all, and thirdly how completely they are convinced of the truth of what they hear. If he, firstly, sees that they do not understand him, he will make his explanation so simple and plain that even the dullest among them can grasp it. Secondly, if he feels that they cannot follow him, he will build up his ideas so carefully and slowly so that even the feeblest among the crowd is not left behind. If he, thirdly, suspects that they do not seem convinced of the truth of what he says, he will go on repeating those truths with new illustrations, addressing the unspoken objections he can sense, disproving and shattering them until, finally, the attitude and expression of even the last opposing group shows it has surrendered to his arguments.

With human beings, it is frequently a matter of overcoming prejudices that are not founded on reason, but supported only by feeling; many times these feelings are deep in the unconscious mind. Overcoming this barrier of instinctive dislike, emotional hatred, and pre-existing objections is a thousand times harder to correct than a belief based on faulty facts or mistaken opinion. False ideas and incorrect facts can be eliminated by instruction, but emotional resistances cannot. Only an appeal to these mysterious forces themselves can be effective. Such an appeal can rarely be made by the writer, but almost exclusively by the speaker.

We can see the most striking proof of this in the privileged-class press. Even with their skillful writing and multi-million reader circulation, they were not able to stop the great masses from becoming bitter enemies of the privileged-class world. The flood of newspapers and books produced year after year by the intellectual crowd simply beaded up and flowed off the millions of the lower classes like water off of oiled leather. This proves either of two things. Either it proves the writing of our privileged-class world used the wrong arguments or it proves the hearts of the broad masses cannot be reached by writing alone, especially when the writing has so little psychological appeal, as is the case here.

Never let it be said that this statement is disproved by Marxism itself just because it produces many writings, especially because of the effect of writings by Karl Marx. A great German-Nationalist paper in Berlin tried to make this argument.

Probably a more shallow defense of a flawed view has never been attempted. What has given Marxism its astonishing power over the broad masses is not the formal, written product of Jewish brains, but the enormous wave of speeches filled with propaganda that have taken possession of the masses through the years. Out of a hundred thousand German workers, on an average, not a hundred know about Marx's book. It has been studied a thousand times more by intellectuals and the Jews than by followers of the movement in the great working classes. In fact, the book was not written for the broad masses at all, but entirely for the intellectual leadership of the Jewish machine to guide them in world conquest. The Jewish machine itself was fired by a different fuel, the press. This is what distinguishes the Marxist press from our privileged-class press. The Marxist press is written by agitators and the privileged-class press attempts to campaign using professional writers. The Social Democratic back-alley editor returns to his editorial chair from the meeting hall where he has gained an unparalleled knowledge of his customers. But the privileged-class pen-wielder leaves his study to appear before the broad masses where he is sickened by their smell and finds his written words are useless to him.

What has won the millions of workers over to Marxism is not the way the Marxist Church Fathers write. It is the tireless and tremendous propaganda work of ten thousands of tireless campaigners, from the top all the way down to the smallest union official and the party delegate and the person who answers questions at the end of speeches. It is the hundreds of thousands of meetings at which these speakers, standing on a table in a smoky pub room, have hammered away at the masses, acquiring a wonderful knowledge of this human fodder, a knowledge that has enabled them to choose the right weapons to attack the stronghold of public opinion. It is the gigantic mass demonstrations and the marches of a hundred thousand men that have burned into the shabby little man a proud conviction that, even though he is a poor worm, he is part of a great dragon whose fiery breath will someday send the hated privileged-class world up in flames and bring final victory to the lower class dictatorship.

The propaganda of speeches is what prepared the men and made them willing to read the Social Democratic press, so the press was the next step following the spoken word. In the privileged-class camp, professors, bookworm scholars, theorists, and writers of every kind sometimes tried to speak, while in the Marxist camp, the speakers sometimes tried to write. The Jew deserves special attention because his deceitful skills of twisting the truth and his cleverness made him an effective writer, but his true strength is in his abilities as a provocative speaker.

This is why the privileged-class newspaper world doesn't have the slightest influence on the attitude of the broadest classes of our people. This is also due to the fact that it is largely Jew-controlled and therefore has no interest in truly enlightening the broad masses. It is hard to overthrow emotional prejudices, subconscious beliefs, or feelings and replace them with other beliefs that depend on invisible forces and conditions for them to be accepted. The speaker who senses the mood of the audience well can judge all of these factors and adapt his message. He knows that even the time of day his speech is given is important in determining its effectiveness. The same speech, the same speaker, and the same subject have entirely different results at ten in the morning, at three in the afternoon, and in the evening. As a beginner, I sometimes called meetings in the morning. I still remember a demonstration we staged in the Munichener-Kindl Cellar as a protest "against the oppression of German territories".(*Munichener-Kindl means Munich's Child, the name of Munich's coat of arms.*) At that time, it was Munich's largest hall, and it seemed a very risky venture. To make it easy for the movement's followers to attend and for everyone else who might come, I set the meeting for a Sunday morning at ten o'clock. The result was devastating, but extremely instructive. The hall was full and the impression stunning, but the room was like ice. Nobody warmed up, and I was deeply unhappy at not being able to establish any relationship, not even the slightest connection, with my audience. My speaking was no worse than at other times, but there were no results. When I left the meeting, I was completely dissatisfied, but one experience richer. Similar attempts that I made later led to the same result.

This should not have surprised us. You only need to watch the performance of a play to see the difference in impression and effectiveness at three in the afternoon and the same play with the same cast at eight in the evening. A person with a keen sensitivity and the ability to analyze this emotional state will immediately see that the magnificence of the afternoon performance is not as strong as the evening's performance. The same statement holds true for film. In the case of the theater, it might be possible to say the actor does not work as hard in the afternoon as in the evening, but the movie does not change between the afternoon showing and the nine in the evening showing. No, the time itself has a definite affect on the room as well as on me. There are halls that mysteriously leave one feeling cold and somehow violently resist any generation of warmth. Men's traditional memories and impressions of a place may also decisively influence their reaction. A performance of Parsifal at Bayreuth will always have a different affect from anywhere else in the world. (*Parsifal is an opera about the Knights quest for the Holy Grail, written by Richard Wagner. Bayreuth is a city in northern Bavaria where Richard Wagner lived until his death.*) The mysterious magic spell of the Festival Heights opera house in the old city of The Margrave cannot be equaled or substituted by dressing up another opera house with fancy decorations. (*The*

Bayreuth Festspielhaus, or Festival Heights, is an opera house that was specially constructed for and is exclusively devoted to the performance of Wagner's operas. Margrave is a title of a military governor and here describes Margrave Christian of Kulmbach, who was responsible for constructing many grand buildings in the city when he moved the capital there in 1603.)

All these cases require the invasion of a man's freedom of will. This is the most true when it comes to political meetings. These meetings are attended by people who are already against you, people who have to be won over to a new purpose. In the morning and during the day, people's willpower seems to resist with the greatest energy any imposition of an outside will, and they refuse to recognize an outside opinion. In the evening, on the other hand, that willpower yields more easily to the dominating force of a stronger willed speaker. In truth, every such meeting is a wrestling match between two opposing forces. A man of dominating force, a man who has the character of an apostle, and a man who is an outstanding speaker will be the one who succeeds in winning over men whose resistance has already been naturally weakened. Their resistance is more easily overcome than those who are still in full possession of their force of will and their intellectual strength.

The same purpose is served by the artificial and mysterious twilight of Catholic churches, the burning candles, incense, etc.

This wrestling match between the adversaries to be converted and the speaker will gradually develop his wonderful sensitivity to the psychological requirements of propaganda, a sensitivity the writer will never have. Therefore, the written work, with its limited effectiveness on its own, is better used to preserve, strengthen, and deepen an already existing view or set of principles. Great historical revolutions have never been produced by authors, but accompanied by their written words.

The French Revolution (*1789-1799 was an uprising of the lower economic classes against the aristocracy*) would never have happened through the discussion of philosophic theories. It had to find an army of trouble-makers led by majestic demagogues who inflamed the passions of an already tormented people. Finally, the frightening volcanic eruption that followed made all of Europe freeze in their tracks with horror. Similarly, the greatest revolutionary upheaval of recent times, the Bolshevist Revolution in Russia (*1917*), came about not through Lenin's writings, but through the hate-stirring speeches of countless aggressive apostles, both great and small.

The uneducated masses were not inspired to start the Communist Revolution by reading theoretical ideas of men like Karl Marx, but by the shining heaven promised to them by the thousands of agitators who were working for an idea. So it was and so it always will be.

It is just like our German intellectual class, with their stubborn isolation from life, to believe that a writer must be intellectually superior to a speaker. This idea is wonderfully illustrated by a review in a nationalist paper, which I already mentioned, which said that one is often disappointed when they see a great orator's speech in print. That reminds me of another review I saw during the war. It put the speeches of Lloyd George (*who was British Prime Minister in the last half of the First World War and for four years afterward*), Munitions Minister at that time, painstakingly under the magnifying glass to arrive at the "brilliant" conclusion that these addresses were intellectually and philosophically inferior, they were unoriginal, and their conclusions were obvious. I picked up a copy of these speeches myself in a tiny booklet, and I could not help laughing out loud at the way these masterpieces were able to psychologically and spiritually lead the masses. It left the ordinary German pen-pusher completely blank. This man judged the speeches simply by the impression they made on his own detached nature, while the great English demagogue successfully influenced the mass of his listeners and the entire lower classes of the English nation as much as possible. From that standpoint, this Englishman's speeches were marvelous performances because they displayed an absolutely astonishing knowledge of the soul of the lower levels of the common people. Their effect was, in fact, tremendous.

Compare these speeches to the futile babble of a Bethmann-Hollweg (*German Chancellor until 1917*). His speeches did appear to be more intelligent, but in reality, they showed only the man's inability to speak to his people. He was a stranger to them. Yet the birdbrain of a common German scribbler whose intellect has been stagnated by scientific knowledge, who does not understand the masses, could only evaluate the intellect of the English Minister by the impression that a speech intended to affect the masses made on his own nature. He naturally compared those speeches with the ones of a German statesman whose intellectual chatter fell on much more fruitful soil with the intellectual writer. Lloyd George was in genius not merely equal to a Bethmann-Hollweg, but a thousand times superior. He proved this by the way he formed and expressed his speeches so that they opened the hearts of his people to him, finally bringing the people to carry out his will absolutely. The very primitive nature of the language he used, the directness of its forms of expression, and the use of easily understandable, elementary examples prove the Englishman's outstanding political ability. I must measure a statesman's speeches to his people by the effect they have on his people and not by the impression they make on a university professor. That alone is the measuring rod of the speaker's genius.

Our movement was founded a few years ago from nothing. Today it is impressive enough to be bitterly persecuted by every enemy of our people, both internal and external. The astonishing development of our movement is to be attributed to the constant awareness and application of these conclusions.

As important as the writings of the movement may be, in our present situation they will be of more value in the training of superior and subordinate leaders within the organization than for winning over the masses from our enemies. Only in the rarest cases will a convinced Social Democrat or a fanatical Communist lower himself to purchase a National-Socialist book or even pick up a pamphlet, read it, and from it gain an insight into our understanding of the universe or study the criticism of his own beliefs. Even a newspaper will very seldom be read unless it bears the stamp of party affiliation from the start. Even if a newspaper were read, it would do little good. The overall impression of a single newspaper issue is so scattered and its effect so disjointed that one cannot expect a result after the reader reviews a single issue. One cannot expect a person who has to count every penny to subscribe to a paper that contains opposing views purely out of a desire for objective enlightenment. Barely one in a thousand will do it. Only the man who has already been won by the movement will regularly read the party journal to keep up with events within his movement.

The leaflet for a speech is different matter. A person is much more likely to look at it, particularly if it is free, and even more if the headline vividly proclaims a subject that everyone is talking about at the moment. When he has read it, he may become aware of new attitudes and points of view, even of a new movement. This impulse gives a gentle push but never creates a strong conviction. The leaflet can only suggest or call attention to something. It only becomes effective in connection with subsequent and more thorough instruction and enlightenment, and that always means a mass meeting.

The mass meeting is necessary because this is where there the individual sees, for the first time, a large fellowship. While, as a budding member of a young movement, he may feel isolated and may fear he will be left alone with his new understanding, the mass meeting has a strengthening and encouraging effect on him. The same man would march to the attack with a unit, in a company, or in a battalion, as long as he was surrounded by all his comrades, and he would do so with a lighter heart than if he had to march alone. In a group he always feels safer, even though in reality there may be a thousand reasons to argue against it.

The community created by the great demonstration strengthens not only the individual, but it also unites the group and creates Esprit de Corps (*Team spirit or group morale*). The man who is the first in his business or factory to express a new doctrine and is subjected to heavy pressures needs the strength found in the conviction that he is a fighter for, and a member of, a great, all-embracing body. He can only get his first impression of this body from a common mass demonstration. When he comes from his little workshop or from a big factory, where he may feel small indeed, into a mass meeting for the first time and finds thousands and thousands of men with similar convictions around him, then he submits to the magic influence of the masses. When he is seeking truth and is swept away into the tremendous stream of hypnotic intoxication and enthusiasm of three to four thousand others, then he surrenders to the magic influence of the mass-mind. When the visible success and the affirmation of thousands confirm the rightness of the new doctrine and awaken for the first time a doubt about the truth in his previous beliefs, then he yields to the magic influence of the mass-suggestion. The will, the longing, and the strength of thousands accumulate in each individual. The man who comes into such a meeting doubting and wavering goes away inwardly fortified and strengthened. He has become a member of a community.

The National-Socialist movement must never forget this. It must never let itself be influenced by the privileged-class idiots who think they know something about everything but have tossed away a great State along with their own existence and the dominating control of their own social class. They are enormously smart, can do anything, and understand everything. There is only one thing they could not do. They could not prevent the German people from falling into the arms of Marxism. Here they were a wretched and pitiful failure. Their present conceit is caused by their cockiness, which is well known to be the companion of stupidity. Ignorance is the mother of audacity. If these people believe the spoken word has no special power, it is because they have already convinced themselves, thank God, that their own ranting words are ineffective.

7. THE STRUGGLE WITH THE RED FRONT

In 1919, 1920, and 1921, I personally visited a number of privileged-class political meetings. They always affected me in the same way as the prescribed spoonful of cod-liver oil from my childhood. One is supposed to take it, and it is supposed to be good for you, but it tastes horrible! If the German people were to be tied with ropes and dragged to these privileged-class "demonstrations", and the doors were barred so no one could leave until each performance ended, maybe then it would bring success within a few centuries. Still, I must frankly confess that I would probably lose all pleasure in life and I doubt I would want to be a German any more. Fortunately, this cannot be done, thank Heavens, and it is not surprising that the sound and unspoiled masses avoid privileged-class mass meetings just as the Devil avoids holy water.

At these meetings I came to know these prophets of a privileged-class World-Concept . From that experience I can say that I am truly not surprised and even understand why they attach no importance to the spoken word. I have attended meetings of the Democrats, the German Nationalists, the German People's Party, and of the Bavarian People's Party, which are actually a branch of the Center Party. The thing that struck one immediately was the uniformity of the audience. It was filled exclusively with their own party members. There was no form of discipline needed because it was more like a boring group of card game players than a meeting of people who had just gone through their greatest revolution. The speakers did everything possible to preserve this peaceful atmosphere. They spoke, or rather they read their speeches aloud as if they were reading a fancy newspaper article or a scientific dissertation. They avoided all rough language and occasionally sprinkled in a feeble professor's joke, at which point the honorable Party Officers would laugh dutifully, but not loudly, while pretending it was a provocative remark. They chuckled with quiet, refined restraint, all very dignified.

I once attended a meeting in the Wagner Hall at Munich. It was to commemorate the anniversary of the Battle of Leipzig. (*In 1813, Napoleon suffered a severe defeat by the Germans ending French occupation of Germany, in this, the largest battle in Europe up to that time.*) The speech was delivered, or rather it was read by a dignified old gentleman, a professor at some university. On the raised platform, at a table, sat the officers of the party. The man on the left had a monocle, the man on the right had a monocle, and the man in between was without a monocle. They were all three in Prince Alberts (*a frock coat, knee length black Victorian era formal coat).* Anyone in attendance would have thought they were either in a court of law about to undertake an execution, or at a solemn baptism or some religious act of consecration. The so-called speech, which might have looked quite nice in print, was simply terrible in its effect. Within forty-five minutes, the whole meeting hall had fallen into a trance that was interrupted only when the occasional observer left the hall, or by the rattle of the waitresses, and always by the ever more frequent yawning of numerous listeners. I stood behind three working men who were attending, either because of curiosity or they may have been sent as appointed lookouts by their own party. They looked at one another from time to time with obvious grins and finally nudged one another before very quietly leaving the hall. One could tell by looking at them that they had no intention of causing any disturbance, and in that company, it was really not necessary to disturb anything.

Finally, the meeting seemed to be drawing to a close. The professor's voice had grown fainter and fainter. After he finished his speech, the chairman of the meeting stood up from between the two monocle wearers and raved in front of the "German sisters and brothers" present about how his feelings of gratitude were so great and how great their feelings must also be, for the unique and splendid speech which Professor X had given in a manner that was so enjoyable and so profound. He went on to say that it was truly an "experience" and even an "achievement", and it would be a sacrilege if this sacred moment, following these logical statements, were befouled with a discussion. So on behalf of all those present, he would omit that part of the evening. Instead, he requested that everyone stand and join in the cry, "We are a united nation of brothers", etc. Finally, in conclusion, he asked everyone to sing Deutschland Über Alles.

They did sing, but it seemed to me that by the second stanza, the number of voices grew fewer. They swelled again tremendously in the refrain. Then, on the third stanza, my feeling was confirmed. I do not believe everyone was quite sure what the words were. But what difference do the words make, as long as such a song resounds to Heaven with all the fervor of a German-Nationalist heart?

Then the meeting broke up and everyone rushed to get out quickly, some for a beer, some to a cafe, or or some just to the fresh air.

Yes, out, out into the fresh air! That was my feeling. Was this how they glorified a heroic struggle by hundreds of thousands of Prussians and Germans? For shame, for shame!

No doubt, the government is fond of things like this "peaceful assembly". The Minister for Peace and Good Order need not fear that the billows of enthusiasm will suddenly burst the legal limits of civil decency. There is no chance that these people, intoxicated with enthusiasm, may suddenly stream from the hall and rush, not to the cafe or the pub, but to march in step by fours side-by-side through the streets singing Deutschland Hoch in Ehren (*Oh, Germany High In Honors*), and annoy a peace-loving police force in need of rest. No, the government is satisfied with these kinds of citizens.

Then, there were the National-Socialist meetings. I must admit, they were not "peaceful assemblies". There, the waves of two World-Concept s collided. They ended with a fanatical outburst of racialist and national passion and not with the dull drum of some patriotic song.

From the very beginning, it was important to introduce unquestioned discipline in our meetings and to absolutely assure the authority of the meeting's chairman. What was spoken in those meeting was not the lifeless slop of a privileged-class speaker. It was always engineered in substance and form to rouse a reply from the challengers. And there were adversaries in our meetings. Often they came in large crowds with a few appointed agitators among them and all their faces reflected the same conviction: Tonight, we'll take care of you!

Oh yes, often the agitators were literally led in by rows, our Red friends, with their duty carefully drilled into them and their instructions to smash the whole affair that evening and orders to put a stop to it! Often, everything hung precariously in the balance, and only the ruthless energy of our meeting chairman and the brutal recklessness of our hall-guard halted the enemy's intentions! They had every reason to be provoked too.

The red color of our posters alone attracted them into our meeting-halls. The ordinary privileged-class was quite horrified to see us using the red of the Bolsheviks and regarded it as very curious scandal. The spirits among German-Nationalists kept whispering to one another their suspicion that basically, we were only a variation of Marxism, maybe even Marxists or some kind of Socialists in disguise. These brains have still not grasped the difference between Socialism and Marxism. When they discovered that we omitted the standard greeting "ladies and gentlemen" and instead used "comrades" and that among ourselves we spoke only of "Party comrades", many saw this as proof of the Marxist ghost. How often we shook with laughter at these simple-minded, scared privileged-class rabbits with their clever guesswork about our origin, our intentions, and our aim.

We chose the color red for our posters after careful and thorough consideration. It was in order to provoke the political Left wing, to drive them into fury, and to lure their members into our meetings. If nothing else we could at least break their people away and gain a chance to talk to them.

It was enjoyable during those years to follow the confusion and helplessness of our adversaries as they constantly shifted their tactics. First, they called on their followers to ignore us and to stay away from our meetings. They mostly complied. But later, a few people did come. The number increased slowly but constantly, and the impression made by our doctrine was obvious. The leaders gradually became more nervous and uneasy. Finally they made the mistake of convincing themselves that they could not continue to watch this development in silence, but must put an end to it by terrorism.

Then came the appeals to those "class-conscious" working people to attend our meetings as a group in order to strike at those responsible for "monarchist, reactionary agitation" and to strike hard with the fists of the lower class.

All at once it seemed our meetings were filled with workmen a full forty-five minutes before the meeting's start time. They seemed like a powder keg that might blow up at any moment and the fuse had already been lit. But it never turned out that way. People came in as our enemies and went out, if not as our supporters, at least as thoughtful and critical examiners who were ready to question the soundness of their own doctrine. Gradually through the night it happened, and after my three-hour speech, followers and opponents would be joined into one single enthusiastic mass. By then, any signal to break up the meeting was useless.

Now the leaders really did become frightened. They sided with those who had originally said it was a bad idea to send workers in large groups to our meetings. After making some pretense to justify the change, they went back to their previous opinion and declared that the only sound thing to do was to forbid workers from attending our meetings at all. Then most of those workers quit coming. But within a short time, the whole game started over again.

The ban was not observed after all. More and more of the comrades came and finally, those in their party who supported the use of radical tactics gained dominance again and decided our meetings must be broken up. It turned out that after members attended two, three, or eight or ten meetings, breaking them up was more easily said than done. Every single meeting we held resulted in a further crumbling of the Red shock troops. Their previous slogan was suddenly heard again: "Working class people! Comrades! Stay away from the meetings of the National-Socialist agitators!"

The same indecisive and wavering policy could also be seen in the Red press. First they would try to freeze us out with silence, and when they became convinced that was not working, they would go back to the opposite extreme and refer to us constantly. We were "mentioned" in one way or another every day. Most references tried to explain to the worker how absolutely ridiculous our whole existence was. But after a while, these gentlemen realized that their efforts were not harming us, to the contrary, they helped us because many individuals began to naturally ask themselves why so much press was devoted to something if it was really so ridiculous. People grew curious. Then there was a sudden shift, and for a time the press treated us as absolute criminals against humanity. They wrote article after article explaining our criminal behavior and offering proof again and again, and finally they used false scandalous stories of every kind in an effort to completely turn the public against us. But within a short time, they saw that these attacks were also ineffective. In the end, their efforts helped to concentrate attention on us more than ever.

At that time, I took the position that it makes no difference whether they laugh at us or abuse us, whether they describe us as clowns or criminals. As long as they mention us and continue to concern themselves with us, we will gradually appear in the eyes of the workers as the only force that can put up a fight. They wish to know what we really are and what we really want. Then we will show those pack-hounds of Jewish journalists some fine day.

One reason their plans to break up our meetings never reached even a starting point was because of the unbelievable cowardice of our opposition leaders. In every case they sent their young cubs in and waited outside the hall to watch the scattering.

We were almost always well-informed about the intentions of these gentlemen. For reasons of practicality, we left many of our Party members within the Red party ranks. We also knew what was going on because the Red puppeteers themselves were seized with the gift of running their mouths, which was very useful to us and unfortunately it is still very common among our German people. They could never hold their tongues when they had hatched anything of this sort, and in fact, they usually began cackling before the egg was laid. We often had time to make extensive preparations before the Red dispersion-groups themselves knew how fast they would be thrown out.

This turbulent period compelled us to take protection measures into our own hands. We could not count on official protection. On the contrary, experience had shown that when officials intervene, it never benefits anyone except those causing the disturbance. The police would bring the meeting to an end after any disturbance, and an end to the meeting was the goal of the hostile intruders.

In fact, the police began using a horribly unjust method of control. If the authorities receive a threat or otherwise hear that a meeting is in danger of being broken up, they do not arrest the one who has made the threat, but forbid the innocent parties from holding their meeting. The police mind sees this piece of wisdom, shocking as it may seem, as a proud piece of police work. They call it a "preventive measure against infraction of the law".

This means the determined gangster has the power, at any time, to make the decent person's political activities impossible. In the name of peace and good order, the governmental authority bows to the gangster and asks the other party not to provoke him. So, if National-Socialists wanted to hold meetings at certain places, and the trade-unions declared this would lead to resistance by their members, the police never considered even the possibility of putting these blackmailing crooks in jail but instead forbade us from holding our meeting at all. Indeed these instruments of the law even had the incredible shamelessness to send this notice to us in writing on countless occasions.

If we were to protect ourselves from such censorship, we had to make sure that any attempt made to break up our meetings would be rendered impossible at the start.

We must also consider the fact that any meeting that must be protected by large battalions of police discredits its organizers in the eyes of the broad masses. Meetings that can only be held when a large police detail is present, have no attraction for others. Obvious strength from one's own side is necessary to win over the lower levels of society.

Just as a courageous man can conquer a woman's heart more easily than a coward, a heroic movement will win the hearts of a people sooner than a cowardly movement that survives only through police protection. The young Party had to uphold its own existence, protect itself, and it had to break the enemy's circle of terror itself.

Meeting protection was built in two ways. The first way was through the forceful and psychologically sound management of the meetings. When we National-Socialists held a meeting in those days, we were the only masters present. We sharply emphasized our mastery every single minute and never tolerated interruptions. Our opponents knew that anyone who dared to incite trouble would be harshly thrown out, even if we were only a dozen against five hundred. In the meetings at that time, particularly outside of Munich, there would be fifteen or sixteen National-Socialists facing five, six, seven, or eight hundred opponents. But even so, we would have tolerated no challenges and the audience at our meetings was well aware that we would have been killed before we would surrender. More than once a handful of Party members successfully maintained themselves in heroic fashion against the yelling and thrashing of superior numbers of Reds.

In such cases, the fifteen or twenty men would have undoubtedly been overpowered in the end. But the opponents knew that at least two or three times as many of their own people would have their heads cracked first, and they did not want to risk that.

We wanted to understand Marxist and privileged-class meeting methods, and we learned a great deal by studying their techniques. The Marxists always maintained unquestioned discipline at their meetings, so there was absolutely no possibility of a Marxist meeting being broken up by a privileged-class group. The Reds, however, had their own intentions when it came to disrupting other meetings. They not only developed a fluent skill in this area, but in large sections of the Reich they finally went so far that they declared any non-Marxist meeting itself as provoking the working class. This was especially true when the puppeteers suspected that their own sins might be discussed at a meeting that revealed the treachery of their activity through their corruption and deception of the people. Whenever such a meeting was announced, the entire Red press raised a furious outcry. Even though they have nothing but contempt for the law, they urgently turned to the authorities demanding that they prevent this "provocation of the working class in case worse things might happen". They chose their wording depending on the particular official's degree of foolishness, which also determined how successful they were at accomplishing their objective. However, if the official's post was occupied, for once, by a real German civil servant rather than just a political creature filling an office seat, and he refused such an offensive and bold request, the result would be the familiar appeal to their party members not to tolerate such a "provocation of the working class", but to attend the meeting in a large group on the scheduled date and to "put an end to the shameful plot by privileged-class creatures using the calloused fist of the working class".

There is nothing like watching one of these privileged-class meetings and experiencing the whole disgraceful and dreadful way in which it is conducted. Often, a meeting was simply called off as a result of threats. There was so much fear among them that the meeting scheduled for 8:00 often didn't start before 8:45 or 9:00. When the meeting did occur, the chairman used several compliments in an effort to make it clear to the attending "gentlemen of the opposition", how happy he and all the others present were that they could attend and welcomed men who were not yet on their side of the fence. What an outright lie! He continued by saying it was only through mutual discussion, which from the beginning he would solemnly promise them, that their different ideas could be brought closer together, they could create mutual understanding, and the gap between them could be bridged. At the same time, he assured them that it was not the meeting's purpose to alienate people from their previous views, but that everyone should find salvation in his own way. However, he should also let his neighbor discover his own beliefs. Therefore, he requested that the speaker be allowed to finish his remarks, which he assured the crowd would not be very much longer, so the world would not see again any shameful display of bad blood between German brothers. Ugh!

The brothers from the political Left usually did not take kindly to this sort of talk. Before the speaker had even resumed his speech, he had to stop amid the grossest insults. Often one had the impression that he was even grateful to Fate for cutting short the agonizing process. In the middle of a huge uproar, these privileged-class bullfighters would leave the arena, unless they were thrown down stairs with cracked heads, which often happened.

So, the Marxists found the way we conducted our first meetings to be very unusual for them. They walked in convinced that they could play the same little game with us they had so often played before. "Today, we'll be the ones to finish this up". Many of them yelled this boast as they walked into our meeting, but immediately, they found themselves sitting outside the entrance to the hall before they could interrupt a second time.

In the first place, the way we conducted our meetings was different. We did not beg to be graciously permitted to speak, and we did not start out by promising an endless discussion opportunity for everyone. We simply and abruptly said that we were the masters of the meeting. We were masters in our own house, and anyone who dared to make so much as a single interruption would be harshly thrown out the way he had come in. Further, we were not responsible for what happened to the fellow who spoke out of turn. If there was time and if we felt like it, we would have a discussion. If not, then we wouldn't. The speaker, Party comrade so and so, now had the floor. Such a bold deceleration astonished the Marxists.

In the second place, we had a strictly organized hall guard. With the privileged-class parties, the hall guard or rather their ushers, consisted mostly of gentlemen who thought that they had a right to authority and respect because of their age. Since the masses in their hyped-up Marxist excitement cared nothing about anyone's age or authority and had no respect, there was effectively no privileged-class hall guard at all.

From the very beginning of our serious activity in holding the meetings, I introduced the organization of a hall guard as a group to control the crowds. This group included nothing but young men. Some of them were friends I knew from the army and others were recently recruited members of the Party who were instructed and trained from the beginning to believe that terrorism can only be broken by terrorism; that the bold and determined man has always been the one to succeed in the world; and that we are fighting for an idea so tremendous, so great, and so noble that it deserves to be sheltered and protected with the last drop of blood. They were saturated with the doctrine that if reason remains silent, then violence has the last word. The best defensive weapon is attack. They were also taught that our control troops should have the reputation of being a desperately determined fighting fellowship and we were not a debate club. These young people had been longing for such a battle-cry! This generation of men from the trenches has been disappointed and outraged, filled with disgust and hatred for the actions of the cowardly and unmanly privileged-class!

Here is where everyone really began to understand how the Revolution had been made possible only because of the catastrophic failure of the privileged-class leadership. The fists to protect the German people from the Revolution were available even then, but the heads that were needed to pledge themselves to action were not to be found. How the eyes of my young men used to shine at me when I explained to them how necessary their mission was, and when I assured them again and again that all the wisdom in the world would fail if it is not backed up by strength to protect and defend it. I told them that the gentle Goddess of Peace can only walk beside the God of War, and that every great deed of peace requires the protection and assistance of strength. The necessity and vision of military duty appeared in a much more vivid light! This is not duty in the frozen sense of old, fossilized officials who are serving the dead authority of a dead State, but in a living realization of a duty strong enough that one will surrender his life to defend the existence of his people as a whole, anywhere and anytime. How those young men stood up to accept their duty! They would fly like a swarm of hornets at anyone who disturbed our meetings, not caring if they were met with a superior force or if they had to sacrifice through wounds and blood. They were obsessed with the great idea of clearing the road for our movement's sacred mission.

As early as midsummer of 1920, the organization of the hall-guards gradually began to take on a definite shape. In the spring of 1921, it grew so large it had to be split into divisions of one hundred each, which, in turn, were divided into smaller groups.

This organization was urgently needed because our meeting activity had continued to expand. We did still frequently meet in the Munich Hofbräuhaus Banquet Hall, but more often it was in the larger halls around the city. The Bürgerbräu Banquet Hall and the Munichener-Kindl Cellar were the scenes of greater mass meetings in the fall and winter of 1920-1921, but the picture was always the same. Even then and in those large halls, demonstrations of the National-Socialist German Workers' Party usually had to be shut down by the police because of overcrowding even before the start of the meeting.

The organization of our control troops raised a very important question. Until now, the movement had no party symbols and no party flag. The absence of these symbols was already causing problems and it was not acceptable for the future of the movement to be without them. One immediate disadvantage was that party members had no distinguishing outer mark to show their allegiance. Looking towards the future, it was unacceptable to be without a distinguishing mark that had the emblem of the movement and that could be set against symbols of the International Marxists.

Even in my youth, I had many opportunities to see and understand the emotional impact a symbol has on the mind. After the war when I was in Berlin, I observed a mass demonstration of Marxism in front of the Royal Chateau and Pleasure Garden (*Lustgarten park*). A sea of red flags, red armbands, and red flowers created a tremendous visual spectacle for this demonstration, which had an estimated hundred and twenty thousand marchers. I could feel and understand how easily the average man could give in to the hypnotic spell of such a grand demonstration. The privileged-class, as a political party, represents or maintains no World-Concept of any kind; therefore, they had no flag of their own. This party consisted of self proclaimed "patriots", and for that reason they ran around in the colors of the Reich. If these colors had been the symbol of a definite World-Concept , it would have been understandable how the nobility of the State could see in these colors a flag that was the sign of their own World-Concept , since their World-Concept was the State and Reich flag that came to be through their own efforts.

But this was not the real situation. The Reich had been put together without the help of the privileged-class and the flag resulted from the war. Therefore, it was actually only a State flag that had no meaning in the sense of a particular mission for some World-Concept .

German Austria was the only place in the German-speaking territories where there was anything like a privileged-class party flag. Some of the nationalists from the privileged-class there had chosen the colors of 1848, black, red, and gold for their party flag. (*There were a series of German revolutions in 1848 based on nationalist sentiment and political reform. The black-red-gold flag symbolized unity among the people.*) This created a symbol which, while it had no importance for a World-Concept , it did have a revolutionary character from the perspective of State policy. We should remember today that the bitterest enemies of this black-red-gold flag at that time were Social Democrats and Christian Socialists or the clergy. In those days, the church parties especially were the very ones who insulted, slandered, and soiled those colors. Just as in 1918 when they dragged the black-white-red German flag in the gutter (*the Pre-Weimar flag*). True, the black, red, and gold of the German parties of old Austria were the colors from 1848, and this period may have been fantastic and was represented individually by the most honorable of German souls, even though the Jew stood invisibly in the background as the puppeteer. It was, therefore, treason to the Fatherland and a shameful sell-out of the German people and what they stood for that made these flags so agreeable to

Marxism and the Center party. Today they revere them as sacred and set up militias to protect the flag they once spat upon.

Up until 1920 there was no flag that opposed Marxism, at least not one which would have represented its direct opposite as a World-Concept . Even if the better parties of the German privileged-class, after 1918, would no longer lower themselves to take over the black-red-gold national flag as their own symbol, they still had no agenda of their own for the future that could oppose the new political development of the Revolution. At best, their idea was to reconstruct an Empire that had already vanished.

The black-white-red flag of the old Empire owes its resurrection as the standard of our so-called nationalist privileged-class parties to this idea of restoring a dead Empire.

It should be obvious that the symbol of the government, which Marxism succeeded in overthrowing under shameful circumstances, is not a suitable symbol for those who would see this same Marxism destroyed again. As sacred and dear as the old and beautiful colors must be, especially when they were fresh and youthful, to every decent German who has fought for them and has seen the sacrifices of so many under those colors, that flag is not the symbol for a battle of the future.

In contrast to the privileged-class politicians, I have always maintained the view in our movement that it is a real blessing for the German nation to have lost the old flag. What the new Republic does under its flag is unimportant to us. But we should thank Fate from the bottom of our hearts that it was merciful enough to protect the most glorious battle-flag of all times from being used as a cover for the most shameful prostitution. The present Reich, which sells-out itself and its citizens, must never fly the heroic black-white-red flag of honor.

As long as the November disgrace lasts, let it wear its own outer garment and not steal one from a more honest past. The conscience of our privileged-class politicians should tell them that anyone who desires the black-white-red flag for the current State is stealing from our past. The old flag really was beautiful, but only for the old Empire, just as the Republic has chosen a new one that is suited to itself.

This was the reason why we National-Socialists could not consider raising the old flag as a symbolic expression of what we were working for. After all, we did not want to awaken the old-dead Empire, which was destroyed by its own faults. We wanted to build a new State.

A movement that fights against Marxism today must show the symbol of the new State everywhere, even in its flag. The question of the new flag and its appearance occupied our minds a great deal at that time. Proposals came from all sides, although they were more well-intended than they were acceptable. The new flag had to be a symbol of our own battle and have a striking poster-like effect. Anyone who has been involved with the masses will realize that these things that seem unimportant are actually very important matters. An effective emblem may ignite the first spark of interest and create a desire to know more about a movement in hundreds of thousands of cases.

For this reason, we had to decline the suggestion that we use a white flag. That recommendation came from many areas. A white flag would have surely identified our movement with the old State and with those feeble parties whose sole political aim is to restore the old Empire. Besides, white is not a compelling color. It is suitable for innocent societies of maidens, but not for rebellious movements in a revolutionary age.

Black was also suggested. It was appropriate for the time, but there was no significance that suggested our movement's intent. Also, this color is not compelling enough either, so it would not attract attention. Blue and white were out of the question, despite their wonderful aesthetic effect. Those are the colors of one German State (*Bavaria*) and represent a political attitude of narrow interest and very state-specific ideas, which did not have a great reputation. It would have been difficult to associate any significance with our movement in these colors. The same was true of black and white. (*Black and white were the dominant colors on the Prussian flag.*)

Black, red, and gold were out of the question. (*Those were the colors of the despised Weimar Republic.*) Black-white-red, in the familiar form (*the form of the old German Monarchy striped flag*) was out of the question for reasons that have been mentioned. However, this color combination is the most effective of all. It is the most striking and harmonious combination there is.

I was also inclined to retain the colors of the old flag because they are the most sacred thing to me as a soldier and because their aesthetic effect appeals far more than any other to my artistic sense. Nevertheless, I had to decline all of the countless sketches that came in from the members of the young movement. Most of them incorporated the swastika into the old flag. As the Leader, I did not want to immediately present my own design to the public since it was quite possible that someone else might produce one equally good or perhaps even better. In fact, a dentist from Starnberg (*a town in Bavaria Germany near Munich*) brought in a design that was not bad at all. It was a lot like mine, but had one flaw, the swastika; it had curved ends and a thin white circle around the swastika.

Meanwhile, after countless attempts, I had finally drawn the final form. It was a flag with a red background, and a white disk with a black swastika in the middle. After many experiments, I also established a balance between the size of the flag and the size of the white disk as well as the shape and thickness of the swastika lines.

And that's how it remained. Arm bands for the guard troops were ordered immediately. They were red bands bearing the white disk with the black swastika. The party badge was designed along the same lines. It was a white disk on a red background with the swastika in the middle. A Munich goldsmith, Mr. Füss, produced the first practical design and that is the one we have kept.

In midsummer of 1920, the new flag appeared in public for the first time. It suited our movement perfectly. The movement and the flag were both young and new. No one had ever seen it before and its effect was like a firebrand (*a person who stirs up trouble or kindles a revolution*). We were all childishly delighted when a faithful woman Party member completed the design for the first time and delivered the finished flag. Within a few months, we had half a dozen of them in Munich. The constantly expanding guard troops were mostly responsible for the spread of the new movement's symbol. And this is truly a strong symbol.

Our respect for the past is demonstrated by each color, and it is passionately loved by us all because it calls forth so much honor from the German people. It was also the best image to show the desire of the people who were driving the movement. As National-Socialists, we see our political program in our flag. In the red, we see the socialist ideas of the movement; in the white, the nationalistic; in the swastika, the mission of the fight for the victory of the Aryan man. At the same time, we see victory for the creative work of a culture, which was anti-Semitic and will be anti-Semitic eternally.

Two years later, when the guard troops had grown in number to many thousands of men who now formed an elaborate Storm Detachment, we saw that it was necessary to give this defense organization of our young World-Concept a special symbol of victory that we called the Standard (*meaning a degree or level of excellence symbolized by a flag or emblem*) I sketched it myself and gave it to the master goldsmith, Mr. Gahr, to execute. Since that time, this Standard has been the symbol and field-badge of the National-Socialist battle.

The number of people attending meetings kept growing in the year 1920. Finally, we began holding two meetings a week during some weeks.

Crowds gathered in front of our posters. The largest halls in the city were always filled. Tens of thousands of those misled by Marxism found their way back to their national community to become warriors for a free German Reich. We were well known in Munich. We were the talk of the town. The word "National-Socialist" was widely discussed and was recognized as a clear political program. The crowd of followers and members began to grow consistently. By the winter of 1920-1921, we were a strong party in Munich.

Except for the Marxist parties, there was no other party at that time that could hold such mass demonstrations as we did. The nationalist parties certainly could not. The Munichener-Kindl Cellar, which held five thousand people, was filled to overflowing more than once. There was only one meeting hall we had not yet dared to try, the Zirkus Krone (*Crown Circus Hall*).

At the end of January, 1921, serious concerns arose again for Germany. The Paris Agreement was to become a reality by signing the London Ultimatum. According to this, Germany had obligated herself to pay the insane sum of a hundred billion gold marks with this deal. (*The London Ultimatum of 1921 eventually set Germany's war reparations at 132 Billion Marks and demanded the first billion to be paid within 25 days.*)

A worker's coalition of so-called racialist societies, which existed for a long time in Munich, proposed sending out invitations for a large general protest over the matter. Time was critical, and I became nervous after seeing the constant hesitation and delays in their decisions. First, they talked about a demonstration in the Konigsplatz (*an open square or parade field in Munich*), but they let it drop because they were afraid of being violently scattered by the Reds. Then they planned a protest demonstration in front of the Field Marshals' Hall, but this was also canceled. Finally, they proposed a joint meeting in the Munichener-Kindl Cellar hall. Days went by, but the big parties ignored the planned protest and the workers' coalition itself could not decide on a definite date for the proposed demonstration.

On Tuesday, February 1, 1921, I demanded a final decision be made urgently. I was put off until Wednesday. On Wednesday, I absolutely insisted on a clear statement when and if the meeting was to take place. Again, the answer was indefinite and evasive. The story was that they "intended" to turn out the workers' coalition for a demonstration a week from Wednesday. I had lost all patience, so I decided to carry out the protest demonstration by myself. On Wednesday afternoon, I dictated the wording for a poster to a typist in ten minutes and had the Zirkus Krone (*Crown Circus*) hired for the next day, Thursday, February 3.

This was definitely a daring move. Not only was it questionable whether the gigantic room could be filled, but there was the further danger that the meeting would be broken up. I feared our hall guard troops were not adequate for this huge room, and I was unsure how to handle the situation if the meeting were broken up. I expected it to be much more difficult to manage a large crowd in the Circus building than in an ordinary hall. As it turned out, the opposite was true. In the giant room, it was actually easier to overpower a dispersion troop than it was in closely-packed halls.

One thing was for sure! Any failure could set us back for a long time. If the Reds were successful just once in dispersing us, it would have destroyed our impression among the people and would have encouraged our adversaries to repeat their success. It might have led to sabotaging our entire meeting activities. It would have taken many months and desperate battles to overcome such an incident.

We only had one day for our posters to work, Thursday. Unfortunately, it rained all morning, which made us reasonably afraid that the weather would cause many people to stay at home rather than hurry through rain and snow to a meeting where there might be violence and killings.

Thursday morning, I felt fear suddenly set in. I was afraid the hall would not be filled. If only a few people showed up, I would have looked like a fool in the eyes of the workers' coalition. I hurriedly dictated a few leaflets with an appeal to attend the meeting and they were printed for distribution in the afternoon. The two trucks I hired were covered in as much red as possible. A few of our flags were attached to them and each one was manned with fifteen or twenty party members. They were ordered to drive around the streets of the city continuously throwing out leaflets and distributing propaganda for the mass demonstration that evening. It was the first time that trucks with flags had ever gone through the city with no Marxists on board. The mouths of the privileged-class fell open as they stared at the cars draped in red and decorated with fluttering swastika flags. In the outer districts where workers lived, countless clenched fists were raised by those who were obviously furious at the latest "provocation of the working class". In their mind, only Marxism had the right to hold meetings and ride around on trucks.

If these kinds of things were done by others, it was the Marxists' holy right to consider it a provocation because, until now, they were the sole owners of this monopoly.

By 7:00 in the evening, the Circus was not filled. I received telephone reports every ten minutes and was uneasy about it because, by 7:00 or 7:15, the other halls were usually half filled or sometimes nearly completely filled. Soon the reason became clear. I had not counted on the new hall's huge size. A thousand people made the Hofbrauhaus Hall look like it was well-packed, while the Circus hall simply swallowed up those thousand people. More encouraging reports followed a little while later and by 7:45, they said that the hall was three-fourths full and there were more large crowds standing in front of the ticket booths. Then I drove to the meeting hall.

At 8:02 I arrived in front of the Circus hall. There was still a crowd of people in front. Some of them were just curious and many of them were opponents who preferred to wait outside. When I went into the enormous hall, I was just as excited as I had been the year before at the first meeting in the Munich Hofbräuhaus Banquet Hall. Only after I squeezed my way through the wall of people and reached the high platform did I see the full extent of the achievement. The meeting hall was in front of me like a giant shell and was filled with thousands and thousands of people. The center of the arena was so filled that it appeared black with spectators. More than 5,600 tickets had been sold and if we count the total number of unemployed, poor students, and our hall-guard troops, there must have been about 6,500 people there.

My theme was "Future or Downfall". I could feel my heart leap with conviction because I saw that the future was right in front of me.

I began and spoke for about two and a half hours. After the first half-hour, I knew the meeting would be a great success. I made a connection with these thousands of individuals. By the end of the first hour, the applause began to interrupt me in growing spontaneous outbursts. After two hours, the applause became less frequent and led into that solemn stillness that I have experienced so many times since then in that hall and which will never be forgotten by a single person who was there. The breathing of the huge crowd was almost the only thing that could be heard. When I had spoken my last word, there was a sudden flood of emotion that found its outlet and its conclusion in a chorus of Deutschland Über Alles, which the crowd sang with ultimate passion.

I waited for almost twenty minutes watching the gigantic hall slowly empty and the tremendous sea of people find their way out through the great central exit. Then

I left my post extremely happy and went home.

Photographs were taken of this first meeting in the Circus Hall at Munich. They show the magnitude of the demonstration better than any words possibly could. Privileged-class papers printed the photos and reports of the meeting but only mentioned that it had been a "nationalist" demonstration and omitted the names of those responsible for making it happen, in their usual modest fashion. For the first time, we advanced far beyond the confines of any of the ordinary parties of the day. We could no longer be ignored. We did not want anyone to think this meeting's success was an isolated stroke of good luck, so I immediately scheduled a second demonstration at the Circus for the following week. That meeting was a success just the same as before. Again the gigantic hall was filled to bursting with masses of people. I decided to hold a third meeting on the same scale the following week. For the third time, the giant Circus hall was jammed with people from top to bottom.

After this successful beginning in 1921, we began holding more meetings in Munich. I now started to hold not just one a week, but in many weeks, two mass meetings. In mid-summer and late fall, there were sometimes three meetings a week. From now on, we always held our meetings in the Circus hall and found to our satisfaction that each evening was a similar success.

The result was a constantly growing number of followers for the movement and a great increase in registered members too. This success naturally kept our opponents from getting any rest. Their tactics wavered between terrorism and a conspiracy of silence. In time they were forced to realize that they could not hinder the movement's development by either method. So, as a last supreme effort, they decided on an act of terrorism they hoped would put a definite stop to any further meetings.

As a show of force, there was a mysterious assault on a parliamentary deputy by the name of Erhard Auer (*a member of the Bavarian Parliament and the Social Democratic Party*). He was allegedly shot at by somebody one evening. That is to say, he was not actually shot, but an attempt had been made to shoot at him. The outstanding presence of mind and the proverbial courage of a Social Democratic party leader thwarted the cunning attack and made those evil perpetrators who were responsible run away in shame. They fled so fast and so far that the police were never able to find the slightest trace of them.

This mysterious occurrence was now used by the Social Democratic party in Munich to arouse public sentiment against our movement in a most extreme way. They hinted at what was to happen next through their standard boisterous ramblings. Measures were taken to make sure we did not get out of hand, that our movement did not grow, and to make sure we were cut down to the root. They said the fists of the lower class would intervene in good time. Within a few days, the time for intervention arrived.

The meeting in the Munich Hofbräuhaus Banquet Hall where I was to speak had been chosen for their final settlement of accounts. On November 4, 1921, between 6:00 and 7:00 in the evening, I received my first confirmation that the meeting would definitely be broken up and that great masses of workers from some of the Red controlled factories were being sent to the meeting to disrupt the proceedings. It was a bit of misfortune that we did not receive this information earlier. That day, we had moved from our respected business office on Sternecker Lane in Munich and were in the process of moving to a new office space. Actually, we were out of the old one, but could not move into the new one because work on it was still in progress. The telephone had been pulled out of the old office and the new office did not yet have a phone installed. There were a number of attempts to inform us by telephone the day of the intended dispersion, but with no phone installed, they were in vain.

As a result, we only had a very small number of hall-guard troops for protection at the meeting. We had forty-six men to do the job of one hundred, and the alert system was not yet developed that could summon any considerable reinforcements in only one hour at night. Besides, that kind of alarmist rumor had reached our ears countless times before without anything coming of it. The old saying that "Announced revolutions seldom take place" had always proved true in the past for us. So, for this reason, everything may not have been done that could have prepared us for a dispersion with vicious determination.

Previously, we believed the Munich Hofbräuhaus Banquet Hall was not well suited to dispersion tactics. We were more concerned about it in the largest halls, particularly the Circus. In that respect, the Circus taught us a valuable lesson. Afterward, we studied the entire security question with a more scientific method and arrived at some surprising and interesting results. These results had fundamental importance later in the organization and in the tactical management of our Storm Troops.

When I came into the lobby of the Hofbräuhaus at 7:45, however, there could be no doubt about their intentions. The hall was overcrowded and for that reason the outside doors were closed by the police and no one else was allowed in. The opponents, who had come very early, were inside the hall and our followers were mostly outside. The little Storm Troop waited for me in the lobby. I had the inside doors to the big hall closed and then I lined up the forty-five or forty-six men. I told the young men that today, for the first time, they would probably have to be true to the movement no matter what. I told them that none of us must leave the hall unless we were carried out dead. I would stay in the hall and did not believe that a single one of them would desert me. However, if I saw anyone turn into a coward, I would personally tear off his armband and take his badge. Then, I instructed them to rush in at the slightest attempt to break up the meeting and to remember that the best defense is an attack. A triple "Heil" which sounded rougher and more hoarse than usual was the answer.

Then, I entered the hall and looked over the situation with my own eyes. They were packed inside, and from where they were sitting they tried to drill into me with their eyes. Countless faces were looking at me with grim hatred, while others had mocking frowns and emitted shouts that were very clear. They would say, "We'll finish you today", and that we should "Look out for our guts", and that they would "Stop our mouths for good", and various other pretty phrases. They were aware of their superior force and felt strong.

Nevertheless, it was possible to open the meeting and I began to speak. In the Hofbräuhaus Banquet Hall, I always stood against one of the long walls of the hall and my platform was a beer table. So, I was actually in the very middle of the crowd. Maybe that was one reason why there was always an attitude of camaraderie in this particular hall that I have never found anywhere else.

In front of me, and especially to my left, there were nothing but opponents sitting and standing. They were extremely tough men and youths, mainly from the Maffei locomotive works, from Kustermann and the Isaria works, etc. Along the left wall of the hall, they had moved close to my table and they now began to collect beer mugs. That is, they kept ordering beer and putting the empty mugs under the table. They gathered whole batteries of them. (*A Battery is a group of similar things placed together to be used.*) I would have been surprised if this meeting had gone off smoothly. I was able to speak for about an hour and a half despite all the heckling and, at this point, it almost seemed as if I would remain in control of the situation. The leaders of the dispersion troops seemed to feel this themselves and they became more and more uneasy. They kept going out and coming back in, then talking very nervously to their people. But then, I committed a small psychological error in trying to prevent an interruption when someone shouted. I realized it the moment it was out of my mouth; I had given the signal for them to cut loose.

There were a few angry shouts, then a man suddenly jumped on a chair and yelled into the hall, "Freedom!" This was the battle-cry of the Social Democrats. On the signal, the fighters for freedom began their work.

Within a few seconds, the whole hall was filled with a roaring and screaming mob. Countless beer mugs flew like howitzer shots over their heads. Chair legs were cracking, mugs were smashing, and there were groans, screaming, and shouting. It was an insane uproar. I stood still where I was and could see my young men doing their duty to the utmost. I would have liked to have seen a privileged-class meeting in that situation!

The game had not started when my Storm Troopers, as they were called from that day forward, attacked. In packs of eight or ten, they fell like wolves on their enemies and gradually began to hammer them out of the hall. Within five minutes, most of them were streaming with blood. In that moment I came to really know many of them for the first time. At the top was my faithful Maurice, my present private secretary, Hess, and many others, who, although severely wounded, continued their attack as long as they could stay on their feet. (*Maurice is Emil Maurice, a watchmaker. As his secretary, Hitler dictated part of Mein Kampf to him as they both served time in prison together.*) The hellish turmoil lasted twenty minutes. By then, my men, numbering less than fifty, had almost finished pounding seven or eight hundred enemies out of the hall and down the stairs. In the left rear corner of the hall, a large group held out, resisting desperately. Suddenly, there were two pistol shots from the entrance towards the platform. Then a wild flurry of gunshots began. My heart leapt as memories of the old war flooded to me.

From then on, there was no way to tell who was doing the shooting. The only thing I can say is from that moment on, the rage of my bleeding young men increased tremendously. Finally, the last troublemakers were overpowered and driven from the hall.

About twenty-five minutes had passed. The hall looked as if an artillery shell had burst in it. Many of my followers were being bandaged and others had to be taken away in cars, but we remained masters of the situation. Hermann Esser, who had taken over as chairman of the meeting that night, said, "The meeting will continue. The speaker has the floor". I resumed speaking.

After we had terminated the meeting, an excited police lieutenant suddenly rushed in madly waving his arms and bragged to the hall, "This meeting is dissolved". I could not help laughing at this come-lately straggler who had such a true policeman's ego. The smaller they are, the bigger they want to appear.

We learned a great deal that evening, as did our adversaries. Until the fall of 1923, the Münchener Post did not warn us again about the fists of the working class. (*The Münchener Post, Munich Post, had a long running campaign against Hitler and closely followed the Nazi party but did not focus on their politics.*)

8. THE STRONG MAN IS MIGHTIEST WHEN ALONE

I have already mentioned the existence of a worker's coalition of German-racialist societies and will take this opportunity to briefly discuss the problem presented by these worker's coalitions.

When we say worker's coalition, we mean that a number of worker societies enter into a certain mutual relationship to assist them in carrying out their work. They chose a common leadership of lesser or greater authority and plan things together. This means the clubs, societies, or parties must always have similar aims and do things in a similar way. The ordinary average citizen is pleased and reassured when they learn that the societies who form such a working coalition have found their "points of agreement" and "put aside their differences". The general belief is that such a union means a huge increase in strength, and that the smaller groups who would be weak on their own suddenly become a power to be reckoned with. But this is usually not the case.

It is interesting and I think important if we are to properly understand this question, to clearly look at how the formation of these societies, groups, coalitions, etc., all claiming to pursue the same end, can come together at all. It would be logical for one issue to be supported by just one society. It does not seem reasonable for several societies to work for the same end. Undoubtedly, that end was originally envisioned by just one society. Somewhere, a man proclaims a truth, summons people to solve a certain problem, sets a goal, and forms a movement to make his purpose a reality.

This is how a club or a party is founded so that it can eliminate existing evils or to achieve a certain state of affairs in the future.

When such a movement comes into existence, it has a certain right of priority. It is obvious that everyone who intends to work for the same end should take his place in the movement to strengthen it and better serve the common purpose. Every intellectually alert mind should consider joining this group as indispensable to the real success of the common struggle of the group. Therefore, assuming they are reasonable and possess a certain degree of honesty, there should be only one movement for one goal. I will prove this later.

There are two reasons why forming a coalition does not gain a small group strength. The first one, I might almost call tragic, and the second one is pitiful and is to be found in human weakness itself. But the bottom line is that I see both as elements capable of strengthening the will, its energy and intensity, and can make a solution to the problem possible. The tragic reason why there is usually more than one society trying to solve a given problem is that any really large achievement on this earth is generally the fulfillment of a wish that has been around for a long time and has been in the hearts of millions of men. In fact, it may be that the problem has been around for centuries and people are moaning and groaning over the intolerable condition, but the desire for change remains unfulfilled. Nations that can no longer find any heroic solution for such distress may be described as feeble and unproductive. However, the best proof of a people's strength and of its being fated to survive is the fact that one day, Fate grants it the brilliant man who can fulfill their long held desire. It may be the release from some great oppression, elimination of bitter distress, or contentment of the people's soul which has become restless from their insecurity.

Great questions of our time naturally lead thousands in their attempt to take part in the solution. Many feel called upon and Fate nominates several choices who are tested by natural forces which only gives victory to the strongest and most capable and entrusts him with the solution to the problem. There may be a people who are dissatisfied for centuries with their religious life and long for a revival. Because of this spiritual pressure, dozens of men arise who believe they are chosen to relieve this religious distress through their insight and their knowledge, either as prophets of a new teaching or as fighters against an existing one.

Here too, the strongest man who is selected by forces of natural order finds himself fated to carry out the great mission, but the knowledge that he alone is called remain unknown to others until much later. On the contrary, they regard themselves as equally entitled to and equally chosen to accomplish this task, and these contemporaries are unable to distinguish the one man among them who is supremely gifted and deserves their sole support, until the very end.

Over the course of centuries or sometimes within a single era, various men arise and start movements to fight for aims which are the same, or at least are felt to be the same by the great masses. The people have vague desires and general convictions so they cannot clearly understand the real nature of a goal, or fully comprehend their own wishes, or even envision how the goal could be achieved.

The tragedy is that all those men are striving toward a single goal by taking different roads without knowing or working with any of the others pursuing the same goal. Therefore, with the purest faith in their own mission, they think it is their duty to go their own way alone.

What at first seems tragic is that such movements, parties, or religious groups, etc., are created independently of each other, from some universal desire of their time, and they all work in a single direction toward the same goal by different paths. Too many people believe that combining the strength used by the groups traveling down different roads into one unified journey would be more certain to bring success and bring it faster. But this is not the case. Nature herself, using pitiless logic, decides who succeeds by putting the various groups in competition with one another and forcing them to struggle for victory. Then, she leads the movement that has chosen the clearest, shortest, and surest road to success to its final goal. The choice between the right or wrong direction can never be decided if the various groups are not allowed to compete freely. The final decision of victory is not in the hands of inflexible human know-it-alls; the decision is left to that most dependable proof—the proof we see through success—and success is what always verifies the justice of an action.

If various groups are marching on separate roads toward the same goal, they will compare their efforts and methods to their competitors. This forces them to test the quality of their own path more thoroughly, shorten it if possible, and draw on their deepest energy to arrive at the goal sooner. This contest improves the breed of the individual fighter. Mankind frequently owes its successes to lessons learned from the mistakes of failed past attempts. What at first may seem like a tragic disjunction, this separation of individual efforts is now recognized as the means that eventually produces the best course and leads to victory.

We can see there was a common opinion in our history that the two possible paths for a solution to German problems should have been united from the beginning. These paths are the policies of Austria and Prussia, and their ruling houses, Hapsburg and Hohenzollern. According to this opinion, one road or the other should have been followed by uniting their forces. If that had been done, the road of the party that was the most impressive would have been chosen, that would be Austria. However, the Austrian purpose would never have led to a German Empire.

The strongest unified Empire of Germany rose from the very thing that millions of Germans despised with all their heart and that same thing which was the final and most frightening result of our internal strife. The German Imperial Crown was brought home from the battlefield of Königgrätz (*which was a decisive 1866 battle in the Austrian-Prussian war where Prussia defeated Austria; the battle is named for the Czech city*) and not from the battles before Paris as most people thought (*this means the real victor between these two ideas or methods was decided in Königgrätz and not in later, smaller battles*). The founding of the German Empire was not the result of common intent pursued along a common road, but the result of a conscious, and sometimes an unconscious, struggle for dominance by separate interests. From this struggle, Prussia eventually emerged victorious. Anyone whose political affiliation does not blind him to the truth must agree that the so-called wisdom of men would never have made the same wise decision that was made by the wisdom of life. Two hundred years ago, who in the German lands would seriously have believed that the Prussia of the Hohenzollerns, and not the House of Hapsburg, would someday be the nucleus, the founder, and the teacher of the new German Empire? On the other hand, who today would deny that Fate made a better choice, which it did. Who could imagine there being a German Empire at all if it were based on the principles of a decadent, cowardly, and degenerate Austrian dynasty? After centuries of struggle, natural conflict finally put the best man in the position he had earned.

That will always be and it will eternally remain as it has always been. For that reason, there should be no regret when different people take separate roads for a single goal. The strongest and swiftest will be recognized and will become the victor.

There is also a second reason why similar movements try to reach similar goals by different methods. This reason is not tragic but is totally pitiful. It originates in the sorry mixture of envy, jealousy, ambition, and a desire to take what belongs to others. This kind of ambition is unfortunately often found in individual members of the human race.

Whenever a man steps out of the crowd who understands fully the nature of the disease suffered by his people, he realizes their distress and seriously attempts to alleviate it; at the moment he envisions a goal and chooses the road that may lead to that goal, all the critical people turn their ears toward him and enthusiastically track the actions of this man who has drawn the public eye. These people are just like sparrows watching a more fortunate bird who has found a piece of bread. They seem to be uninterested, yet they keep a vigilant watch to steal his crumb at the first unguarded moment. A man only has to place one foot on a new road and immediately many lazy loafers become alert, sensing some profitable tidbit that may be at the end of that road. The moment they have found out where their prize is hidden, they eagerly set out to reach the goal by another and, if possible, quicker road.

Once the new movement has been founded and it has established a definite program, these people rise up and claim they are fighting for the same cause, but they don't do this in an honest way by joining the ranks of the movement and acknowledging its priority. Instead, they steal the program and start a new party of their own. They are bold enough to tell their unthinking contemporaries that they had the same idea long before the other man. They are frequently successful in showing themselves in a favorable light instead of attracting the universal contempt they deserve. It is disrespectful for a man to write down another's idea and claim it as his own, or to steal the basic points from another's program and then pretend it was his own creation. This disrespect can be clearly seen among those who originally caused the division by forming their separate new organization. When they think the adversary has too big of a head start to catch up, that is when they shout the loudest about the need for harmony and unity. The current "racialist disunity" is due to this exact process.

It is true that the formation of a whole series of groups, parties, etc., described as racialist resulted entirely from the natural development of affairs in 1918-1919 and the founders of these were not at any fault for their movement's creation. As early as 1920, the NSDAP had definitely surfaced as the victorious party among them all. Nothing was more brilliant or fundamentally honest than the decisions of the various founders of other parties when they made the truly admirable decision to sacrifice their own, obviously less successful movements, to the stronger one and dissolve their smaller groups or unconditionally incorporate them into the larger.

This is particularly true of the leader of the then German Socialist Party in Nuremberg, Julius Streicher, who was also a school teacher in Nuremberg. (*Julius Streicher published an anti-Semitic newspaper of offensive cartoons and anti-Semitic children's books. Streicher had his own personal followers and merged them with the Nazi party. He also participated in the failed 1923 Putsch.*) Our NSDAP and his German Socialist Party had been founded with the same ultimate aims, but they were founded completely independently. At first, he too was filled with holy conviction for his movement's mission and future. But as soon as he saw clearly and beyond any doubt that the greater strength and swifter growth of the NSDAP had made it the mightier force, he discontinued his activity for the German Socialist Party and the worker's coalition. He urged his followers to take their places in the NSDAP, which had emerged victorious from the struggle, and to go on fighting for the common aim within its ranks. This was a difficult thing to do but this decision was totally honorable on his part.

No division remains from these early days of the movement. The honest will and intent of those men led almost without exception to an honorable, upright, and proper outcome. What is now called "racialist disunity" owes its existence exclusively to the second cause I have explained. It is created by ambitious men who never had any ideas or goals of their own, yet felt "called upon" precisely at the moment they saw the undeniable truth that the NSDAP's success had matured.

Suddenly, political programs emerged that were outright copies of ours. Ideas were circulated that had been borrowed from us; aims were set up that we fought for years earlier; paths were chosen that the NSDAP had already traveled. They tried every way possible to explain why they felt compelled to establish these new parties, despite the long-existing NSDAP, but the more noble they claimed their motives were, the more dishonorable these masquerades became.

In reality, only one reason drove their actions. This reason was the personal ambition of the founders who wanted to play a role their own smallness did not allow them to otherwise play. The only ability they had was the great boldness to take the ideas of others, a boldness that in ordinary civil life is usually called stealing.

There was no idea or concept created by others that one of these political kleptomaniacs did not soon collect for his new business. The people who did this were the same ones who later tearfully moaned about the "racialist disunity" and talked constantly about the "necessity of unity" in the secret hope that they could make others so weary of the constant theft accusations and protests, that their counterparts would throw the thieves not only the ideas they had created, but the entire movements meant to carry them out.

But if the thieves did not succeed in that endeavor, and if the profits of their new enterprise failed to keep up with expectations because of the inferior intellect of the owners, they often sold out cheaper and were satisfied if they ended up in one of the so-called worker coalitions.

At this time, all those leaders who could not stand on their own feet united into these worker coalitions in the belief that eight lame men, arm in arm, would create one big gladiator. If there were one healthy man among the lame ones, he needed all his strength to keep the others on their feet and ended up paralyzed himself.

Joining such worker coalitions must always be regarded as a question of tactics, but at the same time we must never lose sight of the following basic conclusion:

The formation of a worker coalition never turns weak organizations into strong ones, but it can and frequently will weaken a strong organization. The belief that a strong unit must result from the union of weak groups is mistaken. Any majority under any conditions has been shown by experience to be the embodiment of incompetence and cowardice so that any group of societies, if they are ruled by an elected governing body of several persons from their own membership, yields to cowardice and weakness. This sort of union also prevents the free play of natural forces, halts the struggle that selects the best man, and forever prevents the healthier and stronger from achieving the necessary and final victory. Such unions are enemies of natural development. They usually interfere far more with the process of finding a solution than they strengthen it.

For purely tactical reasons, the supreme leadership of a movement, with their attention focused on the future goals of the organization, will form some agreement with a similar group on certain questions for a very short time, and will even agree to participate in joint activities or meetings. But this can never lead to a long-term association unless the movement is planning to abandon its mission of salvation. Once it is entangled in such a coupling, it loses the opportunity and the right to use its strength to the fullest, to claim its place through natural development, to overcome its rivals, and to reach its goal as the one and only victor.

It must never be forgotten that nothing truly great in the world has ever been achieved by an alliance. It has always been through the triumph of the individual. The very origin of joint forces carries with it the germ of its own later decay. Great intellectual revolutions that shake up the world are only conceivable and only possible when they are monumental struggles by individuals and never when they are enterprises of coalitions.

Above all, the new race-based state will never be created by the compromising indecisiveness of a racialist worker-coalition, but only by the iron will of a single movement that has fought its way through all that opposed it.

9. BASIC THOUGHTS ON THE MEANING AND ORGANIZATION OF THE STORM TROOPS

The strength of the old State rested on three pillars: the Monarchy form of government, the civil administrative bodies, and the army. The Revolution of 1918 did away with the Monarchy, weakened the army, and brought party corruption to the civil administrative bodies. With that, the fundamental supports of any state authority were smashed to bits. These supports almost always depend on three elements—the same elements that are the fundamental base for all authority.

The first requirement for the creation of authority is popular support. However, if authority depends solely on this foundation, it is shaky, unreliable, and weak. Everyone who is supported by popularity alone must aim at improving and strengthening this authority through the generation of power. Power, through the use of force, is the second fundamental for authority. Authority through power is more stable and reliable, but not always stronger than authority through popularity. If popularity and power are combined and they can survive together for a certain time, then that authority may form an even stronger basis, the authority of tradition. If popularity, power and tradition are united, authority can be considered unshakable.

The Revolution destroyed all authority by tradition. Tradition was rudely torn down with the break-up of the old Reich, the removal of the Monarchy form of state, and the annihilation of its symbols of former grandeur. The result was a heavy blow to state authority.

Even the second pillar of state authority, power, was no longer present. In order to carry through the Revolution at all, it was necessary to remove the organized force and power of the State, which was the army. They had to use pieces torn from the army as the fighting element of the revolution. Although the armies from the front had not been effected by this destruction, the acid of disorganization in the homeland still started to eat away at them when they returned from the fields of glory and left their heroic battle behind. The battle had lasted four and a half years, and their journey ended once they arrived at the garrisons for their discharge papers, and they were faced with the confusion of voluntary obedience, as it was called, imposed in the era of soldier self-government through the Soldiers' Councils.

No authority could be built from this collection of mutiny-minded soldiers who considered military service as an eight-hour day job. Therefore, the second element that guaranteed security for authority was also lost. This leaves the Revolution with only the original one, popularity, on which to build up its authority. This basis was very unreliable. The Revolution succeeded in shattering the old state structure with a single, mighty thrust and this was possible for only one reason. The normal structural balance of our people was abolished by the war.

Every national body can be divided into three classes. First, there is the best of mankind who are good because they possess strong civil virtues and are especially distinguished by courage and take pleasure in self sacrifice. Second, and at the other extreme, are the worst scum of mankind who are bad in the sense that they exist to indulge in every selfish impulse and vice. Between the two extremes lies a third class. This is the large, most broad group that exhibits neither a gleaming heroism nor a mean criminal temper.

When a national body experiences a period of distinct rise, it occurs only through the absolute leadership of the extreme best part of the national body. Periods marked by a normal, steady development or by a stable condition exist when the middle element is dominant and the two extremes maintain an equal balance that cancels each other out. A period ending in the collapse of a national body will certainly result from the work of the worst elements.

It is remarkable to note that the broad mass, the middle group as I call them, makes their presence known only if the two extremes come into conflict. The middle group will then submit to whichever extreme wins. If the best group dominates, the broad mass will follow them. If the worst group wins, the middle group will, at the least, not resist. The intermediate mass will never fight for themselves.

Four and a half years of war—with all its bloody events—disturbed the equilibrium of these three groups. This happened because of the massive sacrifice made by the middle group. This bloodbath almost completely wiped out the best men. The irreplaceable blood these German heroes shed during these four and a half years was a horrible loss. There were hundreds of thousands who gave up their lives. Volunteers were requested in every area: volunteers for the front, volunteers for patrols, volunteers as spies, volunteers for communications, volunteers for construction, volunteers for the U-boats, volunteers for aviation, volunteers for the storm battalions, and so forth, again and again for four-and-a-half years on thousands of occasions, volunteers and more volunteers. And one saw the same result every time: only the very young, even beardless boys, or the very old men stepped forward. They were the ones filled with passionate love for the Fatherland and they volunteered for these duties with great, personal courage and with a strong sense of duty. This was repeated tens and hundreds of thousands of times until, gradually, this part of the human species grew scarcer and scarcer. Those who did not either die or become crippled soon joined their ranks because of the wounds they received as a result of the dwindling supply of replacement soldiers. The most important thing to consider is that in 1914, the whole army was made up of volunteers who, thanks to the criminal corruption of our parliamentary do-nothings, had received no real peace-time training for war and were handed over to the enemy as defenseless men.

The four hundred thousand who fell or were permanently maimed at the battle of Flanders could not be replaced. Their loss was more than just a loss of numbers.

The death of these willing volunteers caused the scale's balance to shift. Now we had too little weight on the good side and too much weight on the bad side. The hostile, vile, and cowardly elements in this mass of the worst extreme became dominant. Add to that the fact that not only did the best extreme group become thinned out on the battlefield in the most horrible way for four and a half years, but the worst group was protected in the most remarkable way. For every volunteer hero who climbed the steps to Valhalla by their holy sacrifice of death, there was a wretched coward who very cautiously turned his back on death so he could prove his usefulness in the homeland by taking the place of the volunteers now serving in battle.

The end of the war presented the following picture. The broad, middle group appropriately sacrificed its share of blood. The best extreme group sacrificed itself with its typical heroism. The worst extreme was unfortunately preserved, completely intact because it was protected by the most stupid of laws and by the failure to enforce the Articles of War.

This well-preserved scum of our nation created the Revolution. It was able to do so because there was no one left to oppose them. The extreme of the best group had ceased to exist. The German Revolution depended on one remaining part of the population. It was not the German people who were guilty of this act of murder against their brother like Cain, but the idiot riff-raff of worthless deserters and pimps, etc.

The man at the front was happy to see an end to the bloody fight so he could return home to his wife and children. He personally had nothing to do with the Revolution itself. He did not like it, and he liked its activists and organizers even less. In four and a half years of the hardest fighting, he had forgotten the political party hyenas. Their bickering had become foreign to him.

The Revolution was only popular with a small part of the German people. Those were the supporters who had chosen a knapsack as the distinguishing sign of honorable citizens in this new State (*possibly meaning pillagers wanting to fill their knapsack with spoils*). Some misguided people believe that these crooks started the Revolution for its own sake, but it was actually because they wanted what would result.

These Marxist pirates had difficulty maintaining an authority that depended on popularity alone, and they knew it would not last very long. The young Republic needed authority immediately and at any cost. Otherwise, after a short period of chaos, it would suddenly be entangled again with another governmental authority linked together out of the last remnants of the extreme good group of our people.

Every supporter of the Revolution was very afraid that in the storm of the chaos they created, their toehold in the position of power would be lost and they would suddenly be captured by a bold iron fist which would place them on a lower footing. This has happened more than once in similar circumstances throughout history. The Republic had to consolidate at any cost. Immediately, the shaky foundation of its weak authority, based in popularity, forced it to again create an organization of power so that it would have a more solid foundation of authority.

During December 1918 and January-February of 1919, the matadors of the Revolution felt the ground wobbling under their feet. They were looking for men who would be ready to use force to strengthen their weak position, which was supported only by the love of their people. The "anti-military" Republic needed soldiers. The first and only support for their government authority, their popularity, was rooted in a society of pimps, thieves, burglars, deserters, cowards, etc., and all those whom we must designate as the worst extreme group. Therefore, finding men from this group who were ready to sacrifice their own lives in the service of the new ideal was Love's Labor Lost; it was impossible. (*Love's Labor Lost is the title of a Shakespeare comedy which came from a Greek poem that says, "To do good to one's enemies is love's labor lost". Doing good to your enemies is futile, and here it is meant as an expression of futility.*) The people who made the revolutionary idea a reality were not ready or capable of inviting the existing soldiers to protect them. This group did not want to risk forming a republican government, but wanted to maintain the disorganization of the existing state so they could indulge in their own desires. Their call was not for order and establishment of the German Republic, but for the plundering of it.

Therefore, the cries for help by the leaders, in their mortal terror, went unheeded by this group of thugs. The cries instead aroused disgust and bitterness. They saw it as a breach of their leader's loyalty and faith in their own group of criminals. The leaders' authority was comfortably resting on popularity, but the group feared that once the leaders gained the strength of power, not just popularity, that this new formation of authority would be the beginning of a battle against those features cherished the most by the Revolution: against their right of theft and the immoral reign of a horde of thieves, plunderers, and trash, a reign by those who had recently been released from their prison shackles, in short, the evil mob would lose its control. No matter how much the leaders yelled, no one came from their own ranks. The call of "traitor" revealed the thoughts from the group that created their popularity.

Countless young Germans found themselves ready for the first time to put on the uniform and steel-helmet, shoulder carbines and rifles so they might defend "Peace and Order" for the destroyers of their homeland. As volunteers, they formed volunteer corps and although they hated the Revolution bitterly, they began to defend and strengthen this Revolution. They did this with the best of intentions.

The organizer of the Revolution, and the actual puppeteer, was the international Jew who sized up the situation correctly when he saw the German people were not yet ripe enough to be pulled into the blood swamp of Bolshevism, as happened in Russia. This was due to the closer racial unity of the German intellectuals and the German laborer. Mass education across all social classes, like what we find in other Western European countries, also played a part in Germany's unity, but such education was not present in Russia. In Russia, the intellectuals were not even of Russian nationality or at least did not have the character of the Slavic race. This created a thin intellectual layer in Russia at that time which could be replaced easily because there was no connecting middle layer to unify the intelligentsia and the masses of the Russian people. The spiritual and moral fiber of the great masses was horribly low.

When the revolutionaries succeeded in Russia by provoking the uneducated masses against the thin intellectual upper layer, which was entirely foreign to the masses and had no connection with them, in that instant, the fate of Russia was decided and the revolution was successful. The Russian illiterate became a defenseless slave of the Jewish dictators. These dictators, however, were clever enough to call this dictatorship a "Dictatorship of the People".

In Germany, there was another factor that affected the outcome. The gradual deterioration of the army is what made it possible for the Revolution to be successful in Germany. This deterioration was not caused by the soldiers at the front. This was the work of the riff-raff, that lowest group, that hid from the light and spent their time either loafing around in home-based military garrisons or working in the homeland somewhere because they were "unfit" for duty. This home-army was strengthened by tens of thousands of deserters who were able to turn their backs on the battlefront without risk. (*German soldiers did desert in the thousands near the end of the First World War and many surrendered to escape the war.*) The real coward fears nothing more than death itself. At the front, he faced death day after day in a thousand forms. If you want weak, indecisive, or even cowardly fellows to do their duty, then there is only one possibility. The deserter must realize that his desertion will always result in what he is trying to escape. At the front, you may die. If you desert, you must die. This severe threat is the only way to halt every attempt to abandon the colors, and this was the only way that weak individuals and the masses could be prevented from deserting. This is the true meaning and purpose behind the introduction of the Articles of War which repealed the death penalty.

It is a noble idea that the struggle for a people's existence could be fought by relying solely on the voluntary loyalty born of and preserved by the knowledge that their actions were a necessity. The voluntary willingness to fulfill a duty has always guided the best among men, but never the average man. Therefore, laws like those against theft are necessary. They were not made for the genuinely honest man, but for the weak and unpredictable elements of the population. By their warning to the evildoers, such laws are intended to prevent a situation where the honest man is considered stupid and where the advantage is assumed to be with one who believes it is better to participate in robbery than to stand by empty-handed or even allow oneself to be robbed. It was a mistake to believe a battle could go on for years and that those time-tested methods, which were proven over hundreds of years, could be pushed aside when those methods alone are able to force weak and withdrawn people to do their duty even in most serious times and in moments which are the greatest test of nerves.

The hero who volunteered needed no threats of the death penalty. Those were needed for the selfish coward who values his own life more than his country when his people need him. This kind of spineless weakling can only be protected from becoming a victim of his own cowardice by the harshest penalty. It is only through the ruthless application of the death penalty that an unreliable fellow can be kept at his post when men around him are constantly fighting against death. They often must hold out for weeks in slimy shell craters with the worst possible food. Threats of prison or even hard labor mean nothing to him. He knows from experience that prison is a thousand times safer than the battlefield. In prison, at least, his "priceless" life is not threatened. It was a terrible mistake to eliminate the death penalty during a time of War and to initiate the Articles of War. When they were passed, in 1918, an army of deserters erupted from the troops, filling the military prisons that were safely behind the lines, and many took trains to return home. They helped form that large, criminal organization which suddenly appeared before us after November 7, 1918 as the Revolution.

The soldiers at the front were really not involved at all. All those at the front longed for peace, but in this desire for peace, there was a danger to the Revolution. After the Armistice, the German armies began returning home which forced the worried revolutionaries to ask only one question: "What will the front-line troops do when they return? Will the field-gray tolerate what we have done?"

During those weeks, the Revolution in Germany had to appear moderate, at least on the outside, otherwise it would face the danger of being suddenly destroyed by a few German divisions. If, at that time, a single division commander had decided to pull down the Red rag with his loyal division and to stand the Revolution leaders up against the wall, and he was willing to break down any possible opposition with trench-mortars and hand-grenades, this division would have grown to an army of sixty divisions in less than four weeks. The puppeteer Jews were more afraid of this than of anything else. In order to avoid this, the Revolution had to present an appearance that made them look somewhat moderate. It could not be allowed to degenerate into full Bolshevism. It had to imitate "Peace and Good Order". This is what was responsible for the numerous great concessions and the appeal to the old civil officials and to the old army leaders. They were still needed, for the time being at least. Only after the old officials had served their purpose as Turk's Heads and had done their duty could the revolutionaries risk giving them the kick they deserved and take the Republic out of the hands of the old servants of the State and deliver it to the claws of the revolutionary vultures. (*Turk's Head is a type of decorative knot; here it means the government officials were kept as decoration.*) They hoped to fool old generals and old state officials in this way and disarm any opposition against them before it started with a disguise of innocence and mildness on the new political situation. The facts of how it turned out show how successful this was.

The Revolution had not been created by elements who were driven by peace and order, but elements motivated by riot, theft, and plunder. For these ruffians, the direction the Revolution was developing in did not match their own desires, and it was impossible to explain the tactical reasons in a way that would make these decisions clear and acceptable to the ruffian crowd.

As the power of Social Democratic Party gradually increased, it lost more and more of its character as a brutal revolutionary party. They never had any other goal besides creating a revolution and its leaders had no other aim. But what finally resulted was just the intention for revolution and a group that was no longer capable of actually making it happen. A party of ten million members can no longer carry out a Revolution. When a movement reaches this stage, it is no longer a group from the extreme of the population, but now it contains the broad mass of the middle group, which is nothing more than a burden because they are inactive.

Even during the war, the Jews realized the masses were weighing down the party and that is when the famous split of the Social Democratic Party took place. While the Social Democratic Party, filled with the inactive masses of the population, clung like a dead weight to the national defense forces, the radical activist elements were extracted from the party and were formed into stronger attack troops. This formed the Independent Socialist Party and the Spartacist League which were the storm troops of revolutionary Marxism. (*The Spartacist League was a revolutionary Marxist group named after Spartacus, leader of the slave uprising.*) They had to prepare the ground for the masses of the Social Democratic Party, which had already been in training for decades, so they could take their positions. The cowardly privileged-class was correctly assessed by Marxism and treated like the scum of the earth. The Marxists did not care how the privileged-class was treated because they realized the dog-like submissive obedience of the political structure, which consisted of an old obsolete generation, would never be capable of serious opposition anyway.

After the Revolution succeeded and the main supports of the old State were broken, the soldiers returning from the front suddenly appeared like a menacing sphinx and the brakes had to be applied in stopping the natural development of the Revolution. (*Here, Sphinx means a mysterious person or more specifically that the intentions of the returning troops were unknown.*) The greater part of the Social Democratic Party had taken over their newly-won official positions and the Independent and Spartacist storm battalions were pushed aside. However, this did not happen without a battle.

The angry ruffian masses were not alone because these activist attack troops of the Revolution felt they too had been deceived. They were not satisfied with the results of the Revolution and they wanted to continue the attack on their own. Their uncontrolled brawling was becoming unpleasant even for those who pulled the strings of the Revolution. The collapse had just barely taken place when two camps became clearly defined. One was the party of peace and order and the other was the group of bloody terror. What could be more natural than for our privileged-class to immediately move into the camp of peace and order and fly their banners there? Now, all of a sudden, these disgraceful political organizations act like they might do something. They had already found the ground prepared for them so that they might gain a footing on it. They had reached some level of solidarity with the power which they hated, but they feared this power even more. The political German privileged-class had received the high honor of being able to seat themselves at one table with the three-times-damned Marxist leaders in order to fight the Bolshevists.

In December, 1918, and January, 1919, the following situation arose:

The Revolution was carried out by a minority of the worst elements, which all the Marxist parties immediately supported. The Revolution then stamped itself so that it appeared as moderate, which aroused the hostility of the fanatic extremists. The extremists began to throw around hand grenades and to fire off machine guns, occupying public buildings, and generally threatening the moderate Revolution.

In order to put these developments in check, a truce was declared between the supporters of the new government and the supporters of the old regime so that they could fight against the extremists together. This resulted in the enemies of the Republic setting aside their battle with the Republic so that they could join forces and subdue those who were also enemies of the Republic, but were enemies for different reasons. This also resulted in avoiding the danger of a battle between the defenders of the old State and those of the new state. This fact cannot be emphasized too much. Nine-tenths of the population did not carry out a revolution, seven-tenths of them rejected it, and six-tenths hated it. Only he who understands this chain of events realizes how it is possible for one-tenth of the people to force a revolution.

Gradually the Spartacist barricade-fighters began to bleed out one side, while the nationalist patriots and idealists began to bleed out the other side as they fought each other. These two extremes soon wore each other down until the mass of the middle group came out victorious. The privileged-class and Marxism found themselves on the ground of common accomplishment and the Republic began to consolidate. This did not prevent the privileged-class parties, especially before elections, from quoting monarchist ideas for some time afterwards. They wanted to be able to conjure up the spirits of the past and, at the same time, renew the smaller spirits of their disciples so they could continue to keep their followers in their net.

This was not very honest. Secretly, in their hearts, all of them had broken away from the Monarchy a long time ago and the filth of the new state also began to make its seductive effects felt in the camp of the privileged-class party. The ordinary privileged-class politician feels more at home today in the mire of Republic corruption than in the clean and decent condition he dimly remembers from the past regime.

As I already mentioned, after the destruction of the old army, the Revolution was forced to create a new agent of power to strengthen its state authority. This agent was only available from the followers of a World-Concept opposed to its own. Only from them could a new army slowly arise, which limited in number by the Peace Treaties had to eventually be transformed into a tool that followed the ideas of the new state.

If we ask ourselves how the Revolution could happen, and we disregard the mistakes of the old State which caused it and focus on how the people could actually allow it, we come to this conclusion:

1. It resulted from our ideas of duty and obedience being paralyzed and
2. It resulted from the passive cowards in those parties who claimed they supported the state.

To this we can add that our ideas of duty and obedience were paralyzed because of our entirely non-national education system which always served the interests of the State and not the nation of people. The result is that no one understands the difference between a means and an end. Being aware of one's duty, the performance of one's duty, and showing obedience are no more ends in themselves than the state is an end in itself. Instead, they should be the means to maintain and protect on this earth a community of spiritually and physically similar beings. When we see the structure of a state collapse and it appears to fall into deep oppression—thanks to the action of a few scoundrels—obedience and performance of one's duty to assist these scoundrels is not a matter of following formal procedures as if everything was normal, it is pure foolish lack of reason to blindly follow some sense of duty in these circumstances. On the other hand, refusing obedience and "performance of one's duty" to them would save an entire nation. According to our present privileged-class concept of state, if a military commander receives the order from higher-up state officials telling him to stop shooting even though he is fighting in a war to protect his people, he believes he is justified when he orders his men to stop shooting. To the privileged-class world, thoughtless formal obedience is worth more than the life of his own people. According to our National-Socialist concept, obedience to the community should come first at such times and not blind obedience to weak superiors. The duty of personal responsibility to a whole nation should come out during these times. The true meaning of these ideas among our people or in our government has been lost in favor of a purely inflexible and formal interpretation—a blind obedient following—and that is why the Revolution was successful!

To the second point I should add that the biggest reason the state-supporting nationalist parties became cowards is because their activist members as well as the best of their group were lost on the field of battle. Apart from this, our privileged-class parties, which were the only political structures standing on the ground of the old State, were convinced that they could represent their views using solely intellectual means and with intellectual weapons, since only the State had the right to use physical force. Not only do we see a gradually developing decadent weakness in such an idea, but the idea itself was absurd at a time when their one political opponent gave up this point of view and openly emphasized that he would pursue his political ends through force. The moment the privileged-class made it clear they had abandoned force and chosen to use intellectual weapons exclusively is when Marxism appeared. Their slogan to fight with intellectual weapons was nonsense and they would have to pay dearly for it someday. Marxism always held the point of view that weapons were to be used if they were expedient and success justified the use of arms. The accuracy of this point of view was demonstrated in the days from the November 7 to 11, 1918. At that time, Marxism did not care at all for parliament or democracy and killed them both through howling and gun firing criminal gangs. The privileged-class chatterboxes were defenseless in this moment.

After the Revolution, the privileged-class parties suddenly appeared again under another name and their brave leaders crept out of their safe dark cellars and drafty attics. However, none of the representatives from the old parties remembered the reasons for their old mistakes and they certainly had not learned anything new. Their political program was just like the old one because they had made no adjustments or changes other than to work with the new state. Their true aim, however, was to participate in the new government and their only weapon was the same as before, just words. After the Revolution, the privileged-class parties constantly collaborated in the most pitiful manner with those who marched in the streets.

When the Law For The Protection Of The Republic came up for a vote, there was no majority to support it. But the privileged-class "statesmen" were so terror-stricken from the two hundred thousand Marxists and their angry demonstration in the streets, that they passed the law even though it was against their convictions. They were afraid they would be beaten to a pulp while leaving the Reichstag if they did not. Unfortunately, because of the passage of the law, this did not occur and they walked away un-accosted. So, the development of the new State ran its course as if there was no nationalistic opposition at all.

The only organizations at this time that would have had the courage and strength to combat Marxism and its stirred-up masses were at first the Free Corps volunteers. Later, the Organization for Self-Defense, Citizens' Corps, and finally, the Traditional Leagues joined in. (*These organizations were militant groups of mostly ex-soldiers.*)

The existence of these counter revolution organizations failed to change the course of German history because the nationalistic parties were unable to exert any influence over them due to the nationalistic parties lacking any form of threatening authority in the streets. The so-called defense units were unable to exert any political influence because they had no political thoughts of any sort and they especially lacked any real political goal.

What made Marxism successful was the skilled combination of political will and activist brutality. What excluded the nationalists from any form of German development was their lack of close cooperation between brutal force and ingenious political desire. Whatever desire the "nationalist" parties may have had, they had no strength to enforce this desire in the streets. The militant defense units had all the strength and they were the lords of the street and the State, but they had no political plan and no political goal that their power might be used to achieve for nationalist Germany. In both cases, it was the clever talk and strength of the Jew which took advantage of the existing situation and worked to maintain it, further deepening this unhappy Fate.

It was the Jew who, very cleverly, used his press to launch the idea that the militant defense units should have a "non-political character". He also cunningly praised political fights of intellectualism and even demanded that such struggles be of an "inner nature". Millions of German blockheads now repeated this nonsense without the faintest realization that they were actually disarming themselves and were surrendering completely to the Jew. There is a natural reason which explains why they did this: the lack of a great reforming concept. When a group has no great concept, the fighting strength of that group is also limited. The willingness of the political right to use the most brutal weapons depends on the existence of a fanatic faith, which gives them a conviction that makes such weapons necessary to achieve victory for a new revolutionary order of things on this earth. A movement that is not fighting for the highest aims and greatest ideals will never reach for the ultimate weapon.

The creation of a new great idea was the secret behind the success of the French Revolution. The Russian Revolution owes its victory to an extraordinary idea. The idea behind Fascism gave it the strength to subject an entire nation, very successfully, to a most positive and comprehensive resurgence. (*The Fascism reference is a glowing compliment to Mussolini in Italy even though he is not mentioned by name.*) Privileged-class parties are not capable of this kind of achievement.

Not only did the privileged-class parties hope to restore the past, but so did the militant defense units, at least in as much as they concerned themselves with political aims. The militant defense units contained the spirit of the old soldiers and those who had faith in Kyffauser, so they all looked towards the past fondly. (*Kyffauser was an old veterans' organization. Kyffauser is also a mountain range in Germany; there is a legend that Emperor Barbarossa sleeps in the mountain and will reawaken at a time of Germany's greatest need. This reference is a snub against those followers of the veterans' group.*) This politically blunted the sharpest weapons possessed by the German nation and allowed them to decay in the hands of the new Republic. They were acting with the best intentions and in good faith, but that does not excuse the foolishness in their actions.

Gradually, Marxism received the necessary power it needed to support its authority through force which was available from the now consolidated Reichswehr. (*Reichswehr was the German National Defense Force formed as a result of the Treaty of Versailles which limited the size and strength of the military.*) It began systematically and logically to eliminate any militant defense units. They could be eliminated now because they were no longer necessary for the Marxist plans and they might become dangerous later. Individual and particularly bold leaders who ignored the order to disband were forced to appear in court and placed behind bars. They received what they deserved because they were to blame for their own Fate.

When we first founded the NSDAP, we created a movement whose aim was not the mechanical restoration of the past—like the aim of the privileged-class parties—but whose aim was to replace today's ridiculous mechanical state with a living state for the people. Our young movement knew, from the very beginning, that their idea must be represented intellectually, but the idea must also be protected and the final accomplishment of this goal must be assured, if necessary, even by physical force. The conviction to this new doctrine carries such a tremendous significance that no sacrifice is too great if it means we can accomplish the goal.

I have already discussed the motives behind movement that intends to win the hearts of the people and why it is necessary to defend itself using its own ranks against the terror attacks of its opponents. Likewise, it has been long shown by history that a terror which is represented by a World-Concept can never be broken by a formal state authority, but such a terror can only be crushed by a new and different World-Concept that is championed by those who are equally bold and determined. This fact will always be unpleasant to the official guardians of the state; however, that does not change the truth of the matter. State authority can guarantee peace and order only when the State's World-Concept and the World-Concept of the people agree. Violent elements promoting a World-Concept , one that differs from the people's, will look like individual criminal groups and will not be seen as champions of a great idea which is opposed to the views of the state. If this were not the case, and the opposition held a World-Concept that matched the people's World-Concept , the State can apply the most violent measures for centuries against the terror threatening it, but, in the end, the state will submit because it is unable to defeat the opposing idea.

The German State is completely infested by Marxism. The State, in its seventy-year struggle, has been unable to prevent the victory of this World-Concept . On the contrary, in spite of jail sentences, which all totaled together are in the thousands of years, and the bloodiest measures which were inflicted on the defenders of the Marxist World-Concept , the State has been forced to almost completely surrender to them. The average privileged-class state leader will try to deny this, but, of course, he is unable to convince anyone.

On November 9, 1918, the State unconditionally surrendered to Marxism so it will not suddenly rise up tomorrow and become its conqueror. On the contrary, the privileged-class simpletons who occupy Ministers' seats already haphazardly discuss how important it is to avoid making any rulings that would be against the workers. Of course, when they say the word "worker" they mean Marxists. By identifying the German worker with Marxism, they are committing perjury in a cowardly and misleading manner, and they also want to hide how they crumbled in the face of the Marxist idea and organization. In view of the fact the privileged-class completely surrendered to the present-day State of Marxism, the real duty falls to our National-Socialist movement in preparing for the victory of our idea and taking up its defense against the terror of International Marxism itself, which is still drunk with victory.

I have already described how our young movement developed a group to protect our meetings out of necessity and how this group gradually assumed the character of a definite military-style troop with its own organization and structure. Although the structure may externally resemble one of the militant defense groups, there was actually no similarity with those groups.

As I have already mentioned, the German defense organizations had no definite political plan of their own. They were actually only units for self-protection. They were more or less suitably trained and organized for that task alone. They really represented an illegal complement to the existing legal military instruments of state power. Their similarity to state military volunteer corps was only due to the nature of their formation and to the unfortunate condition of the State at that time. You could not say they were free units who were formed freely and privately so they might fight for their own individual idea; that is simply not accurate. They had no such idea or conviction in spite of the fact that individual leaders and whole groups were opposed to the Republic. If we are to talk about a conviction in the higher sense of a true belief on the level of faith, that requires more than recognizing that the current system is flawed. The root of a conviction lays solely in the knowledge of a new order, which one can see in the mind's eye and when one knows it must be achieved under any circumstances, and it is our most important task in life to make this idea a reality.

What fundamentally distinguished the storm troops of the National-Socialist movement at that time from all militant defense groups was that our troops were not and did not want to be a servant of the existing state, but instead wanted to fight exclusively for a new Germany.

At first, this troop simply provided security at meetings. Its first task was to make it possible to hold meetings, which otherwise would definitely have been prevented by the opposition. At that time, this troop was trained to attack blindly. However, it did not regard the rubber billy-club as the highest ideal as some stupid German nationalists claimed, but these men understood that the highest ideal can be exterminated if its leader is knocked low by a rubber billy-club. As history has frequently shown, the most important thinkers have died as the result of a blow by the most insignificant slave. Our troops did not consider violence as a goal but wanted to protect the messengers of a spiritual plan from being oppressed by violence. The troop also understood that it was not duty-bound to assume the protection of a State which failed to protect the nation from those threatening to destroy both people and State.

After the massacre at the meeting in the Munich Hofbräuhaus, our small security troop received the permanent name of Storm Detachment in memory of the heroic acts against the attackers. It is obvious from the name itself that this group represents only one part, a detachment, of the movement. Just as propaganda, the press, the scientific institutions, and other aspects are merely single parts of the larger Party.

We could see how important the Storm Troop was not only at this memorable meeting, but also when we ventured to spread the movement from Munich throughout the rest of Germany. As soon as we began to appear dangerous to Marxism, it left no stone unturned in an effort to thwart our National-Socialist meetings or, if that failed, to forcibly break them up. Of course, the Marxist Party organizations of all kinds completely hid anything to do with such attacks from the government's representative bodies. The privileged-class parties, the same ones that were thrashed down by Marxism and did not dare let their speakers appear at certain public places, and in spite of that, those parties show a remarkably stupid satisfaction, which is quite incomprehensible, anytime they hear that our battles against Marxism took a path that was not in our favor. They were happy that Marxism, which could not be conquered by them and was overcoming them, was not being defeated by us either. There were state officials, police-chiefs, yes, even senators, who, indecently and unscrupulously, chose to pass themselves off to the public as "nationalist"; however, in all disagreements which we had with Marxists, they gave the Reds the most reprehensible and underhanded assistance. These people were so disgraceful that, in exchange for the miserable praise of Jewish newspapers, they did not hesitate to persecute the very men whose heroic intervention they should have thanked in part for their own lives; it was these men who prevented their mutilated corpses from being hanged from light-posts by the Red jackals only a few years ago.

These fake-nationalists were such terrible creatures that, on one occasion, they drove our unforgettable late Chief Pöhner to bluntly express his opinion. (*Pöhner is Ernst Pöhner, the Bavarian Chief Of Police who was already mentioned in Volume 1; he died in a car accident in 1925 after his release from serving three months of a five-year sentence for his part in the 1923 Putsch.*)

Chief Pöhner was critical in his straightforward manner and hated all such swindlers, as an honorable man should. He said, "In my whole life, I never wanted to be anything except a German first, and then a public official second, and I never want to be confused with those creatures, who are official whores, they prostitute themselves to whoever their current master may be".

It was especially sad that such people gradually gained power over tens of thousands of the most honorable and upright servants of the State and slowly infected those officials with these creature's own lack of character. They persecuted the honest officials with bitter hatred and finally gnawed them out of office while these lying hypocrites represented themselves as "nationalists".

We can never hope to receive any kind of broad support from such men and what support we have received was only on very rare occasions. Only through the creation of our own protection could our movement protect our activities and at the same time attract public attention and achieve a common respect, the kind of respect that is only received by one who can defend himself when he is attacked.

In the development of this Storm Troop, the guiding idea was to train it to be an incorruptible force that was a zealous representative of the National-Socialist idea, to provide physical training, and finally, to strengthen its discipline to the highest degree. It would not be anything like the militant defense organizations of the privileged-class or any kind of secret organization.

The following explains why I intensely struggled against setting up the S. A. Storm

Troop of the NSDAP like one of the militant defense units: From a purely practical point of view, the defense of a people cannot be carried out by private units unless they have a great deal of support and assistance from the State. Anyone who believes they can do so has an exaggerated opinion of their own ability. It is impossible to develop a military-style organization beyond a certain point when you rely on so-called "voluntary discipline". Authority requires an important support so that it can give orders, which is the ability to punish, and without that ability, authority is gone. In the fall, and more so in the spring of 1919, it was possible to organize "volunteer corps". For a time, this group obeyed like soldiers because they were soldiers who had fought at the front and they completed the school of the old army. That kind of common experience imposed a sense of duty on each individual, at least for a little while.

This sense of duty and discipline is entirely lacking in the volunteer militant defense organizations of today. The larger the organization becomes, the more discipline weakens and the less that can be demanded from individual members and the more the whole thing will assume the character of the non-political associations of soldiers and veterans. Voluntary training for an army without assured, unconditional authority to give orders will never be possible for larger organizations. Only a few individuals will voluntarily give the kind of obedience that is necessary for an army to function.

Inadequate facilities and supplies create a serious obstacle in the training of defense units. The very best, most reliable training must be of prime importance to such an institution. Eight years have passed since the War and, in that time, not a single class of our youth has been trained. A defense unit certainly cannot expect to rely on existing generations who have already been trained. Using this method, we can calculate with mathematical certainty when the last trained member will retire. Even the youngest soldier of 1918 will be too old to fight after twenty years, and that time is quickly approaching. As time passes, every defense unit becomes more and more like the old veterans associations. An institution that does not call itself an association of ex-soldiers can never rely on this source for members. A defense unit, simply through its very name, strives to not only maintain the tradition and solidarity among former soldiers, but also to develop the defense idea and make it a reality by creating a unit that is capable of defense.

Forming such a force demands unconditional training of recruits who previously had no military drill instruction and in practice. This is actually impossible for a small defense force. One cannot create a soldier with one or two hours of training a week. Today, the requirements to turn an individual into a man suited for military service have been enormously increased, and a two-year service period is only sufficient to transform the untrained young man into an educated soldier. We have all seen the terrible consequences on the battlefield when young soldiers are not thoroughly trained in military techniques. Units of volunteers who, with iron determination and infinite devotion, had been drilled for fifteen or twenty weeks at the front only became cannon fodder. Only when the younger recruits are distributed into the ranks of experienced old soldiers and trained from four to six months can they serve as useful members of a regiment. In this way, they were guided by the "old ones" and then gradually grew into their task.

It is discouraging when we compare this with the attempt to raise troops using a one to two hour so-called training session each week where there is no clear power of command, and where there are limited training means! Such training may work to freshen up old soldiers, but it can never turn young men into soldiers. Such a procedure is inferior and completely worthless which is shown clearly when a so-called volunteer militant defense unit, facing difficulty and despair in the process, tries to train a few thousand well-meaning men in the idea of defense, while those who are not so harmonious simply remain untrained. While they try to train these men, the State itself consistently robs millions of other young people of their natural instincts. They do this through pacifist-democratic education that poisons their logical patriotic thought and gradually transforms them into a herd of sheep, tolerant of every tyranny and willing to follow any arbitrary command. How ridiculous in comparison are all the efforts of the defense units to teach German youth when the State teaches the opposite.

Almost more important is the point of view which made me oppose every attempt to use what we call military training for a volunteer unit. Assuming an organization succeeded in training a number of Germans to be men capable of defense in spite of the previously mentioned difficulties, year after year, including proper instruction in their attitude, physical proficiency, and arms training, even then the result would have to be absolute zero in the current State. Based on the way the State acts, it does not want any such defensive abilities at all. They even hate the idea of defense since it completely opposes the innermost aim of its leaders who are actively destroying the State.

In any case, such training would be worthless under regimes whose actions have proven they care nothing about the military power of the nation, and who would never be willing to ask this power for assistance, except of course in the extreme case where they need military force to protect their own cancerous existence. Today, that is how things are. It is ridiculous for an organization to even attempt to train some ten thousand men in the State's twilight of decline when, only a few years before, the State disgracefully abandoned eight and a half million men.

It was not that they simply no longer needed the services of these men, but, as a reward for their sacrifices, these soldiers were subjected to general insults. Do these organizations intend to train soldiers to serve as a regiment of a State which disgraced and spat on those who were once the most honorable soldiers. They ripped their badges of honor from their chests, trampled their banners, and degraded their actions in battle.

Has this present State ever tried to reestablish the honor of the old army, have they tried to hold those responsible for their destruction accountable, and have they brought forward those who freely slandered our troops? Not in the least! On the contrary, we can see these destroyers and slanderers enthroned in the highest state offices. As it was said at Leipzig, "Right goes with might". (This is a *reference to the Battle of Leipzig 1813, Napoleon was defeated and forced out of Germany by greatly superior numbers of troops.*) Today the power in our Republic lies in the hands of the same men who once plotted the Revolution, so there is no reason to increase their power by training a new young army. This Revolution is the most dishonorable type of treason and it represents the most wretched disgrace in all of German history. It is against all reason for them to have any might.

After the Revolution of 1918, any value this State attributed to the military was only related to how that strength could reinforce its position, and this is clearly and unmistakably demonstrated by its attitude towards the large militant defense organizations. They were not unwelcome, as long as they contributed to the personal defense of those cowardly creatures of the revolution. However, as our people gradually fell farther into ruin, the danger for these creatures declined as well. The existence of the defense units was no longer necessary to supplement national political strength; therefore, everything was done to disarm them or even break them up.

History reveals that princes show gratitude only in rare instances. But the new privileged-class patriot could never, not even once, count on the gratitude of revolutionary troublemakers, exploiters of the people, and national traitors. Whenever it was suggested that militant defense forces should be created, I could never resist posing these questions: Who am I training these young people for, for what purpose are they to be used, and when are they to be called upon? The answer provides the best rule for us to follow.

If the present day State did call upon trained militant defense reserves, it would never be to defend our interests in a foreign land. It would always be for the tyrants within the nation who need protection from the general rage of the deceived, betrayed, and sold-out people, which may someday explode. This is why the S. A.

Storm Troop of the NSDAP was not assembled as a military organization. It was a means of education and protection for the National-Socialist movement and its job lay in an area entirely different from that of the so-called militant defense units.

The S. A. Storm Troop was not intended to be a secret organization. The purpose of secret organizations can only be illegal activity, which also limits the size of these organizations. It is not possible, especially considering how loose the lips of the German people are, to build up a large organization and keep it a secret, and it is even more difficult to conceal its aims at the same time. Any attempt to form such an organization will be hindered in a thousand ways. A staff of pimps and similar rabble is at the service of our police officials who will, for the Judas fee of thirty pieces of silver, betray anything they can find and invent anything they cannot find to betray. Even the members of the organization will be unable to observe a rule of silence. Only very small groups can become a true secret organization and then only through years of sorting through members. The small size of such structures would make them useless for the National-Socialist movement. What we needed and do need is not a hundred or two hundred bold conspirators, but hundreds and hundreds of thousands of fanatical fighters for our World-Concept . This work cannot be done in secret shady gatherings, but in mighty mass public processions. The path we walk cannot be blazed by the dagger and poison or pistol, but through the capture of the streets. We have to show Marxism that the future lord of the streets is National Socialism, just as it will someday be the lord of the State.

There is also a danger with secret organizations that the members will frequently misunderstand the magnitude of the task. They believe that through a single murder, the Fate of the nation could be turned around in their favor. Such an opinion does have its historical justification, such as when a nation suffers under the tyranny of some sort of brilliant oppressor, one who has a towering personality, which guarantees the internal strength of his position and enables him to continue his oppression. In such a case, a man ready for the ultimate sacrifice may suddenly spring forth from the crowd to plunge the dagger of death into the heart of the hated individual. Only some petty scoundrel who thinks along the lines of the republic and is filled with self-conscious guilt will see such a deed as repulsive. It was the greatest poet of freedom among our people who took it upon himself to glorify such an action in his "Tell". (*A reference to William Tell who, supposedly in 1307, was forced to shoot an apple off his son's head with a crossbow by the territorial ruler; he assassinated the territorial ruler later. Tell was a popular figure in Germany; however, the story's origin is unclear and it is unknown who Hitler thought was the original poet, but he was likely referring to Hans Schriber who published a collection of stories.*)

442

In 1919 and 1920, there was a danger that some member of one of these secret organizations might seek vengeance against the plunderers of his home, spurred on by the great examples of history and horrified by the unending misfortune of his Fatherland, in the belief that, by his deed, he was setting in motion an end to the misery of his people. Every such attempt was sheer folly. Marxism did not win because of the superior talent and personal importance of any one individual, but because of the sorry and cowardly neglect of the privileged-class world. The most horrible criticism that can be hurled against our privileged-class is that the Revolution did not bring forth a single brain of any distinction, yet, the privileged-class still gave in and submitted themselves to it. It is understandable how one would surrender to a Robespierre, a Danton, or a Marat, but to grovel before a scrawny Scheidemann, a fat Mr. Erzberger and a Friedrich Ebert and all the countless other political dwarves—that thought is overwhelming.

(Mattias Erzberger was one of the officials who accepted the Treaty in 1919 and he was assassinated in 1921 by two soldiers from a militant organization.)
(Maximilien Robespierre, Georges Danton, and Jean-Paul Marat were the three most important figures in the French Revolution of 1789. Marat was also stabbed by a six inch dagger, and this may be the source for Hitler's other stabbing reference. Philipp Scheidemann was the second Chancellor of the Weimar Republic, Matthias Erzberger was a prominent member of the Center Party, and Friedrich Ebert was the first president in the Weimar Republic.)

There was not a single intelligent person present that one could have called the talented man of the Revolution and placed in him the misfortune of the Fatherland. They were nothing more than revolutionary bugs, knapsack Spartacists, one and all. *(A reference to the previous insult about knapsacks, meaning here the Spartacist party or more generally Socialists who were plunderers.)* To squash one of them was absolutely pointless and, at best, the only consequence was that some other bug, just as fat and just as bloodthirsty stepped into the open position more quickly.

In the early years we had to sharply curtail this idea, which was born from and inspired by the truly great happenings of history because it was not suited in the least to our current age where we had so many little politicians running around.

The same argument can be applied when we consider the question of disposing with those who might be called traitors. It is ridiculous and illogical to kill a fellow who has betrayed the location of an artillery storage facility to the enemy while, nearby in the highest positions of authority, sit zeros who sold out a whole country. *(This reference regards executing informers in Germany who revealed arms cache locations to the Allies after the First World War; this is not a reference to betrayal during wartime.*) These zeros have the sacrifices of two million dead on their conscience and are responsible for millions of cripples. Yet, at the same time, they remain spiritually calm and carry on their business of running the republic as usual. To dispose of little traitors is senseless in a State whose government itself frees greater traitors from every punishment. So, someday it will happen that an honorable idealist, who feels he is acting on behalf of his people, does away with a rogue military traitor, then he is held accountable for his actions by bigger national traitors of the first magnitude. There is certainly an important question here: Is one to allow a treacherous little creature to be disposed of by a similar creature or by an idealist? In one case, the larger success, the disposing of villainy, is doubtful and more treachery is sure to follow. In the other case, one little scoundrel is disposed of and, in the process, the life of the idealist who did the act is now put at risk through law or retaliation and if the idealist is lost, he may not be easily replaced.

My position is that one should not hang little thieves while letting the big ones run free. Someday, a German national court of law will have to condemn and execute ten thousand or so of those organizers and criminals who were responsible for the November treason and all the consequences that followed. This would set an example and be a lesson for the petty traitors who revealed arms locations once and for all.

Because of these considerations, I forbade any participation in secret organizations and repeatedly emphasized the need to guard the S. A. Storm Troop itself from giving even the appearance of such an organization. In those years, I kept the National Socialist movement far away from any experiments where those who carried out these plans were mostly made up of gloriously idealistic-minded young Germans. They would become the victims of their own deeds and their sacrifice would not improve the fate of their Fatherland at all.

If the S.A. could not be a militant defense organization or a secret society, then these conclusions result:

1. Its training must not be military style, but must focus on the aims of the Party. In promoting physical health of the members, the chief emphasis was not to be on military drills, but more on sports. Boxing and Ju-Jitsu have always seemed to me more important than any sort of rifle training, which is much less vigorous. If the German nation is given six million athletically-trained bodies, all of which are excited with a fanatical love for their country and all of them trained to the highest pitch of aggressive spirit, then a national state will have the ability to create an army in less than two years time if necessary. At least it would be possible

if a basic army was already at hand which they could be integrated into. But, the situation today means that this basic army stock can only be supplied by the Reichswehr (*National Defense military resulting from the Treaty of Versailles*) and not from a militant defense league which is mired in its own inadequacy. The physical conditioning will make the individual conscious of his own superiority and give him the confidence that is always found through the awareness of one's own power. Also, this training will give him the athletic skills which will serve as a weapon for defense of the movement.

2. The S.A. uniform is recognizable to everyone. However, in order to prevent any confusion of the S.A. with a secret organization, from the very beginning we used the great number of its members to make it clear how it was used by the movement and we maintained that it must be well known to the public. It must not meet in secret, but must march in the open air. This would absolutely destroy all legends about a "secret organization". We had to extinguish any desire the members may have to participate in small conspiracies; it must, from the beginning, be completely indoctrinated with the great idea of the movement and be completely devoted to the task of representing this idea. It must be so completely trained that from its inception, the horizon of every member would be expanded and the individual would see his mission not in the disposal of some smaller or greater rogue, but in his participation in building a new National-Socialist State of the people. In this way, the struggle against the present State was elevated far above the actions of petty revenge and conspiracy to the magnitude of a philosophical war of annihilation against Marxism and its structures.

3. The formation of the S.A., including the choices for its uniform and equipment, was not modeled after the old army, but decided by its own purpose—they were chosen to meet the needs of the task at hand.

These views guided me in 1920 to 1921 as I gradually instilled them into the young organization. By mid-summer of 1922, we enjoyed the success of having an impressive number of groups consisting of one hundred men each. Then, in the late autumn of 1922, one after the other of these groups received their special distinguishing uniform.

There were three events that were supremely important for the further development of the S. A.:

1. The first was the great general demonstration against the Law for the Protection of the Republic, which was held by all patriotic associations in the late summer of 1922 on the Konigsplatz (*King's Place, an open square*) in Munich. The patriotic

associations of Munich at that time issued a proclamation calling for a protest against the introduction of the law through a gigantic demonstration in Munich. Even the National-Socialist movement was going to take part in it. The closed ranks of the Party marched in six groups of one hundred each, which were followed by the political sections of the party. In the parade itself, two bands marched and fifteen flags were carried along. When the National Socialists assembled, the great square was already half full but there were no flags for any other group. Our arrival caused the release of an enormous amount of passion. I myself had the honor of speaking as one of the orators before the crowd of about sixty thousand.

The success of the demonstration was overwhelming largely because it showed for the first time that our Munich branch could march on the street in spite of all the Red threats. The Red republican defense schemers, who tried to terrorize the marching columns, were scattered with bloody heads in only a few minutes by the S.A. Storm Troop. The National-Socialist movement had demonstrated for the first time its determination to claim the right to march on the streets and to wrestle this monopoly from the hands of the international traitors and enemies of the Fatherland. The result of this day was indisputable proof that our psychological and organizational ideas about the structure of the S.A. were correct. It was now enthusiastically expanded based on this successful principle and in only a few weeks, the number of Munich groups of one hundred was doubled.

2. The March to Coburg in October 1922. (*Coburg is a city in Bavaria, which only voted to join Bavaria in 1920 and was previously ruled by a duke in the fief of Saxe-Coburg and Gotha. It lost its ruler as a result of the Revolution.*) A number of "racialist" associations intended to hold a "German Day" welcoming Coburg. I received an invitation with a note that they wanted me to bring along some supporters from my party. I received this request about eleven o'clock in the morning and it came at a very opportune time. The arrangements had been made within an hour. For my supporters, I designated eight hundred men of the S.A., who were to be transported in fourteen groups by a special train from Munich to the village that had only recently joined Bavaria. Similar orders were sent to the National-Socialist S.A. groups that had been formed in other cities along the route. It was the first time that a train of this sort traveled in Germany. At each place where new S. A. men boarded, the transport attracted great attention. Many had never seen our flags before and they were very impressed.

When we assembled at the station in Coburg, a representative of the festival committee for "German Day" received us and gave us a signed order which said it was an "agreement" by the local organizations, which meant the Independent Party and the Communist Party. The agreement said that we would not be allowed to enter the city with our flags waving, we would not be allowed to play music—we had brought our own band of forty-two men—and we could not march through the streets in a group or closed ranks. I immediately dismissed these disgraceful conditions and did not hesitate to express to those gentlemen of the festival committee who were present how astonished I was that these kinds of arrangements had been made and that it was disgraceful they had come to any agreement with these people. I explained that the S.A. would immediately march in company formation through the city and it would be to the sound of music with our flags waving. And that is what happened.

There were already thousands of howling, hooting people to receive us at the depot. "Murderers", "Bandits", "Robbers", "Criminals", were some of the pet names that these outstanding founders of the German Republic graciously showered on us. The young S. A. maintained themselves in perfect order. The squads of one hundred assembled on the square in front of the railway station and, at first, ignored the abuse. We were unfamiliar with the city streets, so the marching procession was directed by a nervous police escort into the Hofbräuhaus Cellar near the center of the town instead of to our quarters on the outskirts of Coburg like we had previously arranged. On both sides of our troop procession, the noise of the masses constantly increased. The last squad had barely turned into the courtyard of the beer garden when large crowds, making deafening shrieks, attempted to rush after them. To avoid a confrontation, the police closed the gates. We could not tolerate this situation, sealed in with everyone hollering, so I told the S. A. to re-assemble. I admonished them briefly for breaking ranks and demanded that the police open the gates immediately. After a rather long hesitation, they complied.

We marched back the way we came to reach our quarters and there we finally had to face the mob. After they were unable to disturb the squads using shouts and insults, the representatives of the true socialism, equality, and brotherhood started throwing stones. Our patience was at an end. For ten minutes we attacked furiously on both sides. Fifteen minutes later, nothing Red was to be seen on the streets any more.

At night, there were more serious attacks. Patrols of the S.A. had found members of the National-Socialist Party who had been attacked and mutilated when they were alone. After that, we quickly took care of our opponents. By the following morning, the Red Terror Coburg had suffered under for years had been smashed.

With typical Marxist-Jewish style, they passed out falsehood-filled flyers and tried again to rally the members of the International laborers into the streets by distorting the facts, saying that our bands of murderers had begun a war to exterminate the

447

peaceful workers in Coburg. At one-thirty, the great "demonstration of the people" was to take place and, according to the flyers, it was hoped that tens of thousands of workers from the area would be present. I was determined to put an end to this Red Terror once and for all so I had the S.A. assemble at twelve o'clock. The S.A. now numbered nearly fifteen hundred. I marched with them to the Coburg fortress across the large square where the Red demonstration was to take place. I wanted to see if they would be so foolish and attempt to assault us again. As we entered the square, there were only a few hundred present instead of the announced ten thousand. As we approached, they remained quiet, although some ran away. There were a few Red troops present who came from outside of the city and, as yet, did not know what to expect from us. Occasionally, they tried to renew hostilities, but any desire to do so was quickly taken away from them. As we watched during the speeches, we could see that the population, which was previously so intimidated, slowly awoke, took courage, and ventured out this time to greet us with shouts. When we left in the evening and marched back through the streets, they broke out in spontaneous loud rejoicing at various places along our route.

When we arrived at the train station, we were suddenly told that the workers refused to run the train for us. At that, I informed a few leaders of the mob that if this was the case, I would seize any Red big shots I could find and that my men would operate the train ourselves. I would also take along a few dozen brothers of international solidarity in the locomotive, the supply car, and in each passenger car. I made it very clear to the gentlemen that a trip managed by our own forces would naturally be a very risky journey and that it was quite possible that we would all break our necks. I let them know it would be a pleasure to enter eternity accompanied by the Red gentlemen who advocated equality and fraternity so highly. After that dissertation, the train left very punctually and we arrived in Munich, safe and sound, the next morning.

For the first time since 1914, the equality of citizens before the law was restored in Coburg. Today, some "ninny" of a higher official may claim that the State protects the lives of its citizens, but it was not true at that time. The citizens had to defend themselves against the representatives of the Republic State.

It was impossible, at first, to see the full significance of this day. Since the S.A. was victorious, they were more self-confident and had more faith in their leader's judgment. Also, the people began to take a greater interest in us and many recognized for the first time that the National-Socialist movement was an institution that probably would one day be used to put the appropriate finishing touches on this Marxist madness. Only the democratic party groaned, complaining because we had not peacefully allowed our skulls to be crushed, but that we instead dared, in a democratic Republic, to strike back against a brutal attack with fists and sticks instead of with pacifist songs.

The privileged-class press was half pathetic and half vulgar. Only a few decent papers welcomed our defeat of the Marxist pirates in at least one city. In Coburg itself, part of the Marxist workers who were simply misled previously in their ideals, had been taught by the fists of National-Socialists that we were also fighting for ideals. Experience proves that a person only fights for something they believe in and love. Without a doubt, the S.A. benefited the most from the events at Coburg. It grew rapidly. On the first Party Day, January 27, 1923, nearly six thousand men took part in the dedication of the flag. For the first time, the companies were dressed in their new uniforms. The experiences in Coburg demonstrated how essential it was to have a unique uniform for the S. A. This not only strengthens the morale, but it also helps our men to identify each other in a dispute which means they can avoid mistakes when it comes to recognizing comrades. Up to this point, the men simply wore armbands, but now, a uniform-coat and the well-known cap were added.

The experiences in Coburg were also significant because it made us determined to systematically break the Red Terror that prevented meetings of opponents in many places for years, and to ultimately restore the freedom to hold public meetings. From then on, the National-Socialist battalions assembled in Red strongholds and gradually, throughout Bavaria, one Red citadel after another fell victim to the Nazi propaganda. The S.A. began to understand its task better and better and it moved farther and farther from the character of an aimless and lifeless defense group. They had risen, transforming themselves into a living organization that was fighting for the establishment of a new German State. This path of development lasted until March 1923. Then, an event happened which forced me to alter the course of the movement and to institute some changes.

3. The occupation in the Ruhr during the first months of 1923 by the French was greatly significant in the development of the S.A. (*The French moved into the Ruhr when the Weimar Republic failed to pay reparations after the First World War. The area included vital coal, iron, and steel production centers.*)

Even today, it is not possible or in the interests of the nation to not talk or write about it publicly. I can only speak of what has been touched on in public discussions already. The occupation of the Ruhr did not come as a complete surprise to any of us. It did, however, give rise to the justified hope that from now on, and once and for all, the cowardly policy of submission would end and the national defense forces would be given a job to do. The S. A. at that time already numbered in the many thousands of powerful young men and they could not help but participate in this national service. In the Spring and Summer of 1923, its transformation into a military fighting organization was completed. The later developments in 1923 can be mostly traced back to this transformation and how they effected our movement. (*In response to the Ruhr invasion, there were strikes and sabotage. The economic problems caused massive unemployment, inflation, and near collapse so the strikes were called off. A state of emergency was declared in late 1923, along with riots and multiple coup attempts including Hitler's Beer Hall Putsch which occurred before Mein Kampf was written.*)

The developments in 1923 are discussed in detail in another section, but I want to state here simply that the transformation of the S.A. at that time, to assume active resistance against France, would have been harmful regarding how it affected the movement if our assumptions about why this restructuring was needed were flawed. The end of 1923 (*The Beer Hall Putsch, which disrupted the party and caused the government to outlaw the Nazi party*) may initially appear as an awful event, but when we look at it from a higher point of view, we see it was a necessity. With a single blow, the transformation of the S.A. into a military unit was ended. The S.A. was made harmless by the arrogance of the German Government's actions, and this weakening of the S.A. in turn damaged the movement. However, this change opened the possibility for us to rebuild one day and where once we were forced to abandon the correct course, we could now follow a new path.

The N.S.D.A.P. was re-founded in 1925. It must set up, develop, and organize the new S.A. according to the principles originally established. It must return to those sound principles, and it must again regard its highest duty to be the development of the S.A. as an instrument of strength in the fight for the philosophy of the movement. It must not permit the S.A. to sink to the level of a militant defense unit or secret organization. It must, on the contrary, build a guard force consisting of a hundred thousand men who will support the National-Socialist Movement and the racialist idea.

10. THE MASK OF FEDERALISM

In the Winter of 1919, and more so in the Spring and Summer of 1920, the young Party was forced to take a position on a question that was greatly significant during the War. In the first volume, I described briefly the symptoms I saw which foretold the threatening German collapse, and I discussed the propaganda that was being spread by the English and French in order to tear open the old gap between North and South Germany. Back in the Spring of 1915, the first organized pamphlet campaign was started which was designed to inflame feelings against Prussia by labeling it as the one and only party who was guilty of starting the War. This propaganda system was developed and perfected, little by little, until the year 1916, and it was as clever as it was wicked. The effort to prod the South Germans and turn them against the North Germans, using their lowest level desires, began to bear fruit quickly. The government deserves a firm reprimand as well as the army and especially the Bavarian leaders for their failure to act and at least attempt to counter this propaganda. This guilt of failure is inescapable; they should have acted. Because they forgot to do their duty, they failed to stop this propaganda with the necessary determination. In fact, nothing was done. In various government positions, they did not even appear to look at this propaganda as a problem. Maybe they were stupid enough to think that this propaganda would somehow build unity among the German people and bring them closer to national unification, and at the same time, somehow the German State powers would automatically be strengthened too. Rarely in history has a malicious neglect been more maliciously avenged. The enemy planned to only weaken Prussia but their propaganda struck all of Germany. The consequence was the acceleration of the collapse which devastated Germany and the individual states themselves.

Against one particular city, the manufactured hatred towards Prussia was stirred up the most violently and that was where the revolution against the ancestral Royal House first broke out. It would be wrong to think this anti-Prussian feeling was exclusively due to the hostile war propaganda or that those who fell for it could not be forgiven. The absolutely insane organization of our war-time economy centralized all of the production resources in one area and that one area not only represented the entire realm, it swindled the Reich, and this was mostly why anti-Prussian sentiment grew so strong. The normal man on the street viewed the companies that handled war production as having their headquarters in Berlin—those profiteers were identical with Berlin—and to him Berlin was synonymous with Prussia. The organizers of this predatory institution of the war profiteers, the so-called War Companies, were neither of Berlin nor Prussians and they were not Germans at all, but this hardly entered the mind of the average person at that time. He saw only the gross failure and the constant encroachments of the hateful financial arrangements from these companies, and it was most pronounced in those who controlled the capital. Of course, he transferred his entire hatred onto the capital of Berlin and thereby to Prussia. This was especially true because the government did nothing to stop it, but instead, this blaming of Berlin was quietly welcomed with a sinister smirk.

The Jew was clever enough to see that his infamous plunder of the German people, which he organized under the cloak of the War Companies, would raise opposition from the public. As long as this opposition did not threaten his throat, he was not afraid of it. To prevent the anger of the rebellious masses from exploding in his own face, there was no better recipe than to let their rage flame up in a different direction and, in this way, he could also use it.

Let Bavaria go on fighting against Prussia and Prussia against Bavaria. The more the merrier! The more difficult the battle was between these two only meant the more secure peace was for the Jew. The public's attention was completely diverted from the international maggot of the nations and they seemed to be forgotten completely. If any enlightened people, and there were many in Bavaria, showed a dangerous tendency to advise caution, to seek insight, or urge restraint in the embittered struggle, or if it there was any threat that the matter would die down, then the Jew in Berlin would provoke the people in a new way and await its success. All of those who profited from the conflict between the North and the South pounced at every opportunity and blew on the flame until the glow sparked to life in a bright fire of revolutionary desire.

It was a clever, subtle game that the Jew played. He kept the German people constantly occupied and diverted their attention which allowed him to steal even more from them. Then came the Revolution.

Up until November of 1918 the average man, especially the narrow-minded middle-class and lower-educated workers, could not yet fully comprehend what was actually going on or the inevitable consequences of the conflict among the German peoples, especially in Bavaria. At least that group which called itself "nationalist" should have been able to comprehend it on the day the Revolution broke out. The dust from the Revolutionary action hardly had time to settle before the leader and organizer declared himself the representative of "Bavarian" interests in Bavaria. This international Jew, Kurt Eisner (*Marxist Premiere of Bavaria*), began to play Bavaria against Prussia. It was obvious that this "valuable gem", who had constantly wandered around Germany as one of the journalist rabble, would be the last person called upon as a protector of Bavarian interests and he was completely indifferent whether Bavaria was even part of God's wide world.

When Kurt Eisner intentionally gave the revolutionary uprising in Bavaria the appearance of a spear point aimed at Prussia, he did not do this from the standpoint of Bavarian interests, but only as a commissioner of Jewry. He used the instincts and dislikes of the Bavarian people in order to more easily break up Germany. He knew the divided nation would easily become the booty of Bolshevism. His tactics continued to be used even after his death. (*Kurt Eisner was assassinated in 1919 by a lone assassin not associated with the Nazi movement, Anton Graf von Arco auf Valley.*) Marxism bathed the individual states and their princes in Germany in the bloodiest mockery, but then they turned around and suddenly called themselves an "independent party", and they appealed to those feelings and instincts among the families of princes and the individual German states.

The struggle of the Bavarian Soviet Republic (*the name of the government formed as a result of the Revolution in Bavaria which declared Bavaria as an independent state*) against the advancing liberation troops sent by the German government was publicized through Marxist propaganda as a "struggle of Bavarian workers" against "Prussian militarism". This claim is the only way we can understand why the overthrow of the Marxist Republic of Councils in Munich was so different from other German regions. In Munich, the overthrow of the Soviet Republic did not lead to the masses recovering their senses, but it caused an even greater bitterness and resentment toward Prussia.

The Bolshevist troublemakers understood how to make the defeat of the Bavarian Soviet Republic look like it was a "Prussian military" victory against the "anti-Prussian" minded Bavarian people and they had great results because the campaign was highly effective. Kurt Eisner did not even have ten thousand followers in the Munich legislative elections and the Communist party had less than three thousand supporters. However, after the collapse of the Bavarian Soviet Republic, both political parties together had risen to approximately one hundred thousand voters.

At this time, my personal struggle against the insane provocation of one group of German people against another began. I don't think I have ever in my life taken on a campaign that was more unpopular than my opposition to the harassment of Prussia at that time. In Munich, the first mass assemblies had already taken place during the Bavarian Soviet Republic period. The hatred against the rest of Germany, especially against Prussia, was whipped up to such a boiling point that it was possible a visitor from North Germany, who made the mistake of attending such a meeting, might be killed. Such demonstrations usually concluded with open insane shouts, "Free from Prussia!", "Down with Prussia!", "War against Prussia!" This was a mood, which an "especially" brilliant representative of Bavarian sovereign interests in the German Reichstag summed up in the battle cry, "I would rather die a Bavarian than rot a Prussian!"

You would have to experience the meetings back then to truly understand what it meant for me to go to a gathering for the first time in the Löwenbräu Cellar in Munich and warn those attending about this craziness, when I was surrounded by only a handful of war comrades who were willing to stand by me. You must remember that the people in this crazy mob are the same ones who wandered around as deserters; they were the ones who shirked responsibility in army bases or hung around at home during that time when we were out defending the Fatherland. So you can understand our feelings when this irrational mob yelled at us and threatened to kill us. These appearances did have some positive benefits. The band of my faithful followers soon felt strongly bound to me for the first time and swore allegiance to me through life and death. These battles were repeated, over and over, through the whole year of 1919, and they seemed to increase in violence after 1920.

I remember one meeting especially well. It was in Wagner Hall in Munich. My group, which had grown much larger by then, had to endure very serious fights that often ended in the mistreatment of dozens of my followers who were beaten, kicked, and finally thrown out of the halls more dead than alive. The battle that I started by myself—back when I was supported only by my war companions— was now continued by the young movement as a holy mission. At that time, we were forced to rely almost exclusively on our Bavarian supporters. However, I am proud to be able to say today that we slowly, but surely, put an end to this mixture of stupidity and treason. I say stupidity and treason because I cannot give the organizers and instigators credit for being simple-minded; however, I am convinced their believers are really good-natured, but stupid followers. I considered and still consider those organizers to be traitors even to this day. They were hired and paid for by France. In the case of Dorten, history has already passed judgment. (*Hans Adam Dorten, attempted a non-violent putsch in the German city of Mainz which was unsuccessful and resulted in an arrest warrant for treason. He took refuge in the French occupied Rhineland, the name for the area on both sides of the Rhine river, and formed a political party there supported by the French; however, due to his treason indictment, the other political parties looked down on the new party.*)

What made this movement especially dangerous was the clever way they concealed their real motives by pushing the federalist intentions to the forefront claiming it was their only motive. (*Here, federalist means forming a weak national state authority to create a union of stronger independent smaller states connected by one central government. This was an important question at the time because before the Revolution of 1918, Germany consisted of 25 independent states and after the revolution the Weimar republic was a stronger nationally-centralized government.*) It is obvious that the stirring up of hatred against Prussia has nothing to do with federalism. A federative activity that attempts to dissolve or divide another state in the federation, at best, seems unusual. A genuine federalist who honestly quotes Bismarck's concept of the Empire could not, in the same breath, want to separate parts from the Prussian State created by or, at least, perfected by Bismarck or even openly support such separatist efforts.

They would have shouted in Munich if a Prussian conservative party had favored or openly promoted the independence of Franconia (*northern part of Bavaria*) from Bavaria. One could only feel sorry for the genuine federalist-minded people who did not see through this reprehensible swindle. They were the first ones who were deceived. By allowing the federalist idea to be twisted to such an extent, its own supporters were actually digging their own graves. One cannot promote a state-centric federative formation of the Empire if one slanders and insults the most important member of such a state structure, namely Prussia. What made this even more unbelievable was that the battle of these so-called federalists was directed against a group of people in Prussia who had the least connection with the November Revolution. The insults and attacks of these federalists were not directed against the fathers of the Weimar Constitution, who for the most part were South Germans or Jews. It was directed against the representatives of the old conservative Prussia who were the exact opposite of the Weimar Constitution. It should not be surprising that the champions of this campaign avoided attacking the Jews, but instead it should reveal the key, the solution to the whole riddle.

Just as before the Revolution, the Jew knew how to divert everyone's attention from his War Companies and from himself and understood how to change the attitude of the masses, especially when it came to directing Bavaria against Prussia. After the Revolution, he had to somehow cover up his new campaign of plunder which was now ten times greater. He was successful again when he incited the "nationalist elements" of Germany against each other by pitting conservative Bavaria against equally conservative Prussia. He did this in the most cunning manner. While holding the fate of the Empire in his hands, he provoked such crude and tactless violations of one against the other that he made the blood of the effected people boil. The anger was never against the Jew, but always between German brothers. The Bavarian did not see the four million people in Berlin who were hard working, industrious people—he saw only the rotten, decomposed Berlin of the west side! (*The west side was predominantly Jewish.*) His hate was not directed, however, against this west side of Berlin, but against the "Prussian" city, which was all Berlin was to him. It was often enough to drive one to despair.

The Jew's cleverness in diverting public attention from himself can be studied by looking at examples today. In 1918, it was impossible to speak of any organized anti-Semitism. I can still recall the difficulties encountered by simply in mentioning the word "Jew". You either received a blank stare or encountered the most violent resistance. Our first attempts to point out to the people the real enemy seemed, at that time, to be practically hopeless. Only very slowly did things take a turn for the better. Although the League of Defense and Offense (*an anti-Semitic league that was banned in 1922*) was organized on a faulty plan and was unsuccessful, it still deserved a lot of credit for having reopened the Jewish question. In any case, in the winter of 1918, something approaching anti-Semitism began to take root. For certain, the National-Socialist movement later brought the Jewish problem to the forefront in a much different manner. It succeeded especially in taking this question out of the narrow circle of upper classes and middle-classes and made it into the main recurring theme of a great national movement. We had hardly succeeded in sharing this great uniting idea of how to combat the problem with the German people when the Jew struck with a counter attack. He used his old methods. With remarkable speed, he hurled the burning torch of dispute into the popular movement and sowed the seeds of disagreement there. In raising the Ultramontane Problem and through the arguments it caused between Catholicism and Protestantism, the public's attention was diverted in order to prevent any organized attack upon Jewry.

(*Ultramontanism is a Catholic religious philosophy giving the Pope massive authority. The Ultramontane Problem refers to whether or not the Pope has authority as a foreign power to dictate local political or church activity. In Germany, the word is more common and basically identifies the conflict between church authority and state authority, Ultramontanes are those who support the Church's authority and independence against the state. The Center Party was also known as the Ultramontane Party, and they were accused of having more loyalty to the Pope than the nation. To oppose Ultramontanism is to oppose Catholicism according to the Church. Protestant Germans who were nationalist accused the Center Party of placing Papal interests ahead of national interests. Otto von Bismark attempted to impede the power of the Catholic Church and limit their influence.*)

The men who introduced the Ultramontane Problem among our people have sinned so grievously against it that they will never be able to make restitution for their transgression. The Jew, however, attained the goal he wanted: Catholics and Protestants carried on a very nice war together while the mortal-enemy of Aryan humanity and of the whole Christian world laughed up his sleeve.

The Jew kept the public preoccupied for years using the struggle between those who wanted independent-state government and central-national government, and he incited them to take sides in this struggle. All of this was happening while the Jew was bartering away the freedom of the nation and betraying our Fatherland to international high finance. He succeeded again by raising tensions between the two German religious denominations and causing them to fight against each other while the foundations of both were being destroyed and undermined by the poison of the international cosmopolitan Jew.

We must remember how much destruction the Jewish bastardization forces on our people every day and realize that this poisoning of the blood can only be removed from the German people after centuries, that is, if it can ever be removed at all. We must also come to understand how this racial disintegration pulls down or even destroys the last Aryan values among our German people. We are the bearers of civilization, but we see our national strength declining and we are in danger, at least in our big cities, of becoming like Southern Italy. This infection of our blood, an infection that hundreds of thousands of our people seem to disregard, is carried out by the Jew according to a methodical plan. According to this plan, these negroid parasites of nations rape our innocent young blond girls and destroy something in this world that can never be replaced. Both Christian denominations are indifferent to this desecration and they ignore the destruction of a noble and unique spirit given to this world by the grace of God. The future of the world does not depend on whether the Protestants conquer the Catholics or vice versa, but on whether the Aryan race will survive or will die out. Yet, the two religious denominations are not fighting against the destroyer of the Aryan race, but they try to destroy each other instead. It would seem that anyone who cared about the nation would see it as his holy duty, each in his own religious denomination, to make certain they do not merely discuss the Will of God, but that they actually perform the Will of God and that they do not allow God's Work to be defiled. The Will of God once gave mankind its form, its soul, and its abilities. Whoever destroys God's work has declared war on all that God created, war upon the Divine Will.

Therefore, every member of his own denomination should take an active role and consider it his first and holiest duty to oppose anyone whose actions, words, or deeds step out of the framework of his own church community and tries to pry his way into the other religious community. Fighting against the little differences in our current religious denominations will lead to a war of destruction between these two major religions in Germany.

We cannot compare conditions here with those in France, Spain, and certainly not Italy (*all predominantly Catholic countries with the second largest group being non-religious*). One can encourage a battle against those who want to give political power to the clergy or Ultramontanism in all three countries without creating a danger that the French, Spanish, or Italian people would fall apart. In Germany, however, this is impossible because the Protestants would also take part in the battle. Therefore, in Germany, any defense would immediately look like an attack of Protestants on Catholicism, while in other countries such a defense of political power would only be carried out by Catholics against political attacks of their own leaders.

What might be tolerated, even if it were considered unjust by members of one's own religious denomination, is immediately and strongly rejected when the attack comes from another denomination. This feeling reaches such extremes that people who might see a disagreement within their own religious community as minor will immediately turn away from that suggested correction and launch a fiery resistance against any outside group that recommends or demands a similar correction. They consider it an unjustifiable, inadmissible, even indecent attempts to become involved in their private internal affairs. Even if such an attempt at change is justified, it is not excused or accepted, not even if the higher right of the nation's interest should be considered first. This is because, today, religious feelings are still deeper than all national and political practicality. This does not change even if the two religious denominations are driven into a bitter war against each other. This antagonism could only be changed if the nation is given a future that is so great, that this greatness itself would calm the religious arena and result in mutual fellowship.

I can, without hesitation, declare that these men who draw the race-centered movements into the crisis of religious controversy are worse enemies of my people than any international Communist. Converting these Communists is the mission of the National-Socialist movement; however, the person who goes outside of his own movement and deviates from their real mission, is a person whose actions are deplorable. It makes no difference whether he is doing this intentionally or unconsciously; he is fighting for Jewish interests. Today, the Jew wants to let the racialist movement use up all its strength and "drain away its life blood" in a religious struggle. It began this crusade as soon as it sensed a danger to the Jew. I emphasize expressly the words "drain away its life blood" because such a fight is clearly futile and only a man completely ignorant of history could ever think he would solve a question today that has remained unresolved for centuries, even when great statesmen have been shattered from their efforts to change another movement.

The facts speak for themselves. The gentlemen of 1924, who suddenly discovered that the supreme mission of the racialist movement was the struggle against Ultramontanism, did not break Ultramontanism but instead shredded the racialist movement. (*This is a reference to Ludendorf who split from the party after the failed Putsch of 1923. His exit and political/religious activity was a major embarrassment and caused reverberations in the party.*) I must also guard against some childish mind within the ranks of our racialist movement who thinks he is capable of succeeding in that which even a Bismarck could not accomplish. (*A reference to Bismark's failed policy of Kulturkampf which attempted to halt Ultramontanism in 1871.*) It will always be the supreme duty of the administration of the National-Socialist movement to sharply oppose every effort that would place the National-Socialist movement in the middle of religious struggles and to immediately remove from our ranks any propagandist who has such a purpose. Actually, our movement had succeeded, without exception up to the fall of 1923. (*This appears to be a reference to Erich Ludendorff and the Beer Hall Putsch. Ludendorf later fell out of favor with Hitler, partly due to Ludendorf's activities against Catholicism.*) In the ranks of our movement, the most pious Protestant could sit beside the most pious Catholic without any conflict of conscience with his religious convictions. Both fought a mighty struggle against the destroyers of Aryan humanity and this fight taught them to respect and to appreciate each other. At exactly the same time, during these years, the movement fought its sharpest struggle against the Center party. This struggle was not about religion, but exclusively for national, racial, and economic goals. We were proven to be in the right by success back then, just as today's elusive success testifies against those "who know better".

In recent years, the racialists, in their God-forsaken blindness of religious squabbles, took the fight so far that they were unable to see how insane the battle was. The Marxist atheist newspapers suddenly became the judge of the religious faithful. Using the most stupid slogans, they defamed one or the other and, in that way, kept the fire blazing. Germans have a history, as is often shown, of carrying on wars for phantoms and they do not stop until they have shed every last drop of blood. Because of this extremism, such a slogan's call to battle will be mortally dangerous to our people. This is how our people were so easily distracted from the real problems threatening their existence. While we tore each other apart in religious squabbles, the rest of the world was divided up by the Jew. While the racialist groups argue whether the Ultramontane danger is greater than the Jewish danger, or vice versa, the Jew destroys the racial foundations of our existence and annihilates our people forever. As far as this type of "racialist" fighter is concerned, I can only say to the National-Socialist movement and to the German people most sincerely, "Lord, guard us from such friends and then we can easily deal with our enemies".

The dispute between federalism (*strong state-level government*) and nationalism (*strong national-centralized government*), which was propagated by the Jews in such a cunning way during the years 1919-1921, compelled the National Socialist movement, even though we opposed the entire argument, to clarify its position. Should Germany be a confederation of states or one national-central government? Exactly what do these terms mean? It seems to me that the second question is the more important one. Answering this question will create a basis for understanding the whole problem and it will also clarify the matter and reconcile the options in the first question.

What is a confederation of states? By a confederacy, we mean a group of sovereign states which come together of their own free will and, in virtue of their sovereignty, create a collective entity. In doing so, they assign selective sovereign rights to the national body that will allow it to safeguard the existence of the joint union.

This theoretical definition does not apply in practice, at least not without some alterations, to any existing confederation of states in the world today. It applies the least to the American Union of States. Most of these individual states never possessed any sovereignty whatsoever. They were gradually brought into the framework of the Union as a whole. Therefore, the various states of the American Union constitute, in most instances, smaller or larger territories that were formed for technical administrative reasons and their borders were frequently drawn with a ruler. These states never possessed any previous sovereignty of their own because that would have been impossible. These states did not come together to create the Union, but it was the Union that created these so-called states. The extensive rights of independence that were relinquished, or rather rights that were granted, to the different territories are in harmony with the whole character of this confederation of states, and with the vastness of its area and overall size, which is almost as large as a continent. So, in referring to the states of the American Union, one cannot speak of their state sovereignty, but only of their constitutionally guaranteed rights, which we could more accurately designate as privileges.

Likewise, our definition does not fully and completely apply to Germany. There is no doubt that the individual states in Germany existed as self-governing states and these were assembled to form the Empire. The formation of the Empire, however, did not take place as a result of free will or from joint cooperation of the individual states, but it was the result of one state, Prussia, achieving dominance over the others. The difference in the size of the individual German states, when compared to American Union states for example, prevents any comparison with the formation of those states. The difference in size between the smallest German federal states and the larger ones, or largest of them, shows that their achievements are not equal, just as their contribution to founding the Empire and the formation of the confederation of states are not equal. As a matter of fact, one cannot speak of most of these states as ever having enjoyed real sovereignty, unless the word "sovereignty" is nothing more than an official catchword. In reality, both the past and the present generations have eliminated many of these so-called "sovereign states", which itself definitely proves these "sovereign" units are frail.

It is not our purpose to go into a detailed historical account of the formation of each state, but I will merely point out the fact that their borders were not the result of racial considerations. These borders are purely a political result, and most of their origins can be traced back into the saddest period of weakness for the German Empire—a time when our German Fatherland was divided into pieces. This inequality was at least partially taken into account by the constitution of the old Empire. It did not grant the same representation to each individual state in the Federal Council, but varied the representation to correspond to the size, the actual importance, and the state's contribution to the construction of the Reich.

The sovereign rights given up by the individual states in order to create the Empire were voluntarily surrendered only in the smallest way. In most cases, these rights were already practically non-existent, or they had simply been taken away through Prussia's superior strength. Bismarck, however, was not guided by the principle of taking away rights just because they could be taken from the individual states. He demanded them to surrender only those rights that were essential in creating the Empire. It was a moderate and wise principle because it took into consideration their customs and traditions, and it also generated a great deal of love and enthusiastic cooperation for the Empire. It would be a mistake to assume Bismarck's intent was to stop at this point and hope the Empire's rights were sufficient for all time. Bismarck never had such a conviction. He actually intended to leave intact rights that would be hard to acquire or tasks that would be difficult to accomplish at the present time and to pursue them in the future. He hoped the passage of time would gradually balance things out. He also hoped that natural pressures, which would result from normal development, would ultimately exert more pressure than any immediate attempt to break the existing resistance of the separate states. This was both a demonstration of and the best proof of his great ability as a statesman. As a matter of fact, the sovereignty of the Empire has continuously increased at the expense of state sovereignty. Time has fulfilled all of Bismarck's expectations.

This loss of state sovereignty was accelerated by the German collapse and the destruction of the Monarchy. The individual German states exist because of purely political reasons and not because of racial reasons; therefore, the importance of these individual states was obviously going to end as soon as the political Monarchy and its dynasties ceased to exist. The Monarchy and associated dynasties were the very embodiment of the political spirit which allowed the existence and development of these states to continue. When a large number of these "state-skeletons" lost their reason to exist, with the collapse of the Monarchy, they automatically gave up their separate existence and united with other states for purely practical purposes or consented to be absorbed by larger states. This was the most striking proof of how exceptionally weak the actual sovereignty of these small states were and it also showed how little value their own citizens held for these states.

The removal of the Monarchy and its representatives was a hard blow to the federal-state character of the Empire, but the financial obligations imposed as a result of the "Peace" Treaty were an even harder blow. Obviously the states lost the right to control their own finances to the Reich at the very moment the Empire was forced to pay-up because of the lost war. This financial obligation could never be met by making separate treaties with each of the individual states. Also, when the Reich took control of postal and railway services, this was the natural result of the gradual enslavement of our people that was brought about by the Peace Treaties. The Reich had to take over more and more sources of revenue in order to meet the ever-expanding extortion payments demanded from it.

The way the unification was carried out within the Reich was frequently absurd, but the process itself was logical and natural. The political parties and the men who previously failed to do everything in their power to end the war victoriously were to blame for it. As far as Bavaria is concerned, those political parties that put their selfish interests first during the war ahead of the Reich, were primarily to blame. They had to pay ten times more after the war was lost than it would have cost if they had just given the Reich the support needed to bring home victory. Time avenges all! Heaven's judgment seldom comes so quickly after sinning as it did in this case. The same parties which had placed the interest of their own states above the interests of the Reich only a few years before, especially Bavaria, now had to witness the suffocation of the individual states by the interests of the Reich. They brought these events on themselves.

It is an unbelievable hypocrisy for the representatives of the different states to complain about the loss of their sovereignty in front of the voting masses, which is the only place our flustered parties direct anything, while at the same time these very parties tried to out-do each other in pursuing a policy of fulfillment—to fulfill the payment terms resulting from the Treaty of Versailles—when it was clear even then that the consequences of this payment would lead to far-reaching internal changes in Germany. Bismarck's Reich was free from international financial obligations and did not owe anyone. At that time, the Reich did not have the heavy and totally unproductive financial obligations that the Dawes Germany of today is subjected to. (*Dawes Germany refers to Germany under the Dawes Plan, which attempted to collect war reparations.*) Even in domestic affairs, Bismarck intentionally limited expenses to a few absolutely necessary costs.

Because of this, the Reich was able to operate without financially dominating the states, and the Reich could function on the contributions made by the individual states. It goes without saying that when the states possessed their own sovereign rights and faced only small financial contributions to the Reich, this made the states very content to be a part of the Reich. It is untrue and dishonest, however, for some to spread the claim that the state's dissatisfaction in being part of the Reich is due exclusively to their new financial obligations to the Reich. No, indeed! The real situation is entirely different. The vanishing joy for the Empire must not be blamed on the loss of sovereign rights by the states, but it is the result of the miserable way the German nation is now represented by its German national government. In spite of all the Imperial Flag Days and Constitution Festivals, the present Reich has not found a place in the heart of any group of the people. The Law For The Protection Of The Republic may be able to frighten people away from voicing their outrage at institutions of the Republic, but the current Reich will never be able to gain the love of even one single German. The Republic's great enthusiasm to protect itself from its own citizens by using laws and jails is the most damning criticism and strongest ridicule of the whole institution.

Certain parties are falsely claiming that states are becoming less pleased with being part of the Reich because the Reich is infringing on the sovereign rights of the states. What if the Reich had not expanded its authority? The love of the states for the Reich would still not have been any better because the total amounts they would have to pay would remain the same. It would have been worse if the various states were required to individually pay the amount needed by the Reich to fulfill the enslaving amounts demanded by the Treaty today and the hatred toward the Reich would be even greater. It would not only be very difficult to collect the contributions from the states, but they would have to be obtained through bureaucratic force by the Reich. The Republic has obligated itself to pay the reparations of the Peace Treaties since it does not have the courage or the intention to break them. Again, the blame rests solely on those parties which constantly preach to the voters about the importance of sovereignty and independence of the states, and then turn around and promote a policy for the Reich that must result in the end of every last one of these so-called "sovereign rights".

I say, "must result" because the present Reich has no other way of shouldering the burdens which resulted from a rotten domestic and foreign policy. Even here we see that one nail drives another deeper still. Every new obligation that the Reich assumes as a result of its criminal mishandling of German foreign interests creates a stronger blow which falls on the states. This requires a gradual elimination, again and again, of all sovereign state rights to avoid the possibility that they would become germ-cells which might sprout resistance.

There is one important difference between the past Reich and the present Reich's policies. The old Empire granted freedom to its people and showed strength to the outside world, while the new Republic displays weakness in foreign affairs and suppresses its citizens at home. In both cases, we can see cause and effect. The powerful national state does not need excessive domestic laws since its citizens love it and are attached to it. The state that is a slave to international interests must resort to compulsory force in order to make its subjects perform the services it demands. Therefore, it is one of the greatest crimes of the new Republic to dare and speak of "free citizens". This could only be said in the old Germany. The present Republic is a slave-colony for the benefit of foreign countries. It has no citizens, but, at best, subjects. For that very reason it does not have a national flag, but only a trademark introduced and guarded by official decrees and regulations. This symbol is the Gessler's hat of German democracy and it will always remain alien to the heart of our people. (*Gessler's hat is a reference to the story of William Tell. Gessler was the local ruler who put his hat on a pole and demanded the citizens bow to it when they passed. William Tell did not bow and was arrested. It is also a play on the name because Gessler is the name of Otto Gessler, the Minister of the Reichswehr.*) This new Republic has thrown the symbols of the past into the gutter, without any respect for tradition and greatness, but the day will come when the new Republic is astonished to find that its subjects were only play-acting and honored its own symbols superficially for they meant nothing to the people. The Republic has made itself nothing more than an intermission; it will be a short, unimportant part in German history.

In order to save itself, this new Republic must constantly restrict more and more the sovereign rights of the individual states, not only for financial reasons, but also to maintain control. Since it drains the last drop of our citizens' blood through its tactics of financial extortion, it must also take away every last one of their rights unless it is prepared to watch as someday general discontent turns into open revolution.

We National Socialists would reverse this trend and create the following basic principle: A powerful national Empire that takes care of and protects its citizens, in the widest sense, through good use of its foreign policy and is able to offer liberty at home without worrying about the stability of the Reich. On the other hand, a powerful national government may intrude on the liberty of individuals and the rights of individual states as long as it can assume the responsibility for these actions without weakening the idea of the Empire. This is possible if every citizen sees that these actions are necessary to make his nation greater.

There is no doubt that all the nations in the world deal with certain unification questions when it comes to their internal structure. Germany will be no exception. Today, it is foolish to speak of "state sovereignty" because of the ridiculous small size of many of these plots. The importance of individual states diminishes as communications and technical administration advances. Modern communication and modern transportation are constantly reducing the obstacles of distance and size. What was once considered a large state is a mere small province today. What we consider small states today were once believed to be as vast as continents. From a technical standpoint, it is easier to govern a nation like Germany (*which is about the size of Nevada*) today than it was to govern the small province of Brandenburg (*approximately the size of Massachusetts*) one hundred and twenty years ago. The distance from Munich to Berlin (*300 miles or 500 kilometers*) has become shorter today than the distance from Munich to Starnberg (*15 miles or 24 kilometers*) was a hundred years ago. Compared with the communication capability that was available one hundred years ago, the entire territory of the Reich today is smaller than any average German state was at the time of the Napoleonic wars. Anybody who refuses to face the consequences of how technology has changed the relevance of our country's size has failed to march with the times. There have been and always will be people who refuse to admit the obvious, but they cannot slow the "wheel of history" and they can certainly never stop it.

We National-Socialists must not be blind to the consequences of these truths. We must not allow ourselves to be caught by the privileged-class party phrases. I use the term "phrases" firstly because these parties themselves do not seriously believe in the possibility of carrying out their intentions. Secondly, they are the very ones who are primarily to blame for the present developments in our country. In Bavaria, the call to stop centralization is nothing but a political maneuver and no one seriously expects it to result in any action. Whenever an opportunity does present itself for these parties to practice what they preach with their phrases, they always fail pitifully. Each time the Bavarian State suffered a "robbery of sovereign rights" on the part of the Reich, it was accepted without any resistance except for some smug barking. But, if any man dared to seriously oppose this crazy system of centralization, the same parties would come forward and ostracize and condemn him as "someone who is not in touch with the current State". They would persecute him until he was silenced either by being thrown in prison or by illegal suppression of his free speech rights. These actions should make the lies of these so-called federalist circles clear to our followers. They use the federalist state idea in the same way they use religion. To them, these are merely means to further their own dirty party interests.

Some activities that involve unification may appear to be natural processes, such as the nationalization of transportation services; however, we as National-Socialists must still oppose such moves in the present Reich if this action is used to hide the real motivation behind it, which is to take over resources so that they can be used to feed a disastrous foreign policy of reparations. The very fact that the Reich of today has assumed control of railways, postal service, finances, etc.—not for the higher purpose of serving national policy, but only to acquire the means to pay for an unlimited fulfillment policy—this should urge us National-Socialists to do everything possible to hinder and prevent such a policy from taking effect. This includes the fight against the present centralization of institutions vital to the existence of our people. Such takeovers have but one objective, and that is to generate the billions of dollars and pay the other guarantees that were agreed to by our leaders when they submitted to the Treaties, and to hand them over for the benefit of countries abroad. This is the reason the National-Socialist movement must oppose any such attempts.

The second reason for opposing a centralization of this sort is because it would establish a dominant domestic power inside a system of government which has previously only brought the greatest disaster on the people of the German nation. The present Jewish-democratic Reich, which has become a real curse to the German nation, is trying to stop the criticism from those individual states that have not fully absorbed the "spirit of today" by demoting those independent states and making them politically and economically insignificant. In contrast to this, we National-Socialists have every reason to support these individual states in their opposition of centralization, and with our support we give them a greater chance of succeeding. Our fight against centralization must be for a higher national German interest. While the Bavarian People's Party works toward their own advantage in obtaining "special privileges" for the Bavarian State, we must fight on the same grounds but in the service of a higher national interest directed against the present November-Democracy.

The third reason for our fight against the present centralization is because much of the so-called "assumption of control by the Reich" does not result in unification and in no way simplifies administration. Often, this centralization is only an excuse to take powers away from the sovereignty of the states in order to transfer assets to the revolutionary parties. Never in German history have we seen a more shameless game of favoritism than the one played in the democratic Republic. Much of the present craze for centralization comes from those parties that once promised to pave the way for the most qualified and talented men, yet they now only consider filling offices or positions with their close supporters. Since the Republic was founded, the Jews have received special attention when it came to obtaining positions in the economic institutions taken over by the Reich, and with centralization, they now find themselves in the national administration. First one, then the other have become realms of Jewry. For tactical reasons, this third consideration is especially important. This consideration makes it our duty to thoroughly study each measure on the road to centralization and, if necessary, to oppose it.

Our position must always be to work toward higher national policy goals, and we must never become tied up in pointless details which support individual state rights merely for the sake of the small state alone. This is necessary so our supporters do not think that we National-Socialists are denying the Reich's right to exercise a higher sovereignty than that of the individual states. We believe this higher right should not and cannot be questioned. To us, the national Reich is just a vessel. What is important is the essential being of the Reich, which means its contents, the nation, and the people. It is clear that all other interests must be subordinated to the sovereign interests of the people. We cannot extend to any individual state a sovereign power or sovereign right which would represent the sovereignty of a nation. We currently have a problem with several federated states maintaining delegations among themselves at home and sending delegations abroad to foreign nations. This must be stopped and it will be stopped. As long as individual states send their own rag-tag delegations to foreign lands, we cannot be surprised when foreign countries doubt the stability of the Reich and act accordingly. The foolishness of maintaining such delegations is even greater because they do more harm than good. If German interests abroad cannot be protected by the ambassador of the Reich, they most certainly cannot be considered protected by the ambassador of a small state whose size and authority is laughable within the framework of the present world order. These little federated states provide nothing but an excuse for others to attempt to break up the Reich from within and without. Efforts that prompt secession are still being welcomed; this is true for one of the foreign nations in particular. As National-Socialists, we must not tolerate it when some senile aristocratic family-tree wants to plant one of its withered branches into new fertile foreign soil in the form of an ambassador's post so it may sprout again. Even in the days of the old Empire, our diplomatic representation abroad was so shameful that it is certainly not something we want to continue experiencing.

In the future, the influence of the individual states will shift to the area of cultural policy. The monarch who did the most in promoting the importance of Bavaria was not some stubborn anti-German who watched out for his own group's interests, but Ludwig I, a man with a great feeling for art and with the ideal of a greater Germany. (*Ludwig the First of Bavaria was king until the 1848 revolutions.*) Since he used the powers of the state primarily for the extension of Bavaria's cultural position and not for the strengthening of its political position, he has rendered a better and more lasting service than would otherwise have been possible. By elevating Munich in his day from an unimportant provincial royal residence to the position of a German metropolis of art, he created a spiritual center which, even today, keeps the Franconians (*northern Bavaria and west-central Germany*) attached to this state despite their differences. (*Munich was the capital of Bavaria and residence of the ruler.*) Suppose Munich had remained what it once was, then the state of Bavaria would have had the same experience as the state of Saxony, the only difference being that the Bavarian city of Nuremberg, which is the equivalent of the Saxony city of Leipzig, would have become a Franconian city instead of Bavarian. It was not the protesters who cried, "Down with Prussia" that made Munich great. The city became important through the efforts of the King (*Ludwig I*), who wanted to give the German nation a treasure of art that would have to be seen to be appreciated. And that is exactly how it turned out. This also holds an important lesson for our future. The importance of the individual states will no longer lie in the state's domain of political power. I see them as important racial and cultural centers. Even here, time will balance things out. Modern transportation throws men together in such a way that slowly, but steadily, the boundaries of provinces and states are being blurred, and even the cultural variations which separate groups by geography will gradually begin to fade and those groups will become more and more uniform.

The army definitively must be kept away from all influences of the individual states. The future National-Socialist State will not repeat the mistake of the past and assign a task to the army that it does not and should not have. It is not the purpose of the German army to be a school for the preservation of provincial cultural quirks, but rather a school of mutual understanding that teaches all Germans to live together. Any element that normally separates different people in the daily life of a nation should be turned into a unifying element by the army. Furthermore, the army should lift each individual young man above the narrow sphere of his own little part of the country and make him conscious that he is a member of the great German nation. He must learn to look beyond the boundaries of his home province and instead see the boundaries of his Fatherland, because the boundaries of his Fatherland are the ones he will someday have to protect. It is, therefore, foolishness to let the young German be trained in his home state. It is more useful to show him all of Germany during his military service. Today, this is even more necessary since the young German does not travel to broaden his horizons as he once did. In view of this fact, it should be obvious that it is unreasonable to leave the young Bavarian in Munich, the Frankonian in Nuremberg, the man of Baden in Karlsruhe, and the man from Wuerttemberg in Stuttgart, etc. (*These were the state's capital cities of the time.*) Wouldn't it be more reasonable to show the young Bavarian the Rhine and the North Sea, the man from Hamburg the Alps, and show the East Prussian the mountains of central Germany? Provincial character may be preserved in a small troop but not the whole garrison. We may disapprove of every attempt at centralization, but we approve when the army is concerned! On the contrary, even if we do not welcome any general attempt at centralization, we would be glad to see this particular one made to unify the army. With the limited size of the present Reich's army, it would be absurd to maintain separate groups representing the different states anyway. However, the unification of the Reich's army that has been undertaken shows a course which we must never abandon, even in the future when the national army will be reinstated.

A young, successful idea must avoid every restriction that threatens to paralyze the power needed to advance the new ideology. National Socialism must claim the right to impose its principles on the entire German nation, without regard to the former limitations of the federated states, and we must educate the nation so they fully understand our ideas and principles. The National-Socialist idea must be just as unrestricted by state boundaries as the churches are unbound by political lines. The National-Socialist doctrine is not the servant of the individual state's political interests, but must dominate the German nation as a whole. It must guide the people to a new life and give them a destiny; therefore, it must claim the absolute right to ignore boundaries drawn by past political forces that we now reject.

The more complete the victory of the National-Socialist doctrine, the greater the freedom it offers to the individual at home.

11. PROPAGANDA AND ORGANIZATION

The year 1921 has become important for me and for the Movement in many ways.

When I first joined the German Workers Party, I immediately took charge of all propaganda. I knew this was the most important area at the time. In the beginning it was not as necessary to rack your brain over the organizational issues, but it was important to distribute the Movement's idea to a larger number of people. Propaganda must come before the structural details of organizing a movement so that we can win over the body of people needed to do the work of the organization. I have never liked to be too hasty or to be overly concerned with book-keeping when it comes to any kind of organization—the result is usually a lifeless mechanical thing instead of a living organization. An organization, or a movement, grows naturally through an organic process of evolution and development. Once ideas have taken hold of a certain number of men, they will naturally form their own order, and this build up is what creates something of great value. Even in this case, we cannot forget about human weakness, which, at least in the beginning, can cause individuals to resist the influence of a superior mind. If an organization is laid out mechanically, this creates a real danger that someone appointed as an officer, someone who has not yet been tested or proven himself, someone who may not be qualified at all, will try to prevent more capable members within the Movement from rising to positions of power out of jealousy. This kind of damage can be fatal, especially if the movement is still young.

For this reason it is best to start off distributing ideas from one central figure. Then, as the body of people who learn about the idea grows to an acceptable point, we can search through them and examine them carefully to find leaders. We frequently see that men who at first appear insignificant turn out to be born leaders.

However, it would be a serious mistake to view an abundance of theoretical knowledge as proof of leadership qualities or as a sign of organizational skill which are both necessary for a leader. The opposite is usually true. Great theorists are rarely great organizers. The greatness of a theorist lies in his ability to understand and establish abstract laws that are correct, while the organizer must primarily be an expert in understanding the human mind. The leader has to take a man as he is, therefore he must understand him. He can neither overestimate him nor under-estimate him, either individually or when looking at a group of men. On the contrary he must try to take weakness and animal-tenacity equally into consideration; the organizer must evaluate all factors in order to create a structure which is filled with animated, constant power as if it were a living being. Then the organization will be capable of embodying an idea and paving the way for its success.

It is even more rare to find a great theorist who is also a great leader of men. A leader is much more likely to be an agitator. Those who have a lighter temperament may not like this assertion; however, the truth in it is obvious. An agitator has to understand human nature if he is able to make the masses absorb an idea, even if he only manipulates their emotions. Such emotional manipulation still makes him better qualified for leadership than the theorist who does not know how men think or how the world works. To be a leader means having the ability to move the masses. The ability to form ideas has nothing to do with the ability to lead. In this connection it is quite pointless to argue over which is of greater importance: to conceive human ideals and aims or to make them a reality. As it happens so often in life, one would be meaningless without the other. The most beautiful theoretical idea has no purpose and has no value unless a leader directs the masses towards that idea. On the other hand, there would be no use for the energy or genius of a leader if the clever theorist did not establish a goal for mankind to struggle toward. The combination of theorist, organizer, and leader in one person is the rarest thing to be found upon this planet; this combination will create a great man.

As already said, I focused my attention on propaganda in the early days of the Movement. It was the means to implant the new doctrine in a small nucleus of men who could be used to form the first elements of an organization. The goals of propaganda usually reached well beyond those of the organizer. If a movement intends to tear down one world order and replace it by a new one, then its leaders must clearly understand the following principles: Each movement must first sift through the body of people that has been attracted and divide them into two large groups—followers and members. It is the task of propaganda to win followers and it is the task of the organization to win members. A follower understands and agrees with the movement's goals; a member is ready to fight for those goals.

A follower is won over to the movement by propaganda. A member is encouraged by the organization to cooperate personally in the winning of new followers, and from those new followers, some may eventually become members. To be a follower only requires the passive acceptance of an idea. To be a member demands that the member actively represent the idea and defend it. Therefore, out of ten followers, we may find only two members. A follower only needs to understand; a member must have the courage to go out and personally represent the newly-found truth so he can spread it to others.

Most followers will be passive in their participation just like the majority of mankind, which is inactive and faint-hearted. To be a member means one must have an active mind, which is found only in a small number of men. Therefore, propaganda must constantly work to win over followers who believe in the idea, while organizers work unceasingly to identify and convert the most valuable of the followers into members. Propaganda does not need to worry about the value of each of the followers it attracts. It is not concerned with their qualities, ability, intellect, or character. It is the task of the organizer to carefully search through these masses for those who can actively help to bring the movement victory.

The propagandist's job is to compel all of the people to accept a doctrine. The organizer's job is to include only those members who will not become an anchor to the further spread of the idea because of their mental attitude. Propaganda attempts to win over the people as a whole to an idea and to prepare them for the time when this idea will be victorious. The followers who are capable and willing to fight create the organized elements and they join together in a massive fighting union which constantly struggles toward their goal of victory. The more completely propaganda has worked its magic among all the masses, and the more the organization which has been built is made exclusive, rigid, and firm, the more likely the final triumph of an idea becomes. This means that the number of followers can never be large enough, but the number of members can easily be too large.

After propaganda has converted the entire population over to an idea, only a handful of men are needed to finish the job. This shows that propaganda and organization, that is to say followers and members, have a mutual relationship of give and take. If the propaganda has worked well, then the organization can be smaller, so that the number of followers can be larger and the number of members can be smaller. However, if the propaganda is weak, the organization structure must be stronger, so in this case the number of followers in a movement remains small, which means a much larger membership is needed assuming the movement expects any success whatsoever.

The first task of propaganda is to win over men who can be used in the organization; the first task of the organization is to select men who can carry on the propaganda. The second task of propaganda is the destruction of existing conditions so the new doctrine can spread more easily, and the second task of the organization is to fight for power. This power will be needed to secure the final success of the doctrine.

A revolution based on a World-Concept will only be completely successful if the new world philosophy is taught to nearly the entire population and later forced upon everyone if necessary. The organization, which is the movement, however, should only be made up of those members who are necessary to take charge of the nerve centers of the coming nation.

In other words, every great world changing movement driven by an idea must first spread this idea using propaganda. The propaganda creator must constantly attempt to explain the new idea to others in a very clear way, which can win them over or at least make them uncertain about their existing convictions. Since the declaration of such doctrine, in the form of propaganda, needs a backbone, the doctrine must be supported by a rigid organization. The members of the organization will be drawn from the number of followers won over by propaganda. The more intensive the propaganda, the quicker the followers will grow, and the members in turn will work better which will make the organization driving it stronger and more energetic.

Therefore it becomes the main task of the organizers to see to it that no internal disagreements lead to an eventual break away of members which would weaken the work inside the movement. The organizers must make certain the spirit that creates a common, determined attack does not die out by constantly making sure it is rejuvenated and strengthened. This does not mean that the membership has to continue growing indefinitely, quite the contrary. Only a limited portion of mankind possesses the energetic and bold qualities a movement needs, so any organization that continues to increase its membership indefinitely would one day become weak and inert. Organizations that continue to grow their membership beyond a certain number gradually lose their fighting power. Then they are no longer able to take the offensive which means they cannot support their propaganda, and if they cannot support it, they cannot benefit from it.

The greater and more revolutionary an idea is, the more active the membership becomes. The revolutionary power of the doctrine spells danger for its ambassador. This danger keeps away the small, cowardly members of the middle or privileged-class. Privately they may consider themselves followers, but they fear to confess their beliefs to the public by openly becoming members. This is how the organization, promoting a truly revolutionary idea, takes in members—only the most active of the followers who have been won over by propaganda. This process of receiving only the most revolutionary membership into the movement, which is a result of natural selection among its followers, guarantees it will actively spread the message in the future and will fight successfully to make the idea a reality.

The greatest danger any movement faces is when the membership grows abnormally fast after a large success by the movement. All the cowards and petty selfish onlookers will shun a movement when it is engaged in a bitter struggle. However, once the movement has either gained a big success or such a success seems likely, these people will usually try to join at that time. The last-minute-joiner is the reason many movements, which are victorious in a battle before they achieve their final success, or rather before the final completion of the idea is achieved, suddenly retreat. They develop a vague, inner weakness, which forces them to suspend the fight and finally the movement dies. Their first victory drew so many bad, unworthy and particularly rotten elements into the organization, that these unworthy creatures eventually superseded the fighting strength of the movement in an effort to force the movement to serve their own interests. They reduce it to their own level of petty heroism and do nothing to achieve final victory for the original idea. The fanatical goal has been erased from their minds, the fighting strength becomes crippled, or as the privileged-class world would rightly say in such cases: "Water has been mixed with the wine". When this happens, indeed, the trees can no longer grow up to heaven (*meaning great things cannot be achieved any longer; the tree has grown as much as it can and decline will follow*).

Therefore, it is essential that a movement interested in self-preservation cease adding members as soon as it has become successful. From that time on, it should exercise the greatest caution before allowing any membership changes and should examine the situation carefully before enlarging its organization. This is the only way it will be able to keep the nucleus of the movement pure, fresh, and sound. It must also be sure that this nucleus is the only group to lead the movement or decide on the propaganda, and as the center of power, this nucleus will perform all actions necessary to make its ideals a reality. All important positions that have been conquered, as well as the internal leadership itself, must be strictly filled from the main body of the old movement. This has to be continued until the old principles and doctrines of the Party have become the foundation and purpose of the new government. Only after this has been accomplished can the reins be gradually handed over to the constitution of this State, and this must be a constitution which is born out of the movement's spirit. Such a hand-over usually takes place only after a mutual struggle between the leaders of the existing movement and those empowered by the constitution. This struggle occurs because it is not so much a question of human insight, as when a leader evaluates those he works with, but it is more about the play and working of powers within the government. Such powers may be clearly seen in the constitution or organization; however, they cannot be guided by the old leadership forever.

All large movements, whether religious or political, owe their tremendous successes to the recognition and use of these principles. Any lasting success is unthinkable if these laws are ignored.

As the leader of the party propaganda, I carefully prepared the way for the future greatness of the movement and through these radical concepts presented in our propaganda, I have worked to recruit only the best quality people as members of the organization. The more radical and inciting my propaganda was, the more it frightened away the weak and timid and prevented them from penetrating the early nucleus of our organization. They may have remained followers, but they certainly did not let the public know; in fact they apprehensively concealed their allegiance. There were many thousands of people who assured me that they were totally in agreement with everything in our program, but under no circumstances could they openly be members! The movement, they said, was so radical that they would be personally subjected to severe criticism and even danger if they became members. So, the honorable, peaceful citizen could not be blamed if he stood aside at first, even though his heart was in full harmony with the ideas of the movement. This was fine with me.

If we allowed people like these, who lack the spirit of revolution, to join our Party as members in the early days, then we would be nothing more than a pious brotherhood because we would no longer be a young movement filled with fighting spirit. The spirited and daring form that I gave our propaganda back then established and guaranteed the radical nature of our movement ever since. From that time onward, only radical people, with a few exceptions, were willing to become members. Nevertheless, our propaganda was so strong that, after a short time, hundreds of thousands not only agreed in their heart with us, but wished for our victory, even though they were personally too timid to make any sacrifices for it and some were too timid to even argue on behalf of it.

Up to the middle of 1921, bringing in new members this way was sufficient and the method was useful to the movement. However, special events during the midsummer of this year, after the success of our propaganda brought the movement into the public eye, made it clear the organization needed to be updated and adapted to deal with this greater visibility in the community.

(This refers to the summer of 1921 when Hitler was away in Berlin giving a speech and, to counter his growing power in the party, Anton Drexler encouraged members to vote to limit Hitler's power in the party. Hitler threatened to leave which would split the party. In order to prevent a split, the party agreed to move Drexler from the position of party chairman and replace him with Hitler, plus, it gave Hitler additional powers. Hitler was then elected as party leader on July 29, 1921, and this was when he was first called Führer of the party.)

A group of racialist visionaries attempted to obtain control of the Party with the help of the president of the Party (*Drexler*). This led to the collapse of this little conspiracy and, during a general meeting of all members, absolute authority over the movement was unanimously placed in my hands. At the same time, a new rule was approved which delegated the complete responsibility of the movement to the leader, did away with the requirement for committees to make decisions, and instituted a system that divided work between the committees instead, and that has since proven to be the greatest blessing. Since the first of August, 1921, I have taken over the inner reorganization of the movement and I found a large number of excellent helpers to assist me. I consider it necessary to mention them and their contributions later in a special appendix.

In my effort to make use of the results we gained from our propaganda so we might improve the organization, I had to do away with many former customs and I had to introduce principles that no existing party possessed or would even have accepted. From 1919 to 1920, the movement was led by a committee which was elected by the members in special assemblies as described in our rules. The committee consisted of a first and second treasurer, a first and second secretary, and the heads were the first and second chairmen. In addition to that, there was a membership secretary, the chief of propaganda, and several other committee members. I found it amusing that the movement was led by a committee, which was the very embodiment of what the movement itself intended to combat, parliamentarianism. It is obvious the organization was functioning by using the same principle that represented the system everyone suffered under and they continue to suffer under today, from the smallest localities, through districts, in the provinces, and the states and all those under the Reich's parliamentary leadership. It was urgently necessary to change this situation so we could prevent the movement from being permanently spoiled and becoming incapable of fulfilling its true mission. When the time came, we could not afford to have such a poor foundation for our organization.

When the majority voted in favor of something, the result was recorded in the written minutes—obviously this represented a miniature parliament. There was no personal responsibility anywhere. The same nonsense and the same foolishness controlled our small committee that controlled the large representative bodies of the State. Men were elected to serve on this committee as secretaries, as treasurers, to manage the membership of the organization, for propaganda, and God knows what else. Yet later, they would all choose a side, for or against each particular question, and then vote on it. For instance, the man who had to look after propaganda voted on a matter that concerned the treasurer, and the treasurer had to vote on matters that concerned the man who looked after other organizational matters, who, in turn, voted on a matter that purely affected the secretaries, etc.

Why is one special man appointed for propaganda if treasurers, secretaries, and member secretaries, etc., also vote on propaganda issues? This appears just as unreasonable to a normal mind as it would if the supervisors or engineers or other workers from other sections in a big factory decided questions that were not in any way related to their department. I refused to submit to such foolishness and after a very short time, I stopped attending the committee sessions. I prepared my propaganda and that was that. I also did not let some good-for-nothing interfere with my work, just as I did not concern myself with their business. As soon as the acceptance of the new by-laws and my appointment to the office of first chairman had given me the necessary authority and the corresponding rights, this foolishness was immediately stopped. The principle of absolute responsibility was introduced to replace the committee resolutions.

The first chairman is responsible for the entire leadership of the movement. He assigns tasks to the members of the committee under him and to the other needed workers. Each one of these men is absolutely responsible for the tasks assigned to him. Each man is accountable to the first chairman, who must make sure that all members cooperate, or he must establish cooperation by choosing men who can work together and by establishing general guiding principles. This law of responsibility has gradually become routine within the movement, at least as far as the leadership of the Party is concerned. In the little local groups and maybe even in the provinces and districts, it will take years before these principles are fully established since hesitant characters and good-for-nothings will fight against responsibility. They will always feel uneasy if they carry the sole blame for a task. They feel more comfortable if every important decision is supported by the majority of a committee. However, I feel it is necessary to strongly oppose such an attitude. I will not make concessions to fear when it comes to responsibility. Even if it takes a long time before this goal is realized, I will ultimately create an understanding among the members that leaves no doubt about the duty and ability of a leader, and this will allow only those who are truly called-forth and chosen to become leaders.

At any rate, a movement that intends to fight against the foolishness of parliamentary institutions must keep itself free from such structures. Only then can it gain the strength needed for its struggle. In a time when majority-rule is the master everywhere, a movement that adapts itself to the principle of one leader who carries all responsibility will someday, with mathematical certainty, overcome the present circumstances and will emerge victorious. This thought led to a complete reorganization within the movement. Its logical effect also resulted in a very strict separation between the financial departments of the movement and the political leadership. This principle was extended to the entire business management of the party. This placed the business section on a sound footing which was free from political influences so it could concentrate on purely economic matters.

When I joined the original six-man Party in the autumn of 1919, it did not have a business office, any employees, printed forms, or rubber stamps. Nothing printed existed. At first, the committee used a room at an inn on the Herrengasse (*or Street of the Lords, a street in Vienna*) and later, a cafe on the Gasteig (*the cultural center of Munich*). This was an impossible situation. Therefore, soon after I joined, I began looking at several Munich restaurants where we could rent a room or another enclosed space for our meetings. In the former Sterneckerbräu Inn Beer Hall in the valley (*a tavern in Munich. The "Tal", or valley, is a shopping street in Munich, stretching from "Isartor" to the Old Town Hall. The Sterneckerbräu used to be an inn. In 1933, Hitler established a small Nazi museum in one of its rooms. In modern times, the building houses offices and the interior has been completely renovated.*), there was a small room with a raised ceiling that had previously served the Imperial Counselors of Bavaria as a place for their drinking bouts. It was dark and gloomy and served its former purpose extremely well, but it was not as well suited for what we needed now. The only window faced an alley that was so narrow, even on the brightest summer day, the room remained dark and gloomy. This became our first business office. Since the monthly rent was only fifty marks, a large sum for us in those days, we were in no position to demand much. We could not even complain when the wooden paneling on the walls that had been put there for the Imperial Counselors, was torn off before we moved in. Now, the room really seemed more like a vault than an office. Nevertheless, this represented great progress. Eventually, an electric light was installed, but it took even longer to get a telephone. A table with a few borrowed chairs was added. Finally, we found an open shelf to use and later, a cabinet for food and dishes. Two sideboard cabinets with shelves and drawers that belonged to the innkeeper served as a storage place for pamphlets, posters, etc.

The former leaders only held one weekly committee meeting. This could not possibly continue in the long run. We needed a full-time, paid party official to manage our business affairs. This was difficult for us back then. The movement had very few members at this time, which made it tricky to find a suitable man among them who could meet all of the movement's demands while requiring very little compensation for himself.

Finally, after an extended search, the first business manager of the party was found in a former comrade of mine, Schüssler. (*Rudolf Schüssler served in the same regiment with Hitler and they worked together in the political department of the Bavarian Reichswehr, national defense force, after the war.*) At first, he worked daily between 6:00 and 8:00 in the evening at our new office and later between 5:00 and 8:00 in the evening. Finally, he began working every afternoon and a short time later he was working full-time. He did his duty from early morning until late at night. He was just as diligent as he was upright and honest. He was a man who personally did all he could and who was a faithful supporter to the movement. Schüssler brought a small Adler typewriter that he owned. (*The typewriter was made by Adler Schreibmaschinen of Frankfurt which was a major typewriter manufacturer. The model was likely an Adler 15. It is interesting Hitler mentioned the brand, possibly out of national pride over a German-built machine.*) It was the first machinery of that kind that our movement used. Later, the movement purchased the typewriter by paying through installments. It seemed necessary to have a small safe in order to protect the card-files and the membership lists from the fingers of thieves. We purchased a safe, though not to deposit any big funds that some might have thought we had at that time. On the contrary, the movement was extremely poor and I had to personally help out frequently with my own scant savings.

One-and-a-half years later, the business office became too small so we moved into a new location on Cornelius Street. This was also a tavern, but this time we had three rooms and not just one room. We also had a large hall. In those days, we thought this was a great achievement. We stayed there until November, 1923. Earlier, in December, 1920, we had acquired the newspaper Völkischer Beobachter (*the Race Watcher*). Its name alone advocated racial ideas and this paper was to be transformed into a vital part of the N.S.D.A.P. In the beginning, the paper was published twice weekly. Early in 1923, it became a daily paper. By the end of August, 1923, it was published as a regular, large-format newspaper which is the format it is commonly known for today. Being an absolute novice in the newspaper business, I frequently had to pay dearly for hard-bought lessons in those early days.

It gives a person food for thought if you notice that, in contrast to the enormous number of Jewish newspapers, there is only one important racial-Nationalist newspaper. Later, I had the chance to learn first hand why this was so. Most of the so-called racialist enterprises were not operated in a business-like manner. They followed the idea that loyalty is more essential than success. This point of view is entirely false. Loyalty in itself is not something that can be seen. It is best expressed through accomplishment. The man who creates something of actual value to his people reveals how valuable his loyalty is. Someone who only acts like they are loyal, but does not actually do anything for his people, is harmful to everyone and a liability to those who are loyal.

As the name indicates, the Race Watcher newspaper we acquired was called a "racial-Nationalist" mouthpiece and it had all the strengths connected with such institutions, but it also had all the faults and weaknesses. The contents of these other newspapers were honorable, but the enterprises were managed in a way that made it impossible for them to function as a business. They believed that racialist newspapers had to be supported by racialist donations. They failed to realize that, in spite of competing with other newspapers, they must still be successful. It is absolutely indecent for their management to cover up their negligence or mistakes using donations from good-intentioned patriots.

As soon as I realized how dangerous these conditions were, I made some changes. Luck was with me when it led me to a man who had since offered the movement extremely valuable services, both as business manager of the newspaper and as business manager of the Party. In 1914 at the battlefront, I met the present general business manager of the Party, Max Amann. At that time, he was my superior officer (*Amann was Hitler's sergeant in the war and later head of Eher-Verlag the Nazi printing office*). During the four years of the war, I had every opportunity to observe the great capabilities and diligence of this conscientious man I would later work with.

In mid-summer of 1921, the movement went through a serious crisis (*apparently another reference to the vote to reduce Hitler's power in the party and the results*). I was no longer satisfied with many of the employees and I had an especially bitter experience with one of them. That was when I accidentally ran into my former comrade from my regiment and, after talking to him for a while, I asked him to become the business manager of the Party. Amann already had a job with a promising future which made him hesitate at first, but he finally agreed. However, he made it clear he would never become the ceremonious servant for some incompetent committee; he would recognize only one master.

The infinite value of our first business manager, who had a strong business knowledge, brought order and integrity into the departments of the Party. This established a method of operation that was unequaled and certainly could not be surpassed by any of the movement's subdivisions. As frequently happens in life, success often causes envy and ill will. The same had to be expected in this case and it was tolerated with patience.

As early as 1922, we established fixed procedures to strengthen the business side of the movement. We already had a filing system containing information on all the Party members. The movement was also financially stable. Current expenses had to be covered by the current income. When we had unexpected or unusually high income, it was used for special expenses. In spite of the hard times, the movement remained practically free of debt, except for a few small current bills. This allowed the movement to steadily increase its assets. We worked just like it was a private business. Employees had to distinguish themselves through success and could not fall back on "the famous loyalty". The conviction of every National-Socialist is demonstrated by his willingness, his diligence, and his ability to do the work that has been given to him by the community of the people. Anyone who does not fulfill his duty cannot brag about his loyalty because he has already committed a sin against it.

Against many influences, the new business manager of the Party energetically defended his position that Party office jobs are not for lazy supporters or members who want to sit around and do nothing. A movement that strongly fights the corruption of our present State administration must keep its own organization clean of such vices.

The management of the newspaper hired employees who formerly belonged to the Bavarian People's Party. However, their achievements alone proved them to be extremely qualified. The result of this experiment was outstanding for the most part. The very fact that the movement honestly and frankly acknowledged real individual successes did more to quickly and fully win the hearts of the employees than would have been possible otherwise. Later on, they became good National-Socialists and they remained loyal. Not only were they loyal in what they said, but they proved it by doing conscientious, good, and honest work in the service of the new movement. It goes without saying that the well-qualified members of the Party were preferred to non-members of the party who were equally well-qualified, but nobody was hired on the basis of his membership in the Party alone. The determined manner in which the new business manager stood for these principles and gradually carried them out in spite of all resistance proved later to be a great advantage to the movement. During the difficult time of economic inflation, when tens of thousands of businesses collapsed and thousands of newspapers ceased to exist, it was possible for the management of the movement to not only continue operating and accomplish its task, but it continued to build up the Race Watcher Newspaper more and more. During this time is when it took its place among the great newspapers.

The year 1921 was significant in another respect. In my position as head of the Party, I was successful in gradually liberating the departments of the Party from the criticism and the lectures of so many of the committee members. This was important because their interference made it impossible to attract a really competent man for a task if he knew committee members, who had no abilities, would constantly interfere because they always thought they knew what was best about everything. All they really did was create terrible confusion. Usually these know-it-alls retired modestly so they could find a new field where they could practice their skills of control and inspiration. These people were plagued with an obvious disease which caused them to find an ulterior motive behind everything and anything. They also seemed to live in a kind of constant pregnancy, always filled with magnificent plans, ideas, projects, and techniques. Their greatest goal was achieved when they appointed a sub-committee, which would have to poke its nose expertly into the work of others and control everything. It never seemed to occur to most of these committee-hounds that it was offensive and non-National-Socialistic for an idiot to continuously lecture the real experts. Anyhow, I considered it to be my duty during these years to protect all assistants who did a good job and carried heavy responsibilities in the movement against such elements, which gave them the necessary backing and freedom to make progress in their work.

The best way to deal with committees that did nothing or only hatched impossible ideas was to give them a real task. It was humorous to watch as the members of such a group quietly disappeared until they were nowhere to be found. It made me think of our greatest similar institution, the Reichstag. They quickly vanish into thin air if they have to do a real job instead of just talk, especially when it was a task that each of these chatterer-boxes would be held personally responsible for.

Even in those days, just as it is done in private business, I always demanded that we continued searching until the most clearly capable and honest person was found to act as an official, administrator, or leader for the movement. He would then be given absolute authority and freedom to act with his subordinates. On the other hand, he would also be completely responsible to his superiors. At the same time, no one was to be given any authority over subordinates unless he was an expert himself in the field of work he supervised. Over the course of two years, I succeeded in establishing my idea and today it is generally accepted in the movement, at least by those in the higher positions of authority. The visible success of this attitude became apparent in 1923. When I came to the movement four years before, not even a rubber stamp could be found. On November 9, 1923, when the party was dissolved and its property was confiscated, the assets, including all valuables and the paper, then amounted to over one hundred and seventy thousand gold marks. *(After the Beer Hall Putsch the NSDAP was banned by the government and their assets confiscated. The Mark suffered hyperinflation and was basically worthless, however here Hitler specifically says Gold Mark, which is backed by gold, as distinguished from Paper Marks which were subject to inflation. The 170,000 Gold Mark value is the equivalent of over sixty kilograms of gold or over 130 pounds of gold.)*

12. THE UNION QUESTION

In 1922, the rapid growth of the movement compelled us to more closely define our position on a question which still had not been fully resolved. In our search for techniques that would quickly and easily attract the masses, we constantly ran into one objection: the working man would never completely belong to us as long as his work-life and economic interests were in the hands of men and union organizations with an opinion that was different from ours. This objection is well founded. It was commonly believed that a worker who was employed in a particular field could not survive if he were not a member of that trade-union. Not only was his job protected, but he could only obtain work if he were a member of the union. Therefore, the majority of workers were members of trade-unions. These unions fought for higher wages and made wage agreements, which guaranteed the workers a certain income. Obviously all workers in this situation profited as a result of the fights, and any honest man was bound to have feelings of guilt if he accepted wages that resulted from the union's struggle but withdrew from the battle himself.

It was very difficult to discuss these problems with the average privileged-class employer. They did not appear to understand and most did not even want to understand the financial or the moral side of the question. From the start, they opposed any effort to organize their workers because they considered it to be against their own economic interests. For this reason alone, most of them are unable to form an unbiased opinion, just as in many cases, they fail to see the forest for the trees. Therefore, we must now turn to disinterested parties. They will be much more sympathetic toward a situation that is so vital to our present and future life if they have the smallest degree of good will.

In the first volume, I gave my opinion regarding the nature, purpose, and necessity of trade unions. As long as there is no change in the relationship between employer and employee, either by government decrees, which are usually ineffective, or by general education, the employee will have no other choice and will be forced to defend his own interests. The employee will have to take a stand, as a participant in economic life, who is equal to the employer. I further emphasized that taking protective measures would be within the interests of the community if those actions prevented serious social injustices that would otherwise harm the entire community. Furthermore, I declared that these protective measures would be a necessity as long as there were employers who personally had no concern for social duties or for the most elementary human rights. From all of this, I drew the conclusion that if self-defense became necessary, it would logically have to come from the uniting of all workers in trade-unions.

My opinion on the subject has not changed since 1922. However, a clear and precise definition regarding these problems had to be found. We could not continue in the satisfaction that we understood the problem. It was necessary to develop a conclusion that we could put into practice.

The following questions had to be answered:

1. Are trade-unions necessary?
2. Should the N.S.D.A.P. take an active part in the trade-unions or direct our members to participate in some other form?
3. What form should a National-Socialistic trade-union take? What are our tasks and what are its goals?
4. How can we establish such trade-unions?

I believe that I have sufficiently answered the first question and shown that trade unions are necessary. It is my belief that, under the present circumstances, we cannot eliminate the trade-unions. They are an important part of the national economic life. Their significance goes beyond social-politics and extends into a much larger area of national-politics. When people receive the necessities of life as a result of their trade-union movement, and the people are also properly educated about the goals of the movement, they will be greatly strengthened and the entire nation's powers of resistance in the struggle for existence will be increased. The trade-unions are indispensable since they are the building blocks for the future council of economics and they will be the equivalent of our current parliamentary groups.

The second question can also be easily answered. If the trade-unions are important, then it is clear that National Socialism must not only take a theoretical side, but must also take a definite stand that will result in action. But how? That is a more difficult question.

The National-Socialist movement is working with one goal in mind: The National-Socialist National State. Without doubt, all future institutions of this coming State must grow out of the movement itself. It would be a great mistake to think that all of a sudden, with nothing in hand but the possession of political power, a reorganization could take place without previously building a foundation of men who are already trained in our beliefs and have proven their loyalty. Even in this case, the spirit that fills the form is more important than the outward form itself which can quickly be created mechanically.

For instance, a dictatorial type of leadership can be imposed on State organizations, however, it will only survive if it has evolved through stages, from the smallest beginnings and gradually developed itself to maturity. After many years of going through the continuous selection process and facing the tests of the hard realities of life, only then will the leaders needed to carry this principle into reality be ready. Therefore, we should never think that we could suddenly pull the constitutional outlines for a new state out of a briefcase and "introduce" them through pressure from above. This can be attempted, but the results will either not survive or it will be dead before it is born. This reminds me of the Weimar constitution, which provided the German people with a new constitution and a new flag that had no connection whatsoever to the changes our people have endured during the last half century. The National-Socialist State must be careful not to try similar experiments. When the time comes, the National Socialist State can only develop out of an organization that has been in existence for a considerable length of time. This organization must possess the National-Socialist spark of life from the beginning so that it can create a living National-Socialist State.

As I have emphasized, those who will seed the council of economics will come from the various bodies that represent the trade-unions. If, however, the future council representing the work guilds and the Central Economic Council are to represent a National-Socialist institution, these important seed-members must also be the agents of a National-Socialist conviction and carry with them our idea. The institutions created within the movement will then be transferred and incorporated into the State. This transfer must take place because the State is unable to suddenly, as if by magic, produce the needed institutions, and if it tried, they would be nothing more than lifeless formations.

When we look at the big-picture, we see that it is necessary for the National-Socialist to engage in activities related to trade-unions. It must do so for another reason too. A genuine National-Socialist education of employers and employees—an education that intends to make both of them members of the new people's community—will not be accomplished by teaching theories, making appeals, or giving warnings. It will only be accomplished through a daily struggle where our members are working among the people. Through this constant struggle, the movement must educate the various large economic groups and bring them closer together on the important issues. If this preliminary work is not done, then the future people's community is just a mere illusion and all hope is lost. Only the great World-Concept ideal that the movement fights for can slowly, but eventually, lead people to create a new order that is seen as firmly united inwardly and outwardly. Therefore, the movement must not only accept the idea of trade-unions, but it must provide its large membership with the necessary education for the coming National-Socialist State by actively participating in this community.

The answer to the third question follows from what we have already discussed. The National-Socialist trade-union is not an instrument of class struggle, but an instrument that represents the different occupations. The National-Socialist State does not recognize any "social classes" and seeks a class-free society. Politically speaking, it recognizes only two groups: "citizens" who have fully equal rights and fully equal obligations, and "subjects" who belong to the State but have no political rights at all.

The National-Socialists do not see it as the trade-union's task to bring certain members of the people into a union in order to gradually transform them into a class that would later fight against other groups which were organized in a similar way. We would never give trade-unions such a mission. But, this was exactly the task assigned to unions the moment they became a tool in the fight of Marxism. A trade-union does not automatically mean "class struggle", but Marxism has turned it into a tool for its own class struggle. It has created this economic weapon which is used by the international world Jew to crush the economic foundation of free and independent national states, and it is used to further the goals of their own national industries and their national trade deals, and finally they use it to enslave free nations into the service of the Jewish super-state of world-finance. (*The Jewish super-state refers to the idea that Jews exist in all major countries, thereby creating a virtual mass state of their own—an extension of the Jewish state within a state idea.*)

In contrast to this, the National-Socialist trade-union must organize groups who participate in the national economic process so that we can increase the safety of the national economy and strengthen its power. We will take corrective actions by removing all those abuses that, in the long run, have a destructive influence on the national community, and those elements that harm the living strength of the people's community and of the state, and we will not overlook those elements that bring destruction and disaster on the economic structure itself.

For the National-Socialist trade-unions, the worker's strike is not a way to destroy or undermine national production, but instead serves to increase and improve it by fighting all those anti-social imperfections which interfere with economic productivity and harm the existence of the people as a whole. An individual's capacity to contribute stands side by side with his legal and social standing in the economic process. This alone shows him how necessary his contribution to the community is towards creating his own prosperity. The National-Socialist employee must understand that the prosperity of the national economic structure means his own material prosperity. The National-Socialist employer must understand that the happiness and the contentment of his employees form the foundation for the development of his own economic strength.

National-Socialist employees and employers are both officer and trustee of the entire national community. They are granted a high degree of personal liberty in their work because experience has shown that when a man is given extensive freedom, his capacity for work increases greatly, much more than it does by coercion from above. Lack of freedom prevents the natural process of elimination from occurring which blocks the promotion of the most capable, able, and diligent people.

The National-Socialist trade-union sees the worker's strike as a method that can, and probably must, be used as long as there is no National-Socialist racially-orientated state. When the National-Socialist State is established, however, it must take over the responsibility for legal protection and eliminate struggles between the employers and employees. This struggle only decreases production and it is harmful to the community. The Central Economic Council will settle disputes and it must maintain a functioning national economy where defects and errors within the system, which are harmful to the economy, are eliminated. Issues today which are decided through the struggles of millions, will in the future be settled in meetings of the Central Economic Council. Then, employers and employees will not fight against each other in their battle over wages, which only damages their mutual economic interests. They will solve these problems together, guided by a higher authority, while constantly considering the well-being of the people and the State which will be in glowing letters as it constantly shines down upon their work.

The iron principle that the Fatherland comes first and then the Party must always apply. The task of the National-Socialist trade-union is to educate and prepare everyone to work together and to maintain and protect our people and their State. This will be done by each individual according to the abilities, capacities, and powers which are either inherent or taught by the community of the nation.

The fourth question: "How can we establish such trade-unions?" seems more difficult to answer. Generally, it is easier to organize something new than to fix something old. It is easy to start a new business in a town where that certain business does not exist. It is more difficult to start that same business if a similar business already exists in the town. It is even more difficult if the economy will only support one of the businesses. Survival would require the new business organizers to not only introduce their own new business, but they must also destroy the older established business so they can continue to exist. Creating a National-Socialist trade-union is senseless if there are other unions operating side by side. Our union must be totally convinced that it alone is necessary to distribute its World-Concept ; it must not tolerate other similar or hostile organizations, and it must emphasize its own importance—it is necessary to the exclusion of all other organizations. There must be no common arrangements and no compromise with similar organizations. We must maintain the absolute, sole right to exist.

There were only two ways that could lead to such a development:

1. We could organize our own trade-union and then, gradually, fight against the international Marxist trade-unions, or
2. We could infiltrate the Marxist trade-unions and try to indoctrinate them with the new spirit of our movement to transform them into followers of our new ideas.

The following problems prevented us from taking the first course of action. Our financial troubles were still rather considerable at that time and we had very little money at our disposal. The gradually-increasing inflation made the situation even more difficult in those years. The increasing inflation made it impossible to say that the trade-unions gave any financial advantage to their members. From the individual worker's point of view, there was no reason to pay dues to the trade-union at all. The already-existing Marxist unions were near collapse until millions of marks fell into their lap because of the brilliant Ruhr-action of Mr. Cuno. (*Wilhelm Cuno was Chancellor of Germany from 1922 to 1923. He is known for promoting passive resistance, or non-work at mines etc., in the occupied territory against the French after they invaded the Ruhr and for creating hyperinflation in Germany by paying the workers to not work.*) This so-called national Reich Chancellor may be titled the savior of the Marxist trade-unions.

In those days, we could not count on receiving such financial aid. No one had any incentive to join a new trade-union which could offer him no advantages because of its own financial weakness. I also had to object strongly to creating a new organization if it would provide nothing more than a plush job with little work to brilliant men. The question of personnel played a very important role. At that time, I did not know of a single man I would have trusted to tackle this huge task. Anyone who could have crushed the Marxist trade-unions in those days and could have replaced their institution of destructive class war by helping the idea of National-Socialist trade-unions to victory would be a man who belonged to the really great men of our nation. A carved bust of him would have needed to find a place in the Valhalla at Regensburg for the sake of posterity. (*Regensburg is a Bavarian city where the Walhalla Temple is located, which is a hall-of-fame type building in classic Roman style built in 1807 to commemorate great figures of the German race/ethnicity in history. It includes a marble interior with busts of famous people.*)

Unfortunately, I did not know of any head that would have been appropriate on such a pedestal. We must not be misled by the fact that the international trade-unions were run by men of only average intelligence. This means nothing because when their groups were created, there were no other organizations in existence. Today, the National-Socialist movement must fight against a gigantic organization that has been in existence for a long time and has developed itself in every detail. A conqueror must always be a greater genius than the defender he wishes to defeat. It is possible today to maintain the fortress of the Marxist trade-union with the help of ordinary bigwigs, yet it can only be stormed by the great energy and brilliant capacity of an overwhelmingly greater man on the other side. If such a great man cannot be found, then it is useless to argue with Fate, and it is even more foolish to force the issue and charge ahead using men who are poor substitutes for greatness.

Here, we must apply the principle that in life, it is sometimes better to let a matter rest for the time being than to start it only halfway or begin badly because of the lack of proper forces. In addition to this, there was another consideration that should not be dismissed. Then and now, I had the firm conviction that it is dangerous to combine a great political world-philosophical fight with economic matters, particularly in the early stages. This is especially true with our German people. An economic struggle will immediately redirect energy away from the political battle. As soon as the people believe that their new economy will allow them to buy a little house, they will devote themselves exclusively to this task. Then they have no more time for a political battle against those who plan to someday, one way or another, take away from these people the pennies they have saved. Instead of fighting in a political battle for the insight and convictions they have gained, they become totally absorbed in their dream of a cottage settlement. In the end, they find themselves sitting between the chairs. (*A reference to a German saying, "Trying to sit on all of the chairs and ending up sitting between them", which actually means "Torn between conflicting interests". However, here it more specifically means "Torn between two interests and ending up with nothing", or "Not sitting on a chair at all".*)

Today, the National-Socialist movement has just begun its struggle. To a large degree, it still has to form and to perfect the image of its World-Concept . It must fight with all its energy to make its great ideals a reality. Success is only possible if the complete power of its collective being is, without reservation, used in the service of this battle. Today, we have a classic example of how a people who have been completely distracted by economic problems will become paralyzed and lose their fighting strength. The Revolution of November, 1918 was not caused by trade-unions, but it prevailed in spite of them. The German privileged-class will not fight for the future of Germany in a political battle because it believes the future is secured adequately through building up the economy.

We should learn from such experiences because the same thing would happen to us if we focused on economic concerns too strongly. The more we gather the complete strength of our movement together for the political battle, the sooner we can count on success in all aspects. The more we prematurely take upon ourselves the load of trade-unions, housing problems, etc., the less our cause will advance as a whole. It is true that these objectives are important, but they can only be realized on a large scale once we are in a position to press the public power into the service of this idea. Until that time, these problems would only paralyze the movement and the earlier it tries to solve them, the worse the condition would become because these economic distractions would lessen its world-political ambitions. This could easily result in the trade-union interests guiding the political movement instead of the World-Concept forcing the trade-unions to march along with it.

However, a National-Socialist trade-union can only benefit the movement and our people if it has already been influenced by our World-Concept and national ideas so strongly that there is no danger of it following Marxist ways. If our National-Socialist trade-union saw its mission as merely competing with the Marxist trade-unions, it would be worse than having no trade-union at all. The National-Socialist trade-union must declare war against the Marxist trade-union, not only as an organization, but, above all, as an idea. In striking at the Marxist union, our trade-union must also challenge their promotion of the class struggle and even the very class idea and set them aside so that we can become the guardian of the professional and occupational interests of German citizens.

All these points made a clear argument against the organization of our own trade-unions, at least, until an individual suddenly appeared who was obviously called by Fate to solve this very problem.

So, there remained only two other possibilities: We could recommend to our own Party members that they quit the trade-unions or recommend that they remain there and cause as much damage as possible. Generally, I recommended the second choice.

We could easily make this recommendation without much difficulty in 1922 to 1923. During that time, there were no financial advantages offered by the trade-unions due to the high economic inflation rate. This meant that even though our membership was not yet very large—because the movement was so new—our small number of members were still able to cause a great deal of damage. The National-Socialist believers were the severest critics of the Marxist trade-unions and, in spite of our small numbers, we still caused a lot of damage within the unions.

In those days, I turned down any suggestion that we attempt an experiment that was obviously doomed to failure. I would have considered it a crime to take money in the form of union-dues from the meager earnings of a worker to support an institution—our trade-union—when I was not convinced our union could give its members some kind of advantage.

When a new political party disappears, it is not a disaster, but almost always a benefit, and no one has a right to complain because the contributions of an individual to a political movement are given without any expectation of receiving something in return. But, anyone who pays his dues to a trade-union has a right to expect the benefits which have been promised to him. If organizers do not see this responsibility, then the organizers of such a trade-union are, if not swindlers, then at least reckless men who must be held accountable.

This is the view that guided our actions in 1922. There were others who apparently knew better than we did and they organized their own trade-unions. They criticized us for not having one because they saw it as the most obvious proof of our mistaken ideas and limited insight. But it was not long before these organizations disappeared. The end result was exactly as we predicted, but with one difference: in the end, we had not deceived ourselves or anybody else.

13. GERMAN ALLIANCE POLICIES AFTER THE WAR

The inconsistency and failure to establish sound guiding principles in creating foreign alliances by the leaders of the Reich not only continued after the Revolution, it became worse. Before the war, a general confusion in political ideas caused our state foreign affairs leadership to be very poor. Then, after the war, it was poor because of a plain lack of honest desire for such a policy. It was obvious the groups that had finally achieved their destructive aims by the Revolution were not interested in a policy of alliances which would have strengthened Germany and restored a free German State. Such a development would have contradicted the purpose of the November crime. Not only would it have interrupted or even ended the process of making the German economy and workers dependent on other nations, which was the internationalization of Germany, but beyond that, the political effect within Germany resulting from a battle to make Germany free from dependence on foreign countries would have had disastrous consequences later on for the present representatives of the Reich's government. What they feared the most was any effort that would make the Reich independent of foreign countries. Such an effort could eventually be disastrous to those in power who needed to make the country as dependent on international elements as possible.

A revolution within a nation can never occur unless it is preceded by a period where strong national sentiment is built up and the people's patriotic spirit is nationalized to a fevered pitch. Conversely, huge foreign policy successes have repercussions among the people which can also create patriotic feelings and therefore have the same result. It has been proven by experience that every battle for liberty leads to an increase in self-awareness of national spirit, which is an increase in patriotism. This leads the people to be much more sensitive to elements that are anti-national or trends that appear anti-patriotic. Such trends or people which are tolerated or even ignored during peace times are suddenly met with rejection and resistance in times when national enthusiasm is stirred up, and this often proves to be fatal to those anti-national elements. We only have to look back at the widespread spy-scare that suddenly explodes in the feverish heat of human passions when war breaks out. This kind of patriotic spirit frequently leads to brutal and unjust persecutions during war-time, even though everyone should see that the danger of espionage is even greater during the long years of peace, but no one pays attention to it during those relaxed times.

The parasites which were washed to the surface by the events of November, with their fine instincts alone, have seen in their future the possible destruction of their own criminal existence. If our nation were backed by a wise policy of foreign alliance, it would move the country toward freedom and sovereignty, which would kindle the national passions and this patriotism would result in the end of these parasites. Knowing this, we can now understand why, since 1918, the foreign policy of our "responsible" government officials has always failed and why the national government constantly and intentionally works against the real interests of the German nation. At first this appears to have no purpose, but when it is studied more closely, we see the logical pursuit of a policy adopted in the 1918 November Revolution.

Admittedly, it is necessary to differentiate between those leaders responsible, or rather, those who "should have been responsible" for our national affairs, the average member of our parliament, and the large, stupid flock of our own people who have sheep-like patience.

Some know what they want. The others just follow along either knowingly or because they are too cowardly to fight ruthlessly against something they recognize as harmful. The last group is submissive because of their lack of understanding and their stupidity.

Problems regarding foreign policy were considered by some of our followers to be minor as long as the National-Socialist German Workers' Party was a small and little-known society. This is because our movement must, and always has proclaimed that external national freedom is never given as a gift by heavenly or earthly powers, but it can only be the fruit that results from inner strength of the nation. The external battle for liberty will only happen after we remove the cause of our collapse and those who benefit from the nation's destruction. From this standpoint, it is easy to understand why, during the first days of the young movement, the questions of foreign policy took second place to the vital aims for domestic reform.

However, as soon as the scope of this little, insignificant club grew and finally blew up into the importance of a large association, it became immediately necessary to outline a program about foreign policy. Standards had to be established, which were not only in harmony with our World-Concept , but they also had to flow from of our way of thinking and expand it into foreign affairs.

The lack of foreign policy training among our people creates an obligation for the young movement to educate our internal leaders and the large masses so that they understand the broad ideas behind our foreign policy aims. This is the first step toward carrying out our foreign policy plans which must prepare the nation to regain our people's freedom and to recover real economic sovereignty for the Reich.

An essential principle must always guide us: Foreign policy is just a means to an end and its purpose is exclusively the improvement of our own nation. It is impossible to decide any question in the area of foreign policy from any viewpoint other than this one: Is it now, or will it be in the future, beneficial to our people or will it be harmful to them?

This is the only question that must have any weight in making decisions. Party politics, religious considerations, humanitarian ideals, and all other viewpoints must be completely disregarded.

Before the war, it was the task of German foreign policy to assure that our people and their children on this planet received the food and supplies they needed by opening a path that would lead to this goal and win the needed allies who could also provide additional forces needed in the war. Today's task is the same with one difference: Before the war, the aim was the preservation of the ethnic German people through the forces of the independent power of the State which existed at that time, but today we must give the people strength by reestablishing an independent state power. This power is the basis for any practical foreign policy that aims to preserve, foster, and nourish our people in days to come.

In other words, the aim of Germany's foreign policy today must be to prepare for regaining freedom tomorrow.

To accomplish our goal, we must remember this fundamental principle: The chance of regaining independence for a people does not depend on unifying a territory or region, but it depends more on the existence of at least a small part of those people, and they must have the necessary freedom and capability to take over the leadership of the spiritual union of their people and to make the necessary preparations for a military battle to win their freedom.

If one hundred million men together accept the yoke of slavery in order to prevent the breakup of their state territories, that is worse than if this government and people had been crushed, leaving only a part of them enjoying full liberty in a smaller territory. At least this is true if this last group has a vision of its holy mission and it constantly proclaims its spiritual and cultural unity with those they are separated from, and it is ready to prepare the weapons needed for a final liberation so they can reunite with the unfortunate oppressed parts of their community.

We also must remember that regaining lost territories, which once belonged to the people of a state, primarily requires regaining political power and independence for the mother country. In other words, the desire to regain lost territories must be ruthlessly postponed, and the primary interest of regaining liberty for the main territory of the country must be the only immediate goal. The liberation of oppressed and cut-off splinters of a nation—or of provinces of an empire—cannot be accomplished through a strong desire by the oppressed population or through a heartfelt protest by those who have been left behind; it is accomplished only through the power of the surviving pieces of the sovereign Fatherland.

Therefore, the first step in regaining lost territories is the intensive development and the strengthening of that part of the State which remains. The people must be motivated and filled with unwavering resolve so that, when the time comes, they will use the entirety of the newly-earned power they have created to liberate and unify the entire nation! We must ignore the interests of the lost territory for it is secondary to the one interest, which is to gain the needed political power and strength that will be required to correct that which has been done by the enemy. Oppressed lands are not brought back into the lap of a common Reich by fiery protests, but by a mighty sword.

It is the responsibility of the national leaders to forge that sword through their foreign policy. The purpose of this foreign policy must be the securing of weapons and finding allies.

Previously, I discussed the half-hearted policy of alliances which was pursued before the war. Of the four possible ways of preserving and feeding our nation, the fourth and least practical was the one chosen. Instead of a sound European territorial expansion policy, we concentrated on expanding colonies and making trade agreements with other countries. What made this even worse was the leadership's way of thinking; they believed these policies would help them avoid any armed conflict. They tried to sit on all the chairs at the same time and the result was the proverbial fall between the chairs. The First World War was only the final bill marked payment-due which was presented to the Reich in testimony of its ill-conceived foreign policy.

Even at that time, the third path would have been the right one: strengthening the power on the European continent by winning new territory, which would make solving colonial problems more practical and easier at a later time. We could have only achieved this policy either through an alliance with England or through an abnormal strengthening of military power, but that would require us to ignore cultural development for forty to fifty years. Even so, one could have taken the responsibility for such a plan of military expansion if it were necessary to assure independence. The cultural importance of a nation is almost always derived from its political freedom and independence. Independence is required in order for great culture to exist or even be established. No sacrifice is too great if it maintains the political independence of a nation. Whatever is withdrawn from cultural development today, and diverted to an exceptionally strong development of military powers, will later be fully paid back. It is safe to say that after such a concentrated effort toward preserving the independence of a nation, it is usually offset afterwards as the nation becomes at ease and relaxed. This relief of pressure generates an astonishing situation where the previously neglected cultural energies of the nation flourish. The distress of the Persian wars led to the bloom of the Periclean Age, and even in between the Punic wars, the Roman State began to devote itself to the service of a higher culture. (*The Periclean Age, or the Golden Age, is a period in ancient Grecian history which began after the end of the Persian Wars in 448 B.C. Pericles was an outstanding personality in politics, philosophy, architecture, sculpture, and literature. The Punic Wars were between Rome and Carthage and were one of the largest wars up to that time in the ancient world. The wars ended in 146 B.C.*)

It is true that putting all the interests of a nation in the background in order to focus on the one task of preparing for a coming war and fighting for the future protection of the State, is a decision which cannot be trusted to a majority of parliamentary fools and good-for-nothings. The father of Frederick the Great was able to prepare for war by ignoring everything else, but the Jewish brand of fathers participating in our parliamentary foolishness are not able to do what is needed. Because of this failure, preparing arms in order to acquire new land in Europe could only be done in moderation during the prewar days; that is why we could not advise against accepting the help of proper allies.

Since they did not like the idea of systematically preparing for war, they quit thinking about acquiring new territory in Europe. By turning to the development of colonies and trade policies, they sacrificed any possibility of forming an alliance with England, but then, the next logical thing to do would have been to seek support from Russia if we could not ally with England, and that too was ignored. Deserted by all would-be allies except the Hapsburg shysters, we finally stumbled into the

First World War.

The character of our present foreign policy shows no evidence of a plan or standards at all. Before the War, the fourth method was wrongly chosen and then it was pursued only half-heartedly. After the Revolution, there is no evidence that any plan was applied to foreign policy no matter how closely we look. There is less careful planning today than there was before the War, except possibly for the plans attempting to crush the last chance we have to make our nation rise again.

A cold, unprejudiced review of the distribution of power in Europe of today leads to the following conclusions:

For the last three hundred years, the history of our continent has been decisively influenced by England's attempt, in roundabout ways, to maintain the balance of power among European countries which ensures no one becomes too powerful and she has the necessary protective covering for her great world political aims. Since the days of Queen Elizabeth, British diplomacy has traditionally been deliberately aimed at preventing, by any means necessary, the rise of any European country beyond the scope of an established balance of power. If necessary, any rising power would be blocked by military force. The path of British diplomacy can be compared to Germany's traditional use of the Prussian army.

England used whatever methods were called for by the situation, but the iron will and the determination to use these methods were always the same. As England's position became more difficult over time and the mutual rivalry grew over the individual greatness of countries, the more the British government felt it necessary to paralyze the powers in Europe. The political fracture of the former North American colonies from England led to an even more concentrated effort to maintain its support in Europe. After England crushed Spain and the Netherlands as great sea powers, the efforts of the British State were concentrated against the rising power of France. (*There were four Anglo-Dutch wars but this reference is most likely about Britain's defeat of the Dutch Navy in the Battle of Camperdown, 1797, during the French Revolutionary Wars, and the French Navy and Spanish Navy in the Battle of Trafalgar, 1805, during the Napoleonic Wars.*) Finally, with the fall of Napoleon I, the danger of a domination from this military power appeared to be definitely broken and this had been the most dangerous threat to England.

The position of British statesmanship changed very slowly before eventually developing a hostile attitude towards Germany. For a time, the German nation's lack of any internal unity presented no obvious threat to England. Also, public opinion, which is influenced in a certain direction by government propaganda, is rather slow in changing attitudes toward the new objective. The sober realization the statesmen developed was taken and converted into an emotional sentiment of the people, and this sentiment is stronger in its effect and does not change over time. A statesman can redirect his thoughts toward new aims immediately after he has reached his goal; however, the masses can only be won over as tools of the new idea presented by their leadership through the slow work of propaganda.

By 1870-71, England had already taken a definite new position. Unfortunately, Germany did not take advantage of the occasional waverings in England that were caused by America's growing importance in world economics and Russia's development of political power. The failure of Germany to act at this critical time allowed the historic tendency of British policy to become more and more firmly established.

England came to regard Germany as a power whose influence in trade and world politics, which resulted from her enormous industrial build-up, was growing frighteningly fast. The two countries began to contend with each other in certain areas. The conquest of the world by "peaceful economic expansion", which appeared to our statesmen to be the last and greatest word in wisdom, became Britain's reason to organize resistance against us. This resistance assumed the form of a well-organized attack which was totally consistent with their statesmanship because their aims were never maintaining world-peace, but strengthening British world dominion. England's effort to secure as allies all the states that could eventually provide military assistance was the natural result of her traditional caution in estimating the strength of her opponent and her own weakness at the time. This cannot be termed as "unscrupulous" because the organization for war must not be judged by heroic standards, but by how efficient it is in reaching the goal. It is not the task of diplomacy to see that a nation dies heroically, but to make certain it survives using any practical means available. Every road that leads toward that goal of survival is valid, and failure to follow that path is a criminal neglect of duty.

With the Revolution in Germany, the British's worries about a threatening German world domination ended in redemption, and the British felt their fears had been justified. However, at that time, England had no interest in seeing Germany completely exterminated from the map of Europe. On the contrary, the disastrous collapse of November, 1918 put British diplomacy face to face with a new situation that at first had seemed impossible.

For four and a half years, the British Empire fought to break an alleged superior continental power. All of a sudden, a total collapse occurred that seemed to wipe out this power entirely. The lack of even the most primitive spirit of self-preservation became so apparent that within forty-eight hours the European balance of power seemed to have been taken off its hinges. Germany was destroyed and France became the strongest political power in Europe.

The huge amount of propaganda that was spread during the War, influencing the British people to persevere and maintain their ground and at the same time greatly incited them by stirring up primitive instincts and passions, now became a lead weight restricting the British statesmen's power to make decisions. The British achieved their war aim when Germany's colonial, economic, and trade policies were destroyed, but anything beyond this was harmful to British interests. Only England's enemies would profit by wiping out German power in continental Europe. In spite of all this, from November of 1918 until late in the Summer of 1919, the position of British diplomacy was fixed and immovable. A sudden change was not possible because the emotional strength of the masses had been exploited more than ever during the long war, and the temperament of the military powers had been established firmly. France had taken the opportunity into her own hands and was in a position to dictate orders to everyone else. Germany was the only power that might have brought about a change during those months of bargaining and negotiating, but she was in the middle of civil war. Germany announced through her mouthpiece statesmen repeatedly that she was ready to accept each and any dictate imposed on her.

If one nation ceases to be an "active" ally because its spirit of self-preservation disappears, it usually degenerates into a nation of slaves and its country becomes more like a colony. In order to prevent the power of France from becoming too great in Europe, England had no other choice than to participate in France's lust for more and more of what they could take.

In fact, England failed to achieve her war aim. The rise of a European state beyond the balance of power among the countries of Europe had not been prevented, but firmly established.

In 1914, Germany, as a military state, was wedged in between two countries—one of them being equal in military power, the other having greater military power. Then, we faced the superior strength of England on the sea. France and Russia were the only countries who placed obstacles in Germany's path and excessively resisted the development of Germany's expansion. In addition to this, the unfavorable geographic position of the Reich, from a military point of view, created a safety-factor which prevented an excessive increase in our country's power. The coastline was also unfavorable for military battle with England because it was small and cramped, but, the battlefront of the interior was wide open to the other countries.

France's position is very different today. From a military standpoint, she is the greatest power, without any serious rival on the European continent. Her borders in the south near Spain and Italy are protected. She is protected against Germany by the helplessness of our Fatherland. The French coastline runs in a long front parallel to the vital nerve center of the British Empire. Not only are these British centers potentially important targets for airplanes and long-range artillery, but most of British trade would be wide open to the danger of submarines. A submarine war would have disastrous effects because France has an advantage with the long stretch of the Atlantic coast and the equally long stretches of the French territories bordering on the Mediterranean in Europe and North Africa where they have military bases.

So, the political result of the battle against Germany's developing power was the creation of French dominance on the continent. The military result was the consolidation of France as the greatest military power on land and the acknowledgment of the American Union as an equally strong sea power. The economic result was the surrender of large areas of British influence to their former allies. To the same degree that traditional British political aims wanted to see Europe broken apart into smaller units, France strove to break Germany into smaller parts. England's long-term desire is to prevent the rise of one continental power to world importance above others. They want to maintain a certain balance of power among the European states because this is what is required for British world domination.

France has always wanted to prevent Germany from becoming a united power by maintaining the system of small German states with well-balanced military powers and no central unified leadership, and they want to occupy the left bank of the Rhine which is essential in order to secure her dominance in Europe. The ultimate aims of French diplomacy will forever be in opposition to the ultimate aims of British statesmanship.

From the previous point of view, anyone who examines the present alternatives for countries that can ally with Germany must be convinced that the only possible connection we can make is with England. Although the results of British policies during the war have been disastrous for Germany, we must not overlook the fact that England is no longer interested in completely crushing Germany. On the contrary, as the gears of British policy turn in the years ahead, it is bound to aim more and more at inhibiting the endless French desire for dominance. An alliance can never be made by looking at past disagreements, but alliances are made productive by the knowledge gained from past experience. And, experience should have taught us all that alliances with negative goals are inherently weak. The Fate of nations become welded together by the promise of common success in the sense of common gains, mutual conquests, and in short, an expansion of power for both allies.

It is obvious that our people are not accustomed to thinking in terms of foreign policy. When our people read current press reports concerning the great "friendliness toward Germany" displayed by various foreign statesmen, the people assume these individuals have an attitude toward our people that somehow guarantees they will support us politically. This is incredibly foolish and an example of the unparalleled simplicity of the average small-minded middle-class German who dabbles in politics. There is not a single British, American, or Italian statesman who could be called "pro-German". As a statesman, every Englishman is, of course, an Englishman first; an American is an American first, and no Italian will ever be ready to pursue a policy that is not pro-Italian. Therefore, anyone who expects to build up alliances with foreign nations because they feel there is a pro-German attitude among their statesman is either an ass or a deceiver. The fates of nations are never linked together by mutual respect or even affection, but only because both nations expect to gain something useful. For instance, an English statesman will always pursue policy that benefits the English and never one that benefits the Germans. Yet, it is possible that some particular elements of this pro-English policy are identical to pro-German interests. This unity may only exist to a certain degree and it may someday change; however, this is where a statesman will show his masterful hand. If he wants to carry out plans vital to his own nation, he will, when necessary, find those partners who must travel the same road in order to promote their own interests.

Knowing all of this, we can now focus on a result that will benefit us the most and this can be found in the answers to the following questions. What countries currently do not want to see France's military and economic power increase until it attains absolute domination, which would be the result if the German influence in Central Europe is eliminated? Based on their current situation and their traditional policy up to now, what other countries will see the rise of France as a threat to their own future?

One must be perfectly clear about this matter: France is and remains the unappeasable enemy of the German people. Whoever rules or will reign in the future in France, whether they are Bourbons, Jacobins, bourgeois followers of Napoleon, clerical Republicans, or red Bolsheviks, the final aim of their foreign policy will always be to take possession of the frontier along the Rhine river and to make this river secure for France by breaking up Germany and keeping it broken.

England does not desire Germany as a world power, however, France does not want a Germany at all, as a world power or not. There is a big difference in these two ideas! Today, however, we are not fighting to regain our position as a world power because we have to struggle for the very existence of our Fatherland, for our national unity, and for the daily bread of our children. When we look around from this standpoint in search for European allies, only two countries are left for us—England and Italy.

England has no desire to see a major power develop in France, whose military fist is unrestrained by the rest of Europe, and who can implement a policy which sooner or later is bound to clash with British interests. England can never desire to see France in possession of the huge western European iron and coal mines because that could easily give the French a dangerous economic world position. Furthermore, England can never desire a France whose political status on the continent is so well protected that it can begin expanding French world policy. This will not only become possible by crushing the rest of Europe, but inevitable. If France pursued this policy, the old Zeppelin bombers might be multiplied a thousand times every night. (*Germany attempted to use Zeppelins in the First World War as bomb and gun platforms, but they proved to be very vulnerable to gunfire. Only thirteen crafts existed at the start of the war and five of those were shot down before their offensive use was abandoned.*) France's military power presses greatly on the heart of Great Britain's world empire.

Italy cannot desire to see the French control of Europe strengthened. Italy's future will always be affected by changes in the territories close to the Mediterranean basin. Italy's motive for entering the War was not a desire to make France more powerful, but it joined the War to give a deathblow to her hated rivals along the Adriatic Sea. Any further increase in France's strength on the continent will hinder Italy in the future. We would be deceiving ourselves if we believed that any kind of kinship which exists among the nations would eliminate rivalries.

A cool and unbiased analysis shows that England and Italy are the two states whose own natural interests are the least opposed to the existence of a German nation and, to a certain degree, their goals are along the same path as Germany's goals.

In evaluating our options for an alliance, we must remember three things. The first one lies within ourselves, the other two with England and Italy.

Can you imagine any state wanting to be an ally with the Germany of today? How can a country wanting to pursue their own aggressive goals possibly ally itself with a state whose leadership has for years presented a picture of the most deplorable weakness and shown themselves to be pacifist cowards? Who would want to ally with people whose participation in the Marxist delusion has caused them to blatantly betray the interests of their own people and country? How could any power that hoped to unite in a fight for joint interests someday, expect to enter into a valuable relationship with a state that apparently lacks all courage and has no desire to lift even one finger to defend its own life? Will any power that sees an alliance as something more than a treaty to maintain a steady state of decay, like the disastrous former Triple-Alliance, risk its very existence by obligating itself to a state that has shown its character by creeping into a corner in shy submission from those forces outside the country and shameful oppression of nationalistic virtues at home? Will a world power risk an alliance with a state that has lost all greatness since it no longer deserves it, a government that cannot even boast of respect by its own citizens, or leaders who find no greater admiration in other countries? No, never.

A power that has any self-respect and expects more from an alliance than to pay commissions to interest-hungry parliamentarians will not enter any agreement with the Germany of today; this is something they simply cannot do. After all, our present unfit condition for any alliance is the main and ultimate reason for the unity of our enemies who are dominating over us. Germany never fights back except by a few fiery protests from our parliamentary elite. The rest of the world has no reason to fight for our protection. As a matter of principle, God never liberates cowardly people, no matter what the continued whining of our patriotic societies may claim—the fight for freedom is the obligation of the states themselves. Even those countries that do not directly seek our complete destruction see no other option except to participate in France's looting expeditions. They can at least prevent France from gaining all of the spoils by agreeing and participating in the robbery.

Secondly, we can see that it would be difficult to change the attitude of the majority of people in former enemy countries. After all, they have been influenced by mass propaganda to think a certain way. It is impossible to condemn a nation as "Huns", "Robbers", "Vandals", etc., for years and then suddenly discover the opposite is true and recommend their previous enemy as a future ally.

Even more attention must be paid to a third fact that will be essential in future European alliances. While it is not in England's interest to crush Germany any further, such a fall greatly interests the Jews of international finance. The difference between the official or rather, the traditional British statesmanship and the leading Jewish financial powers, can be seen clearly by looking at the different attitudes about British foreign policy. The Jewry of finance wants to see the complete economic destruction of Germany and her absolute political enslavement. This is contrary to England's welfare interests. The internationalization of our German economic system, by transferring control of German working strength into the possession of Jewish world finance, can only be completed through a state that is politically Bolshevik. However, in order for the Marxist shock troops of the international Jewish capitalists to finally break the backbone of the German National State, it needs the kind cooperation from outside forces.

Therefore, they must have France's armies storm the structure of the German State and continue to batter it until the Reich falls victim to the Bolshevik soldiers controlled by the Jew of international world of finance. Today, the Jew is the driving force behind the complete destruction of Germany. Wherever in the world we read offensive articles about Germany, the Jews have manufactured them. During peacetime, as well as during the war, the Jewish financial and Marxist press intentionally incited the hatred against Germany until one state after another gave up its neutrality and joined the World War coalition, ignoring the real interests of their people in the process.

The thought process of the Jew is clear. The conversion of Germany to a Bolshevik State requires the extermination of the nationalistic ethnic German intelligent sector and then the exploitation of German workers under the yoke of Jewish world finance. This is just the beginning, then the Jewish strategy for conquering the world will spread further. As it has happened so often in history, Germany is again right in the middle of the huge struggle. If our people and our state become victims of these money-obsessed Jewish bloody tyrants, then the whole world will be ensnared by this octopus. If Germany succeeds in liberating herself from its clutches, the greatest danger facing all the nations of the world can be considered smashed. We can be certain the Jews will undermine our efforts as much as possible in order to maintain or increase the hatred of the world toward Germany. The interests of the nations that are being poisoned are hidden from their own eyes so that they are confused by the Jewish press and do not realize that they are not acting in their people's real interests. In general, Jewry will fight in different nations using different weapons. The Jew chooses the weapon that appears to be the most powerful based on how the people in that particular nation think and he always chooses the weapons that promise the most success.

Our own national body lies severely torn from the standpoint of "blood" (*meaning the Aryan race is split, and the bloodline is impure*). Jewry uses this condition to spread a pacifist way of thinking through these "cosmopolitan" circles (*cosmopolitan means "world-citizen" or Jewish*) in their battle to gain power, which comes from their international ideologies. In France, its weapon is easily recognized and they have evaluated its power correctly, it is the fanatical patriotism of the French. In England, its weapon is the economic and world-political viewpoints. In short, the Jew always employs a method that targets the way the respective nation thinks. Only after it has achieved a certain overshadowing influence in economic and political power can it throw off the shackles of such traditional weapons so it may operate unrestricted. This is when it reveals its true intentions and the goals it is fighting for. The destruction then progresses more and more quickly—it destroys state after state, creating the ruins on which the sovereignty of the eternal Jewish Empire is to be established.

In England, as well as in Italy, the difference between the views of the old and more solid statesmanship, and the goals of the Jewish financial world is so obvious and even crude, it jumps out at your eye.

Today, only France shows a fundamental agreement between the intentions of the stock exchange, as represented by the Jews, and the desires of the fanatical patriotic members of their nation's statesmanship. The fact that both views are along the same lines constitutes a huge danger for Germany. For this reason, France is and will remain absolutely the worst enemy of Germany. Because of its corruption by the negro and its agreement with the aims of the Jewish world dominion, France represents a constantly-lurking danger to the existence of the white race in Europe. The heart of Europe has been infected by negro blood on the Rhine. This corruption matches the sadistic perverse vindictiveness of this fanatically-patriotic, arch-enemy of our people; they are just like the icy-cold calculating Jew who uses this method to begin the bastardization process starting from the heart of Europe, and through infection by inferior people, they plan to deprive the white race of the foundations for a sovereign existence.

The present actions of France, which sprang from her own desire for vengeance and were carried out under the leadership of the Jews, is a sin against the existence of the white man. Someday, their actions will cause all the avenging spirits of a generation, which has recognized the degeneration of a race, to be unleashed on that nation for their sin against mankind.

For Germany, however, the danger posed by the French means we have a duty to forget about bad feelings of the past and join hands with those who are also threatened as long as they are unwilling to suffer or tolerate France's lust for power. In the foreseeable future, there will only be two possible allies for Germany: England and Italy.

If we bother to look back at Germany's foreign policy after the Revolution, we are shocked by the constant failures of our government. A man who sees the constant and incomprehensible decline of his government can only drop his head in despair or feel the beginning of an internal desire for a flaming rebellion against such a regime. These acts cannot be dismissed as the result of poor understanding. The mental Cyclops of our November parties have done things that would be inconceivable to anyone who had a working brain. (*The Cyclops has one eye; this reference means the parties are functioning on half a brain.*) They actually solicited France's favor. (*The reference to soliciting France's favor refers specifically to a parliamentarian named Walther Rathenau, who was The Foreign Minister of Germany at the time and a Jew with some connection to the Freemasons. He met with representatives of French industrialists where he made a number of agreements in 1922.*) Yes, indeed, with touching simplicity only seen in these visionaries, who never seem to learn, they have repeatedly tried to offer themselves to France. They have bowed to the "great nation" and, in every cunning trick of the French executioner, they thought they saw the first signs of France's change of heart. The actual puppeteers behind our politics were not so foolish. For them, the pursuit of France's affection was nothing more than a means to block every effort that could lead to a sound alliance policy. They were never in the dark about the aims of France and her backers. However, their cool calculation forced them pretend they honestly believed it was possible to change the Fate of Germany by cuddling up with France, otherwise our people would probably have chosen a different path.

It is not easy for us to present England to the rank and file of the Nationalist-Socialist movement as a possible future ally. Our Jewish press has been too successful in concentrating hate against England. Many good and stupid German gimpel willingly landed on the sticky twig which was specially pruned by the Jew to capture them. (*Gimpel is a German name for the bullfinch, little birds, also meaning one who is so extremely foolish they are saintly. The birds are known for becoming trapped on a species of tree with sticky branches.*) They chatted about "reviving" German naval power; they protested against the plunder of our colonies and recommended taking our colonies back. The Jewish scoundrel then took this information to his tribe in England so they can use it for their propaganda. It should by now become clear to even our privileged-class simpletons playing in politics that our fight is not over "power on the seas" etc. Even before the war, it was crazy to concentrate the forces of Germany on the sea without first protecting our position in Europe. In politics today, such foolishness is called a crime.

It often drives one to despair looking at the way Jewish puppeteers have successfully kept our people preoccupied with unimportant matters and agitating them into demonstrations and protests. While they were distracted, France carefully removed one piece after the other from the body of our nation, destroying the foundation of our independence.

I must mention one particular hobby-horse which the Jew rode with special skill during those years: South Tyrol. Yeah, South Tyrol. (*South Tyrol was part of the Austrian-Hungarian Empire and was annexed by Italy at the end of the First World War including ethnic German areas. Many Germans were angry at the loss of the territory; however, Hitler was not as concerned about it and considered the area unimportant. This annexation by Italy was not part of Wilson's Fourteen Points Plan for the division of territory, but nothing was done to stop it.*)

Can you not look at any of the faces of our intellectual fools and see the flame of utter indignation burning? If I take up this question here, at this point, I do so in order to settle an account with that same lying crowd which counts on the forgetfulness and the stupidity of the masses of our people. This group pretends they are upset over South Tyrol's loss, but the feeling of anger when it comes to abuses of the nation is more foreign to these parliamentary rascals than the idea of property rights is foreign to a magpie.

I wish to state here and now that I personally was one of those who actually defended this territory through my service in the army. The fate of South Tyrol was decided from early in August, 1914 until November, 1918. I did my share of fighting in those years not because I thought South Tyrol should be lost, but because I felt that South Tyrol, together with every other German territory, should be preserved as part of the Fatherland.

The parliamentary tramps took no part in the fighting. Not this gang of sneaking thieves who spent their time playing party politics instead. On the contrary, while we fought, believing that only victory could preserve South Tyrol for the German people, the mouths of these Ephialtes schemed and plotted so long against this victory until finally Siegfried yielded to the stab in the back.

(*Ephialtes was a soldier who betrayed the Spartan army. He is said to have told the Persians about the pass of Thermopylae around the mountains, which they used to attack in the Battle of Thermopylae in 480 B.C., so this reference means a traitor. This reference could also refer to a Greek Ephialtes who made major government changes, taking power away from some, and was assassinated as a result, which would mean a big talker who damages the government in this context. This is the second reference to Ephialtes so it is possible Hitler meant to balance the first mention with a second of a different person as an intellectual joke to see who would understand the second reference or if they would assume it meant the same as the first reference. Siegfried is a German way of saying 'the average Joe' or 'John Smith', or a Germanic German; it is the name of a character in Wagner operas but may have been used earlier as an 'everyman'.)*

The possession of South Tyrol by Germany was not guaranteed by the lying and inflammatory speeches from those elegantly-dressed parliamentarians on the Vienna City Hall Square or in front of the Field Marshalls' Hall in Munich, but only by the battalions fighting at the front. Those who broke up this front not only betrayed South Tyrol, but also betrayed all the other German territories. Anyone who believes today that the question of South Tyrol can be solved by protests, speeches, local parades, etc., is either especially mischievous or a typical German middle-class citizen.

It must be completely understood that, at this point, the lost territories will never be won back by prayers to the dear Lord or by pious hopes in a League of Nations, but only by force of arms. Therefore, there is only one question left to ask: Who is willing to regain the lost territories by armed force?

Personally, as far as I am concerned, I can assure anyone that I have enough courage to put myself at the head of a newly-formed parliamentary storm-battalion consisting of parliamentary chatterboxes and party leaders and their various counselors, who can all take part in the victorious conquest for South Tyrol. The Devil knows I would be glad if all of a sudden a shrapnel shell burst over the heads of these demonstrators in this "fiery" protest. I am convinced that if a fox broke into a henhouse, the cackling could not be any worse and the chickens could not run for safety any faster than what would occur at this "protest-rally".

The disgraceful part of it all is that these gentlemen know they cannot gain anything by such protests. They know better than anybody else that all their fuss is harmless and hopeless. They do it only because, naturally, it is easier to chatter about recovering South Tyrol today than it would have been at one time to fight for its preservation. Everyone does his part: then we sacrificed our blood; today these people sharpen their beaks.

It is pleasing to watch those in Vienna, who support the Monarchy system, when their comb swells up to express their outrage in their efforts to regain South Tyrol. Seven years ago, however, the noble and illustrious dynasty, the Royal House of evil—with the lying deceit that they are so proud of—is the very one that helped the world coalition take, among other things, South Tyrol. In those days, these same men were happy to support the policy of their treacherous Monarchy and did not care a bit about South Tyrol or anything else. Today, of course, the battle for these lands has become much easier. Now the battle is fought with "mental" weapons. It is much easier to talk oneself hoarse in a "protest meeting" expressing righteous anger or to get a sore finger writing newspaper articles than it is to blow up bridges during the occupation of the Ruhr territory. (*This is a reference to the saboteurs in the Ruhr after the First World War who blew up railroad tracks etc. after the French took control of the region.*)

The reason why certain groups recently made the question of "South Tyrol" the focus of German-Italian relationships is very obvious. Jews and supporters of the old Monarchy are deeply interested in preventing a German alliance policy that might eventually lead to the rebirth of a free German Fatherland. It is not the love for South Tyrol which prompts all these fake protests. These calls-to-action do not help the interests of South Tyrol, they harm them. What drives these people is not the hope of regaining South Tyrol, but it is the fear of a possible German-Italian agreement if tensions between our countries should subside.

The general tendency to lie and slander is part of the nature of these groups who coldly attempt to make themselves appear as if they are filled with impudence and pride and that their indignation implies we somehow "betrayed" South Tyrol. These gentlemen should be told as plainly as possible that, first, South Tyrol was "betrayed" by every healthy German who from 1914-1918 could not be found anywhere at the front or did not offer his services to the Fatherland. And second, South Tyrol was betrayed by everyone who failed to strengthen our nation's endurance so we could finish the war and those who failed to build up the determination of the people to see this struggle through to the end. Third, South Tyrol was betrayed by all of those who participated in the November Revolution, either by direct action or indirectly by cowardly tolerance of it. Those who allowed it to happen destroyed the only weapon that might have saved South Tyrol. In the fourth place, South Tyrol has been betrayed by all those political parties and their supporters who put their signatures to the treaties of shame: The Treaty of Versailles and St. Germaine. Yep, my "courageous" Mr. Word-protester, this is how things are! (*The Treaty of St. Germaine, 1919, between the Allies and the new Republic of Austria made vast territories independent or otherwise took them from Austria and included reparations to be paid by Austria.*)

Today, I am guided by the cool reasoning that lost territories cannot be conquered by the words of our parliamentarians, whose tongues are sharpened by constant babbling, but they can only be conquered by a sharp sword through a bloody battle. I do not hesitate to say that the die has now been cast and I believe it is impossible to regain South Tyrol through war. I would also personally decline to take such an action because I am convinced that it would be impossible to generate enough passionate national enthusiasm among the German people to guarantee a victory. On the contrary, I believe that if such blood has to be sacrificed, it would be a crime to do so for two hundred thousand Germans while next door seven million are suffering under a foreign regime and the vital lifeline of the German people has become the playground of hordes of African negroes (*meaning the occupation of the Ruhr where the French used black races in some areas as troops*).

If the German nation is to end a condition that threatens to exterminate it from Europe, it must not fall into the errors of the pre-war period and make enemies of God and the world. It must, instead, determine who the most dangerous enemy is and strike at him with concentrated force. If sacrifices in other areas must be made to achieve this victory, future generations of our people will not condemn us for it. The more glowing our success, the more they will be able to appreciate the serious distress we are under and the deep concern which leads to such a decision.

Today, we must be continuously guided by the principle that regaining lost territories is primarily a question of regaining the lost political independence and power for the mother country. A wise foreign policy that allows us to form strong alliances is the first step toward creating a powerful foreign policy for our State. We National-Socialists must be especially careful not to be taken in by our Jew-led privileged-class patriots who prefer to battle with words. Our movement will be in trouble if it indulges in protest speeches, like they do, instead of preparing to fight!

One reason for the ruin of Germany was the "fantastic" idea to create a Nibelungen-alliance with the corpse of the Hapsburg State. Holding onto our enormous feelings of allegiance from the past when it comes to our foreign policy of today is the best way to definitely prevent our rise to power. (*Nibelungen is a Germanic name from mythology, however, here it appears to be cited from Wagner's opera, The Ring of Nibelung, where it means "dwarf" as well as additional details from the opera storyline including how the dwarves had their treasure stolen, or in this reference, a possible meaning is "forming a dwarf-like alliance of no value between the naive Germans with the corpse of the Austrian State".*)

I feel compelled to take this opportunity and deal briefly with objections the previous discussion raises. First, would anyone be willing to enter an alliance with the present Germany in view of her obvious weakness? Second, would it be possible to change the attitudes of enemy nations toward Germany? Third, is the existing influence of Jewry stronger than all reason and good will, which would make it impossible to follow through on any plans, no matter how good the intentions?

I believe I have already answered the first question sufficiently. It should go without saying that nobody will seek an alliance with present Germany. No nation in the world would dare to link its fate with a State whose government gives no reason for them to have any confidence in it. Many of our fellow countrymen may attempt to condone or even excuse the acts of the government by pointing out the pitiful mindset of our people, but we must strongly object to this.

There is no doubt that for the last six years, the decline in our people's character has been pitiful. Their indifference toward the most important national interests has been depressing, and the cowardliness has become so bad it frequently cried out to Heaven for relief. However, one must not forget that in spite of all our troubles, these are the same people who only a few years earlier gave the world a wonderful example of the highest human virtues. Beginning in the days of August, 1914 until the huge struggle of nations ended, no people on earth have shown any greater manly courage, any stronger perseverance, any better endurance, or a greater patience than our German people—our people who have now become equally miserable. However, nobody can claim that our present shame is an accurate representation of our people's character.

What we find today, in us and around us, is only the dreadful, unreasonable, and illogical result from that act of perjury on November 9th, 1918. We can easily apply the word of the poet when he says evil begets evil. (*A theme from Shakespeare's Macbeth and other plays—evil creates further evil, however, this is not an actual quote.*) Yet even in these days, the fundamentally good elements of our people have not been totally lost. Those qualities are sleeping underneath the surface and once in a while, like lightning against the dark curtain of night, virtues flare up that the future Germany will someday remember as the first signs of an approaching recovery. More than once, thousands and thousands of young Germans have united voluntarily and joyfully, all of them determined to once again sacrifice their young lives on the altar of the Fatherland as they did in 1914. Even today, millions of men are working industriously and diligently as if no revolution had ever brought destruction. The blacksmith is again standing at his anvil, the farmer is at the plow, and the scholar sits in his study. All of them are working hard in an effort to do their duty.

The oppression coming from our enemies is no longer met with indifferent laughter, but now it is met with bitter and worn faces. There is no doubt that a great change in our attitude has taken place.

If all this has not sparked a resurgence of the desire for political power and of the spirit of self-preservation in our people, then the blame can be placed on those men who, since 1918, have ruled our people to death. They do not rule by the call of Heaven, but by their own self-appointment. If anyone disapproves of the state of our nation today, he must be asked, "What has been done to improve it? Is the tiny amount of support received by the people as a result of the few decisions our government has made significant enough to deal with the weakness of our people, or is it just a sign of the government's complete failure to handle its most precious treasure? What did our government do to restore the national spirit of proud independence, manly defiance, and wrathful hatred?"

In 1919 when the Peace Treaty was forced on the German people, one could have easily hoped this tool of unlimited oppression would make the cry for German liberty louder. Peace treaties which strike demands upon the people, like lashes from a whip, frequently turn out to be the first drumbeat signaling an approaching rebellion.

How easy it would have been to make use of the Treaty of Versailles! It would have been simple to take this tool of endless extortion and shameful humiliation and, with a determined government, turn it into a tool that could be used to stimulate national passions to a fevered pitch! How easy it would have been to use a targeted system of propaganda to turn the indifference of a people into resentment, and the resentment into flaming rage because of these sadistic cruelties!

How easy it would have been to burn every single one of these Treaty points into the brain and into the heart of our people, over and over, until finally, it was branded on sixty million heads of men and women, and the commonly felt shame and hatred would have become one flaming sea of fire! Out of its glow an iron will would have emerged and a cry would have come forth, "We want arms again!"

Yes sir, such a peace treaty can very well serve this purpose. The excessive measures it contains, the oppression and the shamelessness of its demands—those are the greatest weapons which can be used for propaganda to arouse the dormant spirit and spark the life of a nation.

For this to happen, everything from children's books to every last newspaper, every play, every motion picture show, every billboard and every available space must be used for this one great mission. In this way, the fear-stricken prayers of our patriotic social clubs, "Lord, make us free!" will transform in the mind of even the smallest boy into the burning plea, "Almighty God, bless our arms when the day comes; be as just as Thou hast been always; judge now as to whether we deserve the freedom or not; Lord, bless our struggle!"

But, every opportunity was missed and nothing was done. It is no wonder that our nation is not what it should be or what it could be. How could it possibly be anything else since the rest of the world sees us as their attendant who might be a more obedient dog and gratefully lick the master's hand after it has been beaten.

There is no doubt that the attitudes of our people do not help our ability to enter into alliances, but our governments are the greatest drawback. Their corruptness is to blame for the fact that, after eight years of unending oppression, there is little desire for liberty left.

A strong alliance policy depends on our nation receiving the necessary amount of respect from other countries. This respect depends on the existence of a powerful government that refuses to be nothing more than a collaborator with foreign states or the caretaker who finds it unpleasant to manage its own strength, but instead it should be the voice of the national conscience. If our people had a government that understood this as its mission, six years would not have passed without the champions of a daring foreign policy for the Reich appearing who could gain the support of a daring people who long for freedom.

To the second question regarding the great difficulty in changing the previous enemy nations into friendly allies, we offer the following answer:

The general anti-German psychosis that war-time propaganda has created in other countries will continue to exist until the German Reich can appear as a State again through a clear and visible revival of German Will and a revival of the spirit of self-preservation. The State must be able to take its place on the European chessboard and show that it can also play the game with others. Only after the government and the people can guarantee the security that is necessary for alliances will it be possible for one or the other powers, someone who has common interests, to consider changing the opinion of their people through their own propaganda efforts. This, too, will require years of continuous, clever work. The very fact that a change in public opinion requires so much time is the reason for undertaking it carefully. No country wants to start these activities unless they are confident that such work will be valuable and bear fruit in the future. The empty talk of a more or less creative foreign minister is not a valid reason for changing the mental attitude of a nation if they have no guarantee that such an attitude change will be valuable. Otherwise, this approach would only divide public opinion. The security that makes future alliances possible is not created by smooth talking members of the government, but by the visible stability of a government and a corresponding support in the form of public opinion. The faith of our people in this policy will be even stronger if the government is visibly active in propaganda that supports its work, and the public opinion is clearly reversed through this effort, which will then be reflected in the actions of the government.

Any nation that is in our position will only be considered fit for alliances when government and public opinion jointly and fanatically proclaim their determination to fight for liberty and uphold that determination through action. This will form the foundation that will be later used to change the public opinion in other states. These states understand the realities of the world and desire to pursue their own interests which causes them to willingly join hands with a suitable partner and enter into an alliance.

There is still another important matter to be considered. It is very difficult to change a certain mental attitude of a nation and the new attitude will not at first be understood by many; therefore, it is a crime and foolish to make mistakes that your opponents can use as weapons against you later.

It is important to understand that this change will require a certain length of time before the people fully grasp the intentions of the government. This is because the ultimate aims of certain political moves cannot be revealed to the public and must be accepted based on the blind confidence of the masses or the intuitive understanding of the more intellectually-developed leading groups. Not many people possess this clairvoyant visionary political understanding. Since, for political reasons, the motives behind these political actions cannot be explained, there will always be a portion of the intellectual leaders who will oppose the new trend and they will call it an experiment, because to them the goals appear vague and they cannot see where these actions are leading. This makes the conservatives in the state oppose anything they do not understand.

However, it is critically important to remove all potential weapons as soon as possible from the hands of these people who might disturb a policy that will lead to mutual understanding. This is especially true when the problem results from purely fantastic ideas dreamed up and chattered about among puffed-up patriots, would-be politicians, and small town coffeehouse politicians, as in our case. If we look at the situation from a cool, logical standpoint, we see that any call for a new war fleet or the restoration of our colonies etc. is obviously just silly talk that has no chance of actually happening.

In England, these foolish statements are used against us politically. Sometimes by harmless, sometimes by insane political warriors, but either way, they always serve the purposes of our mortal enemies. This is not good for Germany. A man becomes exhausted battling this threat through his antagonizing demonstrations against God and the rest of the world, and he forgets the first, essential principle to all success: Whatever you do, do it thoroughly. When we howl at five or ten countries, we cannot concentrate on all the intellectual and physical forces needed for a shock to the heart of our wicked enemy. Such howling sacrifices the chance to strengthen ourselves for the final struggle by securing alliances. The National-Socialist movement has a mission in this area as well. It must teach our people to disregard insignificant objectives and to keep in mind the greater objective. We must not divide ourselves over unimportant matters, but remember that today we are fighting for the basic existence of our people and we must strike against the sole enemy that is robbing us of that existence.

This may hurt us, sometimes bitterly. But we must not abandon all common sense by fighting with the whole world and foolishly yelling at them instead of concentrating all our powers against the deadly enemy. In addition, the German people have no moral right to criticize the rest of the world until the criminals who sold out and betrayed their own country are brought to justice. There is no holy justification for howling and protesting from far away against England, Italy, etc., when we turn around and allow the scoundrels to continue about their business who reaped the rewards from the enemy's war propaganda and who took our weapons away, and who shattered our moral backbone, and who sold the resulting paralyzed Reich for thirty pieces of silver.

The enemy only did what could have been expected. We should learn from his attitude and actions. Anyone who cannot rise above the situation to see this must then admit we have to give up any possibility of forming an alliance because that chance has definitely been eliminated. If we cannot enter into an alliance with England because she robbed us of our colonies, or with Italy since she took South Tyrol, or with Poland or Czechoslovakia for obvious reasons, that leaves only France, who incidentally stole Alsace-Lorraine, which means nobody else is left in Europe.

There can hardly be any doubts about how an alliance with France would serve the interests of the German people. When someone does propose this idea, there is only one question to ask: Is this opinion being expressed by someone who is a simple drip or by cunning crooks out to deceive us? When this suggestion is made by political leaders, I always choose to believe they are of the cunning crook variety.

Therefore, a shift in the disposition of previously hostile nations may occur if their future interests are along the same lines as our own, and if they can see the domestic power of our State and its determination to defend our existence, only then will we once again appear as a worthwhile ally. This change in attitude can only occur if those who oppose an alliance with our former enemies are not fed weapons as a result of our clumsiness or even criminal acts on our side.

The answer to the third objection is the most difficult one. Is it conceivable that the representatives of the true interests of those nations we could form an alliance with will be able to carry out their intentions against the will of the Jew who is the mortal enemy of free people and nations?

Will the powers of British statesmanship, for instance, be able to break the disastrous Jewish influence or not? This is a very difficult question because it depends on too many factors to reach to a conclusive answer. One thing is certain, there is one state where the present government has firmly established itself and the government exclusively serves the interests of that country to such a degree that international Jewish groups cannot prevent political necessities—their interference has been made impossible.

The fight waged by Fascist Italy against the three main arms of Jewry is the best indication that, indirectly at least, the venomous fangs of this Jewish super-state are being pulled out. Some may believe this was unconscious on the part of Italy, but I do not. Suppression of the secret Freemason Lodges, persecution of the Jewish super-national press, and permanently ending international Marxism along with steadily strengthening the fascist state idea will eventually allow the Italian government to serve the interests of the Italian people more and more without paying any attention to the hissing of the Jewish world hydra.

The situation in England is more difficult. In this country of "free democracy", the Jew dictates his will almost without any limitations today through the indirect means of public opinion. Yet, there is still a constant struggle between the representatives of the British State's interests and the advocates of a Jewish world dictatorship. The contrasting viewpoints became clear for the first time after the war when the attitude of the British government toward the Japanese problem conflicted openly with the press. (*After the First World War, the U.S. and Japan became growing naval powers and Britain had to choose an ally. They chose not to continue an existing alliance with Japan and signed the Washington Naval Treaty of 1922 between Britain, the U.S., Japan, France, and Italy. This decision limited the British Navy size and was hotly debated in Britain for many years afterward.*)

As soon as the war was over, the old irritations between America and Japan appeared again. It was impossible for the great European powers to remain indifferent to this new threat of war. Even the old ties of kinship cannot prevent England from feeling envy and anxiety when it comes to the constant growth of the American Union in every area of international, economic, and power politics. It seems as though the one-time colonial territory—the child of the great mother—is growing up to become a new master in the world. It is easy to understand why England today reviews her old alliances with caution and why British statesmanship anticipates fearfully the time when the slogan will not be "England rules the seas", but will become, "The seas belong to the Union".

It is much harder to confront the gigantic American State with its enormous wealth of virgin soil than to confront the German Reich wedged in-between various countries. If the dice were thrown to decide Fate today, England would face disaster if she found herself alone. Therefore, she anxiously reaches out for the yellow fist and all hope is based on an alliance that is irresponsible from a racial standpoint, but which offers the only possibility for strengthening the British world position against the growing influence of the American continent.

Even though they shared the battlefield in Europe, the British government could not make up its mind whether or not it should loosen the alliance with their Asian partner. On this question, the entire Jewish world press suddenly attacked the possibility of an alliance.

How is it possible that the newspapers of a Northcliffe, who were the faithful shield-bearers in the British battle against the German Empire, suddenly broke ranks and chose a path of their own? (*This idea and much of the following about America came from carmaker Henry Ford's newspaper, Dearborn Independent. Hitler was very interested in Henry Ford's theories. Northcliffe was a title Baron Northcliffe bestowed on Alfred Harmsworth, a newspaper magnate who was also called Lord Northcliffe. He controlled the Times and other papers and was known for influencing propaganda against the Germans in the First World War.*)

The British did not seek the destruction of Germany; that was a Jewish interest. Today, the destruction of Japan is not in the political interest of England, but it does match the desire of the Jewish leaders and their longing for a Jewish world-empire. While England over-exerts herself to maintain her position in the world, the Jew is organizing an attack in order to conquer it.

The Jew already sees the present European states as tools in his fist, controlled by either the indirect means of western democracy or in the form of direct control through Russian Bolshevism. The old world is not the only one that he holds in his net. He also threatens the new world with the same fate. The Jews rule the financial powers in the American Union. Each year they become more and more the master, controlling the working power of one hundred and twenty million people. Today, there is one great man, Ford, who has preserved his independence and is still irritating the Jews. (*Later editions of Mein Kampf omitted the name Ford, which referred to carmaker Henry Ford. This reference may have been removed at the request of Henry Ford due to social and political pressure he received because of his anti-Semitism; however, it is more likely it was removed by order from Hitler because of a public apology Henry Ford made to the Jews in 1927, which was issued after he was forced to shut down the newspaper, and in court Ford claimed he had no idea what his anti-Semitic newspaper had been publishing.*)

With cunning skill, the Jew molds public opinion and forms it into a weapon used in the battle for their own future. The top leaders of Jewry already see the time approaching when their proverbial prophecy of the Old Testament will be fulfilled and they will completely devour the nations of the earth. Yet, if one single independent state remains within this large flock of Jewish-controlled colonial territories, which have been stripped of their national qualities, that one state can still ruin all of their work in the last hour because a Bolshevized world can only exist if it completely encompasses everything. If just one state preserves its national strength and greatness—the Jewish ruling world empire, like every tyranny in this world—is bound to succumb to the power of the national idea.

The Jews have sinned for a thousand years, which has taught them how to adapt. He knows very well that he can undermine European nations and turn them into generic race-less bastards, but he can hardly do the same to an Asian nation such as Japan. Today, he presents himself like a mime, pretending to be a German, or an Englishman, or an American, or a Frenchman, but he cannot create a bridge to reach the yellow Asian. Therefore, he must instead try to destroy Japan using other nations in order to rid himself of this dangerous adversary before he has taken the last bit of political power into his fist and completed his tyranny over the helpless masses. He is so nervous over having a Japanese national state in his Jewish thousand-year empire that he wishes to destroy it even before establishing his own dictatorship.

For this reason, the Jew is today inciting the nations against Japan as he once did against Germany. While British statesmanship is trying to build an alliance with Japan, the British-Jewish press is already fighting against the ally and preparing their war of annihilation while pretending to fly the flag of democracy and shouting the war slogan, "Down with Japanese militarism and imperialism!" The Jew in England has today become defiant. Because of this, the struggle against this Jewish world menace on Japan will start in England.

The National-Socialist movement has its biggest task to fulfill here. It must open the eyes of the people in all foreign nations and show them the true enemy of our world today. Instead of directing our hatred against fellow Aryans, whom we may be separated from in every way, and with whom we must remember that we are bound together by blood and by a traditional common culture, and therefore we must expose the mortal-enemy of humanity as the actual cause of all suffering so that everyone will hate him. But above all, the movement must make sure the deadly enemy is recognized in our own country and that the fight against him becomes a flaming symbol that leads to a brighter time. Our actions will then show other nations the path to salvation for the struggling mankind of the Aryan.

May reason be our guide and Will our strength. May the sacred duty that drives our actions give us perseverance and may our faith remain our supreme protection.

14. EASTWARD ORIENTATION VS. EASTERN POLITICS

I have two reasons that cause me to examine the relationship between Germany and Russia more closely.

1. This question could be the most significant matter of German foreign policy in general.
2. This question is the touchstone, which will test the ability of the young National-Socialist movement to think clearly and act rightly. (*A touchstone is a black stone once used to test the quality of gold or silver by scraping and comparing the stone to a sample. The reference often means to test for genuineness, quality, or courage.*)

I must confess that the second point has caused me especially great worry. Our movement's supporters do not come from groups who are indifferent to politics, but they come from groups with radical points of view. It is only natural that they come to us already burdened with prejudices and possess the narrow understanding held by those groups with which they were previously politically and ideologically connected. This does not only apply to the man who comes to us from the political left-wing. On the contrary, his previous education in politics may have been subversive; however, it was balanced by a natural and healthy instinct which remained within him. Therefore, it was only necessary to replace the influence planted in him previously by a stronger and better one. Very often, the healthy instinct and spirit of self-preservation that still existed could be transformed into a very good ally.

But it is much more difficult to teach clear political thinking to a man if his previous education was in fact reasonable and logical, but he sacrificed the last shred of his natural instinct on the altar of objectivity. [He wants to look at every argument from both sides, even when the other side is his enemy, even when doing so is contrary to his or his people's interests.] The members of our so-called intellectuals are the ones who are especially slow when it comes to representing their own interests and those of their people in a clear and logical way. Not only are they weighed down by perverse attitudes and foolish prejudices, but they have lost their natural urge for self-preservation. The National-Socialist movement has to fight hard battles with these people because, in spite of a complete obsession with their fantasy ideas, which makes them incompetent, they believe everything they do is perfect. This conceit makes them look down on other usually more sound people when they have no reason to do so. They are snooty know-it-alls who actually lack all capacity for reasoning and judgment, which is critically important in all foreign policy plans and actions.

Today, these very groups are starting a dangerous trend by diverting our foreign policy from a true representation of the racial interests of our people so that it can instead serve their ideology and make their "fantastic" dream come true. Because of this, I feel it is necessary for me to discuss with my supporters as completely and clearly as possible the most important question of foreign policy, and that is our relationship with Russia.

I will start by making this general remark: If foreign policy is the guideline for the relations of a nation to the rest of the world, those guidelines must be determined by certain facts. As National-Socialists, we want to make the following statement about the meaning of foreign policy in a racial state: The foreign policy of a racial state has a duty to protect the existence of the race which forms the state on this planet by creating a natural, strong, and healthy relationship between the number and growth of the people and the quality of the soil and the size of the territory occupied.

A healthy relationship only exists when the nutritional needs of a nation are met through its own territory and soil. Every other condition, even though it may last centuries or even thousands of years, is an unhealthy situation and, sooner or later, it will lead to harm or destruction of the nation. Only a sufficiently large space on this earth guarantees a nation is free to continue to exist.

The amount of land needed for expansion cannot be determined by the present needs of the people and it cannot even be determined by the production that might be possible based on the number of people. I have already stated in the first volume of this work in the chapter titled "German Policy of Alliances Before the War" that the territory of a state is important to the people as a military and political asset, not just a resource to feed the people. (*There was actually not a chapter by that name in the first volume though the topic was discussed.*) Even after a people possess territory and soil in proportion to their numbers, it is still necessary to protect the land itself through the vastness of that territory. This safety lies in the general political power of the state and that power, to a large extent, is determined by the military value of the geography.

Therefore, the German people will be able to defend their future only if they are a world power. For almost two thousand years, the defense of our national interests has been a matter of world history, if we can call our more or less fortunate activities in foreign policy a defense. We ourselves have witnessed the gigantic struggle of the nations during the years 1914 until 1918, which was only the struggle of the German nation for its existence on earth, but the event itself is called the World War. The German people entered this war presumably as a world power. I use the expression presumably because, in reality, we were not ready. If in 1914 there had been a different ratio between the square footage of our territory and the population in Germany, then Germany would have been a real world power. Apart from all other factors, it would have been possible to end the war in our favor.

It is neither my task nor even my intention to point out the "If" in case the "But" had not been present. I do, however, feel that it is absolutely necessary for us to see conditions as they truly existed, without coloring them, and to point out their terrible weaknesses, if only to deepen the knowledge so the situation may be understood within the ranks of the National-Socialist movement.

Today, Germany is not a world power. Even if we could overcome our present military weakness, we still could not claim this title any more. How much importance could there be in a structure on this planet that has such a pitiful proportion between its population and the available area as the present German Reich? In an age when the earth is gradually being divided among nations, many of which are so large they almost span entire continents, it is not possible to speak in terms of a world power when our political motherland is restricted to the ridiculous area of hardly five hundred thousand square kilometers (*193,000 square miles, slightly larger than California*).

From a purely territorial point of view, the area of the German Reich absolutely disappears when compared to that of the so-called world powers. England does not prove the statement to be incorrect because the British mother country is really nothing but the giant capital of the British World Empire which possesses almost one-fourth of the entire globe. There are other gigantic states like the American Union, Russia, and China. Some of these countries are ten times the size of our present German Reich. Even France has to be included in these states. Not only does she constantly increase and replenish her army out of the negroid livestock from her enormous Empire, but also, from a racial viewpoint, her infiltration with negro blood is increasing so rapidly that we could call it the creation of an African state on European soil. The present colonial policy of France cannot be compared with the Germany of the past. If the present development of France continues for another three hundred years, the last bit of French blood will sink into the European-African half-breed state [a mulatto state] that is now being formed. It is a huge continuous settlement from the Rhine to the Congo and will be populated by a lower race that has been gradually created by continuous bastardization.

This was the difference between the French and the old German colonial policy. The former German colonial policy was a half-hearted effort at best, just as was everything we did. It did not try to enlarge the territory for settlement by the German race or try to increase the power of the Reich through the use of black blood, which would have been a criminal act itself. The African Askari (*name for African soldiers serving in European armies*) of German East Africa (*now called Tanzania*) represented a small, hesitant step in that direction. However, they were only used to defend the colony. No one had ever considered using black soldiers on a European battlefield, of course, realistically it was impossible during the World War, and it never came up as an option during more favorable times. In contrast, the French saw the recruitment of black blood as another reason for their colonial activity.

So, today we find a number of powers on the earth who have a considerably larger population than Germany and who have greater political support for their powerful positions. When we compare the area and population ratio of the German Reich with other rising world powers, Germany has never seen such unfavorable conditions, not since the beginning of our history two thousand years ago, not until today. At that time, we were a young, bold nation entering a world of large political structures that were already crumbling and we helped to dispose of one of the last giants, Rome. Today, we find ourselves in a world where large power states are again developing while our own Reich gradually sinks deeper and deeper into insignificance.

It is necessary for us to coldly and calmly keep this bitter truth in our mind. It is necessary for us to study and compare the area and population of the German Empire throughout the centuries with that of other states. I am convinced that everyone will come to the same alarming conclusion that I have already pointed out. Germany is no longer a world power, regardless of whether she is strong or weak in the military sense.

We are no longer in proportion when compared to the other great states of the world. That is thanks to the disastrous leadership of our nation in matters of foreign policy, thanks to the absolute lack of a clearly-defined foreign policy, and thanks to the loss of all natural instincts and loss of the desire for self-preservation.

If the National-Socialist movement wants to shine brightly in history and show it is ordained to pursue a great mission for our people, it must fully recognize and feel deep pain over their situation on this earth. It must take up the fight, with courage and purpose, against the aimlessness and ineptitude that has guided our foreign policy. Without regard to "tradition" or bad past experiences, it must find the courage to organize our people and unite their strength in a march forward on the road that will lead our people out of their present narrow living area to new territory and new soil. We must liberate them forever from the danger of perishing from the face of this earth, and we must not allow them to serve others as slaves.

The Nationalist-Socialist movement must attempt to remove the mismatch between our population and the size of our territory, the inequality between our historic past and our present weakness. Our land must be seen as the source of survival and the pivotal point of political power. In doing so, the movement must always keep in mind that we are ambassadors of the highest level of humanity on this earth and are bound by a solemn duty. We can meet these requirements if we work to make the German people race-conscious so they not only breed dogs, horses, and cats carefully, but they show mercy toward their own blood.

When I call the former German foreign policy aimless and inept, the proof of that statement lies in the actual failure of this policy. If our people had been intellectually inferior or cowardly, the results of their struggle on earth could not have been worse than what we see today. The developments of the last decades before the war must not mislead us on this issue. (*Before the First World War, Germany embarked on an imperialistic policy expanding its colonies in Africa.*) You cannot measure the strength of an empire by comparing that empire to itself; instead you must compare it to other states. This comparison furnishes the proof that not only have other states steadily increased in power, but they have ultimately become more powerful. In spite of any apparent rise in German power, the road that Germany traveled actually led farther and farther away from the other states. Eventually she was left far behind and the increasing difference was not in our favor.

We fell more and more behind, even in our population we continued to fall behind. Our nation is certainly not surpassed by any other people on earth when it comes to heroic courage. Considering everything, our people have sacrificed more of their own blood to secure their existence than any other people on earth. Our failure can only be blamed on the way that courage was used.

If we examine the political experiences of our people during the last thousand or more years, review all the countless wars and battles that have passed before our eyes, and examine the final results, we must confess that out of this sea of blood, only three phenomena have appeared that we might identify as the lasting fruits of a foreign policy:

1. The colonization of the Ostmark, which was accomplished mainly by the Bavarians of old. (*Ostmark means the Eastern March or the eastern border land.*)
2. The conquest and the push into the territory east of the Elbe. (*The Elbe is a major river in Germany that defines the upper eastern third of the country.*)
3. The organization of the Brandenburg-Prussian state by Hohenzollerns, which was a model as a nucleus and the crystallization of a new empire. (*The Hohenzollern or Prussian Royal Dynasty operated the Brandenburg-Prussia territory which was formed when the Duchy of Prussia and the Margraviate of Brandenburg were united in 1618. The name of the territory later became Prussia, and this union ultimately resulted in the formation of the German Empire in 1871.*)

This illustrates something that we should take as a warning for the future! The first two great successes of our foreign policy have become the most long lasting. Without them, our people would not play any part in the world today. They represent the first and, unfortunately, the only successful attempt to match the increasing population with the available territory and soil quality. It is a tragedy that our German historians have never appreciated these two facts because they represent the greatest importance to future generations. Instead, historians glorified everything else under the sun, including fantastic heroism, and praised the adventures of many battles and wars rather than recognize the insignificance most of these events had when we look at the vast development of the nation.

The third great political success was the formation of the Prussian State. Through it, a special idea of state was cultivated and the modern spirit of self-preservation was grown through the German army. This Prussian State, and its newly-formed ideas about how a state should operate, did away with the belief that individual provinces should defend themselves and required the formation of a national defense force. It is impossible to overemphasize the importance of this event. Even with the excessive bleeding of Germany, caused from being torn by the extreme trend toward individualism of states, which caused the German people to rot, the discipline that was established by the Prussian army allowed Germany to at least recover part of the long-lost ability to organize the province states. Other nations may still have a primitive need to group together in a flock, but our nation regained its structure as a result of the process of military training, which was a great accomplishment even if it was in part artificial and not a natural process. The termination of required military service may not be important to dozens of other nations, but was of vital significance to us. If it had not been for the educational influence of military training, ten generations would have been delivered over to the evil effects of their disunity, to vice and a corrupt world view, they would be without the ability to correct themselves, and then our nation would have lost the last remaining passion for independent existence on this planet. The German spirit would then have made its contributions to civilization only in the shadow of foreign nations without anyone knowing where such contributions originated. We would have become nothing more than cultural fertilizer until the remainder of Aryan-Nordic blood in us was finally spoiled or wiped out.

It is important to note that the significance of these real political successes, which our people gained in their battles over a period of more than a thousand years, are recognized and appreciated more by our opponents than by us. Even today, we rave about a heroism that robbed our nation of millions of its most noble members and, in the end, accomplished nothing (*meaning the First World War.*) It is very important for our present and future that we learn the difference between the real political successes of our nation and the events where the spilling of national blood gained us nothing.

We National-Socialists must never ever become involved in the empty cheering patriotism that is common in the privileged-class world. It is deadly dangerous to believe the last developments before the war will in any way guide our own course. The entire historical period of the nineteenth century does not contain a single undertaking that we would be justified in pursuing today. In contrast to the behavior of representatives of that time, we must make the only goal of all foreign policy once again the expansion of land so that it matches the population. Yes, we can see from the past that we must have two aims for our political actions: Obtaining new land and soil must be the aim of our foreign policy, and the aim of our domestic policy must be the formation of a new, ideologically solid foundation for the interior of the country.

I would like to briefly explain my position on whether the demand for territory and soil appears to be ethically and morally justified. As terrible as it is to have to justify this argument, it is necessary since even in the so-called race-conscious circles, all kinds of suave but insincere speakers appear who try to tell the German people the injustice of 1918 is the justification for their foreign policy and they only want to recover what was lost. But then, they turn around and assure the rest of the world that they only want racial brotherhood and sympathy.

Let me anticipate objections and propose the following idea. To demand the frontiers of 1914 be restored is political foolishness which is so severe it appears criminal. This idea does not consider the fact that the Reich's old borders were not drawn logically. In reality, the old borders were incomplete because they did not include all Germans and they were certainly unreasonable when we consider the military value of the geography. Those borders did not result from a carefully-considered political plan, but they were drawn at the spur of the moment during a political struggle that is still not over and some were even drawn by random chance. It would be equally right, and in many cases more just, to randomly select any other year in German history and reconstruct conditions from that time and use that to justify our foreign policy goals. This would make our privileged-class world happy. They do not possess a single constructive political idea for the future. They only live in the past, actually, they live only in their own recent past because they cannot see beyond their own lifetime. Inertia compels them to continue along their current path and makes them resist any change, which explains why they never go any faster in their opposition. It is, therefore, obvious the political horizon of these people does not reach beyond the borderlines of 1914. When they proclaim they want those borders restored, they again repair the crumbling alliance of our opponents. That is the only thing that explains why the alliance of the victors is able to maintain itself intact even eight years after a world struggle in which nations with the most diverse desires and goals came together to take part.

All these nations profited by Germany's collapse. Their fear of our strength pushed the greed and the envy that existed between them into the background. They saw the complete dismemberment of our Reich's heritage as the best protection against any future uprising. Their troubled conscience and their fear of the strength of our people has proven to be the most durable cement for keeping the members of this coalition together. We did not disappoint them when our privileged-class world set up a political program for Germany that restored the boundaries of 1914. Everyone in the alliance of enemies who might think of pulling out has to jump back in as a partner because he fears that if he withdraws he will be isolated and the others may turn on him. Then he would no longer have the protection of the individual allies so he merrily goes back to the alliance. Every single nation feels threatened and intimidated by this privileged-class slogan.

At the same time, their plan is doubly foolish. First, because they lack the strength to move their idea from the haze of night clubs into reality, and second, even if it could happen, the result would be so pitiful that, by God, it would not be worth the bloodshed of our people again. It is unquestionable that the restoration of the borders of 1914 could only be accomplished by bloodshed. Only someone with a childlike naive spirit would think the Versailles Treaty could be changed by a plot or by begging for handouts. Such an attempt would require the character of a Talleyrand, and we do not have a Talleyrand on our side. (*Charles Maurice de Talleyrand-Périgord was an influential French diplomat under Napoleon I and other rulers. He also established many of the borders of the Prussian empire. These borders allowed Prussia to create a powerful position, eventually resulting in German unification, and the borders remained until the start of the First World War. Here the reference means Germany does not have such a Frenchman who would act in favor of Germany.*)

Half of our politicians are shrewd individuals lacking any character and who are hostile to our people. The other half are kind, harmless, and agreeable morons. Furthermore, times have changed since the Congress of Vienna. Princes and princely mistresses no longer bargain and haggle about borderlines of states; now the relentless world Jew fights for domination over the people. No nation can remove this fist clutching at its throat except by the sword. Only the united strength of a powerfully concentrated national passion can rebel against this international enslavement of the nations. However, such a process is and remains a bloody one.

However, if we have a strong conviction that the future of Germany requires the greatest risk, no matter what the outcome may be, then we must choose a goal, regardless of political considerations, and devote ourselves completely to a struggle that is worthy of our sacrifice.

The frontiers of 1914 mean nothing to Germany's future. They offered no protection in the past and they would give us no strength in the future. They will not provide the German people with unity, and they will not meet our food requirements. The military value of the old frontiers are not practical or satisfactory either. They certainly will not improve our present standing among other world powers, or rather our standing with the real world powers. The distance to England is not shortened, the vastness of the American Union is not reached, and France would not experience a substantial decrease in her world political importance. One thing, however, would be certain. Even if we were successful, any attempt to restore the borderlines of 1914 would lead to further bloodshed for our people, but this time it would be to such an extent that no one would be left to make decisions and plan actions necessary to guarantee the life and the future of the nation. The alternative would be that once Germany was intoxicated by such an easy success, any further goals would be rejected since the "national honor" was already restored and, at least for the moment, all attention would focus on the few doors which would open for commercial progress.

In contrast to all this, we, as National-Socialists, must hold tightly to our goals in foreign policy. We must secure the territory and soil that is due for the German people for their place on this earth. This action is the only one that could justify bloodshed in the eyes of God and of future German generations. It would be justified before God because we are placed on this world to eternally struggle for our daily bread. We are beings who are given nothing and who owe their position as lords of the earth to the ingenuity and to the courage that they use to fight for and preserve their position. This sacrifice would be justified in the eyes of future German generations because they will know we did not shed the blood of one single citizen without the gift of a thousand others to the future. The securing of territory and soil will justify the risk of the farmer's sons of today, for the future sons of Germany. Even though statesmen may be persecuted for their decisions today, someday in the future, the responsible statesmen will be absolved of all bloodshed and of all guilt for those sacrificed.

I must sharply oppose those racialist writers who pretend to think that taking land like this is somehow a "breach of sacred human rights", and who oppose it through their penmanship, of course such written protests are in keeping with their beliefs. You never know who is truly behind such fellows. One thing is certain; however, the confusion they create is welcomed by the enemies of our people who look upon it most favorably. Their attitude provides a criminal level of help in the weakening of our people and it removes from within our people the desire for the one and only possession that can provide the necessities of life. No people on the earth hold even one square meter of territory and soil as the result of any heavenly wish or higher right. The frontiers of Germany were laid down by chance and they are only temporary during the current political struggle, likewise, so are the frontiers of other nations. A thoughtless fool may believe that the earth's surface is unchangeable like granite, but it actually represents only a pause in a slow development involving constant change, which affects the people living along the boundaries of these lands. Perhaps by tomorrow it may even be destroyed or changed again by the greater forces of nature.

State frontiers are made by men and changed by men. The fact that a nation successfully gains an immense territory does not establish a holy right to keep it for eternity. Gaining this territory only proves the might of the conquerors and the weakness of those who tolerate them. This strength alone establishes the right to keep the territory. The German people are crowded on an impossibly small territory today and facing a pitiful future, however, this situation has not been decreed by Fate, and to revolt against it is not an insult to Fate. A higher power has not granted more territory to some other nation instead of Germany, just as no higher power is offended by such an unjust distribution of territory. Our ancestors did not receive the land we live on as a present from Heaven, but they had to risk their lives and fight for it. In the future, we will not obtain the land and the life it offers for our nation through any act of Heavenly generosity. We will only obtain the land we need through the might of the victorious sword.

We all recognize that a confrontation with France is necessary; however, it would be pointless if this were the limit of our foreign policy. The only sensible foreign policy is one that expands our people's living space in Europe. Acquiring colonies is not a solution to this problem. We must gain settlement territory to enlarge the mother country itself. This will keep new settlers in close communion with the land of their origin and also guarantee the entire nation experiences the advantages that only come from a large and united territory.

The race-based Nationalist Movement must not defend the rights of other nations, but act as the spearhead of its own people's rights. If it does not do that, then it serves no useful purpose. It is not entitled to gripe about the past because then it would be repeating the past. The former German policy mistakenly followed interests of the royal dynasty; however, the future should not be guided by such commonplace sickening sentimentalism. Specifically, we should not act as policemen for the well-known "poor, small nations", but instead we should act as soldiers guarding the interest of our own people. (*This may be an argument against colonization, meaning Germany should not act as policemen in foreign colonies—such colonies require a lot of effort to control—but it is more likely that it is a reference to the idea of joining the League of Nations which later resulted from the Treaty of Versailles.*)

However, we National-Socialists must go even further. The right to possess territory and soil can turn into a duty if we see a great nation which suddenly appears doomed if it does not acquire more territory. This is especially true when we are not talking about just any little negro tribe, but about the Germanic mother of all life and the cultural image of the world. Germany will either be a world power or cease to exist. In order to become a world power, she needs the vastness that will give her the importance needed today and provide life to her citizens.

So, we National-Socialists must scratch out the foreign policy practices of the pre-war period. We will begin our work where it was left off six hundred years ago. (*A reference to the Old Prussia of the 13th and 14th century when Teutonic Knights conquered regions and brought in ethnic Germans.*) We will stop the eternal Germanic migration to the south and west of Europe we have seen in the past and look toward the land in the east. (*Russia and Austria-Hungary territory.*) We will finally end the colonial and trade policy of pre-war times and move forward into the land policy of the future.

However, when we say territory and soil today in Europe, we can only think about Russia and the border-states under her control.

Here, Fate seems to have given us a clue. By surrendering Russia to Bolshevism, it deprived the Russian people of that intelligent group responsible for creating the state and which guaranteed their existence as a state up to that time. The Russian State did not result from the political abilities of the Slavic race in Russia, but its creation was a wonderful example of the state-forming ability possessed by the Germanic element that still exists within an inferior race. Numerous powerful empires on the earth have been created this same way when inferior races, led by Germanic organizers and masters, have grown into huge states and they continued to exist as long as the racial nucleus of the state-forming race survived.

For centuries, Russia has fed on this Germanic nucleus of her leading upper classes. Today, that group is in danger of being exterminated because it has been almost entirely wiped out. The Jew has stepped into their place. It is equally impossible for the Russians to rid themselves of the Jewish yoke of bondage using their own strength as it is impossible for the Jew to maintain the huge empire in the long run. The Jew is not an organizer, but an enzyme of decomposition. The gigantic empire in the east is ripe for collapse. The end of Jewish domination in Russia will also be the end of the Russian state. We have been selected by Fate to witness this catastrophe and it will be the strongest confirmation that the national race theory is true and correct. (*Hitler worked with anti-communist Russians who assured him Russia was near collapse in the mid 1920s. Hitler expected to be invited in to put down a revolution and was not planning an invasion.*)

The mission of the National-Socialist movement is to give our people the political insight needed so they do not see their future aim in the romantic image of a new campaign by Alexander the Great, but they see their future working busily at the German plow for which the sword will provide the soil.

It goes without saying that the Jew has proclaimed his violent opposition to the eastern expansion policy. He can feel, more than anyone else, how these actions will impact his future. The fact alone that he opposes the plan should convince all truly nationally-minded men that this new direction is the correct path. Unfortunately, the exact opposite is the case. German national and race-conscious circles have declared a hostile war against the very idea of an eastern expansion policy and, as always happens, the people listen to the one who has the most famous name. In order to justify a different policy, which is just as absurd as it is impossible and very harmful for the German nation, the spirit of Bismarck is summoned. They claim that Bismarck, during his time, had always stressed the importance of maintaining a good relationship with Russia. That is correct for the most part. Yet, they completely forget to mention that he also stressed the importance of a good relationship with Italy. The same Mr. von Bismarck even made an alliance with Italy so he could settle matters with Austria. (*Bismarck made a secret alliance with Italy to gain Austrian-controlled land in 1866, which split Austrian forces resulting in the defeat of Austria at the battle of Königgrätz, the largest battle until that time in history.*)

Why do they not continue to promote the Italian policy, too? They will say, "because today's Italy is not the same Italy from those days". All right, then, honorable sirs, permit me to raise the objection that the Russia of today is also no longer the Russia of those days. Bismarck never intended to create a political course that would become a permanent strategy. He was the master of the moment and would not want to tie himself down like that. The question should not be, "What did Bismarck do in his days?" but we should ask, "What would he do today?" This question is much easier to answer. His political wisdom would never have permitted him to unite with any state that is doomed to destruction.

Also, Bismarck regarded the German colonial and trade policy with mixed feelings since his main focus was on uniting and internally strengthening the State he had created. That was the only reason he welcomed the Russian support, so he could have a free hand for his work in the west. However, what was useful to Germany then would be harmful to her today.

As early as 1920-1921, the young National-Socialist movement was slowly brought into the forefront on the political horizon and was, to some degree, considered as a German movement for independence. Our Party was approached by various sides who attempted to establish a relationship between their people and the independence movements of other countries. This was actually quite similar to the widely advocated League of "Oppressed" Nations proposed at the time which mainly consisted of representatives from certain Balkan states and those of Egypt and India. To me, they all seemed like pompous windbags without any actual experience. There were many Germans, especially among the nationalists, who allowed themselves to be dazzled by these proud Orientals. They immediately believed any worthless student was a "representative" of India or Egypt. These fools failed to realize that not only did most of these "representatives" have no support, but they had not been authorized by anyone to decide on any kind of treaty with anyone. Therefore, the practical result of all relations with these people was zero. I have always resisted these kinds of pointless dealings. I not only had better things to do with my time than to waste weeks on such fruitless "discussions", but even if these representatives had been authorized by their respective nations, I would have considered the whole thing to be pointless or even harmful.

It was bad enough during peace times that the German alliance policy lacked any aggressive intentions and ended up as nothing more than a defensive society of old states, long since retired from world history. The alliances made with Austria and Turkey were not at all satisfactory. While the greatest military and industrial states of the earth united in an active aggressive League, the rest gathered together a few old, weak states and tried to confront an active world coalition with this trash that was doomed to destruction from the start. Germany was bitterly repaid for this foreign policy error. However, this repayment was apparently not bitter enough because it did not prevent those eternal visionaries among us from immediately committing the same error again. Their attempt to disarm the almighty victors of the First World War with a League of "Oppressed" Nations was absurd and ultimately became disastrous. It is disastrous because it constantly distracts our nation from what we could do. Instead of accomplishing something fantastic, the nation yields to unproductive hopes and illusions. The Germany of today is like the drowning person who grasps at every straw. They may otherwise be very intelligent, but just as soon as a ray of hope can be seen, no matter how elusive, these people immediately run to catch the ghost. No matter whether it is a League of "Oppressed" Nations, a real League of Nations, or any other kind of fantastic invention, it will, nevertheless, find many thousands of souls who are willing to believe.

I still remember the childish and incomprehensible hopes that suddenly arose in 1920-1921 in nationalist circles that England was supposed to be on the verge of collapse in India. Some Asian impostors, or for all I care perhaps even real "fighters for the independence of India" who were loitering about in Europe at the time, had successfully filled the heads of otherwise sensible people with the mistaken idea that the British World Empire was about to collapse in the very part of India where she had her central cardinal position. Of course, it never occurred to them that their own desire had fathered all of their ideas. Nor did they see the paradox of their own hopes. How could they expect that the collapse of English rule in India would somehow lead to the end of the British World Empire and British power? They admitted that India was of the greatest importance to England, so if the Empire was not ended then why would she abandon India so easily?

The native German prophet may consider this vital question as the deepest secret known to man, but it is, presumably, known by those who guide the history of England. It is childish to assume that England does not realize the value of the Indian Empire to the British World Union. It is another negative indicator of our absolute refusal to learn a lesson from the First World War when we blindly misunderstand the strong Anglo-Saxon determination, and we let ourselves think that England would let India go without doing everything possible to prevent it. Furthermore, it is proof that Germans do not understand the methods used by the British in their penetration and administration of the Indian Empire. England will only lose India if she falls prey to racial breakdown through her own administrative machine, something that is unlikely in India at this time, or if she is conquered by the sword of a powerful enemy. Indian rebels will certainly never successfully conquer her. We Germans know from experience how difficult it is to conquer England. Apart from this, I, as a member of the Germanic race, would prefer to see India under English rule than under the control of any other nation.

The hopes for a mythical uprising in Egypt are just as miserable. The promise of a "Holy War" gives a strange, yet pleasant sensation to our German sheeps-head players when they think others are now willing to shed their blood for us. (*Schafkopf or Sheepshead is a card game common in Bavaria.*) Cowardly speculation has always been the silent father of these hopes. In reality, any such uprising would come to a hellish end under the concentrated fire of English machine guns and the barrage of explosive bombs.

It is impossible to successfully attack a powerful state that is firmly determined to risk its last drop of blood for the sake of its existence and especially foolish to launch such an attack with a coalition of cripples. As a nationalist who knows how to evaluate humanity based on its racial foundations, I cannot link the fate of my own nation with that of the so-called "Oppressed Nations", which I can see are racially inferior.

We must take the very same position today in regard to Russia. At the present time, Russia has been stripped of its Germanic ruling layer and therefore cannot be an ally in the struggle for an independent German nation. From a purely military standpoint, the situation would be disastrous if Germany and Russia should find themselves in a war against Western Europe, which would likely mean a war against the rest of the world. The fighting would not take place on Russian soil but in German territory, and Germany would not be able to receive any effective support from Russia. The military might of the present German Reich is so disgraceful and so inadequate that we could not even protect our borders against Western Europe, including England. Even the German industrial territory would be exposed to the direct fire from our enemies and we would have no way to defend it. Another problem is that between Germany and Russia lies the Polish State, which is entirely in French hands. In the event of a war with Germany and Russia both fighting against Western Europe, Russia would first have to flatten Poland in order to bring the first soldier to the German front lines.

In reality, it is not so much a question of soldiers as a question of technical armaments. In this respect, the conditions of the First World War would be repeated, except it would be even more terrible. German industry had to supply our notorious allies so Germany had to bear the burden of producing the technical armaments all by herself during the First World War. If we faced combat together, Russia would likewise be useless when it came to the technical equipment of war. There would be no way we could oppose the general motorization of the world, and the ability to mobilize with vehicles will be an overwhelmingly decisive factor in the next war. Germany has remained disgracefully far behind even in this important field and then she would have to also support Russia out of what little she has. Even today, Russia does not own a single factory in which an automobile that actually runs can be manufactured. Combat under these conditions would be nothing but a massacre. The youth of Germany would bleed many times more than they did before because the burden of the actual fighting would lie only on us, as it always does, and the result would be unavoidable defeat.

Even if a miracle should happen and combat under these circumstances did not end with the utter destruction of Germany, the final result would still mean we had been bled white. Afterwards, Germany would be the same as she was before, and we would remain surrounded by large military states—there would have been absolutely no change in conditions at all. The objection that a Russian alliance does not necessarily mean there will be war is in itself an empty claim and to claim that the purpose of such an alliance is simply to be prepared in the event of war is equally useless. No. An alliance that is not ultimately about war is foolish and worthless. Alliances are made for the purpose of battle. Even though the friction is not apparent when the alliance is formed, war is the fundamental motivation and the expected result. Never think that other powers will view such an alliance differently. Either a German-Russian alliance would take place only on paper, in which case it would serve no purpose and have no value for us, or the words of the treaty would become a visible threat which would warn the rest of the world. It is utterly naive to think that England and France would react by waiting a decade until the German-Russian alliance had enough time to complete its technical preparations for war. No, the storm would break out over Germany with lightning speed.

Therefore, the formation of a new alliance with Russia would lead in the direction of a new war and the result would be the end of Germany. Additionally, we must also consider the following.

1. The present rulers of Russia have no intention of entering into a genuine alliance or of honoring it if they did. We must not forget that the rulers of present day Russia are bloodstained common criminals. We are dealing with the scum of humanity who used the conditions of a tragic hour to overrun a large state, kill and root out millions of its leading intellectuals in a wild thirst for blood, and now, for almost ten years, they have exercised the cruelest tyranny of all times. We must also not forget that these rulers belong to a people who possess the rare combination of inhuman cruelty and an incomprehensible skill of deception. Today these people, more than ever before, feel called upon to impose their bloody suppression on the whole world. We must not forget that the international Jew, who completely dominates Russia today, does not see Germany as an ally, but as a state destined for a similar fate. You do not form an alliance with a partner whose only interest is your destruction. Above all, one does not form an alliance with creatures to whom no contract is sacred. They do not live on this world as representatives of honor and truth, but as representatives of deceit, pilfering, and robbery. A man who believes he can enter into a contract with parasites is no different from a tree trying to make a favorable agreement with mistletoe. (*Mistletoe is a parasitic plant that slows the growth of a tree and sometimes kills it. It was considered as a pest in the 20th century and is also poisonous to many animals.*)

2. The danger that Russia was once subjected to is constantly hanging over Germany. Only a privileged-class fool could dream that Bolshevism has been banished. In his shallow thinking, he does not realize that this is an act of instinct. It is the Jewish nation striving for world domination, a phenomenon that is as natural as the Anglo-Saxon's urge to dominate the world. Just as the Anglo-Saxon pursues this course in his own way and fights his battle with his own weapons, so too the Jew fights with the weapons he knows best. His way is sneaking into nations and undermining their inner structure. He fights with his weapons of lies and slander, poison and decay, intensifying the battle until he has achieved the bloody extermination of his hated opponent. Russian Bolshevism represents the Jew's twentieth century attempt to gain world domination just as they tried by different, though closely related means throughout history. His desire is too deeply

rooted in his nature for him to change.

No nation would voluntarily stop following their natural impulse to expand its own kind or to enhance their power. They are forced to do so by outside circumstances or it is the result of old age as they become a victim of weakness. In the same way, the Jew will not voluntarily relinquish his road to world dictatorship by simply suppressing his eternal urge. He can only be thrown off his course of world domination by outside powers or when his efforts expire with his own death. The weakness of the nations and their demise through senility is caused by their surrender of racial blood purity. The Jew guards his racial purity more than any other nation of the world. So, he continues in his disastrous way until another power confronts him and in a huge struggle throws this attacker of Heaven back again to Lucifer.

Today, Germany is the next great objective of Bolshevism. We will need all the strength of a young missionary idea to again rescue our nation from the entanglement of the international serpent and to stop the contamination of our blood. Only then will we be able to protect our nation and prevent the last catastrophe from ever again being repeated (*meaning the Revolution.*) If we pursue this goal, then it would be madness to unite with a power that is ruled by the very enemy who means death to our own future. How can we free our nation from the slavery of this poisonous embrace if we willingly walk into it? How can the German worker come to understand that Bolshevism is a damnable crime against humanity when we choose as our allies the very organizations of this evil plan and acknowledge it as an equal? How can we condemn a member of the broad masses for his sympathy toward a world philosophy when the leaders of the State choose the representatives of that World-Concept as an ally?

The struggle against the Jewish effort to convert the world to Bolshevism requires that we clarify our attitude toward Russia. After all, we cannot drive out Satan by using Beelzebub. If race-aware circles today are enthusiastic over the idea of an alliance with Russia, they need only to look around Germany to realize whose support they have. Or do the recent racialists think anything that is recommended by the Marxist international Jewish press is going to be beneficial to the German nation? Since when do racialists go to battle with a weapon offered by the Jew? Has the Jew become our shield-bearer?

There is one main criticism that can be made against the old German Reich concerning its policy of alliances: It ruined its relations with everyone because it constantly swayed back and forth in an unsound and weak effort to preserve world peace at all costs. There is also one thing it could not be criticized for; it did not maintain a good relationship with Russia. I admit that even before the First World War, I already believed it was a wiser course for Germany to renounce her foolish colonial policy, renounce her commercial and naval fleet, and ally herself with England against Russia. This would have taken Germany from a weak international policy to a definite European policy of continental territorial conquest.

I have not forgotten the constant insolent threats that the former Pan-Slavic Russia dared to make against Germany. (*Pan-Slavics are those who wanted to expand Russia and unite all Slavic people.*) I have not forgotten the constant military practice drills that were only intended to provoke Germany. I cannot forget the public attitude in Russia, even before the war, that was filled with hateful attacks against our nation and Reich. And I can never forget how the great Russian press was always more favorable toward France than toward us.

There could still have been a second path we might have taken before the war. We might have relied on Russia in order to direct our attack against England. Today, of course, conditions are different. Even if we had choked down all kinds of bad feelings and been able to side with Russia before the war, we can no longer do that today. Since the war, the hand of the world clock has moved on and the hour has struck loudly announcing to us the time when the Fate of our nation must be decided in one way or another. The large nations of the world are joining together and this is our last warning signal to put a stop to all the nonsense, to bring our people back out of the dream world and into harsh reality. We need to point the way into a future that will lead the old Reich to blossom into a new era of prosperity.

In pursuing this huge and important task, the National-Socialist movement must free itself of all illusions and allow reason to be its sole leader. Ultimately, the catastrophe of 1918 may prove to be an infinite blessing for the future of our people. Out of this wreckage, our nation can change the direction of its foreign policy and stabilize its position in the world once it has been strengthened by its new World-Concept at home. Then, it can finally adopt a "political testament" like England possesses and that even Russia once possessed, and like the one that enabled France over and over again to make correct decisions that benefited her.

The political testament of the German nation concerning its foreign policy shall and must always contain these following ideas. We must never allow two continental powers to form in Europe! We must consider every attempt to organize a second military power on the German borders as an attack against Germany, even if it is just the formation of a state which could potentially be a strong military power. We must consider it our right and our duty to prevent such a state in every way possible, even if it means using arms to prevent the formation of this kind of state or to break its back if it is already in existence! We must be certain that the strength of our people is maintained by preserving the soil of the homeland in Europe and not in colonies. We must never consider the Reich to be truly secure until it can guarantee every individual descendant of our people his own piece of land for centuries to come. We must never forget that the holiest right on this earth is the right to the soil that one wishes to till oneself, and that the holiest sacrifice is the blood that one sheds for this soil.

Before I end these deliberations I must again point out the only possible alliances for us in Europe today. Previously, regarding the problem of German alliances, I named England and Italy as the only two nations in Europe that we should strive to develop closer relations with and those are the only nations that hold a promise of success. I will only briefly touch on the military importance of such an alliance here.

The military consequence of such an alliance would be the opposite from an alliance with Russia. Most importantly, closer relations with England and Italy will not bring any danger of war. The only power that might be against the alliance, France, would not be in a position to go to war against such an alliance. Therefore, the alliance would give Germany a chance to quietly make all those preparations that would be necessary in order to later settle the account with France. The true significance of such a coalition lies in the very fact that once it is finalized, not only would Germany no longer be exposed to the possibility of a hostile invasion, but with the enemy alliance itself broken, the previous Peace Treaty agreement is automatically dissolved, thus isolating the deadly enemy of our people, France. Even though this success would initially only have a psychological result rather than a physical result, it would be enough to give Germany today an unimaginable amount of freedom to act on its own. The new European Anglo-German-Italian alliance would be the one making the decisions and it would decide what to do, while France would no longer be in control.

Suddenly, Germany would no longer be in such an unfortunate strategic position. This new order would give us a powerful protector on one border and on the other border we would be completely guaranteed secure supply-lines for our provisions and raw materials. What is even more important is that the new coalition would be made up of nations that, in many respects, would compliment each other in their technical abilities. For the first time, Germany would have allies who were not leeches sucking on our economy, but instead they could and would greatly contribute to the technical build-up of our armament.

There is another final fact that must not be overlooked. In both cases, we are dealing with allies who cannot be compared with Turkey or present Russia. The combination of the greatest world powers on earth and our young national state would create a different balance on European battlefields than we saw with the decaying national corpses that Germany was allied with in the last war.

I have already pointed out the great difficulties we would face from those who attempted to prevent such a League. However, can anyone say it was easier to form the Entente? What the ingenuity of King Edward VII achieved, which in part was against the natural interests of certain people [the Jews], here we must and shall also achieve. (*Edward VII was King of the United Kingdom until 1910. The Entente refers to the Entente Cordiale between England and France, which reached agreements on colonies in Africa and settled ongoing conflicts. It later led to the Triple Entente between England, France, and Russia.*)

When we realize these actions are necessary, it must inspire us to follow a wise self-determined course. This will be possible the moment we become conscious of the impending need and choose one single, methodical road to follow instead of continuing along the aimless path our foreign policy followed in recent decades.

The future goal of our foreign policy must not be to favor the east or the west, but rather an eastern expansion policy that will acquire the necessary farmland for our German people. For this we need strength, but the deadly enemy of our people, France, is mercilessly choking us and robbing us of our power. Therefore, we must be willing to make every necessary sacrifice if it will result in the destruction of the French desire for dominance in Europe. Today, every national power that feels France's lust for domination on the continent is unbearable—those nations are our natural allies. We must not consider any road that leads us to the strength we need as being too difficult, nor should we say that giving up any old alliances is unspeakable if the final result offers merely the possibility that we could overthrow the fierce hatred of our enemy. We will then leave the smaller scratches to quietly heal over time after we have cauterized and closed the biggest wound.

Of course, today, we face the destructive barking of our nation's enemies at home. But we National-Socialists should never be swayed from our course of proclaiming what is absolutely necessary based on our inherent convictions. It is true that we must endure the flow of public opinion, which has been misled by the cunning Jewish exploitation of German thoughtlessness. It is true that sometimes the waves around us roar with evil fierceness, but those who swim with the current are more easily overlooked than the one who swims against the current. Today, we are just a rock sticking out of the flowing current. However, in only a few years Fate will elevate us to become a dam which will direct the flow of the current into a new riverbed.

Therefore, it is necessary for the National-Socialist movement to be recognized and established in the eyes of the rest of the world as the representative of a definite political idea. Whatever Heaven may have in store for us, let everyone know who we are by the caps we wear.

As soon as we understand how greatly our intervention is needed in foreign policy, that is when this knowledge will make us absolutely determined and the strength of perseverance will flow through us. This strength will become important when one of us is under the drumming fire of the hostile pack of dogs known as the press and he becomes frightened. This is the time he will feel the urge to make concessions here and there so that everyone is not against him, and in this moment he will want to howl with the wolves.

15. SELF-DEFENSE AS A RIGHT

When we laid down our arms in November 1918, it established a policy that anyone should have seen would gradually lead to complete submission. Similar historical examples show that people who stop fighting without a compelling reason will eventually accept the greatest humiliation and demands rather than try to change their fate by using force again.

This human quality is easily understandable. If at all possible, a wise conqueror will always impose his demands step by step on the conquered. He can count on the fact that a nation that has lost its strength of character—which is true of every nation that voluntarily surrenders—will not see a strong reason to reach for a weapon as each small separate act of oppression is forced on them, one at a time. The longer such demands are willingly accepted, the less the people see them as a reason to resist. When they consider the individual oppression, it seems unimportant when compared to the collective oppressions against them, then they realize they have already tolerated much more and suffered a much greater misery in silence, so one more makes little difference.

The downfall of Carthage is a terrible demonstration of how a people can become the victims of a slow execution brought about by their own fault.

In his Three Beliefs, Clausewitz emphasizes this thought in a manner like no one else could and immortalizes it when he says, "The stain of cowardly submission can never be wiped out. This drop of poison in the blood of a people is transmitted to posterity and will paralyze and undermine the strength of future generations", and that, on the other hand, "even the destruction of this freedom after a bloody and honorable struggle assures the rebirth of a nation; it is the essence of life from which a new tree is sure to take root some time in the future".

(*Carl Philipp Gottlieb von Clausewitz was a Prussian soldier, historian, military theorist, and author of the book* On War *about military theory. The reference here is not from* On War *but from* The Creed of 1812, *which was a program for German national liberation. It is also known as the* Three Statements of Belief, *and in it Clausewitz said "...a people can value nothing more highly than the dignity and liberty of its existence; that it must defend these to the last drop of its blood; that there is no higher duty to fulfill, no higher law to obey; that the shameful blot of cowardly submission can never be erased; that this drop of poison in the blood of a nation is passed on to posterity, crippling and eroding the strength of future generations".*)

Of course, a nation that has lost its honor and character will not care about this doctrine. Whoever does take it to heart can never sink below a certain point. Only he who forgets or no longer chooses to acknowledge it can be broken down. Therefore, you cannot expect someone who has willingly surrendered their character and who is responsible for the submission of his people to suddenly repent and act differently than they did before simply because he is confronted by a logical statement or even as a result of his own experience. On the contrary, these are the people who will reject this very idea until either the population has become accustomed to their enslavement or until greater forces come along and take power from the hands of the current corrupter. In the first situation, these people do not feel miserable like they should because they are often given the job of overseeing the slaves by the clever conquerors. These people of weak character usually exercise this office without mercy over their own people and it is much worse than any foreign bully who might be put into the same office by the enemy.

Events in Germany since 1918 show that our hope to possibly gain the mercy of the victors through voluntary subjugation has unfortunately proven to be disastrous. This willing submission has caused the wide masses to form a fatal political notion. Here I would like to emphasize the words "wide masses" since I do not believe that all actions and the constant failure to act by our people's leaders can be credited to the same disastrous mistake. After the war, the direction of our fate changed and it became obvious that it lay in the hands of Jews. You cannot possibly assume that a flawed understanding is the only cause of our misfortune. On the contrary, we must now be convinced that a conscious intention is destroying our people. As soon as one looks at the problem from this viewpoint, the obvious insanity in the foreign policy practiced by the leaders of our people becomes clear; it is actually the result of that highly cunning, ice-cold logic which serves the Jewish thought process and is part of their struggle for world conquest. Knowing this, it is then easy to understand why such a long period of time has elapsed without any improvement in our situation; to the contrary, in this time our state has steadily become weaker. This same span of time is comparable to that from 1806 to 1813 but in that case, the time was sufficient to put the completely broken Prussia back together with new energy and a determination to fight.

It has been seven years since November, 1918 and they just signed the Treaty of Locarno! (*The Locarno Treaties were seven agreements made at Locarno Switzerland in October 1925 and signed in London that December. The western borders of Germany were fixed but the eastern borders were still open to be changed. German nationalists saw the treaty as an unnecessary loss of land and resources. Here Hitler seems to say seven years have passed and Germany is still losing valuable territory, which is further weakening the country. Losing this territory with its natural resources obviously made it more difficult to pay reparations, too.*)

Here is the sequence of events that we have experienced. After the disgraceful Armistice was signed, no one had the energy or the courage to suddenly stand up and oppose the oppressive measures inflicted by the enemies, who returned over and over with more demands. The enemy, however, was clever enough not to ask for too much at any one time. They always limited their extortion to a level that they, and our German leadership, believed would be just enough to bear at the moment so that they did not have to fear a possible explosion of public opinion as a result. The more these individual demands were signed and choked down our throats, the less any resistance could be justified. This degradation was just one more extortion, so why would we suddenly do what had not been done so many times before, why would we resist? This is the very "drop of poison" Clausewitz talks about when he mentions the first deed which lacks integrity, and it is this deed which is bound to grow until it gradually becomes the worst possible heritage which hinders every future decision. This lack of character becomes a terrible lead weight that a people cannot shake off and that ultimately pulls them down to become a race of slaves.

In Germany we faced disarmament and enslavement rulings, our political system was made helpless, and we suffered economic plunder. All of these alternated until they finally produced a moral spirit that somehow could see the Dawes Plan as a blessing and mistook the Treaty of Locarno for a success. When viewing the situation from a higher point of view, we can see that at least one good thing has come out of this regrettable situation. It has been our good fortune that, although men may have been deceived, Heaven could not be bribed. For us, our blessing was misery and worry, which have since become the constant companions of our people and misery is our only true ally. Fate has not chosen to make an exception in this instance—we are judged the same as all others and because of this—Fate handed out what we deserved. We may no longer know how to value honor, but we have at least learned to value freedom when it comes to bread. Our people have now learned to cry for bread, and some day they will learn to pray for freedom.

The bitter collapse of our people in the years after 1918 was apparent even before it arrived. At that time, anyone who dared to foretell what actually did take place was later violently persecuted. The leadership of our people was just as miserable as it was conceited. This was especially true when it came to removing disagreeable and undesirable prophets. At that time, it was likely to happen, and it is still happening today, that the greatest parliamentarians, those simple-minded straw-heads who actually are members of the glove-maker's guild and master saddle-makers, that is not to say their profession makes them dunces; it is simply that they have no training or experience in what they are trying to do, and they were suddenly elevated to the pedestal of a statesman and allowed to rebuke the ordinary mortals from their lofty heights. (*The saddle-maker remark was directed to Friedrich Ebert, German Chancellor in the Weimar Republic, who was a saddle-maker before turning to politics.*) It made no difference that, after six months of practicing his craftsmanship, such a "statesman" is generally revealed to be the most miserable good-for-nothing windbag and he is then showered with scorn and ridicule by the rest of the world. By this time, he is at his wits' end. He doesn't know what to do next and has already shown himself to be completely incompetent! That makes no difference to him. The more these parliamentary statesmen of this Republic lack real accomplishments, the more furiously they persecute those who expect accomplishments from them and those who have the audacity to expose their failure and predict their future failure. If anyone has cornered one of these parliamentary gentlemen, and if this tradesman can no longer deny that everything he has tried to do crumbled, then he finds thousands and thousands of excuses for his failures. One thing they will never admit, however, is that they are the main cause of all the evil themselves.

During the winter of 1922-23, everyone should have seen the iron determination France displayed as she continued to pursue her original war aims even after peace was declared. (*France attempted to obtain more severe concessions in the period 1922-1923 before deciding to take military action and occupying the Ruhr in 1923.*) No one could believe that during four and a half years of the most decisive struggle in her history, France would have risked the meager blood of her people simply to be compensated evenly for previous damages. Even the Alsace-Lorraine territory would not explain the energy driving the French war tactics, not unless their aim was only part of a larger political program for the future of French foreign policy. This policy goal is the break up of Germany into a jumble of small states. That was the real goal this fanatical patriot France fought for, but in going after this prize, she actually sold her people out as slaves to the international world Jew.

This war goal of the French could have been achieved during the First World War if it had been fought on German soil as they had originally hoped in Paris. Let us suppose that the bloody battles of the First World War had not been fought on the Somme (*Somme is named after the Somme river and is a province in France*), in Flanders, in the Artois (*a province of northern France*), near Warsaw, Nishnij Novgorod (*Nizhny Novgorod the fourth largest city in Russia*), Kowno (*the second largest city in Lithuania*), Riga (*capital of Latvia*), and wherever else, but had been fought in Germany, on the Ruhr, on the Main, on the Elbe, near Hanover, Leipzig, Nuremberg, etc. Then, you quickly see that Germany's complete destruction would have been at hand. It is very doubtful that our young federal State of States would have endured the same difficult ordeal for four and a half years as well as France did. France had been rigidly centralized for centuries and looked to the indisputable center, Paris, for leadership. The fact that this great struggle between nations took place outside the boundaries of our Fatherland was to the immortal merit of the old army, but it was also the greatest piece of good fortune the future of Germany could have received. Though the idea sometimes causes me great suffering, it is my unshakable conviction that if the war were fought on German soil, the German Reich would have long since ceased to exist, and today nothing but a crowd of Germanic "states" would remain. This is the only reason why the bloodshed of our friends and brothers who have died on the battlefield has not been completely in vain.

Fortunately for us, it turned out differently! Germany did collapse quickly in November, 1918, but when the disaster happened at home, the armies of soldiers were still deep in enemy countries on the front lines. France's main concern at that time was not breaking up Germany, but how to rid France and Belgium of the German armies as quickly as possible. Therefore, the first task of Paris politicians was to disarm the German armies and to force them as quickly as possible back into Germany. Only after soldiers were out of their lands could they return to work on their original and real war aim. In this effort, however, France had already been paralyzed. For you see, England believed the war had been won the instant the colonial and commercial power had been destroyed, and Germany had been reduced to the rank of a second-class state. Not only did England have no interest in destroying the German State completely, but she had every reason to see it become a future rival of France in Europe. The French policy had to continue during peacetime with stronger determination than what the war had started. Now,

Clemenceau's declaration that, as far as he was concerned, peace was merely a continuation of the war and had a greater significance. (*Georges Benjamin Clemenceau was a French statesman and journalist who was the prime minister of France from 1906 to 1909 and again in 1917 to 1920. He strongly influenced the Treaty of Versailles.*)

The fabric of the Reich was shaken at every opportunity. In Paris, they hoped that by imposing ever-new reparation costs, disarmament demands and through the economic damage those caused, they could gradually loosen the fabric of the Reich's structure. The more national honor died out in Germany, the sooner economic pressure and our unending need would cause political destruction. If this policy of political control, which trained our people to be submissive, and of economic plunder were pursued for ten or twenty years, it would have ruined even the best state and would eventually dissolve it. The ultimate war goal of the French would have then been achieved.

Everyone must have recognized this as France's intention long before the winter of 1922-23. (*The French occupied the Ruhr on January 11, 1923*). Knowing this, there remained only two possibilities. One is that we could hope to blunt the will of the French with the toughness of the German people. The other is to finally do what must eventually take place, that is, to turn the helm of the Reich's ship during some especially drastic situation and ram the enemy. This would mean a struggle for life and death, and the only chance we might have for life would be if we succeeded in isolating France before the struggle and isolate her well enough so that this second conflict would not be a struggle of Germany against the world, but a defense of Germany against a France which was constantly disrupting world peace.

I must emphasize that I am firmly convinced this clash will eventually come, either in one way or another. I could never be convinced that France's intention toward us will change. Their actions are deeply rooted in the French nation's thoughts of self-preservation. If I were a Frenchman and if the greatness of France was as dear to me as the greatness of Germany truly is sacred to me, then I would act no differently from Clemenceau. The French race is gradually dying out, not only in the number of her people, but especially in regard to her best racial elements. France can only retain her continued importance in the world through the destruction of Germany. French policy may make a thousand detours, but somewhere at the end, this will always exist as the ultimate goal—it is their greatest desire and deepest longing. It would be a mistake to think that a purely passive will, seeking to preserve itself, can withstand an active attack from an enemy with an equal or stronger will in the long run. The everlasting conflict between Germany and France will never be decided as long as that conflict is limited to a German defense against French aggression.

Century after century, German borders will continue to fall back farther and farther. If you look at the wandering frontier that defines the German language from the twelfth century up to the present time, you will lose faith in the old attitude of development because you will see, up to this time, it has caused us so much harm. This must be made clear in Germany so we will no longer allow the German nation's will-to-live to degenerate into a mere passive defense, but rather concentrate this will toward an active confrontation with France and use it in a final decisive battle so we can reach the greatest ultimate goals for Germany. Only then will we be able to end the eternal and fruitless struggle between Germany and France. Through the destruction of France, Germany can finally give our people the means to expand. Today, there are eighty million Germans in Europe! After one hundred years, when there are two hundred and fifty million Germans on this continent, this foreign policy will be appreciated much more. Our people will not be crowded together like factory coolies working for the rest of the world, but we will be farmers and workers who use their labor to support each other and help their fellow man earn a living. (*Coolies is an offensive term for unskilled Asian workers.*)

In December, 1922 (*just before the Ruhr occupation by France*), the friction between Germany and France had again reached a dangerous peak. France had her eye on new unprecedented extortions and needed a way to justify them. Political pressure led the way for this economic plunder and the French believed only a violent grip on the nerve center of our entire German livelihood would be sufficient to put these unruly people under a heavier yoke of burden. France hoped the occupation of the Ruhr territory would not only break Germany's moral backbone, but that it would also force us into an economic position where we would have to accept even the heaviest obligations, willy-nilly, whether we wanted it or not.

It was a matter of bending or breaking. In the beginning Germany bent, only to break completely at the end. The occupation of the Ruhr caused Fate to once more reach out to Germany, offering her an opportunity to rise again. What, at first, looked like a terrible misfortune proved on closer examination to be the great promise of the possibility to end all of Germany's suffering.

The occupation of the Ruhr had, for the first time, deeply alienated England from France. It was not only British diplomatic circles who entered and maintained this alliance with their eyes wide open and based their decisions on cold logical calculation who disliked these events, but this occupation also estranged large circles among the English people. The English business world felt the continental strengthening of France's power the most and they had an obvious resentment. Aside from the fact that France now occupied a military position in Europe that Germany had not enjoyed even before the war, she also gained economic resources that practically gave France an economic monopoly. The greatest iron and coal mines in Europe were now united in the hands of a nation that, unlike Germany, had looked after her own interests in a decisive and active manner, and this was a nation that had reminded the world of its military ability during the Great War, and here again their action caused alarm all over the world. France's occupation of the Ruhr and the coalmines deprived England of all her diplomatic success. Now, the industrious and active British diplomacy was no longer the winner, but Marshal Foch and the France he represented was the winner. (*Ferdinand Foch was a French soldier and military theorist who was a general during the First World War, then became Supreme Commander of the Allied Armies. After the end of the war he wanted to impose heavy limits on Germany to prevent them from becoming a world power. He also pushed to prevent German control along the Rhine River, which goes through the Ruhr area where the Ruhr and Rhine rivers cross.*)

Italy's relations with France had not been exactly rosy since the end of the war; however, feelings toward Italy now turned into outright hatred. This was the great historical moment when former allies might be future enemies. The fact that this did not happen and that the allies did not suddenly fight among themselves—like what happened during the second Balkan War—is due to the fact that Germany had no Enver Pasha, but merely a Chancellor Cuno.

(*The Balkan Wars were two wars involving Bulgaria, Montenegro, Greece and Serbia conquering Ottoman-controlled Macedonia and Albania and much of Thrace in 1912 to 1913. After the war, the victors had severe disagreements about how to divide the spoils. Pasha was a high-ranking title in the Ottoman Empire similar to being called an English Lord. Ismail Enver or Enver Pasha was a Turkish military officer and the leader of the Ottoman Empire during the Balkan Wars and The First World War. Cuno refers to Wilhelm Cuno, Chancellor of Germany from 1922 to 1923 who is known for passive resistance to the French invasion of the Ruhr area.*)

The invasion of the Ruhr territory by the French opened up great possibilities for Germany's future in terms of our foreign and domestic policies. A large number of our people were suddenly cured of the delusion, which was fueled by the lying press that France was the champion of progress and liberty. The Spring of 1923 became just like 1914 when all the dreams that there existed an international solidarity between nations were banished from the minds of our German workers. Suddenly, they were brought back to the world of eternal struggle. Everywhere, we can see how one being fed upon another and the death of the weaker means life for the stronger.

When the French carried out their threats and finally began to march into the German coal territory, though at first they did so with great caution and hesitation, a decisive hour for Germany had struck. (*The French were very cautious about entering the Ruhr Area and feared they might have to retreat if they met any resistance at all.*) If our nation, at this moment, had changed their frame of mind and taken action, then the German Ruhr territory might have become for France what Moscow was to Napoleon. (*Napoleon suffered severe French losses in his attempt to take Moscow and when the Russians withdrew leaving the city open, they ordered the city burned rather than allow the French to take it intact. Napoleon eventually left Moscow when he realized taking it would not end the war and he had to return to deal with political problems in France. Ultimately the French suffered catastrophic losses and gained nothing.*)

When the French moved into the Ruhr, there were only two possible courses for us to take. The first was that we could submit to this injustice, just as we had before, and do nothing or, the second option was that with our eye fixed firmly on the territory of the flaming smelting-furnaces and the smokestacks, we could see an image that would create in the German nation a flaming desire to liberate itself from this eternal shame and become willing to take on the horrors of the moment rather than to endure the unending daily horror any longer.

A third way can be immortally credited to Chancellor Cuno, then in office, and our German privileged-class world deserves even more glorious credit for their admiration of him and their willingness to endorse his plan. (*This refers to Chancellor Cuno's plan of passive resistance by paying workers not to work.*)

Before I discuss that, I would first like to examine the second path as briefly as possible.

When France occupied the Ruhr, she became guilty of a notorious breach of the Treaty of Versailles. At the same time, she placed herself in opposition to those powers who guaranteed the Treaty, especially England and Italy. France could no longer hope that they would continue to support her own selfish raids. This adventure, and that was what it was at the beginning, had to be handled by her and ended satisfactorily by her alone. The German national government had only one option, and that was the honorable one. One thing was certain: we could not yet actively oppose France using armed force. It is important to realize that any form of negotiation that is not backed up by force is ridiculous and the result would be worthless. However, it was equally absurd to take the position of, "We are not negotiating" when we could not actively resist either. But it was unbelievably absurd to negotiate anyway in the end without creating a military force in the meantime.

This does not mean that it would have been possible to prevent the occupation of the Ruhr territory by military means. Only a madman could even recommend such an idea. However, our reaction to this French occupation should have been to do everything possible to secure the military force that we would need later so we could strengthen the hands of our negotiators. This would have to be done without considering the limitations of the Treaty of Versailles. Besides, France had already torn it to shreds. From the very beginning, it was clear that someday, at some conference table, a decision would have to be made about this French occupied territory. It is also important to realize that before negotiations start, even the best negotiators could not expect success when the ground they stand on and the chair they sit in is not protected by the shield arm of their nation. A feeble little tailor could never expect to fight with trained athletes, and equally so a negotiator who has no power backing him has always been made to graciously submit to the sword of Brennus on the hostile side of the scale if he had no sword of his own to throw in the opposite balance. (*Brennus refers to the Leader of the Gauls who, in approximately 390 B.C., invaded part of Rome and agreed to withdraw in exchange for a ransom. The Roman capital delivered the gold ransom and as the Gauls were weighing the gold, the Romans complained the weights being used were inaccurate and unfair. Brennus threw his sword on the weight side of the scale and proclaimed "Woe to the conquered". The moral is: the sword settles all disputes.*)

It was a shame to watch the comedies called negotiations that, ever since 1918, were always held before each new decree was imposed upon us. This degrading spectacle was presented to the whole world, and we were only invited to be mocked so everyone could see us walk up to the conference table where we were told what decision had been made in a long program. The resolution had already been previously drawn-up and approved. These negotiations were supposedly open to discussion, but from the very start the final ruling had already been made and it could not be changed. Our negotiators were rarely above the most modest intelligence of the average person, which justified too well the insolent remark of Lloyd George who had said scornfully in regard to the former German Reich Minister, Simon, "The Germans did not understand how to elect men of intellect as leaders and representatives". (*David Lloyd George was a British statesman and Prime Minister in the last half of the First World War and for four years afterwards.*) However, even a genius would have achieved very little at these negotiations considering the strong will of the enemies and the pitiful state of his own nation which was defenseless.

In the Spring of 1923, anyone who intended to use the occupation of the Ruhr by France as an excuse for the reconstruction of military power would first have to supply the nation with its spiritual weapons, strengthen its will power, and remove those who destroyed our military for it was our most valuable strength.

We failed to crush the head of the Marxist serpent once and for all in 1914 and 1915, and in 1918 this was bloodily avenged. In the same way, terrible results were certain to follow if we did not take advantage of the opportunity that presented itself in the Spring of 1923 to stop the Marxist traitors and murderers of our nation.

The very thought of actual resistance against France was foolishness as long as war was not declared against those powers that had, from the inside, broken German forces on the battlefield just five years earlier. Only those from the privileged-class could entertain the outrageous idea that Marxism might now somehow be different from what it was before and that these villainous want-to-be-leaders in 1918 would suddenly be ready to do what was right for the nation in 1923. In 1918, they had been willing to trample over two million dead just to step up into various government seats. This hope that former national traitors would suddenly become defenders of German liberty was an incredible and totally absurd thought! They never even considered protecting Germany! Just as a hyena will not turn loose a carcass, a Marxist will not turn away from high treason. No one should make the most stupid objection by saying many workers had once died for Germany in the war. German workers, yes, but at that time they were not international Marxists. If in 1914 the German workers had consisted of dedicated Marxists, then the war would have ended after three weeks.

Germany would have collapsed before the first soldier stepped across the border. No, the fact that Germany was still fighting in 1918 was proof that the Marxist delusion had not yet penetrated the entire national mind. To the same degree that the German worker and German soldier returned to the hands of the Marxist leaders was the same degree that he was lost to the Fatherland. If at the beginning and during the war twelve or fifteen thousand of these Hebrew corrupters of the people would have been put under poisonous gas, like hundreds of thousands of our very best German workers of all classes on the battlefield had to endure, then the sacrifice of millions at the front would not have been in vain.

On the contrary, if we could have removed twelve thousand crooks in time, we might have saved a million valuable Germans for the future. It was a part of the "art of statesmanship" demonstrated by the privileged-class to deliver millions of our people to a bloody death on the battlefield without batting an eye, but at the same time, they regard ten or twelve thousand traitors, parasites, usurers, and swindlers as sacred national treasures and openly proclaim their sanctity. It is hard to know what quality is considered greater in this privileged-class world, hard-headedness, weakness, cowardice, or through and through ethical corruption. It is truly a class destined by Fate to perish; unfortunately it is dragging the whole nation along with it into the abyss of tears.

The very same situation that existed in 1918 stood before us again in 1923. Regardless of what kind of resistance was chosen, the first step was always the elimination of the Marxist poison from the body of our nation. It was my conviction, even at that time, that the first duty of a real National government was to find forces determined to declare a war of destruction against Marxism and to give these forces free reign. It was not the National government's duty to worship the nonsense of "peace and order" at a time when a foreign enemy was dealing the most destructive blows to the Fatherland and when treason lurked around every corner at home. No, a real nationalistic government would have wished for unrest and disorder. Under the confusion, a final settlement with the Marxist mortal-enemies of our nation would at last be possible and it would finally happen. The failure to take out this enemy meant any thought of resistance was pure madness. A settlement of real world-historical importance never results from the scheme of some secret counsel or from the withered mind of an old state minister. True resolution happens according to the eternal laws of nature on this earth which is the unending struggle for existence. It is important to realize that often, out of the bloodiest civil wars, a robust national body, which is as hard as steel, springs forth, yet, more than once, artificially maintained conditions of peace have produced a foul stench of decay so strong that it reached up into Heaven.

The Fates of nations are not changed with kid gloves. Therefore, the greatest brutal steps should have been used in 1923 to seize the vipers that were feeding on our national body. Only after this was successful would there be any sense in preparing for active resistance.

At that time, I spoke again and again until I was hoarse in an effort to make it clear to the so-called national circles what was at stake this time if the mistakes of 1914 and the years following were repeated. They were bound to result in an end like that of 1918. I have asked them again and again to let Fate take its course and to give our movement free reign so we could bring a reckoning to Marxism. I preached to deaf ears. They all thought they understood the situation better, including the Chief of the Defense Force. Finally, they found themselves in front of the most miserable submission of all time.

It was then when I became fully aware that the German privileged-class had reached the end of its mission and had no reason to complete any task. At that time, I saw that all these parties were doing nothing more than competing with each other in their arguments over Marxism, with no true desire to wipe it out. They had long since accepted the idea of the destruction of the Fatherland. The only thing that motivated them was their deep concern over whether or not they would be allowed to participate in the funeral feast. This is the only thing they are still "fighting" for.

I openly admit that during this time, I developed the deepest admiration for the great man south of the Alps. His passionate love for his people did not permit him to make pacts with Italy's internal enemies, but he struggled in every way possible to destroy them. The reason why Mussolini will be ranked among the great men of this world is his determination not to share Italy with Marxism, but to save his Fatherland from Marxism by sentencing Internationalism to destruction. On the other hand, how pitiful and small our German pygmies of statesmen seem in comparison to such a great man. We must choke back disgust when these disrespectful, conceited zeros dare to criticize a man who is a thousand times greater. It is even more painful to realize this is happening in a country that just fifty years ago called Bismarck its leader.

The attitude of the privileged-class in their willingness to spare Marxism in 1923 meant that the fate of any armed resistance in the Ruhr territory had already been determined in advance. To fight against France, with a deadly enemy in our own ranks, was foolish. Whatever else was done could only be called shadow-boxing (*a reference to the passive resistance campaign in the Ruhr*). It was nothing more than a staged fight to pacify the nationalistic elements in Germany and to calm the "boiling anger of the nation's soul", or rather to deceive it. If they were serious, they would have been forced to recognize the fact that a nation's strength lies primarily in its will and not in its weapons. Before one can conquer foreign enemies, the enemy within must first be annihilated. Otherwise, if victory does not crown the battle on the very first day, then all is lost. As soon as even the shadow of defeat passes over a nation that is not free from internal enemies, its resistance will be shattered and the enemy will be the final victor.

This could have easily been predicted as early as the Spring of 1923. It is useless to discuss whether or not there was any chance of a military success against France! If our reaction to the French invasion of the Ruhr territory had resulted only in the destruction of Marxism in Germany, that alone would have brought us success. A

Germany that has been delivered from the deadly enemies of her existence would possess a strength that no power in the world could ever strangle again. The day that Marxism is totally crushed in Germany will mark the complete shattering of her shackles. Never in our history have we been conquered by the forces of our enemies, but we have only been conquered as a result of our own faults and by the enemy in our own camp.

Since the German government could not pull themselves together at that time and commit to such a heroic action, their only option was to follow the first road: do nothing and let things take their own course. At this momentous hour, however, Heaven gave the German nation the gift of a "great" man, Mr. Cuno. He was not a statesman or politician by profession and he certainly was not one by birth, but he represented a sort of political yes-man that could be used for the completion of certain tasks. Otherwise, he was more skilled in business than politics. This politicized merchant was a curse for Germany because he regarded politics as an economic undertaking and began to act accordingly. Mr. Cuno said to himself, "France occupied the Ruhr territory and what is found there? Coal. Therefore, France is occupying the Ruhr territory for its coal!" Knowing this, what other idea would possibly seem more natural for Mr. Cuno than to call for a labor-strike so that the French could no longer take any coal? At this point, at least according to Mr. Cuno's thinking, they would certainly evacuate the Ruhr territory some day because the enterprise did not prove to be profitable. This was the train of thought of this "outstanding national statesman" who was permitted to speak to "his people" in Stuttgart and other places and whom this entire nation blissfully admired so deeply.

To hold a strike, the Marxists were needed, since it was primarily the workers who had to strike. It was necessary to bring the worker into a unified front with all the other Germans. In the mind of a privileged-class statesman, there is no difference between the worker and a Marxist. You should have seen how these moldy privileged-class party-politicians lit up in response to such an inspired slogan! Cuno was nationalistic and inspired at the same time, and with this plan the privileged-class finally found what they had been searching for all along! The bridge to Marxism had been revealed to them. Now, it was possible for the nationalistic impostor to extend a respectable hand to the international traitor creating a "German-esque" face that was shouting nationalistic phrases. The Marxist grasped that hand immediately. Cuno needed the Marxist leaders for his "unified front" as much as the Marxist leaders needed Cuno's money. So, both sides benefited. Cuno received his united front consisting of national babblers and anti-national swindlers, and the international swindlers were able to serve their most lofty fighting mission: they were able to destroy national economy and make the government pay them to do it. The idea of saving a nation through a paid general strike was so obviously "brilliant", it was a slogan that even the most indifferent good-for-nothing could get behind with great enthusiasm.

It is generally known that a nation cannot be liberated through prayers alone. Whether or not it could be liberated by laziness has not yet been proven by history. If Mr. Cuno had only demanded two more hours of work from every German instead of calling for a paid strike, then the fraud of this "united front" would have revealed itself on the third day. Nations are not liberated by doing nothing, but by sacrifice.

This so-called passive resistance could not continue very long. Only a man completely ignorant of war tactics could imagine that an occupying army would be driven out by such absurd means. This was the only reason for starting this campaign that cost billions and which essentially aided in the total devaluation of the national currency. (*Cuno's labor strikes contributed to the hyperinflation in Germany making the Mark basically worthless.*)

The French were able to calmly establish their military bases in the Ruhr territory once they saw resistance would only be passive. We had already given them the best recipe for bringing a stubborn civilian population back to its senses if its activities could have seriously endangered the occupation forces. Nine years ago, did we not quickly chase the bands of Belgian guerrillas out, making it clear to the civilian population how serious the consequences would be if their activities endangered the German armies? The moment passive resistance in the Ruhr territory became dangerous to France is the moment the occupying army could have, with playful ease, put a gruesome end to this entire childish nonsense in less than a week's time. This question always remains: What do you do when passive resistance finally wears out the patience of an enemy and he begins to fight it with brutal force?

Do we continue to resist? If we do, then we must be prepared to suffer the most severe and bloody persecutions. The result is the same as if we started an active resistance, an outright battle. For this reason, every so-called passive resistance only has value when it is backed up by a determination to continue resistance through open war or covert guerrilla warfare. Generally speaking, every struggle should be evaluated based on its chance of succeeding. Whenever a fortress is fiercely attacked by the enemy and overwhelmed, it is forced to give up its last hope that it might be saved and it has effectively surrendered at that time. This is especially true when the defender has a certain desire to remain among the living instead of facing the high probability of dying. If the garrison soldiers of a besieged fortress lose their faith in a possible deliverance, all strength of resistance would break down at the very same instant.

Therefore, the final consequences that were bound to result from a successful passive resistance at the Ruhr would only matter if they were supported by an active front line building up behind it. In that case, we could have obtained an endless commitment from our people. If each of these Westphalians had known that their Fatherland was building up an army of eighty or one hundred divisions to support them, the French would have been walking on thorns. (*Westphalia is the general region encompassing the Rhine area, here meaning the people in the Ruhr area.*) You can always find more courageous men who are ready to sacrifice themselves for success than you can find men who wish to sacrifice themselves for nothing.

This was a classic situation that forced us National-Socialists to oppose this so-called nationalist slogan with the sharpest weapons we could. During these months, I was frequently attacked by people whose total nationalist convictions consisted of a mixture of stupidity and showy displays intended to enhance their self image. These were the people who shouted with others because it gave them a thrill to suddenly act like a "nationalist" without putting themselves at risk. I considered this "united front" as the most miserable and most ridiculous demonstration possible and history has proven me right.

As soon as the unions filled their treasuries with Cuno's contributions and the passive resistance campaign faced the possibility that it might have to change from a lazy defensive act to an active offense, the red hyenas instantly broke away from the national flock of sheep and returned to what they had been all along. Without a whimper, Mr. Cuno sneaked back to his ships. Germany had been enriched by an additional experience and made poorer of a great hope.

Up to late mid-Summer, many officers, and not the worst of the lot, could not accept that such a shameful development would be allowed to continue. They all hoped that, if not openly, perhaps at least secretly, preparations would be made to change this bold invasion by France into a turning point in German history. Within our own ranks, there were many who placed their trust in the defense forces of the Reich. This conviction was so strong that it influenced the actions and even encouraged the training of countless young people.

Back when the dreadful and disgraceful 1918 surrender took place, an intense revolt flared up in a blaze at the betrayal of our desperate people. Now, after a fortune of billions had been spent and many thousands of young Germans were sacrificed—who had been foolish enough to take the promises of the Reich leaders seriously—the millions of people suddenly saw their conviction burning brightly and clearly and they knew that only a radical step could save Germany, the removal of the whole ruling system.

Never was the time so ripe and never did it cry so strongly for a solution than it did at this moment. On one hand, the naked shameless betrayal of the Fatherland clearly showed itself. On the other hand, a nation had been delivered over to death through gradual economic starvation. Since the State had trampled on all laws of good faith, had scorned all the rights of its citizens, had cheated millions of its most faithful sons out of their sacrifice, and had robbed millions of their last penny, it no longer had the right to expect anything but hatred from its subjects. This hatred against the destroyers of the people and of the Fatherland was bound to explode. Here, I can refer to the final sentence of my last speech at the great trial in the Spring of 1924: "The judges of this State may calmly condemn our actions, yet history, as the goddess of a nobler truth and of a more perfect law, will someday smile as she tears up this judgment and frees us from all blame and guilt".

History will, however, also call before her tribunal those who are in power today, those who trample on justice and law, those who have led our people into suffering and misery, and those who during the Fatherland's humiliation, placed their own interests ahead of the community's life.

I will not go into the details that led to, and finally decided, the events of the 8th of November, 1923 (*The Beer Hall Putsch.*) I do not see any point in it because I do not think it will benefit the future and, primarily, because it is useless to tear open wounds that have only begun to heal. Besides, there is no point in talking about the guilt of people who, maybe, deep down in their hearts, cling to their nation with a love equal to mine, but who strayed from the path or did not recognize the common road.

In view of the great troubles in our Fatherland we all share, I would not want to offend and thus alienate those who someday in the future will have to form a great united front made up of all true Germans against the common enemies of our nation. I know the day will come when even those who once were hostile to us will respect those who died bitterly for the sake of the German nation.

I dedicated the first volume of my work to those eighteen fallen heroes whom I want to present to the supporters and defenders of our doctrine as the champions who knowingly sacrificed themselves for all of our sakes. Their memory must bring the man who has become indecisive and weak back to the fulfillment of his duty. This duty is one they themselves fulfilled in good faith and to the very end.

Along with them, I must include a man who has dedicated his life to the awakening of his and our nation through his words and thoughts and finally, by his acts: Dietrich Eckart.

(*Dietrich Eckart was involved in the Beer Hall Putsch but was released from prison and died soon after due to a heart attack.*)

AFTERWORD

On November 9, 1923, in the fourth year of its existence, the National-Socialist German Workers Party was dissolved and forbidden throughout the entire Reich. Today in November, 1926, it is free again throughout the entire Reich and is stronger and more solid internally than ever.

All persecutions, blasphemies, and slander the movement and its leaders have suffered could not affect it. The truth of its ideas, the purity of the supporter's will to sacrifice for it caused it to break free from all restraints and become stronger than ever.

In our present world, filled with parliamentary corruption, if our movement concentrates more and more on the deepest essence of its struggle, and feels that it embodies the pure values of race and personality and, as that personification, it positions itself accordingly, it is bound, with almost mathematical certainty, to be victorious in its battle when the time comes. Germany must also gain her deserved place on this earth if she is organized and led by the same principles.

A nation that works to cultivate its best racial elements during this era of race-poisoning is bound to someday become the lord of earth. May the supporters of our movement never forget this, especially in those times when they may have misgivings about the magnitude of the sacrifices they face and when they question the chance of success.

(*In the final dedication, Hitler says 18 heroes, however only 16 were listed in the Volume 1 Dedication, and only 16 party members were killed in the Putsch. It is interesting that such an error was overlooked or even made. Hitler was likely thinking of the original 16 plus the following deaths of Pöhner and Eckart.*

This error was corrected in later German language editions. You can find out more about this and other unusual facts about the various translations in the eBook **Mein Kampf: A Translation Controversy** *which is available for free at www. HitlerLibrary.Org.*)

Download Your Bonus

This concludes Mein Kampf, the Ford Translation. You can download a free bonus gift that supplements this edition at

http://Bonus.HitlerLibrary.com

You can find more information about Adolf Hitler and find analyses of Mein Kampf at our literary archive. Go there now at

http://www.HitlerLibrary.org

Listen To This Book

When you have finished reading Mein Kampf, listen to it once more and re-discover everything you missed.

Now you can listen to Mein Kampf in your car, on your MP3 player, or with your computer. This is the full, uncensored Ford Translation. Audio includes many extras and bonus material not available in the printed book. Listen again after you finish reading the book. Rediscover parts you missed so you can gain the most from this work.

Visit www.Mein-Kampf-Audio.com to listen to a free sample from Mein Kampf.

FREE BONUS:

As a special thank-you for purchasing this book, you can download a bonus gift at

http://Bonus.HitlerLibrary.com

This special page contains additional updates and audio information so go there now.

CPSIA information can be obtained at www.ICGtesting.com
Printed in the USA
LVOW121927210512

282645LV00019B/268/P